MILE = 1609 METERS

THE CROATIA

CRUISING COMPANION

A yachtsman's guide to Croatia –
The Dalmatian Coast and Islands

Jane Cody and John Nash

Published by John Wiley & Sons Ltd, The Atrium, Southern Gate, Chichester,
West Sussex PO19 8SQ, England
Telephone (+44) 1243 779777
Email (for orders and customer service enquiries): cs-books@wiley.co.uk
Visit our Home Page on www.wileynautical.com
Edited and designed by Nautical Data Ltd

Reprinted January 2010

Photographs by Jane Cody and John Nash

Additional photography:
Page 85 ©ACI dd Opatija; Pages 22, 25, 29, 38 (top), 54, 98, 101 (right), 104 (bottom), 112 (top and bottom), 132 (top), 145, 164 (bottom), 188, 207, 225 (top), 241© Croatian National Tourist Board; Page 41 ©Illirija dd; Page 185 ©Le Méridien Grand Hotel Lav; Pages 12, 160 (top) ©Mike Forbes; Page 56 ©Plava Vala doo; Pages 4, 5, 108, 206, 238 by Pat Collinge ©Sunsail

For Wiley Nautical
Executive Editor: David Palmer
Project Editor: Lynette James
Assistant Editor: Drew Kennerley

For Nautical Data
Cartography: Jamie Russell
Art Direction: Vanessa Bird and Jamie Russell
Cruising Companion series editors: Vanessa Bird and Lucinda Roch

ISBN-13: 978-1-904358-28-2

IMPORTANT NOTICE

This Companion is intended as an aid to navigation only. The information contained within should not solely be relied on for navigational use, rather it should be used in conjunction with official hydrographic data. Whilst every care has been taken in compiling the information contained in this Companion, the publishers, author, editors and their agents accept no responsibility for any errors or omissions, or for any accidents or mishaps which may arise from its use.

Neither the publisher nor the author can accept responsibility for errors, omissions or alterations in this book. They will be grateful for any information from readers to assist in the update and accuracy of the publication.

Readers are advised at all times to refer to official charts, publications and notices. The charts contained in this book are sketch plans and are not to be used for navigation. Some details are omitted for the sake of clarity and the scales have been chosen to allow best coverage in relation to page size.

Correctional supplements are available at www.wileynautical.com and on request from the publishers.

ACKNOWLEDGEMENTS
The authors would like to thank the many people who helped them to uncover the essential facts and essence of one of the best cruising grounds in the world, onshore and at sea. Special thanks go to the following for a wide variety of input, over and above the call of duty: Radovan Solarić – Hydrographic Institute of the Republic of Croatia; Zdeslav Bošcović – Croatian British Society; Jon Wilson – Sunsail; Radovan Kečkemet – Translations and Language; Trvtko Trlek – Croatian Post Office; Bill and Niang Amos, John Tillisch and David Lindsay – sparkling, good-humoured and ever ready crew.

Printed by PrinterTrento in Trento, Italy

Cruising among the islands of the Dalmatian Coast

Looking towards Split peninsula from Podstrana

Introduction

The Dalmatian Coast is widely held to be one of the best and, until recently, one of the least discovered cruising areas in Europe. Jacques Cousteau described the Adriatic as 'one of the cleanest seas on earth', while George Bernard Shaw suggested 'those who seek paradise on earth should come to Dubrovnik'. Croatia is now a 'hotspot' for land-based tourism and is also becoming very popular as a charter destination, so the waters are much busier than they were, particularly in August. However, it is still possible to come across a quiet, away from it all anchorage, as easily as it is to find a buzzing town full of music and nightlife. It is the variety and diversity of destinations, set against such a spectacular natural backdrop, that makes Croatia a hard place to beat.

The Croatian Adriatic includes 1,185 islands, islets and reefs and a stretch of coastline 1,778km (1,111 miles) long. The mainland and islands are dotted with fishing villages, apparently unchanged in many years, and the otherwise uninhabited islands come alive in the summer as the restaurants and café-bars open up for passing sailors. There is much to be said for northern Croatia, particularly the peninsula of Istria with its strong Venetian influence, but this Cruising Companion covers the sailing heartland of Croatia – the Dalmatian coast – from Zadar down to Molunat, south of Dubrovnik, and all of the islands and islets in between.

CRUISING STRATEGIES

Dalmatia provides something for everyone, from the novice sailor to the expert, and from the party-goer to the tranquillity seeker. For those who prefer the comfort of marinas, these are well spaced along the coastline and on the islands. Many of the bigger ports and harbours also have good facilities and are improving them steadily. Alternatively, there are sheltered anchorages in abundance, often with restaurants and basic facilities, and you are never too far away from civilisation if you need it.

If you lean towards the nightlife then you should take in Trogir on the mainland near Split, Hvar Town on Hvar Island and certainly Dubrovnik. All have great summer music festivals and plenty of other entertainment. More recently, Zadar is also developing a name for itself for nightlife. If you like the civilisation and facilities of the bigger towns but would prefer to stay a little bit away from the madding crowds, then include Vis Town on Vis Island, Jelsa or nearby Vrboska on Hvar and Pučišća on Brač. If watersports and beaches are your thing then Bol on Brač is a must. For picture postcard settlements, it's hard to beat Korčula Town on Korčula Island, Komiža on Vis, Cavtat, south of Dubrovnik, or Primošten between Šibenik and Trogir. For peace and quiet and beautiful unspoilt scenery, the Kornati Islands are top of the list, closely followed by the island of Mljet. For the best sailing take a route through the Pašman Canal and visit the islands of Pašman and Ugljan. For spectacular waterfalls, head up the estuary at Šibenik and visit Skradin and the Krka National Park, and for history and architecture explore Zadar, Šibenik, Split, Trogir and Dubrovnik.

You could spend an entire week just circumnavigating one of the larger islands of Brač or Hvar, or another week discovering the indented coastlines of Ugljan or Dugi Otok. A base for a few days on the Pakleni Islands might give you the best of all worlds, with Hvar Town in easy reach, and the calm of the islands to soothe your spirits after a night on the town.

Although it's all relative, the places of least interest are the south-west coast of Pašman, Ugljan and Dugi Otok, which offer little protection, and the mainland south of Split as far as Ston. This part of the coastline does have the tourist resorts of Makarska and Omiš, a few beaches, probably the most spectacular of the karst mountain scenery directly behind Omiš, and the onshore delights of Ston and Mali Ston, but there are few marinas or ports of significant interest, and you come to a dead end where the Pelješac Peninsula joins the mainland.

If you can avoid the high season, especially August, do so. If you can't, then try to book your night stops in advance to avoid having to get there too early. You'll find Hvar Town and Vis particularly difficult to get into in the high season. We tend to sail in the shoulder season – June, early July and September – and while the marinas and main ports are busy, particularly Hvar, we can generally always find somewhere to stay without too much effort. If you prefer anchorages, then the many organised anchorages are best for basic facilities, though try and line up a couple of options to cater for different weather conditions.

Apart from the tourist traffic in the high season, the other thing to watch out for is the ferries. Dubrovnik, Split and Zadar are busy international ferry ports, as well as serving a number of local destinations. The islands have frequent ferries, particularly in the summer, so keep an eye-out on the charts for the ferry routes. Some of the fuel stations can also get busy in the summer and a few are sited close to ferry piers. This can make the somewhat disorderly queuing system hazardous and frustrating, so it's a good idea to fuel up at the less popular spots. Biograd, Zadar and Dubrovnik are among the worst, while Vis Town, Rogač on Šolta and Preko on Pašman are among the best. Fishing fleets are smaller than they were and are only a problem when it comes to finding space in the harbours that accommodate them.

Navigationally, there are no tides of any significance to worry about, so the biggest issue is the density of the islands and islets and the indentation of the coastline, together with the shoals, rocks and other natural hazards. This is a cruising area where attention to charts and visual navigation are much more important than electronic technology. We have therefore been circumspect with the provision of approach waypoints in many areas. The Croatian Hydrographic Institute is an up-to-date and forward-looking organisation and Croatia is a seafaring nation. Consequently, the area is well-buoyed and charted and lights are generally good, though notably still lacking in some areas. However, we would not recommend sailing at night or in restricted visibility, as it is often confusing enough counting off the islets or finding the harbour entrance in clear daylight. The density of the islands and islets around this coastline

The picture postcard town of Primošten, situated between Šibenik and Trogir

means that distances between ports are relatively short.

In the event of a minor problem, it is probably best to head for the nearest marina, which will always try and accommodate a boat needing assistance. Similarly, one of the permanently open marinas is the best place to leave your boat if you want to go inland for a few days or lay up over winter. Please do check your insurance cover, however, as we have heard of a couple of isolated hard-luck stories over what is and is not covered by the marinas.

If entering Croatian waters from another country, you should take the shortest route to the nearest port open for international traffic. Similarly, before leaving Croatian waters, you should complete Customs formalities and so forth at the relevant port. A friend of ours stopped for a swim entering Croatian waters from Montenegro recently, and was politely but firmly asked to proceed directly to Cavtat by a watchful official. Dalmatian ports permanently open to international traffic are Zadar, Šibenik, Split, Vela Luka on Korčula, Ploče, Metković, Dubrovnik and Ubli on Lastovo. Seasonal maritime border crossings are fixed for each year and normally open from 1 April to 31 October. These currently comprise Sali and Božava on Dugi Otok, Primošten, Stari Grad and Hvar on Hvar, Komiža and Vis on Vis and Cavtat. Cavtat is one of the newest and most 'user-friendly' ports of entry and far preferable to Dubrovnik. Split, Cavtat, Dubrovnik and, to a lesser extent, Zadar are all near to airports with good internal connections and some international routes.

You can get full contact details from www.pomorstvo.hr, which is the government website for the Ministry of Sea, Tourism, Transport and Development. There are English pages but, as yet, harbourmaster details are not translated, so stay on the Croatian pages and click on '*more*' (sea), and then '*lučke kapetanije*' and then select the port. '*Lučke kapetanije*' (harbourmasters' offices) should not be confused with '*lučke uprava*' (port authorities). The former is a government agency concerned with the implementation and monitoring of maritime legislation, while the latter is a commercial body empowered to run a port. Crew changes, permits and so forth are dealt with by the harbourmasters' offices; mooring fee collection, waste disposal, etc, are carried out by the port authorities or their appointed agents or concession holders. If in doubt, staff at one of the marinas should be able to help you with all the paperwork or at least direct you to the best port.

Note that the rules on foreign vessels have recently changed quite radically and are still being amended in the face of a certain amount of controversy. The aim of the new rules was to try and outlaw the black market charter business but there is some speculation that the laws have missed their target and instead may be damaging tourism, specifically multiple ownership or frequent crew changes. In essence, the law limits the number of people allowed on each boat each year to 2.3 times the maximum number of crew permitted to be carried on the boat. The crew should be named in advance and, with limited exceptions, the owner must remain on board at all times. In practice, the suggestion is that if you leave Croatian waters, you can start again, but the situation is less than ideal and the law is changing in detail as more and more 'special cases' present their position to the government. The English pages of the website in the immediately preceding paragraph should have up-to-date details on the current requirements.

CHARTS, MAPS AND DATUMS

The Croatian Hydrographic Institute (HHI) has a comprehensive range of charts available from its authorised resellers, located in the main towns. Full details can be found on its website, www.hhi.hr. These charts are updated by monthly notices to mariners in both Croatian and English, which can be downloaded or ordered from the same site. As well as the charts, the Hydrographic Institute produces a series entitled 'Living Archipelago', which are A3-sized flip charts covering different areas. They include less detailed versions of the charts, useful local information and descriptions of some of the key tourist areas. Last, but by no means least, the Hydrographic Institute has recently issued a two-volume Pilot series in English. These are factual books with good harbour plans but lacking in detailed onshore information.

The area is also covered by the British Admiralty standard nautical charts and the Admiralty (UKHO) has recently published a Leisure Folio for Southern Croatia. Covering Zadar down to Dubrovnik (SC5767), this folio contains 21 charts that are printed in a practical A2-sized format. For more information on the Admiralty charts and how to buy them, go to www.admiraltyleisure.co.uk.

All the Croatian charts and the Admiralty charts on Croatia are drawn to the Hermannskogel datum, which differs slightly from WGS 84, most commonly used in GPS systems. The Hydrographic Institute is, where practical, updating to WGS 84 but this is a slow process. In the meantime, each chart shows the adjustment to be made to convert to WGS 84. We have used WGS 84 in the text, but you will be able to plot the waypoints on the Croatian charts by reversing the instruction included on the Croatian chart.

For land-based maps, the main tourist offices have a good road map of the country with a tourist map on the reverse. This is great for putting all the various places into perspective, as well as providing much useful background, tourist and travel information. The local tourist offices in destinations of any size mostly, but not always, have town plans but seldom harbour plans.

There still seems to be a firm divide between land-based tourism and nautical tourism, and we often found that any questions about harbour facilities and depths were not within the knowledge base of the local tourist office. Where there is one, the harbourmaster is the best person to talk to, though harbour plans can often be found in the form of big billboards in town.

The marinas invariably have marina plans and brochures readily available. The chain of government-owned ACI marinas has its own brochure with prices and details of each marina, while another brochure, available from the tourist office, includes details and prices for all the marinas. The ACI website is also a good source of reference for detailed approach notes to its marinas – www.aci-club.hr. The national tourist office's website is www.croatia.hr and it has an office in London at 2 Lanchesters, 162-164 Fulham Palace Road, London W6 9ER, Tel: 0044 (0)208 563 7979; Fax: 0044 (0)208 563 2616, email: info@cnto.freeserve.co.uk. From this website you will find the details of the local tourist offices but don't be too despondent if you don't get many replies to emails, especially during the winter months. Email still does not seem to be a favoured communications medium and some of the offices are only manned in the summer season.

Note that the chartlets in this book should not be used for navigation and are for reference only. For an explanation of the abbreviations and symbols used, see page 28. All the marked depths are shown as metres and tenths of metres.

The chart information in this product is reproduced with the permission of the UKHO.

BEARINGS AND COURSES

All bearings and courses are True and given in degrees. The magnetic variation in Croatia ranges from 2 to 3°E (2007), increasing annually by 5'E. It is advisable, however, to check the compass rose on an up-to-date chart to be completely accurate. Note that anomalies have been recorded in the area between the island of Vis and the islets of Svetac and Jabuka, west of Vis, due to geological factors.

WAYPOINTS

Please remember that all waypoints should be plotted on a chart before use to check their relevance to your passage plan and that the only safe way to sail is to use your charts and your eyes over and above any electronic instruments.

We have supplied safe water waypoints in WGS 84 datum, to two decimal points of a minute, from which you should be able to easily visually navigate to the suggested berth, mooring or anchorage. Note, though, that positions must be altered on charts referenced to the local datum. The range of error to two decimal points is about 18.5m.

COASTGUARD

Croatia has no direct equivalent of the Royal National Lifeboat Institution (RNLI), with Coastguard services provided by individual harbourmasters under the overall co-ordination of the Maritime Rescue Co-ordination Centre based in Rijeka (MRCC- Rijeka). The MRCC provides a 24-hour watch service and covers the whole of Croatian territorial waters. The territory is divided into sub regions – 'Maritime Rescue Sub-Centres' (MRSC) – which share responsibility for their region with Rijeka. Ultimately, Coastguard services come under the responsibility of the Ministry of Sea, Tourism, Transport and Development.

In an emergency, call 9155, free of charge, from both fixed lines in Croatia and Croatian mobile phones. If dialling from abroad, dial 00 385 51 9155. Alternatively use VHF Channels 10 and 16.

Croatia is a signatory of the International Convention on Maritime Search and Rescue, and is therefore part of the Global Maritime Distress and Safety System (GMDSS). In addition to MRCC Rijeka and the MRSCs there are three shore-based radio stations combining to operate GMDSS on both terrestrial and satellite technology. All services operate 24 hours a day.

The three radio stations transmit weather reports and

- MRCC Rijeka: Tel: 051 312 253, Fax: 051 312 254, email: mrcc@pomorstvo.hr, VHF DSC MMSI 002387010 or 002387020
- MRSC Pula: Tel/fax: 052 222 037, MMSI 002383050
- MRSC Senj: Tel: 053 881301, Fax: 053 884 128, MMSI 002383150
- MRSC Zadar: Tel: 023 254 880, Fax: 023 254 876, MMSI 002387400 or 002387401
- MRSC Šibenik: Tel: 022 217 214, Fax: 022 212 626, MMSI 002387500 or 002387501
- MRSC Split: Tel: 021 362 436, Fax: 021 346 555, MMSI 002387040 or 002387030
- MRSC Ploče: Tel/fax: 020 679 009, MMSI 002383350
- MRSC Dubrovnik: Tel/fax: 020 418 989, MMSI 002387800 or 002387801

- Rijeka Radio: Call sign 9AR, Tel: 051 217 332, Fax: 051 217 232, MMSI 002380200, VHF Channels 04, 16, 20, 24, 81, VHF-DSC Channel 70. Weather reports at 0535, 1435 and 1935 UTC on VHF Channel 24.

- Split Radio: Call sign 9AS, Tel: 021 389 190, Fax: 021 389 185, MMSI 002380100, VHF Channels 07, 16, 21, 23, 81, VHF-DSC Channel 70. Weather report at 0545, 1245 and 1945 UTC on VHF Channels 7, 21, 23 and 81.

- Dubrovnik Radio: Call sign 9AD, Tel: 020 423 665, Fax: 020 423 397, MMSI 002380300, VHF Channels 04, 07, 16, 85, VHF-DSC Channel 70. Weather reports at 0625, 1320 and 2120 on VHF Channels 4, 7 and 85.

navigational warnings in Croatian and English three times a day. For Split Radio, these reports are at 0545, 1245 and 1945 UTC. Weather reports are broadcast by the harbourmaster's offices in Croatian and English: Šibenik – VHF channel 73, Split – VHF channel 67.

On entering Croatian waters, the harbourmaster should supply you with an information pack including HHI Chart 101, which provides extensive information on the Coastguard service as well as details of marinas, harbourmaster's offices and embassies, rules for foreign yachts entering and leaving Croatian waters, notes on buoyage systems, collision avoidance rules, etc.

WEATHER

Croatian weather is a fascinating subject. Every local is an expert, although you will often get a different view from each of them. That's partly down to the micro climates that exist here, so you can experience very different weather even in the same small village, and a lot down to the mighty Bora wind, which is treated with the greatest respect by locals and is notoriously difficult to anticipate. It's less of a problem in the summer, but it can still arrive with little warning and make sailing conditions very uncomfortable indeed. Compounding the problem are isolated local Boras which can just occur in one bay, caused by cold air rushing down the mountains. So, wherever you are, pay attention to the weather forecasts for the area you are in, but always try and ensure that your overnight stop provides protection from the north-east. If the mainland-facing coast of an island has no vegetation, or the trees in a bay are leaning towards the south, take these as signs of a Bora-prone area and avoid overnight stays in all but the most settled of weathers.

The Adriatic coast enjoys a Mediterranean climate, with warm dry summers and wet autumns and winters. Winters can also be cold but the temperature seldom drops below freezing on the coast. Fog is relatively rare in the Adriatic, except in the Gulf of Trieste and the west coast of Istria.

Adriatic weather is particularly affected by anticyclones (high pressure) from the Azores and Siberia, and cyclones and depressions (low pressure) from Iceland. The weather systems are influenced by the geography of the coast but there are essentially three main types of weather – fair settled weather with northwesterly winds, dry cold weather with northerly winds, and humid warm weather with southerly winds. The Maestral (northwesterly) is the predominant wind in the summer months, with the Sirocco (blowing from east-south-east to south-south-east) and Bora (northeasterly) mainly evident between October and April. Southerly winds in general are referred to as the 'Jugo', though Jugo is often used as a direct substitute for the Sirocco, and are much disliked for the effect they have on people. Many, many years ago, it was apparently possible for a prison sentence to be significantly commuted if a crime was committed while

The effects of a particularly strong Bora wind – the locals treat the Bora with the greatest respect

the Jugo was blowing, on the grounds of something similar to diminished responsibility. Now people just complain of headaches.

The northeasterly Bora blows across the land down to the sea. The cold air descends from the mountains towards the sea and can give rise to violent and sudden 'local' Boras, sometimes with gale force strength. In the summer, a Bora may only last for a couple of hours, although may continue for three days. In the winter it can last for much longer and gives rise to a choppy sea rather than large waves. An approaching Bora can be difficult to spot but cloud caps over the highest mountains (Velebit and Biokovo) are an indication. If the cloud cap increases, it's a sign that the Bora is strengthening. If the cloud formations on the peaks move downward and disperse then a Bora can be expected imminently. The Bora blows particularly strongly in the Šibenik and Zadar areas, in Kaštela bay, along the coast between Split and Makarska, and around Pelješac. It's at its worst in the Velebitski Kanal, north-west of Zadar but, in general, loses its strength as it heads across the open sea towards Italy.

The approach of a Sirocco is easier to identify as it is normally accompanied by thick clouds and rain. It can occasionally reach gale force but normally has a strength of up to Force 5. It generally lasts up to three days in summer and nine days in winter. Unlike the Bora, the Sirocco gains strength slowly and blows constantly rather than in gusts.

Maestrals are most common in the summer months and blow from sea to land, effectively following the sun in direction. Starting around 9am, reaching full strength at about 2pm, and dying away by early evening, the Maestral is great for cooling down on a hot summer's day and normally heralds fair weather.

Storms can arise quite quickly during the summer, with little apparent warning, and in a number of weather conditions. Treat them with respect as they can be accompanied by short but violent gusts.

A strong Sirocco/Jugo wind in Kaštela Bay

Of the less prevalent winds, the Lebić or Libeccio, from the south-west, probably causes most problems. It can last for several days, depending on the speed of the accompanying anticyclone, and occasionally causes large waves and reaches gale force.

Indications of a change in the weather for the worse include cirrus clouds moving across a clear sky (wind direction following that of the movement of the clouds); cumulus clouds at dawn; the Sirocco increasing in force in the evening (rain likely); irregularities in the Maestral wind in the summer months, eg, calm at midday or starts late or finishes early; wind from the south-west quadrant, especially at sunset (rain); eastern wind after fair weather; southeasterly wind after fair weather (possible storm); and unusually high sea levels.

Short storms or squalls, known as Neveras, occur mostly between June and September, normally originate from Italy, especially the north, and tend to approach the Croatian coast from the north-west, west or south-west. They can travel at speeds of up to 20 knots and usually bring violent winds, thunder, rain or hail. Neveras can develop very quickly in varied weather conditions and cannot always be forecast in time. Look out for sultry mornings, a hazy sky and clouds building up with high clouds from the north-west. That suggests an afternoon storm. If it remains sultry after the storm, or if there is any kind of wind from the east or south-east, there is likely to be another Nevera the following day. If, however, the Nevera is followed by cooler air and a northwesterly wind the next day, then there is less likely to be another one.

We've witnessed a number of these storms, fortunately mostly from land, and they need to be treated with respect. They can be very localised and some will pass elsewhere, but it's best to take shelter if you suspect one is coming.

Waterspouts (*tromba*) can also occur periodically in the Adriatic, normally in unstable atmospheric conditions, or in otherwise calm weather with thunder clouds in the sky. They look like tall narrow vases opening upwards at the mouth and can travel at speeds of between 0 and 60 knots, but usually blow themselves out after about 6 miles. They mainly approach from the west or south-west and are immediately followed by heavy rain. They can occur anywhere but are most common off the west coast of Istria, around Palagruža, and in the channels of the central Adriatic (between Brač and the mainland, Brač and Hvar, etc). Clearly the best action is to avoid the path of the waterspout by turning at an angle of 90° to it.

SEA TEMPERATURE

Sea temperatures in the Adriatic show the greatest variation in the winter, ranging from 7°C in the north-west to 14°C in the Strait of Otranto, south-east of

Dubrovnik. As you'd expect, the range of fluctuations start to even out in the spring, averaging around 17°C. In the summer, temperatures are between 22°C and 25°C, with temperatures ranging between 14°C and 18°C in the autumn. Maximum temperatures are in July and August, while minimum temperatures are in February.

SEA SWELLS

Heavy or long swells are rare and the sea state is most affected by the Maestral in the summer and by the Bora and Sirocco in the winter. Waves caused by the Sirocco are higher than those resulting from a Bora of similar strength. Wave lengths tend to be shorter than in British waters for a similar speed of wind, but heights are a little higher. The sea state can change quite quickly, going from one area to another. Confused choppy seas often result from a change of wind direction and/or when two channels meet. These can be very uncomfortable and, in severe conditions, dangerous but shelter is normally never very far away.

TIDES AND CURRENTS

Tidal ranges in the Croatian Adriatic are generally so small as to be insignificant. Sea levels are more susceptible to weather (air pressure) than tides. The increase in air pressure caused by a strong persistent Bora or Tramontana may cause a fall in the sea level of up to 0.5m, while strong winds from the south can increase sea levels by up to 1.4m in extreme conditions. Variations are at their most severe in the Northern Adriatic. Given the low sea-walls in many cities, these conditions may cause floods.

In cases of extremes of barometric pressure, a phenomenon called a *seiche* can occur, particularly in enclosed basins of water. Winds running along an enclosed basin can pull up the level of the water at the closed end. If the wind then changes its direction or speed, the equilibrium is restored by oscillations of the sea levels. The severity of the change in levels is determined by the amount the wind speed or direction has changed, while the length of the oscillation depends on the size and topography of the basin. On rare occasions, and notably in bays open to winds from the west, like Stari Grad on Hvar and Vela Luka on Korčula, *seiches* with amplitudes of between 3 and 5m have been reported with oscillation periods of just a few minutes.

Currents also have little impact on navigational safety, averaging 0.5 knots. However, currents can rise up to 4 knots in narrow channels or near river estuaries. Croatians suggest that the surface current is one of the most influential factors in the clarity of their waters with clean water coming in along the Croatian coast, travelling around the north-west head of the Adriatic and flowing out along the Italian coast.

ROUTES

In an ideal world, the less of a fixed itinerary you have, the better your sailing is likely to be as you can pick your destinations according to the conditions. As you will see from this Cruising Companion, in Dalmatia you are never very far away from a safe harbour or a great restaurant, and part of the fun is letting the wind decide where to take you. If you want to plan ahead then the prevailing Maestral in the summer suggests that you start from the north-west end of the area and head south-east along the mainland coast. However, with such a wealth of diverse islands along the coast you are bound to want to explore in all directions. So if you are relatively flexible, our suggestion is that you pick out a few 'must see' destinations, according to your preferences (see pages 5 – 7) and incorporate them into a loose schedule that allows you to explore elsewhere, depending on weather conditions. The sea is generally still warm enough for swimming in late September and early October but clearly the further south you are the warmer it will be.

BUOYAGE

The IALA Buoyage System A has been in place in Croatia for many years and is generally well maintained and provided for. However, there are notable gaps in a small number of areas so it does pay to study the charts well, particularly around the more remote island groups. In contrast, there are some remarkably well-buoyed areas, particularly in some of the shallow channels between islands.

HARBOURS, MARINAS AND ANCHORAGES

The marina industry suffered a little from having been ahead of its time in the early days of development, when yachts were smaller. The tourist board marina brochure lists 49 marinas, although in fact there are now 50. Of these, 45 were officially categorised but only four were given category I status, denoting that they were 'marinas of the highest standard'. Twenty one of the listed marinas form the ACI network, constructed in the mid-sixties, and are owned by the state. These marinas are well located along the coast

The small, unspoilt harbour at Lopud

At anchor in Uvala Rasotica

and islands, and well equipped and managed, but will need to rethink their layouts and facilities if they want to accommodate larger yachts on a regular basis. One of the newest marinas in Croatia, Kaštela Marina, has made a point of including a superyacht pier in its design and construction. Yachts of 10 to 15m (33 to 50ft) in length will generally have no problems berthing in marinas.

Marina rates vary and are generally much cheaper out of the main tourist season. In 2007 the price rise for some marinas was around 15-20%, unusually high for Croatia. Certain daily rates include 'normal' use of electricity and water and some marinas charge extra for all use. From time to time, and sometimes in conjunction with third parties, ACI offers discounts or special rates for using its marinas so it's worth checking its website, www.aci-club.hr, for what's on offer and also for detailed information on approaches, prices and much more. If you need longer term berths, many of the marinas will claim to have a waiting list but it's not too difficult to get into most of them if you persist.

Individual marina facilities are itemised in detail in the text within their section, but as a general guide all marinas have good toilet and shower facilities, a laundry service and rubbish disposal. Almost invariably they also have electricity and water available to all berths, though supplies may be restricted on some of the islands. Electricity connections are normally standard 240 Volt, 16 Amp, and water taps occasionally come with hoses provided, but it's best to take your own. Most have some form of boat lift, crane or hoist and repair facilities, and should be able to tell you where to find a specific facility or service if it exists within the area. Some have fuel stations, supermarkets, cash points, bars and restaurants and a handful, such as Frapa Marina in Rogoznica, have on site deluxe facilities, including swimming pools, nightclubs and apartments. Several of the newer marinas such as Kaštela Marina (between Trogir and Split on the mainland), Olive Island Marina (Sutomišćica Bay on Ugljan Island), Le Meridien's Marina Lav (Podstrana, just outside Split) and NCP Marina Mandalina (Šibenik) have not yet been featured in a selection of the brochures and guides, but full details are included in this Cruising Companion. There are others in the concept stage and several that have been 'planned' for a number of years. However, some new developments may take years to be realised so we have been circumspect with speculation. Readers should note, however, that despite much contrary information on the internet there is, as yet, no Marina Zirona on Drvenik Island and, in spite of a number of stops and starts, Vinišće Marina, near the town of Marina, now appears to be operating.

Some marinas are more popular than others and most marinas have a number of charter companies using annual berths, which means they do sometimes get extremely busy on changeover days – normally weekends – in the middle of summer. Marinas in the big cities such as Dubrovnik and Split can be difficult to get into at any time of year, but at least in the summer the charter boats are out during the week and their berths are available. Most marinas are open throughout the year but a notable few, normally on the more remote islands, are closed in the winter.

The majority of town harbours of any size will provide berths and the bigger ones have electricity and water pedestals available for use, with rubbish disposal facilities never too far away. The day-to-day management of berths and facilities is normally franchised out to a commercial operator, with the harbourmaster retaining responsibility for harbour rules and regulations. Fees vary but are generally about half the price of an equivalent berth in a marina and sometimes, especially out of season, it's not always easy to find someone to take your money from you.

With both marinas and harbours, staff will want to take your passport in order to prepare your invoice and register you for tourist tax. In some cases, you may be able to negotiate a special rate if you are staying for a few days.

Some entrepreneurial restaurant owners in the more popular island destinations have laid down pontoons outside their establishments to facilitate berthing. A few have also installed electricity and water and normally expect no more than that you eat at their restaurant. Occasionally you will find an enterprising boatman acting as a mobile grocery shop and rubbish disposal service.

If you prefer anchoring then you will find few restrictions apart from in National Parks, where only some bays are 'approved', and around the Zadar district (including the Kornati Islands) where there are organised anchorages (many with mooring buoys provided) and you will be required to pay a fee. Again, some restaurants have laid down mooring buoys and will expect you to eat with them if you use their facilities.

Berthing and lazylines

With no major tidal fluctuations to worry about, berthing will almost invariably be on lazylines, whether in a marina, a harbour or on pontoons provided by restaurants. Normally someone will be waiting for you, ready to raise a line out of the water to make pick-up easier. To those readers who have no previous experience of lazylines, berthing is bows- or stern-to. Assuming you intend to moor bows-to, as you approach the berth someone needs to be at the bow end to pick up the line with a boat hook. The line is attached to the shore at one end and runs to a concrete block below the surface of the water, behind where your stern will be, at the other end. Once you've picked up this line, walk around to the stern and pull it in until the thicker rope at the end, attached to the block, is taut, and make this fast to your stern. There will normally be two cleats on the harbour wall or marina pontoon that you can use to secure both sides of your bow.

Anchoring

We include details, wherever possible and relevant, of the reliability of the anchorage, depths, prevailing winds and weather, etc. It is always sensible to take a line ashore where this is practical.

BOAT REPAIRS AND MAINTENANCE

Wherever possible we have included details, within each location, of facilities for repairs and maintenance. There is, as yet, no comprehensive catalogue of repair and maintenance facilities for boats within Croatia, though there must be hundreds of skilled technicians and specialist suppliers working from garages or small outlets all over the country. If you have a specific need then it's best to ask the harbourmaster or a member of the marina staff where the nearest solution can be found. In many cases, the marina itself may be able to help as most have workshops on site. However, below is a selection of suppliers and service providers that we have discovered and this should be of help.

The Dubrovnik ACI Marina. Berthing throughout Croatia is generally bows- or stern-to with lazylines

Engines

AD Mehanic Nautic, ACI Marina Korčula, Tel: 091 507 4635
ABP Diesel, Obala Kralja Tomislava bb, Kaštel Gomilica, Tel: 021 660 454
AD Mehanika, Obala Kneza Branimira 8, Zadar, Tel: 023 305 738
Adriatic Service, Mate Leoni 23, Šibenik, Tel: 098 757 135
Argosy, Iva Dulčića 15, Dubrovnik, Tel: 020 435 005
Basadura, Badnje 9, Tribunj, Tel: 022 446 861
Bilan Ecio, Put Jamin 12, Jezera, Tel: 098 266 031
Boltano, Stinice bb, Split, Tel: 021 490 565
Boltano, Put Kard, Alojzija Stepinca 1, Stari Grad, Hvar Island, Tel: 021 766 211
Brodomehanika, Put Gradine bb, Hramina, Murter Island, Tel: 022 435 950
Cipulin, Silvija S Kranjčevića 7, Vis, Vis Island, Tel: 022 287 527
F Bobek, Put Gaćeleza bb, Vodice, Tel: 022 444 478
Gerry Nautika, Kod Bralića bb, Bibinje-Sukošan, Tel: 023 261 675
Gringo, Vrboska, bb, Vrboska, Hvar Island, Tel: 098 387 878
Honda Marine, Ind Trg Zona bb, Vodice, Tel: 022 443 300
Ive Commerce, Put Blata 28, Kaštel Stari, Tel: 021 231 690
KW Nautik Servis, Obala Kneza Trpimira 61, Zadar, Tel: 023 332 394
Kaštela Auto, Put Kupališta 44, Kaštel Gomilica, Tel: 021 222 880
Matadur, Uvala Baluni 1, Split, Tel: 021 398 561
Moto Marina Servis, Ivana Meštrovića 2, Zadar, Tel: 023 204 870
Nautika Centar Nava, Uvala Baluni 1, Split, Tel: 021 398 430
NCP-Remontno Brodogradilište, Obala Jerka Šižgorića 1, Šibenik, Tel: 022 312 900
Orsan Marin, Ivana Zajca 2, Dubrovnik, Tel: 020 436 147
Polaris Yacht Service, Artina 2, Vodice, Tel: 022 443 021
Servis Bruno, Put Kapelice 9, Trogir, Tel: 021 882 264
V- Marine, Zanatska 1, Kali, Ugljan Island, Tel: 023 282 456

Sails

DB Sails, Sustjepanska Obala 31, Dubrovnik, Tel: 020 450 110
Elvstrom Sails, Uvala Baluni bb, Split, Tel: 021 398 572
Jetto Sails Service, Marina Kornati, Biograd na moru, Tel: 023 384 507
Martin, Eugena Kvaternika 15, Šibenik, Tel: 022 218 830
North Sail, Bana Jelačića 6, Split, Tel: 021 661 156
Olimpic Sails Croatia, S Batušića, Zadar, Tel: 023 340 698
Pinet, Jadranska Cesta 109, Bibinje-Sukošan, Tel: 098 927 5756
Tamara, Ivanje Gomile bb, Stari Grad, Hvar Island, Tel: 021 765 737
UK Sailmakers, Lučica 4, Split, Tel: 091 787 6852

General – boat repair workshops, etc

GBN Marine Service, Agana Marina, Marina, Tel: 021 889 055
Jaht Servis, Marina Kornati, Biograd na moru, Tel: 098 878 068
Nautički Servis, Dražanac 3a, Split, Tel: 021 314 300
NCP – see engines

Accessories

Bocel, Peričićeva 12, Split, Tel: 021 389 795
Hermes Nautica, Obala Kneza Branimira 28, Zadar, Tel: 023 205 189
Nautica Vis, Vukovarska 10, Vis, Vis Island, Tel: 091 584 0126
Orka Korčula, Kovački Prolaz 7, Korčula, Korčula Island, Tel: 020 715 121
Penul – in most major cities and distributors of Croatian charts – go to www.hhi.hr for a list of contacts

Electrical appliances

Brodel, Sradinska 5, Split, Tel: 021 453 258
CTM, Liechtensteinov Put 28, Dubrovnik, Tel: 020 456 290
Riz-Itea, K Branimira 18, Zadar, Tel: 023 305 777
Tea-Nautes, Marina Kornati, Biograd na moru, Tel: 023 385 656

Electronic equipment

ETS, Put Brodarice 2, Split, Tel: 021 332 477
Kimer, Vladimira Nazora 47, Šibenik, Tel: 022 212 118
Pomorski Centar za Elektroniku, Zrinsko-frankopanska bb, Split, Tel: 021 361 463

Refrigerators and air-conditioning

Sea Way Co, Obala Hrvatske Mornarice 1, Šibenik, Tel: 022 212 055
Srđan Karuza, Matije Gupca 14, Vis, Vis Island, Tel: 091 251 0266

FUEL

Fuel stations are reasonably well scattered along the coast and around the islands and we've supplied full details in the text. Opening hours vary and change between summer and winter, but most are open between 0600 to 2200, seven days a week in high summer, though some may restrict opening hours on Sundays and Bank Holidays. We've included telephone numbers so that you can check opening times and any special requirements. The majority of fuel stations take most credit cards and supply most types of fuel.

A new fuel station at Sumartin on Brač Island

LANGUAGE

Croatian is a southern Slavonic language and not too dissimilar to Russian, an eastern Slavonic language. A number of different dialects are spoken around the country and it is not a language that an average adult can expect to pick up quickly. However, it is an easy language to spell and pronounce once you know the rules, as each letter is pronounced and the pronunciation is generally consistent.

Fortunately most Croatians, especially those involved in the marine industry, speak good English and almost all marina staff and harbourmasters will very happily converse freely in English. For Croatians aged 50 and older, the first foreign language is normally German; for younger generations it is English.

While it is not necessary to know any Croatian, understanding the alphabet will help you pronounce place names and use dictionaries. Mastery of a few basic phrases will bring great pleasure to your hosts.

For the purposes of this book, we have used the Croatian alphabet for proper names as this will help readers pronounce them correctly. For indexing purposes, for ease of use, we have grouped all 'c's' together rather than following the strictly correct Croatian practice of listing, for example, 'c', 'č' and 'ć' separately.

There are 30 'letters' in the alphabet. These are listed below, with some tips on pronunciation where it differs markedly from English pronunciation. The emphasis on syllables is also a little different from English. In words of two syllables, the stressed syllable is always the first but otherwise it's just a question of listening to the patterns.

The glossary on page 250 incorporates a few standard useful words and phrases that will at least help you to get started, along with a few more specialised phrases that you are unlikely to need but will impress your hosts.

Letter	Pronunciation
A	like the 'a' in 'cat'
B	similar to English pronunciation
C	like the 'ts' in 'hats'
Č	like the 'ch' in 'chink' eg, čarape = socks, pronounced charaper
Ć	like the 'tch' in 'catch' – slightly softer than č
D	similar to English pronunciation
Dž	like the 'j' in 'judge' eg, džip = jeep; džemper = jumper (pronounced jemper)
Đ	like the 'g' in 'page' – softer than dž
E	like the 'e' in 'fell'
F	similar to English pronunciation
G	like the 'g' in 'golf'
H	a guttural sound like the 'ch' in 'loch'
I	like the 'ee' in 'yippee'
J	like the 'y' in 'yahoo'
K	like the 'c' in 'cap'
L	similar to English pronunciation
Lj	like the 'll' in 'millionaire'
M	similar to English pronunciation
N	similar to English pronunciation
Nj	like the 'ny' in 'canyon'
O	like the 'o' in 'tot'
P	similar to English pronunciation
R	always 'rolled'
S	like the 's' in 'sing'
Š	like the 'sh' in 'shine'
T	similar to English pronunciation
U	like the 'oo' in 'moo'
V	similar to English pronunciation
Z	like the 'z' in 'crazy'
Ž	like the 's' in 'pleasure'

COMMUNICATIONS

VHF communications are covered on page 8. In the age of mobile telephones, readers will be pleased to note that this industry is probably further advanced than landline telephony in Croatia. Despite the nearby mountains, you can get a good mobile phone signal almost anywhere in Croatia, though the downside is that diverted calls on a UK mobile will be quite expensive. If you intend to use a mobile phone heavily in Croatia it may be worth investing in a Croatian handset (£60 to £90) and taking one of the pay-as-you go packages. Also note that contact details for hotels, restaurants, tourist offices, etc, frequently give a mobile number (09...) as a contact telephone number, instead of, or as well as, a landline number. This is partly because the size of most operations is quite small and

therefore the main office is not always manned, and partly because Croatians tend to use their mobiles much more than landlines.

Telephone kiosks can be found almost everywhere. The most isolated villages tend to have a kiosk and a bus timetable even if there is nothing else. However, you can make calls more cheaply from a post office. In this companion we have given landline telephone numbers in the following format: 021 203 020, where 021 is the local dialling code, in this case the Split region, and 203 020 is the local number. If you are dialling from abroad or using a foreign mobile, you will need the international dialling code for Croatia, which is 00 385, followed by the code without the zero, followed by the number, ie, 00 385 21 203 020. If you are dialling from a Croatian mobile anywhere in Croatia, or from a landline outside the Split region, you should dial the full number with code, ie, 021 203 020. If you are dialling from a landline within the Split area in this example, you just dial the last six digits, ie, 203 020. More generally, using a landline, if the code of the number you are dialling is the same as the code of the number you are dialling from, then drop the first three digits/local code. Zagreb, the capital city, is the exception to a three-digit area code, having just two digits – 01.

Croatian mobile numbers always have 09 as the first two digits and wherever you are within Croatia, regardless of whether you are dialling from a landline or a mobile, you will need to dial the full number.
In summary:

Landline number	**021 203 020**
00 385 21 203 020	If dialling from abroad or using a non-Croatian mobile.
021 203 020	If dialling from a landline outside the 021 area or from a Croatian mobile anywhere in Croatia.
203 020	If dialling from within the 021 area on a landline.
Mobile number	**098 953 8162**
00 385 98 953 8162	If dialling from abroad or using a non-Croatian mobile.
098 953 8162	If dialling from a Croatian landline or mobile anywhere.

NB Please do not practise on the above numbers as we have made them up and they may well belong to someone who may not appreciate your call!

Emergency numbers, such as police, ambulance, etc are normally given as if dialling from a Croatian phone. For example the telephone number quoted for police is 92. If you are dialling from abroad or on a non-UK mobile, you will need to dial 00 385 1 92. The 1 is for Zagreb (dialling code 01).

Internet

The internet is reasonably well developed within Croatia, although only the newer hotels have rooms equipped for internet connection or internet facilities. Wireless internet access is becoming increasingly available at marinas and there is generally an internet café in the larger settlements. However, it is only a year or so ago that we used to struggle to log on in our travels around the country, sometimes having to use the phone line of local restaurants. Though the situation is improving quickly, don't rely on being able to log on around the less developed areas.

The telecoms industry in Croatia has been subject to a number of takeovers and mergers like everywhere else. This has meant frequent changes to email addresses as

each change of ownership has resulted in rebranding. T-com is the current owner of the main network, prior to which it was HTnet and before that Hinet. Old email addresses still appear in many of the tourist guides and leaflets and we have updated these where the old email address would have been inaccessible. If you see the following format of email addresses, you can change them as follows:
abc-address@zd.tel.hr or abc-address@zd.hinet.hr both become abc-address@zd.htnet.hr

In fact, the more correct email address would be abc-address@zd.t-com.hr but, as email addresses have only recently just changed to 't-com', and as we have been assured by T-com that in view of so many changes over the last few years 'htnet' addresses will be valid indefinitely and interchangeable with t-com addresses, which are otherwise identical, we have left all email addresses in the htnet format.

CURRENCY

The Kuna is the official currency of Croatia (literally 'marten', the bird). The Kuna is subdivided into 100 Lipa (literally 'linden-tree' or 'lime-tree') but you will rarely see prices in anything other than whole Kuna. The exchange rate of roughly 10.5 Kuna to £1 has been relatively stable over the past few years but the value of the Kuna is more directly linked to the Euro with occasional central bank intervention to prop it up or weaken it in line with the Euro. The natural tendency is for the Kuna to become stronger in the summer months, at the height of the tourist season, though again the central bank tries to smooth out this peak to ensure tourists do not suffer markedly higher prices than they are expecting.

Cash machines are ubiquitous, except in unpopulated areas and the most deserted islands. Even the smallest settlements have post offices where you can easily change money or withdraw cash on debit or credit cards. Cash is still king in Croatia and a higher proportion of restaurants, bars, etc, than in the UK will not take credit cards. If you're exploring the more remote islands then don't count on any of the local traders taking anything other than cash. Euros are widely accepted and in many cases prices are quoted only in Euros. Sterling is also accepted in some places.

Cash machines are reasonably widespread in Croatia

The banks in Croatia are still a little bureaucratic, though it's easier to open a bank account than in many other places, provided you have a fixed address. International transfers from Croatia are still subject to some exchange controls, particularly from business accounts, and you generally need to open a separate account for each currency in which you want to transact money. Cheques do not really exist – if you want to make a payment by post and the recipient does not take credit cards, then you need to go to the post office, hand over the money and fill in a type of giro credit form which you can then send off. If you want to change money at a bank then you will almost invariably be asked to produce your passport.

TRANSPORT

If you're looking for a good one-stop shop to try and plan your travel to Croatia, Visit Croatia has a very easy-to-follow travel section with most of the information you might need – www.visit-croatia.co.uk. Of course the situation is dynamic and ever-changing, so below are general details with other useful sources to get the most up-to-date information. The website www.croatiaonline.blogspot.com is also a good means of finding out the latest travel and destination news.

By air

The Croatian skies have at last opened up. In 2003 Croatia Airways was the only carrier operating all year round from Split with very few direct flights to the UK, especially outside the summer season. Now British Airways, Wizz Air, easyJet, Ryanair and a whole host of other airlines are operating and increasing their scheduled routes to Croatia, not to mention the myriad charter and tour operators that appear in the summer.

As we write in early spring 2007, Ryanair has just announced that it will be operating flights to Zadar airport, so far largely overlooked. Zadar aside, the major international airports are the country's hub in the capital city of Zagreb as well as Split and Dubrovnik along the coast. Pula and Rijeka, in the north, now also have international low-cost flights and there are smaller airports at Osijek and on Brač Island.

Split is probably the ideal airport for accessing the best of the sailing areas, with a number of marinas and charter operations within an hour's drive. The new marina in Kaštela is just 10 minutes away from Split airport and 20 minutes from Split city centre. From here, Hvar, Brač and Vis are all within easy sailing range, as well as a number of smaller islands. From Dubrovnik, the Elaphite Islands, Korčula and Mljet are within easy reach, but the neighbouring settlements on the mainland are arguably of less interest. With Zadar now more accessible by air, this is the best airport for reaching Zadar Town and Biograd, good starting bases for the Kornati Islands and the smaller undiscovered islands around Šibenik. Bear in mind that public transport from airports to the city, and vice

Zadar airport – Ryanair's latest Croatian destination

versa, is not always straightforward and Split can be a particular problem. Croatia Airlines lays on buses but these are normally timed to coincide with the airline's departures and arrivals. This year, however, we're told that they will also be meeting other airline departures and arrivals.

Internal flights within Croatia, using Croatia Airlines, are relatively inexpensive, especially outside the business peak days of Monday and Friday, so that's another option. Don't overlook Croatia Airlines either when trying to get a good deal in the summer at relatively short notice. While British Airways and the low-cost airlines can ratchet up their prices in the peak season, Croatia Airlines may have seats available at more reasonable prices.

Below are a selection of websites and UK telephone numbers for some of the carriers:

Croatia Airlines	www.croatiaairlines.com Tel: 020 870 4100 310
British Airways	www.britishairways.com Tel: 0870 850 9 850
easyJet	www.easyjet.com Tel: 0905 821 0905
Wizz Air	www.wizzair.com see website for call centres
Ryanair	www.ryanair.com Tel: 0871 246 0000

For airport information, including travel links to town and scheduled flights online, each airport has its own website which we have listed below, together with the Croatian telephone number.

Zagreb	www.zagreb-airport.hr Tel: 01 456 222
Split	www.split-airport.hr Tel: 021 203 555
Dubrovnik	www.airport-dubrovnik.hr Tel: 020 773 333
Zadar	www.zadar-airport.hr Tel: 023 205 800
Pula	www.airport-pula.hr Tel: 052 530 105
Rijeka	www.rijeka-airport.hr Tel: 051 842 040

By rail

The mountainous terrain and other factors mean that the railway system is not particularly well developed. Coaches are often faster and more comfortable and are the preferred means of national long-distance travel. However, new 'bendy' trains are being brought in and the system is gradually being improved.

There are direct international connections, mostly from Zagreb, with Bosnia and Hercegovina, Serbia, Montenegro, Slovenia, Germany, Austria, Hungary and Italy. Within Croatia there are links between Split, Zagreb and Rijeka, but there are no trains along the coast between Split and Dubrovnik. Croatian Railways has a website, www.hznet.hr, where you will find a network map if you look hard enough. That's probably the best place to start to decide whether it's worth contemplating using rail transport for your journey. You can search the timetable online or call 060 333 444 for more information.

By sea – ferry

This can be one of the most overlooked forms of long-distance travel within Croatia by visitors. We regularly use the overnight ferry from Split to Rijeka to get a head start on the day and cut down on driving and hotel costs. There are regular ferries up and down the coastline as well as internationally to Italy and, of course, connecting the many islands to the mainland and vice versa. The government-owned ferry line Jadrolinija is heavily subsidised to attempt to provide a regular service to the inhabitants of all the islands. The schedules tend to be geared to islanders who work on the mainland rather than visiting tourists, but additional services in the summer cope reasonably well with the crowds. As well as Jadrolinija, there are a number of Italian companies that operate services and some smaller local private organisations on specific routes. For short trips to the islands in the summer season, there are plenty of agencies and local operators who will compete for your fares. Some of the main websites and Croatian telephone numbers are included below:

Jadrolinija	www.jadrolinija.hr Tel: 051 666 111
SEM Marina (Blue Line)	www.sem-marina.hr Tel: 021 352 533
Venezia Lines	www.venezialines.com Tel: 060 351 351
Snav	www.snav.it Tel: 021 322 252

By road – general

Croatia's first motorway was opened in June 2005 and connects Zagreb with Split. It's a remarkable feat of engineering, given the country's mountainous geography, and appears to have been a great success, although it can become very congested at peak weekends. There's a toll system, plenty of tunnels, generally well-netted rocks and a number of good motorway services. The Krka service station is a particularly interesting stop-off point as you get a great view of Skradin marina, up the Krka river, as well as a good restaurant for lunch.

Before the construction of the motorway, the main option for travelling by road along the coast was the Magistrale, a windy (sometimes in both senses of the word), mostly single carriageway. The views in some places are spectacular, but a long journey along this road is not for those of a nervous disposition. The cliffs drop away vertically to the sea very close to you in many places, sometimes with no crash barrier for comfort, and Croatian drivers are not always too cautious when attempting to overtake. Local Croatian roads can leave a lot to be desired and the signage is not always comprehensive, although it is improving. You can therefore find yourself quite unexpectedly at a dead end or in a very narrow street that was probably designed for much smaller modes of transport than yours!

Croatia has quite recently toughened up on its driving laws from a fairly *laissez-faire* approach. Seat-belts are now compulsory, you must have dipped headlights on at all times, there is zero tolerance to

Another car ferry heading into Zadar's busy port

drinking and driving and the use of mobile phones is not permitted while driving. There are also quite strict requirements about what safety equipment you need to carry. Speed limits are relatively low in certain areas and tightly enforced by police with speed cameras who will levy on-the-spot fines for speeding and other traffic regulation infringements. In certain cases we have heard that the size of the fine can be negotiated, but it's best to carry enough cash around to pay them immediately as the alternative might be having your passport taken and appearing at a local court in a few days time. The average fine is around 200 Kunas, approximately £20. In the case of an accident, especially if someone has been injured, call the police and, unless totally unavoidable, do not move your car.

The Croatian Automobile Club has an informative website – www.hak.hr – including details on fuel and toll prices, current traffic conditions, route advice, radio stations that give traffic reports in English and ferry information. If you are unlucky enough to break down in Croatia, it provides roadside assistance at various standard prices depending on distance and whether a repair is practical or the vehicle needs to be towed. A list of prices is on the website. For roadside assistance, call 987 (or 00 385 1 987 if dialling from abroad or from a non-Croatian mobile phone).

If you're travelling in your own car, the considerations are the same as crossing most international borders, and you may be able to buy the relevant green card at the frontier crossing. Make sure you keep your insurance documents and driving licence with you as the police will want to inspect them if you get stopped for an offence or just a routine paperwork check.

By road – car hire

If you're thinking of hiring a car then Croatia is not cheap. Holiday Autos, part of lastminute.com, has bases in the main towns and seems to provide good value for money – www.holidayautos.co.uk, Tel: (UK) 0870 400 4461. Most of the international organisations such as Avis, Thrifty and Dollar operate in Croatia. If you are booking a hire car locally, head for the nearest airport, if that's practical, or get a selection of local operators from the ubiquitous tourist board offices.

By road – fuel

Petrol prices in Croatia are generally cheaper than in the UK though petrol stations are perhaps not quite so widespread and not all, even on the main roads, are open 24 hours a day. The more usual opening times are 0700 to 0100.

By road – coach

The national coach network is generally faster and more comfortable than the train, with all the main

coastal towns connected by coach. We tend to use our local Atlas travel agency to find out the times and to book our journeys, but any tourist office should be able to help you out. Note that it's often easier to travel between neighbouring towns by coach rather than bus. For example, you can get between Trogir and Split using both forms of transport but the coach takes the main coastal road and has no stops in between, whereas the bus takes the local road and stops frequently. You can travel internationally by coach but journey times are long.

By road – bus

A number of different companies operate the bus routes and their websites are not often in English. www.ak-split.hr is an exception and will give you an idea of the Split service. However, bus timetable posters are pinned up in key points, even in the most isolated of villages.

By road – taxis

The normal caution applies when getting a taxi in a foreign country. Mostly there should be a taxi sign somewhere on the car and it's preferable to ask for an idea of the cost before you embark on your journey. Croatian taxis are not particularly cheap and can sometimes be hard to find – in some small villages, they're just one-man bands. Ask staff at the local tourist office if they have a particular favourite or head for the main transport link stations in bigger towns. Not all taxi drivers speak English so if you can get a number from the local tourist office, hotel or restaurant, ask them to make the call for you.

By road – motorbike or scooter

Almost all the local tourist agencies operate or have links with a scooter hire company and that's probably the best way of exploring short distances onshore. Pay no attention to the blasé attitude of many locals who drive around without crash helmets, sometimes talking away on their mobile, and occasionally with a young child 'on board'. They tend to know when the police are making spot checks on all these illegal activities and you generally don't!

By road – bicycle

Not recommended for anything other than short trips or for fitness fanatics on account of the severe gradients almost everywhere. The Croatian Tourist Board site, www.croatia.hr, has a special section on cycling for those who want to incorporate it into their sailing holiday. Bikes are cheap to buy in Croatia so that might be a better bet than hiring. Finally, note that while petty crime in Croatia is rare, bicycles do go missing from tourist centres.

By road – walking

Better saved for exploring the National Parks or walking round small settlements. Croatian roads are not designed with walkers in mind and many have no pavements, with narrow single lane carriageways, not much of a hard shoulder and sometimes a steep drop nearby.

PROVISIONING

Opening hours

Opening hours vary widely, according to the season, the size of the settlement and the whim of the shop owner. Opening hours for the larger supermarket chains are more reliable, but for the smaller shops you need to check out any handwritten or, sometimes, printed note on the door and don't expect these to be cast in tablets of stone. In the summer, shops may open for a few hours in the morning, eg, 0800 to 1200, and then close for siesta time until around 1600, normally staying open until 2000. Saturday is usually a half day, with shops and post offices typically closing around 1300. The rules on Sunday trading have followed the pattern established some years ago in the UK – for a while everywhere was open, then the government tried to enforce closing and now it's a bit of a free-for-all with a tendency to open late and close early. Some shops (and restaurants) may close on a Monday – either for just the morning or all day. As stated earlier, opening times vary according to the time of year and shops are most accessible in the height of the tourist season. However, the length of the season varies from place to place and between

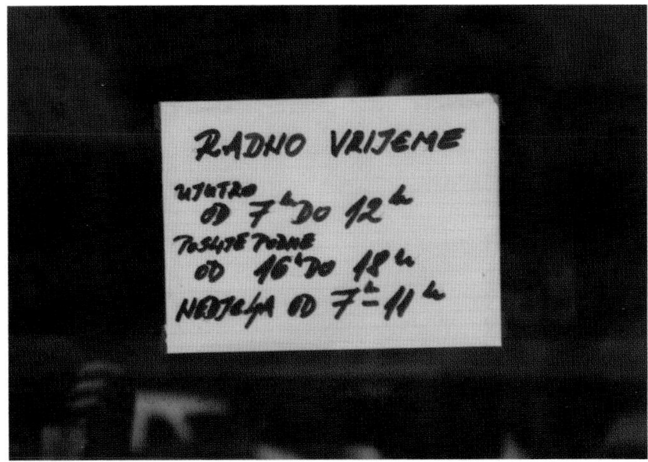

individual retail outlets. As a rule of thumb, the most generally held dates for 'the season' in bigger towns are from 1 June to 30 September. For smaller settlements that effectively only come to life to serve tourists, the season can be as short as from mid-July to the end of August. In many cases 'the season' may end when the owner is exhausted and thinks he has earned enough money for the year. No doubt, with the opening up of the Croatian skies all year round, the season will extend everywhere but it's likely to be a slow process.

Because of the unpredictability of opening times, together with the regularity at which they seem to change, we have been circumspect in providing too much detailed information in the body of this book. Where such information has been given, it may well have changed and is intended as a guide only.

PRODUCE AND AVAILABILITY

Fruit and vegetables

Croatia is a nation of small holders and great tasting fresh produce is widely available if you know where

A small section of Split's vibrant open-air market

to look. The best places for fresh fruit and vegetables are the markets (*'tržnica'*). In big cities and towns like Dubrovnik, Split and Trogir, these are open seven days a week. The hypermarket selections of fruit and vegetables are reasonable, with increasing amounts of imported produce, but the medium-sized supermarkets do not offer a great choice in terms of quality or range. Also keep an eye-out for sole traders on the roadside but, as with the markets, try to find out the price before you commit. In most places you'll generally have to accept whatever is in season, although the hypermarkets may offer a larger choice. Fruit and vegetables are generally much cheaper than in the UK but watch out for the occasional greedy market trader.

Fish

The Adriatic is, like most seas, not as abundant in fish as it once was but most of the restaurants have a tame local fisherman who brings them a regular catch of Class 1 fish. There are fish markets in the larger towns – if these are not a daily event then Thur, Fri and Sat seem to be the most popular days. As for the supermarkets, they generally tend to have a good selection (especially on Thursdays) or none at all. Prices are a little cheaper than in the UK. Some of the fish available is farmed (Class 2).

Meat

There's not much difference between the price of UK meat and its Croatian equivalent, although the cuts can be quite different. Beef has less flavour than in the UK as it tends to be very young meat that has not been hung. The medium-sized supermarkets generally have mince, chicken breasts and sausages; the larger hypermarkets usually have a good range and their own butcher's counter. There are plenty of small local butcher's shops (*'mesnica'*) around if you are brave enough to try and specify exactly what you want.

Bread and cakes

Almost every village, no matter how small, has its own bakery (*'pekarnica'*) with fresh bread and cakes made or delivered daily. White bread in large loaves is the most common, but you can ask for a half (*'pola'*). Bread is very cheap.

Dairy

Local cheeses are varied and good, and foreign cheeses (with the exception of English ones) are generally available. There's little fresh milk around but you can buy homogenised in varying types, roughly equivalent to skimmed, semi-skimmed and full fat. Croatian eggs

Fishermen at work. The Dalmatian Coast, with its numerous islands, is an area well known for its wide variety of fish

are special and the UK equivalent will seem pale and flavourless in comparison.

Local specialities

In Dalmatia, plain grilled fish and meat predominates. However, look out for *'prsut'*, the local smoked ham, similar to Palma ham but often a little chewier. Good local cheeses are *'livno'* and *'paški'*. Grilled squid and octopus salad are local favourites, as is black risotto.

Wines and spirits

Croatian wine is generally inexpensive but varies greatly in quality. We've found a couple of local brands at about 20 Kunas a litre (£2), which are very drinkable and there are some more expensive ones which would give medium-priced French brands a good run for their money. You'll find a number of home-made wines in the market or on little stalls outside houses. Some of them are fine, but ask to taste them first. There's not too much in the way of imported wines on the shelves and where there is it's generally from Germany or Italy. If you like dessert wines or sweet martini, try the local Prošek at about 45 Kunas a litre.

Foreign imported spirits are about the same price as in the UK. Reasonable local brandies such as Stock are about 75 Kunas a litre, with home-made versions also available. Rakija and Travarica can taste a little like fire water to start with and are often offered free before or after a meal.

POST OFFICES (HRVATSKA POŠTA OR HP)

The Croatian post office network may make you nostalgic for how the UK system worked many years ago. If there are no other facilities in a small settlement there will be a post office – very soon after our arrival in Croatia we learnt to judge the size of a settlement that we didn't know, and how big its summer tourism industry was likely to be, by the opening hours in the on and off seasons. Apart from buying stamps and sending letters, you can make cheap phone calls, change money, withdraw cash on your credit card, pay bills, send money by giro and often buy a mobile phone. Note that there are normally separate booths for stamps, so before you join a long queue in a city post office, check that you're in the right one.

We've provided quite a lot of detail on opening times in the text as these can normally be counted on and the post office may be the only facility in the more remote settlements. The details include off-season and on-season opening times, though the definition of 'the season' again varies from area to area. Usually 'the season' is from around mid-June to mid-September, but for some outlets it's just July and August. The website www.posta.hr has English pages, including details of all the services and locations of post offices as well as a zip file of postcodes.

TISAKS OR KIOSKS

You will see *Tisaks* or newspaper kiosks all around Croatia. Apart from newspapers, they sell tobacco, sweets and telephone cards. In the summer, in the larger towns and villages, many of them have foreign newspapers, though these are normally a couple of days old and cost between 30 and 40 Kunas.

TOBACCO

If you are a smoker, cigarettes in Croatia cost between 15 and 20 Kunas per packet with the local brands being cheaper. Croatia is beginning to go the way of western Europe in terms of smoking in public places but has a long way to go. At the moment you're challenged to find no-smoking areas in restaurants or bars and if you do, enforcement is not always strict. However, given that eating and drinking takes place mostly outdoors in the summer, non-smokers should not despair.

RESTAURANTS AND BARS

Croatia abounds with restaurants and bars in the summer, a few of which stay open all year round. Bars normally do not sell any kind of food or snacks and it's quite acceptable to take your croissant from the bakery along with you to eat with your morning coffee. In many places it's difficult to find somewhere to sit down for just a sandwich or a snack, but there are plenty of fast food kiosks around for takeaways. Croatian coffee is very good, with several varieties to choose from.

Restaurants come in many shapes and sizes, from the cosy informal *'konobas'* to the more formal *'restorans'*. On some islands you will just find makeshift shacks. Plain grilled fish or meat is the Dalmatian norm, although several new restaurants are becoming a little more adventurous with sauces and international cuisine. Don't, however, expect the scampi you order to turn up in breadcrumbs like it does in England – whether it arrives plain or in tomato sauce (*buzara*), you will normally have to remove the shells yourself. There

The impressive view from Restaurant Foša, Zadar

A café in Trogir's ACI marina complex overlooking Kamerlengo Castle

are pizzerias everywhere and the pizzas are normally of very good quality and value. The pastas are perhaps slightly less appealing compared to western European standards.

You can eat out in Croatia for much less than in the UK. Typically a main course, coffees and wine for two will cost around 200 Kunas (about £20). If you have steaks, starters and especially fish, expect to pay more. Octopus salad or black risotto are favourite starters and the choice of desserts is normally either pancakes or ice-cream.

Fish is sold by the kilo, with a typical large fish for one weighing just under half a kilo. Fish prices are higher on the islands and can be open to manipulation. Try and pin down the price of your fish before you commit – most restaurants will let you pick your individual fish and then weigh it for you. Finally, on choosing fish, there are normally three menu options – Class 1 is generally used to mean fresh fish caught locally the same day, Class 2 usually implies farmed or imported frozen fish and small fish means what it says – a small selection of smaller fish.

Croatian restaurateurs are on the whole an honest and straightforward breed but, as anywhere, there are a few exceptions, usually in highly-developed tourist areas where there is a lot of competition for passing trade. The areas most rife for exploitation are wine, where you may be served an expensive bottle when you really want the local (*domaći*) wine, normally served in a carafe, fish (see above) and water. Partly down to the German influence, restaurants have a tendency to assume tourists want bottled water unless you clearly specify otherwise. Croatian tap water is highly drinkable almost everywhere except on the remotest island with no mains or local water supply. We've tried all sorts of gestures and requests to ensure that we get local tap water and finally discovered that the only almost foolproof way of getting it is to ask for '*voda iz spina*', literally water from the tap. After five years in Croatia, eating out regularly all around the country, we've only had a couple of occasions when we believe a deliberate attempt was made to inflate the bill. The embarrassed proprietor quickly made the necessary adjustment, but might well be tempted to try again another time.

Expect to leave a tip of around 10% if you are happy with your service and don't be afraid to ask for advice on what the owner recommends, though it will normally be fish, which just happens to be the most expensive item on the menu. If you're a late eater, be aware that not many restaurants stay open past 11pm or 12am in the smaller towns and the coffee machines in the bars tend to get switched off early. Similarly, there won't be too many bars open if you want to go partying into the small hours.

CLUBS AND NIGHTLIFE

Thankfully, so far, Croatia has resisted the temptation to go down the Ibiza route. You'll often hear a cacophony of music from adjacent bars playing different radio stations but generally not disco music all night long, although occasionally the summer festivals can be noisy. If you're into nightlife then Hvar is the party town, with more modest offerings available in the big cities. Some of the best clubs in Croatia include Aurora, near Primošten, The Garden in Zadar, and Hacienda in Vodice.

SUMMER FESTIVALS

Almost every Dalmatian coastal settlement with a tourist industry has a summer festival of some sort, usually in the height of the tourist season from mid-July to the end of August. The local Klapa Music is a favourite feature – multi-part male harmony singing, usually unaccompanied – but you may also find theatre, disco, rock and roll and jazz. The local tourist board is the best source of information and it's also worth finding out from them when the local saints day is as that's normally a big event.

BEACHES

Most of Croatia's beaches consist of pebbles, although there are a few sandy ones about. Those in any tourist settlement of any size mainly have roped-off swimming areas in the summer and a beach bar or two plus a restaurant. Increasingly portable changing rooms and toilets are provided and most have a freshwater shower. Watersports on a serious scale only take place in a few areas, particularly Bol on Brač, and you won't hear too much throbbing from jet ski engines as you head around the coast. Naturism is quite popular in Croatia with many designated separate beaches. See the Health section on page 27 for the few hazards to watch out for and look at www.croatia-beaches.com for the complete lowdown on beaches.

PUBLIC HOLIDAYS

Some bank holidays seem to pass by without much of a change in day-to-day life, while others are observed fervently and almost everything closes. Most settlements have their own local saint's day, which are normally celebrated on a grand scale. Below are the national public holidays:

1 January	New Year's Day
6 January	Epiphany
March or April	Easter Sunday
March or April	Easter Monday
1 May	Labour Day
May (variable dates)	Corpus Christi
22 June	Anti-Fascist Resistance Day (commemorating 1941 Anti-Fascist Uprising)
25 June	National Day
5 August	Known locally as Victory Day (the Homeland War), described with more political correctness as National Thanksgiving Day
15 August	Assumption
8 October	Independence Day
1 November	All Saints Day
25 December	Christmas Holiday
26 December	Christmas Holiday

One of Croatia's most popular beaches at Bol on Brač Island

DOCUMENTATION AND VISAS; RULES AND REGULATIONS

General

You do not need a visa to travel to Croatia if you have an EU, Canadian, American, Australian or New Zealand passport, but you will need official permission to stay there for more than three months or to work at any time. That means going to your local police station for the relevant forms and obtaining various certificates from the UK. Wherever you stay – in a hotel, with friends or on a boat – you must be registered with the police as a visitor and pay your tourist tax. If staying in a hotel or on a charter holiday, the hotel or charter company will register you and include the tourist tax in their charges. If you are travelling independently, it is your responsibility to register at the nearest police station, though if you stay at a marina or at one of the larger ports, tourist tax and registration will often be included within the overnight mooring fee. Historically these regulations have not always been strictly enforced but we are increasingly hearing that this is going to change.

Foreign vessels entering Croatian waters

Foreign vessels may not engage in 'cabotage', the commercial transport of goods and/or passengers. See page 7 for the effects of the new regulations on foreign vessels. The regulations change fairly frequently in detail and their interpretation, but the government website www.pomorstvo.hr should have the latest information. However, below is a brief summary of the current requirements:

On entering Croatian waters you must take the shortest route to the nearest port of entry to obtain a 'vignette' from the harbourmaster's office. This vignette must be valid for as long as the vessel remains in Croatian waters, up to a maximum of one year, and will be issued on presentation and inspection of the documents listed below. Vignettes are not required for vessels under 2.5m (8ft 2in) in length, those with an engine power of less than 2.5kW, kayaks, canoes and rowing boats, vessels left in a marina or harbour, or vessels attending a bona fide sports competition or nautical fair.

1. Crew list

This will be certified by the harbourmaster. Boats not equipped for overnight stays on board are exempt from the requirement for a crew list.

2. List of persons

This should contain the names of everyone who is intended to be on board for the period of the validity of the vignette. Children under the age of 12 do not need to be listed and do not count towards the total. The total number of persons shall not exceed 2.3 times the maximum carrying capacity of the vessel as determined by its documents. Visitors to the boat while moored or at anchor need not be entered and it is possible to update the list of persons at a later date, although changes must be made and certified by the harbourmaster as soon as a new person embarks. If an inspection results in a discrepancy then the vessel will be deemed to be engaging in cabotage.

3. Certificate of seaworthiness

This should be drawn up in accordance with the national regulations of the flag state. In the absence of a certificate, the harbourmaster will carry out an inspection and may well charge for this.

4. Certification of skipper's competence

Drawn up in accordance with the national regulations of the flag state. If the flag state does not require a competence certificate, and there is no suitable alternative, the skipper needs to obtain the appropriate Croatian certificate of competence. The skipper must also have a VHF licence or equivalent and VHF systems are compulsory.

5. Certificate of insurance

6. Certificate of ownership

Fees for the vignette include a safety of navigation fee, light dues (use of navigational lighting), information chart and government administration fee. In 2007 a vignette for a 12m (39ft) boat cost 1,716 Kunas and a 15m (49ft) boat cost 2,060 Kunas. A 10% discount is available for annual consecutive renewals up to a maximum of 50%.

Foreign vessels leaving Croatian waters

The skipper must pass through the border control and have the crew list certified by the nearest HM.

General maritime rules

Motor boats and yachts should cruise at least 50m (164ft) away from the shore where there is no beach, 50m (164ft) away from the seaward perimeter of roped-off swimming areas and 150m (492ft) away from beaches. Swimming is not allowed at a distance of more than 100m (328ft) from the coast.

Although there are extremely limited pump-out facilities as yet, discharge into the sea is apparently forbidden. In practice, however, discharge into the open sea, away from beaches, is unlikely to be challenged.

Divers require a valid diver's card issued by the Croatian Diving Federation and a licence is also needed for fishing. Special rules apply in some passages and in National Parks. These are highlighted, where applicable, in the main text.

Consulates and embassies

The British Embassy is in Zagreb and there are Consulates in Split and Dubrovnik. **Split (Riva):** Obala Hrvatskog Narodnog Preporoda 10/3, 21000 Split, Croatia, Tel: 021 341 464, Fax: 021 362 905, email: british-consular-st@st.htnet.hr. **Dubrovnik:** Bunićeva Poljana 3, 2000 Dubrovnik, Tel/fax: 020 324 597, email: honcons.dubrovnik@inet.hr.

Customs

Customs formalities are generally pretty straightforward but you should have all the information and documentation available that you would need for the harbourmaster plus a list of anything you have to declare. If you are a non-Croatian national using your boat for private/pleasure purposes you are effectively temporarily importing your boat into Croatia. Briefly, the rules are that you can use your boat for a continuous or broken period of six months in any twelve months but the maximum period the boat can stay in Croatia is 24 months. Periods of non-use can be achieved by placing the boat in bond at a marina or harbour. The 24-month period can start all over again if the boat leaves Croatian waters and re-enters. There have been the occasional horror stories of crews being heavily interrogated and boats thoroughly inspected but these are rare and sometimes exaggerated. Normally, provided your crew list and list of persons are in order and there are no signs that you are engaging in illegal charter, Customs entry and exit is just a formality. However, it is important to head directly for an approved port of entry when you first come into Croatian waters and to have your papers stamped at an approved port immediately before leaving Croatian waters.

Port Police

The job of policing Croatian waters normally falls to Croatian Naval patrol vessels, which are probably most active at the south-east perimeter of Croatian waters, near Dubrovnik and Cavtat. Do make sure that you head directly to the nearest authorised port of entry and you will have no problems.

SECURITY

Croatia is generally a safe country and the marinas, on the whole, have good security systems. However, it does make sense not to flaunt your valuables and to keep your boat locked up. There have been odd reports of motor boats stolen to order, and occasional tales of minor accidents happening to boats while in marinas along with petty thefts to apparently abandoned boats in local harbours. In the cities, there is isolated news of locals flagging down foreigners, under the guise that their car has broken down or there is some sort of problem, and then robbing them. In out-of-the-way places there are still some landmines left over from the Homeland War and an English mine was recently found near a submarine cave on Lastovo Island. Generally, however, you are less likely to come across problems than in most parts of Europe. Sensible precautions include checking insurance cover if leaving your boat at a marina for any length of time, not walking off the beaten track in remote areas, not leaving your boat unattended in a deserted bay or harbour for too long and not stopping to help strangers personally on the roadside – perhaps call the police instead if you are worried that they might genuinely need help. The big cities obviously have more crime than the smaller towns and villages.

HEALTH

As a sweeping generalisation it's probably fair to say that the general level of training, qualifications and experience of the Croatian medical profession is as high as many countries in Europe. However, the infrastructure, also like many other places, could do with some investment and the facilities are perhaps not as modern and extensive as in the UK, for example. There is a reciprocal agreement between Croatia and the UK for treating each other's citizens free of charge in the event of an emergency, but the greatest risk is needing specialist attention when you are in a remote area where the local facilities are limited. Insurance is therefore advisable. If you decide to go for private treatment then it will be much less expensive than in the UK, though you may have to pay in advance. For dental treatment, Croatia is a bargain and the standard of skills and technology are generally high. Opticians are also readily available. Pharmacies are widespread and usually have a good range of drugs and well-qualified staff equipped to advise on minor ailments.

Mosquitoes can be a nuisance in the summer so it's advisable to take repellents or buy them locally. Sea urchins are probably the biggest marine hazard and are fairly common. Fortunately, given the clarity of the water, you can usually spot them – tennis ball-sized with black spikes lurking on the rocks, near the shore, just below the surface of the water. However, given the pain a prick can inflict and also the discomfort of the normally pebbly beaches, it's advisable to wear plastic sandals when swimming. You are also more likely to see a snake in Croatia than in the UK, but only the horned viper and the common adder are poisonous.

DOGS AND OTHER ANIMALS

Croatia recently joined the pet passport scheme, which means that if you comply with the rules and regulations, dogs and some other animals can travel freely between the UK and Croatia. Note, however, that Montenegro is not yet part of the scheme.

SYMBOLS AND ABBREVIATIONS

AC	Admiralty Charts (UKHO)
	Airport
	Anchoring
	Anchoring prohibited
	Berthing stern/bows- to
	Boat hoist
	Boatyard
	Chemist
	Church
	Crane
	Customs office
	Direction of buoyage
ECM	East cardinal mark
	Ferry terminal
	Fishing boats
	Fish farm
	Fuel berth
	Harbourmaster
HHI	Croatian Hydrographic Institute
	Hospital
Hr	Hrid (Rock)
	Information bureau
	Isolated danger mark
J	Jezero (Lake)
	Launderette
Ldg	Leading
L	Luka (Harbour)
	Marina
	Mooring buoy
NCM	North cardinal mark
Plič	Pličina (Shoal)
PHM	Port-hand mark
PA	Position approx.
	Post office
	Public telephone
	Restaurant
SWM	Safe water mark
	Shipwreck
	Shore power
	Showers
	Slipway
SC	Small craft folio (UKHO)
SCM	South cardinal mark
SHM	Starboard-hand mark
	Submerged shipwreck
	Supermarket
Sv	Sveti (Saint)
SS	Traffic signals
U	Uvala (Bay)
	Water
	Waypoint
WCM	West cardinal mark

LIGHTS AND FREQUENCIES

FR	Fixed red light
FG	Fixed green light
Fl	Flashing light, period of darkness longer than light. A number indicates a group of flashes, eg: Fl (2). Most lights are white unless a colour follows the number of flashes, eg: Fl (2) G. The timing of the sequence, including light and darkness, is shown by the number of seconds, eg: Fl (2) G 10s.
L Fl	Long flash, of not less than two seconds
Oc	Occulting light, period of light longer than darkness
Iso	Isophase light, equal periods of light and darkness
Q	Quick flashing light, up to 50/60 flashes per minute
VQ	Very quick flashing, up to 120 flashes per minute
Mo	Light flashing a (dot/dash) Morse single letter sequences, eg: Mo (S)
Dir	A light, usually sectored, RWG or RG, usually giving a safe approach within the W sector. Either fixed or displaying some kind of flashing characteristic

Marina Dalmacija, Bibinje – Sukošan

Chapter one

The Northern Dalmatian mainland – Zadar to Biograd na Moru

The northern Dalmatian mainland is notable for the historic medieval town of Zadar. A major ferry port with its own international airport, Zadar makes a good starting point from which to explore the Zadar archipelago and the Kornati Islands. Zadar has three marinas in the vicinity and this stretch of mainland boasts six marinas in total, including the largest marina in Croatia, Marina Dalmacija: based at Sukošan, it is equipped with 1,200 sea berths.

Joined together by a bridge, the long thin islands of Ugljan and Pašman run broadly parallel to the mainland, which makes them popular weekend spots for the city dwellers of Zadar. These islands are covered in Chapter two on pages 45 to 61. The northern half of this stretch of mainland is separated from the island of Ugljan by the Zadar Canal (Zadarski Kanal), while the southern half is separated from the island of Pašman by the Pašman Canal (Pašmanski Kanal). The area is a favourite spot for sailors in the summer, with relatively challenging conditions, particularly in the Pašman Canal – see page 31.

Zadar itself is a bustling town and a busy harbour. Marina Zadar, on the north-east side of the main harbour, is the marina closest to the town and ferry port. A fuel station, situated nearby, can become very busy in the high season, although alternatives are at Marina Dalmacija and Biograd.

Marina Zadar, independently owned, was one of the more expensive marinas we visited. The main alternative to Marina Zadar is Marina Borik, a mile further north-west up the coast. Marina Vitrenjak, about half a mile north-west of Marina Zadar, is a municipal marina and predominantly used by locals. If there are places available here, beware of depths as the marina is shallower towards its inner end and near the pontoons.

Although there is plenty to see along the mainland coast, in practice, and depending on the winds, you will probably want to flit between the mainland and the islands of Ugljan and Pašman. If you prefer to berth in marinas, the mainland is for you. For unspoilt town harbours and anchorages use the twin islands, particularly Ugljan.

Heading south-east from Zadar towards Bibinje you will notice a large industrial site and, just before the headland, Bibinje's small town harbour with a café/restaurant. It's too shallow to be safe for larger yachts, but could provide a suitable anchorage for a lunchtime stop just outside.

After Bibinje comes Marina Dalmacija and the town of Sukošan. The marina itself is one of the more recently built in Croatia, covers 125 acres and has a wide range of facilities. It is set apart from the town and is a settlement in its own right.

Travelling south-east from Sukošan, towards Biograd na Moru, you will come across a number of quiet, mostly sandy beaches as well as small settlements and towns. Turanj has a tiny harbour, appropriate for shallow-draught craft, but is not sheltered from the Sirocco. Sveti Filip i Jakov, a reasonably-developed tourist village for its size, also boasts a little harbour, sheltered from all winds, where smaller craft can moor against the breakwater.

Arriving at Biograd, there is a choice of two marinas within the breakwater but, apart from being a good base from which to visit the Kornati islands and Lake Vrana (Vransko Jezero), the largest natural lake in Croatia, Biograd is essentially a traditional resort town though modernising rapidly.

Marina Dalmacija, Sukošan

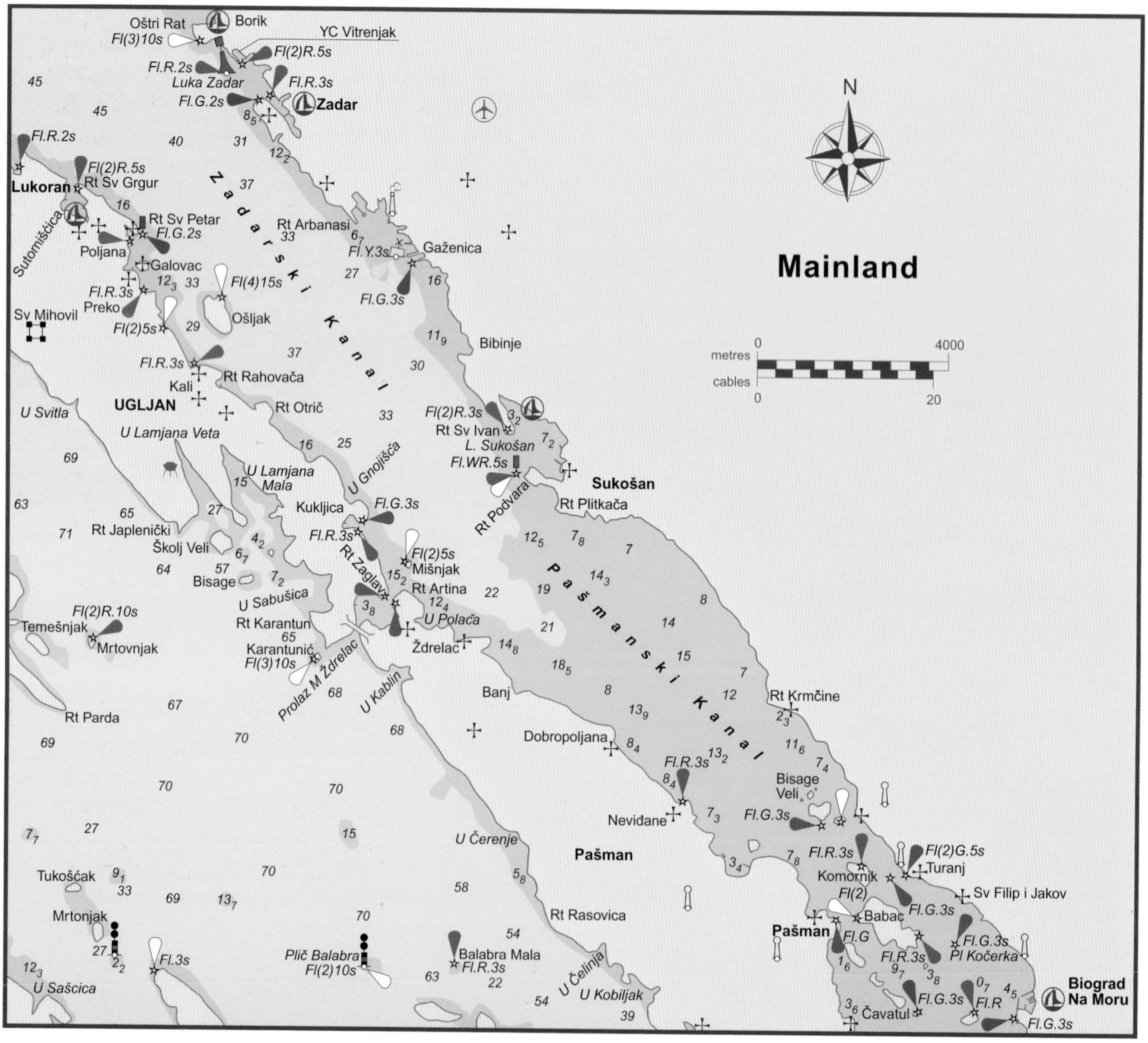

The Pašman Canal

Heading south-east from Sukošan you enter the Pašman Canal (Pašmanski Kanal) which, running the length of the island of Pašman, stretches between Sukošan and Pakoštane on the mainland. The channel extends for about 12 miles and is one of the more challenging cruising areas covered by this book. If your vessel draws over 4m (13ft), the Pašman Canal is best avoided, though guides indicate it is navigable for draughts of up to 6m (20ft). The western passage is deeper than the eastern passage (see below).

The white light on Sv Katarina Islet

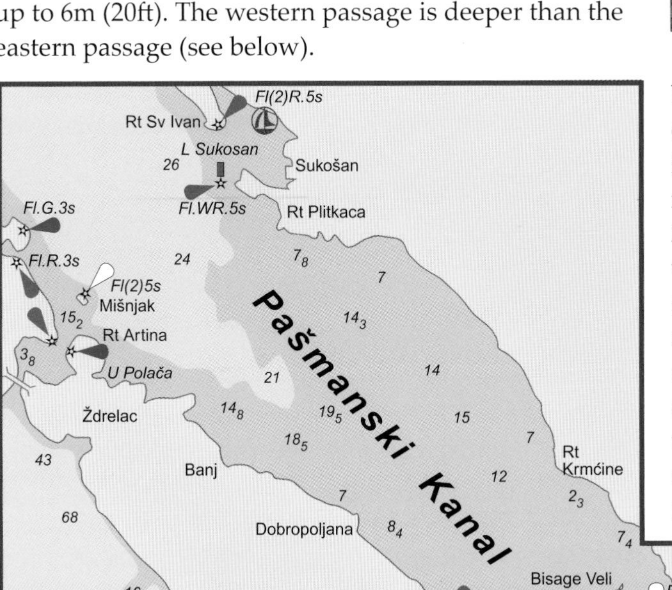

It is not advisable to navigate here in the dark and navigation is anyway prohibited when visibility falls below 0.2 nautical miles. The speed limit is 10 knots and anchoring or stopping is forbidden in the fairways or on the approaches.

As you enter the canal, the channel narrows and visual navigation and careful observation of charts becomes even more important. There are many islets and shoals, the channel shallows significantly in its narrowest part, roughly at the centre, and depths vary considerably.

The combination of wind and currents can also add to the demanding cruising conditions. The Bora, the Sirocco and northwesterlies are known to blow strongly here. The southwesterly wind changes direction in the channel and blows from the south or south-south-east. Northwesterlies may cause high seas. Currents can be as high as 2 to 2.5 knots, depending on the direction of the tide and winds, and are strongest in the narrowest part of the channel and by Turanj and Sv Filip i Jakov. So make sure you know exactly where you are on the chart at any moment in time and keep an eye on your depth as well as your surroundings. The water is very clear with a sand/shell bottom, but this can mean depths appear shallower than they really are. Better this than the other way round!

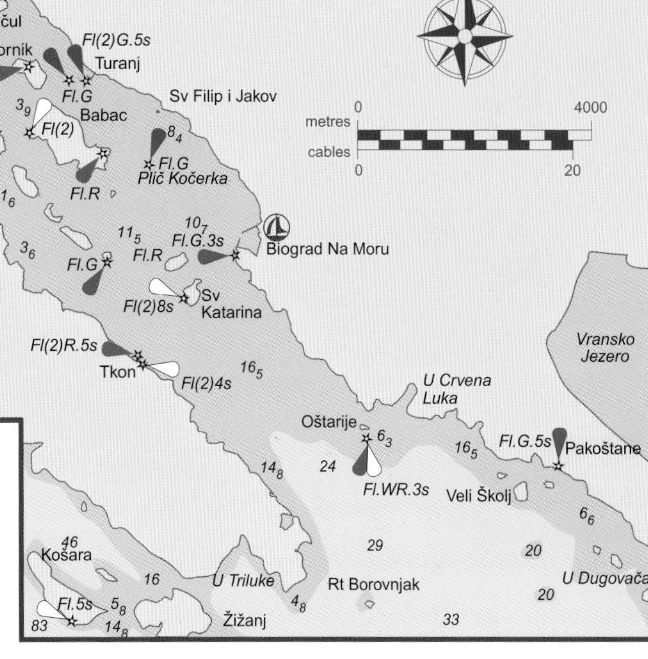

In fact, the Pašman Canal divides into two, in its narrowest part, around a number of islets – the western channel and eastern channel. We tried both of them, using the eastern channel heading south-east along the mainland (see page 32), and the western channel heading north-west along the coast of the island of Pašman (see page 45 of Chapter two). Vessels up to 50 tons can use either channel and swap freely between them. Our choice of channel would have led us in the opposite direction from vessels over 50 tons, which are required to use the eastern channel heading north-west and the western channel heading south-east. We suspect, however, that larger vessels are rarely encountered here as there are better alternative routes to reach the main towns in this part of Croatia. Smaller vessels were a rarity too when we took this route.

Pašman Town to Sukošan; white light on Ričul Islet

Sukošan to Biograd, on the eastern fairway of the Pašman Canal

The passage is relatively clear of obstacles as far as Rt Krmčine (Krmčine Point), next to the village of Sv Petar na Moru on the mainland. Aim to be in the centre of the passage as you pass Rt Krmčine, leaving the first islets of Bisage Mali and Bisage Veli about 400m to port. These two islets lie side by side, the larger islet to port of the smaller one, with another small rock further to port, so you should see three as you approach.

Immediately after is the islet of Galešnjak, about four times the size of the largest islet in the first group of three, with two conical peaks. This should also be left to port. As you pass this islet, you will see a green light beacon (Fl G 3s) on its south side and, further to port, the smaller islet of Ričul with a white light (Fl G 3s). Straight ahead of you will be the islet of Komornik and to port of this islet, on the mainland, is the town of Turanj. Komornik Islet has a red light (Fl R 3s) on its north-eastern tip. If heading for Turanj or Biograd, it is best to turn to port before Komornik Islet, leaving this and Babac Islet to starboard.

Once in the eastern fairway, if you intend sailing on past Biograd, leave Pličina Kočerka (Kočerka Shoal) to port. This is marked by a green light. Aim for the gap between Biograd, to port, and the islet of Planac to starboard. Past Planac, note that there is a 3.5m shoal just south-east of the northern tip of the islet of Sv Katarina. Otherwise, if heading for Biograd harbour and marinas, leave Pličina Kočerka to starboard.

Zadar

Marina Zadar entrance: 44°07'.19N 15°13'.30E

Bombed but by no means browbeaten, Zadar's architecture reflects its rich, varied and often troubled legacy. With a Roman layout, the town was a main base for the Byzantine fleet in the Middle Ages and prospered under early Venetian rule. Formally signed over to the Italians in 1921, it endured 72 bombings in World War II, became part of Yugoslavia on its formation in 1947 (when most of the Italian population left) and suffered again between 1991 and 1995

The medieval church of St Donat's, on the site of the Roman Forum, Zadar

when Serbian irregulars and the People's Army of Yugoslavia (JNA) initially nearly captured it but then continued to bombard it from the outskirts of town.

This eclectic history gives the old town of Zadar a hotchpotch of architectural styles, a Latin flavour and a comfortable, lived-in feel. It's the main town between Rijeka in the north and Split, further south, and the Zadar region can provide most of the best that Croatia has to offer.

Zadar is a bustling international ferry port with plenty of commercial traffic and, in the high season, a number of craft vying for position to refuel. It is also a permanent port of entry for foreign vessels. Only commercial vessels and fishing boats are allowed in the main town harbour.

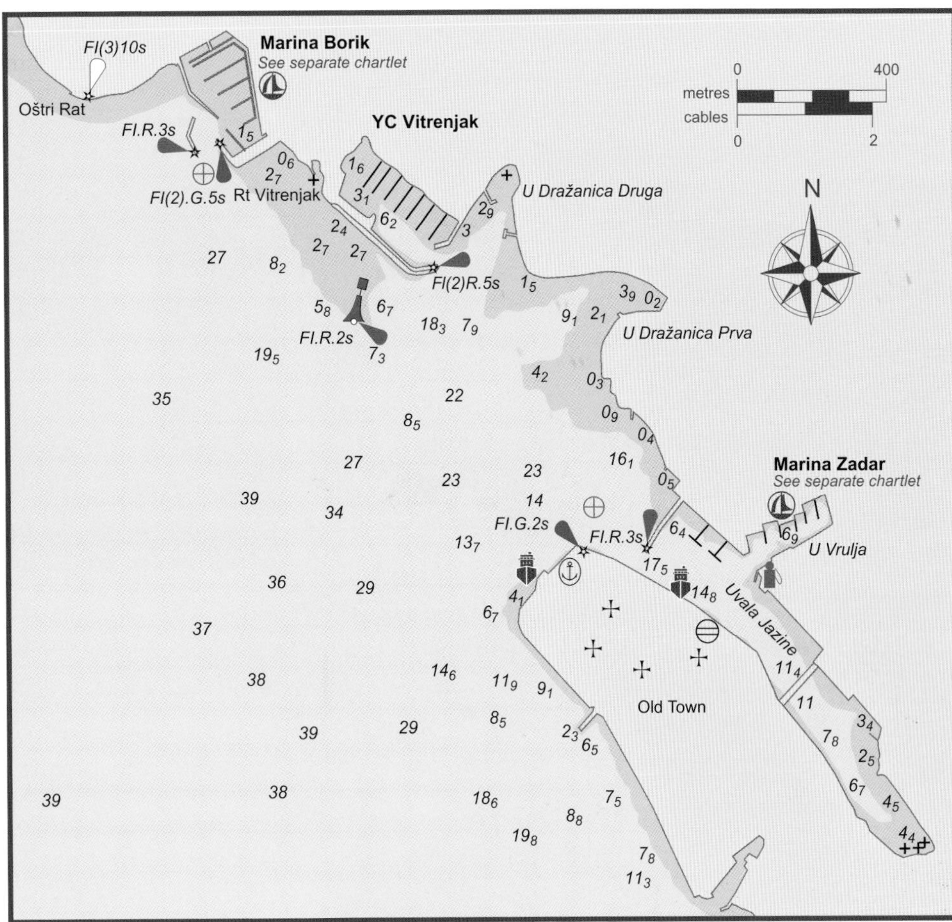

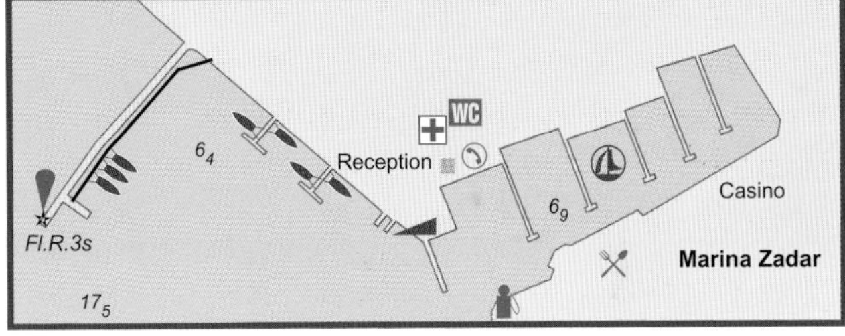

Of the three marinas in the area, Marina Zadar (Tankerkomerc) is the only one within relatively easy walking distance of town – 10 minutes using the footbridge. It is well sheltered from winds, but has a fairly tight entrance, especially when it is at full capacity. The ferry terminal, although recently partly transferred to a less congested area of the harbour, is still operating from opposite the marina entrance and departing ferries have to turn to port in front of this entrance.

There are no good anchorages for non-commercial vessels around Zadar and anchoring of any sort is prohibited in one area north and one area south of the harbour, where underwater cables and pipelines are laid. These areas are clearly indicated on the charts and stopping in or between them is also prohibited.

Zadar – the green light (Fl G 2s) at the end of the Old Town peninsula, and the new location for part of the ferry terminal

NAVIGATION

Charts: HHI 100-20, MK-12, MK-13; AC 515, AC 2711, SC5767

Approaches: From the north-west, look out for the Oštri Rat white light (Fl (3) 10s) on the mainland, which is followed immediately by Marina Borik. The marina has an external, low-lying floating breakwater with a red light (Fl R 3s) and, just to the east, a stone breakwater extending from the shore with a green light (Fl (2) G 5s). The outer breakwater of Marina Vitrenjak follows soon after and you need to look out to port for the red buoy (Fl R 2s) that marks the shallow areas. Ahead of you should be the peninsula of the old town with two belfries visible.

From the south and south-east, the conical islet of Ošljak, to port, can normally be seen from some distance and has a white light on its north-east point. To starboard is the deep-water port of Luka Gaženica and a large industrial area. Then follows the peninsula on which the old town lies.

The only other alternative approach is between Ugljan and Pašman, from the south-west, but this is not recommended for anything other than small craft. The bridge opens in the morning for an hour at 0900, but the channel is shallow and when the bridge is closed, clearance is only 16.5m (54ft).

Pilotage: At a waypoint of 44°07'.03N 15°12'.91E, Marina Vitrenjak will be directly to the north and Marina Borik to the north-west. Head due east from this waypoint for about 400m, across the tip of the peninsula, and you will see, to starboard, the channel between the old town peninsula and, to port, the marina breakwater. Keep close to the breakwater side to avoid the ferries. Immediately after passing the breakwater you should see the inner entrance to Marina Zadar to port. The entrance to the marina is narrow, as is the space between the piers, and the water shallows considerably towards the innermost parts of the marina.

Zadar – a traditional rowing boat takes passengers from the Old Town to the breakwater

BERTHING

You should be met by a member of the marina staff, even if you haven't called ahead, but make sure he or she knows your draught. The maximum depth is 8m.

The marina (VHF Channel 17; Tel: 023 204 700) is open all year round and listed as 'Category II' (see page 11 in the main introduction). It has 300 berths and 200 dry berths ashore. The charge per metre per day for boats between 10 and 20m (33 and 66ft) is about €4.4. Long stays, over 30 days, are charged at approximately 50% of the daily rate but are unlikely to be available in the high season. A water connection will cost an extra 10% while a power connection will be a flat rate of €7. The marina is well protected from all winds.

Useful information – Zadar

FACILITIES

Electricity and **water** pedestals are available to all berths and there are plenty of **rubbish** bins in the marina complex. The **showers** and **toilets** are in good working order, having recently been refurbished. Other facilities include a **café, exchange office, restaurant, chandlery, car hire** agency and a **casino** on site, and a couple of small **supermarkets** just outside. **Weather reports** can be obtained from the marina office, **ice** can be bought on site and there is also a **laundry service.** Parking is adequate and **telephones** are available.

The marina has two **cranes** on site – 7 and 15 tons – as well as an automatic 50-ton **slipway.** The **fuel** station (Tel: 023 265 962) is just outside the marina entrance, but does get busy. The queuing system is erratic and not helped by passing ferries and traffic in and out of the marina. The depth is 2.5m.

There are a number of **boat repair** and **supply shops** nearby, which include: Marina Stores, Jurja Biankinija 8, Tel: 023 254 458.
Mikeli Trade, Zrinsko Francopanska 27a, Tel: 023 224 860.
Adrijana Sport Internacional, Liburnska obala 6.
Ri Riz Itea Nautika Commerce, Obala Kneza Branimira 8, Tel: 023 305 888.
AD Mehanika, (equipment and motors), Obala Kneza Branimira 8, Tel: 023 305 738.

PROVISIONING

There are plenty of **cash points** close to the marina. The town has numerous **banks, travel agencies** and a wide range of shops. The **post office** is in Kralja S Držislava 1 Tel: 023 316 552.

EATING OUT

The locals tend to head towards Borik to eat. A good fish restaurant is Albin, on the road to Borik, 5km outside the centre, Put Dikla 47, Tel: 023 331 137. The town itself is bustling with restaurants and pizzerias but it's probably best to avoid the restaurants right by the marina, which can be expensive. In town, try Foša, Kralja Dimitra Zvonimira 2, Tel: 023 314 421, a fish

Useful information - continued

restaurant by the small harbour outside the Land Gate, or Konoba Marival, Don Ive Prodana 3, Tel: 023 213 239, which is pretty cramped but informal and popular with the locals.

ASHORE

The **tourist office** is situated in the south-eastern part of the old town, Ilije Smiljanića 5, Tel: 023 212 412/212 222, email: tzg-zadar@zd.htnet.hr, website: www.zadar.hr. There are also many private agencies with more limited information.

The attractions are too numerous to list in full, but a couple that can be recommended include the Renaissance façade of the Church of St Mary in the old town, along with the Byzantine architecture of the Church of St Donat. In a park in the suburb of Brodarica lies the Maritime Museum (Pomorski muzej) of the Institute of the Croatian Academy of Sciences. The archives, established in 1625, incorporate the history of shipping and fishing in the Eastern Adriatic.

Zadar is becoming a popular hub of entertainment, with two city centre venues, the Garden (www.thegardenzadar.com) and the Arsenal (www.arsenalzadar.com), both of which attract international visitors and guest performers.

The Zadar summer festival takes place, all around the town, between mid-July and mid-August and includes concerts, theatre performances and a few fringe events. As well as this there is a wide variety of cultural exhibitions and museums.

Beaches: North-west of the town is the tourist complex of Borik with its own beaches. Further north, a short car drive away, is the beach of Diklo. Zaton has a good beach and a tourist village, still further north, 15km from town. The beaches are a mixture of pebble and sand.

TRANSPORT

Flights: Zadar airport is 10km south-east of town. Since early 2007, Ryanair has been flying directly to Zadar from London Stansted three times a week. Most other international flights are via Zagreb but the connections to London are generally good except on Mondays. Croatia Airlines buses operate between the town and the airport and are timed to leave 60 minutes before the Zagreb flights take off and shortly after they land; Tel: 023 205 800.

Trains: The train station is about 1km east of the town and there are regular trains to Zagreb, via Knin, though the coach service is normally quicker; Tel: 023 212 555.

Ferries: Jadrolinija, the state ferry company, runs a multitude of services to and from Zadar. These cover most of the inhabited islands as well as international routes. For timetables and so forth, visit the website www.jadrolinija.hr; local office Tel: 023 250 555.

Buses: The bus station is situated near the train station; Tel: 023 211 555. There are good connections to most major western European cities.

Car hire: Budget is closest to the marina at Obala Kneza Branimira 1, Tel: 023 337 103.

Bike hire: Super Nova, Obala Kneza Branimira 2a, Tel: 023 311 010.

Motorcycle hire: Bugonvilija tours, Kraljice 11, Tel: 023 385 900.

Taxis: Liburnska Obala 8, Tel: 023 251 400 or Ante Starčevića 2, Tel: 023 317 288.

OTHER INFORMATION

Port Authority Zadar: Liburnska Obala 8, PP 226. Tel: 023 254 888.

Harbourmaster: Tel: 023 250 758; Fax: 023 250 235.

Tankerkomerc Marina Zadar: (to use the official name!) Ivana Meštrovića 2, Tel: 023 332 700; Fax: 023 333 917/333 871; email: tankerkomerc@tankerkomerc.htnet.hr; website: www.tankerkomerc.hr.

Hospital: Bože Peričića 5, Tel: 023 315 677.

Pharmacy: Plenty around but this one claims to have a 'non-stop' phone! Centar, Jurja Barakovića 6, Tel: 023 302 929.

Borik

Marina Borik entrance: 44°07'.65N 15°12'.58E

Borik is really a residential and tourist suburb of Zadar. It's a half-hour walk into town but there are plenty of good restaurants and open spaces here. The marina is easier to access than Marina Zadar and has more up-to-date facilities. Be aware that there is a relatively new, arrow-shaped breakwater protecting the entrance between the two main breakwaters that extend from the mainland. This may not be marked on some charts.

NAVIGATION

Charts: HHI 100-20, MK-12, MK-13; AC 2711, SC5767

Approaches: See Zadar on page 34.

Pilotage: The approach waypoint is 44°07'.32N 15°12'.43E, from where, between north and north-east, you should see the three breakwaters defining the marina entrance just over 400m away. Do not be confused by Marina Vitrenjak, which lies a little further east.

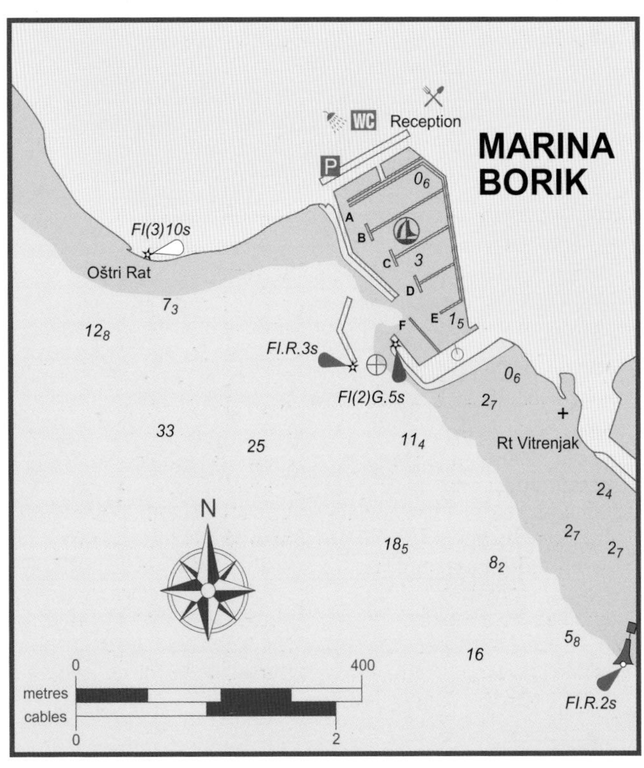

BERTHING

The marina (VHF Channel 17; Tel: 023 333 036) is open all year round and has 165 berths and 50 dry berths. The maximum depth is 5m. Borik is currently a Category III marina, mostly because the facilities are just outside the marina complex. Still, it's not very far to walk to get to them and the rating does not really do justice to the modern facilities, which include fingers for each double berth – a rare commodity in Croatia. Rates are between €3.5 and €4.2 per metre per day for boats between 10 and 20m (33 and 66ft), with a 30% discount between 1 October and 31 March. Now that the new breakwater is in place, the marina is well protected in all conditions.

Marina Borik

Useful information – Borik

FACILITIES

New finger pontoons and bollards make this one of the more modern marinas in the region. **Water** and **electricity** are available from well-sited bollards, which also have the capability to provide **phone, television** and **satellite** services. Just outside the marina is the reception area with **showers, toilets, weather reports, laundry** service, a **supermarket, phones,** a **café** and a **bank** with **cash point**. The marina has a 5-ton **crane** and is intending to purchase a 90-ton mobile crane in the near future. **Fuel** can be obtained at Marina Zadar (see page 34).

PROVISIONING

Apart from the **supermarket** by the reception, there are a few **grocery shops** nearby and some **tourist shops**. Head into Zadar if you need more intensive retail therapy.

EATING OUT

You will find no shortage of restaurants within a short walking distance of the marina and there's also a cluster on Put Dikla, which includes Albin (see page 34), and Roko, Put Dikla 74, Tel: 023 331 000.

ASHORE

See Zadar on page 35.

TRANSPORT

There's an hourly ferry to Zadar costing around 10 Kunas per single trip.

OTHER INFORMATION

Marina Borik: Obala Kneza Domagoja 1, Tel: 023 333 036; Fax 023 331 018; email: info@marinaborik.hr; website: www.marinaborik.hr.

One of the many good restaurants on Put Dikla, the road between Borik and Zadar

Otherwise, see Zadar on page 35.

Marina Vitrenjak: Entrance wpt: 44°07'.52N 15°13'.10E. Mostly used by the locals, operated as a club and rarely appearing in any tourist information brochures and guides, the marina has 250 berths for small yachts and is relatively shallow.

Jedriličarski Klub 'Uskok', Obala Kneza Trpimira bb; Tel: 023 331 076; Fax: 023 333 888; email: office@uskok.biz.hr; website: www.uskok.biz.hr

Bibinje

Town Harbour entrance: 44°04'.19N 15°16'.92E
Charts: HHI MK-13; AC 515; AC 2711, SC5767

Bibinje is a small town of not more than 4,000 inhabitants, but makes a refreshing contrast to the city bustle of Zadar and the somewhat antiseptic feel of the enormous Marina Dalmacija complex at Sukošan, further south.

With a straightforward approach, it has a small (and quite shallow) town harbour and an anchorage just outside. The harbour is exposed to northerly, westerly and southwesterly winds, so it's not recommended for

Bibinje Harbour

an overnight stay but looks like a relaxing and peaceful lunchtime stop in clement weather conditions. There are a few restaurants and cafés and some long, deserted stretches of beach.

Tourism is obviously quite well developed for such a small town, no doubt aided by its proximity to Zadar and Sukošan. With its own website, www.tzo-bibinje.hr, Bibinje's facilities include a tourist office, a post office with an exchange service (Tel: 023 261 010, open 0800 – 1400 weekdays only), a local store, a doctor, dentist and a repair shop for cars and boat engines.

There are five churches in Bibinje, of which two are still in use. The parish church of Sv Roka was built in 1673 on the location of an earlier structure and extended in 1854. St Rocco, to use the English translation, is the patron saint of Bibinje and this is celebrated on 16 August. The town has a long history and, formerly named Bibano/Bibanum, dates as far back as the 11th century.

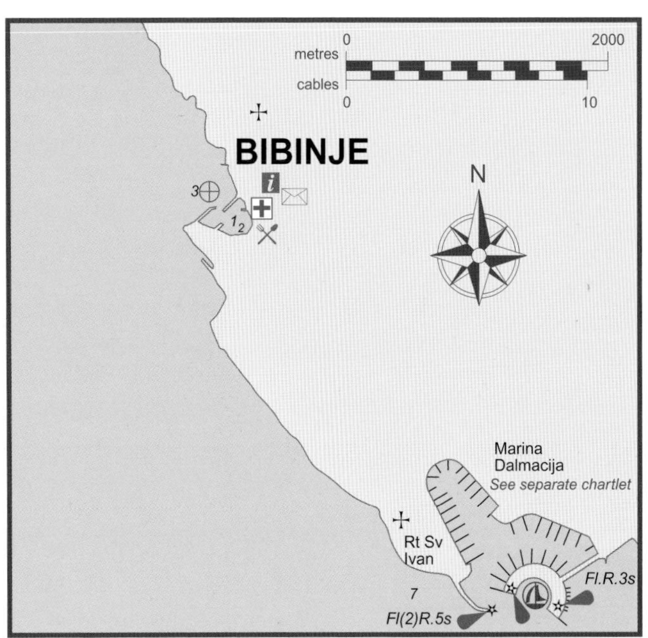

Sukošan

Marina Dalmacija; entrance to bay: 44°02'.94N 15°17'.57E

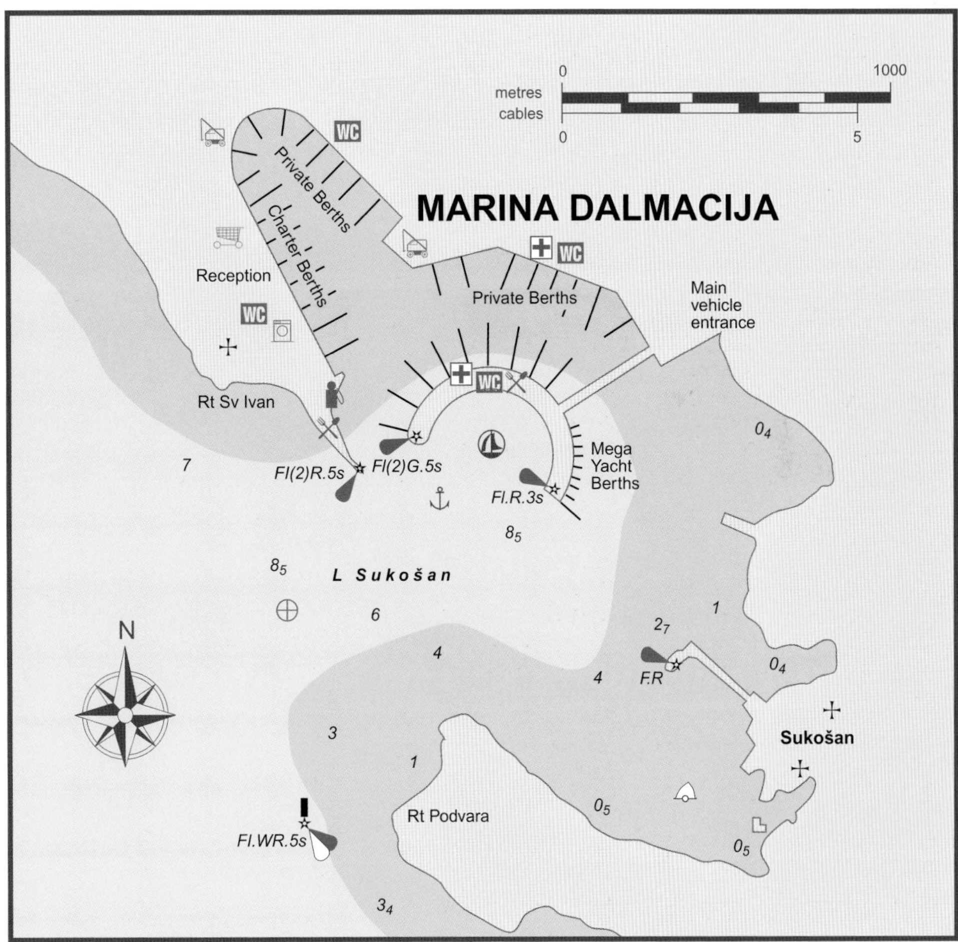

Sukošan, the town, is somewhat overshadowed by the enormity of Marina Dalmacija, which lies to the north-west.

Missing only a cave to make it an ideal *Thunderbirds* location, the marina is the biggest in Croatia, covers 125 acres and has an eerie feel to it.

The town itself, to the east of the bay, is a more manageable size and has plenty to offer in terms of restaurants, ruins and good sandy beaches.

NAVIGATION

Charts: HHI MK-13; AC 515, AC 2711, SC5767

Approaches: The approach to the waypoint (see page 38) is relatively hazard-free from both directions. Approaching from the south-east, look out for a red/white light (Fl WR 5s) approximately 200m west of Rt Podvara on the south side of the entrance.

There is a shallow bank either side of the bay (inside and outside) and a 6m bank across the entrance. The eastern part of the bay, where the town and town harbour are situated, shoals rapidly, which means that the head of the long breakwater (depth 3m) is really the only suitable mooring for yachts other than in the marina.

The marina entrance itself is well marked. An approach from the south-west between Ugljan and Pašman is not recommended due to limited clearance under the bridge and shallow waters.

Pilotage: Just one approach waypoint is needed for

the marina, whichever direction you are coming from, although when approaching from the south you will pass most of the harbour entrance before you get to the waypoint. This is to give you a clear view of the entrance to the marina and the town harbour from the middle of the Zadar Canal. East of the waypoint you should see the town, and on a bearing of about 73°T you should make out the red light (Fl R (2) 5s) marking the end of Rt Sv Ivan as well as the semi-circular pier of the marina, the eastern end of which is identified by a red light (Fl R 3s) and the western end by a green light (Fl (2) G 5s). The waypoint is 44°02'.83N 15°16'.09E and lies approximately 1.3 miles from Rt Sv Ivan.

As you approach the marina, watch your depths and be ready to turn sharply to port after the red light on the breakwater extending from Rt Sv Ivan, in between this light and the western end of the semi-circular pier, marked by a green light. If you do decide to moor at the town end of the bay, though this is not advised, watch out for the shallows and the ruins.

Marina Dalmacija, Bibinje – Sukošan

BERTHING

The marina can be contacted on VHF Channel 17 or Tel: 023 200 300. Open all year round, it is listed as a Category II marina. There are 1,200 berths and 500 dry berths, with a maximum depth of 8m. A 10m (33ft) boat will cost €4.2 per metre per day plus tourist tax, reducing to €3.7 per metre per day for a 20m boat, with a 30% discount between 31 October and 31 March. The marina is well protected from winds, but in a strong southwesterly some swell can enter the harbour.

Useful information – Sukošan

FACILITIES

The marina (Elizabete Kotromanić 11/1, 23000 Zadar, Tel: 023 200 300, Fax: 023 200 333; email: info@marinadalmacija.hr; website: www.marinadalmacija.hr) covers a large area and all berths have access to **electricity** and **water. Rubbish** bins are widely available and the complex has four **toilet/ shower** blocks as well as a **restaurant, cafés,** a **laundry, chandlery, supermarket, sailmakers,** a diving centre, reception and exchange office. There is a **repair/ service** workshop along with 30 and 65-ton **travel lifts.**

The **fuel** station lies towards the end of the west pier and can accommodate boats of up to 55m (180ft) in length – minimum depth 4.5m; opening hours 0630 to 2200 every day.

PROVISIONING

The marina **supermarket** has most things and is probably a better bet than the long walk to Sukošan. There is a **post office** in the village.

EATING OUT

If you want to get away from the restaurant in the marina, there are a couple of reasonable restaurants, serving most things, on the road just outside the main entrance. We tried Restoran Tomislav, Tel: 023 393 866. The food was good and cheap but they insisted on selling us bottled water, which nearly doubled the size of the bill! Otherwise, if you fancy a longish walk, there are some good *konobas* in Sukošan serving the normal Croatian fare. Try Konoba Kod Guste, Tel: 023 393 303 or Joso, Tel: 023 393 144.

ASHORE

A small **tourist office** is located in the village – Tel: 023 393 345; email: tzo-sukosan@zd.t-com.hr; website: www.sukosan.hr. Note that the website was in Croatian only at the time of writing. The islet in the south-eastern corner of the bay plays host to the ruins of the 15th century summer villa of M Valaresso, archbishop of Zadar. Sv (St) Kasijan Church, though renovated in 1673, is thought to date back to the 11th century and contains fragments from its earlier form in the door posts and at the front. Sukošan has several long sandy beaches.

Marina Dalmacija – the red light (Fl R 3s) near the megayacht berths

Turanj

Town Harbour entrance: 43°57'.94N 15°24'.35E

Turanj is a sleepy settlement connected to Sv Filip i Jakov by a seafront promenade. It's probably one of the more attractive villages along this stretch of the coast and has some good beaches, a smattering of restaurants and bars, and a church dating back to the 15th century. Yachts can berth in the town harbour or along the outer end of the breakwater (depth 3 to 4m), but the harbour is not protected from the Sirocco, which can cause waves to break over the inner part of the larger mole.

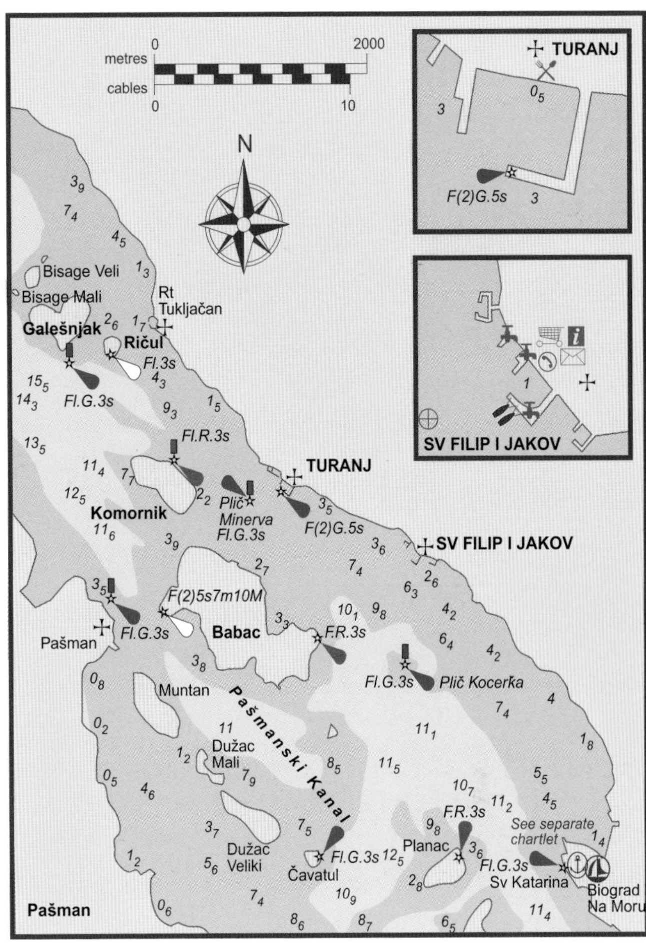

NAVIGATION

Charts: HHI MK-14; AC 2711, AC 2773, SC5767

Approaches: From the north-west, leave the islets of Bisage (Veli and Mali), Galešnjak and Ričul to port and the islet of Komornik to starboard (see Pašman Canal notes on pages 31–32). From the south-east, keep clear of Pličina Kočerka, identified by a green light (Fl G 3s). From both directions watch out for Pličina Minerva, depth 4.3m, just off the harbour entrance, also marked by a green light (Fl G 3s), and a group of detached shoals. The church tower is conspicuous, as is the long dog leg shaped breakwater marking the eastern boundary of the harbour, with a green light (Fl (2) G 5s) at its tip.

BERTHING

Small craft can berth along the inner side of the breakwater, marked by a green light, though this is mostly used by fishing boats and local craft. Anchoring is not recommended and the harbour is only protected from northerly and northeasterly winds.

ASHORE

A post office and tourist information office can be found at neighbouring Sv Filip i Jakov, about 1km's walk along the coast (see below), along with a couple of small shops for provisions. There are a few restaurants to choose from in the high season – try Afrodita, Tel: 023 389 463, Roko, Tel: 023 388 117, or Palma, Tel: 023 389 263.

Sv Filip i Jakov (St Phillip and Jacob)

Harbour entrance: 43°57'.64N 15°25'.28E

A compact, well-cared for settlement with a thriving tourist industry centred around some large hotels on the outskirts of the town.

NAVIGATION

Charts: HHI MK-14; AC 2711; AC 2773, SC5767

Sv Filip i Jakov lies three quarters of a mile south-east of Turanj (see above). Approaches and pilotage considerations are as for Turanj. Landmarks include a white belfry behind the harbour, with a more traditional belfry further west.

The harbour is well protected from all winds but is only suitable for smaller craft – depths are up to 2m on the inner side of the breakwater and the inner end of the west pier outside; up to 4m on the outside of the breakwater. It is advisable to berth bows-to here, due to a projecting ledge below the surface of the water.

ASHORE

Facilities comprise a tourist office, post office, two cash points, a couple of grocery shops and a market on the main street, as well as a smattering of cafés and restaurants and a pebble beach. The town is named after the original medieval church.

The present day church of St Mihovil (St Michael) was built in the 14th century, but was reconstructed

in the 18th century after the Turks withdrew. Also of interest are the ruins of a Benedictine monastery in Rogov, while a summer festival takes place each year in August.

OTHER INFORMATION

Tourist office: Tel: 023 389 071; Fax: 023 389 239; email: tzo-sv.filip-jakov@zd.htnet.hr; website: www.sv-filipjakov.hr.
Post office: Tel: 023 389 922; Fax: 023 388 627. Open from 0800 to 1400 weekdays, closed Saturdays and Sundays.

Left: Sv Filip i Jakov

Biograd na Moru

Approach to entrance to Marina Kornati and Marina Šangulin: 43°56'.51N 15°26'.28E

Biograd is the first largish town heading south from Zadar and has a town harbour, two marinas and some large, package-type hotels. Unusually there are two separately-owned marinas within the same breakwater boundaries. If arriving by car, make sure you know which part of the marina you are heading to as there are a number of different routes by road. The approach by sea also requires attention as it can be busy, with a ferry pier and a popular fuel station close to the entrance to the marinas. Biograd is a good base for visiting the Kornati Islands and Lake Vrana, but there's not much of an old town, the beaches are average (and often crowded) and it lacks the character found in most Croatian towns and villages. The Venetians are partly to blame for this, razing the settlement to the ground in 1126.

NAVIGATION

Charts: HHI 515, MK-14; AC 2711, AC 2773, SC5767
Approaches: From the north-west, past Sv Filip i Jakov, leave Pličina Kočerka (shoal) to starboard and see the navigational notes on Turanj on page 39 for the preceding parts of the approach. From the south-east, leave the islet of Sv Katarina to port and watch out for the 3.5m shoal on the south-east side of the northern tip. Continue past the headland so that you have a good view of the harbour as you will have to turn back on yourself for the entrance to the marina. Useful landmarks include the church belfry, the green light (Fl G 3s) at the head of the town harbour pier, the two lights on either side of the marina entrance

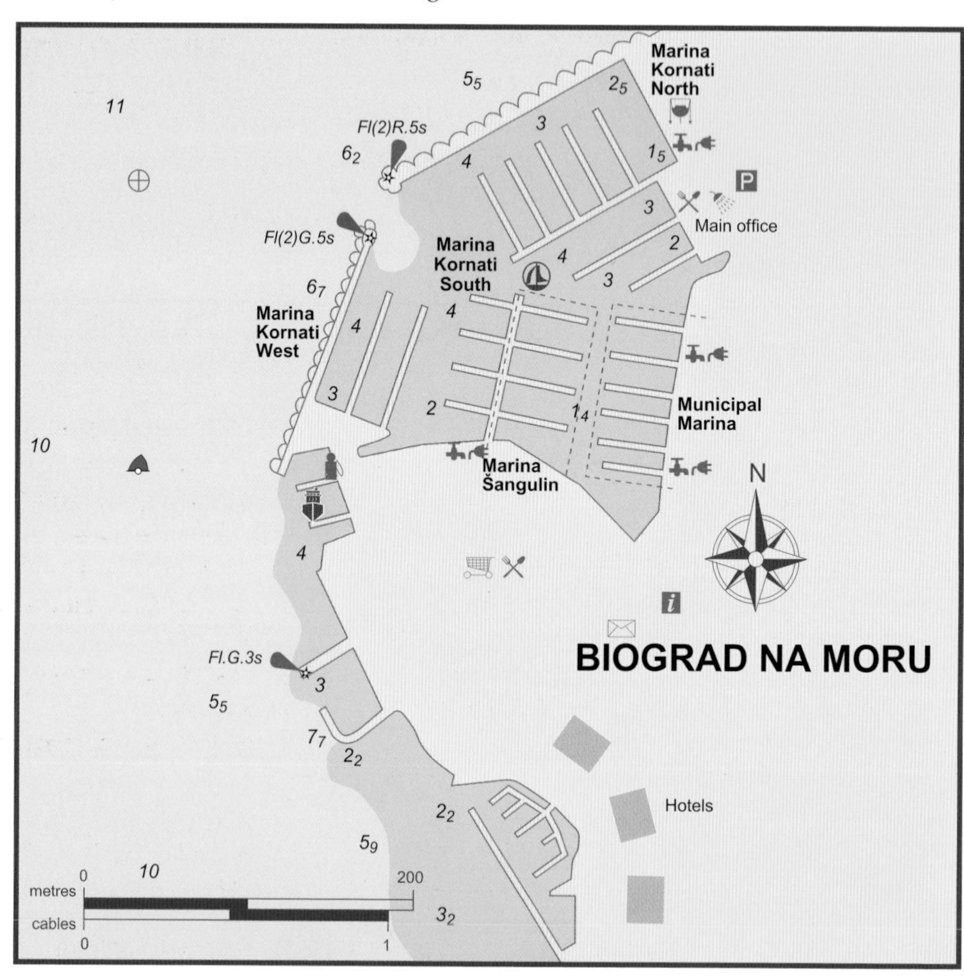

The marinas at Biograd na Moru

on the end of the breakwaters (port side – Fl (2) R 5s; starboard side – Fl (2) G 5s) and the large Marina Kornati sign in front of the red light.

Pilotage: If you're in the deepest part of the channel between the mainland and Pličina Kočerka, you should see the two long breakwaters ahead of you, between which is the entrance to the marinas. Similar considerations apply when approaching from the south-east. If you stay in the deepest part of the channel between Sv Katarina (and its off-lying shoals) to port and the mainland to starboard, you can start checking off the landmarks listed under the approach section.

The stone L-shaped breakwater marks the southern and western boundaries of Marina Kornati west. The entrance to Marina Kornati (north, south and west) and Marina Šangulin is at the far end of the long part of the 'L'. As you enter, Marina Kornati west is immediately to starboard (breakwater and two pontoons running parallel to the breakwater). The outer half of the concrete pier, which follows on the starboard side, is Marina Kornati south and the inner side of this pier is Marina Šangulin. The pontoons closest to the mainland on the starboard side as you enter are reserved for locals. The area to port and attached to the mainland is Marina Kornati north (see chart on opposite page).

BERTHING

Marina Kornati, which can be contacted on VHF Channel 17, Tel: 023 383 800, incorporates 600 berths and 60 dry berths, all with water and power supplies. A Category II marina, open all year round, with a maximum depth of

Biograd ferry pier and town harbour

5m. The cost is around €4.3 per metre per day for boats between 10 and 20m (33 and 66ft).

Marina Šangulin (VHF Channel 17, Tel: 023 385 020/385 150) has 150 berths and 10 dry berths. Maximum depth is 4.5m. Prices are only quoted up to 16m (52ft). A 10m (33ft) boat will cost €3.9 per metre per day. The marina has not currently been given a category.

Both marinas are well protected in all conditions.

Useful information – Biograd na Moru

FACILITIES

Marina Kornati: Electricity and **water** are available to all berths and there are plenty of **rubbish** bins. Facilities include **showers**, **toilets**, a reception area, a **restaurant/bar, laundry** facilities, a **chandlery** and a **supermarket**. A **service** and **repair** workshop, a 10-ton **crane** and 50-ton **travel lift** are also on site. The **fuel** station can be found next to the ferry pier on the east side of the entrance:

Marina Šangulin: Electricity and **water** for all berths, **rubbish disposal, showers** and **toilets**. There is a **repair/servicing workshop** and a 12-ton **crane**. More extensive facilities are available in the Marina Kornati complex.

PROVISIONING

There are plenty of shops around and a well-stocked **supermarket** is situated on Trg Kralja Tomislava near the hotel Kornati, which is open from 0630 to 2000 weekdays and Saturdays, and from 0700 to 1300 on Sundays. A **cash point** can be found next door to the supermarket with a number of others around town. The **post office** is on Zagrebačka 1, Tel: 023 383 110; Fax: 023 383 112. Open 0700 to 2100 weekdays, 0700 to 1400 Saturdays, closed on Sundays.

EATING OUT

Restaurant Guste is a reasonably-priced rustic seafood restaurant situated on Obala Kralja Petra Krešimira IV, Tel: 023 383 025, but there's a wide choice of eating establishments serving up all the normal dishes.

ASHORE

The **tourist office** is in a courtyard a five-minute walk from the seafront on Trg Hrvatskih Velikana 12, Tel: 023 383 123/385 382; Fax: 023 383 123; website: www.tzg-biograd.hr. There are also a number of private tourist agencies in the town that will sort out most of your needs. If you decide to take an organised boat trip to the Kornati Islands, get them to show you where you are going to avoid any disappointment. Some of them go to Dugi Otok, which is attractive enough but not part of the Kornati Nature Park.

The town is now somewhat dominated by the large hotels. As far as churches go, only the Basilica of St John survived the Venetian destruction, although the early Romanesque Church of Saint Anthony dates back to the 13th century. The Town Museum houses an archaeological collection with prehistoric, antique and early Croatian finds, as well as a collection of ships' cargo from the end of the 16th century.

Any one of the numerous private tourist agencies will be able to organise activities such as diving and provide bikes, scooters, car hire details and so forth. Better **beaches** can be found in Sv Filip i Jakov or Turanj (see page 39).

TRANSPORT

Buses: The bus station is near to the tourist office, Tel: 023 383 022.

Ferries: There is a regular ferry service to Tkon on the island of Pašman, Tel: 023 384 589, with a ticket office by the ferry terminal.

Taxis: Tel: 091 518 54 79 or 098 286 495.

Car, scooter and bike hire: Check out the rates with one or two of the tourist agencies.

OTHER INFORMATION

Harbourmaster: Obala Kralja Petra Krešimira bb, Tel/fax: 023 383 210.

Marina Kornati: Šetalište Kneza Branimira 1, Tel: 023 383 800; Fax: 023 384 500; e-mail: marina-kornati@zd.htnet.hr; website: www.marinakornati.com.

Marina Šangulin: Kraljice Jelene 3, Tel/fax: 023 384 944; email: info@sangulin.hr; website: www.sangulin.hr.

Pharmacy: Matije Ivanica 2, Tel: 023 385 444.

Sali, Dugi Otok

Chapter two

Islands off the mainland between Zadar and Biograd Na Moru, including the Kornati Islands

If you remember your geometry and can still visualise a parallelogram, imagine the shorter of the two parallel sides stretching between Zadar and Biograd Na Moru and the longer one stretching between the north-west tip of Dugi Otok and just beyond the south-west tip of the island of Kornat to include the islands of Smokvica and Kurba Vela. Nature clearly did not intend the Croatian coastline to be neatly divided into boxes and chapters and this particular part of the Companion could fill a book in its own right. We'll tell you the highlights and essentials and give you a flavour of all the different pleasures on offer, but there's plenty to explore and the contrasts are stark.

Much has been written about the Kornati Islands, and almost every bit of tourist information you can find will quote (or misquote) George Bernard Shaw's effusive appreciation of them. For us, they provided an amazing but slightly bleak lunar landscape emerging from azure waters, with occasional bursts of lush green vegetation and small pockets of civilisation. A visual spectacle of rare unspoilt beauty to sail through, a number of seasonal restaurants, but generally not too much to do or see if you go ashore.

North-west of the Kornati National Park is the long thin island of Dugi Otok. The south-west side of the island faces the full force of the elements and has little to offer in the way of civilisation, comfort or shelter. It's a different story around the other side and we fell instantly for the modest charms of Sali.

Lying in between the islands of Dugi Otok and Kornat

and the mainland, the islands of Ugljan and Pašman provide a balanced transition from the suburban life of mainland Zadar. Leave the city gently behind here before exploring the wilderness of the Kornati Islands, discovering the scattered settlements on the islands of Dugi Otok, Žut and Iž and revealing the bounty of the smaller neighbouring islands and islets. In this cruising area you can truly find your retreat to nature one day and then, the next, return to whatever scale of civilisation and creature comforts you seek.

This is a popular sailing area in the high season so choose your night stops carefully and aim to be there by 1600 if you can. Keep a good eye on the winds and the weather and line up a couple of overnight options in the less protected areas, so you have a choice depending on the conditions. There are marinas on the islands of Iž, Žut and Piškera, a good scattering of organised anchorages and some idyllic town harbour berths. Of the three marinas, only Iž Veli Marina stays open all year round and don't expect to find many restaurants and shops open on the islands outside the main tourist season. The 'high' season in Croatia is still very short (generally from mid-July to the end of August) and once the locals deem that there aren't enough tourists to merit opening or staying open, that's it. The bigger settlements and towns may have one or two eateries open all year round for the indigenous population but, beyond the more cosmopolitan towns and settlements, many of the local entrepreneurs return to the mainland outside the main tourist season. So, if you like to get away from it all between November and March (and sometimes even May, June, September and October!) don't be surprised if you find a ghost town instead of a thriving, buzzing mini metropolis.

Water, fuel and electricity can be found on some of the islands but it's best to fill your tanks before leaving the mainland. Water can be scarce and is therefore often more expensive where available. Similarly, expect to pay a little more for provisions and eating out – there's less competition on the islands and the transport costs add to the overheads of the restaurateurs and shop keepers.

Geographically, there's no 'best' way of covering the entire area if that's your objective. The areas of least interest, protection and facilities are the south-west coasts of Pašman, Ugljan and Dugi Otok. We found the north-east coast of Ugljan preferable to that of its twin island Pašman, the latter appearing relatively deserted and less cared for. As for Dugi Otok, it's a fair distance to travel in order to cover the length of its north-east coast, with relatively little protection and interest in return. So, to get the best flavour of the area if time is limited, one option is to head north-west along the north-east coast of Ugljan, around its north-west tip, and then south-south-east and along the north-east coast of Iž. From here, head south to Sali, on Dugi Otok, then south-east to the island of Žut, maybe staying overnight in the marina before doubling back on yourself a little to round the north-west tip of Žut. From this point, head west through the gap between Dugi Otok and Katina, then follow the south-west coast of Kornat, sailing on through the National Park that encapsulates the best of the Kornati Islands.

If time is shorter still, then save the north-east coast of Ugljan for another occasion as it's an easy day-trip by ferry from Zadar on the mainland. Instead, head out to the other islands from Biograd or from further south along the mainland.

Navigationally, as with much of the Croatian coastline, this is not really an area to sail at night. The islands and islets are densely packed and the best way to be sure of a safe passage is to know where you are on the chart at any moment in time and maintain good visual identification of the landmarks, islets and islands.

Given the richness of this cruising area and its geographical layout, it is very hard to construct any one passage to cover all the ports and harbours in a logical order, particularly considering the number of islands and islets. So this chapter deals with each main island separately, with the group of smaller Kornati Islands following below the section on the main island of Kornat. Finally, we look at the group of islands between Ugljan and Dugi Otok. Our overview of each island, in the context of the whole area, will help you decide whether to fit it into your itinerary. Our summary of the ports will then help you choose where to visit and/or stay. At the end of the chapter, we provide you with some pertinent facts on the numerous smaller islands and islets to help you decide whether to include them in your trip as well. Otherwise, this chapter follows the structure of the rest of this Cruising Companion.

Pašman Island

Pašman runs parallel to the mainland between Crvena Luka, south-east of Biograd, and Sukošan, north-east of Zadar. It is joined to the island of Ugljan, further north-west, by a bridge, and is separated from the mainland by the Pašman Canal (Pašmanski Kanal); see page 31. Being close to the mainland, it has a number of villages and settlements on its north-east coast, but most of them appear a little run down and deserted in contrast to the generally well-kept towns and villages of the neighbouring island of Ugljan. Many of the settlements stretch back to the main road and, unusually,

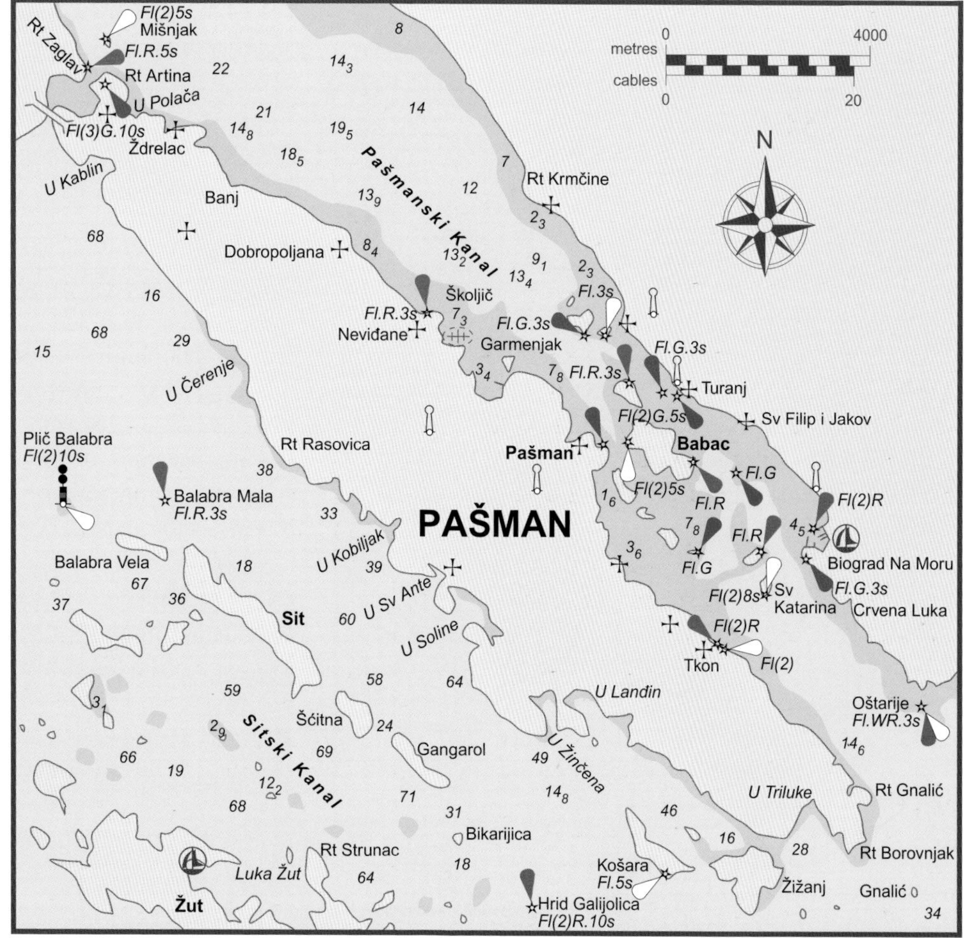

you will often find shops and post offices, where they exist, a reasonable walk from the coast. The south-west coast has a few anchorages, Soline being the best, but is otherwise predominantly uninhabited and inhospitable. If you like mountain biking or trekking then Pašman has a number of mountain trails and tourist walks to offer. It's also a good centre for watersports and boasts plenty of sandy beaches.

If these are not your priority, and given what else is on offer in this particular area, we wouldn't make a special detour for Pašman. However, if you're navigating the Pašman Canal and looking for a stop-off point, you may prefer some of the settlements on Pašman to those on the mainland. Below we explore the options available clockwise from the north-west tip of the island.

Pašman town harbour, Pašman Island, with the mainland in the background

Prolaz Mali Ždrelac

PASSAGE BETWEEN PAŠMAN AND UGLJAN

Centre of bay: 44°01'.12N 15°15'.41E

The passage itself is not recommended for yachts as it is shallow, narrow and the bridge has a clearance of only 16.5m (54ft). However, for yachts not exceeding

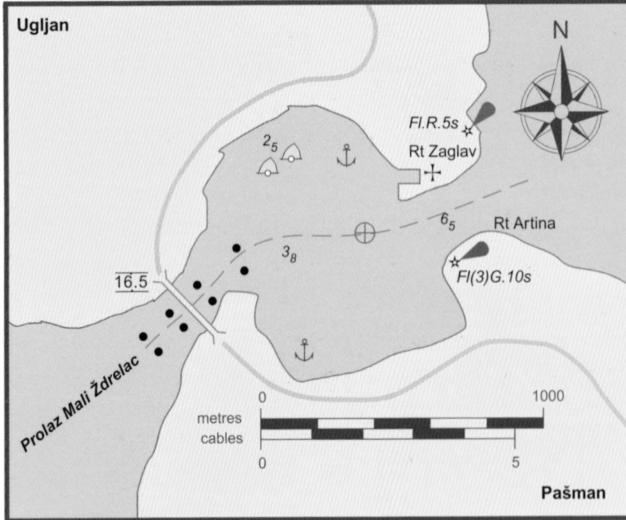

4m (13ft) in draught, there is a good, well-sheltered anchorage on the south side of the bay. Anchoring is also possible on the north-west side of the bay and a number of mooring buoys have now been installed. Vessels drawing less than 1.5m (4ft 9in) can berth at the mole. This stretch of water claims to be the cleanest in the Adriatic with a change in tidal streams every six hours. However, there are not many facilities available unless you head into Ždrelac itself.

NAVIGATION

Charts: HHI MK-13; AC 515, SC5767

Approaches: The bridge between the two islands is not clearly visible until you get to the entrance of the bay. The islet of Mišnjak lies just north-east of the entrance. It has a white light (Fl (2) 5s) on its north-eastern side, but the islet can be difficult to spot from a distance. From the south-east you will pass the stone chapel of Ždrelac village, about a mile before the entrance to the

Prolaz Mali Ždrelac and the Pašman/Ugljan road bridge

Leaving Ždrelac anchorage, heading towards the mainland

bay. From the north-west, the village of Kukljica, on Ugljan Island, is a similar distance from the entrance. There's a red light (Fl R 5s) just off Rt Zaglav, which signifies the north-west boundary of the bay on the Ugljan side. On Rt Zaglav itself is the chapel of Gospa od Sniga. The Pašman side of the bay is bounded by Rt Artina, which has a green light (Fl (3) G 10s) sited on the inner edge of the channel entering the bay, just before the bay opens out. On the mainland, on a bearing of 40°T from the approach waypoint, lies Marina Sukošan (see page 37). Keep an eye-out for the regular ferries passing under the bridge and note the speed limit of 8 knots. Anchoring, fishing and stopping are prohibited in the channel and vessels entering from the north-east have right of way. The tidal streams can run as high as 4 knots under the bridge and are affected by the winds.

Pilotage: The approach waypoint of 44°01'.93N 15°16'.51E brings you to within a mile of the entrance, well clear of Mišnjak Islet. Looking at the entrance, which lies on a bearing of 224°T, you should be able to see the islet of Mišnjak just to starboard, the green and red lights on either side of the entrance, and the bridge at the far end of the bay. Although this waypoint should give you a clear view of the bay, be prepared to adjust your course to port to avoid the shallow water around Mišnjak Islet. The inner part of the bay shelves quite rapidly so keep an eye on the depth gauge.

MOORING/ANCHORING

This is an organised anchorage under a concession granted by the local authority, so a fee will be payable whether you use one of the mooring buoys or anchor. Someone will come round for your payment and may also offer to take your rubbish. You should get an official receipt but, if in doubt, ask for some identification. The mooring rings are just underneath the buoy and it is recommended that you use at least 3.5m (11ft 5in) of rope. The anchoring blocks weigh 700kg and the polyamide lines linking the blocks and the buoys are 20mm in diameter. There have been reports of these types of moorings parting in bad weather, perhaps due to lack of maintenance, so be warned. If you anchor, the holding is good on a mud bed.

ASHORE

Limited facilities are available at this anchorage. The settlement of Ždrelac has a supermarket, café and restaurant as well as a post office and tourist information office.

Banj

Anchorage: 44°00'.28N 15°17'.81E

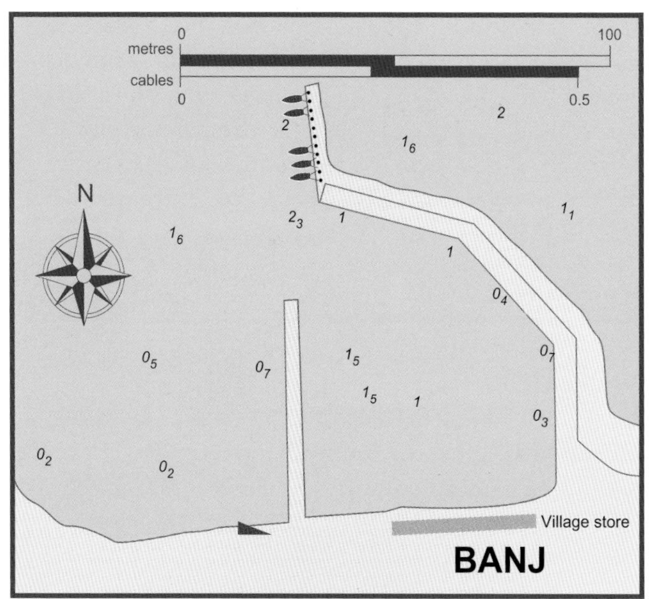

Banj is a small, quiet village surrounded by olive groves and vineyards and containing a number of springs. The church of Sv Kuzme dates back to 1356. The bay offers a good anchorage for smaller vessels, and there is a tiny village harbour with maximum depths of 2m, but it is exposed to the Bora so we would not recommend it for anything other than a short stop.

NAVIGATION

Charts: HHI MK-13 & MK-14; AC 515, AC 2711, SC5767

Approaches: There are no particular hazards a mile either side of the bay. The church, high on the hill behind the village, is clearly visible. The stone harbour wall was undergoing extensive work at the time we visited it.

ASHORE

Water and provisions are available in the village store that looks out onto the sea from the harbour.

Dobropoljana

Harbour entrance: 43°59'.63N 15°19'.69E

Another small village with a harbour that appeared almost deserted when we passed through. However, it has a lovely sandy, gently sloping beach. The harbour is exposed to the Bora and is only suitable for small craft drawing up to 2.5m (8ft 2in).

NAVIGATION

Charts: HHI MK-13, MK-14; AC 515, AC 2711, SC5767

Approaches: If approaching from the south-east, watch out for the sunken wreck just off the coast by Neviđane. The town harbour has a stone breakwater and there is currently a roofless stone building just behind it.

Dobropoljana harbour

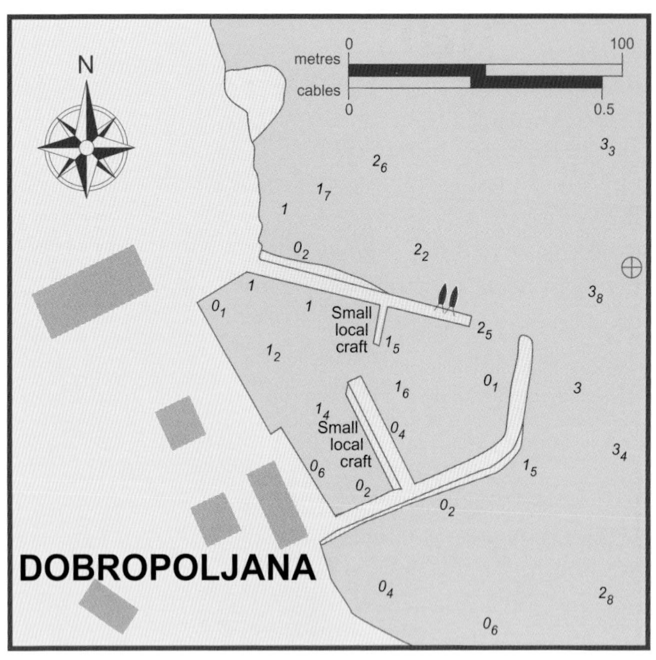

ASHORE

Apart from a few boats in the harbour and some limited building activity, we saw no signs of life but there is a large restaurant – Restaurant Zrinski, Tel: 023 269 142 – a short walk towards the main road, which is presumably vibrant during the short Pašman season.

Neviđane

Harbour entrance: 43°58'.92N 15°20'.65E

From the sea, Neviđane appeared to be another ghost town when we passed it. Despite its good sandy beach, we understand that tourism is relatively new to the inhabitants, and it shows. The population is concentrated a few hundred yards inshore by the main road, where the post office is situated, and it may be that there is a thriving village here in the high season. However, the deserted waterfront and empty harbour do not entice you to explore further and are exposed to the Bora.

Neviđane fishing boats and local craft

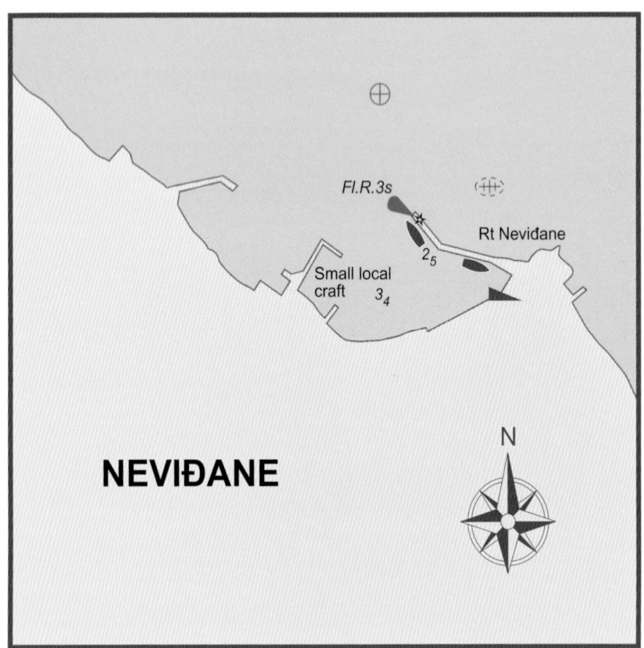

NAVIGATION

Charts: HHI MK-13, MK-14; AC 2711, AC 2773, SC5767

Approaches: Watch out for the dangerous sunken wreck just off the harbour entrance and Školjić rock, about three quarters of a mile east-south-east of the entrance. There's a red light on the end of the breakwater and the church belfry is visible.

Pašman

Harbour entrance: 43°57'.48N 15°23'.28E

This may be the 'capital' of the island, but it appeared just as deserted as all the other settlements on Pašman. It has a town harbour, but there are strong currents at the entrance and it is exposed to northwesterly winds. If you do decide to stop, you can berth along the main breakwater in depths of around 2m.

NAVIGATION

Charts: HHI 515, MK-14; AC 2711, AC 2773, SC5767

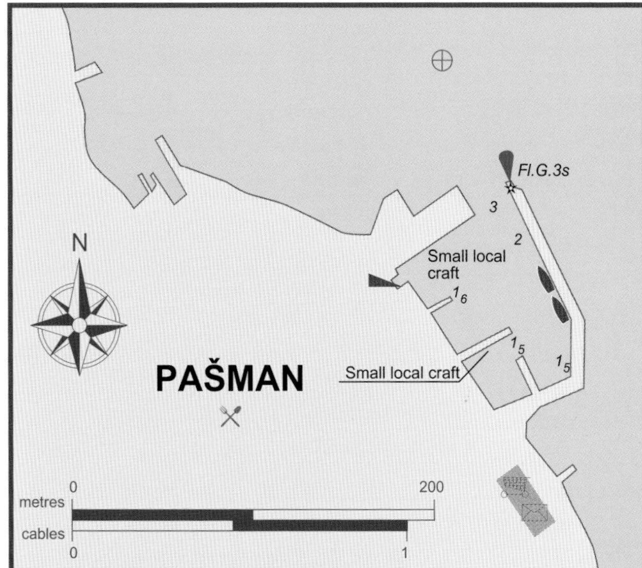

One of the cafés in Pašman Town

Approaches: Pašman lies in the narrowest part of the Pašman Canal and there are a number of shoals and islets nearby, as well as currents, winds and tidal streams to watch out for (see Chapter one, page 31). Landmarks include the green light (Fl G 3s) at the head of the breakwater and the belfry behind Uvala Lučina, west of the harbour.

ASHORE

The large building by the harbour houses a supermarket and a post office. Along the front are some bars and a couple of restaurants – Tamaris and Lanterna. Otherwise there are few signs of life.

Tkon

Harbour entrance: 43°55'.44N 15°25'.23E

Of all the possible stop-off points on Pašman, Tkon is the only one with any real signs of life to it. This is because it's the main ferry port on Pašman linking the islanders to Biograd on the mainland.

If you want to explore the beaches, mountain trails and cultural heritage of Pašman without navigating the most difficult parts of the Pašmanski Kanal, Tkon is the best place to head for. That being said, berths are scarce, limited to vessels drawing up to 2.4m (7ft 9in), and the harbour is not well protected. A few new berths have been created inside the westerly breakwater, at the seaward end, with lazylines, electricity and water provided.

NAVIGATION

Charts: HHI 515, MK-14; AC 2711, AC 2773, SC5767

Given shallow coastal waters, the proximity of a number of islets and the ferry route, an approach waypoint is not helpful. Instead, look out for the chapel on top of a small hill behind the village, and a monastery and belfry higher up. There is also a prominent mobile telephone mast. At the head of the ferry pier is a white light (Fl (2) 4s) and the harbour entrance is identified by a red light (Fl (2) R 5s).

ASHORE

Ashore you will find a restaurant, café, post office, two private tourist offices and a supermarket by the harbour.

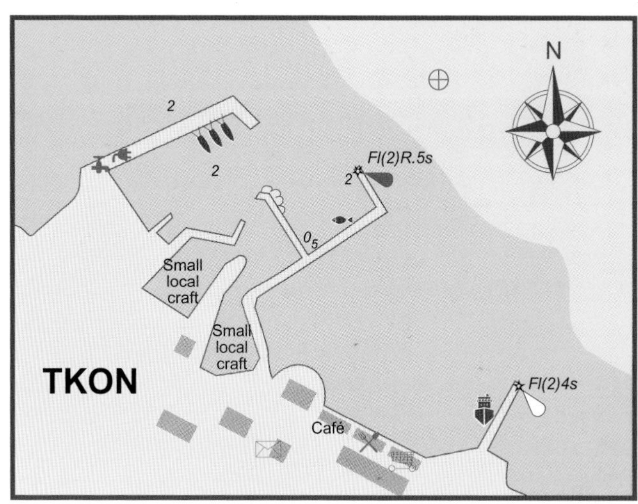

Triluke

Anchorage: 43°53'.57N 15°26'.54E
Charts: HHI MK-14; AC 2711, SC5767

A well-protected but uninhabited cove inside the southernmost tip of the island. Although sheltered from all winds, a Sirocco causes heavy seas. Only suitable for large vessels as depths are around 30m (98ft) in the centre of the bay. Good holding on a sand and gravel bottom. No facilities.

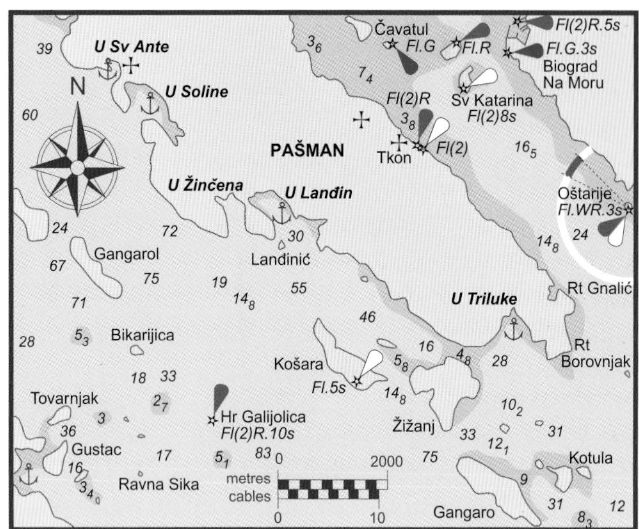

Uvala Lanđin

Entrance to bay: 43°54'.35N 15°23'.50E
Charts: HHI MK-14; AC 2711, SC5767

As with Triluke above, this bay is not suitable when a Sirocco is blowing, but provides sufficient shelter from the Bora.

Holding is good on a sand/weed bed, with depths of between 5 and 8m. Watch out for the low-lying islet, Otočić Lanđinić, just off the headland that forms the western boundary of the bay.

This is a popular anchorage but has no facilities.

Uvala Žinčena

Entrance to bay: 43°54'.48N 15°22'.62E
Charts: HHI MK-14; AC 2711, SC5767

This bay lies immediately west of Uvala Lanđin and is normally a little less frequented, partly due to the greater depths – 10 to 13m at the head of the bay. Shelter is similar to Uvala Lanđin (see above). No facilities.

Uvala Soline

Entrance to bay: 43°55'.64N 15°21'.05E
Charts: HHI MK-14; AC 2711, SC5767

Northwesterly winds can cause a swell, but otherwise the anchorage is sheltered from all winds and offers good holding on a sand and weed seabed in depths of 3 to 7m. Avoid the centre of the bay, which has a rocky bottom.

The unspoilt nature of the bay and the protection afforded make this one of Pašman's best anchorages. Expect to pay a fee whether you use one of the mooring buoys or drop your own anchor (see organised anchorages below).

Uvala Sveti Anti

Entrance to outer bay: 43°56'.01N 15°20'.63E
Charts: HHI MK-14; AC 2711, SC5767

This bay is immediately north-west of Uvala Soline. Sv Ante Chapel lies on the north-east side of the cove, well hidden by trees, and the best anchorage is west of the chapel in a sand and gravel bed in depths of 3 to 8m. The bay is only partially sheltered, being exposed to southerly through to westerly winds, so Uvala Soline is a safer bet for an overnight stop. Beware of rocks off the promontory halfway along the north-western shore as well as off the inner part of the eastern shore.

Again, expect to pay a fee whether you opt for a mooring buoy or drop your anchor (see organised anchorages below).

Pašman – useful information

Pašman falls under the jurisdiction of the Zadar harbourmaster's office (see page 35).

ORGANISED ANCHORAGES

Zadarska Županija: Božidara Petranovića 8, Zadar; Tel: 023 350 350; website: www.zadarska-zupanija.hr. They weren't too forthcoming with information when we contacted them and very little of the website is in English.

TOURIST BOARDS

Zadar County Tourist Board: S Leopolda Mandica 1, Tel: 023 315 316; email: tz-zd-kn@zd-htnet.hr; website: www.zadar.hr.
Pašman Municipal Tourist Board: Tel: 023 260 155.
Tkon Muncipal Tourist Board: Tel: 023 285 213; email: tz-opcine-tkon@zd.htnet.hr.

MEDICAL CENTRES

Pašman: Tel: 023 269 298; Tkon: Tel: 023 85 408.

Ugljan Island

Ugljan, immediately north-west of Pašman, runs parallel to the mainland between Rt Skala, to the north-west, and Sukošan, to the south-east. In contrast to Pašman, Ugljan is well populated and full of life. Kukljica, towards the south-eastern tip of the island, was one of our favourite town harbours and the many villages along the north-east coast are well worth a visit.

The south-west coast has little in the way of shelter or life other than at the top and bottom of the island. Part of Ugljan's charm is that, despite its proximity to Zadar, it is far from overwhelmed by the trappings of the tourist industry and still retains its local rural character. Olive Island Marina, in Sutomišćica, opened in May 2007 – see page 56. Preko, Ugljan's principal town, has the island's only fuel station, is also the site of the ferry port and the branch harbourmaster, and, in August 2007, a small new marina was in the course of construction.

North-east of Kali is the islet of Ošljak – see page 53.

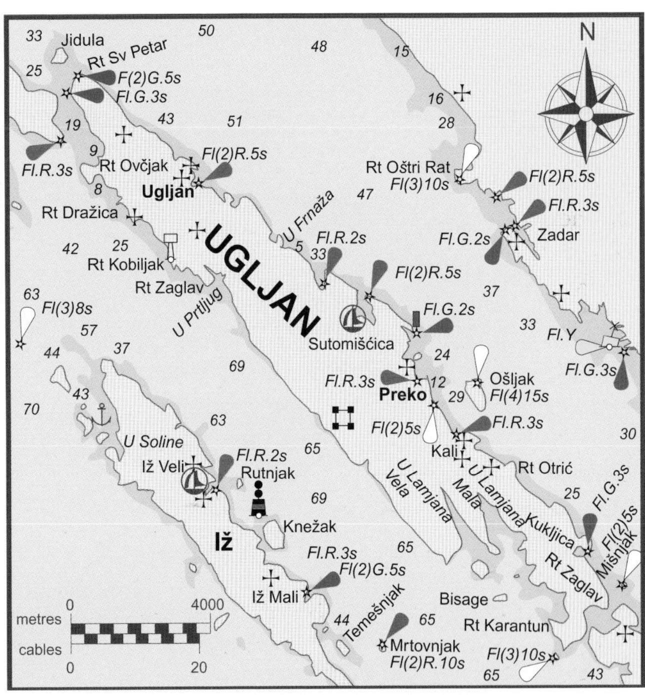

Below we explore the possible stop-offs anticlockwise from the south-eastern tip of Ugljan.

Ugljan Town on Ugljan Island

Prolaz Mali Ždrelac

The passage between Pašman and Ugljan

Ugljan shares this passage and anchorage with Pašman – see page 46 for full details.

Kukljica

Entrance to bay: 44°01'.97N 15°15'.32E

Kukljica has a biggish natural harbour which, by local standards, has been well developed. The local tourist board brochure claims 180 sea berths, but many of these are occupied by fishing vessels while some are reserved for visiting tourist boats from Zadar. It's a good place for an overnight stop, providing southeasterlies aren't sending a swell into the harbour. There's a large hotel complex on the eastern tip of the bay, but this is far enough away from the centre of the village for it to retain its local character.

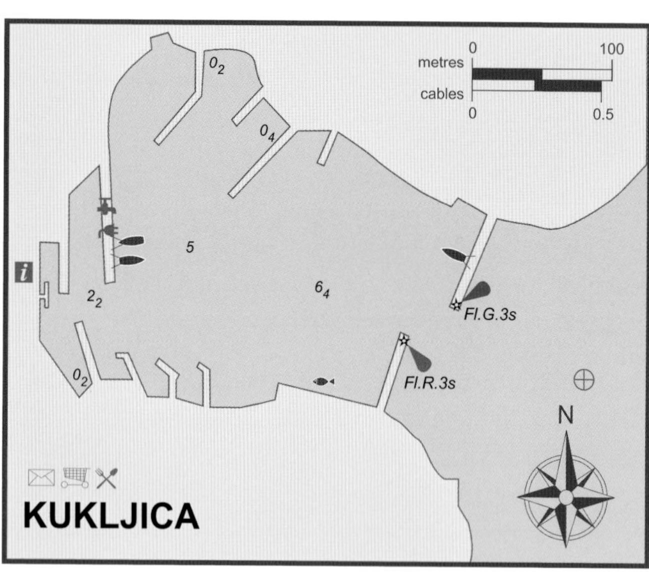

Kukljica Harbour

NAVIGATION

Charts: HHI MK-13; AC 515, AC 2711, SC5767

Approaches: The islet of Mišnjak lies about 0.8M south-east of the harbour entrance and has a white light (Fl (2) 5s) on its north-eastern tip. Otherwise there are no particular hazards. The harbour itself has green (Fl G 3s) and red (Fl R 3s) lights marking the entrance. The north side of the entrance (green light) is quite heavily forested and in the village the church belfry is visible.

BERTHING

When we visited Kukljica in mid June, there was no one to direct us to a berth or to take a fee from us. We berthed alongside the first pontoon on the north side of the harbour and were shortly joined by a day-tripper boat full of tourists from Zadar. Watch your depths on the shore side of the inner pontoons. The harbour is sheltered from all winds.

ANCHORING

Given the recent increase in berthing capacity and the potential volume of traffic in the high season, anchoring is probably not as common or advisable as it used to be. Kukljica is, however, identified as an organised anchorage in the Zadar municipality *Anchorages and Marinas* brochure. The depth in the centre of the harbour is 5m, but the holding (rocky bottom with thin layer of mud) is unreliable.

Useful information – Kukljica

FACILITIES

Kukljica looks like a village and harbour awaiting further investment, so facilities may improve. Some of the inner pontoons already have **electricity** and **water** and there is a **boatyard** and **slipway** for repairs to traditional wooden craft. **Rubbish** bins are reasonably well distributed and we are reliably informed that **showers** and **toilets** have now been built. The harbour is run by Sabuša d.o.o. Contact name Ivo Joja Tel: 023 373 840; Fax: 023 373 229; email: sabusa@zd.htnet.hr.

PROVISIONING

The **post office** and a sizable **supermarket** are located in the main square. The nearest **bank** and **cash point** are in Preko, although money can be exchanged at the post office.

EATING OUT

Konoba Stari Mlin (Tel: 023 373304) and Konoba Kod Barba Tome (Tel: 023 373 323) have the normal selection of standard Croatian restaurant food at reasonable prices. A few cafés and pizza places and another restaurant can be found in the hotel complex.

ASHORE

The **tourist office** is in the main square, Tel: 023 373 276; email: kukljica@kukljica.hr; website: www.kukljica.hr. It did not have much information available when we visited, but its website is one of the best we've come across for a village of this size.

There are plenty of walking trails – one of them takes in a few quiet beaches on the south-western side of the island and the Chapel of Our Lady of the Snow (Gospa Snježna). This chapel, and a big festival on 5 August involving the whole village, commemorate a miraculous August snowfall some 400 years ago. The walk is 6.5km (4 miles) long and is said to be 'easy'.

OTHER INFORMATION

Medical: The nearest emergency hospital is in Zadar but there are four ambulances on Ugljan, and one is based in Kukljica, Tel: 023 373 379.

Kali

Approx 100m from the northern harbour: 44°04'.08N 15°12'.16E

Kali is reputed to have the biggest fishing fleet in the Adriatic and, when the fleet is in, it may be difficult to find a berth. There are two harbours on either side of Rt Rahovača, the main one being to the north. Both are exposed to northerly winds, which can cause a swell. Perhaps due to the decline in the fishing industry, the village appears a little run down.

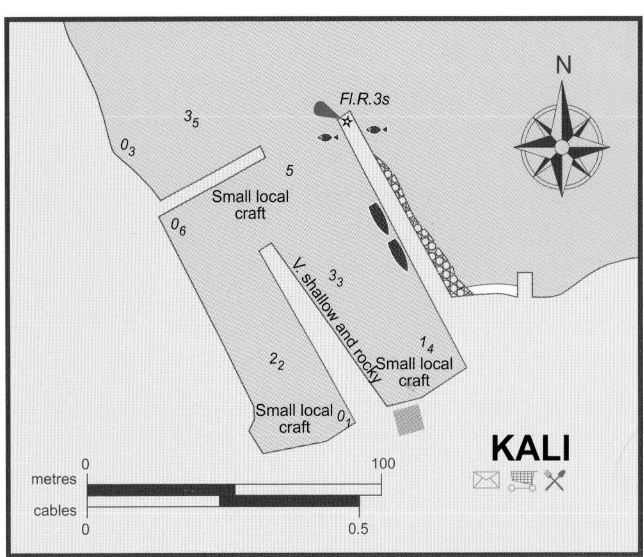

NAVIGATION

Charts: HHI MK-13; AC 515; AC 2711, SC5767

Approaches: The islet of Ošljak lies half a mile to the north-east of the harbour and has a white light (Fl (4) 15s) on its north-eastern tip. The church belfry is visible above the rooftops and there's a red light (Fl R 3s) on the head of the east mole of the northern harbour.

BERTHING

The fishing fleet takes up most of the inner harbour. The best berthing for yachts (depths 2 to 5m) is on the inner side of the breakwater in the north harbour.

ANCHORING

Anchoring is not recommended and there is an underwater power cable about 200m north-west of the harbour, running to Ošljak Islet.

Useful information – Kali

FACILITIES

The nearest **fuel** is in Preko. There is a branch **port authority** (harbourmaster) also in Preko, Tel: 023 286 183.

PROVISIONING

There's not much tourism here though there are shops for provisioning and a **post office** (post office opening hours as Kukljica on page 52). The nearest **bank** is in Preko.

EATING OUT

Eating facilities include Franov, Tel: 023 281 715, and a number of cafés.

ASHORE

The centre of the village is full of narrow streets and traditional houses. A Fisherman's Festival, comprising a regatta and other competitions, takes place in August.

OTHER INFORMATION

Medical: The nearest hospital is in Zadar, but there are four ambulances on Ugljan, and one is based at Kali, Tel: 023 281 142.

Kali's main breakwater, usually dominated by the fishing fleet

Ošljak Islet

Charts: HHI MK-13; AC 515, AC 2711, SC5767

This islet lies about half a mile off the island of Ugljan, between the villages of Kali and Preko, and claims to be the smallest inhabited island in the Adriatic.

It has limited facilities but might make a good lunchtime stop. Yachts drawing up to 3m (9ft 8in) can berth alongside the breakwater on the south-west side of the islet.

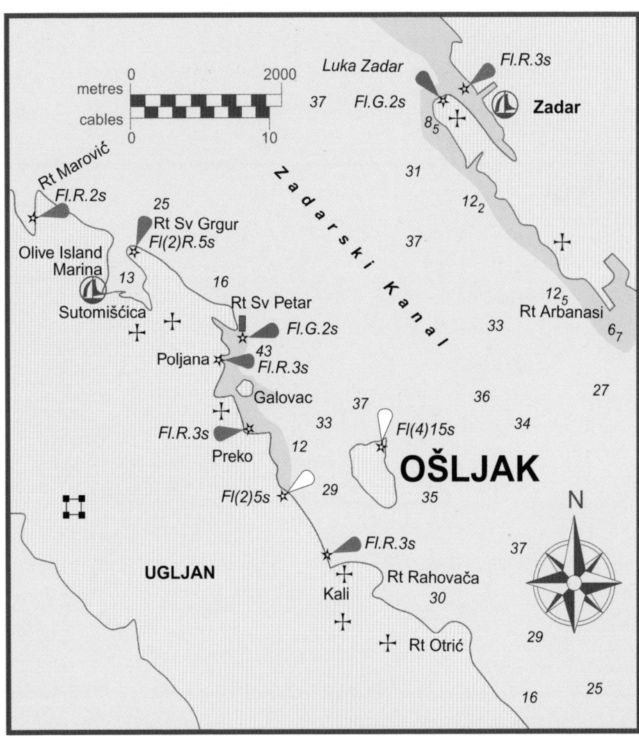

Preko

Just outside south harbour entrance: 44°04'.97N 15°11'.33E

Preko is the largest village on Ugljan, strategically placed opposite Zadar, and is also the site of Ugljan's ferry terminal. Its name means 'opposite' and it is somewhat in the shadow of its mainland neighbour. It has a fuel station and greater facilities than other villages on the island, but otherwise not too much to attract the passing yacht. However, a new marina was under construction in the summer of 2007. There are two harbours: the south harbour is the main one and closest to the town; the inner north-west harbour is the most protected, but depths may not be suitable for yachts in many places.

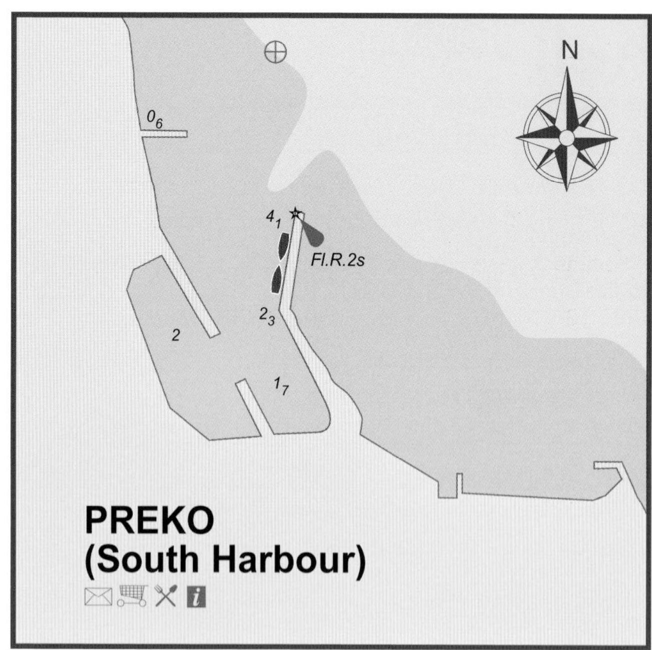

NAVIGATION

Charts: HHI MK-13; AC 515, AC 2711, SC5767

Approaches: It is not possible to pass between the island of Ugljan and the islet of Galovac due to shallow depths and overhead cables. Galovac lies between the north and the south harbours. Approaching from the south-east, you may pass either side of Ošljak Islet (see page 53). Approaching from the north-west, the light beacon on Rt Sv Petar (Fl G 2s) marks a 2m shoal between the beacon and Ugljan Island.

Pilotage: The larger conical islet of Ošljak, south-east of Preko, can be spotted at some distance from both directions. Looking further towards the island of Ugljan, Galovac Islet should be visible to starboard from the north-west, once you are about 550m past Rt Sv Petar. From the south-east, you should see Galovac almost directly ahead of you if you take the middle of the channel between Ugljan Island and Ošljak Islet. Approaching from the south-east, there is a white metal tower (green light) at the head of the ferry pier and just past this is the fuel station. Continuing the approach from the south-east, the head of the breakwater at the entrance to the south-east harbour has a red light and the main part of the village lies behind this harbour. Then, immediately past Galovac Island, which you leave to port, is the entrance to the north harbour. The top half of the church tower, currently painted a light burgundy, and a large factory building behind it, become visible as you pass the main part of the village approaching from the south-east.

Looking north over Preko's harbours

BERTHING

Either berth alongside on the outside of the southern pier in the north-east harbour (about a 2m depth) or alongside the breakwater on the south-eastern harbour. Watch depths carefully as they fluctuate significantly in different parts of the harbour.

ANCHORING

Depths of 5 to 8m can be found north-west or south of Galovac, but look carefully at the chart to avoid the prohibited area. Anchoring is not recommended as both locations are exposed to the Bora.

Useful information – Preko

FACILITIES

Fuel and **water** are available at the fuel berth, Tel: 023 286 214, depths 2 to 2.7m, and you'll find **rubbish** bins scattered around the village. The **branch harbourmaster's office** is also here, Tel: 023 286 183.

PROVISIONING

There are plenty of shops in the village as well as a **chemist**, a **post office**, a **bank** and a few **cash points.**

EATING OUT

Konoba Barbara is by the ferry terminal and is good for fish, Tel: 023 286 129. Also worth a try are Restoran Jardin, Tel: 023 296 358, and Restoran Preko, Tel: 023 286 194. There are plenty of cafés and bars around the harbours.

ASHORE

The **tourist information office** is in the main harbour square, back from the waterfront; Tel/fax: 023, 286 108; email: tz-preko@zd.htnet.hr; website: www.ugljan-pasman.com/preko.

In the high season you can get a boat to Galovac where you will find a Franciscan monastery. The Fortress of St Michael, which lies behind the village to the west, is about an hour's walk away and well worth a visit. On a clear day it offers spectacular views of Zadar to the east and Dugi Otok and Italy to the west.

TRANSPORT

The **Jadrolinija office** is by the ferry port, Tel: 023 286 008. The municipal **tourist office** or the private tourist agencies will be able to help you with **renting bikes, scooters** and **cars.**

OTHER INFORMATION

Medical: The nearest emergency hospital is in Zadar, but there is an ambulance station in Preko, Tel: 023 286 181.

Poljana

Entrance to bay: 44°05'.51N 15°11'.20E

Poljana has two breakwaters and a number of small jetties, but is exposed to easterly and southeasterly winds. Note too that the Bora causes a moderate swell.

Facilities are limited to one small supermarket and a couple of pizza restaurants (one delivers – Tel: 023 268114), although the village is the main supplier of vegetables to Zadar market thanks to numerous wells that irrigate the produce.

NAVIGATION

Charts: HHI MK-13; AC 515, AC 2711, SC5767

Approaches: Beware of the shoal that lies south-east of Rt Sv Petar, marked by a green light (Fl G 2s) at its south-eastern extremity. Also watch out for the submerged rocks off the north coast of the cove. Landmarks are the church belfry and the red light (Fl R 3s) on the breakwater south of the entrance.

BERTHING/ANCHORING

Depths by the main pier are too shallow for most yachts so anchoring is a safer bet in about 7m of water just south-east of the pier.

Poljana – exposed to easterly and southeasterly winds

Sutomišćica

Entrance to bay: 44°06'.17N 15°10'.10E
Charts: HHI MK-13; AC 515, SC5767

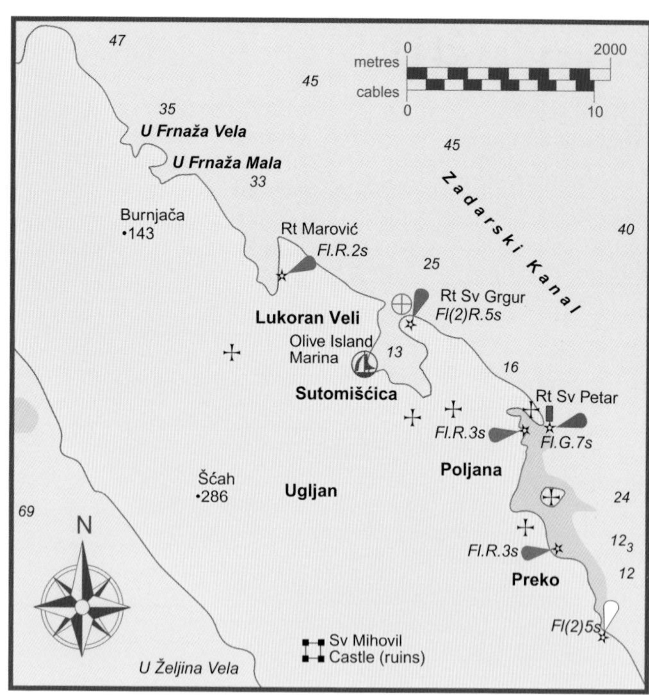

Sutomišćica is a sleepy settlement with a large bay. However, it may not remain sleepy for much longer as a 200-berth marina was opened in May 2007. Among its facilities are an on site restaurant, shop, chandlery and yacht repair services. The bay is exposed to the Bora and Tramontana, but otherwise is well protected and has a number of quays and moles. There's a red light on Rt Sv Grgur on the south-east side of the bay, and the church belfry is prominent. Facilities include a restaurant, Bei Schloss, sign-posted from the harbour, plenty of cafés and a grocery shop in the village.

BERTHING/ANCHORING

Up to date details of the new marinas facilities can be found at www.oliveislandmarina.com or call the marina on Tel: 023 335 809. In the bay depths vary by the various moles and quays, with probably the deepest water on the south side of the pier on the east side of the bay – between 2 and 3m. Alternatively, you can anchor north of this pier on either the east or west side of the bay. The holding is good on a sand and mud bottom.

Olive Island Marina in Sutomišćica Bay, Ugljan

Lukoran Veli

Harbour entrance:
44°06'.49N 15°09'.13E

Another bay with a few piers, but these are mostly for small craft. New apartments mix with attractive old houses and the village has a restaurant, post office, store and sandwich bar. It even has its own tourist office but it's only open on Thursdays and Sundays between 0900 and 1100.

Lukoran Veli – the red light is on the main pier on the east side of the bay

NAVIGATION

Charts: HHI MK-13; AC 515, SC5767

Approaches: Watch out for shallow banks on the west side of the bay and also, if approaching from the south- east, those along the headland to the east of the bay. There's a red light (Fl R 2s) on the main pier on the east side of the bay and the church on the hill is clearly visible.

BERTHING/ANCHORING

Depths are shallow by the pier so anchoring is recommended. The holding is good on a sandy bed. The bay is exposed to the Bora but otherwise well sheltered.

Uvala Frnaža (Mala and Vela)

Just north-east of Lukoran Veli, and before Čeprljanda, are two small deserted bays. They are not as sheltered as Lukoran Veli or Čeprljanda, further north-east, but provide a good place for a short stop away from it all. Uvala Frnaža Mala, the first of the two bays when approaching from the south-east, is shallow.

Čeprljanda Harbour – recommended only for a short stop in settled weather

Čeprljanda

Charts: HHI MK-12, MK-13; AC 515, SC5767

The village of Čeprljanda straddles two small shallow bays up to 3m in depth. There's little in the way of facilities, but the bays are sheltered from all winds except those from the north and north-west.

It is not recommended for anything other than a short stop in good weather conditions.

Ugljan

Harbour entrance: 44°07'.91N 15°06'.54E

Ugljan is a reasonably well-developed tourist village with some pretty bays and a hotel that also doubles up as a recreational centre for watersports and cycle hire. Unfortunately, the harbour itself is quite shallow and exposed to the Bora, and the anchorage holding is unreliable, so it's not the best place for an overnight stop.

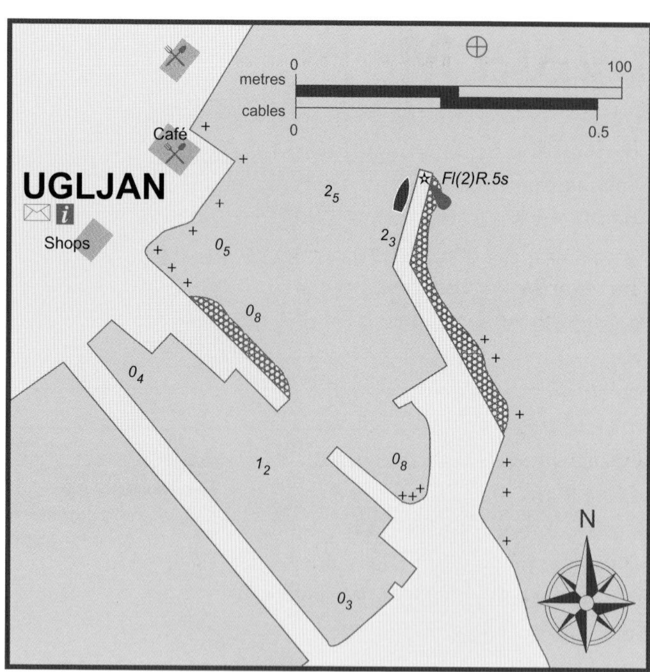

Ugljan, with the white cross in the background

NAVIGATION

Charts: HHI MK-12, MK-13; AC 515, SC5767

Pilotage: Depths in the approach to the bay reduce to 4m in places and there is a shoal north-west of the entrance. Landmarks include a distinctive monastery and stone cross on the headland, north-west of the harbour entrance, and a red light (Fl (2) R 5s) at the head of the main pier/breakwater. The Hotel Ugljan, with a prominent statue in front of it, is situated close to the seafront.

BERTHING/ANCHORING

Ugljan is really only suitable for shelter from the Sirocco. Depths in the harbour are about 1m and, along the north-west side of the pier, a maximum of 2.5m. Anchoring is possible outside the harbour, but is not recommended.

Useful information – Ugljan

FACILITIES

No nautical facilities worth noting. Preko is the main 'nautical' town of the island.

PROVISIONING

There are a few shops in the village, including a large hardware store, as well as a **post office** and a **cash point**, but the nearest **pharmacy** and emergency **medical services** are in Preko.

EATING OUT

There are plenty of bars, pizzerias and restaurants for a village of this size. Try Konoba Ankora, Tel: 023 288 622, or Restoran Apollo, Tel: 023 288 394, both on the front and offering standard Croatian fare.

ASHORE

Ugljan has its fair share of ancient monuments, including the Franciscan monastery and the ruins of a Roman villa. There's a **diving centre** offering a range of options; Tel/fax: 023 288 022; email: diving.center.ugljan@zd.hinet.hr. Check out the **tourist office** (Tel: 023 288011; email: info@ugljan.hr) or the Hotel Ugljan (Tel: 023 288 024) for **bike hire** and other activities. The best **beaches** are Cinta and Mostir.

The red light (Fl (2) R 5s) at the head of the main breakwater

Uvala Muline

Entrance to bay: 44°08'.37N 15°04'.17E
Charts: HHI MK-12, MK-13; AC 515, SC5767

The bay of Muline and the village of Donje Selo lie on the north-west end of the south-east coast of Ugljan. The approach from the north is via the Veli Ždrelac passage, between the islands of Ugljan and Rivanj, which can have strong currents. Otherwise the approach is relatively straightforward. The bay is well protected from all winds by the surrounding islands. Berthing, with caution, is possible alongside the seaward end of the main pier for yachts drawing up to 3m (9ft 8in). About 10 mooring buoys have been laid and there are a number of suitable anchorages, mostly in sand, away from the main channel, although check the charts for the position of underwater cables.

Facilities are limited, with just a makeshift café and a transportable toilet, but it's a great spot with some interesting ruins, including the mill from which the word Muline is derived.

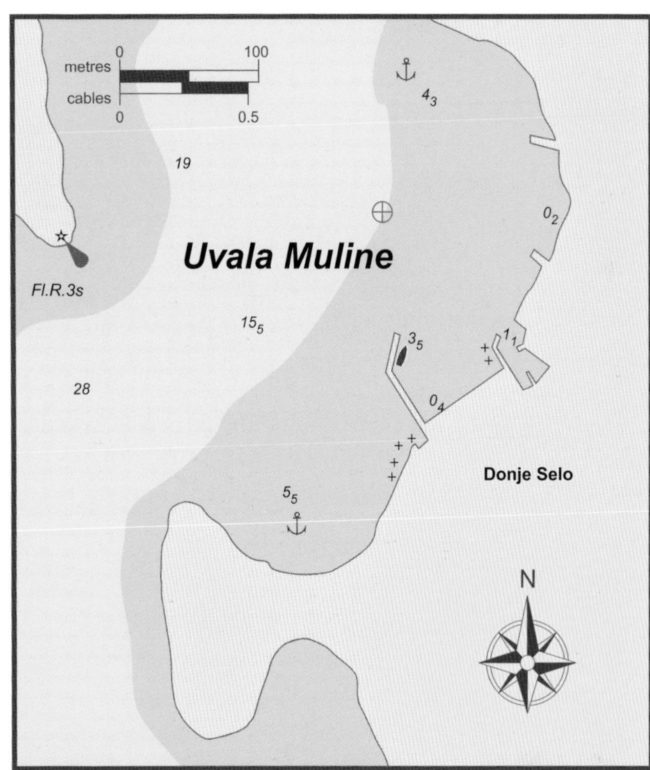

The breakwater and temporary toilet facilities in Uvala Muline

Uvala Prtljug

Entrance to bay: 44°06'.29N 15°06'.83E
Charts: HHI MK-13; AC 515, SC5767

This bay provides a peaceful anchorage of varying depths, with good holding in a sand and weed bed. It's sheltered from all winds apart from those from the south-east, which cause a swell.

There are no facilities at Uvala Prtljug, but this is the last good stop-off opportunity before reaching the south-east tip of Ugljan.

Uvala Lamjana Vela

Entrance to bay: 44°02'.14N 15°12'.67E
Charts: HHI MK-13; AC 515, SC5767

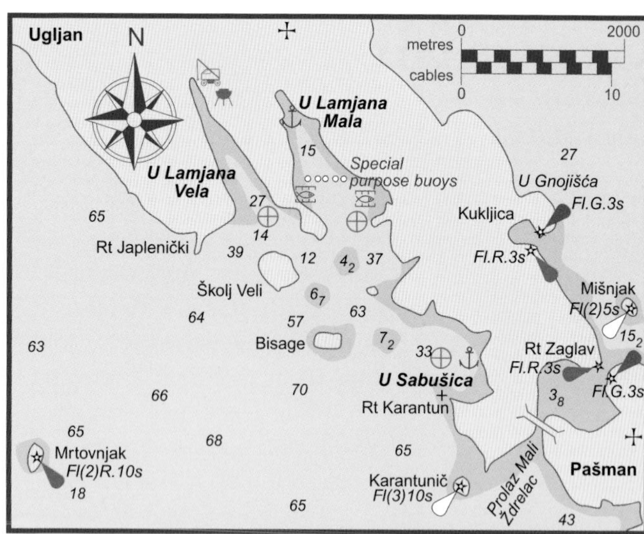

The most westerly of the two bays at the south-east tip of Ugljan, Uvala Lamjana Vela was originally the home of Zadar shipyard and holds little attraction for the passing recreational sailor. The land has now been taken over by a commercial operation which plans to develop the area into a marina and residential complex.

There are a number of islets and shoals to watch out for as well as a rock, visible above the water, close to the south-west entrance to Uvala Lamjana Vela.

The shipyard at Uvala Lamjana Vela

Uvala Lamjana Mala

Entrance to bay: 44°02'.11N 15°13'.41E
Charts: HHI MK-13; AC 515, SC5767

This bay provides a well-protected anchorage that lies beyond the mooring buoys allocated to fishing vessels. The holding is good in a bed of weed, with a depth of 3 to 6m. Look out for the shoals and islets when approaching the bay and stay clear of the fish farm on the western side of the bay. The speed limit is 7 knots and no night-time navigation is permitted for vessels over 16m (52ft) in length and with engines of over 80hp.

One of Uvala Lamjana Mala's fish farms

Uvala Sabušica

Entrance to bay: 44°01'.38N 15°13'.99E
Charts: HHI MK-13; AC 515, SC5767

A good anchorage in sand, in depths of between 2 and 8m, and well protected from both the Bora and the Sirocco. Stay clear of the sandbank extending north-west from Rt Karantun (clearance about 3.8m).

Useful information on Ugljan

ORGANISED ANCHORAGES
Zadarska Županija: Božidara Petranovića 8, Zadar **Tel:** 023 350 350; **website:** www.zadarska-zupanija.hr

ZADAR COUNTY TOURIST BOARD
S Leopolda Mandica 1 **Tel:** 023 315 316; **email:** tz-zd-kn@zd-htnet.hr;
website: www.zadar.hr

LOCAL TOURIST BOARDS
Ugljan: Tel: 023 260 155; **email:** tz-ugljan@zd.htnet.hr
Preko: Tel: 023 286 108; **email:** tz-preko@zd.htnet.hr; **website:** www.ugljan-pasman.com
Kali: Tel: 023 282 406; **email:** kalionline@hotmail.com
Kukljica: Tel: 023 373 276; **email:** kukljica@kukljica.hr

Hotel Ugljan, 23275 Ugljan, **Tel:** 023 288 004; **email:** hotel@hotel-ugljan.com; **website:** www.hotel-ugljan.com

MEDICAL CENTRES
Preko: Tel: 023 286 181; **Kuklijica: Tel:** 023 373 379; **Kali: Tel:** 023 282 655 & 023 281 143.

Ugljan falls under the jurisdiction of the Zadar harbourmaster's office (see page 35).

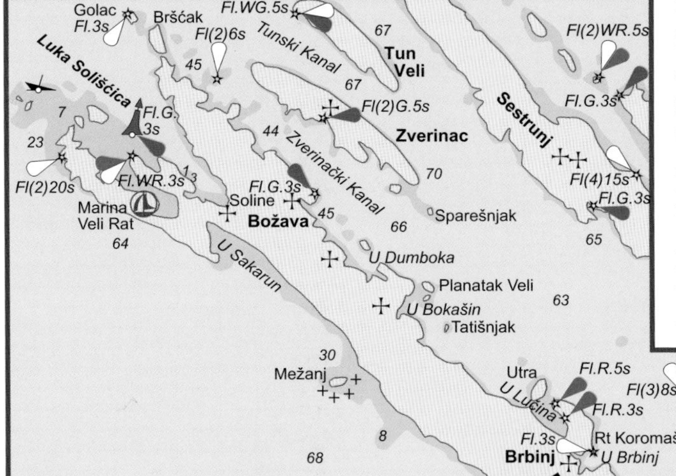

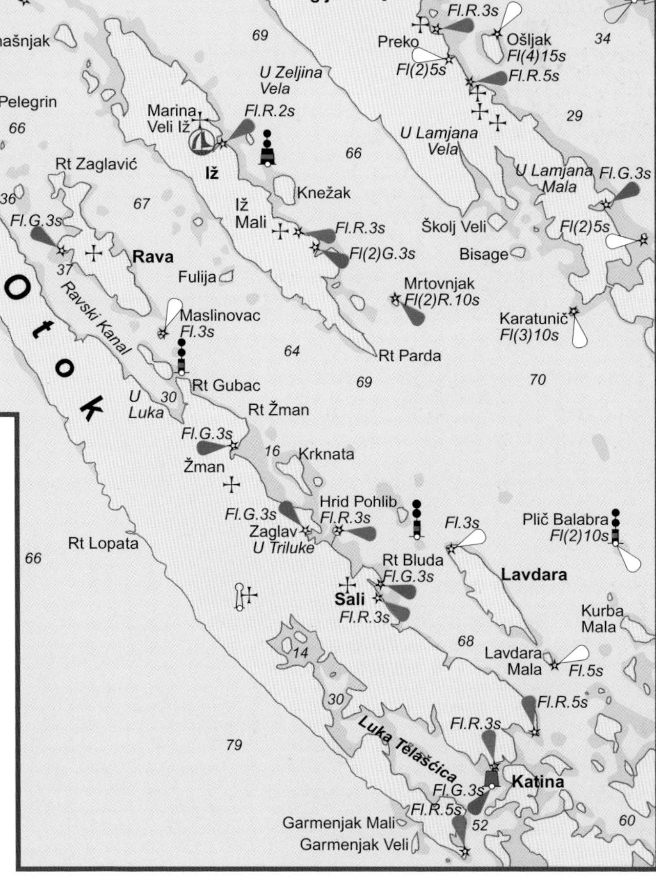

Dugi Otok

The long thin island of Dugi Otok, with the Kornati Islands further south-east, protects the inner islands of the Zadar Archipelago from the worst of the onshore winds. The south-west of the island has the barren, rocky, largely inaccessible coastline to prove it. In contrast, the north-east coast of the island has a number of bays, islets and villages, many of which are worth a visit. There are no natural sources of water on the island so water can be a scarce commodity. The island is thinly populated, which leads to a slower pace and more limited facilities than you will find on Pašman and Ugljan. The principal settlement on the island is Sali and the main attraction is the Telašćica Nature Park, both at the south-east end of the island. The nature park used to be part of the Kornati National Park before it received its own Nature Park status. It is accessible from the sea and has a salt-water lake popular with the locals. A rare species of carnivorous sponge can also be found in these waters.

In exploring Dugi Otok, we start with Luka Telašćica at the south-east end of the island and work our way anticlockwise, around the north-east coast, concluding with a summary of what little shelter lies on the opposite side. Useful information for the whole island, including transport and the fuel station in Zaglav, is incorporated at the end of all the individual port summaries.

Luka Telašćica

Entrance to main bay: 43°52'.97N 15°12'.28E

Luka Telašćica is a long, heavily indented bay at the southeastern end of the island. Designated a nature park, the area is largely uninhabited and, although perhaps not as stunning or dramatic as the Kornati National Park, it still has considerable intrinsic beauty. Unfortunately, there was a devastating fire in 1995, although reforestation has since taken place. The bay divides into a number of connected basins and there are several anchoring options for boats of various sizes.

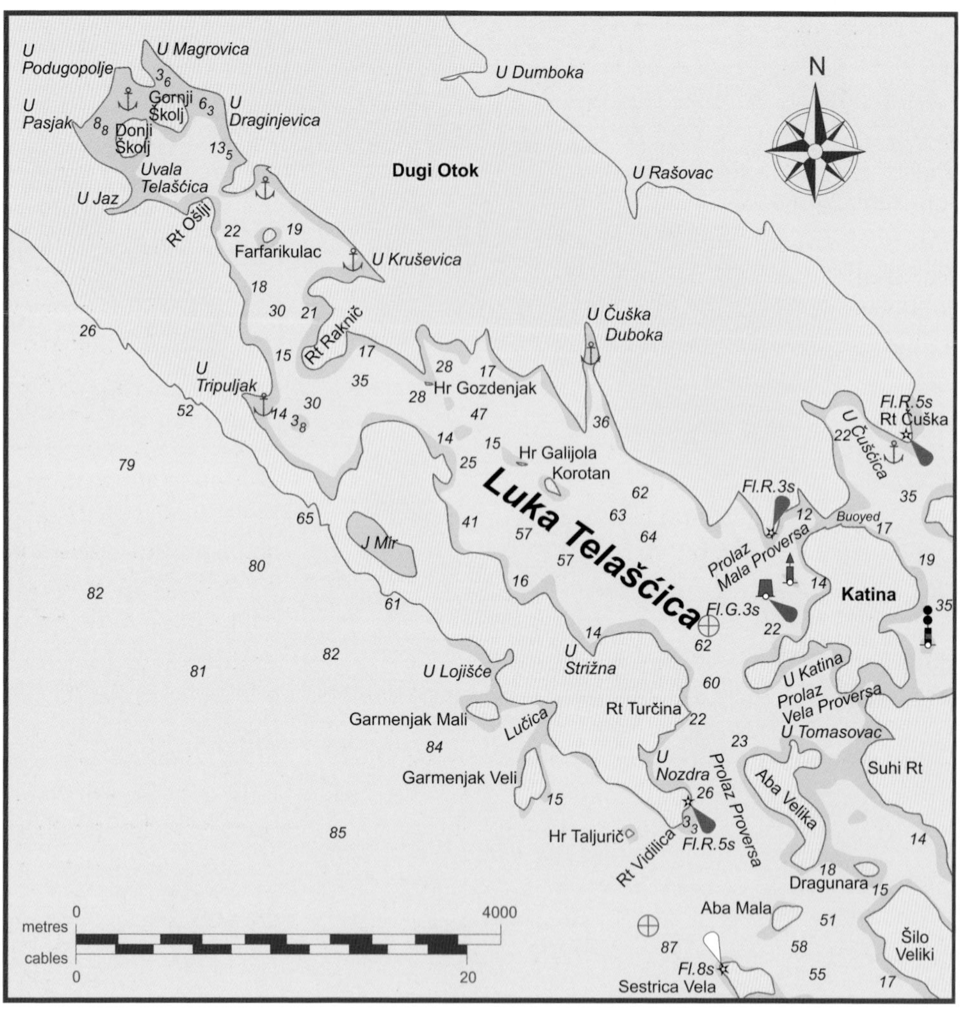

NAVIGATION

Charts: HHI MK-14; AC 2711, AC 2773, SC5767

Approaches: The approach from the open sea, south-west of the entrance to the bay, is the best route in. Heading north-east towards the gap between Dugi Otok and Aba Velika, the islet of Sestrica Vela lies to starboard and has a distinctive lighthouse (Fl 8s) on its north-west point. To port, on Dugi Otok, is a red light (Fl R 5s) on Rt Vidilica. Extending from Rt Vidilica, for about 200m, is a shoal with a 3.3m clearance and south-west of the same point is an above-water rock (Hrid Taljurič). If approaching from the north-east, avoid Prolaz Vela Proversa, between the islands of Kornat and Katina, which is very shallow. Instead, use Prolaz Mala Proversa, between Katina and Dugi Otok. Although this channel is much narrower, it is well buoyed and deeper. The currents in the channel can reach up to 4 knots and tend to follow the direction of the wind.

Pilotage: From the west, a course of 44°T from an approach waypoint of 43°51'.38N 15°11'.84E should allow you to see the two lights mentioned above and head you directly towards the middle of the south-east coast of Aba Velika, about a mile away from the waypoint. As you head towards Aba Velika, you will see the entrance to the bay opening up to port. Approaching from the east, there are a number of islands and islets to avoid so, rather than using an approach waypoint, approach just north of the islet of Gornja Aba, with the red light (Fl R 5s) on Rt Čuška to starboard. Follow the curve of the islet round to the west until you see Prolaz Mala Proversa. The channel has been dredged to a depth of over 4m and is well marked with green and red buoys. To port, on Katina Island, is Restaurant Aquarius, while in a bay to starboard you will see some mooring buoys. As you exit the narrowest part of the channel, continue keeping a look-out for two rocks west of Katina Islet. The inner rock is identified by a beacon and the outer rock by a green light beacon (Fl G 3s). The bay itself stretches inland for about four miles, with a few more rocks and islets to navigate, all of which are clearly identified on the charts. Korotan Islet marks the start of a mostly submerged rock ridge extending north-west to Dugi Otok.

BERTHING/ANCHORING

A strong Sirocco causes a swell and the effects of the Bora can be severe in many parts of the bay. The best shelter from all winds is found in the innermost bays – Uvala Magrovica and Uvala Pasjak – north-west of the two islets. The holding is good in a mud bed in depths of between 3 and 10m. A deeper anchorage for larger yachts can be found on the other side of the two islets. This location also has the added advantage of being close to the popular restaurant Taverno Goro, and has a grocery store on a boat that normally does the rounds in the morning and evening.

Uvala Čuška Duboka lies to the north of the outer basin and is well sheltered from everything but a strong Sirocco. Protection is best if you head towards the end of the inlet but it does become quite shallow. Holding is good in a mud bed. Mooring buoys are available further out, but note that you will be more exposed here.

Uvala Tripuljak lies on the north-west side of the second basin and affords good protection on its southern shore, except in a strong Bora, though depths do not start to reduce until quite close in. Watch out for the 3.8m shoal clearly marked on the chart and avoid the mooring buoy in the centre of the bay, which is reserved for Croatian naval vessels. Anchor in good holding on a mud bed in depths of between 2 and 20m, or use one of the mooring buoys. The nearby campsite has limited facilities (see below).

Uvala Kruševica, on the north-east side of the third basin, also has visitors' mooring buoys and affords good shelter from all winds except those from the south-west sector, through west, to north. Use one of the buoys or anchor in 3 to 9m in good holding on a mud bed.

FACILITIES

Whether you take a mooring buoy or not, you'll still be charged for staying in the National Park. Last time we checked, the fee was 50 Kunas a head and entitled you to two nights in Telašćica and one in Kornati National Park. You should also get your rubbish collected. The campsite in Uvala Tripuljak has a café and a restaurant. Taverno Goro, in the innermost bay, does traditional Croatian food cooked under a bell (*peka*); however, it's best to order this in advance. The grocery boat concentrates on the inner bays but might be persuaded further afield. For anything else you'll need to go to Sali (see page 64). Look at the website www.telascica.hr for the most up-to-date information on the park, though there were no pricing details in August 2007.

ASHORE

The park has plenty of natural beauty to offer and the mud from the salt-water Lake Mir, where the water is warmer and saltier than the sea, is alleged to have great natural healing powers.

Prolaz Mala Proversa

Sali

Entrance to bay: 43°56'.13N 15°10'.14E

Sali is a cosy town with a real heart and a bustle of its own that is far from dependent on tourists. It's a fishing centre and has its own fish-processing factory. With plenty of shops and restaurants, it must be one of the few places in the area that you could visit well out of season and expect to find reasonable facilities.

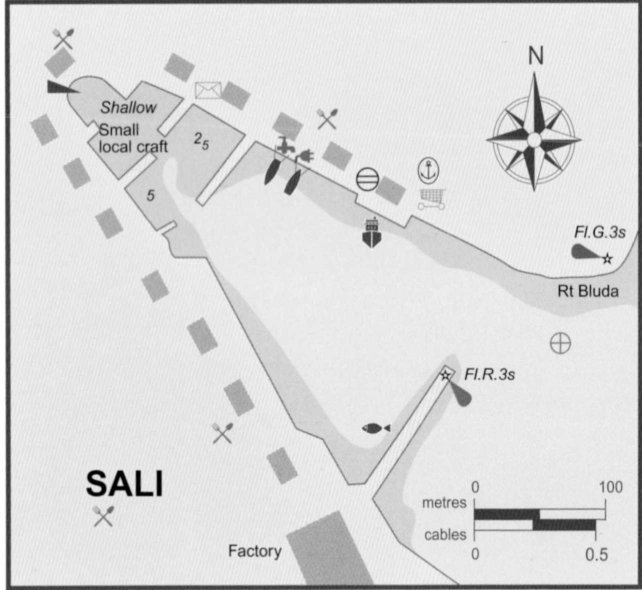

Sali's inner harbour at sunset

Pilotage: The low, long building with a tall chimney is the fish-processing factory and provides the best landmark for Sali. Just east of this is a pier with a red light (Fl R 3s), which is used by fishing boats, while a green light (Fl G 3s) sits on the headland (Rt Bluda) on a square brick tower. Don't be confused by the larger red-domed object behind it that has a cross on the top. As you pass between the two lights, head for the quay to starboard, situated before the breakwater that protects the inner harbour.

NAVIGATION

Charts: HHI MK-13, MK-14; AC 2711, SC5767

Approaches: There's little to worry about when approaching from the south-east. From the north-west or the east you need to watch out for the shoals, rocks and islets west and north-west of the northern tip of the island of Lavdara. These are clearly marked on the charts and the shallowest area, at 2.2m, is identified by an isolated danger beacon. Watch out for the ferries.

BERTHING/ANCHORING

The harbour is sheltered from all winds apart from those from the south-east. As you approach, the quay to starboard, located between the ferry quay (also to starboard) and the inner harbour, has lazylines and depths of about 3m. The inner harbour is usually full of fishing boats and smaller local boats.

Anchoring is possible in the outer part of the harbour but this is more exposed. Uvala Saščica is a better bet when southeasterly winds are blowing and lies around the other side of the headland from Sali, heading north-west.

Useful information – Sali

FACILITIES

The visitors' moorings are operated by a private company by concession – Mulik d.o.o Tel: 023 344 250. We were told it was not possible to book ahead. Facilities comprise **water** and **electricity** bollards, as well as **rubbish** bins. **Yacht services** include a workshop next to the fish processing plant, for engine repairs and maintenance, and a boatyard in the nearby Saščica bay for hull and engine repairs.

PROVISIONING

There's a large **supermarket** by the ferry terminal, a **cash point** just west of it, a **post office** a little further west and then a Jadrolinija ferry kiosk. You'll find plenty of other **shops** and **mini-markets** in the town, which incorporates everything that the indigenous population of about 1,200 needs to avoid too many trips to the mainland.

EATING OUT

Sali has plenty of bars and cafés and a number of good restaurants dotted around the harbour.

Our favourite, for its rustic atmosphere and good simple Croatian food, is Konoba Marin, tucked up a side street just off the north-west corner of the harbour, Tel: 023 377 500; Mobile: 098 843 202.

The Pub on the Moon was full of tourists when we visited, but lacked atmosphere. Otherwise there's Grill Tamaris and Grill Toni, both of which are situated on the south-west side of the harbour towards the fishing boat pier.

ASHORE

The **tourist office**, Tel: 023 377 094, is on the south-west side of the harbour, on Obala Kralja Tomislava. Opening hours vary according to the season. When we visited, the handwritten note said 0800 to 1400, Mondays to Fridays, with a break between 1100 and 1130, Saturdays 0800 to 1200.

Useful information – Sali continued

There's also a **diving centre** based in the nearby Saščica bay, Tel/fax: 023 377 079; email: info@dive-kroatien.de; website: www.dive-kroatien.de. Sali has its fair share of old churches, ruins and historic buildings, and a very lively festival during the first weekend of August.

Zaglav (Uvala Triluke)

Entrance to bay: 45°57'.24N 15°09'.06E

Zaglav is a small ferry port connecting to Zadar on the mainland via Sali. It has the only fuel berth on Dugi Otok and this can lead to a fair amount of congestion in the high season.

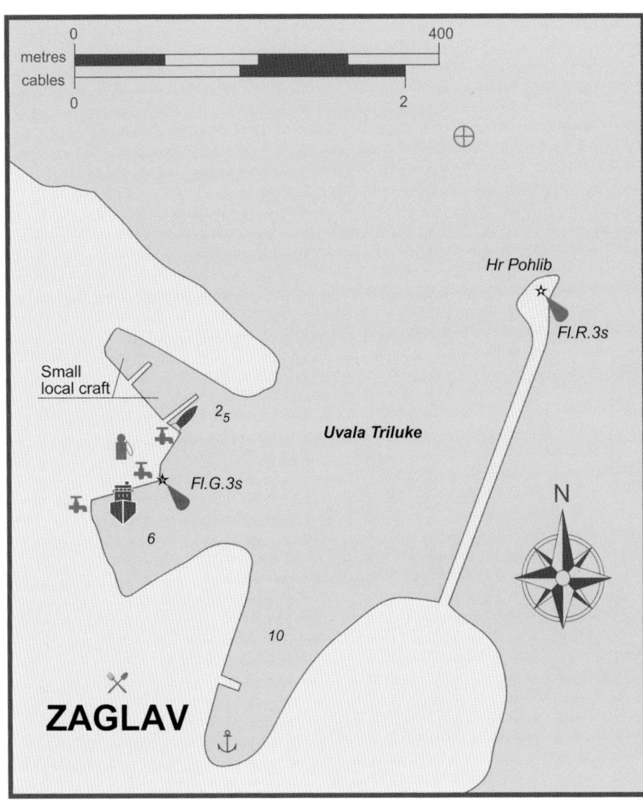

Zaglav fuel station and green light (Fl G 3s)

BERTHING/ANCHORING

Anchoring is the best option given the ferry traffic and the fact that the harbour is mainly used by local fishing boats. The most southerly inlet is sheltered from all winds except the Bora and provides good holding in sand, in depths of 7 to 13m. The fuel station, Tel: 023 377 234, has depths of 2m.

ASHORE

Ashore you will find two shops, a bakery and two restaurants, along with tourist information, Tel: 023 377 094, bus and ferry services.

Zaglav's tourist office

NAVIGATION

Charts: HHI MK-13, MK-14; AC 2711, SC5767

Approaches: On the eastern side of the entrance, the rock, Hrid Pohlib, is joined to the mainland by a breakwater and marked by a red light (Fl R 3s). Further north-east are a group of shoals, islets and islands that are identified clearly on the charts. The ferry quay is marked by a green light.

Pilotage: The approach waypoint, if coming from the north-west, through north, to the east, is 43°58'.05N 15°10'.36E. This is about 1.5 miles from the harbour entrance. On a bearing of 227°T you should be able to see the entrance, leaving the shoals and islets well to port. If approaching from Sali, you will need to chart a course that takes you inside the group of islets and shoals.

Žman (Uvala Žmanšćica)

Entrance to harbour:
43°58'.29N 15°07'.06E

Žman is a tiny fishing port that affords partial shelter. The islet of Krknata lies just east of the bay and its south-west coast provides alternative shelter as well as a small harbour.

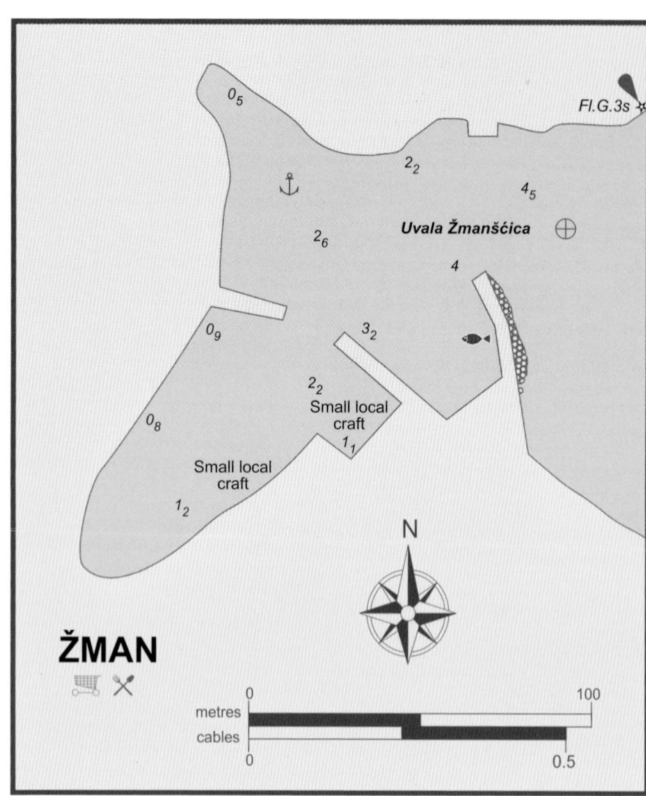

NAVIGATION

Charts: HHI MK-13, MK-14; AC 2711, SC5767
Approaches: There are no specific hazards and a green light (Fl G 3s) marks the north of the bay.

BERTHING/ANCHORING

Fishing boats tend to monopolise the breakwater and harbour, but there is an organised anchorage in the small bay north-east of the harbour. Depths are around 2m over a mostly sandy bottom. The harbour only provides shelter from winds from the north, through west, to south-west. If the Bora is blowing, the best anchorage is on the south-west coast of the island of Krknata.

ASHORE

Mooring fees will be charged and water and rubbish disposal may cost extra. You will find a shop and restaurant in the village.

Luka

Anchorage: 43°58'.86N 15°05'.78E

A tiny village of only 160 residents, with a number of small bays and beaches, situated around a harbour that is protected by the islet of Luški.

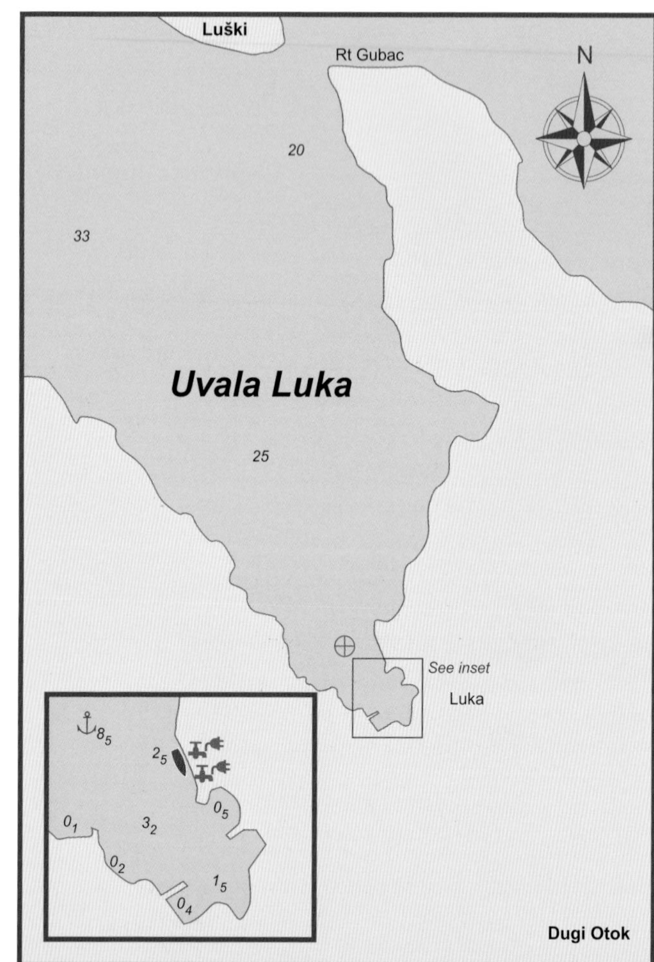

NAVIGATION

Charts: HHI MK-13 and MK-14; AC 2711, SC5767
Approaches: From the east or south-east, avoid passing between the islet of Luški and Rt Gubac on Dugi Otok as there can be strong currents, although depths are between 3m and 7m. Just north-east of this gap, watch out for a rock marked by an unlit isolated danger beacon. Half a mile north-west of this beacon is the islet of Maslinovac, identified by a white light (Fl 3s), just beyond which is a small rock off the south-east tip of the island of Rava.

Approaching from the north-west, you can pass either between Dugi Otok and Rava or further east between Rava and the island of Iž. The first alternative, closest to Dugi Otok, features a number of small rocks and islets but these are clearly marked on the charts. There is less to watch out for with the second option and the same approach waypoint as below applies.
Pilotage: The harbour entrance is not lit and entry at night is not recommended. Approaching either from the

south-east or north-west between Iž and Rava, a bearing of 258°T from an approach waypoint of 44°00'.47N 15°06'.11E should allow you to see the gap between Hrid Ravica to starboard and the islet of Maslinovac to port and leave you one and a half miles from the mainland. As you approach on this bearing you will pass Maslinovac and then the island of Luški to port. After Luški the harbour entrance will be to port.

Approaching from the north-west between Dugi Otok and Rava, visual navigation and charts are more useful than an approach waypoint in order to avoid the rocks and islets. If you stay close to Dugi Otok, you should see the harbour entrance from a good distance away.

BERTHING/ANCHORING

There are a number of moles where smaller boats can tie up alongside in depths of around 2m. Larger yachts may be able to find space alongside the quay where water and electricity are available.

Anchoring is possible just outside the harbour in depths of between 8 and 12m, but beware of rocky areas.

The harbour is exposed to the Bora and northwesterly winds but is otherwise well protected.

ASHORE

Facilities comprise a hotel with a restaurant and a shop.

A lone yacht alongside Luka's quay

Uvala Savar

Harbour entrance: 44°03'.85N 15°01'.37E
Charts: HHI MK-13; AC 515, AC 2711, SC5767

Even smaller than Luka, with just 85 residents, Uvala Savar has a small harbour and a village, up the hill, with limited facilities. The harbour has no lights and the rock Hrid Po Hliba lies about a mile south-east of Ront Pelegrin. The bay is deep and Brbinj, about a mile further north-west, has more to offer nautical visitors.

For land-based tourists, however, the church on Rt Pelegrin, built between the 7th and 9th centuries, is an impressive example of medieval architecture, and the stone quarry was the source of building material for Zadar's Roman forum, palaces and churches in Rome and Venice, and the UN building in New York.

The nearby cave of Strašna Peć, which translates to 'scary cave', is also of significant interest and was one of the first Croatian caves to be opened up to tourists. Among those to have visited the cave are Prince Edward and the Austro-Hungarian Emperor Franjo Josip.

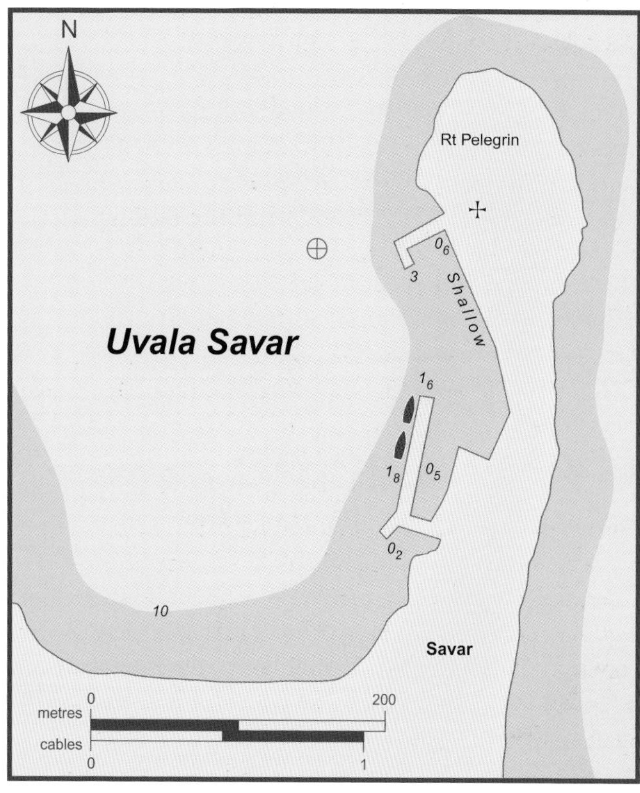

Brbinj (Uvala Brbinj)

Entrance to bay: 44°04'.42N 15°00'.68E

Brbinj is a small, unspoilt village, with a ferry connection to Zadar, although the ferry actually berths in the neighbouring bay, Uvala Lučina (see below). It's one of the organised anchorages and a good place for an overnight stop. Whether you anchor, berth or pick up a mooring buoy, you will have to pay a fee.

Stern-to at Brbinj quay

NAVIGATION

Charts: HHI MK-13; AC 515, AC 2711, SC5767

Approaches: There are no major hazards in the immediate vicinity of the harbour but there are two submerged rocks 2 miles and 2.5 miles north-east of it. The rock nearest to the harbour is lit by a white light, as is the northern boundary of the bay (Rt Koromašnjak – Fl 3s).

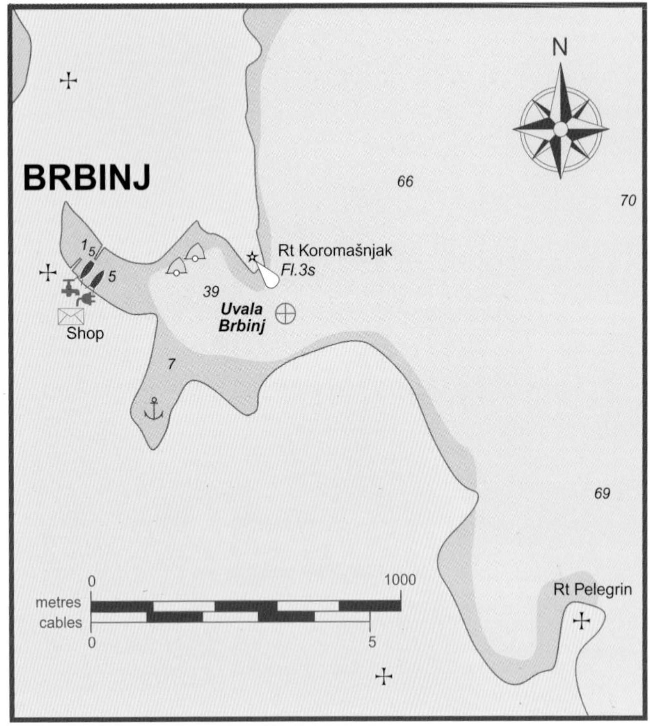

Pilotage: A bearing of 255°T from an approach waypoint of 44°04'.73N 15°02'.26E will give you a good view of the entrance to the bay from a distance of about a mile.

BERTHING

The harbour is in the north-west part of Uvala Brbinj, and it is possible to berth here on lazylines. Water and electricity are available. This area of the bay is sheltered from all winds, although it may be more comfortable anchoring in the south-west part of the bay in a strong Sirocco.

MOORING

Mooring buoys and stern lines to shore are provided in the northern part of the bay, just west of the light at the entrance. There is some exposure to the Bora here, so be prepared to move to another part of the bay if necessary.

ANCHORING

The south-west part of the bay offers a good anchorage in a combination of sand, weed and mud in depths of 3 to 7m. This area affords protection from the Sirocco and other winds from the south.

ASHORE

You will find rubbish disposal, a shop and post office on the quayside, as well as a few bars and restaurants.

Uvala Lučina (Zaglav)

Entrance to bay 44°05'.25N 15°59'.50E

Confusingly, Uvala Lučina is the location of the second settlement called Zaglav on Dugi Otok (see page 65 for the first). This is not the Zaglav where the fuel station is situated. More confusingly, the ferry from Zadar stops here and calls the destination Brbinj, which is in fact adjacent to this bay (see above).

NAVIGATION

Charts: HHI MK-13; AC 515, SC5767

Approaches: The islet of Utra guards the entrance to the bay and there is an 8m shoal about half a mile north-west of the islet, but otherwise there are few hazards.

Pilotage: You can pass either side of Utra but the south-eastern channel is safer, particularly at night. Prominent landmarks include a red light (Fl R 5s) on Rt Lučina on Dugi Otok and a church at the inner end of the bay. If you take the channel on the east of Utra, bear in mind that the ferry pier, displaying a red light, is immediately to port as you round the headland, so head well into the bay before turning. The village harbour is further past the ferry pier and the visitors' mooring buoys are on the other side of the bay.

BERTHING/ANCHORING

It may be possible to berth in the village harbour in depths of between 2 and 4m. The best option, however, is to pick up one of the buoys in the south-west part of the bay in depths of around 7m. Alternatively, anchor in the middle of the bay in depths of between 4 and 12m. Expect to pay a fee, whichever way you choose to moor. The bay provides good shelter from the Sirocco, but north and northwesterly winds can cause a considerable swell.

ASHORE

Ferry connection to Zadar, supermarket and restaurant.

Uvala Bokašin (Dragove)

Entrance to bay: 44°06'.67N 14°56'.58E
Charts: HHI MK-13; AC 515, SC5767

Lying roughly midway between Brbinj and Božava, Uvala Bokašin (sometimes spelt Bukasin) is partially protected by the islets Planatak Mali and Planatak Veli and offers an anchorage in sand in varying depths. The village of Dragove is just inland.

Uvala Dumboka (Dragove)

Entrance to bay: 44°07'.26N 14°55'.94E
Charts: HHI MK-13; AC 515, SC5767

Heading north-west, Uvala Dumboka is just around the headland from Uvala Bokašin and provides a reasonable anchorage and good protection from the Sirocco.

Božava

Entrance to bay: 44°08'.29N 14°54'.59E

Božava is probably the most touristy settlement on Dugi Otok. It has a large hotel and is regularly visited by tripper boats. It is a seasonal border crossing (see page 7 in the main introduction), an organised anchorage and has a ferry terminal with connections to Zadar.

NAVIGATION

Charts: HHI MK-11, MK-13; AC 515, SC5767

Approaches: Approaching from the north-west through the Zverinački Kanal, beware of the shoals and rocks at the northern entrance to the canal. The hazards are well marked on the chart, but only one rock is lit. If you would prefer to avoid this stretch, pass through the Tunski Kanal on the other side of Zverinac Island and approach Božava from the east.

From the south-east, you should be able to easily spot the hotel on the north-west side of the bay. The green light (Fl G 3s) on Rt Sv Nedjelja should be visible from both directions, as should the church, also on the point.

Pilotage: Head for the centre of the bay and assess the mooring options. Someone will probably come out and help you.

BERTHING/ANCHORING

The bay is protected from all but southeasterly winds, in which case Uvala Dumboka offers better shelter (see above).

The most sheltered berths are inside the breakwater in depths of 2 to 12m. Tie up bows- or stern-to using the lazylines provided.

Alternatively, it is possible to berth at the quay on

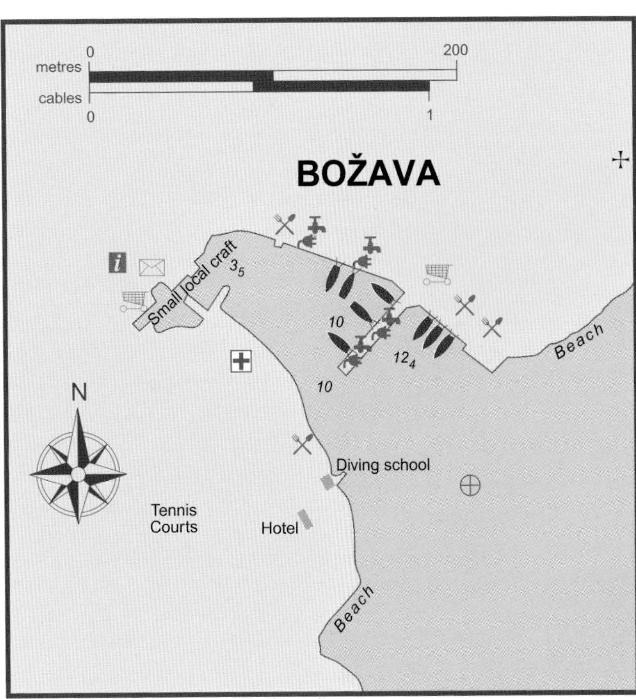

Božava is a popular tourist destination and often visited by tripper boats

the eastern side of the bay before you reach the breakwater. The quay in front of the hotel is generally reserved for diving boats, but you can anchor in the outer part of the bay. Both water and electricity are available on the quay.

ASHORE

You will find plenty of shops, restaurants and bars, a post office, a diving centre and other sports facilities available in the hotel (www.bozava.zadar.net).

Uvala Dobra

Entrance to bay: 44°10'.09N 14°52'.56E
Charts: HHI MK-11, MK-13; AC 515, SC5767

This is a good, well-sheltered anchorage with a sand and mud bottom, but it is not without its share of hazards. The head of the bay is shallow, and a submerged rock lies about 550m west of Rt Zaglavič. There are also a number of shoals and rocks to watch out for when approaching from the north-west.

Luka Solišćica
(Veli Rat Marina)

Anchorage at Soline: 44°08'.63N 14°52'.39E

Luka Solišćica is, in effect, two expansive bays on the north-west tip of Dugi Otok with plenty of navigational hazards to watch out for. The westernmost bay has an inner and outer basin and, although the inner basin is totally protected, the channel between the two basins can experience strong currents and the depths drop to 2m. The approach to the westernmost bay is also tricky, with a number of islets, shoals, rocks and wrecks. The eastern bay has two anchorages, of which Soline is preferred. The alternative is in Uvala Lučica, to the west of the eastern bay but, as there is an exposed wreck in the area, it is best avoided. In summer 2007 Veli Rat Marina opened at Luka Solišćica. For more information, see 'Berthing' below or go to www.baotic-yachting.com.

NAVIGATION

Charts: HHI MK-11, MK-13; AC 515; AC 2773, SC5767
Approaches: From the north-west, the approach to the eastern bay is relatively straightforward. If you are approaching from the south-east along the north-east or south-west coast of Dugi Otok, study the chart carefully to avoid the shoals, islets, wrecks and rocks. Heading along the north-east coast, do not turn back towards the approach waypoint (see below) until you are clear of Golac Islet (Fl 3s), as there are rocks and shoals between the islets prior to this point. If sailing along the south-west coast, the safest route is to leave the last islet of Mali Lagniči well to starboard before turning north-east for the north-west tip of the islet of

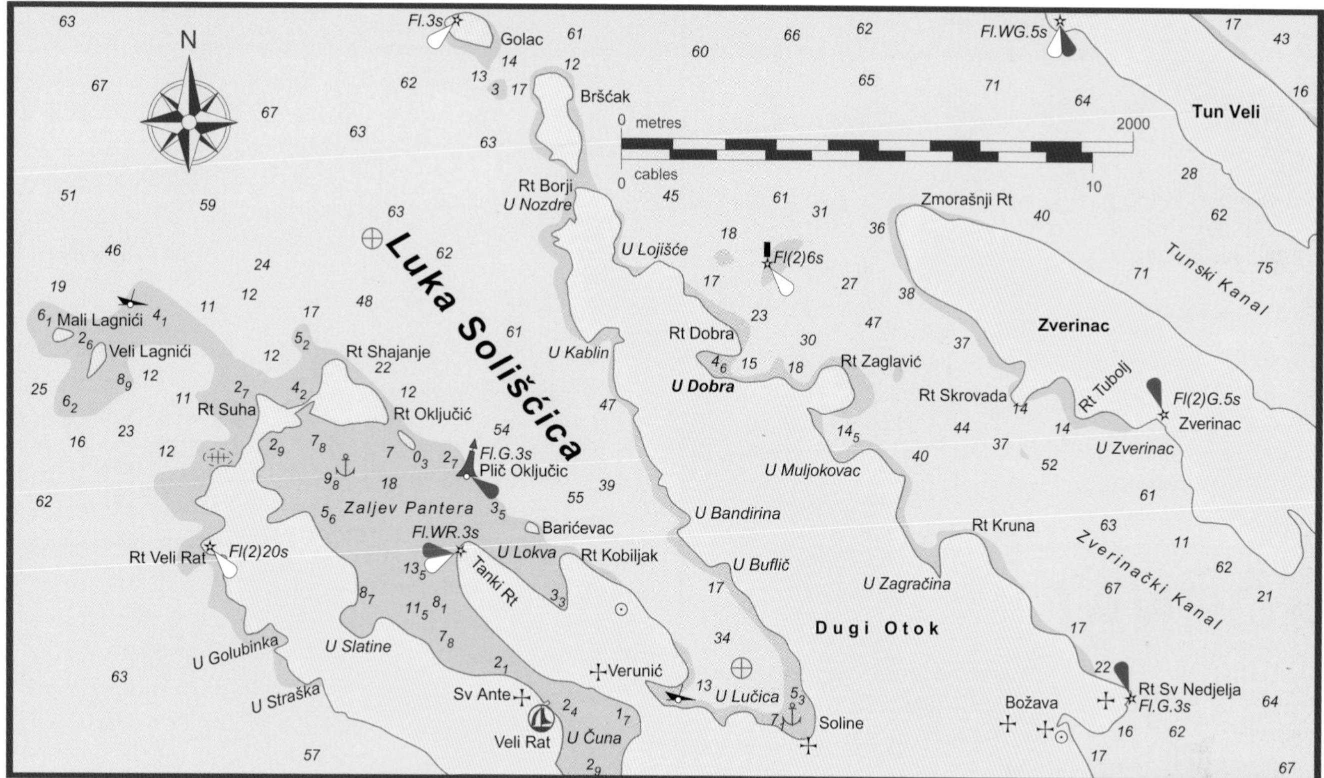

Golac. This avoids another wreck and a rock just north-east of the larger of the two Lagniči islets (Veli Lagniči). It is, however, possible to turn north- east before these two islets, but beware of a submerged wreck about 550m south-west of Rt Suha and a 5.2m shoal about the same distance north-east of Rt Suha.

Pilotage: From an approach waypoint of 44°10'.77N 14°49'.94E, on a course of 139°T, you will be just outside the entrance to the bay, in the centre and heading to Soline, which is about 3 miles away. You will see the preferred anchorage straight ahead of you, just off the village harbour, and the alternative anchorage and wreck to starboard when you are about 400m away from the village of Soline.

BERTHING

Veli Rat Marina provides 110 berths for yachts up to 20m (66ft) in length and among its facilities are a reception, toilets and showers. Electricity and water are available on the pontoons and there's an exchange office nearby.

ANCHORING

The organised anchorages, with buoys available, are in the western bay but are not recommended for larger yachts. Zaljev Pantera and Uvala Čuna provide good holding in mud in depths of over 5m and about 3m respectively. However, note the shallow entrance and avoid anchoring in the entrance to Uvala Čuna, which is rocky.

Both locations are well protected from swell but the former can be uncomfortable in strong winds from the west, north-west and north. The best anchorage is just off the village harbour of Soline. The sandy bottom affords good holding in depths of 5 to 9m, but is not comfortable in the swell caused by northwesterly winds.

Uvala Lučica offers more shelter in these conditions, but beware of the wreck in the bay. Depths are between 6 and 10m on a mud bed, although make sure your anchor is dug in well, as the bottom can be rocky in places.

FACILITIES

In the western bay, the two organised anchorages provide rubbish disposal facilities. The village of Veli Rat has a supermarket, post office, restaurant and bar, while another restaurant can be found at Uvala Čuna.

The south-west coast of Dugi Otok

There's very little to offer on the stark south-west coast of the island and none of the places below are so special as to make them worth a detour. However, for the sake of completeness, starting from the north-west tip:-

Uvala Sakarun, near Soline, has a good sandy beach, one of the best on the island.

Cavonjine, situated east of the islet of Mežanj, is a suitable anchorage in calm, settled conditions and has a reasonable beach.

Uvala Brbišćica and **Uvala Samotvorac** have good beaches, but are not suitable anchorages.

Useful information on Dugi Otok

PORT AUTHORITIES (SEASONAL): **Sali: Tel:** 023 377 021; **Božava: Tel:** 023 377 021.

POST OFFICES: **Božava: Tel:** 023 377 616; **Sali: Tel:** 023 277 027; **Žman: Tel:** 023 377 008.

TOURIST OFFICES: **Božava: Tel:** 023 377 607; **Sali: Tel:** 023 377 094; **Telašćica: Tel:** 023 377 096.

FUEL: **Zaglav: Tel:** 023 377 234.

MEDICAL CENTRES: **Božava: Tel:** 023 377 604; **Sali: Tel:** 023 377 032; **Žman: Tel:** 023 372 050.

DIVING CENTRES: **Božava: Tel:** 023 377 619; **website:** www.hoteli-bozava.hr;
Sali: Tel: 023 377 079; **website:** www.dive-kroatien.de; **Zaglav: Tel:** 023 377 167; **website:** www.kornati-diver.com

FERRY SERVICES (BRBINJ AND SALI): **Tel:** 023 378 713; **website:** www.jadrolinija.hr
Note that services to Sali are for foot passengers only. Buses on the island are scarce and irregular.

KORNAT

The Kornati Islands take their name from the largest island in the group, though Kornat is only just over 13 miles long and not much more than a mile across at the widest point. In contrast to Dugi Otok, it is the north east side of the island that is relatively barren and uninteresting. The south west side of the island is much more indented and attractive, providing a number of good anchorages, though it is the numerous islands and islets lying off this coast that gives it its unique character and National Park status. These islets provide a spectacular sailing backdrop but demand careful use of charts and visual navigation. Also note that if passing from the north-east between Dugi Otok/the islet of Katina and Kornat, you should use Prolaz Mala Proversa and not Prolaz Vela Proversa (see page 62).

National Park status comes with some additional rules and regulations and, despite our details of all the possible stop-offs on Kornat, there is an 'approved' list of overnight stops in the park that comprises Suhi Rt, Šipnate, Lučica, Kravljačica, Strižnja, Vrulje, Gujak (Uvala Lopatica), Opat, Stiniva and Statival. See pages 77 to 79 for more details on the Kornati National Park, including where to buy tickets.

There are no marinas on Kornat itself, the two nearest

being Piškera ACI marina, on the islet of Panitula Vela, to the south, and Žut ACI marina, on the island of Žut, to the north. Both marinas are open from April to October.

Like the majority of the islands in the area, Kornat has no permanent residents, most of the land belonging to the inhabitants of Murter. Nor does it have many natural springs – only fresh rain-water collected in basins. This means that facilities are sparse and there are few signs of life out of season. During the summer months, however, the island is a hive of industry to cater for the many tourists that visit it. Kornat is also something of a gourmet's paradise, with at least three notable restaurants geared up for visiting nautical tourists. We start from the north-west tip of the island and head anticlockwise around it.

The Kornati Islands

Suhi Rt

Anchorage: 43°52'.35N 15°13'.31E
Charts: HHI MK-14; AC 2711, AC 2773, SC5767

Suhi Rt lies on the north-west tip of the island of Kornat, just north of which is a small bay and fisherman's village. In some guides this bay is referred to as Uvala Tomasovac, but is called Uvala Valica on HHI MK-14.

It's exposed to Bora gusts and depths at the jetties are no more than 1.5m. Depths reduce to 2m in the inner bay but anchoring is possible further out.

There is a Kornati National Park reception centre here where you can buy tickets in the season, but overall Suhi Rt is not recommended for an overnight stop. If you do decide to try it, watch out for the rocks close to the coast between Suhi Rt and the bay. Otherwise there are no hazards in the immediate vicinity of the bay, although there are a number on the approach (see the navigation section for Luka Telašćica on page 62 and the approach notes for Šipnate below and on page 74).

Although the mud bed provides good holding, for more shelter it would be best to choose one of the neighbouring bays.

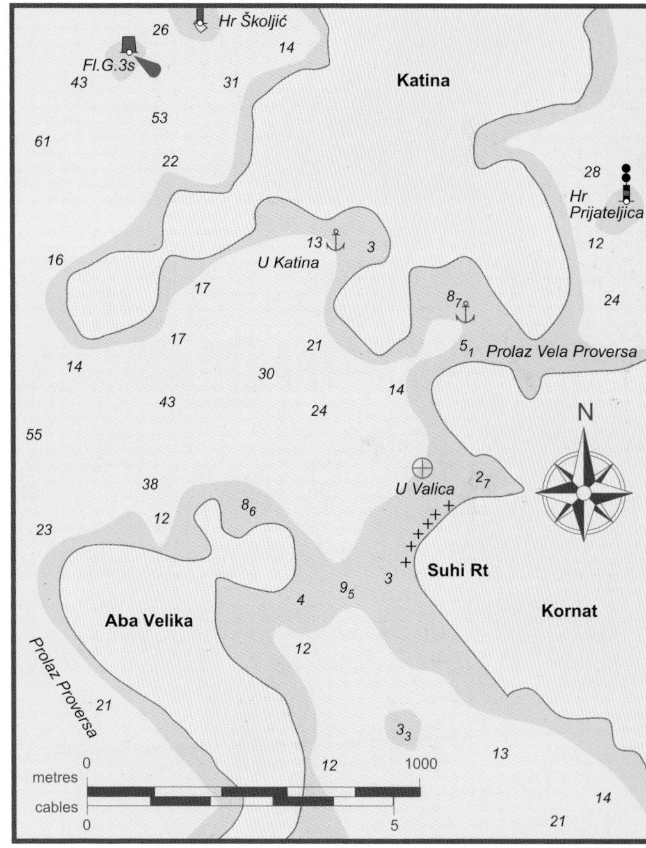

Šipnate

Entrance to bay: 43°51'.12N 15°14'.58E

Heading south-east along the south-west coast of Dugi Otok, with the islet of Šilo Velo to starboard, is the village of Šipnate. Nearly two miles from Suhi Rt, this is a great anchorage with a good restaurant.

NAVIGATION

Charts: HHI 512, MK-14; AC 2711, SC5767

Approaches: If approaching from the north-west, beware

A starboard hand buoy marks a rock between Aba Velika and Dragunara

of a 3.3m shoal just past Suhi Rt and a small islet just off the bay. From the south-east, watch out for a rock and a 3.7m shoal about halfway between Lučica and Šipnate. Between Aba Velika and Dragunara lies a rock marked by a green starboard hand buoy.

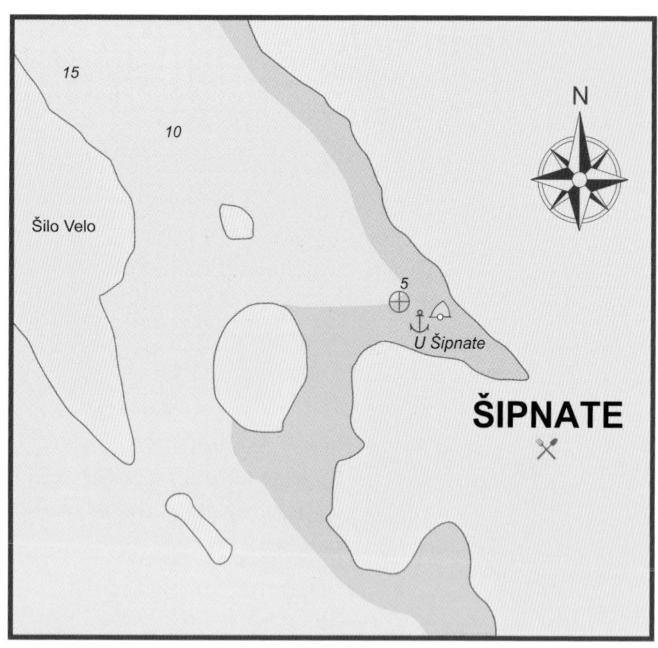

ANCHORING

You can anchor here, in depths of 5 to 10m, on a sand and weed seabed. The anchorage offers good shelter and is exposed only to northwesterly winds. Alternatively, take one of the mooring buoys.

ASHORE

Restaurant Solana is open from mid June until the middle of September, Tel: 022 435 433. It's owned by Smima and Vita Ramesa and serves all the normal Croatian dishes, including a local speciality, Kornati stew.

Lučica

Entrance to bay: 43°50'.29N 15°15'.33E
Charts: HHI 512, MK-14; AC 2711, SC5767

Lučica lies between Kravljačica and Šipnate, on the south-west coast of Kornat. It is partially protected by the islet of Levrnaka but is exposed to winds from the west and north-west. The small town harbour has depths of less than a metre, but it is possible to anchor off the outer pier in depths of 3.5m. However, the bay is really too deep to provide a good anchorage and is exposed to westerly winds, so we wouldn't recommend it as an overnight stop.

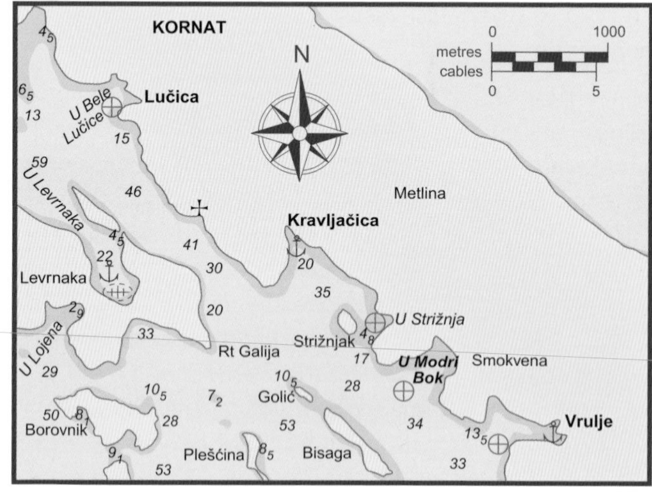

Kravljačica/Strižnja

Uvala Strižnja: Entrance to bay: 43°49'.20N 15°17'.06E

Kravljačica is at the north-west end of a large bay, with the settlement of Strižnja at the other end. There are two restaurants here, but not much else in the way of facilities.

NAVIGATION

Charts: HHI 512, MK-14; AC 2711, SC5767

Approaches: The approaches from either direction, along the coast of Kornat, are relatively straightforward. Heading south-east past Lučica towards Strižnja, you will see a ruin and the chapel of Sv Gospa.

Pilotage: Heading along the coast from either direction, keep between Kornat Island and the first layer of islets. It's a good idea to mark off the islands and islets as you pass them to avoid confusion. From the open sea, the best route is between the islets of Levrnaka and Borovnik.

MOORING/ANCHORING

The two restaurants are situated in the south-east part of the bay and it is possible to pick up one of the mooring buoys off the piers in depths of between 1.7m and 2.7m. The longer pier has the deeper water where you can berth alongside the inner side in depths of around 2m. The main jetties belong to the restaurants so your choice of where to eat will be decided for you once you berth! Alternatively anchor nearer Kravljačica in depths of up to 10m.

The bay is sheltered from all but southeasterly winds, but the level of protection varies in different parts of the bay.

ASHORE

Konoba Strižnja (Tel: 098 563 278) managed by Darko and Branka Simat, offers traditional fresh fish and lamb. Quattro (Tel: 022 435 187) run by Peter and Jere Skracic, provides similar fare. Both claim to be open from 1 May to the end of September/beginning of October.

Uvala Modri Bok

Entrance to bay: 43°48'.88N 15°17'.37E
Charts: HHI 512, MK-14; AC 2711, SC5767

This bay has no facilities ashore, but is a good overflow anchorage if you are determined to eat at Vrulje and the bay is full. Good holding on a sand bed in depths of 6 to 10m, although avoid the rocks in the east of the bay and just off the north-west shore. This bay is not on the official National Park list of approved overnight stops.

Uvala Modri Bok

Vrulje

Entrance to bay: 43°48'.63N 15°17'.95E

Vrulje, deemed the capital of Kornat by the locals and often spelt without the 'l', is a popular anchorage with a number of restaurants. It takes its name from the underwater springs, which cool down the water and can be seen in the bay, particularly in winter after heavy rain.

Vrulje – a popular destination for hungry sailors

NAVIGATION

Charts: HHI 512, MK-14; AC 2711, SC5767

Approaches: Heading along the coast of Kornat, from either direction close to shore, there are no real hazards. Heading north-east from the open sea, beware of the Kamičići reefs between the islets of Rašip Mali and Mana. From the south-east, there's a stone cross on Rt Prvčena, before you round the headland to Vrulje. The restaurants mostly have their own jetties and mooring facilities.

MOORING/ANCHORING

Restaurant Ante has a concrete pier with six moorings in depths of between 1.5 and 2.9m. Alternatively, anchor in the middle of the bay in depths of between 8 and 18m or use the visitors' mooring buoys provided. Check depths carefully in the south-east part of the bay as the water shoals rapidly here.

ASHORE

There are an increasing number of small restaurants vying for business. Ante's, Tel: 022 435 025, has a great atmosphere and serves traditional fish and meat dishes.

Uvala Lopatica

(Gujak)

Entrance to bay: 43°47'.26N 15°20'.30E

About two miles south-east of Vrulje, Uvala Lopatica is a good anchorage, with a restaurant at the head of the bay. It is sheltered from all winds except southeasterlies and southwesterlies.

NAVIGATION

Charts: HHI 512, MK-14; AC 2711, SC5767

Approaches: From the south-east, watch out for a submerged rock off the east coast of Gustac Islet, and another rock about 400m north-east of the first, but stay on the north side of Gustac to avoid the small islets and rocks on its south side. From the open sea, pass between the island of Piškera and the islet of Rašip Veli.

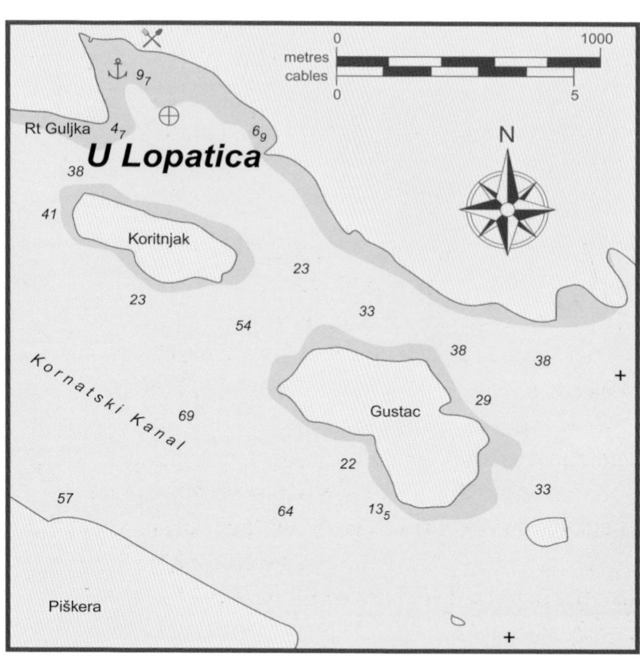

ANCHORING

There is a mole for small yachts (depths 1 to 1.5m), but you can anchor in the bay, in depths of between 5 and 10m, on a sand and weed bed that provides good holding.

ASHORE

Restaurant Beban, Tel: 099 475 739 (Marin Mudronja), serves traditional lamb and fish dishes and is open from the middle of April right through until the end of December.

Opat

Entrance to bay: 43°44'.24N 15°27'.12E

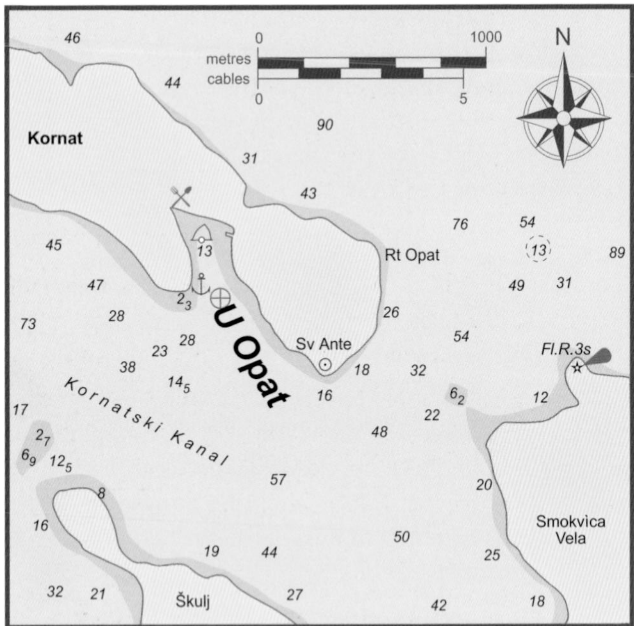

Opat is at the south-east tip of Kornat and has two rustic restaurants with moorings for visitors. A challenging, but rewarding, sign-posted walk up the shale hills will give you a fantastic panorama of the surrounding islands and islets.

Opat Bay, from halfway up the sign-posted walk

NAVIGATION

Charts: HHI 512, MK-14, MK-15; AC 2711, SC5767

Approaches: There are two shoals in the area to be aware of: the shallowest, at 2.3m, lies just off the western boundary of the bay. About 550m south-west of this shoal is a 2.7m shoal. The stark conical hill to the west of the bay is easily distinguished.

BERTHING/MOORING/ANCHORING

The bay shelves quickly to the shore, reducing to about 1.5m in depth off the jetties, in the north-eastern corner of Opat. Lazylines have been provided for visiting boats. Mooring buoys are also available or you can anchor off the western shore of the bay. The bay is exposed to the Sirocco, but provides shelter from the Bora.

ASHORE

There are rubbish disposal facilities as well as a shop. You can get a good, reasonably-priced meal at either of the two restaurants, which predominantly serve fish. You can even pick your lobster from the fish hole. We chose Restoran Matteo in preference to Konoba Opat, although both looked equally inviting.

Lazyline berths in front of Opat's two rustic restaurants

Uvala Statival

Entrance to western inlet: 43°51'.60N 15°15'.51E
Charts: HHI 512, MK-14; AC 2711, SC5767

On the north-east side of Kornat, at the Dugi Otok end, Uvala Statival has no facilities but makes for a peaceful, 'away from it all' anchorage, providing there are no south-easterlies blowing. The best anchorage is in the western inlet in depths of 5 to 10m.

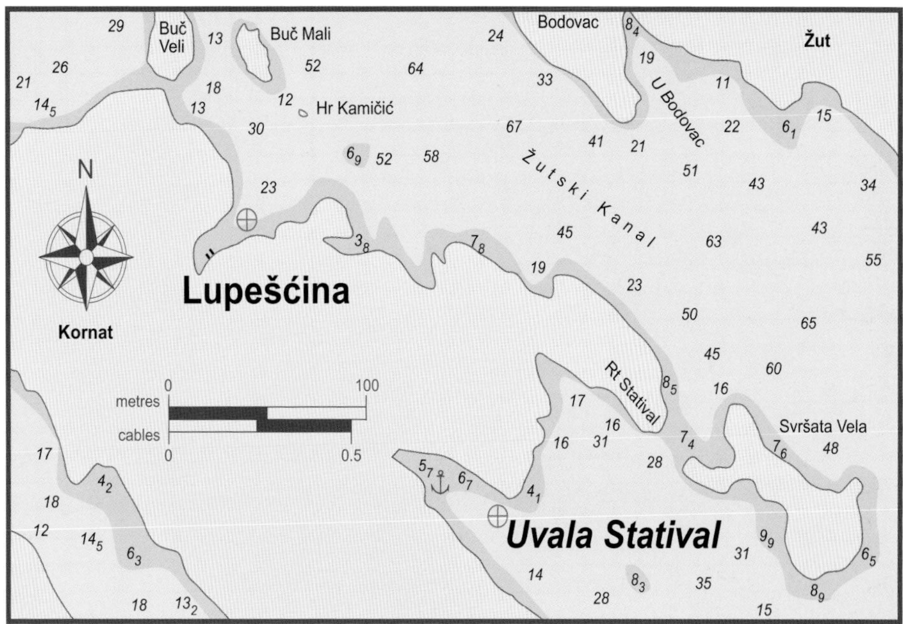

Lupešćina

Entrance to bay: 43°52'.34N 15°14'.49E
Charts: HHI 512, MK-14; AC 2711, SC5767

This bay is exposed to the Bora and has shoals and a rock off the entrance. There are a number of jetties with depths of up to 1.6m.

It is not recommended for an overnight stay and is not an approved overnight stop under the National Park regulations.

Useful information – Kornat

As there are no permanent residents on Kornat, facilities are scarce apart from a small selection of restaurants geared up for tourists in the summer season. See below for useful information on the Kornati Islands as a group.

The Kornati Archipelago

The Kornati Archipelago is the densest group of islands in the Mediterranean. There are 152 islands, islets and rocks and they are normally geographically split into two parts: Upper Kornati, north-east of Kornat and Dugi Otok, comprising Sit, Žut and the surrounding islands, and Lower Kornati, consisting of Kornat and the islands around it, mostly to the south-west. The Kornati National Park, designated as such in 1980, includes 89 islands, islets and rocks in Lower Kornati. The National Park website, www.kornati.hr, has a map and a list of the islands, islets and rocks included in the park, as well as prices and basic information. The rules and regulations are not too onerous, but are aimed to ensure the protection of the area. The park is open continuously, but most of the park reception centres on the islands are seasonal (June to September), except for the main office in Murter, which is open all year round. If you enter the National Park area you will normally need to pay a fee, although out of the holiday season it's not always easy to find someone to whom you can pay it.

The characteristic features of the area are the lack of vegetation, an almost eerie, deserted quality and a barren landscape. The islands were originally owned by the Zadar nobility but they hit bad times about a century ago and sold 90% of the land off to the residents of Murter, with the remaining 10% going to the inhabitants of Dugi Otok. The new owners built dry stone walls to protect their boundaries and burnt the forests to provide pasture for their sheep. Kornat was inhabited by the Romans and Piškera was a permanent settlement in the Middle Ages. Now, however, both the sheep and the permanent residents have long since gone and the development of the islands is led by the yachting fraternity and 'Robinson (Crusoe) tourism'. You will, therefore, find little in the way of facilities, other than seasonal restaurants and shops clustered around the most popular bays. The seas have been over

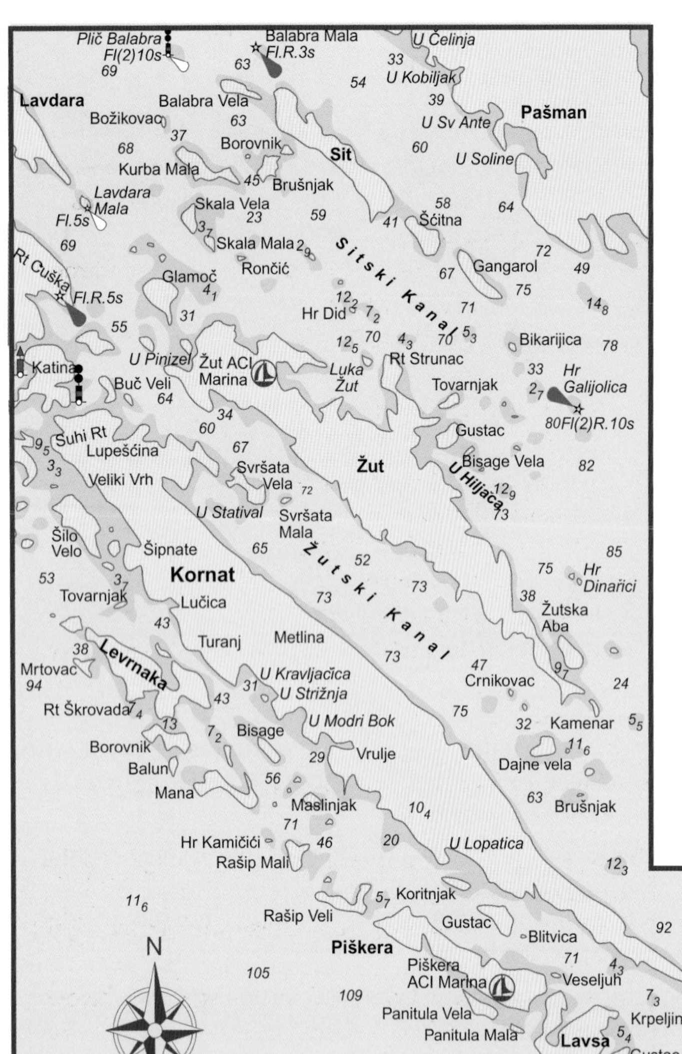

fished but that does not deter the restaurant owners from providing a wide variety of fresh fish to tourists.

It goes without saying that the density of the islands and islets requires very careful concentration to navigate safely through them. All the various hazards are well-marked on the charts which, along with constant visual navigation, are vitally important.

Counting off the islands and islets as we passed them proved crucial to our safe and trouble-free passage and, for this reason, as well as the lack of lights in the area, we would not recommend sailing by night or in limited visibility. Also watch out for strong flows in the channels between the islands and beware of the Bora, which blows hard here. In this section we have restricted navigational tips and approach notes to the bare minimum – there are so many different ways of approaching each destination and there is so much to watch out for on the charts that trying to condense it all in this section could be confusing at best and dangerous at worst. Instead, we leave you to concentrate on the charts and we help you to pick the best destinations according to your preferences.

This section begins with the islands around Kornat and, as with the section on Kornat, starts at the north-west tip and proceeds in an anticlockwise direction. Next, we explore Žut, Lavdara and Sit, finishing with the smaller islands and islets of upper Kornati. As mentioned on page 44, there are two marinas in the area – Piškera in Lower Kornati and Žut in Upper Kornati. At the beginning of the islands sections, we give you an at-a-glance guide to all the islands and their main features. We have supplied heights of the islets where this is a helpful aid to navigation.

Islands around Kornat
(most of the National Park)

Navigation is permitted throughout the park, with the exception of the specially protected areas around Purara and Hrids Klint and Volić, and the islets of Mrtovnjak, Klobučar, Obručan Mali and Obručan Veli. However, under National Park regulations, overnight stops are only officially permitted at Smokvica, Ravni Žakan, Lavsa, Piškera – Panitula Vela and in the bay of Anica on the island of Levrnaka.

Katina – two restaurants and a few anchorages – for more detail see below.

Aba Vela, Aba Mala and Dragunara – beware of spits and shoals.

Sestrica Vela and Sestrica Mala – white light on the larger of the two islets.

Šilo Velo and Šilo Malo – beware of shallows, rocks and shoals.

Obručan Veli and Obručan Mali Mrtovac – specially protected area which you need permission to visit.

Levrnaka – two anchorages, a wreck and shallow water – for more detail see page 80.

Sušica – do not pass through the channel between Sušica and Levrnaka.
Borovnik and Balun – shallow water between the two islets.
Plešćina (27m high) and Bisaga (22m high) – beware of shoal patches.
Mana – 7m shoal between Mana and Plešćina.
Bisagica (2m high), Babuljaši Mali (7m high) and **Babuljaši Veli (11m high)** – a group of three very small islets.
Hridi Kamičići – two above-water rocks lying on a bank. The southern rock is 2m high; the northern rock is 5m high.
Maslinjak – 39m high.
Arapovac – 5m high; beware of shoal patches.
Rašip Veli, Rašip Mali and Rašipic – beware of shoals.
Piškera – Piškera ACI Marina situated on off-lying islet.
Panitula Vela – Piškera ACI Marina, see below.
Panitula Mala – beware of the two rocks and shallow bank off the north-west tip.
Koritnjak – no notable features.
Gustac (sic), **Blitvica and Hrid Kamičić** – beware of shoals and rocks.
Veseljuh – 4m high surrounded by a shallow bank.
Lavsa – anchorage and restaurant – see below for more details.
Gustac (sic), **Klobučar and Kasela** – Klobučar is a protected area that you need permission to visit.
Krpeljina – no notable features.
Prišnjak Mali (14m high), Prišnjak Veli (35m high) and Hr Kaselica (12m high) – beware of shallows.
Ravna Sika (30m high) and Bisaga (13m high) – shallow banks and off-lying 4.8m shoal.
Vodenjak – shallow bank and 2.9m shoal.
Gominjak – shallow banks and shoals.
Lunga – anchorage on the south of the islet in 12m, but exposed to all winds from west through south to east.
Ravni Žakan – restaurant and anchorage – see pages 82 to 83 for more details.
Žakanac, Jančar and Kameni Žakan – shallows and rocks.
Škulj – 2.7m shoal off north-west tip.
Prduša Vela and Prduša Mala – beware of shoals and rocks.
Garmenjak Veli and Garmenjak Mali – beware of shoals and rocks.
Purara and Hrid Klint – protected area – approach and anchoring prohibited.
Kurba Vela – no notable features.
Oključ – no notable features.
Lukmarinjak – no notable features.
Puh, Gornji Puh, Kameni Puh and Vodeni Puh – shallow banks and rock.
Samograd – no notable features.
Vrtlič – no notable features
Skrižanj Mala and Vela – shallow banks around the two islets.
Mrtovnjak – specially protected area; white light on the north-east tip.
Babina Guzica – shallow banks, shoals and a green light 550m off west tip.
Smokvica Vela – restaurant and anchorage – see below for more details.
Smokvica Mala – shallow bank and off-lying shoals and rocks.

The peace and tranquillity of the Kornati Islands

Katina Island

Charts: HHI MK-14; AC 2711, AC 2773, SC5767

Katina lies between Dugi Otok and Kornat and is not part of the Kornati National Park. The two channels of Prolaz Mala Proversa and Prolaz Vela Proversa separate Katina from its neighbouring islands, and both have conveniently placed restaurants. However, see page 62 regarding navigation through the channels and only choose Prolaz Vela Proversa if you have a very shallow draught. Either of the restaurants would make a good lunchtime anchorage, but we preferred to find an overnight stop away from the challenges of the channels.

Prolaz Vela Proversa has a number of anchorages offering varying degrees of shelter, and there is a restaurant in the arch of the south-facing foot of Katina Island. Mare, owned by Vjekoslav and Nela Seselja (Tel: 098 273 873) is open from the beginning of May until the end of December and offers modern Kornati cooking, specialising in fresh fish. There's a 20m (66ft) concrete pier and a quay outside the restaurant. Depths at the pier are between 2 and 3.5m.

Prolaz Mala Proversa, on the other side of the island, is well buoyed and has depths of over 4m. We passed Restaurant Aquarius, also with a pier and jetty, but there were no signs of life at the end of May. There are mooring buoys in the bay on the north side of the channel.

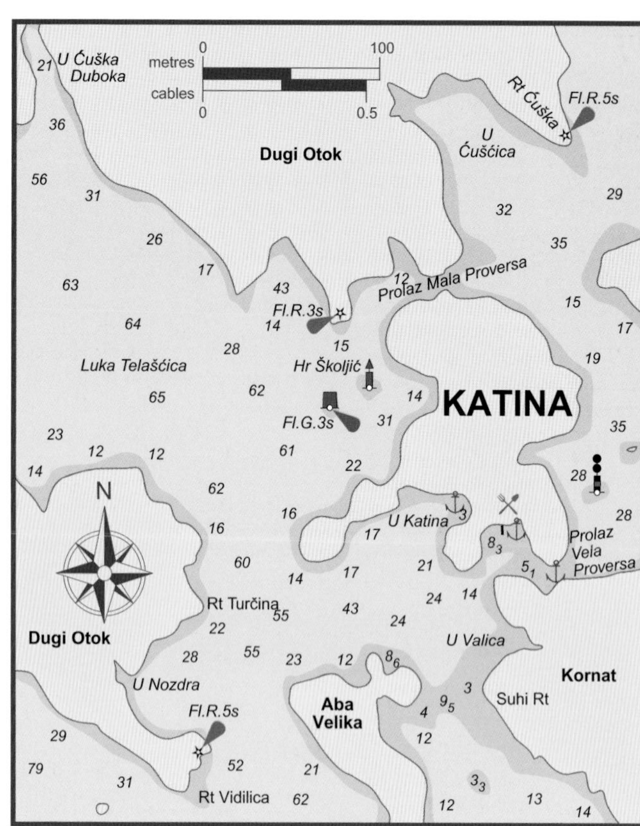

Levrnaka Island

Anchorage on north coast: 43°49'.50N 15°15'.21E
Anchorage on south coast: 43°49'.10N 15°14'.91E
Charts: HHI 512, MK-14; AC 2711, SC5767

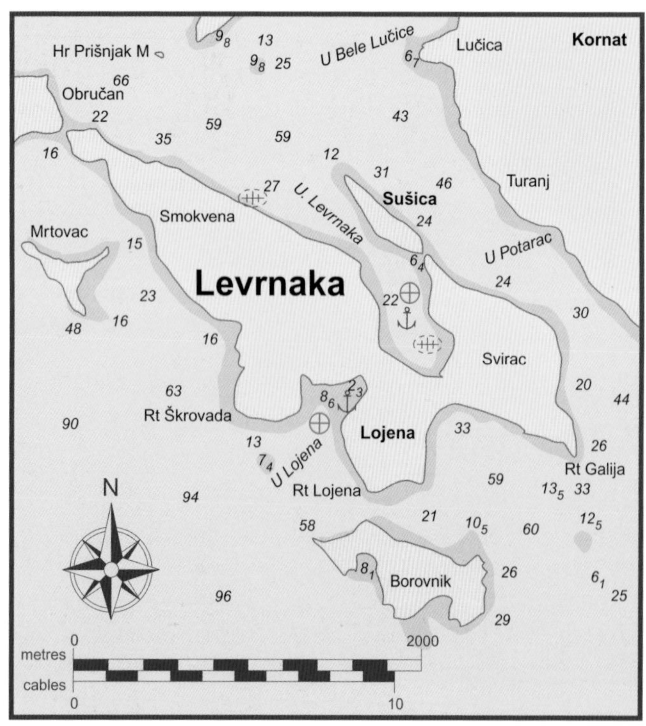

Levrnaka Island – the anchorage on the north coast

Although the anchorage on the north side is popular, it is deep (10 to 24m). In addition to this, there is a submerged wreck to avoid and do not, on any account, try to approach between the south-east tip of Sušica and Levrnaka where depths drop to under half a metre. The anchorage is protected from all winds except those from the north-west.

On the south side of the island, you can anchor in Uvala Lojena on a sand bed in depths of around 5m. The anchorage is exposed to winds from the south.

Piškera ACI Marina

Entrance to bay: 43°45'.46N 15°20'.99E

Piškera ACI Marina is on the island of Panitula Vela, off the south-west coast of the larger island of Piškera. It is open from April to October and is exposed to southerly winds. There are no signs of life away from the marina complex.

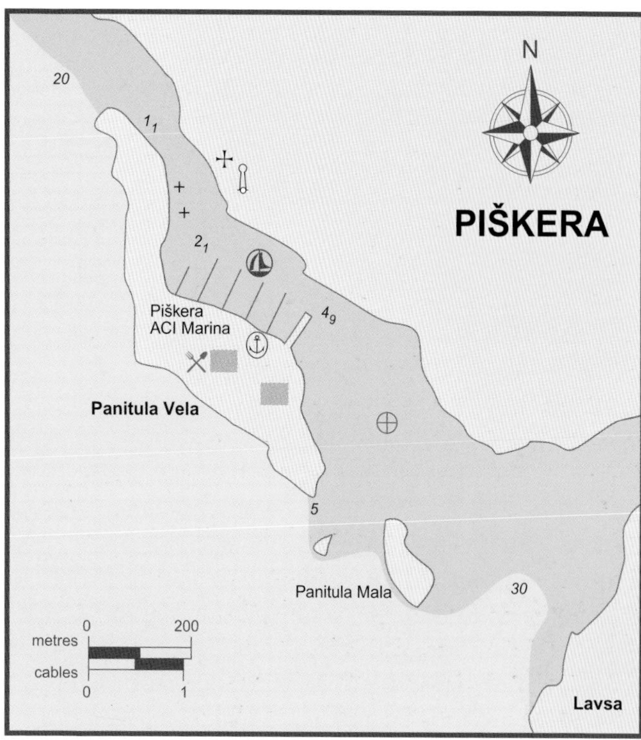

NAVIGATION

Charts: HHI 512, MK-14; AC 2711, SC5767

Approaches: Approaching from the south-east between Kornat Island and the main group of Kornati Islands, pass between the islands of Lavsa and Piškera. From the north-west or south, the safest route is to turn north-north-east for the channel between Lavsa and Piškera and then west-north-west just after Panitula Mala. You can pass between the reefs (just west of Panitula Mala) and Panitula Vela in depths of 7m, but do not attempt to approach from the north-west between Panitula Vela and Piškera as the water is shallow and there are a number of rocks here.

Piškera ACI Marina buildings

BERTHING

The marina, which can be contacted on VHF Channel 17; Tel: 091 470 0091/92, has 120 berths in depths of between 2.5 and 3.5m. Berthing is on lazylines. A 10m boat will cost €3.8 per metre outside July and August. Add 10% in the high season.

FACILITIES

Limited water and electricity supplies – water available from 0800 to 1000; electricity from 0800 to 1200 and from 1800 to 0000 – reception, exchange office, restaurant, telephone, toilets and showers.

Piškera ACI Marina can accommodate 120 yachts in depths of up to 3.5m

Lavsa Island

Entrance to bay: 43°45'.48N 15°22'.27E

Situated to the south-east of Piškera, Lavsa has a popular anchorage in the bay on its north coast. There are mooring buoys and a restaurant here, but very little else.

Anchorage and mooring buoys in the sheltered bay on the north coast of Lavsa Island

NAVIGATION

Charts: HHI 512, MK-14; AC 2711, SC5767

Approaches: From the south and west of Lavsa, pass through the channel between Lavsa and the islet of Gustac to its east, watching out for the 5.4m shoal just north of Gustac. The channel between Lavsa and Piškera is 6m deep. From the south-east, take the middle of the channel between Kornat and the group of larger islands along it, staying clear of the shoals just south of Opat and north of Škulj, and leave the tiny islet of Bisaga well to starboard. As you enter the bay, there is a lone house to starboard along with some mooring buoys. Further into the bay, to port, is Konoba Idro.

MOORING/ANCHORING

There was a full set of buoys when we passed through Lavsa, though there have been reports that the buoys are sometimes taken away for maintenance. If that's the case and you don't mind a 3.5m dive, you can loop your rope through the ring attached to the concrete base. Alternatively, find an area clear of the mooring buoys and bases, and drop your anchor. The inner part of the bay is well protected but might be uncomfortable in strong northerly winds.

ASHORE

Konoba Idro, run by Tedi Juraga, offers the normal Croatian fare of fresh fish and grilled meats and is open from the beginning of June to the end of September – Tel: 099 438 726.

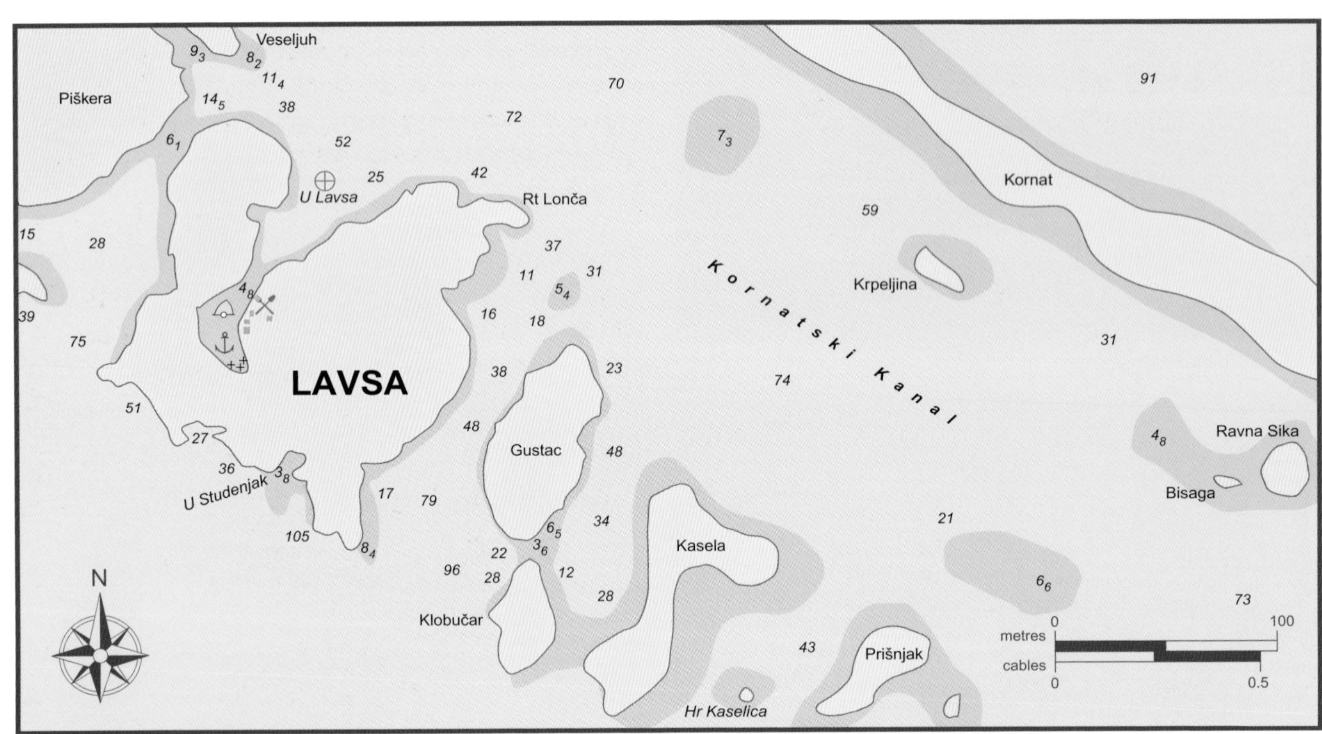

Ravni Žakan Islet

Entrance to bay: 43°43'.49N 15°25'.96E

The islet lies a mile west-south-west of the south-east tip of Kornat. The bay on the south of the islet is another popular anchorage and incorporates a small village harbour for shallow draught boats. It's exposed to winds from the west through to the south. It used to be a seasonal port of entry and had a Kornati National Park reception centre, but this was closed in 1999.

There is also an anchorage on the north-west side of the island, which provides shelter from the Sirocco and the Bora and has a seasonal restaurant.

NAVIGATION

Charts: HHI 512, MK-14, MK-15; AC 2711, SC5767

Approaches: From the east, north of Škulj Islet, watch out for the two shallow shoals. The channel between Lunga and Ravni Žakan is 6m deep. From the south, south-west and west, pick your route carefully from the chart to avoid the rocks, shoals and islets.

MOORING/ANCHORING

There is a pier where you can berth bows or stern-to, in depths of between 1 and 2m. Alternatively anchor further out on a sand bed, with depths of up to 10m. The bay is sheltered from the Bora, but exposed to winds from the southern quadrant.

ASHORE

Konoba Larus, a traditional fish restaurant, run by Melina Turcinov, is open between the beginning of June and the end of September – Tel: 098 230 383.

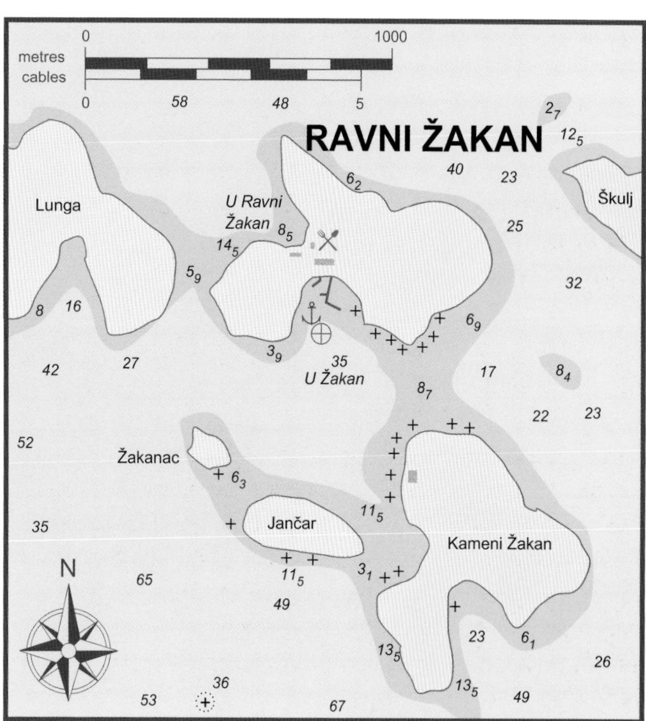

Smokvica Vela Island (Uvala Lojena)

Entrance to bay: 43°43'.25N 15°28'.77E

This bay has a seasonally inhabited village and fishing harbour and another great traditional fish restaurant. Although it's an officially approved overnight stop, it's exposed to winds from the south-west, through south, to the south-east.

NAVIGATION

Charts: HHI 512, MK-14, MK-15; AC 2711, SC5767

Approaches: There are a number of shoals and rocks around the island to look out for, particularly to the east. The best approach is from the south-east, leaving the islet of Babina Guzica and the 3.6m shoal to port.

MOORING/ANCHORING

There is a pier outside the restaurant, with depths of 2 to 2.5m, where you can berth stern- or bows-to.

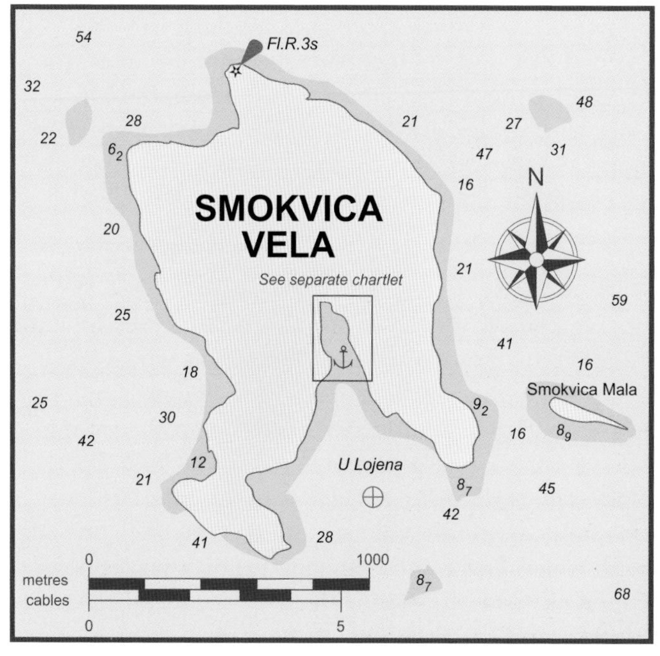

The jetty has depths of less than 1.3m. Anchor in the bay, in varying depths, on a bed of sand and weed, or take one of the mooring buoys, but note the lack of protection from winds from the south.

ASHORE

Piccolo restaurant (Tel: 022 435 106 and 099 541 280), run by Ante and Tomo Turcinov, is open between May and October and serves good fresh fish. Rubbish bins and signs of a new restaurant under construction are on the opposite side of the bay from Piccolo.

Piccolo restaurant, Smokvica Vela

Useful information on the Kornati National Park

NP OFFICIAL WEBSITE – www.kornati.hr
NP MAIN OFFICE – 22 243 Murter, Butina 2. **Tel/fax:** 022 434 662, 022 434 166
NEAREST AMBULANCE SERVICE – Murter or Sali on Dugi Otok
NEAREST HOSPITAL – Šibenik
NEAREST HOSPITAL SPECIALISING IN DIVING INJURIES – Split
DIVING – Only approved companies can arrange diving in the park – the official website (above) has full contact details
TRANSPORT – There are no ferries operating in the area – only tours and private boats

Park fees depend on the size of boat. A 10m (33ft) yacht will cost 120 Kunas if you buy the ticket before entering the park, or 200 Kunas once you are in the park. Scuba diving costs 150 Kunas per person per day, including the entrance fee, as part of an approved organised group; otherwise it costs 300 Kunas per person per day. Fishing permits also cost 150 Kunas per person per day, including an entrance fee, or 300 Kunas if you buy the ticket once inside the park.

Upper Kornati Islands

This section deals with the islands and islets north-east of Dugi Otok and Kornat – the largest islands being Žut, Sit and Lavdara. There are still a number of hazards, but not quite as many to watch out for as with the Lower Kornati Islands.

There's one marina in the area, on the north-east coast of Žut, and not too many restaurants, apart from a cluster around Dragišina (Uvala Hiljača) on Žut. Good anchorages are also more scarce. We begin with Žut, Lavdara and Sit and then pick out any suitable places on the smaller islands.

Žut Island – Luka Žut

Entrance to bay: 43°52'.90N 15°17'.99E

Luka Žut is a wide bay on the north-east coast where you can anchor or berth at the ACI marina. You will find shelter from most winds in different parts of the bay.

The stop is worth it if only to talk to the very enthusiastic owner of the Festa hotel/restaurant. He has big plans to develop out-of-season eco tourism here, has already installed pontoons for guests which are equipped with water, electricity and showers, and has opened a small grocery market to supply passing boats. He also intends to put in a breakwater in the not too distant future and claims to have the first ever privately owned desalination unit in Croatia to provide fresh water. This is in addition to extensive solar power panels as there is no mains electricity or water on the island as yet.

NAVIGATION

Charts: HHI 512, MK-14; AC 2711, SC5767

Approaches: From the open sea, use Prolaz Mala Proversa and take the channel between Glamoč and Žut, leaving well to port the rock (Hrid Krbarić) off the northern headland of Žut. From the north and north-east, there are a number of shoals and rocks to look out for so pick your route carefully. The Festa sign is clearly visible to port as you enter the bay and, just past Festa, the flags outside identify the marina reception, which is hidden behind trees.

Žut ACI Marina and the Upper Kornati Islands

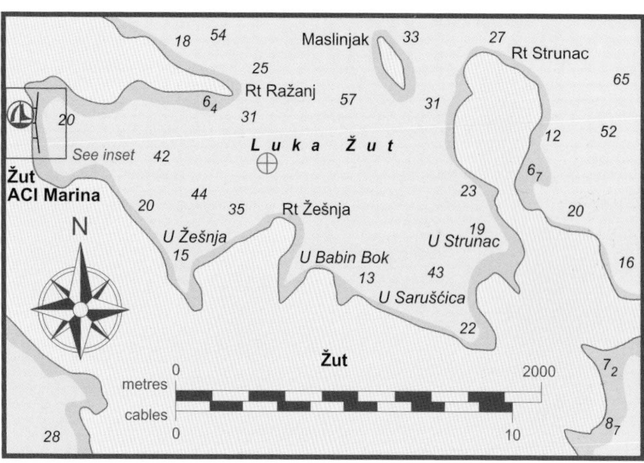

MOORING/ANCHORING

The ACI marina can be contacted on VHF Channel 17; Tel: 022 786 0278/099 470 028. Open from April until October, it has 120 berths. Depths at the one long pontoon vary between 0.5 and 3m, so wait for help if you are uncertain. Prices are the same as Marina Piškera

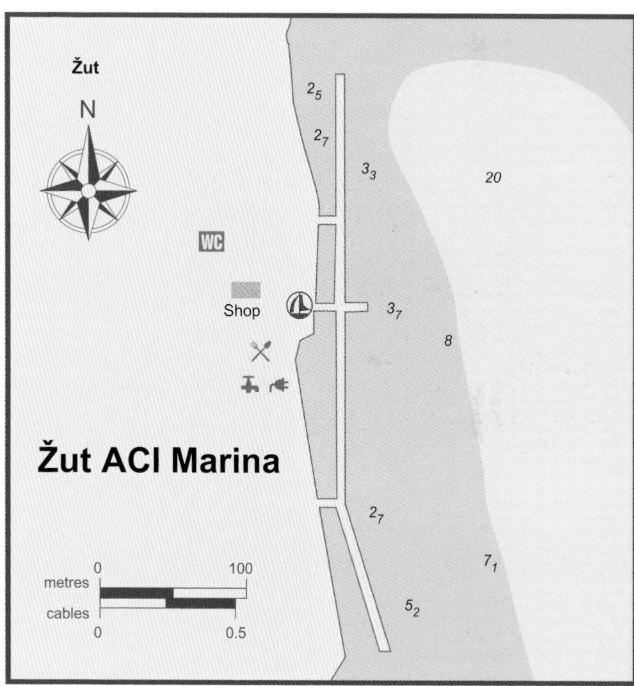

(see page 81). There are two inlets in the southern part of the bay where you can anchor in depths of between 7 and 12m. Website: www.aci-club.hr.

ASHORE

Electricity and water supplies in the marina are limited: water is available from 0800 to 1000; electricity from 0800 to 1200 and from 1800 to 0000. The marina complex incorporates a restaurant, exchange office, toilets, showers and a small supermarket.

Outside the marina is Festa with a restaurant, grocery supplies and some newly refurbished guest accommodation. Telephone (the owner) Krešimir Mudronja on 022 786 0410 or 098 425 229. Konoba Sandra also serves up traditional fish dishes – Tel: 098 492 340.

Uvala Hiljača

Entrance to bay: 43°52'.06N 15°19'.60E

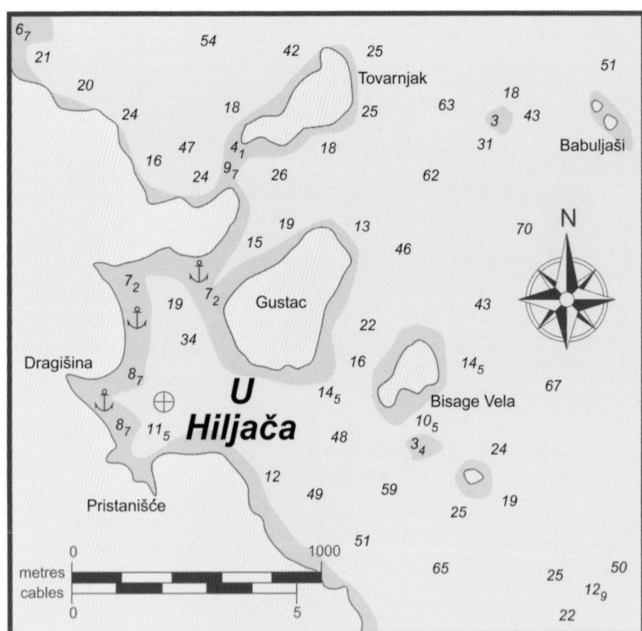

Uvala Hiljača is another popular anchorage with plenty of shelter in varying conditions in different parts of the bay.

NAVIGATION

Charts: HHI 512, MK-14; AC 2711, SC5767

Approaches: Three quarters of a mile east of the bay and south of Bisage Vela is a 3.4m shoal, while further east are a number of tiny islets, rocks and shallows to watch out for. The island of Gustac shelters the bay to the north-east, half a mile north-east of which is another 3m shoal.

Approaching from the north-west or the south-east, beware of more rocks and shoals. Other than a light (Fl (2) R 10s) marking the rock Hrid Galijolica, approximately two miles east of the bay, there are no navigational lights, so it is advisable not to approach when visibility is poor or at night and study the charts carefully.

ANCHORING

There are a couple of options available for anchoring, depending on the weather conditions. The northern part of the bay, west of Gustac Islet, provides suitable protection in a Bora, but is exposed to southeasterly winds. The holding is good on a sand bed, in depths of between 5 and 10m. Alternatively, the southern part of the bay, by the village of Pristanišće, offers more all-round protection, although is not recommended in bad weather.

ASHORE

There is a seasonal traditional restaurant by each of the anchorages, with another two located in Uvala Strunac, north-west of Uvala Hiljača.

Uvala Pinizel

Entrance to bay: 43°53'.14N 15°15'.62E

A well-protected anchorage, though no restaurants or other facilities were spotted. The village of Pinizel is inhabited only during the summer months.

NAVIGATION

Charts: HHI MK-14; AC 2711, SC5767

Approaches: From the north, north-east and east, note that there is a 3.8 and 4.1m shoal as well as a rock to watch out for. There are fewer hazards on approach from the south and west, though see pages 62 and 80 for navigational information on the channel around Katina Island.

ANCHORING

Although there is a small town harbour, depths are below 1.3m. Anchor close to the islet of Pinizelić in depths of around 10 to 20m, but avoid the middle of the bay, which has a rocky bottom. The anchorage is sheltered from all winds apart from northwesterlies.

Lavdara Island

Charts: HHI MK-14; AC 2711, SC5767

Lavdara is a yellow rocky island with no real facilities and no mains water or electricity. However, it does have its own website, www.lavdaraturist.com, and a couple of possible anchorages offering partial protection – these are in Uvala V Bok, halfway along the south-west coast, and Uvala Škrovada on the south-east end of the island. The website is built around apartment lets, but does offer motor boat rentals, shopping trips to Sali on Dugi Otok, diving and fishing. If you want an 'away from it all place', then Lavdara Island can be highly recommended. Contact Branko Filipi on Tel: 023 321 884/098 9387 733, or email info@lavdaraturist.com to get local advice, a few days in advance, on the suitability of the anchorages and what he can provide to visiting yachts. Watch out for the 2.2m shoal half a mile off the north-west tip of the island. Otherwise there are no major hazards in the immediate vicinity of the island's coast.

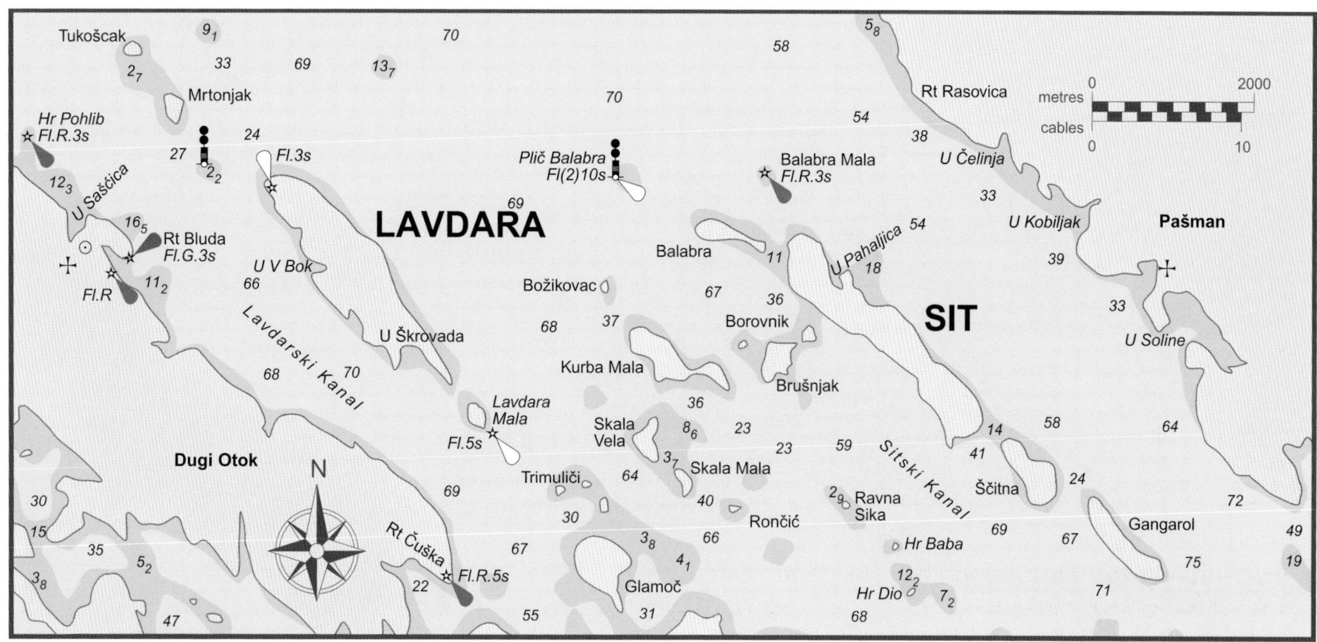

Sit Island

There's not too much to say about Sit Island apart from identifying a possible anchorage in Uvala Pahaljica on the north-east coast.

This side of the island is, however, pretty barren and there are no facilities.

Islands and islets around Žut, Lavdera and Sit

There are many islands and islets in Upper Kornati, but we did not identify any that were worth a special visit or could provide good shelter. As there are so many other places to explore and this area has more than its fair share of shoals, rocks and other hazards, it's probably best avoided.

Islands between Ugljan and Dugi Otok

The main islands between Ugljan and Dugi Otok, working anticlockwise from the north-west tip of Ugljan, are Rivanj, Sestrunj, Tun Veli, Zverinac, Rava and Iž. Rivanj has a small harbour on its western side where you can tie up alongside the harbour wall in depths of about 5m, but you will be competing with the ferry and the tidal streams are too strong for safe anchoring in the channel further out. Sestrunj has a reasonable anchorage in Uvala Hrvatin, but this only provides limited protection. Tun Veli has nothing to offer, but Zverinac has a harbour and anchorage. Rava has three possible stop-offs on its west coast, while Iž has a marina and a number of sheltered bays.

This cruising ground is less hazardous than the Kornati Islands, but perhaps less attractive to visitors. We look at the islands of Zverinac, Rava and Iž in more detail below.

Zverinac Island – Zverinac

Entrance to bay: 44°09'.61N 14°54'.87E

Zverinac is a pretty fishing village with a ferry to Zadar, on the mainland, and modest facilities.

NAVIGATION

Charts: HHI MK-13; AC 515, AC 2773, SC5767

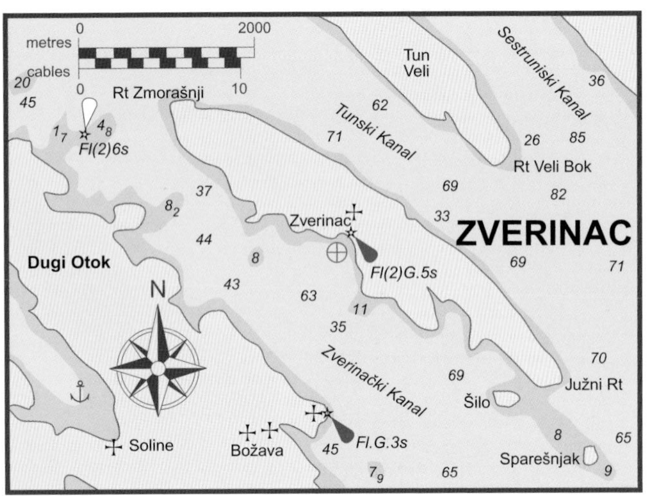

Approaches: There are a number of shoals and rocks on the north-west approach. The central shoal is marked by a white light (Fl (2) 6s). The houses are predominantly situated near the church, the belfry of which can be seen from some distance.

BERTHING

The bay is quite deep (12m plus), so it's best to use the lazylines provided on the outside of the north quay. A mooring fee will be payable.

ASHORE

Water and electricity are available on request to the harbourmaster. A small supermarket and a restaurant are in the village.

Rava Island – Mala Rava

Entrance to bay: 44°02'.27N 15°03'.28E

Mala Rava is a small village that is situated on the north-west end of the island, by Uvala Lokvina, and has a ferry service to Zadar. There is an organised anchorage here with the normal fees and facilities. Limited amenities are available in the village.

NAVIGATION

Charts: HHI MK-13; AC 515, SC5767

Approaches: When approaching the harbour, beware of a rock about half a mile west of the bay.

The village is on the east of the bay, as is the ferry quay, while a fishfarm is situated in the next bay to the south.

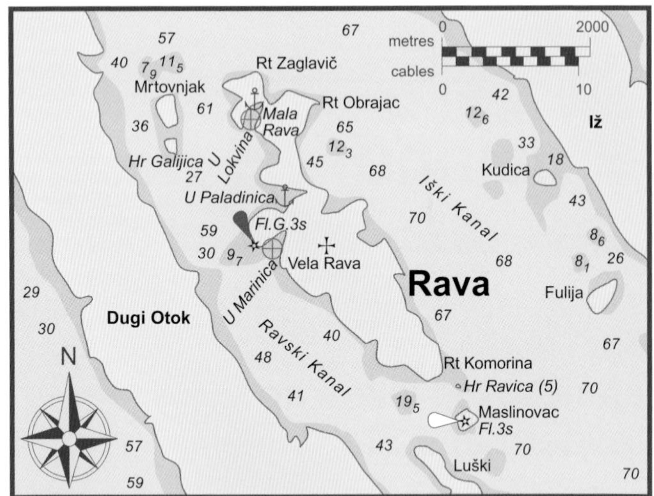

MOORING/ANCHORING

The mooring buoys are on the west of the bay or you can anchor in the middle of the bay in depths of between 6 and 12m. It is exposed to southwesterly winds, but is otherwise well protected.

Mala Rava, where you can anchor in the middle of the bay in depths of between 6 and 12m

Uvala Paladinica

Entrance to bay: 44°01'.76N 15°03'.38E
Charts: HHI MK-13; AC 515, SC5767

A large, quiet bay, with no facilities, on the west coast of Rava between Mala Rava and Vela Rava. The bay is exposed to winds from the south-west through west to north-west, but otherwise provides a tranquil anchorage in depths of between 5 and 10m. For approaches, see Mala Rava (above) and Vela Rava on page 89.

Vela Rava

Entrance to bay: 44°01'.30N 15°03'.41E

Vela Rava is the largest settlement on Rava and is about 400m south-east of Uvala Marinica, where you can berth or anchor.

NAVIGATION

Charts: HHI MK-13; AC 515, SC5767

Approaches: From the south-east, pass between Hrid Ravica and the islet of Maslinovac (Fl 3s) at the foot of the island. At the top of the island, approaching from the north-west, leave Hrid Galijica well to starboard. From this direction there's a green light (Fl G 3s) on the headland immediately before the bay. Note that there is no anchoring either side of the bay where there are underwater cables.

BERTHING/ANCHORING

The bay is sheltered from all winds except those from the south-west. The breakwater, just past the ferry berth, is reserved for visiting yachts and has depths of between 1 and 5m. Berth bows- or stern-to. Alternatively, anchor on a mud bed with good holding in depths of 5 to 12m, although make sure you are out of the path of the ferry.

ASHORE

You will find a post office, restaurant and supermarket on the quayside, with more shops in nearby Vela Rava. Ferry service to Zadar.

Iž Island – Iž Veli

Entrance to bay: 44°03'.21N 15°06'.78E

Iž Veli lies about a third of the way down the north-east coast of Iž, and has a small marina open all year round. One alternative to Iž Veli Marina (see below), just north-west of Iž Veli, is the village of Drage in the bay of Uvala Maslinčica. It has a small harbour with depths of 2 to 3m, where you can berth stern- or bows-to.

NAVIGATION

Charts: HHI MK-13; AC 515, SC5767

Approaches: The islet of Rutnjak lies to port approximately 800m away from the harbour. Half a mile further to port and roughly the same distance from the shore is an isolated danger mark indicating a shoal. Otherwise the approaches from either the north-west or south-east are relatively straightforward.

Pilotage: An approach waypoint of 44°03'.77N 15°07'.91E lies roughly halfway between the islands of Ugljan and Iž. A bearing of 238°T from this point should give you a clear view of the entrance to the bay. There's a hotel on the north-west side of the bay and a red light on the south-east side. Keep to the centre of the entrance where depths are around 5 to 7m, shallowing gradually to 2m at the far end of the harbour.

BERTHING

The marina, contactable on VHF Channel 17/Tel: 023 277 006, is equipped with 45 sea berths and 150 dry berths, has the same owners as Marina Zadar and is listed as Category II. It quotes prices on vessels of up to 20m (66ft) in length and has depths of between 3 and 6m. A 10m (33ft) boat will cost €3.3 per metre per day. Add €6 for a power connection and a flat rate of 10% on the cost of the berth for water. Berthing is stern- or bows-to at the quay. The harbour is not well protected from northeasterly and easterly winds, which can send in an uncomfortable swell.

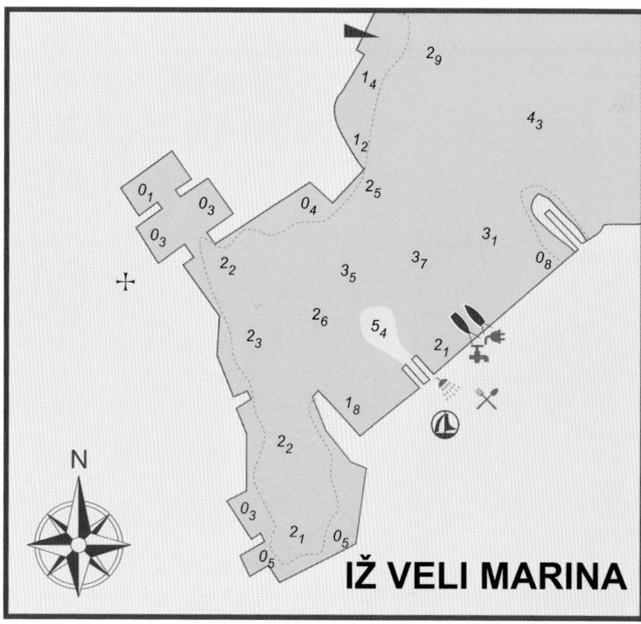

Useful information – Iž Veli

FACILITIES
All berths have **electricity** and **water** supplies. Other facilities include **reception, exchange office, showers, toilets, café, restaurant, repair workshop**, a 24-ton **travel lift** and a 50 ton **slipway**. In the town around the harbour are a **post office, supermarket, bread shop, medical centre** and **hardware store.**

USEFUL INFORMATION
Marina contact details: Tankerkomerc Marina Veli Iž, 23284 Iž Veli. Tel: 023 277 006. Tel/ fax: 023 277 186. VHF Channel 17. Email: marina.Zadar@tankerkomerc.htnet.hr; website: www.tankerkomerc.hr
Tourist information: 23284 Veli Iž, Tel: 023 88 491.
Medical centre: Tel: 023 88 312 .

Iž Island – Iž Mali

Uvala Komoševa harbour: 44°01'.81N 15°08'.45E

There are three bays around Iž Mali – from the north-west these are Uvala Knež, Uvala Komoševa and Uvala Bršanj. Uvala Bršanj provides a quiet, sheltered anchorage inside a relatively new breakwater, in depths of about 6m, and has a green light on the western side of the bay. Uvala Knež has a town harbour where you can berth bows- or stern-to to one of the jetties on the northern side in depths of around 2m. Probably the best option, however, is Uvala Komoševa, closest to the village, which we explore in more detail below.

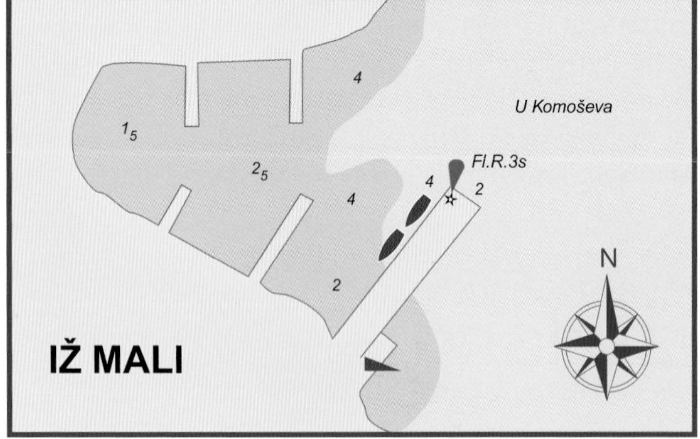

NAVIGATION

Charts: HHI MK-13; AC 515, SC5767

Approaches: From Iž Veli, to the north-west, beware of the rock close to the shore, about 550m from Iž Veli. Half a mile east-south-east of the rock is an isolated danger beacon marking a shoal. The depths between the islet of Knežak and the island of Iž drop to 3.5m. From the south-east, the small islet of Mrtovnjak is identified by a red light (Fl (2) R 10s). The harbour itself has a pier with a red light (Fl R 3s) on it.

BERTHING

You can berth alongside the inner side of the ferry pier in depths of 4m, but check that you will not be in the way of the ferry. The harbour is protected from winds from the north through west to south-east.

ASHORE

Uvala Komoševa and Uvala Knež have a restaurant, shop and café.

Uvala Vodenjak Veli

Entrance to bay: 44°01'.00N 15°09'.32E
Charts: HHI MK-13; AC 515, SC5767

Uvala Vodenjak Veli is a quiet anchorage situated a mile or so as the crow flies south-east of Iž Mali. Beware of the small islet of Školjić and the reef that connects it to the shore. Depths in the bay reduce from 15m to 1m at the inner end. The bay is sheltered from winds from the north-east, through north, to south, and the sea bed is sand. You will find no facilities here.

Uvala Soline

Entrance to bay: 44°03'.74N 15°04'.30E

This bay lies on the north-west coast of the island, about one and a half miles south of the north-west tip, and provides a quiet, protected anchorage. There are no facilities.

NAVIGATION

Charts: HHI MK-13; AC 515, AC 2711, SC5767

Approaches: On the approach from the north and north-west are a number of shoals, rocks and islets. It is safest to leave all these to port, starting with the northernmost rock identified by a white light. From the south-east, note that there is a rock off the islet of Kudica, so keep well in the centre of the channel. Other hazards to be aware of are fish farms off the entrance to the bay, a rock between the islet of Glurović and Iž, and a 2m shoal just south-south-west of Glurović.

ANCHORING

Anchor in depths of between 3 and 7m on a sandy bed. The bay is well protected from all winds, but strong northwesterlies can produce a swell.

Šibenik

Chapter three

The mainland between Biograd Na Moru and Primošten and the off-lying islands

The first stretch of the mainland from Biograd, heading south-east, is not particularly inspiring. Pakoštane is a fairly run-down village, although it springs into life in the tourist season and it looks like there is some money going into improving the infrastructure. Murter, though actually an island, is linked to the mainland. It has a good selection of light industry, as well as three marinas and a tourist industry geared towards exploring the Kornati Islands. Further down the coast, Tribunj is a lovely small village with a rapidly developing marina aimed towards the top end of the market, while Vodice is a bustling tourist town with an ACI marina. Šibenik is an industrial suburb, reached by passing through a long estuary. It is not, as yet, highly developed for tourism, nautical or otherwise, but the sprawling conurbation hides a striking old town rich in history and architecture. There are, however, big plans for Šibenik, including three possible new marinas. Its first marina, Mandalina, opened in 2006 and is expanding rapidly. Šibenik is also en route for a trip further upstream, along the Krka River, to the spectacular waterfalls and the ACI marina, just before them, at Skradin. It's well worth the detour.

Primošten is the most picturesque settlement of this area, connected to the mainland by a man-made road link. The town is entered through a walled gate and densely packed onto a conical hill with a church on the top. It's a popular place for land-based tourists in the season but the nearest marina (Kremik) is in the next bay south (Luka Peleš), which is somewhat isolated and over a mile away by road or two miles by sea.

The main islands off this coastline fall into two groups – the cluster of small islands around Murter, the largest of which is Vrgada, and the group that radiates out to sea from Šibenik, which includes Žirje, Kakan, Kaprije, Zmajan, Tijat, Prvić, Zlarin and Krapanj. These islands are not as developed for tourism as others, but have spawned a number of new, good quality, boutique hotels and you can still find some lovely bays with the occasional good restaurant.

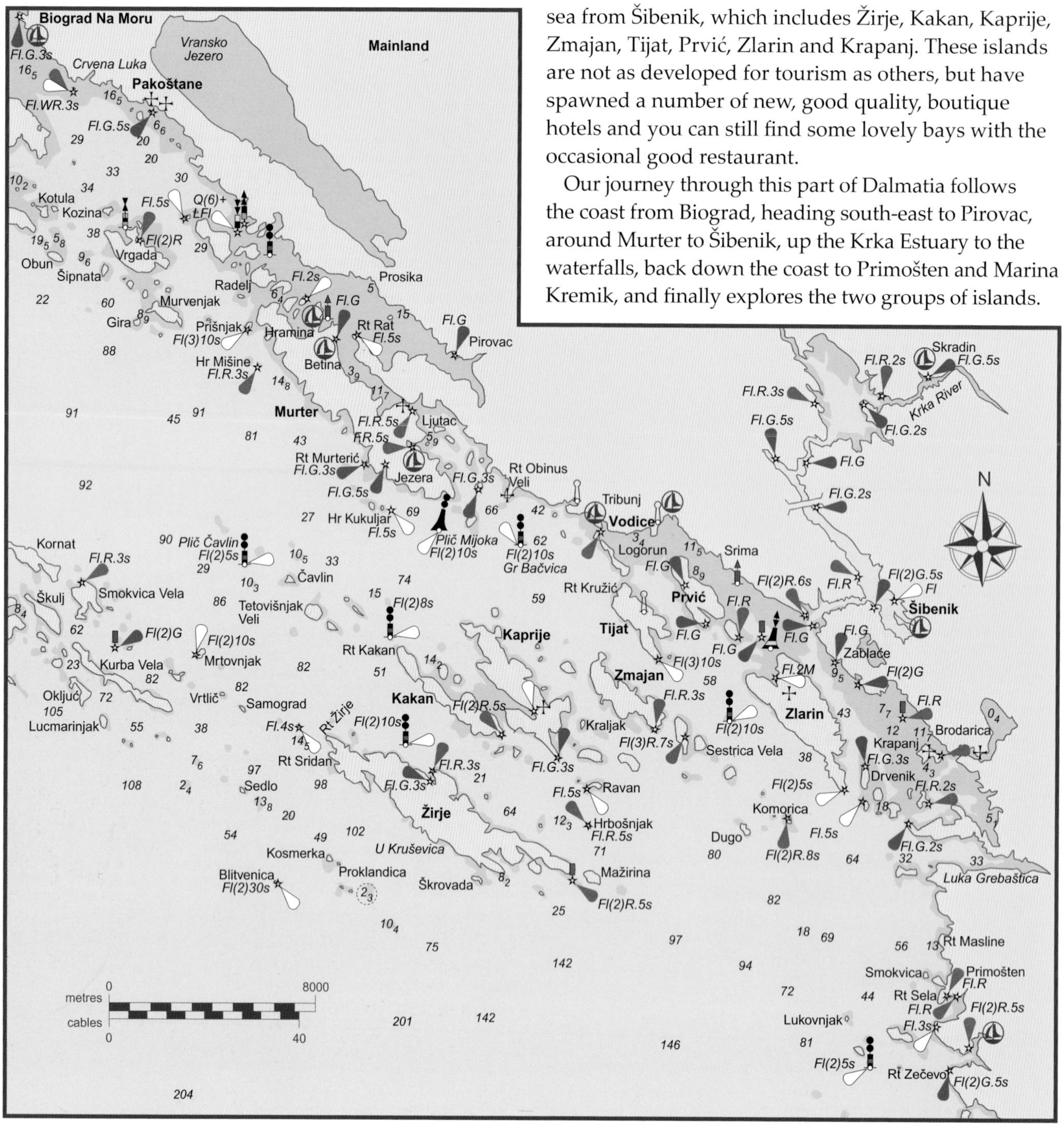

Our journey through this part of Dalmatia follows the coast from Biograd, heading south-east to Pirovac, around Murter to Šibenik, up the Krka Estuary to the waterfalls, back down the coast to Primošten and Marina Kremik, and finally explores the two groups of islands.

Crvena Luka

Entrance to bay: 43°54'.90N 15°28'.47E
Charts: HHI MK-14; AC 2711, AC 2773, SC5767

Although Crvena Luka is a possible anchorage, we wouldn't recommend it. It's really just a holiday resort full of not very attractive apartments, with much of the bay roped off for swimmers and watersports. There is, however, a lovely sandy beach about 300m north-west of Crvena Luka, in the direction of Biograd.

If you do decide to anchor here, it is not protected from the Sirocco and beware of the rocks and islet on the western side of the entrance to the bay.

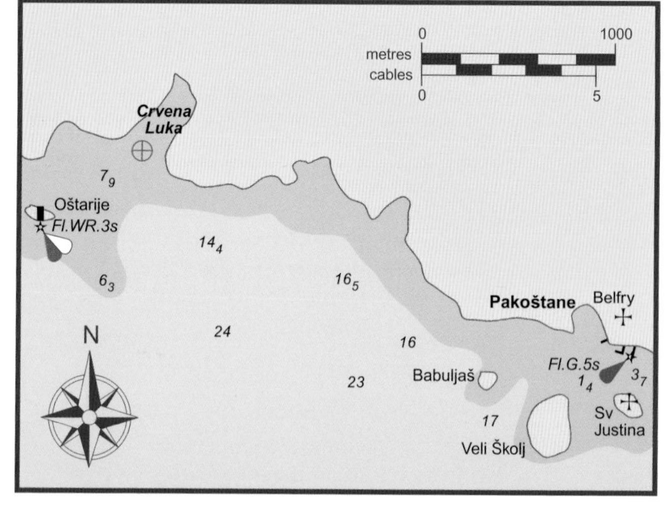

Pakoštane

Charts: HHI MK-14; AC 2711, AC 2773, SC5767
Harbour entrance: 43°45'.38N 15°30'.48E

Pakoštane harbour

We're keeping a close eye on Pakoštane as there seems to have been a steady programme of improvement over the last year or so. However, at the moment it's still principally a package holiday centre. The small harbour and anchorage are not particularly well protected and the bay is full of sunbathers and swimmers. The approach is hazardous, with three islets just off the entrance, a marked shoal and depths falling to below 2m between the two most easterly islets. The village itself has a post office, a market, a supermarket and a small selection of bars, cafés and restaurants.

Velika Luka

Entrance to bay: 43°51'.47N 15°34'.20E

Although there are no facilities on shore, this bay is well protected and provides good holding on a sand bed, in depths of between 3 and 7m. Care is, however, required when approaching and entering the bay.

NAVIGATION

Charts: HHI 512, MK-14; AC 2711, AC 2773, SC5767
Approaches: About a mile north-west of the entrance to the bay, there are two cardinal markers, the southerly one of which is lit (Q (6) + L Fl 15s) and marks a shoal and rock Plič Kušija. Half a mile off the entrance to the bay, towards the islet of Arta Mala, is an isolated danger beacon. Beware of a number of rocks on the inner sides of the bay and you'll need to watch depths carefully, particularly on the northern and western sides of Velika Luka.

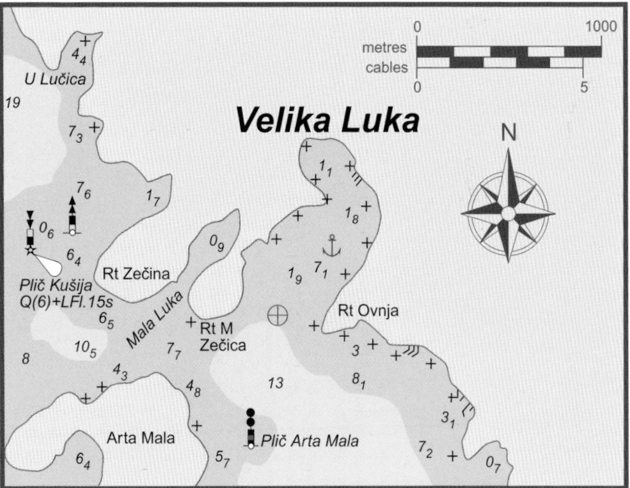

Cardinal markers approaching Velika Luka from the north-west

Pirovac

Entrance to bay: 43°49'.11N 15°39'.50E
Charts: HHI 512, MK-14; AC 2711, SC5767

If you hug the coast heading south-east from Velika Luka you will end up at Pirovac, after which you will have to head back on yourself before sailing around Murter to reach the next part of the mainland. It's not really worth a special visit in our view and the harbour is shallow, quite busy and only partially

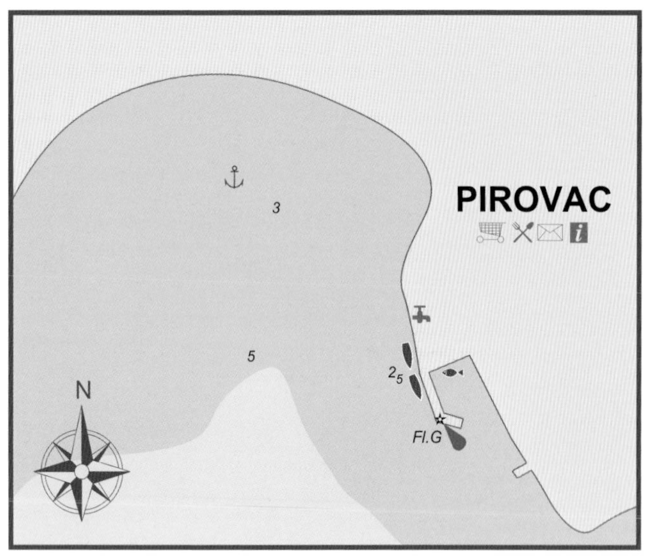

protected from winds. Alternatively you can anchor to the west of the harbour on sand and weed in depths of 3 to 5m.

The approach is straightforward, although note that there is a 5m shoal just west-north-west of the harbour. A green light (Fl G) marks the end of the breakwater enclosing the harbour.

The facilities in the village are good and include a range of shops, medical centre, post office, tourist information office as well as a number of bars and restaurants. In the future, it may well be that Uvala Makirina, the bay to the south-east of Pirovac, will play an important part in the development of the town. Its curative mud covers an area of 414,800 square metres and is believed by many to have considerable potential for health tourism.

Tisno

Entrance to bay: 43°47'.98N 15°38'.93E
Charts: HHI 512, MK-14, MK-15; AC 2711, SC5767

Tisno road bridge connects the island of Murter to the mainland and the village has grown up around the quay. Although the bridge opens twice a day between mid-May and the end of August (0900 to 0930 and 1700 to 1730), depths reduce to under 2m in the eastern approach to the bridge and currents can reach up to 4 knots. Air clearance is 2m (6ft 6in) when the bridge is closed. An anchorage and the town harbour lie on the east side of the bridge, with the anchorage situated on the north side of the channel. The holding is good on a mud and sand bottom and the depth in the centre of the bay is about 4m.

The harbourmaster's office is on Velika Rudina 1, Tel: 022 439 313. Facilities in the village include a post office, tourist office (Tel: 022 438 604), medical centre, shops, bars and restaurants. However, with all that's on offer elsewhere and given the navigational restrictions, there does not seem much point in going out of your way to visit Tisno.

The church on the Murter Island-side of Tisno

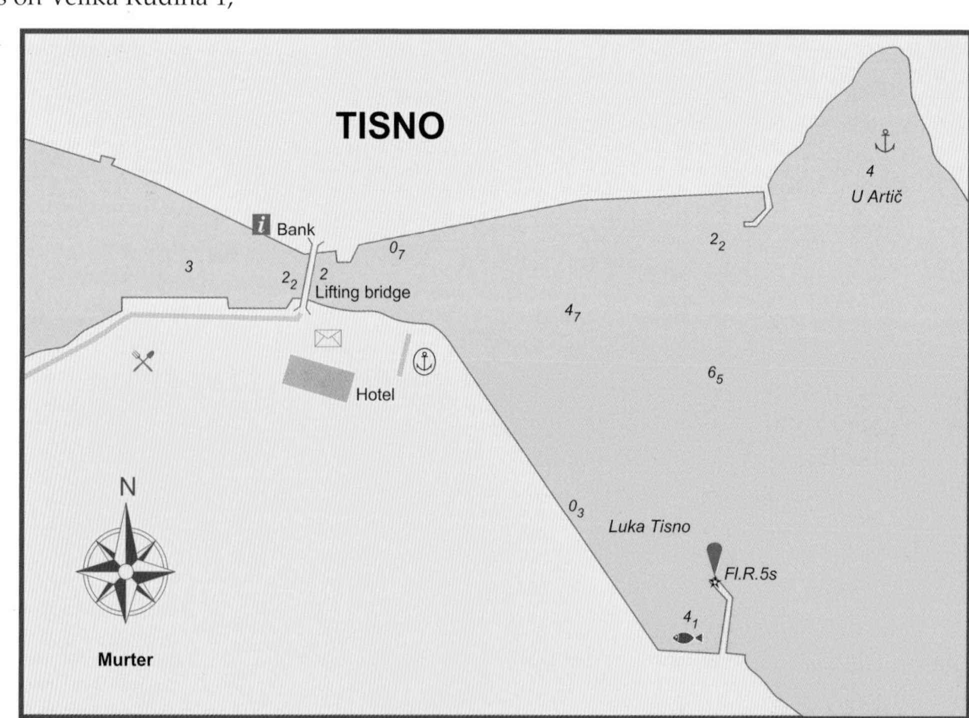

Tisno's lifting bridge

Betina

Entrance to bay: 43°49'.78N 15°36'.09E

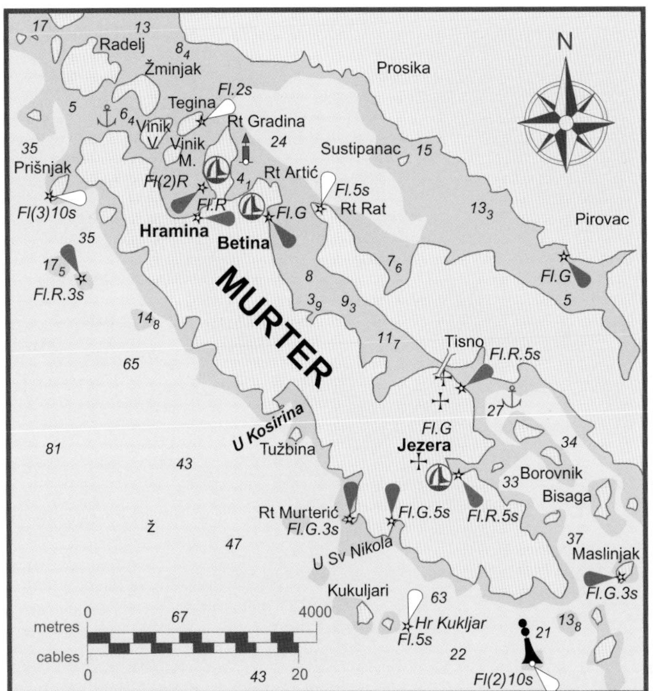

Betina is a small but busy village with a marina, a town harbour and an active boatyard. The development of Betina has not been over influenced by tourism and it therefore has great local character and bustle. It may be possible to tie up alongside the middle wall of the town harbour, but depths are less than 2m and there is a water polo area in the outer half of the harbour. The best bet is therefore to use the marina, which is just around the headland. Note that the marina has recently added a new breakwater that extends out from one of the existing piers and then runs north-east to south-west. This may not be marked on some charts and guides.

NAVIGATION

Charts: HHI 512, MK-14; AC 2711, SC5767

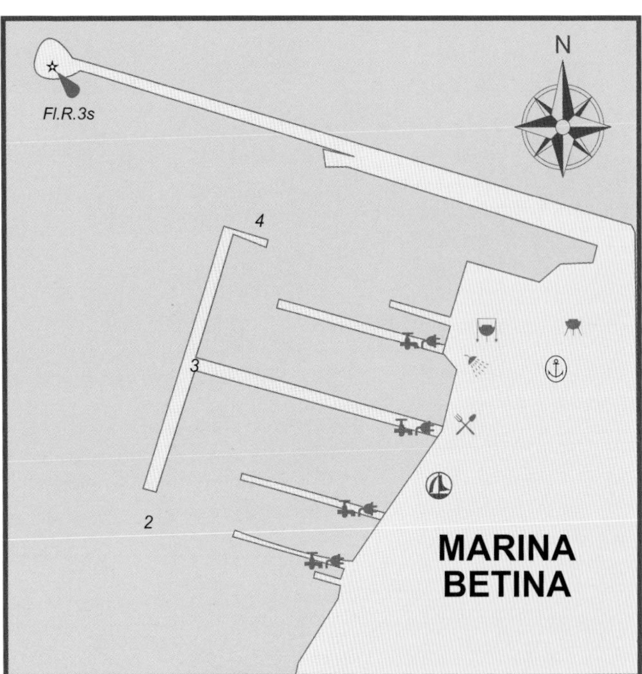

Approaches: From the south-east, see page 94 for details of passing under the Tisno bridge. From the north-west, see page 93 for the approach notes to Velika Luka.

Pilotage: As you continue south-east, past Velika Luka, you will leave to starboard the white light (Fl 2s) on the islet of Tegina, Rt Gradina on Murter, then a green beacon, before turning to starboard towards the marina. Pass between the stone breakwater, with a red light at its head, and the concrete breakwater.

BERTHING

The marina, contactable on VHF Channel 17; Tel/fax: 022 434 497, is Category II, open all year round and has 180 berths where you can berth bows- or stern-to on lazylines.

The daily berthing rate of about €3.5 per metre includes water and electricity, which is available to all berths. With the new breakwater, the harbour is even better protected now and well sheltered from all winds.

Approach to Marina Betina

Useful information – Betina

FACILITIES

The marina has a modern reception and outer buildings, a 50-ton **crane,** two **travel lifts** (20 and 260 tons), a **repair/service workshop, chandlery, reception, exchange office, showers, toilets, laundry** service, a **restaurant** and **café**. Nearby is a working **boatyard,** Brodogradilište, which can offer additional **repair/workshop facilities,** Tel: 022 435 234.

The nearest **fuel** station is less than half a mile from the marina as the crow flies, at Marina Hramina (see page 97).

ASHORE

The village boasts a **supermarket, post office, tourist office** and **internet café**, as well as a number of **bars** and **restaurants.** Try Restoran na Moru, Trg na Moru, Tel: 022 435 177, or Restoran Kalafat, right by the marina, Nikole Škevina bb, Tel: 022 434 497. The main town of Murter has more extensive facilities (see page 97).

OTHER INFORMATION

Marina Betina: Nicole Škevina bb, 22244 Betina, Tel/fax: 022 434 497; email: marina-betina@si.htnet.hr; website: www.marina-betina.hr
Post office: Trg na Moru bb, Tel: 022 434 315.
Tourist office: Trg na moru 2, Tel: 022 434 996; Fax 022 435 218.
Diving centres: Mistral Real, Varos 87, Tel: 022 434 269; email: info@mistralreal.com; website: www.mistralreal.com, or Nautilus Diving Centre, Branimirova 19, Tel: 022 435 893; email: nautilus@siol.com; website: www.diving-adria.com.

Hramina

Marina entrance: 43°49'.58N 15°35'.37E

Marina Hramina is another privately owned marina in a large bay at the top end of Murter. As you enter the bay, don't be confused by the shipyard to starboard – the marina is to port. The marina is within walking distance of Murter, the main town on Murter Island. Tourism in Murter is mostly focused on excursions to the Kornati Islands but the town has a good selection of shops, cafés, bars and restaurants, as well as tourist agencies, etc. The main tourist office for the Kornati National Park is in Murter and open all year round.

NAVIGATION

Charts: HHI 512, MK-14; AC 2711; AC 2773, SC5767

Approaches: See Betina on page 95 for general approach notes.

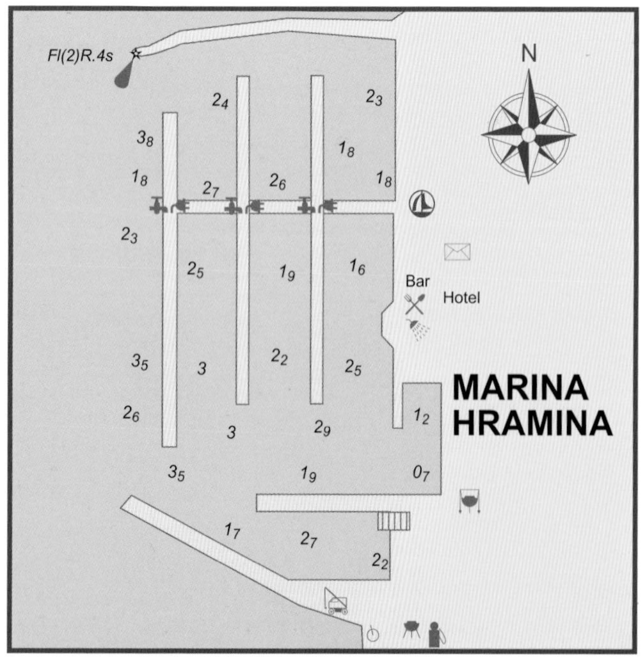

The distinctive cemetery on the approach to Marina Hramina

Pilotage: Enter the bay with the islets of Tegina (Fl 2s) and Vinik Mali to starboard where depths are about 8m. You will pass a big cemetery to port and then, as you round the headland, you will see the stone breakwater of the marina with a red light at the end.

BERTHING

This 400-berth, category III marina is open all year round and can be contacted on VHF Channel 17; Tel: 022 434 411. The berths, equipped with lazylines for berthing bows- or stern-to, are all supplied with electricity and water. Prices average about €4 per metre per day, but note that electricity and water are charged separately for boats over 16m (52ft).

Marina Hramina's boat hoist and crane area

Useful information – Hramina/Murter

FACILITIES

The marina has a **reception office**, exchange facilities, **restaurant, hotel, internet café, laundry** facilities, **showers, toilets**, 15-ton **crane**, 70-ton **travel lift, repair/service workshop, supermarket** and **nautical shop**. There is also a **diving school** and **boat charter** service. Just past the marina is a **fuel** station (depth 2.5m) and the marina can organise the refilling of **gas** bottles. The marina also hosts a number of **repair/maintenance/marine** distribution companies and displays full details on its website (see below under 'Other information').

PROVISIONING

Murter has a good range of **supermarkets, bakeries** and **butchers** as well as a **fish** and **fruit and vegetable market**, all packed into a small area by the seafront. Try Slastičarna Zelena on Trg Rudina for pastries, cakes and ice cream. The **post office** is open from 0730 to 2100 Monday to Saturday in the season, otherwise from 0800 to 1500 Monday to Friday, 0800 to 1300 on Saturday. There are also plenty of **cash points**.

EATING OUT

Murter has numerous bars, cafés and restaurants to choose from. Tic Tac – Luke 25, Tel: 022 435 230 – is a popular, traditional up-market restaurant while Konoba Co, also on Luke, caters for the other end of the market, offering cheap stews and good fresh fish. The restaurant in the marina – Butina – is also worth a visit.

ASHORE

The **tourist office** is at Rudina 3, Tel: 022 434 995, while a number of travel agencies are situated on the front. The Kornati National Park HQ is also at Butina 3, Tel: 022 434 662; website: www.kornati.hr. There's not a great deal to see in Murter itself and the beach by the town is not particularly inspiring. A better beach, however, can be found at Slanica bay, a 15-minute walk west of Murter, although it is very popular in season.

TRANSPORT

Buses run fairly regularly between Šibenik and Murter, with connections at Vodice. Rent a boat or a scooter at Eseker Tourist Agency, Tel: 098 480 950, or at one of the other agencies, which may also be able to help with **car hire**.

OTHER INFORMATION

Harbourmaster: Trg Rudine 8, Tel: 022 435 190.
Marina Hramina: Put Gradine bb, 22243 Murter, Tel: 022 434 411; Fax: 022 435 242; email: info@marina-hramina.hr; website: www.marina-hramina.hr
Medical centre: Tel: 022 435 262.
Pharmacy: Pharmacy Skračić, Luke bb, Tel: 022 434 129.

The Harbourmaster's office in Murter Town

Uvala Kosirina

Entrance to bay: 43°47'.58N 15°36'.57E

Uvala Kosirina is a popular anchorage in the middle of the south-west coast of Murter Island. Facilities are limited, although there is a campsite shop open in the season.

NAVIGATION

Charts: HHI 512, MK-14, MK-15; AC 2711, SC5767
Approaches: From the north-west, the approach is straightforward. From the south-east, avoid the sunken rock about 400m south-east of the islet of Tužbina.

ANCHORING

Good holding in sand and weed in depths of 3 to 13m. The bay is well protected from westerly winds, the Bora and easterlies. However, strong southerly winds can send in a swell.

For a suitable spot for a lunchtime swim, take a short trip to Uvala Vučigrade, a mile north-west of Uvala Kosirina. Here it is possible to anchor in around 7m of water, but the bay is not well enough protected for an overnight stay.

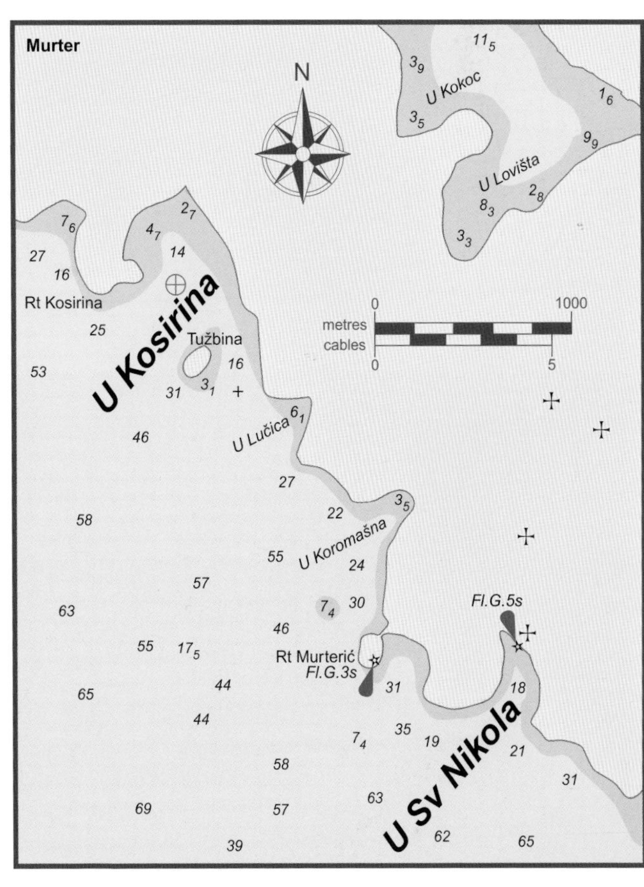

Jezera

Entrance to bay:
43°47'.04N 15°39'.08E

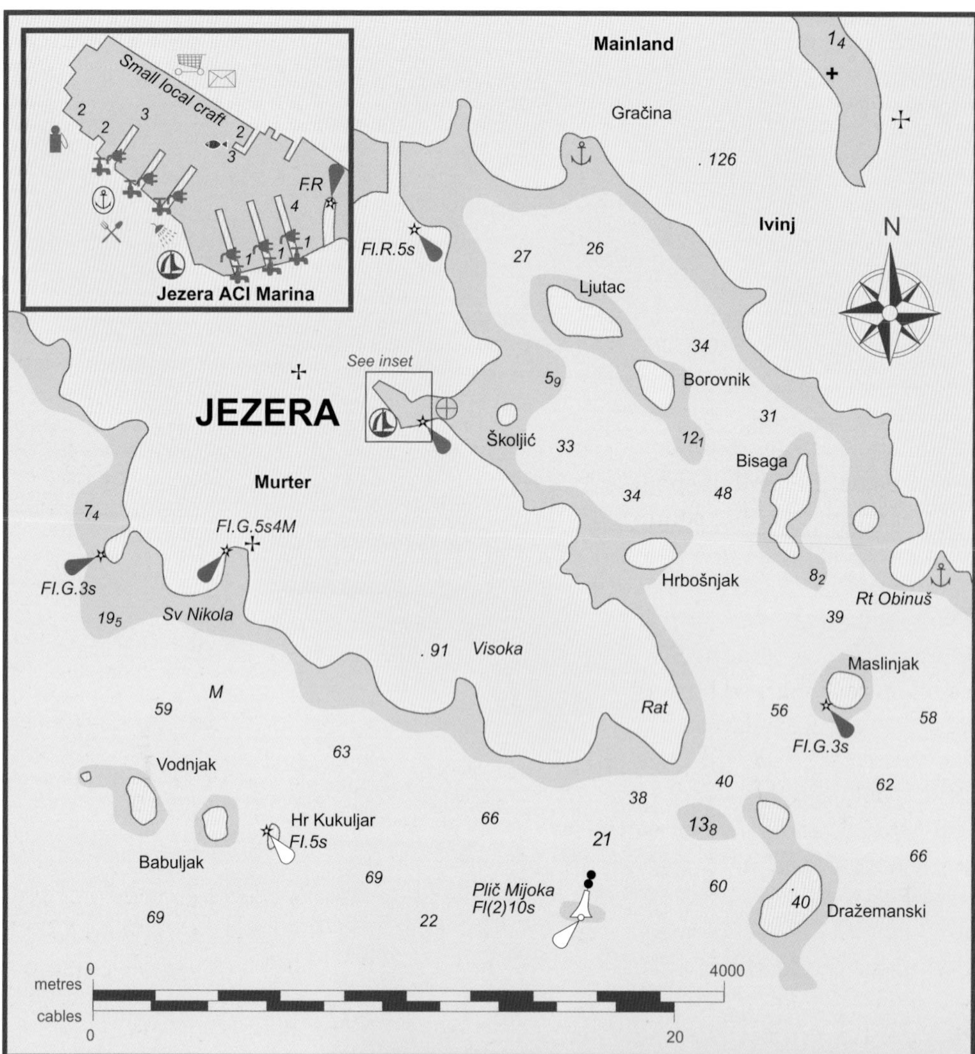

Jezera is a small village on the north-east coast of Murter, not far from Tisno on the mainland, with an ACI marina open all year round.

NAVIGATION

Charts: HHI 512, MK-14, MK-15; AC 2711, SC5767

Approaches: Just under a mile from the southern tip of Murter is a shoal with an isolated danger mark and a white light (Fl [2] 10s). Two miles east-south-east of the shoal is a rock that is also marked and lit (Fl [2] 10s). As you head into the bay from the south-east, with the islet of Maslinjak (green light Fl G 3s) to starboard and the islet of Hrbošnjak to port, the small islet of Školjić lies just outside the entrance to the bay. Pass either side in depths of 7m to the north and 15m to the south. Just north-east of the islet is a 5.9m shoal. The marina is located in the southern part of the bay with a fuel station past the marina and a town harbour further on. At the head of the marina breakwater is a fixed red light.

BERTHING

The marina (contactable on VHF Channel 17; Tel: 022 439 315) is open all year round, listed as a Category II and has 189 berths and 60 dry berths. It is well protected in all conditions. Moor bows- or stern-to on lazylines as directed by the marina staff. Daily berthing rates are €3.8 per metre for a 10m (33ft) boat, rising slightly as boat length increases. You will pay another 10% in July and August, as is the case with most other ACI marinas.

FACILITIES

All berths have power and water supplies. Facilities include a fuel station, a repair workshop, 10-ton crane, sailing school, reception, exchange office, toilets, showers and a restaurant. Marina contact details are ACI Jezera, 22242 Jezera, Tel: 022 439 315; Fax: 022 439 294; email: m.jezera@aci-club.hr; website: www.aci-club.hr.

Jezera ACI Marina

ASHORE

The main street in Jezera has a post office, tourist office, supermarket and butcher, all of which are next door to one another.

Tribunj

Marina entrance: 43°44'.95N 15°44'.86E

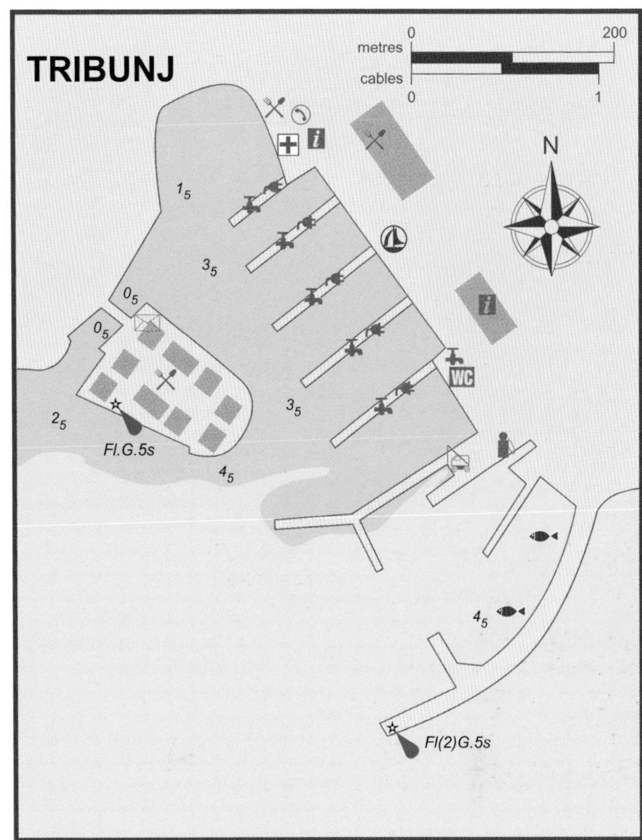

In 2002, Tribunj was a quiet, pretty fishing village with a huge, half-built marina building that had dominated the area for some time. Now that the marina and outlying buildings have been developed, the village is growing and prospering. However, the tranquillity of Tribunj is still a good antidote to the bustle in the neighbouring, more established, tourist town of Vodice. The old town is connected to the mainland by a stone bridge and has a more rustic feel than on the other side of the bridge. Enjoy the fairly strenuous walk up the hill to the church at sunset.

NAVIGATION

Charts: HHI MK-15; AC 2711, AC 2773, SC5767

Approaches: From the west, look out for Gr Bačvica, a sunken rock marked by a white light, three miles west of the marina entrance. Further inland, just off the west coast of the village, is a rock and a 2.5m shoal. Depths between the islet of Lukovnik and the mainland shelve to 2m, and to 3m between Lukovnik and the larger islet of Logorun. From the east be aware that the water shoals rapidly from a depth of 10m half a mile away from the shore, between Vodice and Tribunj and around the island of Prvić. The chapel on its own at the top of the hill is identifiable from a distance.

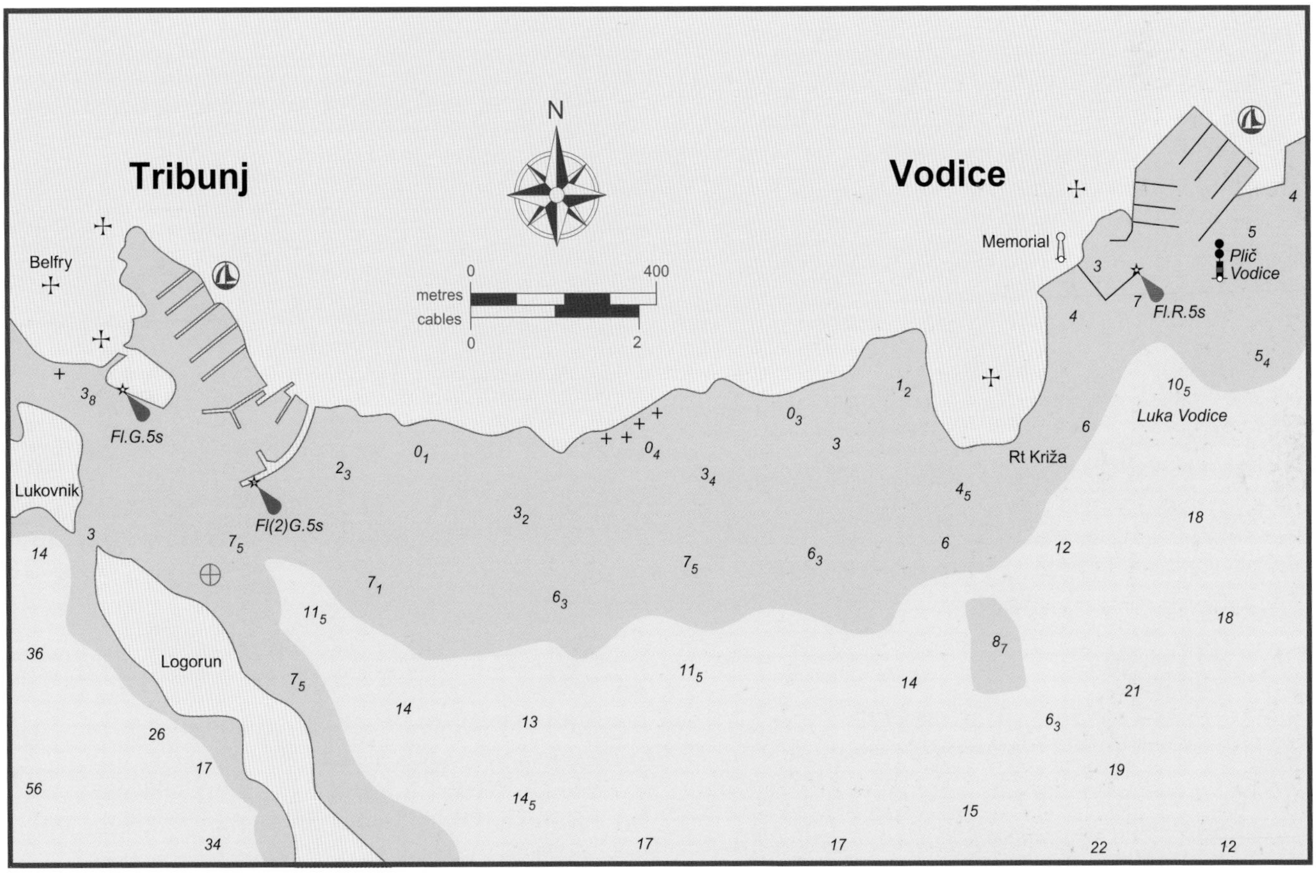

Pilotage: The two islets of Lukovnik and Logorun protect the harbour entrance. Arriving from the west, if you draw less than 3m take the channel between the two islets. More safely, from the east and south-east, take a course roughly parallel to the north-east coast of Logorun, aiming for the gap between the two green lights on either side of the harbour entrance. The first breakwater to starboard, with the green light, marks the outer boundary of the harbour, which is reserved for fishing boats. The next breakwater to starboard forms the entrance to the marina.

BERTHING

The marina can be contacted on VHF Channel 17, Tel: 022 447 140. A category I marina, it is open all year round and has 260 berths and 160 dry berths. The daily rate per metre is €4.2 for a 10m (33ft) boat, rising to €6.05 for a 20m (66ft) boat, although there's a 20% price increase in July and August.

Tribunj Old Town. The marina building is to the right in the background

Useful information – Tribunj

FACILITIES

Water and **electricity** are available to all berths and the now very smart **reception** area has an **exchange office, showers** and **toilets, laundry** facilities and a **pub/restaurant.** Everything else you might need is close by in the village. Yacht services include an 80-ton **travel lift** and a **slipway.** The **fuel station** is towards the shore end on the outside of the breakwater enclosing the marina.

PROVISIONING

The **post office** is in the old town on a street called Badnje – over the bridge on the right-hand side. Just off the harbour front you will find a large **supermarket**, a **market** and a **bank.** Several **mini-markets** are also dotted around, along with a **bakery** and a **butcher.**

EATING OUT

There are a few restaurants, pizzerias and bars to try, including those within the marina complex itself. Tribunj is considered to have one of the biggest fishing fleets in central Dalmatia so there's no shortage of fresh fish on offer. Restoran Tople has been there for a long time and the Grubelić family who owns it have watched the marina in its various stages of development. The restaurant is more posh than rustic and serves great fish and meat. You can find it by walking along the road that runs parallel to the main marina quay, roughly opposite the central pontoon – Uvala Vladimira Nazora 9, Tel/fax: 022 446 403.

ASHORE

There's not that much going on in Tribunj itself apart from the relaxed ambience of the old town and the glitz of the new marina, but you can walk to Vodice in under an hour along the shore. The main tourist office is by the post office, Tel: 022 446 020, and there's a tourist agency and a bus stop as you exit the marina on the corner before turning left towards the old town.

OTHER INFORMATION

Marina Tribunj: Jurjevgradska 2, 22212 Tribunj, Tel: 022 447 140; Fax: 022 447 141; email: marina-office@marina-tribunj.hr; website: www.marina-tribunj.hr
Medical centre: Tel: 022 446 11.

Tribunj Old Town, with its distinctive church at the top of the hill

Vodice

Entrance to bay: 43°45'.11N 15°46'.77E

Vodice is a well-developed tourist town, crammed with restaurants and bars as well as its fair share of large package-type hotels. There are a few good beaches but these are mostly concrete and full of tourists. The town itself becomes very lively in the high season but still manages to retain some intrinsic charm.

The ACI marina holds a number of regattas during the year and Vodice is a good base from which to explore inland, either by bike or on foot, following the established trails.

NAVIGATION

Charts: HHI 533, MK-15; AC 2711, AC 2773, SC5767

Approaches: Approaching from Tribunj, be aware of shallow water near the coast (see page 99). From the west, further out to sea, head between the islands of Logorun and Tijat; from the south, pick a route between the islands of Zmajan and Obonjan, then Tijat and Prvić, leaving well to port the tiny islet of Kamenica, just east of the southernmost point of Tijat; from the south-east, it's best to leave the island of Zlarin to starboard if you want to avoid the sometimes heavy commercial traffic using the Šibenik estuary and the shallow water off the coast. If approaching from Šibenik, with the islet of Prvić to port, note that there is a starboard-hand lateral mark roughly halfway between the estuary leading to Šibenik and Vodice. This marks a bulge in the 2m contour line, away from the shore. The tall Punta Hotel is clearly visible above the tree line, on the point south-west of the marina. In the town itself, landmarks include the church tower, with a grey pyramid roof and, south-west of the church, a concrete statue that looks like a gigantic, nose-down, World War II bomb, but allegedly represents a torch. The town harbour has a breakwater with a red light on it and just north-east is the ACI marina. About half a mile south-east of the entrance to the marina is a rocky shoal indicated by an unlit isolated danger mark. It is safest to leave this to starboard and only approach the marina during daylight hours.

BERTHING

Open all year round, the marina (VHF Channel 17; Tel: 022 443 086) is listed as Category II and has 290 berths and 60 dry berths. It will cost you between €3.8 and €4.3 per metre per day for boats between 10 and 20m (33 and 66ft), plus the normal extra 10% in July and August. The marina is well protected by its two breakwaters, but the Sirocco and Bora can blow strongly in the area.

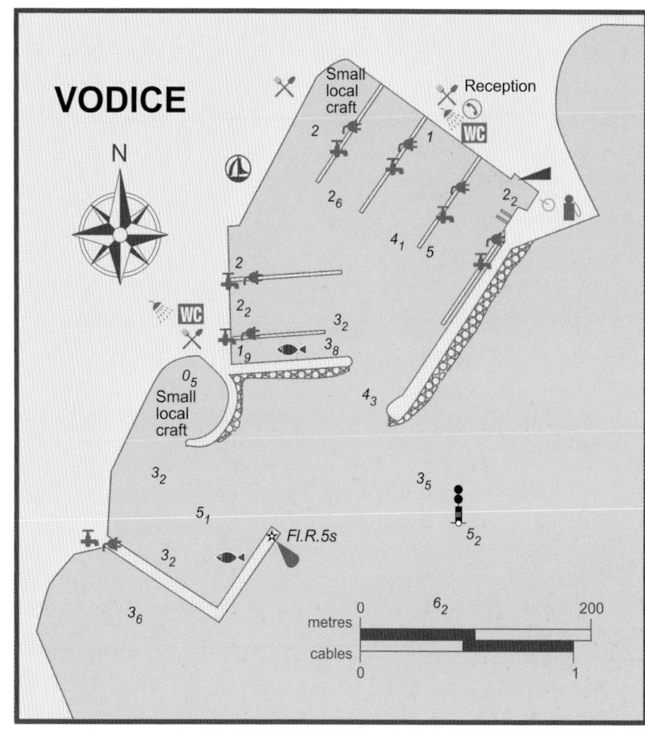

Vodice's municipal harbour. The statue on the left is said to represent a torch

Vodice ACI Marina, with the tall Hotel Punta in the background

Useful information – Vodice

FACILITIES

The marina has the normal comprehensive ACI facilities with 10-ton **crane**, 40-ton **travel lift** and **slipway**. Good **showers** and **toilets**, including an irritating but eco-friendly timer switch on the showers. The **fuel** station, depth 3.3m, Tel: 022 443 024, is on the outside of the south-east-facing breakwater. Opening hours are from 0800 to 2000 every day in the season (1 June to 30 September) and from 0800 to 1400 the rest of the year, except for Sundays and bank holidays when it is closed. **Petrol** and **diesel** are available. **Yacht repair** and service companies in the area are as follows:

Polaris Yacht Service (Yanmar, Volvo Penta, Tohatsu, Mercury, Mariner, Mercruiser, Perkins, Suzuki), Artina 2, Tel: 022 443 021.

F. Bobek d.o.o. (Yamaha), Put Gačeleza bb Tel: 022 444 478.

FDO NAV Centar (Yanmar), Artina 2 Tel: 022 443 221.

PROVISIONING

There's no shortage of **cash points, banks, travel agencies** and **shops** close to the marina and in town. Turn left out of the marina, along Herfordska, to find the post office. Open 0700 to 2100 Monday to Saturday in the season; otherwise 0700 to 2000 Monday to Friday and 0700 to 1500 on Saturday.

EATING OUT

Restaurants in Vodice tend to have a greater choice of food on their menus than a lot of other places. We had traditional Dalmatian roast beef in sauce with dumplings (*pasticada*) at Arausa, Trg Hrvatskih Mučenika, Tel: 022 443 152. Otherwise try Santa Maria Restaurant Pizzeria, Kamila Pamukovića 9, Tel: 022 443 319, for some local atmosphere, vivid decoration and a Mexican flavour.

ASHORE

It used to be a bit of a walk to the main **tourist office**, but in June 2007 it was due to move to the seafront, not far from Hotel Penta (Obala Vladimira Nazora - Tel/fax: 022 443 888; email: info@vodice.hr; website: www.vodice.hr). The new Aquarium, (Obala Matice Hrvatske 33, Tel: 098 214 634; open in summer 1000–1400, 1700–2400, in winter by arrangement) claims to be the largest exhibition of its kind in Dalmatia. On display, in eighteen individual tanks, are more than 60 kinds of fish and other organisms from the Adriatic, including a shark, a sting ray and a tuna.

There are a number of churches and ruins to visit, plenty of summer concerts and six footpaths and cycle paths to explore if you are feeling energetic – you can hire bikes via most of the tourist agencies. Neptun diving centre is based at the Hotel Punta, Tel: 022 200 493/098 266 279; email: neptun@neptun.com.hr; website: www.neptun.com.hr.

TRANSPORT

Vodice is about halfway between Zadar and Split airports and ferry ports and is well connected by **bus** to other towns along the coast. The bus station, Tel: 022 443 627, is just outside the marina entrance, near to a **taxi rank. Car, bike** and **motorcycle hire** can be arranged through the large number of private agencies or the main tourist office.

OTHER INFORMATION

Harbourmaster: Trg Marine bb, 22211 Vodice, Tel: 022 443 055.
ACI Marina Vodice: 22211 Vodice, email: m.vodice@aci-club.hr; website: www.aci-club.hr.
Ambulance: Tel: 022 443 152 (the nearest hospital is in Šibenik).
Medical centre: Tel: 022 443 169.
Pharmacy: Tel: 022 443 168, just west of the bus station.

Santa Maria's terrace

Šibenik

**Approach to town quay:
43°43'.83N 15°53'.40E**

Šibenik is probably one of the most underrated towns in Dalmatia. Like Zadar and Split, it has sprawling and not very attractive industrial suburbs, but the long estuary leads to a charming and atmospheric old town. You have to pass Šibenik to visit the Krka waterfalls but it's worth a detour in itself if you want to absorb some culture and history. It's a busy commercial port but has a town quay,

Looking out to sea from behind Šibenik Old Town

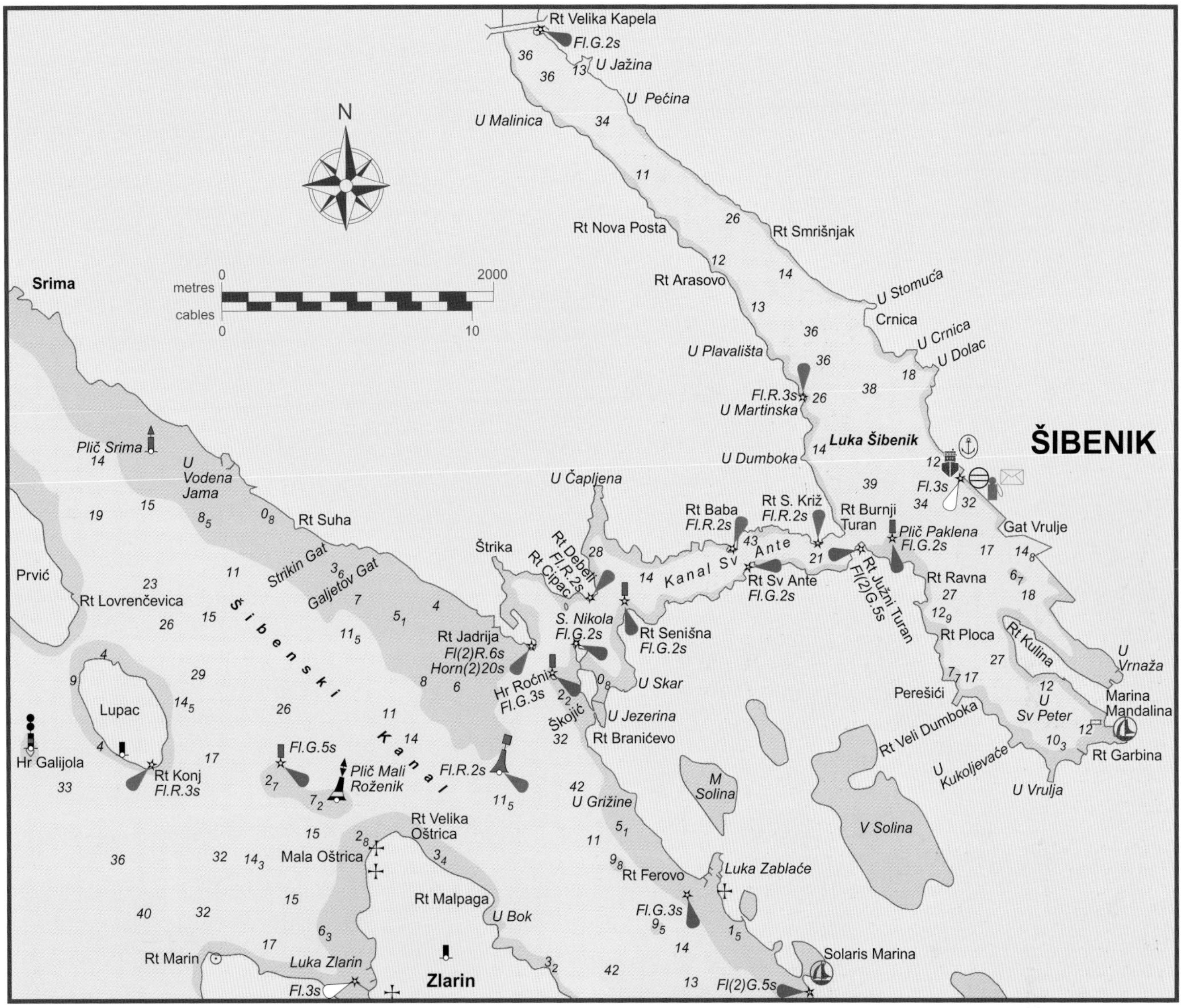

one new marina, Mandalina, one in the course of development and at least another one planned, so it's definitely a place to watch. On the downside, the town quay only offers limited shelter and the approach can be tricky, in a channel about 1.4 miles long, with plenty of commercial traffic and currents of up to 3 knots. It's trickier still in a Bora or a southwesterly when the canal acts like a funnel.

NAVIGATION

Charts: HHI 533, MK-15; AC 2711, AC 2773, AC 2774, SC5767

Approaches: Approaching Kanal Sv Ante, from the south-east, stay close to the north-east coast of Zlarin to avoid a number of islands, islets and shoals; from the north-west, take the middle of the channel between the island of Prvić and the mainland to stay clear of the shallow water on either side; from the south-west, look out for the shoal between the islands of Zlarin and the islet of Lupac, marked by a green light (Fl G 5s). On the north-west side of the entrance to the canal is a lighthouse with a big house behind it, visible from the north-west at some distance; on the south-east side of the entrance, discernible from closer up, is a large fort off which lies a rock marked by a green light (Fl G 3s). Once you are in the canal, it's hard to miss the town, which is situated at the far end, but heading for the fort at the top of the hill will take you to the town quay.

Fort and starboard hand light at the mouth of the estuary leading towards Šibenik

Pilotage: An approach waypoint of 43°43'.17N 15°50'.96E will give you a clear view of the entrance to the canal but you must use visual navigation to get there. The channel is well lit at night, there are special regulations for navigation and signals control commercial vessels over 50 tons, which must obtain permission to enter. The speed limit is 10 knots, overtaking is generally prohibited except if required for safety reasons and vessels under 50 tons must keep to the starboard side and not impede commercial vessels. Anchoring in the channel is prohibited. Look out for the well-camouflaged submarine caves to starboard as the channel narrows in the middle.

As you approach the town, the ferry berth is directly to port of the pier marked by a white light (Fl 3s) and the fuel station is to starboard. There are berths for approximately 50 boats on either side of this pier.

BERTHING

Berthing is normally bows- or stern-to on lazylines or alongside if space permits. Depths are between 2 and 3.8m north-west of the ferry pier and between 2 and 7m south-east of the pier. In the season someone will come along quickly to extract a mooring fee from you; otherwise go to the harbourmaster's office just left of the ferry quay, as you face the town with your back to the water. The only real shelter is from northerly and easterly winds.

Berthing at Šibenik's town quay

Useful information – Šibenik

FACILITIES

Water is available from hydrants but there's no electricity or heavy duty rubbish bins. The **fuel** station, depth 7m, Tel: 022 213 868, is open between 0600 and 2200 every day in the summer (June to September inclusive) and between 0600 and 2100 every day in winter. **Petrol**, **diesel** and **eurodiesel** (blue) are available and most credit cards are accepted. A number of services are carried out in the nearby boatyard, Luka Šibenik, Hrvatske Mornarice 4, Tel/fax: 022 337 989; email: zimovnik@lukasibenik.hr; website: www.lukasibenik.hr. **Repair/service** shops situated nearby include:
Remontno brodogradilište (Caterpillar and MTU) Tel: 022 333 399, 091 333 5111.
Nauticki centar Šibenik (Johnson, Evinrude, Volvo Penta, Tohatsu, Tomos) Tel: 022 217 357, 098 266 018.
Intermotor (Lombardini) Tel: 022 339 888.
Martin (Sail Repairs) Tel: 022 218 830.

PROVISIONING

As you'd expect from a town of this size, you can find just about anything here. The **post office** is on the corner of Put Splita and Vladimira Nazora, just behind the ferry pier. Opening hours are from 0730 to 2100, Monday to Saturday, between 1 June and 30 September, otherwise from 0700 to 2000.

EATING OUT

To soak up the atmosphere of Šibenik and sample traditional food in style, try Gradska Vijećnica (Tel: 022 213 605) in the old Venetian town hall building in the main square opposite the cathedral. One of the most well-known restaurants in Šibenik is Uzorita, situated at Bana Josipa Jelačića 50, Tel: 022 213 660. Specialising in seafood, its prices are reasonable. It's about half an hour's walk uphill from the centre, near the football ground, and is set in a traditional Dalmatian building dating back to 1898, suitably decorated, with courtyard.

ASHORE

The **tourist office** is just by the church of Sv Frane and the ferry pier – Obala Dr Franje Tuđmana 5, Tel: 022 214 411; Fax: 022 214 266; email: tz.grada.sibenik@si.t-com.hr, website: www.sibenik-tourism.hr. It used to be a good walk away, on Fausta Vranjica, so don't be misled by older guide books. As always, there are plenty of private agencies dotted around the town.

Šibenik's UNESCO-protected cathedral

Historically, Šibenik is unusual as it was founded by the Slavs rather than the Greeks and Romans, though it came under Venetian control in the 15th century. It suffered significantly in the Homeland War due to infighting between the indigenous Croats and Serbs and has taken longer to recover than other towns. That being said, its location and natural assets make it ripe for further development. The spectacular cathedral took over a century to build due to lack of funding, disputes on location, plagues and a fire, and is therefore a fascinating mixture of architectural styles. Outside, carved in stone, are the faces of those people who allegedly refused to contribute to the cost of building the cathedral. Inside, the baptistery is an example of intricate carving and the vaulted roof of interlocking stone slabs is considered to be unique. The roof was badly damaged during the war in 1991 and it

Useful information – Šibenik continued

took a team of international experts to rebuild it. If you have time, take a trip to St Anne's fortress for breathtaking views of the old town and the estuary and islands beyond. The first Croatian falconry centre is within 7km of town, on the road that leads to the village of Dubrava. It's open to visitors in the summer between 0900 and 1900, Tel/fax: 022 215 169, and there are plenty of excursions to the nearby Krka waterfalls further up the estuary from Šibenik. Through the summer, there are numerous music evenings as well as the renowned international children's festival. For **diving** try Neptun-Sub, Draga 4, Tel/fax: 022 331 444, 098 642 009 or Otok Mladosti, Trg Republike Hrvatske 3a, Tel: 022 216 089; Fax: 022 212 551; email: ured@otok-mladosti.hr; website: www.otok-mladosti.hr. **Beaches:** It's best to head out of town for beaches, ideally to the pristine waters of the nearby islands of Zlarin and Prvić, or in the Hotel Solaris complex, 4km away on the mainland.

TRANSPORT
The nearest **airports** are Zadar and Split.

The **train station** is at Milete bb, Tel: 022 333 696, close to the seafront, with connections to Zagreb and Split. The **bus station**, Tel: 022 216 066, is on Draga bb with connections to Zagreb and most of the main coastal cities, as well as less frequent trips to a number of towns in Austria and Germany. The public and private tourist offices will have the normal choice of **taxis** and **car**, **boat** and **bike hire** or try Budget Car Rental, Trg P Šubića 1 br 1, Tel: 022 200 330; Fax: 022 216 761 or Tel: 970 for radio taxis.

OTHER INFORMATION
Port Authority Šibenik: Obala Dr. Franje Tuđmana 8, PP 51, 22000 Šibenik, Fax: 022 217378.
Harbourmaster: Tel: 022 214 261.
Hospital: Between Stjepana Radića and Matije Gupca, east of the old town, Tel: 022 212 499.
Pharmacy: Varos, situated at Kralja Zvonimira 32, Tel: 022 212 249.

Marina Mandalina

Entrance to bay: 43°43'.44N 15°53'.85E

South-east of the old town is a district called Mandalina where there is an existing boatyard that has recently extended its premises to include a new marina. Mandalina now has 118 berths, predominantly used by charter yachts. It is hoped that by March 2008 a further 180 berths will have been added, with the final stage of the project bringing the capacity to 400 berths. Facilities currently include a 50-ton travel hoist and service area. Water and electricity are also available.

Šibenik shipyard has a 900-ton lift, a 1,600-ton floating dock and can undertake most repair and maintenance work – Tel: 022 312 900; Fax: 022 312 901; email: ncp@ncp.hr; website: www.ncp.hr. Contact details for the new marina and the existing charter company are Tel: 022 312 999; Fax: 022 312 988; email: booking@ncp.hr; website: www.ncp.hr.

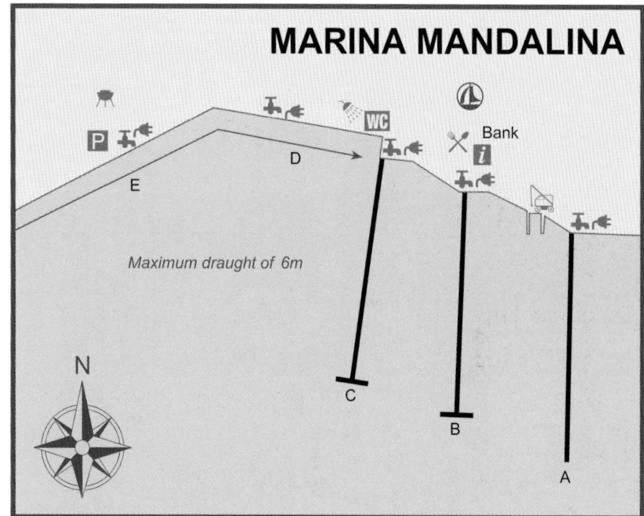

Marina Mandalina, opened in 2006, is already expanding

The Krka Estuary and National Park

Heading north-west along the estuary past Šibenik, then north-east, you will eventually come to a large lake. Exiting the lake to the east will lead you to the small village of Skradin and the site of the ACI marina. From here you need to take an organised boat trip to see the Krka waterfalls and explore the National Park, as private boats are no longer allowed there. The park covers an area 2km downstream from Knin, to Skradin, and the lower course of the Čikola river which joins the Krka river at Skradinski buk. Skradinski buk is probably the most spectacular part of the falls, at a total height of nearly 50m (164ft) and with 17 steps, but Roški slap is the widest and perhaps the most impressive for its surrounding canyons.

In this section, we start with general navigation, followed by specific information for the marina and a summary of the other possible stop-off points as you leave Šibenik, and finally, a useful lowdown on the area.

GENERAL NAVIGATION

Charts: Please note that the Male Karte (small charts) supplied by the HHI do not extend the whole way up the estuary, so make sure you have an alternative. HHI Plan number 518, on a scale of 1:15,000, covers this area, as does AC 2773 (1:30,000) and SC5767.

Approaches and pilotage: See Šibenik on page 103 for general approach notes on the entrance to the estuary and as far as Šibenik town. Note that there are power cables and a road bridge at Rt Velika Kapela, with a height restriction of 27m (88ft), and a road bridge just past Skradin with an 8m (26ft) height restriction.

Although the estuary is well lit, there are some tight bends that curb visibility. As well as a number of shellfish farms close to the shore to watch out for, in addition be aware of a couple of shoals and rocks, all of which are clearly marked on the charts.

The speed limit here is 3 knots, minimum depths for navigation are 7m (though depths on the outer parts of the lake reduce to 3m) and currents can reach up to 3 knots. The Bora is known to blow very strongly along the river.

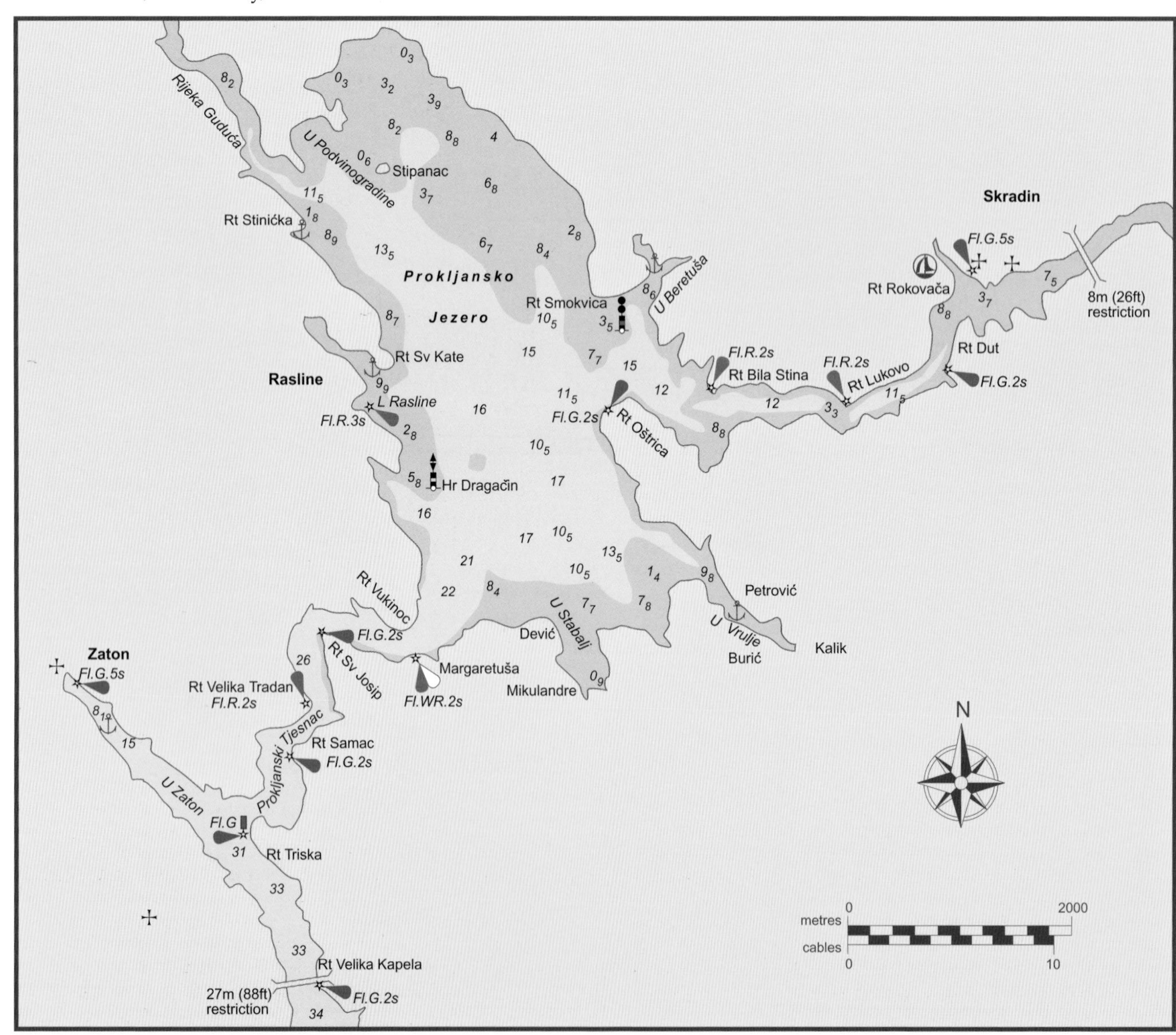

Skradin

Entrance to bay: 43°48'.89N 15°55'.53E

Situated in a small inlet north-west of the pier in Skradin, the marina (VHF Channel 17; Tel: 022 771 365) lies about 8 miles upstream from Šibenik. Take a direct north-east route across the lake to avoid the rocks and shoals. The north-east quay has a green light (Fl G 5s) and the tall church tower is visible from a distance. Anchoring is prohibited just before the inlet.

The marina, with depths of between 2 and 8m, is a popular place to leave a boat in the winter, out of salt water. Listed as Category III, it has 153 berths and the standard ACI facilities, although it's not equipped with lifts or cranes. Charges are €3.8 per metre per day for a 10m (33ft) boat (plus 10% in July and August). Shelter is good from all winds except the Bora. There's a restaurant in the marina and Skradin itself has a few bars and two great traditional restaurants. Zlatne Školjke, Grgura Ninskog 9, Tel: 022 771 022, is open all year round and specialises in seafood. Konoba Toni, Trgovačka 46, Tel: 022 771 177, which closes around Christmas and reopens around Easter, is well known for traditional dishes such as lamb and veal cooked under a 'peka' (metal dome) and fish stew, which is more delicious than it sounds.

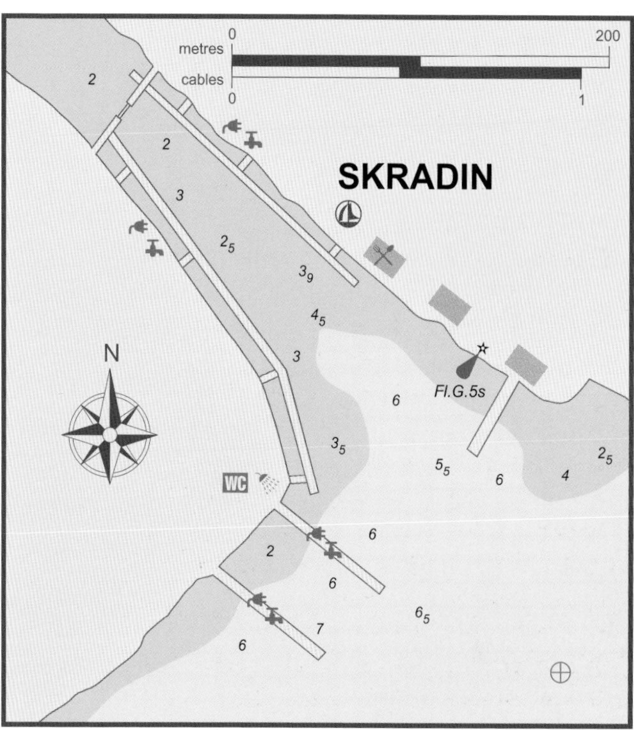

Skradin boasts a good range of grocers, bakers, butchers, a post office, market, bank, medical centre, pharmacy and a tourist office as well as a traditional wine cellar, Vinarija Bedrica, which is well worth a visit, Tel: 022 771 095.

The ACI Marina at Skradin is set in beautiful surroundings on the Krka River

Zaton

Approach to bay: 43°46'.96N 15°49'.67E

Heading upstream, north-west from Šibenik, Zaton is at the end of the creek past the turning you would take to head north-east to Skradin. Halfway along you will pass under the taller of the two road bridges (height restriction 27m [88ft]) and you'll need to watch out for the shellfish farms close to the shore. There's an active rowing club here with lanes often marked by unlit buoys and no anchoring is allowed off the pier, which is identified by a green light (Fl G 5s). However, you can anchor in the outer part of the creek or tie up alongside the quay in depths of about 2.2m.

Winds from the south or south-east are at times problematic, but otherwise the harbour is well protected. Zaton has a similar range of shops and facilities to Skradin.

Rasline

Entrance to bay: 43°48'.41N 15°51'.61E

Although the through-route of Prokljansko Jezero (the lake) is safe, apart from the marked shoal just north of the exit upstream, the shores are shallow, with many detached rocks and shoals making navigation around the lake hazardous. Rasline is in the middle of the western side of the lake. Approaching from the south, about halfway between the entrance to the lake and Rasline, there is an unlit east cardinal mark indicating an above-water rock. The rock lies in the obscured sector of the red harbour light (Fl R 3s). Navigation north of Rasline is not recommended due to shallow water and rocks, although the north-west inlet to the lake, fed by the Guduće river, provides a sheltered anchorage in depths of 6 to 10m on a mud bed (anchoring in the inner part is prohibited), as does the inlet just north of Rasline (depths 3 to 6m on a mud bed). Berthing at the harbour is not recommended in a Bora or Sirocco. Depths are 4m at the outer end of the harbour, shallowing rapidly. Provisions are limited in the local shop.

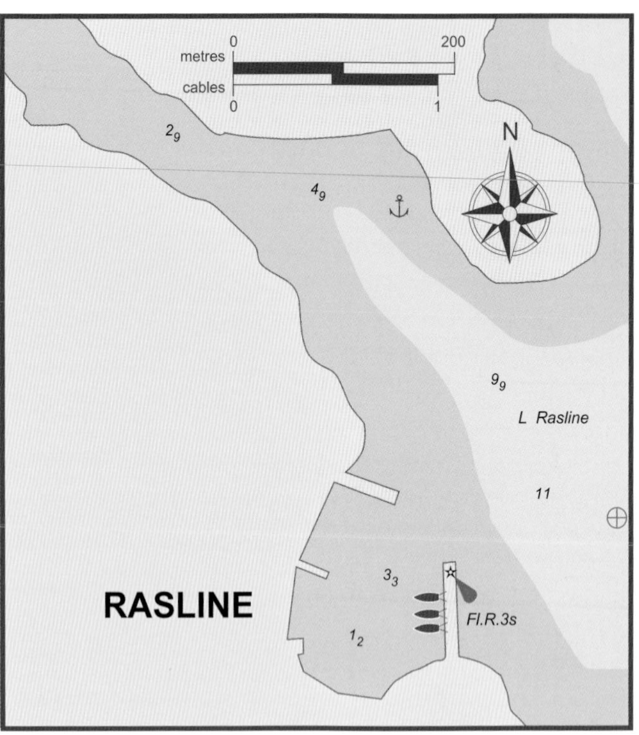

Uvala Beretuša and Uvala Vrulje

These two bays offer good, sheltered anchorages on a mud bed, but there are a number of hazards to watch out for so they are not recommended.

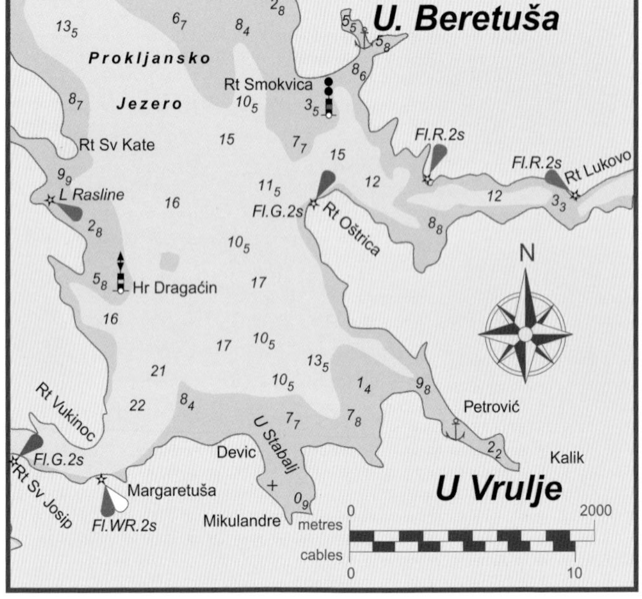

Useful information – the Krka Estuary

The Krka waterfalls

SKRADIN ACI MARINA: 22222 Skradin, Tel: 022 771 365; Fax: 022 771 163; email: m.skradin@aci-club.hr; website: www.aci-club.hr

KRKA NATIONAL PARK: Trg Ivana Pavla II, Br 5, 22000 Šibenik, Tel: 022 217 720; Fax: 022 336 836; email: turizam.npk@npkrka.hr; website: www.npkrka.hr

POST OFFICE SKRADIN: Dr Franje Tuđmana 8, 22222 Skradin, open 0800 to 1200 and 1800 to 2100, Monday to Friday in July and August, otherwise 0800 to 1500.

POST OFFICE ZATON: Hrvatskih Branitelja 1, 22215 Zaton.

TOURIST OFFICE SKRADIN: Trg Male Gospe 3, 22222 Skradin, Tel/fax: 022 771 306; email: tz-skradin@si.htnet.hr; website: www.skradin.hr.

AMBULANCE SERVICE SKRADIN: Tel: 022 771 099.

PHARMACY SKRADIN: Tel: 022 791 019.

Zablaće

Entrance to bay: 43°42'.34N 15°51'.98E
Charts: HHI 533, MK-15; AC 2773, AC 2774, SC5767

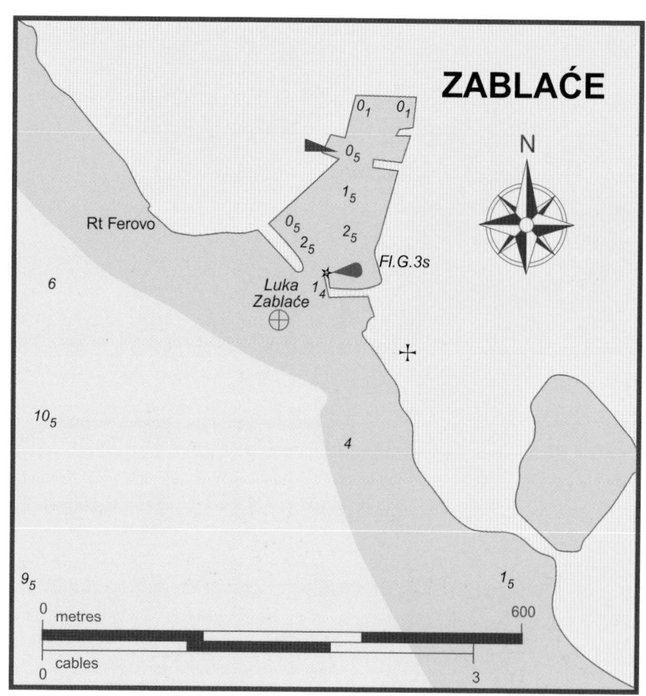

A mile south-east of the channel leading to Šibenik, Zablaće is a small town with a few shops. The inner part of the town harbour is shallow, but there are depths of between 2 and 3m on the inner side of the breakwaters, from halfway along the breakwaters to the outer end. The harbour has a slipway and is exposed to the Sirocco. There's a green light (Fl G 3s) at the end of the breakwater and no particular approach hazards.

In the 15th century, Zablaće had an important salt works but, like Biograd, the town was destroyed twice; once in 1510 and again in 1537. Salt production, agriculture and fishing have largely been replaced by tourism, although history lives on in the names of Zablaće's two main lakes – Velika Solina and Mala Solina (big salt works and small salt works).

Solaris

Entrance to bay: 43°41'.91N 15°52'.50E
Charts: HHI 533, MK-15; AC 2711, AC 2773, AC 2774, SC5767

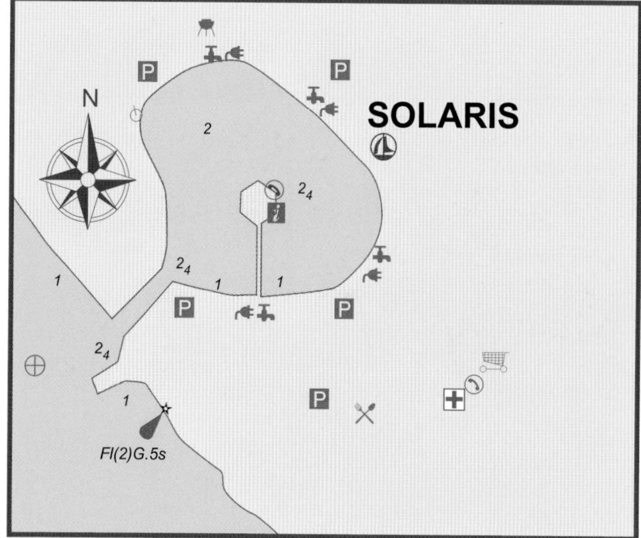

Just over half a mile south-east of Zablaće lies Solaris – a huge tourist complex with hotels, apartments, campsites and a marina. If you like resort holidays then this is the place for you. The marina itself is shallow – maximum depth of 2.4m – but is well protected with 320 berths and 200 dry berths. The maximum length quoted for is 11m (36ft), which will cost just under €3.2 per metre per day. It's a Category III marina equipped with toilet and shower facilities, a pet washing area (sic), outdoor seawater pool, shops and sports facilities and a 5-ton crane. The approach is straightforward, the marina easily identified amid the apartment blocks and there is a green light (Fl (2) G 5s) on the south-east side of the entrance.

Solaris Yacht Marina: Hotelsko naselje Solaris bb, 22000 Šibenik, Tel: 022 361 024/091 100 1068; Fax: 022 361 801; email: prodaja@solaris.hr; website: www.solaris.hr.

Entrance to Marina Solaris

The reception at Marina Solaris

Brodarica

Village harbour:
43°40'.53N 15°55'.16E
Charts: HHI MK-15; AC 2711, AC 2774, SC5767

Brodarica is a small village with one of the best traditional fish restaurants in the Šibenik region. It's also right opposite the island of Krapanj (see page 123), which is famed for being the smallest inhabited island in Croatia and also the lowest lying. Brodarica has a small town harbour, completely exposed to the Sirocco, but has recently installed a floating pontoon for visiting yachts. The fish restaurant, Restoran Zlatna Ribica, is also a hotel and mini-tourist office. (Zlatna Ribica Hotel, Restaurant and Tourist Agency: K Spuzvara 46, 22010 Brodarica, Tel: 022 350 300/022 350 695; Fax: 022 351 877; email: tudic@si.htnet.hr; website: www.zlatna-ribica.hr). It is open throughout the year and easily spotted on the seafront. Canoes and boats are available to hire here.

Opposite the fish restaurant, on Krapanj, is a new, very plush hotel and restaurant with two floating pontoons. It can be reached via one of the several small boats ferrying people across this short stretch of water. Brodarica is probably a lunchtime stop rather than an overnighter, but well worth a visit. There are no particular approach hazards, but facilities are limited.

Zlatna Ribica restaurant, Brodarica

Jadrtovac

Channel entrance: 43°40'.22N 15°55'.63E

The village of Jadrtovac lies on the south-east corner of a small lake, Morinje, which is accessible via a channel about a mile long. The lake has depths of less than a metre but there are some good anchorages along the channel, as well as three small quays near the lake with depths of 1 to 1.5m.

NAVIGATION

Charts: HHI MK-15; AC 2711, AC 2774, SC5767

Approaches: The entrance to the channel is under a road bridge with air clearance of 20.5m (67ft). There are a number of rocks and shoals in the area so the best approach is from the south-west between Rt Oštrica Vela on the mainland and the islands of Oblik and Vela Krbela. The rock just off the east coast of Oblik is identified by an east cardinal mark. Look out, however, for another rock in the large mainland bay facing Vela Krbela, as well as rocks off the south coast of Krapanj and a 1.9m shoal close to the mainland just over half a mile south-east of the entrance to the channel.

ANCHORING

As you pass under the bridge you will see three bays on the northern side of the channel where you can anchor on a mud bed in good holding in depths of between 3 and 10m. Alternatively, head a little further into the channel and anchor by the chapel south of the small islet in depths of between 2 and 7m, or past the islet in depths of 3m. Shelter can be found from all winds, although the inner channel is exposed to the Bora.

ASHORE

A small supermarket in the village.

Luka Grebaštica

Centre of bay: 43°38'.18N 15°56'.10E
Charts: HHI MK-15; AC 2711, AC 2774, SC5767

Luka Grebaštica provides a reasonable anchorage in the inlets on its northern shore, towards the head of the bay. It is completely exposed to winds from the west and the outer part of the bay is open to southerlies.

Note that there is nothing special about this place, and that there are plenty of better places to stop off, most of which can be found nearby.

Primošten

Centre of bay: 43°34'.82N 15°55'.50E

The picture postcard town of Primošten, famous for its Babič wine, is popular with tourists in the season. Joined to the mainland by a causeway, its conical shape, densely-packed with houses, is of classic Croatian style and visible from a distance. North of the town is a wooded peninsula that is home to a large hotel and campsite. Marina Kremik is just too far away to really be able to claim to be Primošten's marina, so if you want to sample the ambience of Primošten close up, use the town harbour or anchor off.

NAVIGATION

Charts: HHI MK-15; AC 2711, AC 2774, SC5767

Approaches: The approach is clear from the north, through north-west, to west, apart from the small islet of Smokvica, about half a mile north-west of the town, with depths of 8m in the channel that separates it from the mainland. From the south, a group of islets, shoals and a submerged rock guard the entrance. These are clearly identified on the charts, the shoal is marked by a red light (Fl R 2s) and the submerged rock has an isolated danger mark and a white light (Fl [2] 5s), so pick your route between the hazards or, safer still, skirt round them all. The church lies at the top of the hill on which the town stands and is prominent from a distance. The breakwater extends from the eastern side of the peninsula and is marked by a flashing red light.

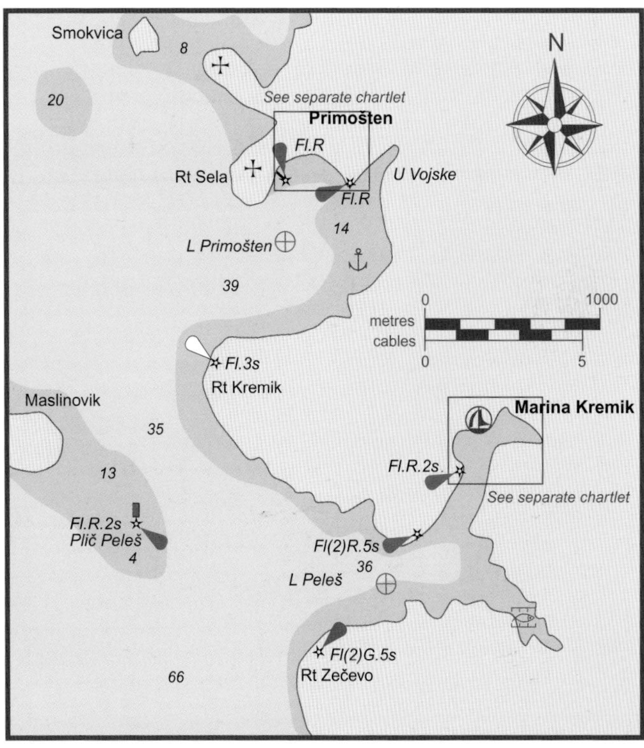

Primošten, a popular tourist destination

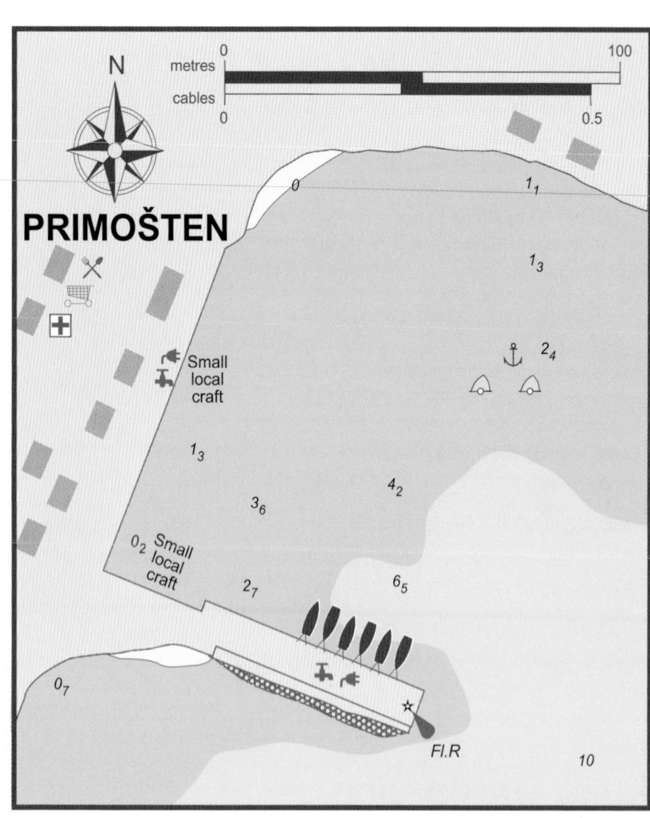

BERTHING

Berth on lazylines, bows- or stern-to, inside the breakwater in depths of between 2.6 and 3.7m. Alternatively, head further into the bay and use the inner harbour in depths of about 2m. There are reports that the holding for anchoring is not good so it's best to pick up one of the mooring buoys in the middle of the bay. Berthing and mooring fees will be payable. Winds from the south-west send in a heavy swell, but otherwise the breakwater affords good protection.

Useful information – Primošten

FACILITIES

Electricity and **water** are provided to most berths.

PROVISIONING

Primošten has a good range of **shops**, a **market**, **bank** and **post office** (Trg S Radića 9, 22202 Primošten), open 0730 to 2100, Monday to Saturday in the season, 0800 to 1500 Monday to Friday and 0800 to 1300 on Saturday outside the season.

EATING OUT

There's no shortage of restaurants to choose from during the season. Restaurant Kamenar (Rudina bis, J Arnerića 5, Tel: 022 570 889), also a small, comfortable hotel, is just inside the main town gate and has a good range of traditional fish and meat dishes at slightly higher than average prices. Konoba Galeb is worth the walk up the hill for the view from the terrace. There are signposts from the western side of the peninsula leading you up to the restaurant – Tel: 098 174 3288.

The picturesque town of Primošten

ASHORE

The main **tourist office** is close to Restaurant Kamenar (Trg Biskupa J Arnerića 2, Tel: 022 571 111; Fax: 022 571 703) and there's a scattering of private agencies. In the town itself, there is not much in the way of things to see or do. For nightlife, however, Aurora, a five-minute drive uphill from the centre of town, is one of Croatia's best nightclubs. It is open 2000 – 0400 from June to September (Tel: 098 668 502; website: www. auroraclub.hr).

BEACHES

A walk around the old town will reveal plenty of concrete and pebble swimming spots, but the best beaches are either side of the hotel complex peninsula. The water is particularly clear and Primošten is famed for its lack of rain.

TRANSPORT

The small **bus station** is at the junction of the roads from the old town and the hotel complex, and will connect you to the towns along the coast.

OTHER INFORMATION

Port Authority Primošten: (Seasonal port of entry) Porat 2, 22202 Primošten, Tel: 022 570 266.
Medical centre: Trg Stjepana Radića 8, Tel: 022 570 033.
Pharmacy: Grgura Niskog 22, Tel: 022 570 305.

Marina Kremik

Entrance to bay: 43°33'.79N 15°55'.52E

Marina Kremik is somewhat isolated and out on a limb, situated in its own bay, and not within easy walking distance of civilisation. Primošten is the nearest town, although there are reasonable facilities within the marina complex. It's a popular charter base but has no soul of its own.

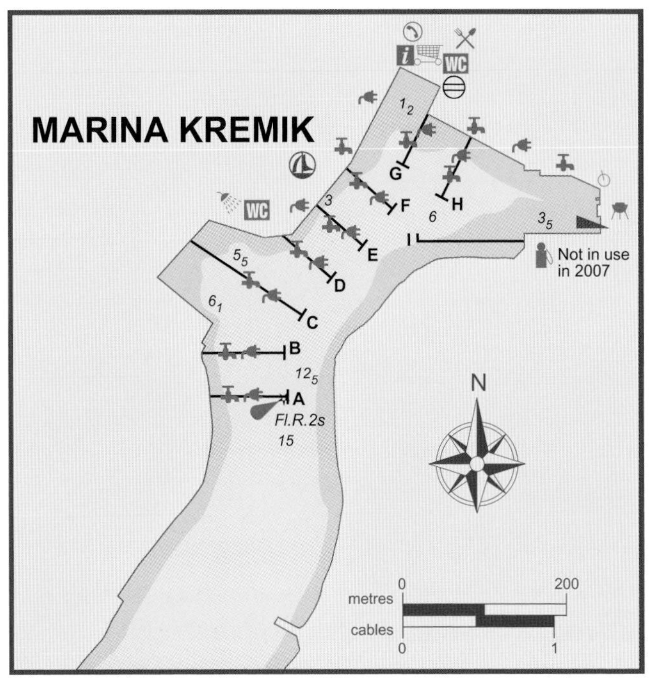

NAVIGATION

Charts: HHI MK-15, MK-16; AC 2711, AC 2774, SC5767

Approach: When approaching the marina from the north-west, hugging the mainland coast from Primošten avoids the hazards mentioned in that section. From the south-east, keep clear of a number of hazards south-west of Rogoznica (see page 127) and Veli Brak shoal, identified by an isolated danger mark. There's a white light (Fl 3s) on Rt Kremik, north of the bay, and a green light (Fl (2) G 5s) on Rt Zečevo to the south. The shoal

A service workshop at Marina Kremik

Marina Kremik offers all the standard facilities

Pličina Peleš, just off the entrance, is marked by a red light (Fl R 2s). The bay divides into two inlets with a red light (Fl (2) R 5s) identifying the north-west bank of the northernmost inlet leading to the marina. No anchoring is allowed in the other inlet where there appeared to be a fish farm last time we passed.

BERTHING

Open all year round, this Category II marina (VHF Channel 17; Tel: 022 570 068) is very well protected, and has 393 berths on finger pontoons and room for 150 boats ashore. The maximum depth is 15m, reducing to 6m. The marina charges a flat rate of €25 per day with a 50% discount between 1 October and 30 April.

FACILITIES

Kremik offers all the standard marina facilities plus restaurant, supermarket, nautical shop, service/repair facilities, a 5-ton crane, 80-ton travel lift and 50-ton slipway. Taxis are available on request at reception. The fuel station (Tel: 022 571 110), in the eastern corner of the inlet, is said to open every day from 0700 to 2000, 1 June to 30 Sep, and from 0800 to 1200 and 1700 to 1900, Monday to Saturday, excluding bank holidays, the rest of the year. Note, however, that it has rarely been in use since 2006. When open, petrol and diesel are available, but there is no eurodiesel. Most credit cards are accepted.

ASHORE

You're pretty well stuck on the marina complex without a car or taxi but the restaurant and supermarket are good. The road out of the marina leads straight onto the main coastal road, and there are no restaurants or shops within walking distance so see information on neighbouring ports, notably Primošten (page 112) and Rogoznica (page 128), for places to visit by car, taxi or bus (a bus service operates along the main road).

Marina Kremik: Splitska 22, 22202 Primošten, Tel: 022 570 068; Fax: 022 571 142; email: marina.kremik@si.t-com.hr; website: www.marina-kremik.hr.

Islands around Murter, between Pakoštane and Tribunj

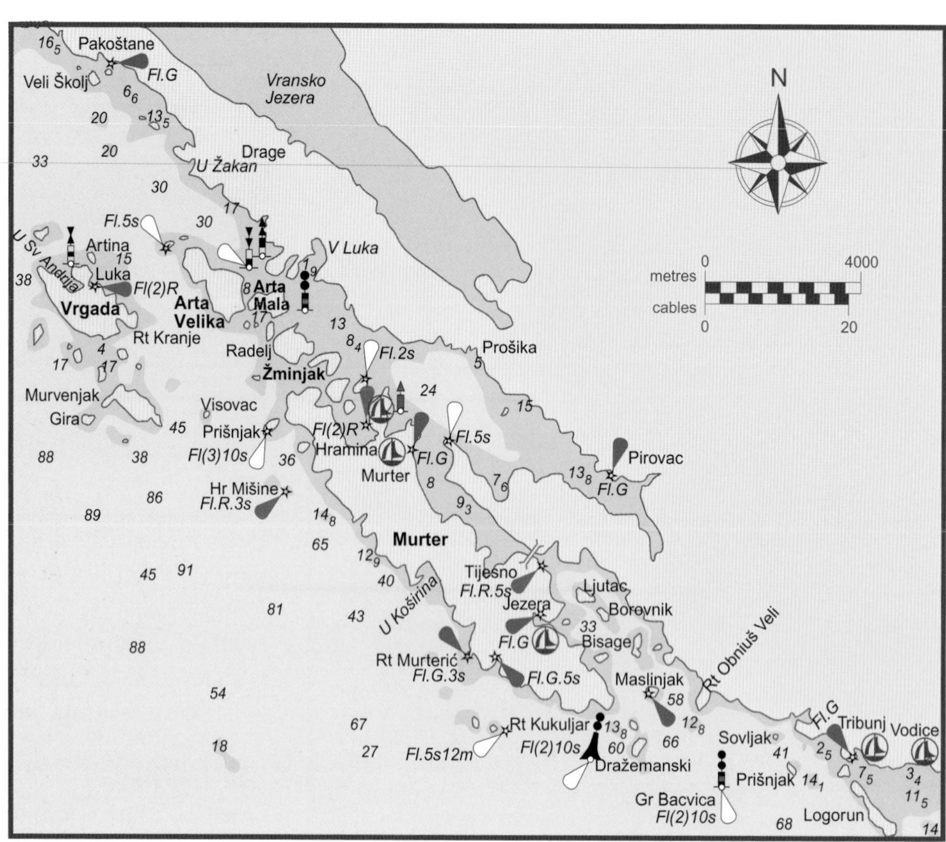

There are a number of islands and islets clustered around Murter, the largest of which is Vrgada. We note the principal stop-off points below, but there are better cruising areas.

Vrgada Island – Uvala Sv Andrija

Entrance to bay: 43°51'.66N 15°29'.62E
Charts: HHI 512, MK-14; AC 2711, AC 2773, SC5767

Lying in the middle of the north coast of the island, this is a shallow bay with a rocky bottom, so anchoring is not recommended. It is possible to berth stern-to the breakwater, but in depths of around only 1.3m. It is also exposed to northwesterly winds and facilities are limited. If you do decide to moor here, however, look out for the rock just off the eastern boundary of the bay, indicated by a west cardinal marker.

Vrgada Island – Luka

Entrance to bay: 43°51'.52N 15°30'.23E
Charts: HHI 512, MK-14; AC 2711, AC 2773, SC5767

This bay is not suitable in a Bora, although provides good protection from westerly and southwesterly winds. Do not pass between the islet of Artina and Vrgada as depths are shallow and the bottom is rocky. Depths on the inner side of the breakwater (which is lit – Fl [2] R 7m 3M) are 1.5m and the moles are only suitable for small craft. Anchoring is possible in depths of between 2.5m and 4.5m north-west of the breakwater. The village incorporates a shop and a restaurant.

Arta Mala Island

Entrance to bay: 43°51'.14N 15°33'.43E
Charts: HHI 512, MK-14; AC 2711, AC 2773, SC5767

This island lies just opposite Vela Luka on the mainland and has a popular anchorage on its south side. It's best approached from the open sea, from the south-west, as shallow water and rocks make an approach from the mainland side of the island hazardous. Go around rather than between the islets of Gubavci and Prišnjak Mali. The bay is exposed to winds from the west, through south, to south-east, but the sand bottom provides good holding in depths of around 7m.

Žminjak Island

Entrance to bay: 43°50'.32N 15°34'.49E
Charts: HHI 512, MK-14; AC 2711, AC 2773, SC5767

Another popular anchorage can be found in the south-west facing bay on the islet of Žminjak. It is exposed to southwesterly winds, but fairly well protected from others, particularly the Bora. The holding is good on a mud bottom in depths of around 5m and there are boulders for attaching lines ashore. Beware of the 5m shoal about half a mile west of the most westerly tip of the island.

Islands off the coast from Šibenik

In an area roughly 10 miles out to sea from the mouth of the channel leading to Šibenik (see chart on page 92) is another densely-packed archipelago. Although as a group not as spectacular as the Kornati Islands, there are plenty of places worth visiting with arguably more character. We start with Žirje, furthest from the mainland, and work our way back in.

Zmajan, though a relatively large island, has no suitable places to put into and is therefore deliberately not included. Logorun Island, just off the mainland coast by Tribunj, is also not suitable for anchoring or mooring, but does have a donkey sanctuary, which might make an interesting visit.

Žirje Island

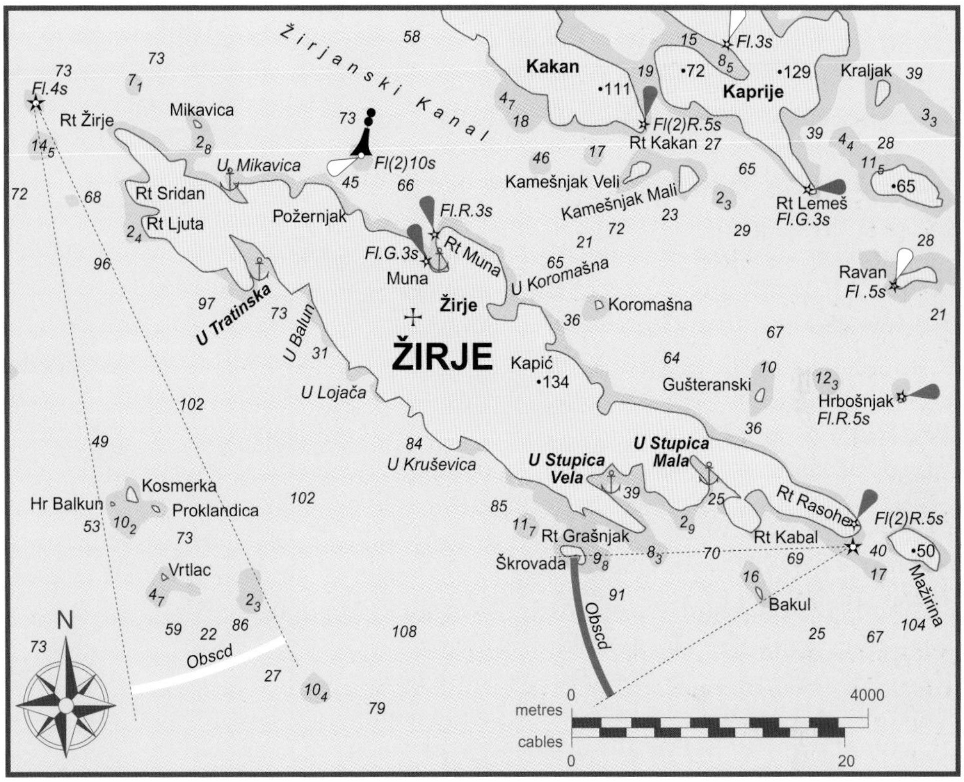

Žirje is the largest of this group of islands and the furthest out to sea, giving it some strategic importance. It was devastated by the Turks in 1572 and has been much fought over by warring dukes.

The south-west coast is exposed to winds from the south-west, south and south-east, which can cause heavy seas.

Unlike other exposed islands, however, the coastline is well indented and shelter for small craft from winds from other directions can be found in Uvala Tratinska, towards the north-west tip of the island, and Uvalas Stupica Vela and Stupica Mala at the south-east end. The north-east coast is exposed to the Bora and the water is deep. Muna and Uvala Mikavica provide shelter in certain weather conditions.

Isolated danger mark off Požernjak, Žirje

Uvala Tratinska

Entrance to bay: 43°39'.49N 15°37'.73E
Charts: HHI MK-15; AC 2711, AC 2774, SC5767

You can berth in depths of about 1m at the quay. Alternatively, it is possible to anchor in depths of 6 to 12m, but this is not recommended. Approaching from the north-west, look out for the 2.4m shoal off Rt Ljuta.

Uvala Stupica Vela

Entrance to bay: 43°37'.68N 15°41'.94E
Charts: HHI MK-15; AC 2711, AC 2774, SC5767

This bay is exposed to the Sirocco, which can cause heavy seas and makes the anchorage unsuitable. However, in other weather conditions the anchorage provides good shelter on a sand bed in depths of around 10m.

It's a popular place, although some reports suggest the holding is unreliable and mooring buoys have now been laid by the one restaurant in the bay. Note that there is a 2.9m shoal between this bay and the neighbouring Uvala Stupica Mala.

If approaching from the east, pass well south of the red light (Fl [2] R 5s) south of Rt Rasohe, marking a rock, to avoid the shallow waters. It's best when you arrive to let the restaurant know in advance that you will be eating there, as they have been known to run out of food.

Uvala Stupica Mala

Entrance to bay: 43°37'.86N 15°42'.36E
Charts: HHI MK-15; AC 2711, AC 2774, SC5767

This is a suitable anchorage for small craft, but is generally overlooked in favour of Uvala Stupica Vela. It is, however, well protected at the inner end of the bay, though depths do not start to reduce until close to the shore. See information on Uvala Stupica Vela (above) for hazards to watch out for on approach.

It is strongly advised when ashore to keep to the established footpaths pending an 'all clear' on the complete clearance of landmines left over from the Homeland War.

Muna

Entrance to bay: 43°39'.92N 15°39'.28E
Charts: HHI MK-15; AC 2711, AC 2774, SC5767

The village of Žirje, where you will find a post office, shop and medical centre, is a strenuous 500m walk uphill from the port of Muna, which has just one restaurant to offer visitors. Here you can berth bows- or stern-to at the quay beyond the ferry pier in depths of between 1 and 5m. Alternatively anchor on a sand bed in depths of 8 to 12m. The bay is exposed to winds from the north-west, north and north-east.

Approaching from the north-west, look out for the isolated danger mark about a mile north-west of the bay. From this direction you will see the red light (Fl R 3s) on Rt Muna, to port of the bay. At the entrance to the bay, the green light (Fl G 3s) on the ferry pier should become visible, as should the road that runs straight up the hill. There is normally at least one ferry a day connecting Žirje to Šibenik on the mainland, via Kaprije, and more in the summer, though on Tuesdays out of season the service starts and ends in Kaprije rather than Žirje. There is a second route operating two ferries every Tuesday, which connects to Šibenik via Zlarin in June, July and September.

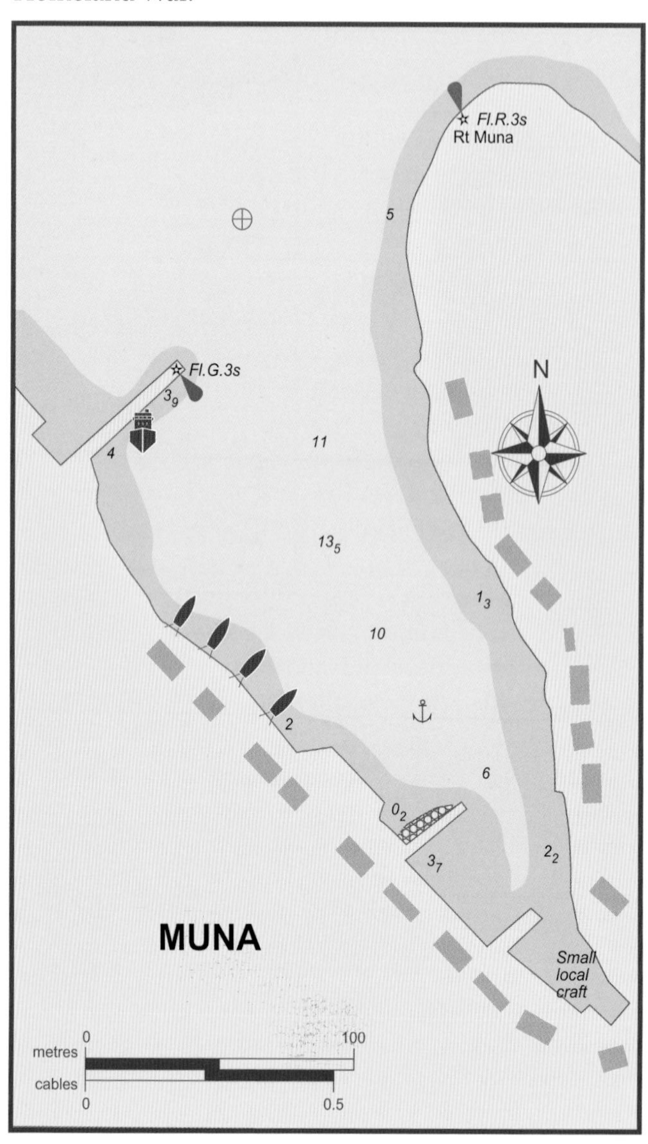

Uvala Mikavica

Entrance to bay: 43°40'.30N 15°37'.25E
Charts: HHI MK-15; AC 2711, AC 2774, SC5767

You can berth at the pier in depths of around 2.5m or anchor just off it in about 6m. The bay is exposed to the Bora along with north and northwesterly winds, so is only suitable as a temporary shelter from southerly winds.

Beware of a 2.8m shoal and an islet just north-west of the bay, as well as a marked isolated danger point about a mile east.

Kakan Island

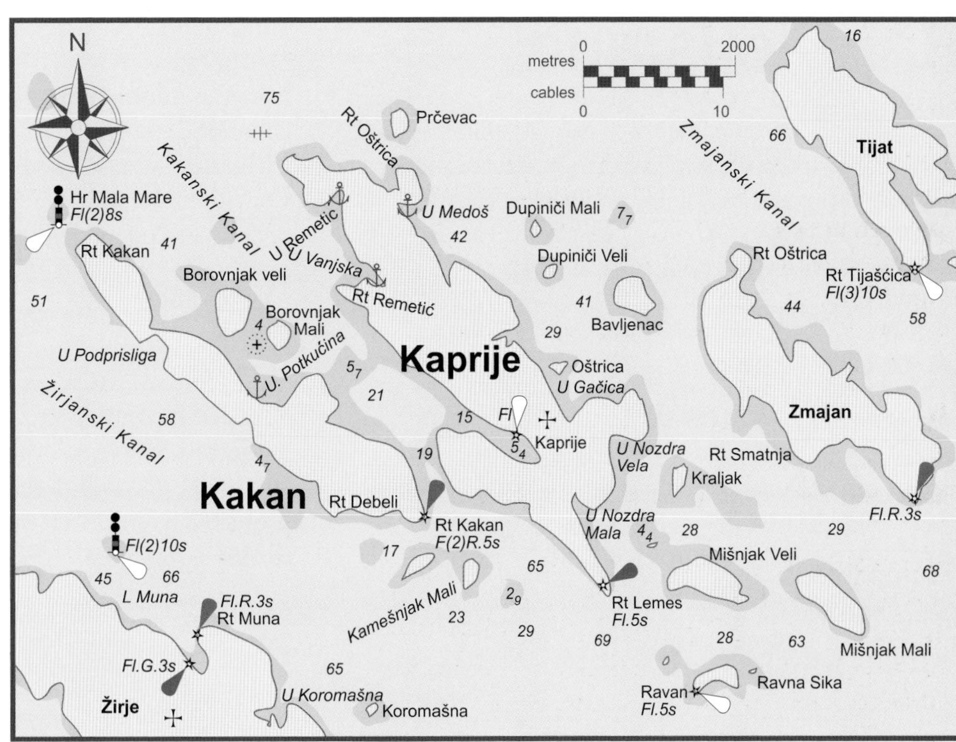

Kakan is uninhabited but semi cultivated by the residents of Kaprije Island. Known as Children's Island, it was part of a United Nations project, started in 1970 to encourage children of all nations to have fun in a natural and unspoilt environment. The south-west coast is inaccessible and its bays are too deep and inhospitable to offer any protection.

Just off the north-west tip of the island is an above-water rock identified by an isolated danger mark with a white light (Fl [2] 8s). About two thirds of the way down the south-west coast is a 4.7m shoal.

The north-east coast is protected by the island of Kaprije from all but the Bora and northwesterly winds. There are two large islets off this coast and a 5.7m shoal just north-east of the south-east headland bounding Uvala Potkućina.

The red light on Kakan Island, with the channel between Kakan and Kaprije behind it

Uvala Potkućina

Anchorage/mooring buoys: 43°41'.63N 15°40'.08E
Charts: HHI MK-15; AC 2711, AC 2774, SC5767

The two islets of Borovnjak Mali and Borovnjak Veli make this a great anchorage, with good protection from all winds in different parts of the bay. Note that depths between Borovnjak Veli and Kakan reduce to 4m or less and look out for the submerged rock off the west coast of Borovnjak Mali, referred to in some guides but unusually not indicated on the HHI or Admiralty charts. See the general notes above for hazards around Kakan and, if approaching from the south-east between Kakan and Kaprije, leave the islet of Ravan and its off-lying rock well to starboard, and the 2.9m shoal, a mile further north-west, to port. Depths in the bay and around the islets vary between 4 and 15m. Holding is good on a sand and weed bed.

Alternatively, use one of the 20 or so mooring buoys, although expect to pay a fee, which will include rubbish disposal, and check that the mooring itself is in good condition.

Kaprije Island

Kaprije (see chart on page 117) is named after the Caper and has just one settlement, of the same name, situated in a well-protected bay on the south-west coast of the island. This is a good stop-off point with reasonable facilities. Shelter is also available in Uvalas Remetič and Vanjska, (south-west coast) in a Bora or Sirocco, and at Medoš (north-east coast) for protection against winds from the south. These three bays are at the north-west end of the island.

The two bays at the south-east end of the island, Uvala Nozdra Mala and Vela, are not really recommended as shelter is limited and there are a number of rocks and shoals on the approach.

Kaprije

Entrance to bay: 43°41'.40N 15°41'.86E

Sleepy, but well cared for, Kaprije has good facilities for a settlement of this size in this location.

NAVIGATION

Charts: HHI MK-15; AC 2711, AC 2774, SC5767

Approaches: See Kakan Island, Uvala Potkućina on page 117 for the approach from the south-east. From the north-west, be aware of the 5.7m shoal between Kakan and Kaprije. Heading south-west from the mainland to the south-east tip of Kaprije, it's best to leave the islets of Ravan, Mišnjak Mali and MišnjakVeli to starboard, thus avoiding the rocks nearer to Kaprije.

As you turn into the channel between Kakan and Kaprije, you will see to port on Rt Kakan a white concrete tower with a red light (Fl [2] R 5s). As you alter course to starboard into the bay, there are a number of houses sprawling away from the town and, as you head further into the bay, you will see the ferry pier with a white light to port.

BERTHING/ANCHORING

The ferry uses the outer part of the pier so you can berth on lazylines on the inner side. Depths are over 2.5m on the part of the pier that lies outside the harbour and less than a metre in the harbour. In order that the ferries have a clear passage, anchoring is prohibited north-west of a line drawn at 205°T from the pier light to the opposite shore, but permitted south-east of this line in depths of between 2 and 5m. The bay is well protected from all but northwesterly winds, when it can be dangerous.

ASHORE

Amenities consist of plenty of cafés and restaurants, a supermarket, post office and a tourist office open in the season (the season starts on 15 June according to the note outside when we last visited). See Muna on page 116 for frequency of ferries to the mainland.

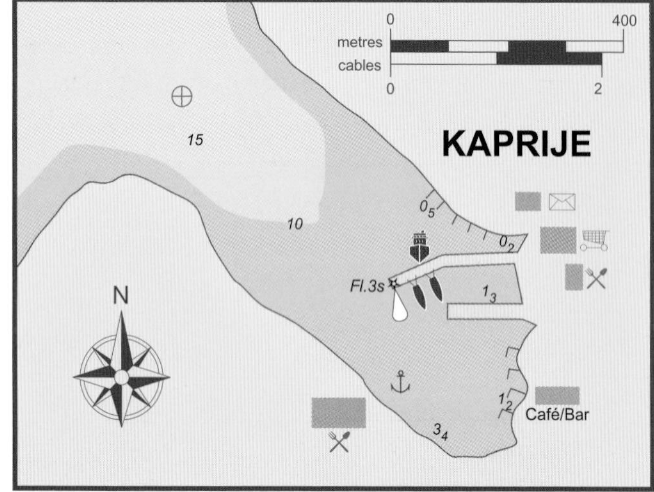

One of the many cafés at Kaprije Harbour

Obonjan Island

Obonjan, also known as the island of youth, has a number of sheltered bays and beaches and is the base for Otok Mladosti, the diving company that operates a head office from Šibenik (see page 105 for contact details).

It's a small island, just east of Zmajan, with a town harbour halfway along its east-facing coast.

The north coast of Obonjan

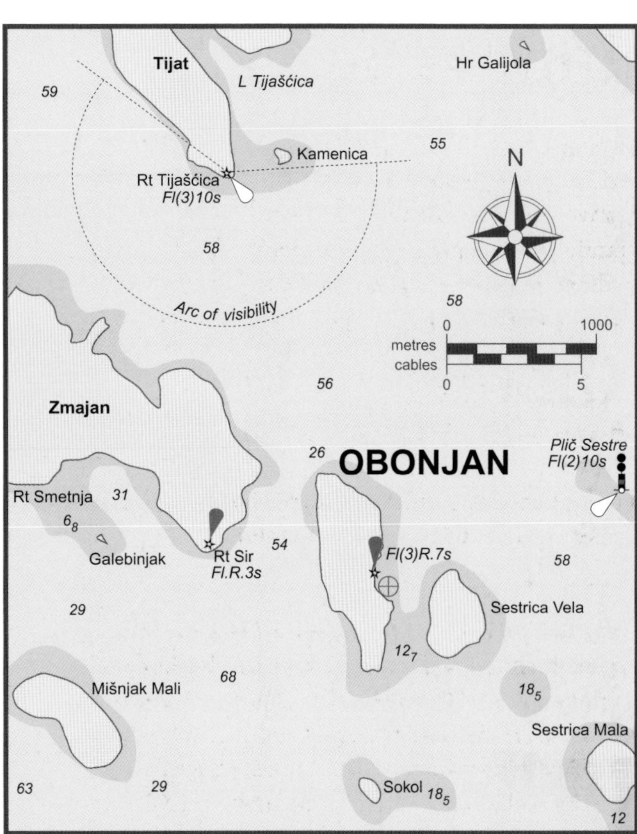

Obonjan

Entrance to bay: 43°40'.70N 15°47'.33E

Charts: HHI 533, MK-15; AC 2711, AC 2773, AC 2774, SC5767

This harbour is not at all safe in a Bora or Sirocco, being completely exposed from the north-east to south-east, but it has a pier (marked with a red light – Fl (3) R 7s) to which you can berth in depths of between 2 and 3.5m.

Tijat Island

Tijat is another uninhabited island, with several conical hills. It is situated between Tribunj on the mainland and the island of Zmajan. Landmarks include an iron cross on the 119m (390ft) summit, Vela Glava, and a white light (Fl (3) 10s) on the island's southernmost point, Rt Tijašćica. The islet of Kamenica, which is surrounded by shallow water, lies just east of Rt Tijašćica in the obscured sector of the light.

Tijat is a favourite spot for game hunters as it is an adopted home to the Mouflon, a wild sheep that is highly prized and now becoming quite rare.

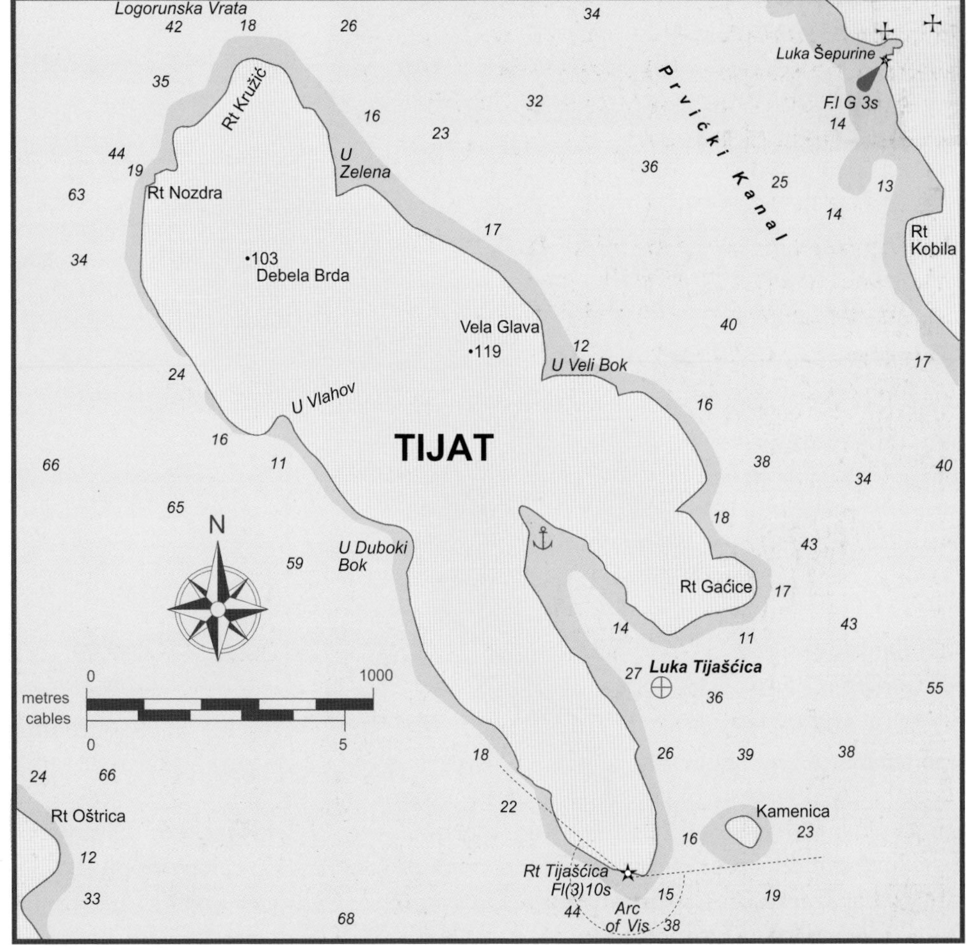

Luka Tijašćica

Entrance to bay: 43°42'.71N 15°46'.54E
Charts: HHI 533, MK-15; AC 2711, AC 2773, AC 2774, SC5767

This is the only possible stopping place on the island, but provides a good anchorage in depths of between 4 and 10m on a sand and weed bed. The approach is clear, apart from Kamenica Islet, and the bay is sheltered from all winds except those from the south, which cause a heavy sea.

Anchorage at Luka Tijašćica

Prvić Island

Prvić lies just off the mainland from Vodice. It has two settlements with small harbours just 20 minutes' walk apart, but is otherwise agricultural and slowly embracing tourism.

Berthing on lazylines on the inner side of Prvić Luka's breakwater

Prvić Luka

Entrance to bay: 43°43'.21N 15°48'.14E

On the south end of the island, the bay is well protected from all winds except the Sirocco, which can be strong but rarely causes a heavy sea. The village is charming and has a relatively new, up-market hotel, which was formerly an old stone schoolhouse. The hotel has installed a 12m (40ft) pontoon for visiting yachtsmen, but this was being used by the locals when we visited.

NAVIGATION

Charts: HHI 533, MK-15; AC 2711, AC 2773, AC 2774, SC5767

Approaches: A low-lying unlit rock (Hr Galijola) lies about half a mile south of the entrance to the bay and has shallow waters around it, as does the islet of Lupac, just south of Prvić, but otherwise there are no particular approach hazards. The channel between Lupac and Prvić is 10m deep in the middle. Lupac has a red light

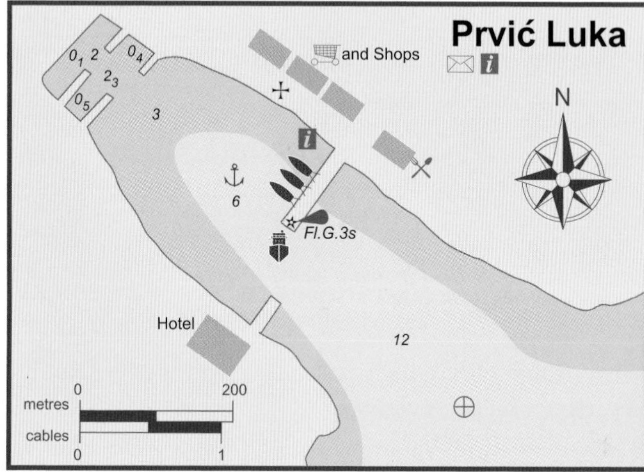

(Fl R 3s) on its southernmost tip, while the breakwater, on the east of Prvić Luka bay, has a green light (Fl G 3s).

BERTHING/ANCHORING/FACILITES

You can berth on lazylines inside the breakwater in depths of 2 to 3m, alongside the hotel pontoon in depths of 2.5m, or anchor inside the harbour in depths of around 5m, although keep clear of the ferry berth and the swimming area.

You will most likely be asked to pay a fee during the season for berthing in the harbour and should eat at the hotel restaurant if you use its facilities, which are available, by agreement, to visiting guests. The hotel plans to install lazylines soon and offers a laundry service (no ironing) for 100 Kunas per load.

Modest municipal toilet amenities are also on hand and include an electric power point inside the toilets as well as a water tap just next door.

ASHORE

A good range of shops and a small market. The post office is on the main street – Ulica 2, Br 1, 22233 Prvić Luka. The tourist office is also on the main street and opens according to demand. Apart from the hotel, there are a couple of restaurants and bars on the front. Near to the hotel is a restaurant specialising in sardines cooked in a variety of ways. The hotel offers marlin on the grill and freshly caught fish at just a little above mainland prices. Hotel Maestral has a number of interesting tours listed on its website, including a visit to the donkey sanctuary on Logorun Island. There are five ferries a day connecting Prvić to either Vodice or Šibenik on the mainland and taxi boats can be arranged.

Speciality Sardine Restaurant in Prvić Luka

Hotel Maestral: Tel: 022 448 300; Fax: 022 448 301; email: info@hotelmaestral.com; website: www.hotelmaestral.com.

Šepurine

Harbour entrance: 43°44'.03N 15°47'.09E

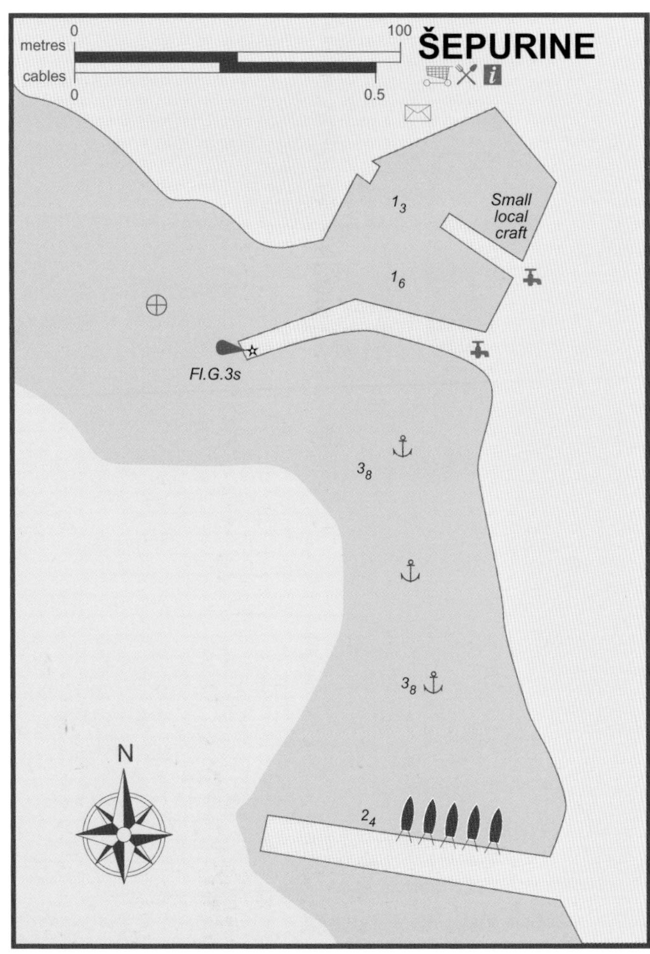

Šepurine, on the west coast of the island, is another attractive sleepy town, with some lovely stone houses and an old summer residence of a famous Šibenik family – the Vrančićs – who are claimed to have conceived the idea for the parachute and wrote the first Croatian dictionary.

NAVIGATION

Charts: HHI MK-15; AC 2711; AC 2773; AC 2774, SC5767

Approaches: A 7.1m shoal lies just south of the bay, but otherwise the approach is clear. Past the breakwater is a green light on the inner pier.

BERTHING/ANCHORING/FACILITIES

Berth bows- or stern-to, either on the inner side of the breakwater in depths of 1 to 2.5m, or just inside the harbour, although depths are shallow – 0.6 to 1.6m – and normally there is not much space. Alternatively, anchor between the breakwater and harbour in depths of between 2 and 5m. Leave room for the ferries. There are water taps at the inner ends of both the breakwater and outer harbour wall. Do not use the harbour when westerlies are blowing. The bay is also exposed to winds from the south, although the breakwater provides limited protection.

ASHORE

Amenities include a post office, a tourist information office, a supermarket and a few bars and restaurants. Ribarski Dvor, which is only open during the season, has a good reputation for seafood.

Zlarin Island

Zlarin Island lies just over a mile off the entrance to the canal leading to Šibenik. It is one of the largest of this archipelago and, though there are a few small bays on the south-east side of the island, Zlarin itself is the only real place for an overnight stay and indeed the only settlement on the island.

No cars are allowed on the island and the largish harbour tends not to get too crowded in the summer. Zlarin is also the one place in Croatia that crafts coral into jewellery and ornaments, and is also famous for being the birthplace of Anthony Maglica who invented the Maglite flashlight. Although one of the numerous émigrés to America, escaping the poverty between the two World Wars, Anthony, now in his seventies, continues to help Zlarin with its infrastructural projects.

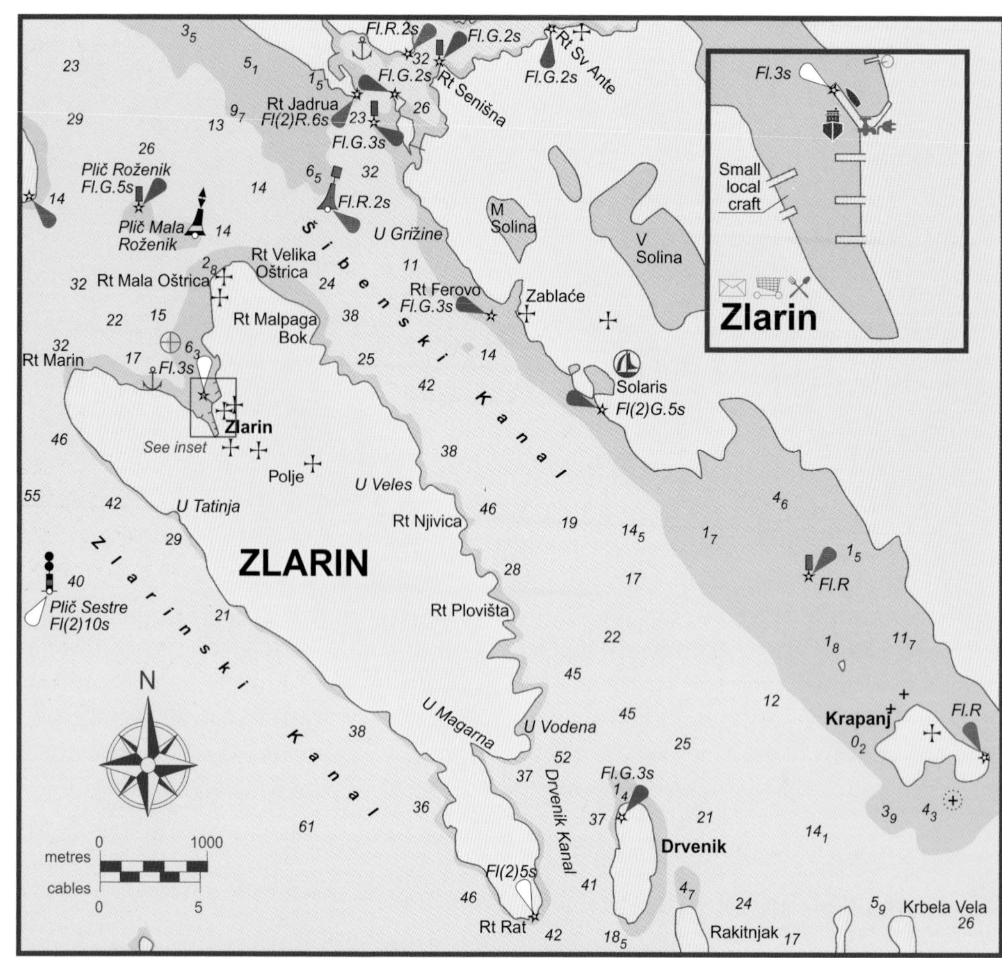

Zlarin harbour

Zlarin

Entrance to bay: 43°42'.25N 15°49'.69E

NAVIGATION

Charts: HHI 533, MK-15; AC 2711, AC 2773, AC 2774, SC5767

Approaches: Note from the charts that depths are less than 5m about 200m or so away from the shore around the northern tip of the island. Approaching from the north, Pličina Roženik is a largish shoal about a mile away from the island. Its northernmost point is marked by a green light (Fl G 5s) and the southernmost point by an east cardinal mark. Just south of the light are the remains of a previous marker. There is a narrow navigable channel between the shoal and the island or you can go the long way round.

If approaching from the south and south-west, another shoal, Pličina Sestre (Fl (2) 10s), lies approximately halfway between the island and the islet of Sestrica Vela. If approaching between Tijat and Prvić, leave the rock lying just south-east of the south end of Prvić well to port.

BERTHING/ANCHORING/FACILITIES

The car ferry uses the inside of the outer pier, but you can berth alongside, on the outside, in depths of about 3 to 4m, although depths at the inner end shallow to 0.3m. Alternatively, try and find a space in the harbour or anchor outside the harbour near the western shore in good holding on a gravel bed in depths of 5 to 10m. Northerly and northwesterly winds cause a swell in the harbour. The harbour and the western side of the pier provide protection from the Bora. Water and electricity are available on the ferry pier.

ASHORE

The post office is on the seafront – Obala Andrije Lučeva bb, 22232 Zlarin, Tel: 123 553 420 – as is the tourist office, Tel: 022 553 557. The village has a hotel, supermarket, shops, medical centre, coral museum, art gallery and a few restaurants and bars. The Four Lions hotel and restaurant, website www.4lionszlarin.com, often acts as the base for organised swimming excursions around the nearby islands, website: www.swimtrek.com. There are four return ferries a day (two on Sundays) from the beginning of June to the end of September, connecting Zlarin with Vodice and Šibenik.

Local boats in Zlarin harbour

Berthing at Zlarin's main breakwater. Yachts on the nearside will have to make way for the ferry

Krapanj Island

Krapanj Island has a tradition of sponge diving and is also noted for being the smallest inhabited and lowest-lying Croatian island. The only settlement on the island, Krapanj, lies just 400m away from Brodarica (see page 110) on the mainland.

The many small piers at Krapanj

Krapanj

Harbour entrance: 43°40'.38N 15°55'.24E

A very small settlement with most activity centered around the new Hotel Spongiola, which has laid down two pontoons for visiting boats.

NAVIGATION

Charts: HHI 153, MK-15; AC 2711, AC 2774, SC5767

Approaches: The island is surrounded by shallow water and rocks and there is also an area of shallow water stretching almost a mile off Zaboričje, on the mainland, as well as islets, shoals and rocks in the approach from the west. See the pilotage below for the safest route. The top half of the church tower is visible from a distance and next to that is the hotel, currently painted orange and yellow. At the end of the quay is a flashing red light.

Pilotage: Approaching from the open sea from the south or west, head between Rt Oštrica Vela (Fl G 2s) on the mainland and the islets of Oblik, then Vela Krbela, leaving them both to port. About 400m off the east coast of Oblik is a rock, marked by an east cardinal buoy. At the mouth of the bay on the mainland peninsula, half a mile on a bearing of 113°T from the red light (Fl R 2s) on Vela Krbela, is an unmarked rock. As you pass the red light take a course roughly parallel to the east coast of Vela Krbela, about 400m away from the shore, heading for an approach waypoint of 43°39'.83N 15°54'.94E. At this point you will be in safe water and will see, on a bearing of 46°T, a road bridge going over a small inlet on the mainland, which leads to Jadrtovac and Lake Morinje. Head directly towards the centre of the road bridge and then turn to port past Krapanj Island, staying just to port of the centre of the channel. If approaching from the north-west, between the mainland and Zlarin, pass well to the west and south of the island to avoid the shallows and rocks. Taking a course due east from a waypoint of 43°39'.83N 15°53'.96E will bring you to the approach waypoint mentioned above and keep you away from hazards.

BERTHING

Anchoring is not recommended due to the narrowness of the channel, the volume of small boat traffic and underwater cables between the island and the mainland. Either berth on the inside of the breakwater, in depths of 2 to 3m, at the head of the pier in similar depths, or alongside the hotel pontoons in depths of between 3.5 and 5m. Note that in summer 2007 Sunsail was using the pontoons for its charter yachts, so expect these to be full on Fridays and Saturdays as charter customers come and go. The Bora and the Sirocco blow strongly in this area, but the harbour has reasonable protection from all but northerly winds.

FACILITIES

A small boatyard lies just north of the village, mostly concentrating on engines and wooden hulls, and the harbour has a slipway for smaller boats. The hotel may charge a fee for berthing, laundry facilities and internet access.

ASHORE

The hotel, built on the site of an old sponge co-operative, has been fitted out to high standards and has an indoor pool, fitness centre and sauna. It specialises in diving trips, but can also offer a range of other watersports and excursions and has a small beach in front of it – Hotel Spongiola, Obala I Krapanj, 22010 Brodarica, Tel: 022 348 900; Fax: 022 348 903; email: info@spongiola.com; website: www.spongiola.com.

Apart from the hotel and the restaurant in Brodarica, just over the water, there's not much at Krapanj besides a couple of bars and shops, although it seems likely that there will be more development in the not too distant future. To get to Brodarica, you can easily take one of the taxi boats, which regularly ply to and fro between the harbour and the mainland.

Hotel Spongiola on Krapanj

Rogoznica

Chapter four

The mainland coast from Rogoznica to Split, including Trogir and Čiovo Island

Heading south from Primošten and Marina Kremik, the first major settlement you come to is Rogoznica. It used to be a run-down town, but has rapidly improved under the influence of Marina Frapa, built in 1998 and aiming at the upper end of the marina market. As you continue along the coast, there are several bays but not much life and few road connections until you round the headland and arrive at Marina (the place!). The exception is Vinišće where there is a relatively new marina. It's in a beautiful, unspoilt bay with a few good restaurants. However, by car it's a lengthy drive along a narrow road from Marina. Marina itself is a charming village with most facilities and its own town marina – Marina Agana.

Heading east again, Seget Vranjica is a well-heeled residential area packed onto a hill on a small peninsula, after which you come to the classic Croatian town of Trogir where you can choose to berth between the superyachts and cruisers on the Riva or in the ACI marina. Trogir itself was originally a natural peninsula, but was turned into an island some years ago when a channel was cut out on the mainland side, over which now runs a small stone road bridge. A longer road bridge connects the old town to the island of Čiovo. It's a swing bridge and supposed to open on request, although we've only seen it open twice in five years. With a maximum air-clearance of 3m (9ft 8in) and depths reducing to 4m, yachts will have to go the long way round Čiovo Island to get to Split or to the seven villages in Kaštela Bay. This is no hardship as there are some beautiful, unspoilt beaches around the island.

From the eastern extremity of Čiovo, it's about 2 miles to Split harbour and the ACI marina in the same bay or, alternatively, you can cruise around Kaštela Bay, visit the marina in Kaštel Gomilica and explore the unspoilt villages west of it. As you head east, past Kaštel Gomilica to Split, the area becomes more industrial, but the old town of Split, within the remains of the Diocletian Palace, is spectacular, and there's plenty of nightlife. There's also the tiny little island of Vranjic, at the eastern extremity of Kaštela Bay, which stands out as an oasis in the industrial desert of Split's suburbs.

We spent our first two years in Croatia living in Trogir. It has a life all year round and the Riva throbs in the summer to the sound of nightly concerts. The single lane bridges are no longer adequate to cope with the ever-increasing tourist trade on Čiovo in the summer, but it's a great place to visit by boat if you can find space to moor or anchor. Since January 2005 we have been based in Kaštel Štafilić, the most westerly of the seven Kaštels. From the road you would think Kaštela is just a tatty suburb of Split, and it tends to get bypassed by most of the tourists. However, along the coast you will find that it is in a very special time warp with a string of good local restaurants and bars, the ruins of an old castle in each village and some attractive beaches well hidden from the road.

Fuel is available in Trogir and Split.

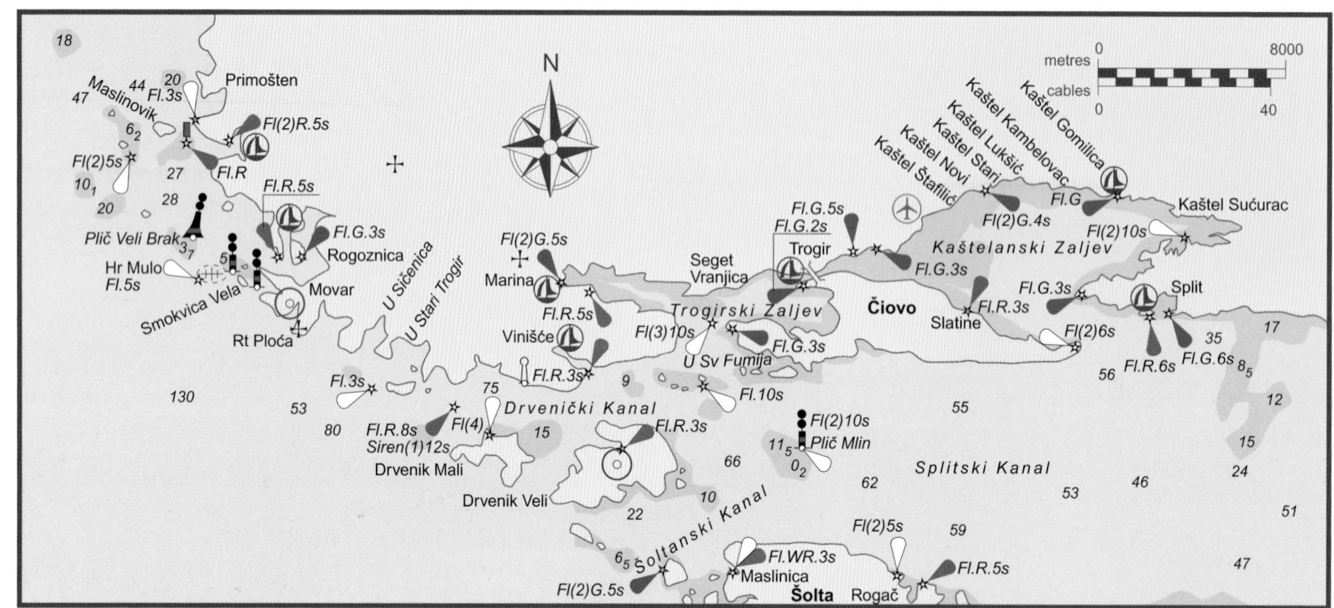

Transport for the area

FLIGHTS: Split airport is situated between Trogir and Split and copes with an ever-increasing number of flights. From 2006 British Airways has been flying direct from London to Split all year round, although there is a strong rumour that the winter flights might be dropped in favour of focusing on Dubrovnik. Wizzair and easyJet now have summer flights to Split, which may be extended. In addition, there are a number of direct flights to other capitals in the season and further international connections from Zagreb, all year round, a half-hour flight from Split. Be prepared for a bit of a melée in the small car park in the height of the season. For more information, contact Split airport on Tel: 021 203 506; email: spu@split-airport.hr; website: www.split-airport.hr.

FERRIES: Split has regular ferry services to Brač, Hvar, Šolta and Ancona in Italy. Trogir has ferry services to Drvenik, and in the summer local ferries operate between Trogir, Slatine (Čiovo Island) and Split, as well as between Okrug, on Čiovo, and Trogir. The telephone number for Split harbour is Tel: 021 338 333. See the introduction for contact details of the various ferry companies.

TRAINS: The train station in Split connects with Zagreb and directly or indirectly with many other Western European cities. The lines, trains and services are being improved, but travelling by coach or bus is still the cheapest and quickest way of getting around. Contact: Domagojeva Obala 9, Tel: 021 338 525, or for information and reservations call Tel: 060 333 444. The left-luggage office is open between 0630 and 2230.

COACHES AND BUSES: There are regular coaches to Zagreb and other major cities. These start just by the ferry terminal in Split, with Trogir being the first stop-off for coach trips along the north-west coast and to Zagreb. The bus station in Split is a fair walk from the town itself and buses from here service the local area. You can also get a bus from Split to Trogir, but you'll go via all the villages on the way, so coach is best. Contact: Ulica Kneza Domagoja 12, Tel: 021 329 180; Fax: 021 329 182; email: info@ak-split.hr; website: www.ak-split.hr.

CAR, BOAT, SCOOTER AND BIKE HIRE: Visit one of the numerous travel agents operating in this area for the best deal or one of the many car hire kiosks at the airport. The following are a couple of car hire companies based in Split: ABC, Obala Lazareta 3, Tel: 021 342 364; Fax: 021 332 471; email: abc-rac@st.htnet.hr; Budget, Obala Kneza Branimira 8, Tel: 021 399 214; Fax: 021 398 220; email: std@budget.hr; website: www.budget.hr.

GENERAL: If you have an international trip to book, try any one of the main travel agents, such as Atlas, to help you navigate through all the various permutations and options. We've found Atlas in Trogir particularly helpful for all our various travel demands (on the same road as the marina entrance, next to Hotel Sikaa). Similarly, a Croatia Airlines flight is normally cheaper and easier to organise through an agent or at the airport than via the website, though the website has recently been much improved.

Rogoznica

Marina Frapa, entrance to bay:
43°31'.29N 15°57'.92E

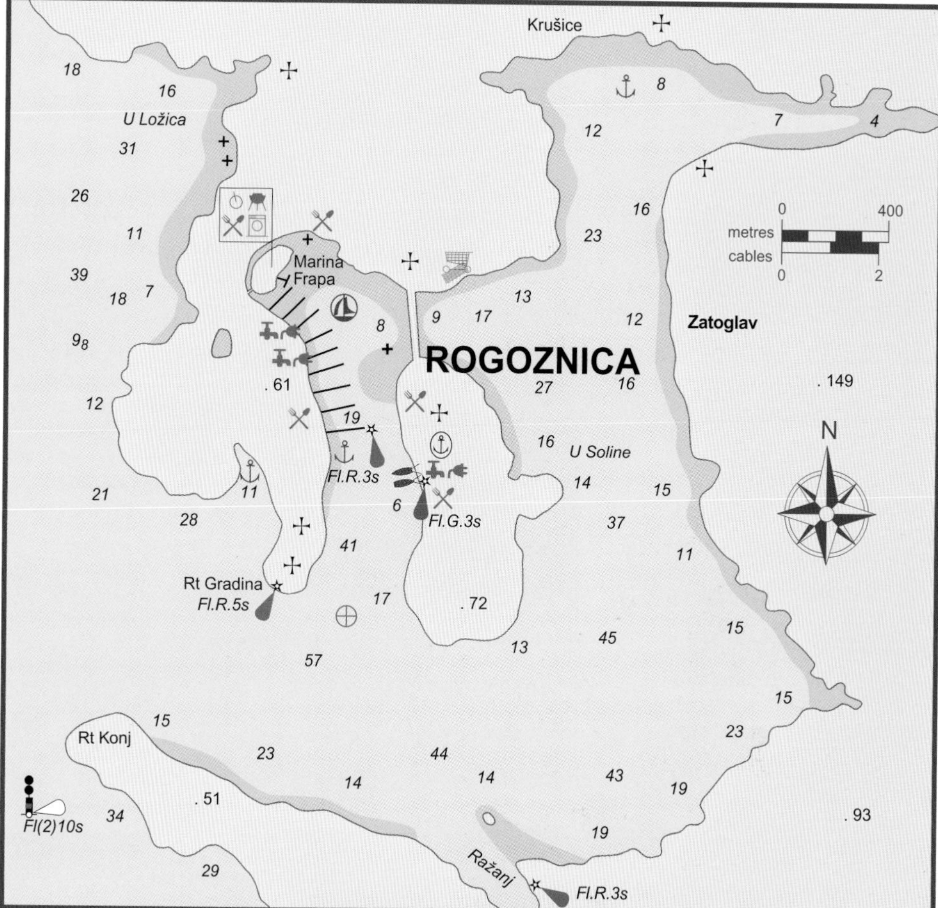

The village is on an island connected to the mainland by a causeway. The marina is set apart from the village, which lies in Soline Bay, but you can walk between the two in about 20 minutes. The marina's facilities include a swimming pool, bar, restaurant, sports amenities and night club. In July 2007 it was in the process of installing a 290m (950ft) visitors' pontoon, with berths for yachts of up to 80m (262ft), and an underwater restaurant that is expected to be fully operational in 2008.

The village is much more rustic, has a number of bars and restaurants and there's a pleasant walk through the woods around the peninsula.

NAVIGATION

Charts: HHI 534, MK-16; AC 2711, AC 2774, SC5767

Approaches: The approach is relatively straightforward from the north-west. From the south-east and south, beware of an unmarked rock just off Rt Ploča, and the rocks, wrecks, shoals and islets off Rt Konj and Smokvica. As you pass between Rt Gradina and Rt Konj, there is a small inlet to port, followed by a larger one with the marina on the western side and the island on the eastern. The outermost pier of the marina has a red light (Fl R 3s), while a green light (Fl G 3s) is situated about halfway along the west coast of the island. Beware of the rock just off the island where it joins the causeway.

Berthing at Rogoznica village

BERTHING

The marina can be contacted on VHF Channel 17, Tel: 022 559 900.

Listed as a rare Category I marina, it has 300 berths and 150 dry berths, all of which are supplied with electricity and water. Prices are around €4 per metre per day, apart from in July and August when they are increased to about €5.3 per metre. This includes electricity and water, but a supplement is charged if you use your air-conditioning or heating. The well-sheltered marina can accommodate a small number of boats up to 40m (131ft) with relative ease and will negotiate on larger boats. It's quite a long walk from the outermost pier to the marina exit, but there's a restaurant near this pier.

As an alternative to the marina, you can berth bows- or stern-to in the village harbour, on the western side of the island, but make sure you stay well clear of the rusting fishing boats and rocks. You can also anchor in the small inlet west of Rt Gradina, but this is less protected.

Useful information – Rogoznica

FACILITIES
The best you can expect in Croatia thus far, though it is irritating to have to pay for parking to leave a car anywhere near the marina if you are visiting. In addition to the normal essential services, there are apartments, **shops** (including a **chandlery**), a **medical centre**, a choice of **restaurants** and **bars**, a **beauty salon, tennis courts**, a **diving centre, sports centre, casino** and **night club**. The **repair/service workshop** can deal with most types of engines, **sail repairs** are undertaken and the marina has a 75-ton **travel lift** and an 'in-house' **fuel** station with a limited choice of fuel – contact the marina to check what's on offer and at what price. At the time of writing, the marina was contemplating the installation of pump-out facilities.

PROVISIONING
The village has a reasonable range of **shops**, a **supermarket** (at the junction of the two roads leading to the marina and the village), a **market** and a **post office** in Obala Kneza Domagoja; opening hours during the season are from 0730 to 2100 Monday to Friday, 0800 to 1200 and 1800 to 2100 on Saturday. Off season: 0800 to 1500 Monday to Friday, 0800 to 1300 on Saturday.

One of Rogoznica many restaurants

EATING OUT
The marina has a good choice of restaurants, and don't overlook the Italian restaurant next to the outermost piers. In the village, a line of cafés and restaurants along the seafront offers a decent choice of the normal Croatian food at reasonable prices. Try Jere, Kneza Domagoja bb, Tel: 022 559 595, or Pizzeria Fortuna, Put Miline 6, Tel: 022 559 676.

ASHORE
The **tourist office** is on the main street running along the seafront – Kneza Domagoja bb, 22203 Rogoznica, Tel: 022 559 253; Fax: 0222 558 030; email: rogoznica@rogoznica.net; website: www.rogoznica.net. The village itself has yet to develop a range of tourist activities but the marina reception will be able to help with most requests, including car, bike hire and diving. There's not a huge amount to see and not much in the way of beaches.

OTHER INFORMATION
Marina Frapa: Uvala Soline, 22203 Rogoznica, email: marina-frapa@si.tel.hr; website: www.marinafrapa.com.
Medical centre: Kneza Domagoja 3, Tel: 022 559 032.

Looking towards Rogoznica from Marina Frapa

Rogoznica to Vinišće

Charts: HHI MK-16; AC 2774, SC5767

This part of the coastline, a long way from the main road, has a barren landscape and is almost devoid of civilisation. However, there are a number of bays that provide sheltered anchorages, although with no facilities worth mentioning. Below are the essential facts.

Smokvica Vela

Entrance to bay: 43°30'.84N 15°56'.61E

This tiny island, lying just off the mainland that curves south around Rogoznica, has a quay on its north-east coast where you can berth alongside in depths of about 3m. See Rogoznica on page 127 for hazards and approaches.

The Sirocco can cause a swell and the bay is exposed to the Bora.

Uvala Movar

Centre of bay: 43°30'.65N 15°57'.38E

East of the south-eastern tip of Smokvica Vela, Movar Bay provides reasonable shelter from the Bora on its north-east shore. Anchor on a sand bed with good holding. Watch out for the fish farms and the hazards around Smokvica Vela.

Uvala Stivančica

Entrance to bay: 43°29'.78N 15°58'.02E

This is only a feasible anchorage in calm weather or for protection in a Bora, and you'll need to watch out for the above-water rocks just off Rt Ploča. A chapel is situated on Rt Ploča's seaward extremity, while the 120m high hill of Movar, on which stands a fortress, is just west of the bay. Be aware that Rt Ploča can act as a dividing line between weather conditions in certain circumstances, such as when a Sirocco and Bora meet, giving rise to confused seas. The terrain in this area is barren and not very inviting, so it is best to choose an alternative anchorage if you can.

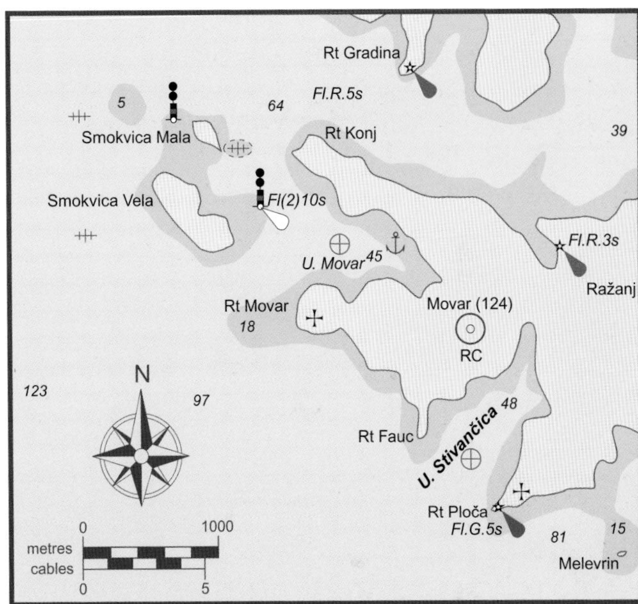

Uvala Sičenica

Centre of bay: 43°29'.45N 16°00'.78E

A deep bay that provides a sheltered anchorage in the most northwesterly inner inlet, in depths of between 5 and 12m. Southwesterly winds can cause a swell, but the bay is otherwise well protected. Beware of the unmarked rock about 750m south-west of the centre of the bay.

Uvala Stari Trogir

Centre of bay: 43°29'.08N 16°01'.87E

This is a large bay afforded some protection from the south by a number of islets. Keep a good eye-out for the unmarked rocks, one just off the western boundary of the bay and one off Uvala Sičenica (see above). There are three possible anchorages – the north-east corner of the bay and the outer part of the bay, to the east, by Merara Islet, both provide good protection from all winds except those from the south-west, although the Bora blows very strongly here. The holding is good on a sand and weed bed. The third anchorage, an area just north of Arkandel Islet, offers better shelter from southwesterly winds, but is exposed to winds from the west and east.

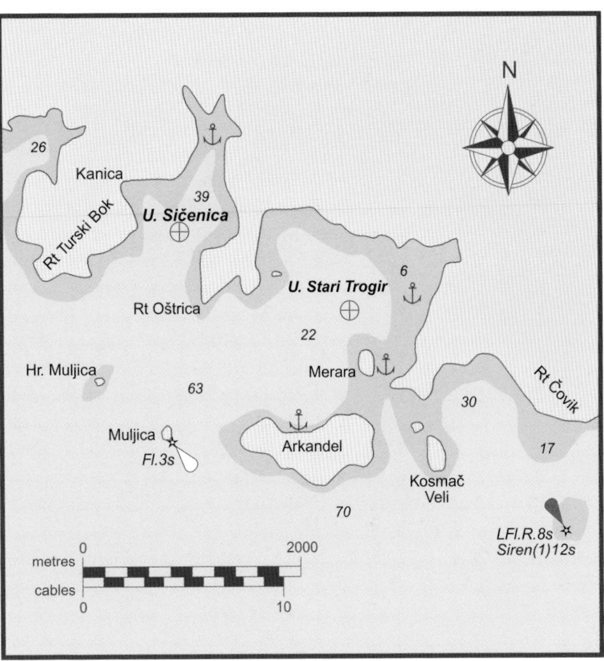

Vinišće

Entrance to bay: 43°28'.70N 16°07'.97E
Charts: HHI MK-16; AC 2712, AC 2774, SC5767

It's difficult to think of a quieter, more secluded spot than Vinišće, a small settlement at the end of a long inlet, opposite the island of Drvenik Veli. After much disruption to the locals, the marina looked to be fully up and running in the summer of 2007, with the pontoons filled with boats, a reception area, a shop and more to come. Contact: Mirna Vala d.o.o., Bačine bb, 21226, Vinišće (Tel: 021 892 109; Fax: 021 796 216). Unusually, prices are fixed at €30 per boat whatever the length, except in July and August. In July and August a 10m (32ft) boat is €33 and a 16m (52ft) boat is €50.

For a settlement this small there are a number of good restaurants, mostly at the head of the bay, and a few shops. We ate well and at a reasonable price in Restaurant Kaktus, Tel: 098 940 7078, whose owner came round to us in a small boat and offered a boat taxi service. Anchoring is possible in most of the inlet in depths of 5 to 15m. The holding is good on a sand and mud bed. The Bora blows strongly here and, in the middle of the bay, easterly winds cause a swell. Landmarks include a red light (Fl R 3s) on Rt Artatur and the above water rock, Hrid Vinišće, about 400m off the entrance to the inlet.

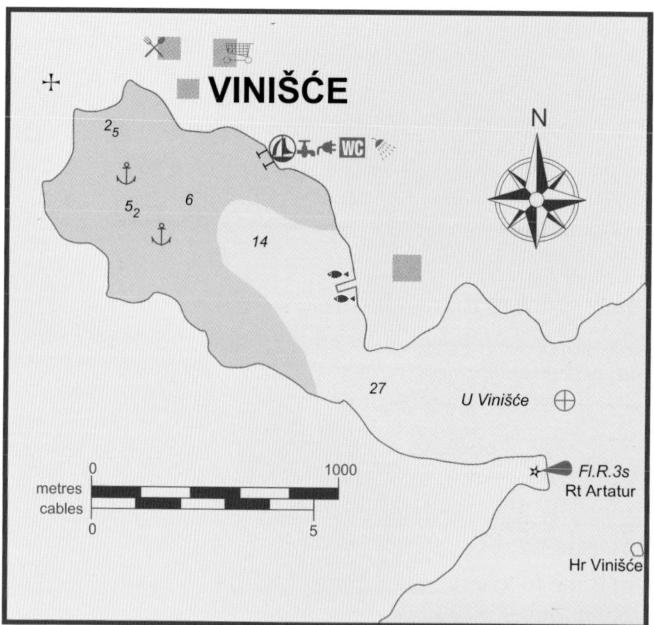

Looking out to sea over Vinišće Bay

Marina

Entrance to marina inlet: 43°30'.69N 16°07'.14E

Marina is a lovely village with a well-protected marina. It's about six miles away from the open sea, but is an extremely picturesque setting for an overnight stop.

NAVIGATION

Charts: HHI 534, MK-16; AC 2712, AC 2774, SC5767

Approaches: The jutting mainland headland and the western arm of Čiovo Island form a bay the shape of a diving whale's tail. To the west is Marina and to the east is Trogir. To get to Trogir's marina and town quay you need to approach from the bay; to get past Trogir going east, head around the south coast of Čiovo. The approach to the entrance of the bay is guarded by rocks, islets, shoals and at least one fishfarm. The most hazardous obstructions are lit at night and the safest approaches are from the south-east, between the two lights on the tiny islets of Balkun (Fl R 3s) and Zaporinovac (Fl G 3s), or from the west, hugging the mainland coast. The waters off the coast do not shallow until after Rt Jelinak, although watch out for the above-water rock just off Vinišće. If approaching further out from the south-east, pay particular attention to the shoal Pličina Mlin, about 2 miles due south of the islet of Sveti Fumija, which itself lies just south of Čiovo. The shoal has a lit isolated danger mark, but it lies in an otherwise clear stretch of water and is difficult to spot. Once you have entered the bay, keep to port to avoid the above-water rock and 4m shoal (Fl (3) 10s). The 16th century tower, the other side of the bay from the marina, is particularly impressive though only four storeys tall and, lying almost at the end of the bay, is not visible from a great distance. The main coast road, the Jadranska Magistrala, runs very close to the coastline all along the northern side of the bay.

Pilotage: The approach waypoint is 43°27'.67N 16°13'.18E. A bearing of 325°T from this point will take you between the two shoals into the centre of Marina Bay. Pličina Mlin is just over 1 mile south-east of the waypoint. As you then head west towards Marina you will see a red light to port on the headland, followed by the green light (Fl [2] G 5s) of the marina.

BERTHING

This Category II marina, which can be contacted on VHF Channel 17, Tel: 021 889 411, has 130 berths and 70 dry berths, with a maximum length of 25m (82ft) and a maximum draught of 6m (19ft 7in). The daily rate varies from €3.2 to €3.6 per metre per day for boats between 10 and 20m (33 to 66ft), with an additional 10% in July and August. The marina is well sheltered from all winds but the Sirocco and easterlies can cause a swell, with a strong Sirocco sometimes generating a sufficient rise in sea level to flood the quay on the southern shore. The Bora and northwesterly winds blow strongly in the area although do not produce heavy seas, and occasional strong summer gales from the west-north-west can be dangerous.

Useful information – Marina

FACILITIES

Electricity and **water** to all berths, a **marina reception** offering the standard services, a **toilet/shower** block, **chandlery, coffee bar, repair** and **servicing workshop** and a 40-ton **crane**. The nearest **fuel** and **harbourmaster** is in Trogir. Boltano, in the marina complex (Tel: 021 889 023), carries out **engine services** and **repairs** and GBN Marine Service (A Rudana 6, 21222 Marina) Tel: 021 889 055, offers general **boat repair** and maintenance services.

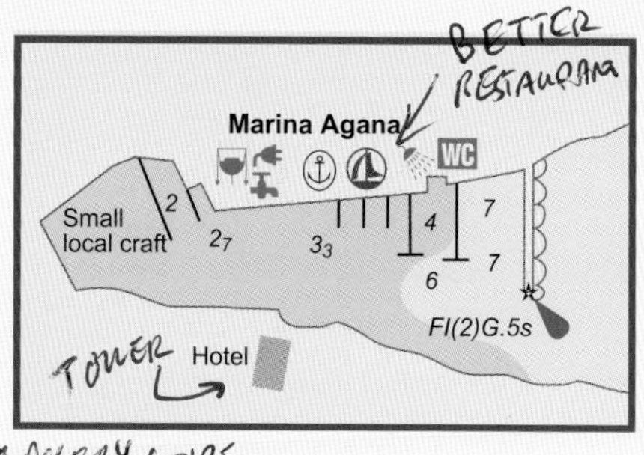

ASHORE

Marina has the essential **shops, post office, market** and **cash point** concentrated in a small area around the seafront. The post office, situated on Ante Rudana 47, 21222 Marina, is open from 0730 to 2100 Monday to Saturday in the season and from 0800 to 1500 Monday to Friday outside the season. The **tourist board** is close to the quay – Trg S Radiča 1, 21222 Marina, Tel: 021 889 015; email: tz.opcine.marina@st.htnet.hr.

There are plenty of **restaurants** and **bars** to choose from and the tower is now a hotel. It recently changed hands and needs to have a little money spent on it.

The best **beach** is on the south side of the bay, well past the marina. Otherwise there are some great little nooks and crannies along the north side if you can scrabble down from the road (which is not too safe to walk along).

OTHER INFORMATION

Agana Marina: Dr Franje Tuđmana 5, 21222 Marina, Tel: 021 889 411; Fax: 021 889 010; email: agana.marina@st.htnet.hr; website: www.marina-agana.hr

Seget Vranjica

Entrance to bay: 43°30'.60N 16°10'.72E
Charts: HHI 534, MK-16; AC 2712, AC 2774, SC5767

Seget Vranjica lies between Marina and Trogir, by Uvala Šašina. The bay is shallow and depths in the harbour vary between 1 and 3m. You can anchor on a bed of sand. The bay is protected in winds from most directions except those from the south, south-west and west. You'll find it a quiet residential settlement with a couple of bars, restaurants and shops, but there is not much else. As you approach, keep well clear of the lit rock (Fl [3] 10s) half a mile south-west of the bay.

Seget Vranjica, a quiet residential settlement

Trogir

Trogir ACI Marina:
43°30'.77N 16°14'.60E

Trogir has few rivals as a base to spend a couple of days exploring and taking in the atmosphere. Declared a World Heritage Town in 1997 by UNESCO, the densely-packed town is rich in history and has all the bars, restaurants, ice-cream parlours, shops, markets and tourist offerings you could want. In season, you can sit in the town square and listen to music or take in an open-air concert in the roofless castle. There are a couple of problems to watch out for during the summer months: Friday night is change-over time for the wooden cruise ships and the town moorings will be chock-a-block until Saturday midday, with the additional complication of a few luxury yachts. The marina is also very busy on Fridays and Saturdays. Moreover, if you want to spend the day on a beach on Čiovo and go there by car, you're very likely to get stuck in a jam coming back over the bridge. The Bora can blow heavily through the channel and can increase currents to 3 knots. There are plans for a second marina in Seget, which lies to port just before you enter the channel.

NAVIGATION

Charts: HHI 534, MK-16; AC 2712, AC 2774, SC5767

Approaches: Although the swing bridge can open, it remains closed other than in exceptional circumstances so for the marina, the Riva (town moorings) and to anchor, approach from the west. East of the bridge

Trogir Old Town. The marina is just out of shot to the right. The jetties on the bottom left are for local craft

is a wall suitable for very small craft and a number of jetties for the local boats. See Marina (page 130) and Seget Vranjica (page 131) for the approach into the bay, but turn to starboard immediately on entering and stay close to Čiovo Island to avoid the rocks, which are buoyed and lit at night. Then head just to port of the green light (Fl G 2s) on Rt Čubrijan, on Čiovo Island, to enter the channel. The marina is on Čiovo Island and can

Trogir old town and the bridge to Čiovo Island

be identified by the large shipyard to starboard, which is situated just before it. To port is the castle and then the Riva where you can berth alongside, space permitting.

BERTHING/ANCHORING

The marina (VHF Channel 17; Tel: 021 881 554) is Category II with 160 berths, 30 dry berths and a maximum depth of 4.5m. Boats have become bigger since the marina was designed and space is limited between the pontoons for the larger boats. Prices are between €3.8 and €4.35 per metre per day for a 10 to 20m (33 to 66ft) boat with a 10% increase in July and August.

If you prefer the Riva (though it can be very noisy in the summer), it's advisable to phone the harbour-master at least a day in advance to check availability. Someone will normally come to meet you or tell you to go away if you turn up on spec. It is possible to anchor just off the old town island, west of the castle, but make sure you stay out of the main shipping channel.

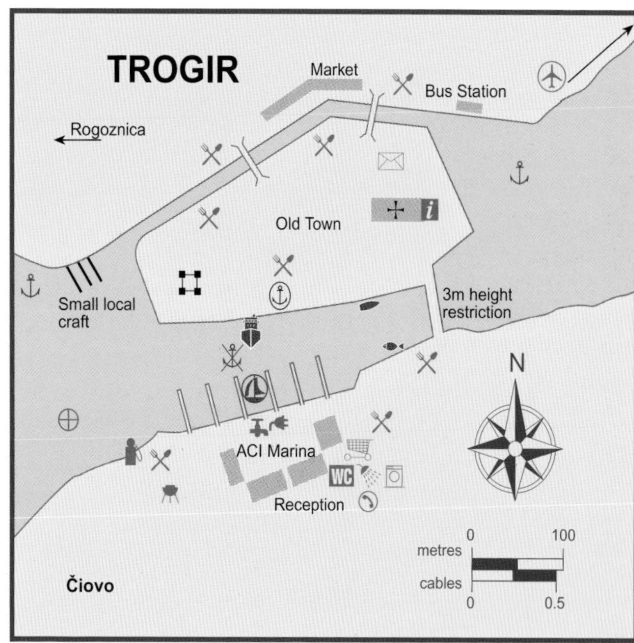

Looking from the mainland towards Čiovo Island, over the channel that takes you (from the west) to Trogir ACI Marina

Useful information – Trogir

FACILITIES

The marina has all the standard facilities plus two **cafés**, a **restaurant**, **supermarket**, **repair/service workshops** and a 10-ton **crane**. The **fuel** station (Tel: 021 885 458) is at the western end of the marina and, from the beginning of June to the end of September, is open from 0800 to 2000, Monday to Saturday, 0800 to 1200 and 1600 to 1900 on Sunday and bank holidays. Outside this period the fuel station is open from 0800 to 1500 Monday to Saturday, closed on Sundays and bank holidays. AIC and Servis Bruno carry out engine services – Put Cubrijana bb, Tel: 021 881 211, and Put Kapelice, Tel: 021 882 264, respectively. During the season the marina operates a **ferry service** to the Riva for a few Kunas, which saves a 15-minute walk over the bridge. For **chandlery** and fishing gear, Barba is just over the bridge to the mainland, by Konzum supermarket.

PROVISIONING

Cash points are everywhere, including in the marina, and there are a number of **supermarkets** on the right-hand side as you walk towards the swing bridge. The best one is just a bit further past the bridge, or else there's a large Konzum supermarket through the town and over the bridge that joins Trogir Island to the mainland. **Bakers** and **butchers** can be found on the walk to the swingbridge, while the bustling **market** (fruit, vegetables, some clothes and souvenirs) is opposite Konzum supermarket, just after you go over the bridge to the mainland. The **fish market** is on the mainland next to Konzum, but you'll need to get there early if you want a good choice. In the old town or at the market you can buy most things, and if you are interested in the traditional suits that stars like Placido Domingo wear, visit Gena in the old town, Ribarska 6, Tel: 021 884 329, who now also has an exhibition in Split.

EATING OUT

There is no shortage of restaurants in Trogir. Brod Čelica, Tel: 021 882 344, the boat restaurant just outside the marina, is reasonably priced but never seems to be that busy. Fontana, Tel: 021 884 811, and Alka,

Useful information – Trogir continued

Tel: 021 881 856, situated near to each other in the old town, are more chic and expensive establishments, used by the locals for special occasions. Our favourites are Konoba Skrapa, Tel: 021 882 344, a little further away from the Riva than Fontana, for its relaxed rustic atmosphere and good value traditional fish and meat dishes, and Pizzeria Mirkec, Tel: 021 883 042, on the Riva by the school, for its great pizzas, efficient and friendly staff, and the location. All the above are open all year round, but there are scores of others that pop up for the season.

ASHORE

The **tourist office** is in the Cathedral Square and there are plenty of private agencies around. Try Portal, which is almost the first office as you walk from the main road along the Riva, or Atlas, on the right-hand side of the road as you walk from the marina to the swing bridge.

Historically and culturally, Trogir is bursting with things to see. Originally settled by the Greeks, Trogir reflects the various influences of subsequent Roman, Hungarian, Venetian, French and Austrian rule. On Trg Ivana Pavla, the three-naved Cathedral of St Lovro (St Lawrence), built over a period of three centuries by the Venetians, is one of the finest pieces of architecture in Croatia. Walking away from the cathedral towards the Riva and turning right at the waterfront, you'll come to the medieval Kamerlengo Fortress, opposite the ACI marina. It's now used as an open-air cinema and events stage, but you can also walk to the top of the towers and get a great view of the surrounding islands. The climb is not for the faint-hearted though, and there's a small entrance fee payable at the gate.

Around the waterfront by the football pitch, one of the castle towers has been converted and has a café terrace on the top, with a music shop halfway up displaying traditional costumes and accessories.

Beaches: If you are feeling energetic, the best beaches and the cleanest water are a good walk to the west side of Čiovo Island.

TRANSPORT

Bus station: For buses along the coast to Split or Šibenik, use the bus station located opposite the market. For coaches to the main cities, wait outside Konzum and check timetables at Atlas.

Ferries: There are daily ferries to the island of Drvenik Veli from the Riva by the castle. In the summer, a local service runs between Trogir, Slatine on Čiovo Island and Split.

Car and bike hire: Atlas or any of the private travel agents will be able to organise this for you.

Quad bike hire: A relatively new activity that takes you through the olive groves on Čiovo Island. Contact: BJ Trogiranina 9, Tel: 021 881 915/091 205 1760; website: www.quad.hr.

OTHER INFORMATION

ACI Marina: Put Cumbrijana bb, 21220 Trogir, Tel: 021 881 544; Fax: 021 881 258; email: m.trogir@aci-club.hr

Harbourmaster: Tel/fax: 021 881 508. The harbourmaster's office is on the Riva, between the school and the fortress, Obala Lazareta 1, PP 317, 21220 Trogir. From June to September it's open from 0700 to 1200 and from 1600 to 2000. Outside the season it's open between 0700 and 1300.

Pharmacy: In the Cathedral Square.

Hospital: The hospital caters for accidents and emergencies – heading out of town, turn left after going over the bridge to the mainland. The hospital is about 150m on your left, after the large car park.

Travel agent: Portal Trogir: Obala Bana Berislavića (Riva) 3, 21220 Trogir Tel: 021 885 016; Fax: 021 885 869.

Čiovo Island

Charts: HHI 536, MK-16; AC 2712, SC5767

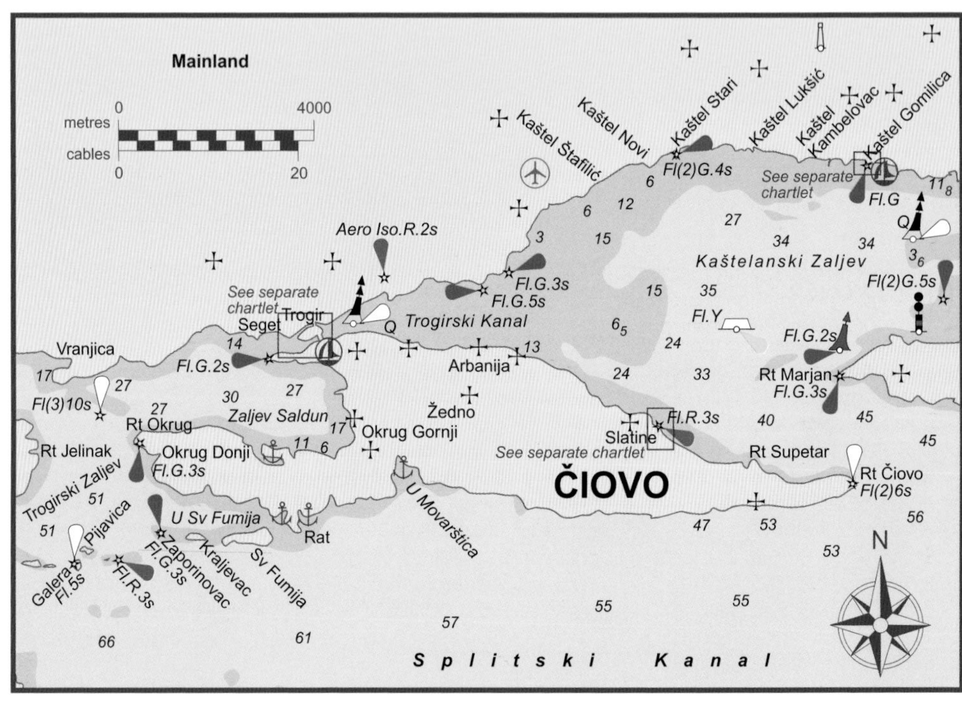

Čiovo Island and the Split Peninsula protect the large bay of Kaštela from the elements. It's a popular tourist spot with an increasing number of holiday apartments and beach bars, as well as a few mainly seasonal restaurants. The tiny settlement of Žedno also has the best walk we've found – through the olive groves with great views of the surrounding coastline. However, it may be somewhat less peaceful now that it is part of the quad bike route – see under 'Transport' above.

There are a few good anchorages away from the crowds and some town harbours. We explore them anticlockwise starting from Trogir.

Zaljev Saldun

Anchorage Uvala Toće, entrance to bay:
43°29'.75N 16°15'.47E

This large bay is immediately south of Trogir, includes the busy resort of Okrug, and has some attractive beaches on the eastern side. There are three smaller bays that provide a reasonable anchorage in depths of 3 to 7m. Holding is good on a mud bed and the bays are well protected from all winds. There are a few beach bars about, a small number of restaurants and a couple of shops. The approach is straightforward from Trogir. See Marina on page 130 if heading from the south.

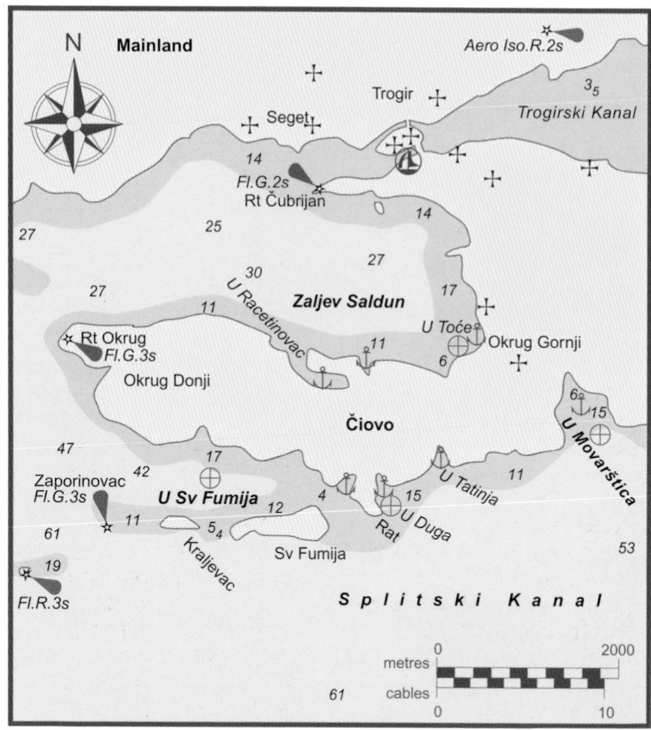

Uvala Sveta Fumija

Centre of bay: 43°28'.84N 16°14'.05E

This is a lovely bay with a campsite and seasonal restaurant (Konoba Duga, Tel: 091 581 8666) that offers great views out to sea – in fact it's a real treat to watch the sun go down over dinner here. To reach the bay by road involves going down a windy track, so fortunately it doesn't get too crowded except when the campsite is in full swing. Other than the restaurant's toilets and an outside freshwater shower on the beach, there are no real facilities on offer. The food is rustic and a little bit more expensive than average, but it's worth it. The bay is exposed to winds from the west, particularly to the afternoon breeze that blows in the summer months.

The rustic charms of Konoba Duga

NAVIGATION

Approaches: At its shallowest point, there is only 4m of water over the bank between the islet of Sv Fumija and Čiovo, and you need to watch out for the hazards at the entrance to Trogirski Zaljev (see page 130).

Approximately 3.5 miles south of the bay is a shoal Plič Mlin, which is lit at night (Fl [2] 10s). It's difficult to spot the Konoba from the sea, but look out for stone-terraced land near the beach.

Part of Konoba Duga's terraced beach area

Uvala Duga

Entrance to bay: 43°28'.77N 16°14'.94E

Next door to Uvala Sveta Fumija, Uvala Duga provides the shelter from the afternoon breeze that its neighbour does not, although it is exposed to winds from the east and south. Holding is good on a sand bed in depths of about 5m. Look out for the shallow bank off Rat and be prepared for a tricky walk if you want to get to Konoba Duga around the coast.

Uvala Movarštica

Entrance to bay: 43°29'.16N 16°16'.60E

This is the last good source of protection from winds from the west, through north to east, heading east along the south coast of Čiovo. The remainder of this part of the coast is barely indented and there are no suitable anchorages. Anchor on a sand bed in depths of 5 to 10m. The bay consists mainly of residential/holiday apartments and has limited facilities.

Slatine

Village harbour: 43°30'.02N 16°20'.70E

On the north-east coast of Čiovo, Slatine itself doesn't have that much to offer but the area is full of beach bars and holiday apartments. Outside the season it is very quiet. The harbour, a good walk from the centre of the village, is quite big, but mostly reserved for locals. Depths vary between 1 and 4m and it is exposed to winds from the north-east quadrant.

The approach is straightforward and there's a red light (Fl R 3s) at the end of the dog leg breakwater. Heading north-west towards Slatine, you'll pass a quarry which provides a reasonable place for a quiet swim, although the bed is rocky.

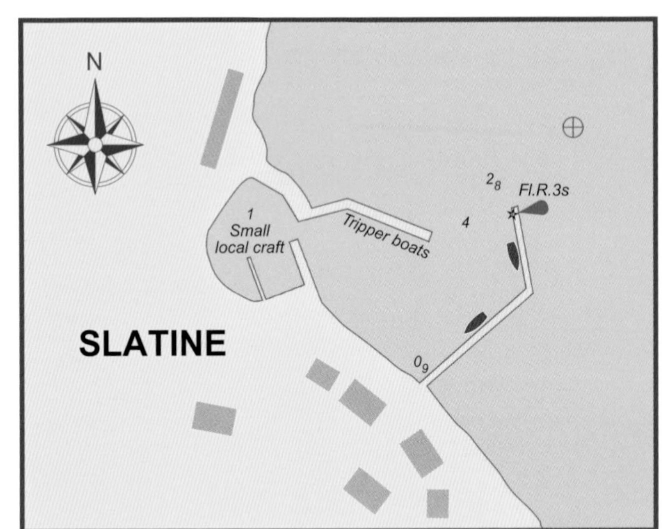

Kaštela

Kaštela is one of Croatia's best-kept secrets. The huge Kaštela Bay has seven established villages, which grew up in the 15th and 16th centuries, each with at least one castle. As you get closer to Split the water becomes less clear and the landscape more industrial, but that will all change as the potential of the area is realised and the new mains sewage system is completed. Kaštel Gomilica is home to one of the newest Croatian marinas, a 10-minute drive from Split airport, and you can find small municipal harbours in most of the villages, but these are really only suitable for shallow draught craft. We start with details of the marina and then give you the highlights of the rest of the area.

Kaštel Štafilić: typical of the castles and harbours around Kaštela Bay

Kaštel Gomilica

Marina entrance: 43°32'.78N 16°23'.74E

Fully open for business in 2006, Marina Kaštela is aiming to provide the very best of facilities to all types of boats, from small cruisers to superyachts.

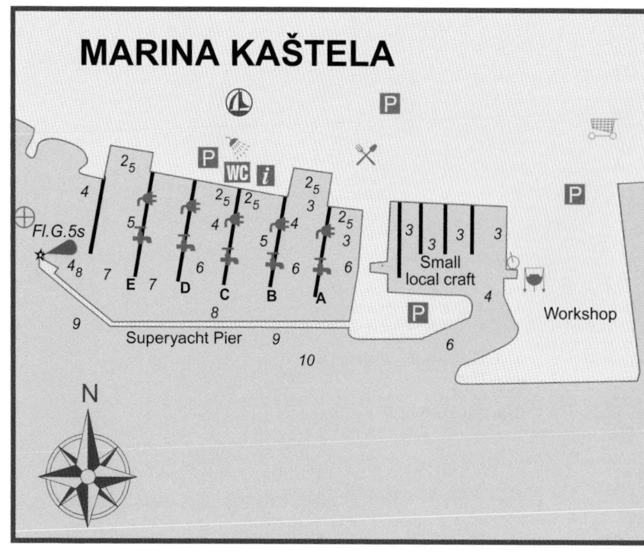

NAVIGATION

Charts: HHI 536, MK-16; AC 269, AC 2712, SC5767

Approaches: The approach to the bay and to the marina is straightforward, although keep well clear of the various well-marked hazards off the Split peninsula. The castle juts out into the sea just west of the marina and the large blue marina building should be visible from a distance, as should the concrete breakwater. To the east of the marina is a sizable factory with concrete chimneys. The breakwater has a green light (Fl G 5s) marking the entrance to the marina.

BERTHING

The marina has 420 berths and 200 dry berths. The outer pier has been designated a megayacht pier, with depths of 9 to 10m and 3 phase power providing up to 125 amps. Inside the marina depths are between 2.5 and 8m. You can berth bows- or stern-to on lazylines or on the outer pier near the green light. Rates are between €3.4 and €4.25 per metre per day for yachts between 10 and 20m (33 and 66ft). This includes 'normal' usage of electricity and water.

The marina is open all year round, but has yet to be categorised. Contact: Šetalište Kralja Tomislava bb, 21213 Kaštel Gomilica, VHF Channel 17, Tel: 021 204 010, 021 204 011; Fax: 021 204 040; email: info@marina-kastela.hr; website: www.marina-kastela.com.

Kaštel Gomilica's castle, with the marina just behind it

Useful information – Kaštel Gomilica

FACILITIES

Power and **water** are supplied to each berth and standard facilities are already available – **toilets**, **showers**, **reception** and a good, reasonably-priced **bar/restaurant**. More amenities, which include a hotel, swimming pool, apartments and **chandlery**, will come about as the development progresses and a **fuel** station and **pump-out** facilities are mentioned in the plans. The marina has a 60-ton **crane**, a 5-ton **lift** and a **boat repair** workshop. **Engine repair** and maintenance services are available at Kaštela Auto, Put Kupališta 44, 21213 Kaštel Gomilica, Tel: 021 222 880, and at ABP Diesel, Obala Kralja Tomislava bb, 21213 Kaštel Gomilica, Tel: 021 660 454.

PROVISIONING

There's a small **kiosk** just as you turn right out of the main entrance, which sells sweets, cigarettes and drinks. A further five-minute walk along the main road, heading east, leads you to Getro, a large **hypermarket**. You will be able to get all your supplies here and it also has a cash point, as does the marina. For more serious shopping, Split and Trogir are about half an hour away by car.

EATING OUT

The on-site restaurant has a wide choice of good, reasonably-priced food and you'll have to walk west along the coast to the other Kastels to find an alternative – see below. As an indication, it's about a 40-minute walk to the Baletna Škola Restaurant in Kaštel Kambelovac.

ASHORE

There is very little in the immediate vicinity of the marina, apart from the lovely castle, but the neighbouring villages are well worth a visit and we give you a sample of what they have to offer below.

TRANSPORT

The marina reception will organise a transfer or **taxi** for you at a price, with Split **airport** being just a 10-minute drive away. There are half-hourly **bus** services to Split or Trogir from the bus stops just outside the marina.

A short guide to Kaštela

The seven villages in the bay, heading from east to west are Kaštel….Sućurac, Gomilica, Kambelovac, Lukšić, Stari, Novi and Štafilić. There are two newer developments, Rudine, just inland from Štafilić, and Resnik, west of Štafilić, which is mostly an old tourist resort in need of modernisation as well as being the location of Split airport. Each Kaštel has a small town quay or harbour mainly used by small local boats with shallow draughts, although you may be able to squeeze in for a lunchtime stop or anchor off, keeping clear of the roped-off swimming areas. If you do try the local harbours keep a very good look out for boulders, ledges, mooring buoys and ropes.

You can walk around the bay in a couple of hours and that's probably the easiest way to take in the villages, but if you haven't got time for that, below is the best of what's on offer. Bear in mind that the main Kaštela road is, at most, a 10-minute walk from the sea and that there are a number of big supermarkets dotted along it, mostly 'Tommy's', where you can find more than that available in the smaller shops along the seafront. Finally, note that there are some great mountain walks starting from Kaštela, with mountain huts at convenient distances.

Kaštela Bay: from left to right is Kaštel Štafilić, Novi and Stari

Sućurac

The closest Kaštel to Split, and the oldest of all the villages, Sućurac is notable for its shopping centre where you can buy most things at reasonably competitive prices. It has a large supermarket, Ipercoop, an even larger furniture shop, Emmezete, and a similarly massive DIY shop, Bricostore. In the main part of the shopping centre are also shoe and clothes shops, jewellery boutiques, a bank and a couple of cash points. Just west of the shopping area is the village itself, which has managed to retain its Dalmatian charm despite the industrial activity around it.

Although the quay is exposed to all winds except those from the north, its western end has depths of up to 3m, but watch out for rocky patches. Alternatively, you can anchor off the quay on a mud bed in depths of around 5m.

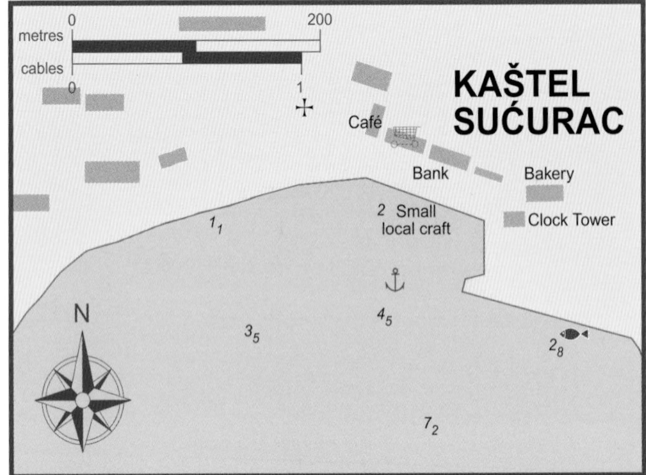

Gomilica

Apart from the Marina, Gomilica probably has the prettiest of the seven castles, built by Benedictine Nuns in the 16th century, but is otherwise a sleepy village with not much to offer tourists except for a couple of bars.

The small harbour by the castle, with depths of around 2m, is exposed to southwesterlies but protected from the Bora and Sirocco.

Kambelovac

Kambelovac is home to one of the best local restaurants we have found, the Baletna Škola (Ballet School), Tel: 021 220 208. The restaurant is not easy to spot from the sea, lying just behind an impressive but derelict house. However, driving along the Kaštela road, which runs parallel to the main coastal road, there is a big white sign indicating the road into which you turn. Drive to the end of this until you can go no further and the Ballet School is on the left. It's a great favourite with the locals and is always busy, but there's plenty of space both inside and out. Offering a good variety of local dishes at very reasonable prices, it's not the place to go to if you are in a rush. Surrounding the restaurant are some pebble and concrete beaches.

The town harbour is normally full of fishing boats but the breakwater, on the eastern side of the harbour, has depths of up to 4m with the same protection as Gomilica. One of the mountain walks starts from Kambelovac – head inland along the marked path that takes you across the two east–west main roads. The first mountain hut, normally open at weekends, is Kolududar, about an hour's walk away, after which the climbing becomes more adventurous.

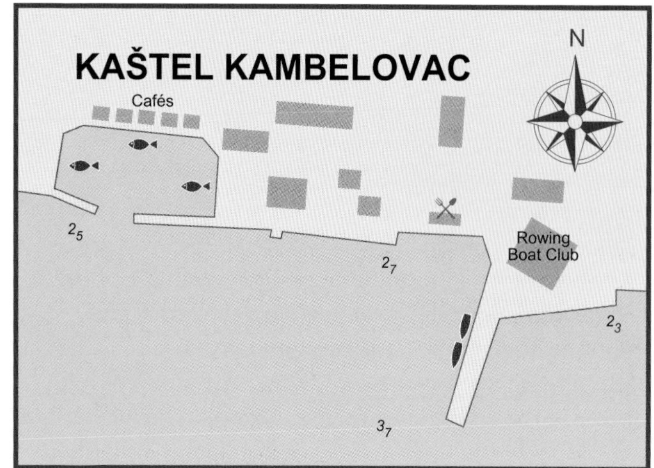

Lukšić

Lukšić is the trendiest village of the group, with a clutch of well-furnished bars around the centre, by the renaissance castle. The castle is home to the main Kaštela tourist office where you can get a treasure trove of information on the castles, the mountain walks, a poignant love story regarding the rival owners of the two castles, and the history of Kaštela. There are also a number of musical events inside the castle during the summer.

The inner town harbour is well protected but shallow. You can berth alongside the main pier in depths of between 2 and 4m, but you will be exposed to winds from the south-east, south and south-west.

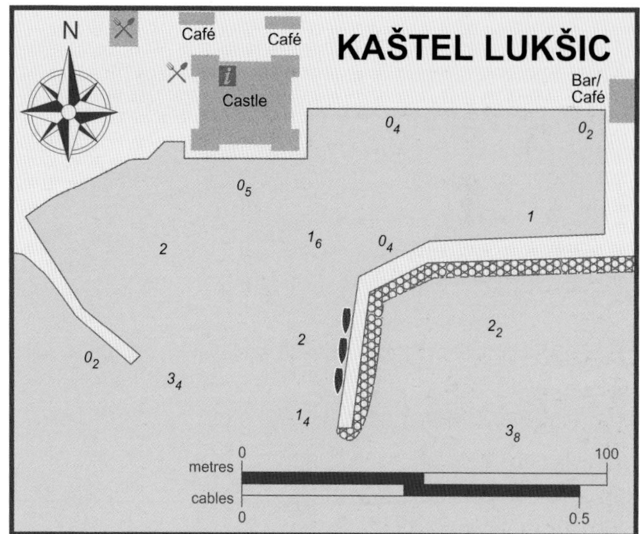

Stari

Stari is the most bustling of all the villages, with plenty of small grocery shops, butchers and bakers. The restaurant, Labinezza, Obala Kralja Tomislava 56, Tel: 021 231 108, situated on the front, can be recommended, serving a good variety of food at reasonable prices. In August 2006, Labinezza extended its outside area by erecting decking over the seafront – the first time we've seen this innovative use of space in Croatia.

You can berth on the western side of the main pier, in depths of 2 to 4m, where you are protected from the Bora, but only partly from the Sirocco, which causes a swell. The harbour is completely exposed to southwesterlies. Dalmacijavino, the local wine and liqueur company, has a depot by the pier and the

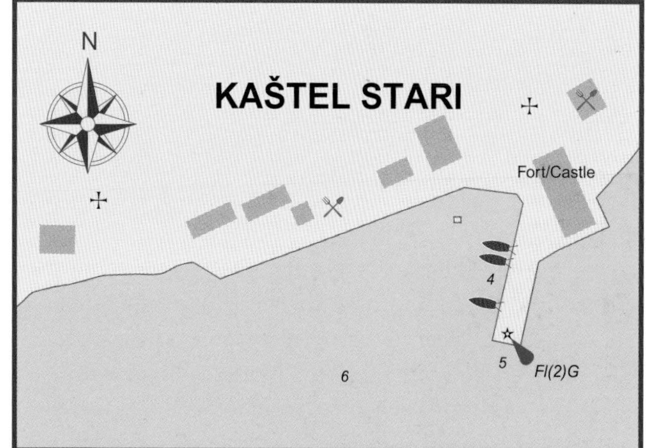

monument of a winged horse, on a tall concrete tower, is prominent from a distance. There's a marked walk towards the mountains from Stari. Head north towards the cemetery and over the railway track to find it.

Novi

Kaštel Novi is typically Dalmatian with its castle, broad seafront walks, palm trees and busy cafés. Intrada – Obala Kralja Tomislava bb, Tel: 021 231 301 – just east of the castle, is a good restaurant, popular with the locals, which serves great pizzas as well as the standard grilled meat and fish. The harbour is chock-a-block with various local boats, so anchoring off is the most feasible option.

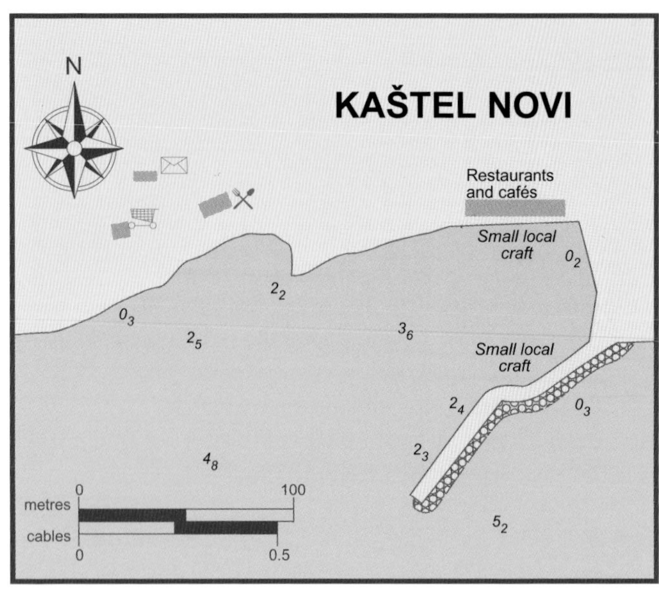

Štafilić

Probably the most residential and rural village of the seven Kaštels, Štafilić has a couple of bakeries and shops, a supermarket and two good beaches to the west of the castle. It also boasts a 1,500-year-old olive tree, allegedly the oldest specimen in Europe. The locals have cobbled together a series of home-made plank walkways to act as a harbour in the area east of the castle. However, depths are shallow and there's little space with limited protection.

Useful information – Kaštela

TOURIST OFFICES: A Beretina 1, Kaštel Novi, **Tel:** 021 232 044, 021 230 955; Dvorac Vitturi, Brce 1, Kastel Lukšić, **Tel:** 021 277 933, 021 228 355; email: tzgkastela@st.t-com.hr; website: www.dalmacija.net/kastela.

MEDICAL CENTRES: Cesta bb, Kaštel Stari, **Tel:** 021 230 708; Cesta bb, Kaštel Sućurac, **Tel:** 021 225 070.

PHARMACY: Starčevićeva 1, Kaštel Stari, **Tel:** 021 230 406.

POLICE: F Careva 7, Kaštel Gomilica, **Tel:** 021 221 170.

TAXI: Airport, **Tel:** 021 895 237.

POST OFFICES: At the airport and in each village, except Štafilić.

BANKS AND CASH POINTS: Cash points are widespread and there are banks in Novi, Lukšić and Sućurac, as well as at the airport.

NEAREST HARBOURMASTER: Trogir or Split.

Split

Entrance to Gradska Luka (Split town bay): 43°30'.04N 16°25'.98E

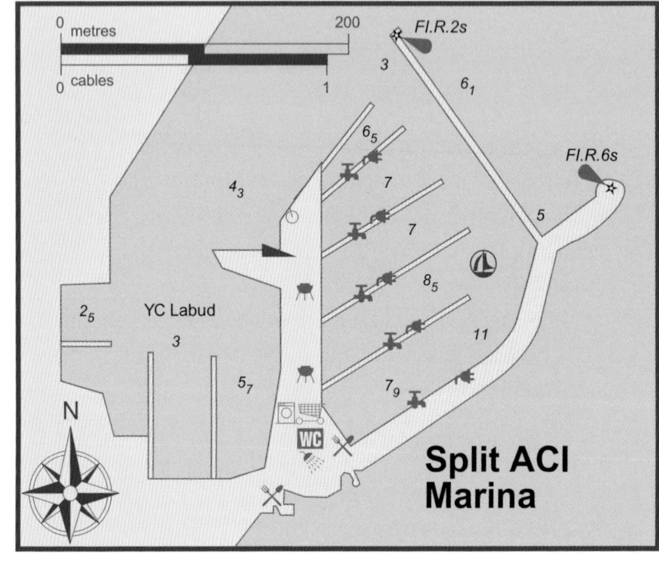

Like Šibenik and Zadar, Croatia's second most important town can seem like an ugly suburb from a distance, with high-rise flats and heavy industry, but again it has a real heart. The remains of Diocletian's palace, built in the fourth century, form the boundaries of the old town, hiding many architectural treasures, while the Riva, recently modernised and now a little too high-tech for many people's liking, is lined with cafés. The lively markets offer fruit, vegetables, fish, clothes and souvenirs and there are plenty of shops around which to browse. The April Boat Show is increasing in size every year and worth a visit if you can find somewhere to berth. Although Split has four marinas, only one of them, the ACI marina, actively welcomes visitors, the other three being mostly run for the locals, although more anchorage space has been made available in the town harbour. Yacht Club Labud, the oldest yacht club in Croatia, established in 1924, occasionally has berths for visitors and is located in the same area as the ACI marina. The two sports clubs, PSD Spinut, on the north coast of the Marjan Peninsula, and PSD Zenta, about a mile east of Split port, are both for locals only. We focus on the ACI marina and the city centre, with a final note about the tiny island of Vranjic, special in that it provides a welcome relief from the heavy industrialisation in the eastern end of Kaštela Bay.

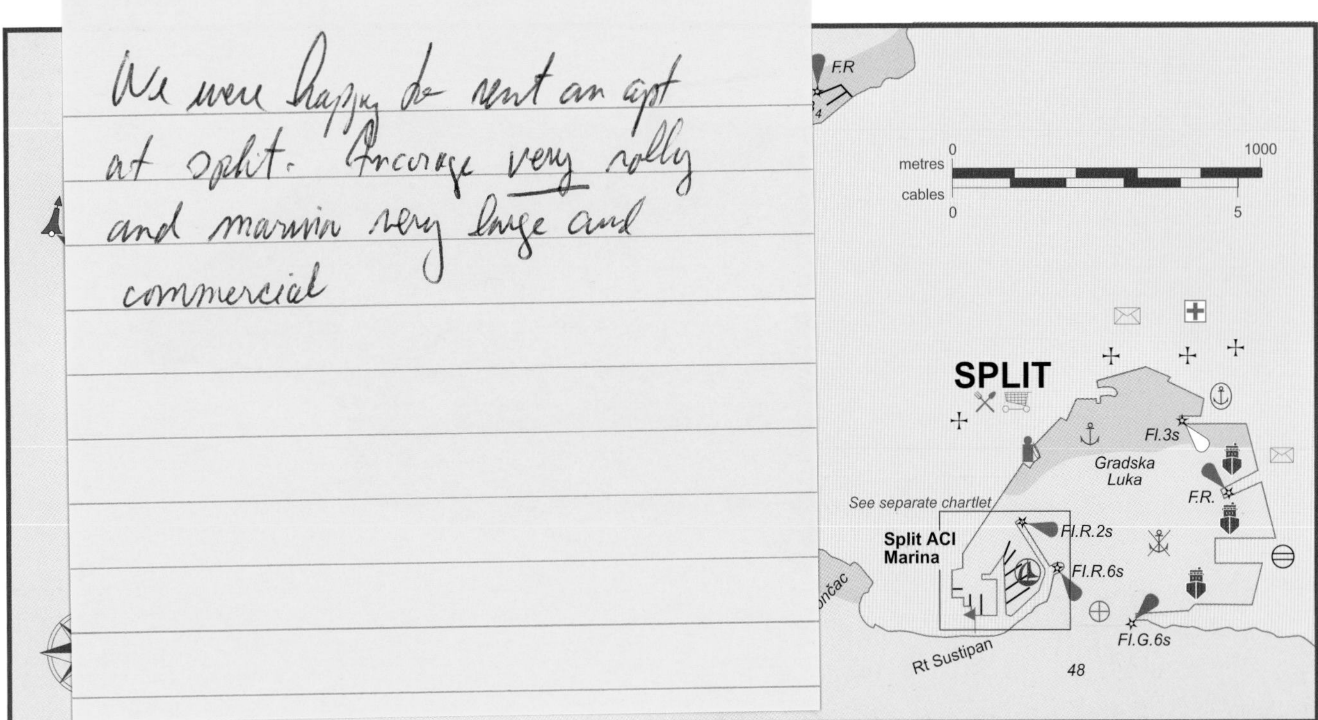

NAVIGATION

Charts: HHI 536, MK-16, MK-18; AC 269, AC 2712, SC5767

Approaches: The approach is clear from all directions, the main hazard being the frequency of ferries in and out of the port. There is a special mark (Fl Y 2s) about 1.2nm south-east of the entrance to the harbour, indicating a pipeline. As you enter the bay, the town harbour is in front of you, the ferry port immediately to starboard and the ACI marina to port. The marina breakwater has a red light (Fl R 6s) at its seaward end and a red light on the inner breakwater (Fl R 2s), while the ferry port breakwater has a green light (Fl G 6s) and a tall square tower at the root.

The green light (Fl G 6s) on the end of the Split harbour breakwater, to starboard as you enter the bay

BERTHING

This Category II marina (VHF Channel 17/Tel: 021 398 556) is open all year round and has 364 berths and 60 dry berths. You will pay between €3.8 and €4.35 per metre per day for a boat between 10 and 20m (33 to 66ft), plus a 10% surcharge from June to September. The breakwater provides protection from southerly winds and the

The Split Boat Show takes place in April each year

Split Riva and the Old Town on the left. The five-storey building with the green dome, at the far end of the bay, houses the harbourmaster's office

marina is naturally sheltered from winds from all other directions. Should you choose to tie up at the town quay beware that the bay can be hazardous in winds from the south and south-west, and that the frequent traffic creates a swell of its own.

Visitors are permitted to berth either side of the harbourmaster's office, keeping clear of the ferries and watching out for protruding ledges.

Useful information – Split

FACILITIES

There is everything you would normally expect from an ACI marina, including a 10-ton **crane**, 35-ton **slipway** and a derrick to step/unstep masts. One **restaurant** is located on site, with a couple more close by. The town harbour has **water** but no electrics as yet. **Fuel** can be obtained to port of the centre of the bay as you head into it, depths 3.5m, Tel: 021 399 484. Charts and accessories are available at Plovput, which shares the harbourmaster's office. There's quite a good choice of service companies in the area, including the following: **Engines**: Boltano, Stinice bb, Tel: 021 490 565; Nautika Centar Nava, Uvala Baluni 1, Tel: 021 398 430. **Electrical equipment**: Brodel, Skradinska 5, Tel: 098 453 258. **Electronic devices**: PCE Elektronika, Zrinsko-Frankopanska bb, Tel: 021 361 463. **Sail repairs**: Elvstrom Sails, Uvala Baluni bb, Tel: 021 398 572; UK Sailmakers, Lučica 4, Tel: 091 787 6862; North Sail, Bana Jelačića 6, Tel: 021 661 156. **General repairs**: Matadura, Uvala Baluni bb, Tel: 021 398 561; Nautella, Lučica 7, Dražanac 3a.

Split also boasts 'Croatia's only automatic laundrette' (sic), situated on Sperun 1 and open from 0800 to 2000 every day. The **launderette** charges 25 Kunas per wash and 15 Kunas for 50 minutes of drying time. You can find it just behind the Church of Sveti Frane, west of the fountain and Diocletian Palace.

PROVISIONING

The **market**, which opens seven days a week, starts on the east side of the Riva, by the car park. It sells the usual souvenirs, clothes, fruit, vegetables and fish although for the best selection of fish you need to get there early. There are plenty of **supermarkets**, **cash points** and **shops** dotted around. The nearest **post offices** are at Kralja Tomislava 9 or by the coach station.

EATING OUT

There's a cluster of restaurants by the launderette and two just by the marina, Restoran Mediteran, Tel: 021 774 323, and Pizzeria Skipper Club, Tel: 021 398 222. Buffet Fife and Kibela are good for their traditional feel. Fife's is not far from the Franciscan Monastery on the seafront – Trumbićeva Obala 11, Tel: 021 345 223; Kibela is within the Diocletian Palace Walls – Kraj Sv Ivana 5, kod Peristila, Tel: 021 346 205. There's also a great new restaurant, Bistro Black Cat (Tel: 021 490 284), a five-minute walk from the market, on the other side of the railway tracks, right on the corner of Petrova and Šegvićeva. Serving enormous salads and a range of good value international cuisine, its Happy Hour is between 1700 and 1800. For the best in traditional pastries and ice-creams, try Tradicija, Bosanka 2, Tel: 021 361 070, just off Narodni Trg, the main town square. There's even a McDonalds on Marmontova, a main street heading north to the theatre.

The fountain and 'piazza' at the west end of the Riva

ASHORE

The **tourist office** is a short walk north from the Riva; Trg Republike 2, Tel: 021 348 600, 021 348 601; email: tz-split@st.htnet.hr. The compact old town is bursting with history and classic architecture and you'll be able to pick up a *Welcome to Split* book, as well as a list of events and details of museums. Split National Theatre, with an eclectic repertoire of ballet, opera and plays, is on the northern boundary of the old town – Trg Gaja Bulata 1, Tel: 021 344 999; email: hnk-split@st.htnet.hr; website: www.hnk-split.hr. The town also incorporates a puppet theatre – contact: Matosićeva 3, Tel: 021 395 958.

Beaches: A 15-minute walk from the town heading south-east then east along the coast will bring you to the Park Hotel where there is a great sandy beach with several restaurants and night spots. A 15-minute walk in the opposite direction will take you near the Hotel Jadran where there is another reasonable beach. The quality of the water is not bad considering the beaches are so close to the town.

TRANSPORT

See the introduction to this section on page 126 for transport details. Also note that there is a new seasonal **ferry** service between Split and Slatine, on the island of Čiovo, and Trogir. It runs about four times a day and embarks from opposite the British Consulate on the Riva.

OTHER INFORMATION

British Consulate: Obala Hrvatskog Narodnog Preporoda 10/II, Tel: 021 362 995. Situated on the Riva, the British Consulate shares the same building with the German and Italian Consulates, and is extremely helpful. **Harbourmaster**: Walking east around the bay past the car park and market, you will see the large stone building that houses the harbourmaster's office – Obala Lazareta 1, Tel: 021 355 488; Fax: 021 361 298. **ACI Marina Split**: Uvala Baluni bb, Tel: 021 398 548; Fax: 021 398 556; email: m.split@aci-club.hr; website: www.aci-club.hr. **Police**: Trg Hrvatske Bratske Zajednice 9, Tel: 021 307 111. **Hospital**: Spinčićeva 1, Tel: 021 556 111. **24 hour pharmacies**: Dobri, Gundulićeva 52, Tel: 021 348 074; Lučac, Pupačićeva 4, Tel: 021 533 188.

Split
Vranjic Islet

Village harbour:
43°31'.88N 16°27'.25E

The traditional Dalmatian settlement of Vranjic, just a stone's throw from industrial Split

In the unlikely event that you would want to head east, past Kaštel Sućurac, to a dead end, you will, for a while, see nothing but mostly disused cement and plastics factories, rusting naval ships and superstores. You will also need to pay close attention to a number of lights and buoys that are relatively densely-packed. However, jutting out from the easternmost part of the bay is a tiny island, linked to the mainland by a causeway. Its traditional character is idiosyncratic and in stark contrast to the rest of the area. The harbour is only suitable for shallow draught boats and we only saw a post office in terms of facilities, but if you want to compare the worst of industrialised Dalmatia as it was, to how it might have been before and could be again, it's worth a trip. It's also not far from Solin, where there are some classic Roman remains, including those of an amphitheatre.

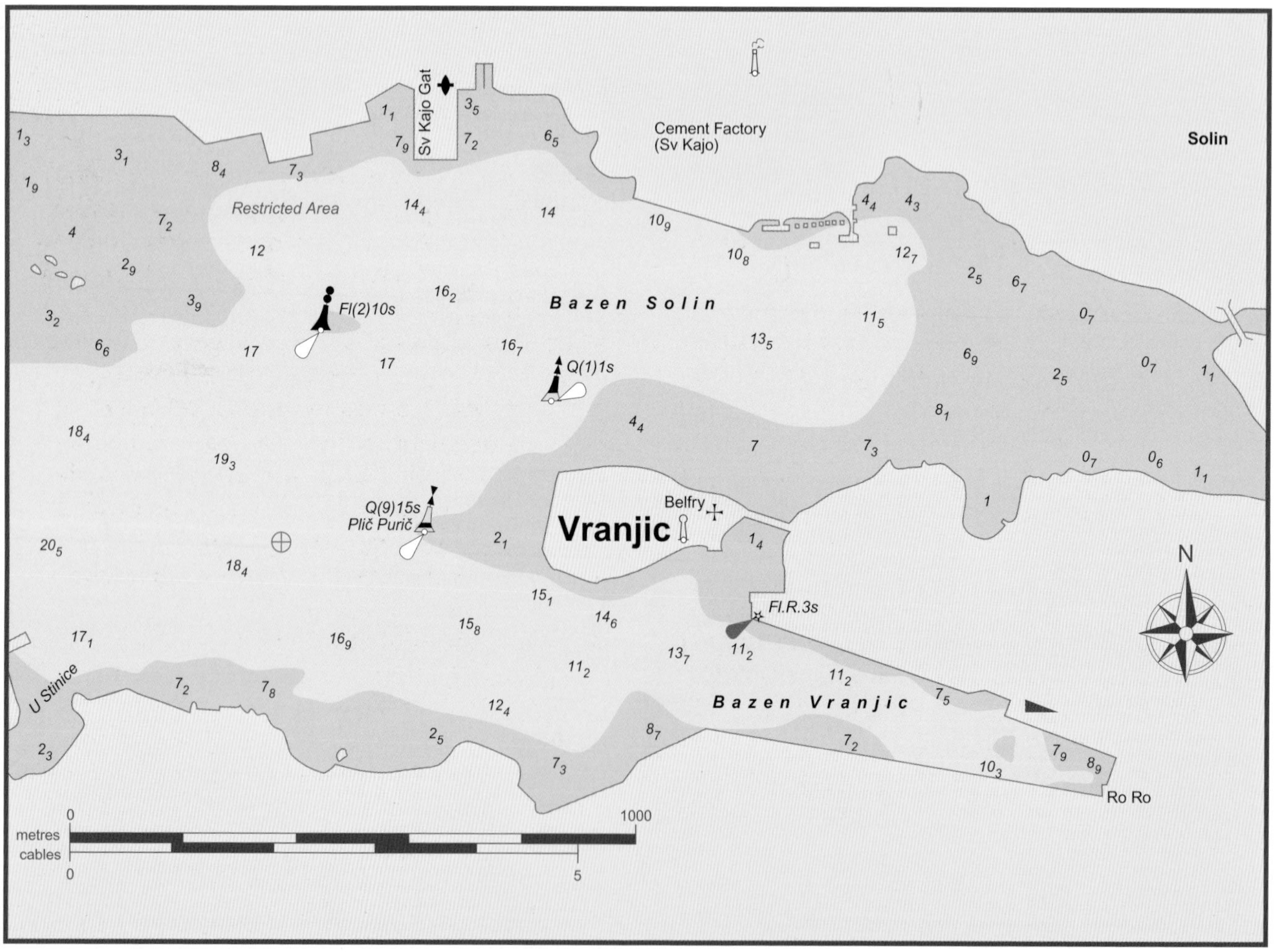

Zlatni Rat, Bol

Chapter five
The islands around Split

The area covered by this chapter is probably one of the most popular cruising regions in Croatia for a number of different reasons. The islands of Brač and Hvar are within easy reach of the mainland and are large enough to have good facilities all year round. Hvar Town has also become something of a celebrity hotspot, with prices to match. Just west of Hvar Town are the Pakleni Islands and another ACI marina, while south of Hvar is the island of Šćedro. Further out to sea, the island of Vis is smaller and less developed than Brač and Hvar, but has two lovely towns – Vis and Komiža – as well as the adjacent islet of Biševo, famous for its blue cave, which glows fluorescently by virtue of a trick of the sunlight. To the west of Brač, Šolta has some beautiful, unspoilt bays and seems relatively untouched by modern tourism. The islands of Drvenik Mali and Drvenik Veli, close to Trogir, have similarly deserted coves but little life.

You could easily spend three or four days around Brač and not get bored. Most of the settlements are on the north coast of Brač but Milna, on the west coast, is a pretty town with two marinas, and Bol, on the south coast, with its famous Zlatni Rat beach, is a great place to visit and now has a quay where visiting yachts can berth. From Bol, it's a short trip to Jelsa or Vrboska, on Hvar Island, which are well equipped for overnight stays. On the north coast, Supetar is a busy ferry and tourist port, Sutivan is a similar size but a little quieter, Splitska is typical of a classic small Dalmatian island village, Postira is a run-down package holiday centre and Pučišća is a real locals' town with a thriving quarrying industry and streetlights made out of the local white stone. Povlja, to the east of Pučišća, is a small settlement built around a long bay, while Sumartin, on the east coast, is a quiet fishing village. If you need to get away from it all, you'll also find plenty of secluded bays, particularly on the west and north coasts.

Hvar Island is longer and thinner than Brač, with most of the settlements concentrated in the western half of the island. If you want to keep up with the jet set, then Hvar Town is for you, but be prepared for most things to cost 50% more than elsewhere and for a degree of opportunism among some of the locals in the tourist industry. It's a fascinating town archaeologically and historically, but in our view is in danger of losing its traditional Dalmatian character. We prefer Stari Grad and Jelsa, although Jelsa is threatening to become the new Hvar Town. Next door to Jelsa is the smaller village of Vrboska, which has an ACI marina, a good town harbour and plenty of charm. At the eastern end of the island is Sućuraj, a smaller ferry port than Stari Grad but a lovely compact, traditional settlement.

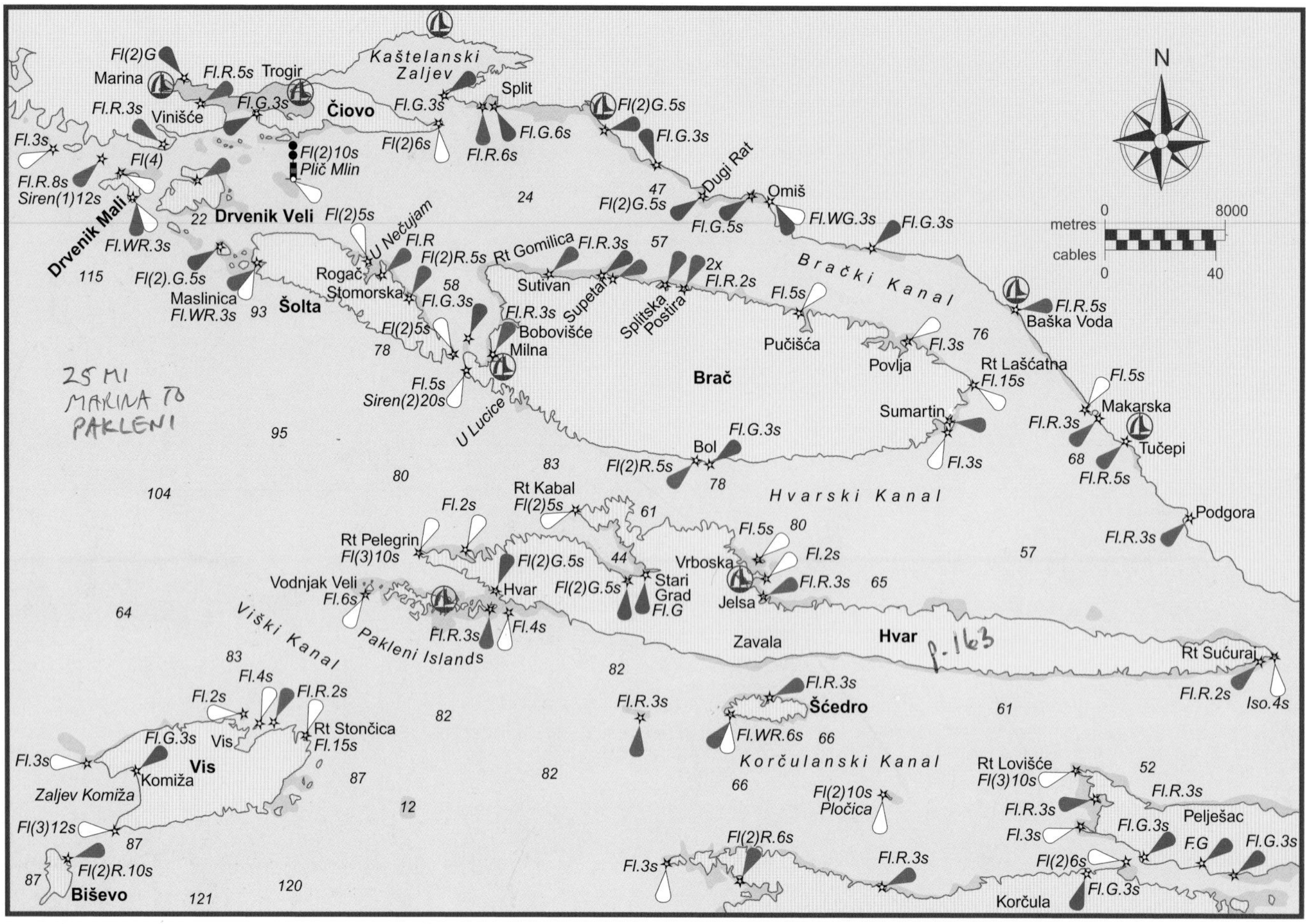

This area is for those who want to explore the islands but need a degree of civilisation close to hand. The principal moorings, especially in Hvar, are packed in the high season, so if you are after a bit more peace and quiet, the islands covered in chapter two are a better bet. Otherwise, make sure you get to your destination early.

Marinas are located on Brač at Milna, on Hvar at Vrboska and just off Hvar Town on the Pakleni Islands. Fuel can be found on Šolta Island at Rogač; on Brač Island at Milna, Sumartin and Bol; on Hvar Island at Hvar and Vrboska and on Vis Island at Vis.

We start from the west, closest to the mainland, with Drvenik Mali and Drvenik Veli, then Šolta, Brač, Hvar and the Pakleni Islands, Šćedro, Vis and Biševo.

Drvenik Mali Island

Charts: HHI MK-16; AC 2712, AC 2774, SC5767

This small island is largely cultivated with olive trees and has two possible shelters – Borak on the east side of the island and Uvala Vela Rina on the south side. There is a small population of permanent

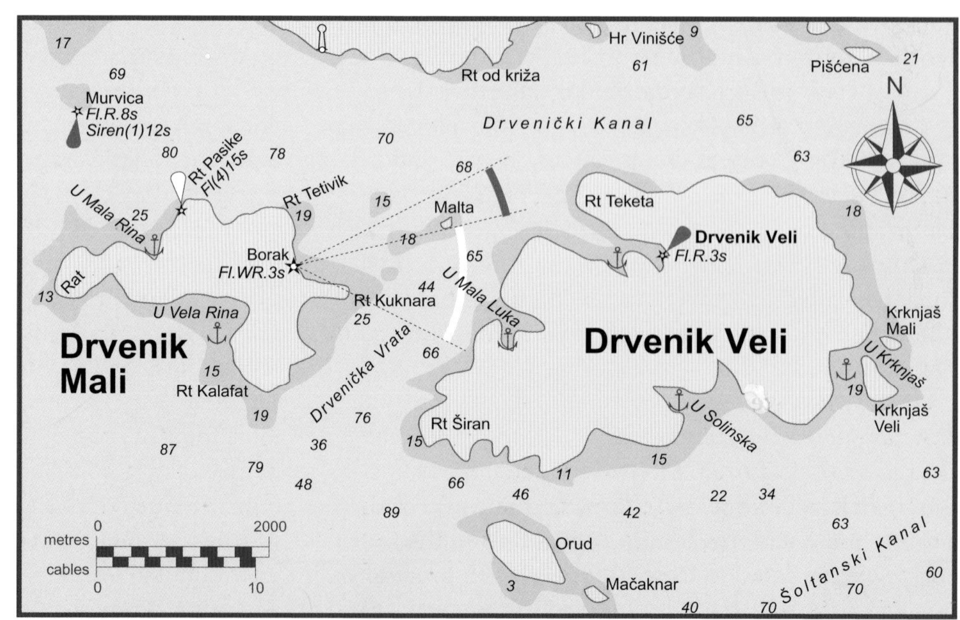

residents, but most do their shopping in Trogir using the ferry from Borak. The approaches to both shelters are straightforward. The nearest fuel is in Trogir or at Rogač on Šolta. There are two to three ferries a day connecting the island to Trogir on the mainland via Drvenik Veli.

Borak

Village harbour: 43°27'.02N 16°05'.57E

You can berth alongside, on the north side of the ferry pier (Fl WR 3s), in depths of 2 to 5m. The ferry uses the south side. You can also anchor off, on a sand bed, but holding is poor. There is some protection from winds from the south and west, but otherwise the bay is exposed, particularly in a Bora. On shore you will find a shop and a ferry service to Trogir.

Uvala Vela Rina

Anchorage: 43°26'.58N 16°04'.71E

This bay provides good protection from the Bora, but does not offer shelter in winds from the south, south-west and west.

You can anchor close to the shore in depths of around 4m, on a sand bed with good holding.

Drvenik Veli Island

Charts: HHI 534 (for Drvenik Veli – see below), MK-16; AC 2712, 2774, SC5767

Rumours of a marina on Drvenik Veli have been circulating for some years now. There's even a website showing Marina Zirona but, so far, all that exists is a fish farm. Latest news is that the project has become live again. In the meantime, there are four possible shelters, which are, clockwise from the north, Drvenik Veli village, Uvala Krknjaš, Uvala Solinska and Uvala Mala Luka. The nearest fuel is in Trogir or at Rogač on Šolta. See above for ferry connections.

Drvenik Veli

Entrance to bay: 43°27'.31N 16°07'.76E

Approaching from the west, look out for the small islet of Malta, otherwise the approach is clear. The bay at Drvenik Veli divides into two parts, with the ferry terminal and harbour in the eastern inlet. The ferry berths alongside the quay, pointing north-west, with the red light (Fl R 3s) just in front of its bows. There is an underwater cable running to the mainland from the eastern head of the western part of the bay.

Yachts can berth along the quay, clear of the ferry area, or on the inner side of the breakwater. Alternatively, anchor on a sand bed in depths of around 7m, south of the quay.

On the oppos[illegible] side of the bay from the red light is a metal statue on a concrete base, and the low- level church belfry is just about visible through the trees.

Three restaurants Jere, Ljubo and Taverna Cantina provide sustenance and there's also a post office and shop. The tourist office (Tel: 021 628 173) is situated on Donja Ubala.

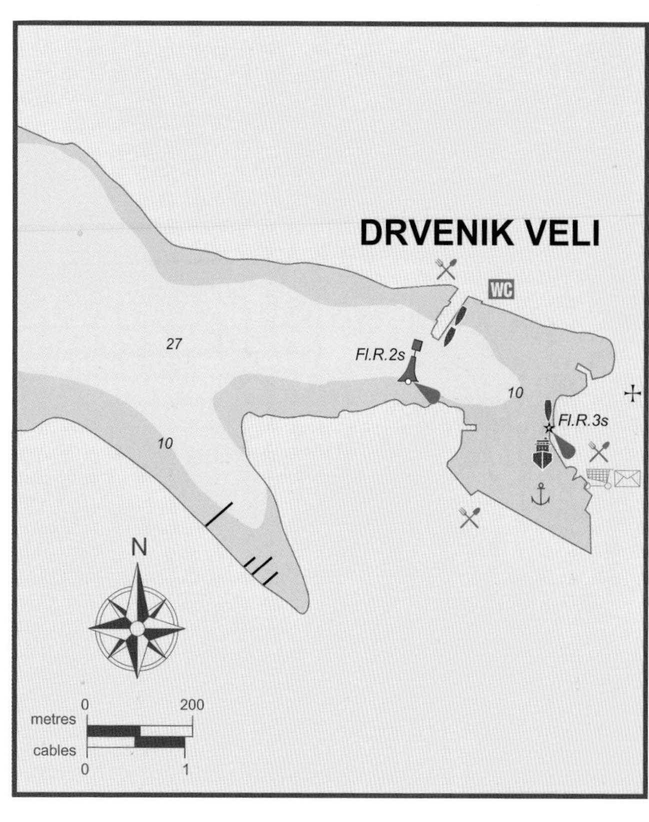

Uvala Krknjaš

Entrance to bay: 43°25'.96N 16°10'.52E

A lovely bay for a day stop, with a good restaurant and crystal clear water but it is not very well sheltered and the holding here is unreliable. It is, therefore, unsuitable for an overnight anchorage except in calm weather. Depths between Drvenik Veli and the islet of Krknjaš Mali are less than a metre and there are rocks in the vicinity, so the safest approach is either side of the islet of Krknjaš Veli. Depths reduce to below 2.5m on the north of the islet. Note that there is an underwater cable west of Krknjaš Veli. You can anchor west of this underwater cable or between the two Krknjaš islets. Shallow draught craft can anchor closer to Drvenik Veli, but watch out for ridges of rock as you get near to the shore. The bed is a mixture of sand, weed and rock.

The seasonal restaurant Konoba Krknjaši (Tel: 021 893 073/091 575 0925) serves up great fish at 360 Kunas per kilo, as well as some meat dishes and good chips, and has built a wooden pier to which you can tie up. However, depths are no more than 1 to 2m on the outer half of this pier and considerably less on the inner half. The restaurant has toilets, but there are no other facilities in the bay.

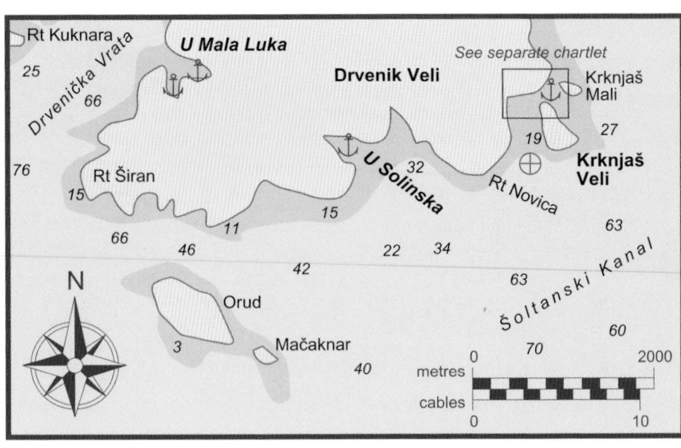

Uvala Krknjaš – a popular anchorage for mainland dwellers

The pier by the restaurant at Uvala Krknjaš for shallow draught boats

Uvala Solinska

Entrance to bay: 43°25'.76N 16°09'.34E

A large bay on the south coast of the island offering good protection from winds from the north, but exposed from other directions, particularly the south. Good holding on a sand and mud bed. Straightforward approach. No facilities.

Uvala Mala Luka

Entrance to bay: 43°26'.68N 16°07'.23E

About a mile south-west of Drvenik Veli, this bay provides good protection from all but northwesterly winds, though the Bora and winds from the south-west can cause a swell. There's a fish farm in the outer part of the bay, but you can anchor in the two inner inlets in depths of 5 to 10m. Good holding on a sand bed. No facilities.

Šolta Island

Charts: HHI 535 (for Maslinica), MK-16; AC 2712, SC5767

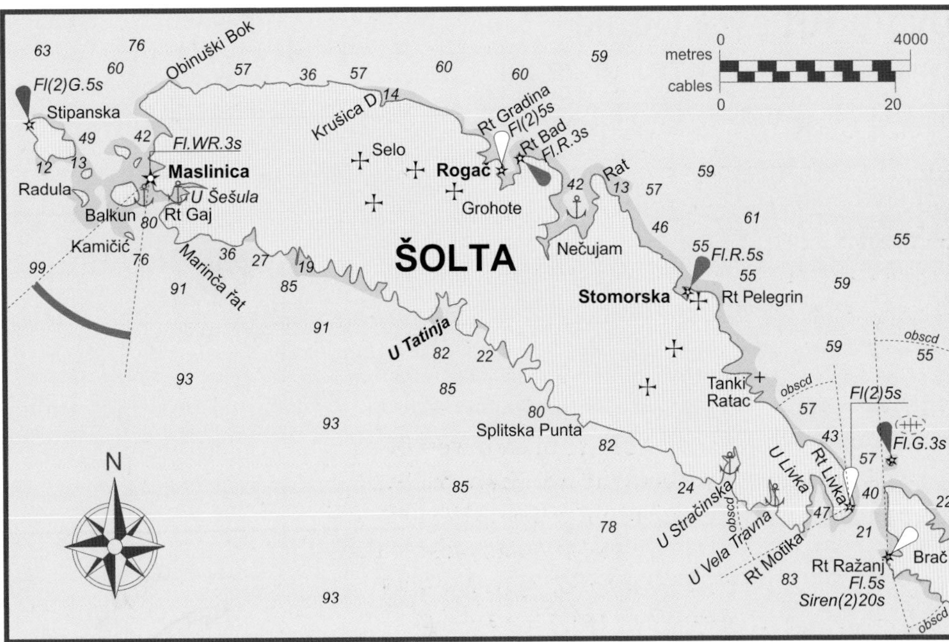

Apart from an out-of-character resort development at Nečujam, Šolta is a lovely traditional Croatian island. The main town, Grohote, is inland from Rogač. One of Šolta's natives, Anthony Paladin, who subsequently emigrated to America, wrote a novel illustrating what life was like on Šolta during World War II, which gives you a real taste of Croatian history. Entitled *The One Who Leaves Never Returns*, it's published by Fithian Press in California.

The south coast is mostly inhospitable, but there are a number of secluded bays and attractive villages along the north coast. We start with Maslinica, to the west, and head east. Fuel is available at Rogač.

There are three to five ferries a day between Rogač and Split, depending on the day of the week and the time of the year. Details of the main facilities to be found on the island are included at the end of the section on Šolta (see page 151).

Maslinica

Entrance to bay: 43°23'.84N 16°12'.08E

Maslinica is the prettiest village on the island, with a bay that provides good all-round shelter, except from the Bora, which does not, however, raise a swell. The fortified villa on the south side of the bay has been a hotel, then a restaurant and now looks poised to become a hotel again.

NAVIGATION

Approaches: The approach is complicated by a number of islets off the entrance to the bay and is not recommended at night. Depths shallow to 2.8m between the islets of Polebrnjak, Saskinja and Šolta, west of the harbour entrance. If approaching from the south, beware of the rock, Kamičić, and a 2m shoal south of Balkun Islet. The fortified villa, with a square tower, is visible from a distance.

BERTHING/ANCHORING/FACILITIES

Space permitting, you can berth at the pier in depths of about 6m on the north side of the bay, watching out for the ferries. In front of the villa, on the south side of the bay, are lazylines, water and electrics. Westerly and northwesterly winds can cause a swell.

Alternatively, you can anchor to the east of Balkun Islet (good protection in a westerly) or the inlet just south of the harbour, Uvala Šešula (not suitable in a southwesterly, which generates a heavy swell). Depths in both anchorages are between 4 and 10m where there is good holding on a sand and mud bed.

ASHORE

Facilities include a supermarket, tourist office, post office and a scattering of restaurants and bars. On the north side of the bay, Konoba Moni claims to be open all year round and specialises in fish. Konoba Saskinja, almost next to Moni, with the tourist office in between, is popular with the locals and open between April and October. There's a pizza restaurant at the head of the bay and a market next to it.

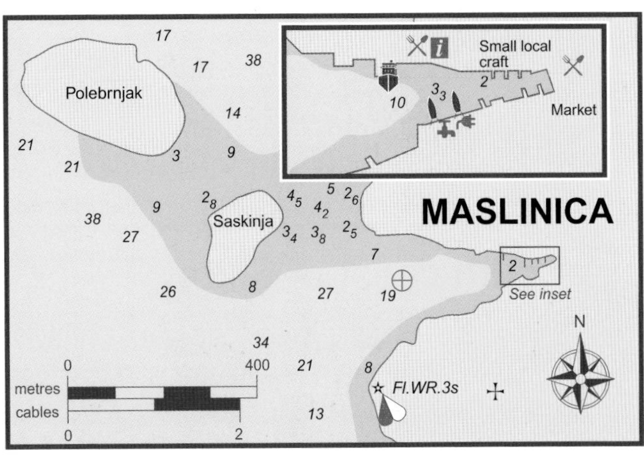

Uvala Krušica Donja

Entrance to bay: 43°24'.72N 16°16'.13E

A small village harbour offering partial protection, but exposed to winds from the north and north-west. You can berth inside the outer wall in depths of up to 3m. The approach is straightforward, but there are no facilities.

Rogač

Entrance to bay: 43°24'.08N 16°18'.07E

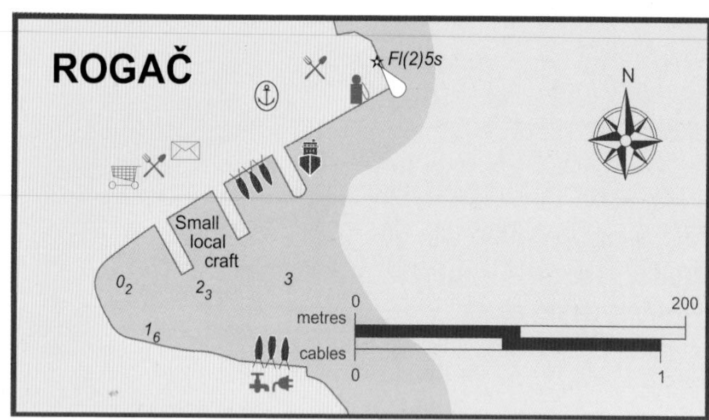

Rogač is a good place to avoid the crowds when refuelling in the high season, but it's a small harbour with not too much going on. The approach is clear, apart from shallow waters around Rt Bad, and you can berth, using lazylines, on the south side of the harbour where electricity and water pedestals have also been installed. The holding is reputedly not good for anchoring. The bay is exposed to winds from the north and a strong Sirocco causes a swell. Rt Bad has a red light, while on the other side of the bay is a white light by the first ferry pier. The fuel station is to starboard as you enter the bay, the second ferry berth is on the same side a little further in, and the road up to Grohote is visible at the head of the bay.

There's a small tourist office on the quay, Restaurant Šolta and a couple of bars. For medical services, the post office and a few more shops, you'll need to go to Grohote, 2km inland.

Nečujam

Entrance to bay: 43°23'.75N 16°19'.31E

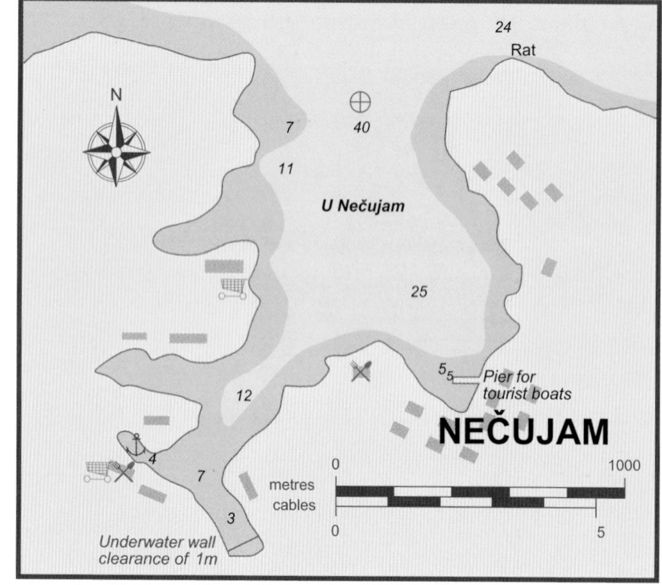

It's not that this relatively new and modern development lacks taste, it just seems completely out of place and a little too visible as you approach from the mainland. The bay is deserted off season, but the long semi-circular beach teems with holidaymakers in high summer. Facilities include swimming pools, beach showers, a restaurant and a supermarket.

The innermost part of the bay has a submerged wall running across it with a clearance of about 1m. Just before the swimming pools is a jetty where you can tie up if it's not taken by day-tripper boats, and the best place to anchor is the innermost of the western inlets.

The bay is exposed to winds from the north and a strong Sirocco causes a swell.

Stomorska

Entrance to bay: 43°22'.52N 16°21'.16E

Stomorska is a small settlement with a relatively new breakwater. Lazylines have been laid on the eastern side of the bay and electricity and water are available. The bay is well protected, although winds from the north cause heavy seas. The approach is straightforward and ashore you'll find a shop, diving centre and a number of restaurants.

The south coast of Šolta

If you are in need of shelter passing along the south coast of Šolta, there are two possibilities for anchoring: Uvala Vela Travna and Uvala Stračinska.

Uvala Tatinja is mentioned in some guides as a good anchorage (see chart on page 149), but the large boulders on the seabed make anchoring difficult. If you do try this bay, you should be aware of the small above-water rock situated just off the western headland and another lying off the land that juts out to divide the bay into two parts.

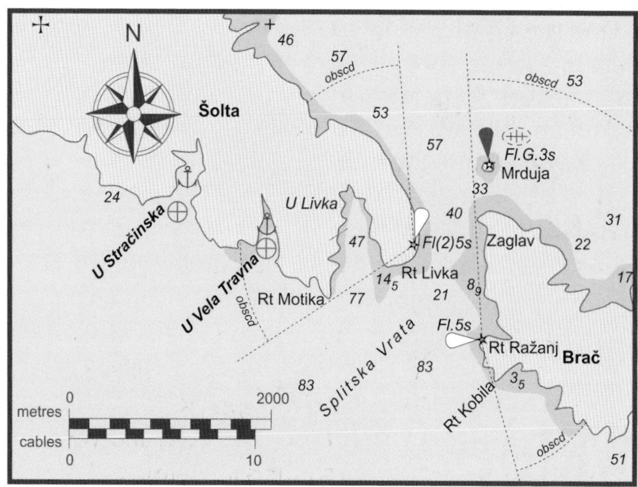

UVALA VELA TRAVNA

Entrance to bay: 43°19'.65N 16°22'.47E

Uvala Vela Travna is exposed to southerly and southwesterly winds, but is a deep bay where it is possible to anchor in depths of around 5m close to the shore. There are no facilities.

UVALA STRAČINSKA

Entrance to bay: 43°19'.89N 16°21'.71E

Uvala Stračinska is another deep bay with a fish farm at its head. However, you can anchor in the inner western inlet in depths of around 10m, sheltered from all winds except those from the south. As with Uvala Vela Travna, there are no facilities.

Useful information – Šolta

HARBOURMASTER: Obala Sv Tereze bb, Rogač, 21430, **Tel/fax:** 021 654 139.

FUEL STATION: **Tel:** 021 654 180, depth 4.5m. Open off season (1 October to 31 May), 0730 to 1100 Monday to Saturday, excluding Bank Holidays. During the season, open from 0730 to 1200 and 1600 to 1930, excluding Sundays and Bank Holidays, except from mid July to mid September when it is open on Sundays and Bank Holidays between 0800 and 1200.

TOURIST OFFICES: **Grohote: Tel:** 021 654 151; **Fax:** 021 654 130; Rogač: Sv Tereze 3, **Tel:** 021 654 491; **Stomorska:** Riva Pelegrin bb, **Tel:** 021 658 404.

POST OFFICE: Grohote bb, 21430 Grohote. Open from 0700 to 1100 and from 1800 to 2100, Monday to Saturday in the season; 0700 to 1400, Monday to Friday in the winter.

MEDICAL CENTRE: 21430 Grohote, **Tel:** 021 654 194.

BUSES: Local buses connect the main settlements with Rogač and are geared towards ferry times.

Brač Island

The third largest island, a 40-minute ferry ride from Split and with some of the highest number of sunshine hours in the region, Brač is a very popular tourist destination. Despite its proximity to the mainland, several settlements still retain their island character, but the recent press hype has led to many foreigners investing in property here, which may result in a change in ambience. Apart from the major tourist destination of Bol, most of the interest is on the northern coastline and at the eastern and western extremities. Milna, to the west, has two marinas,

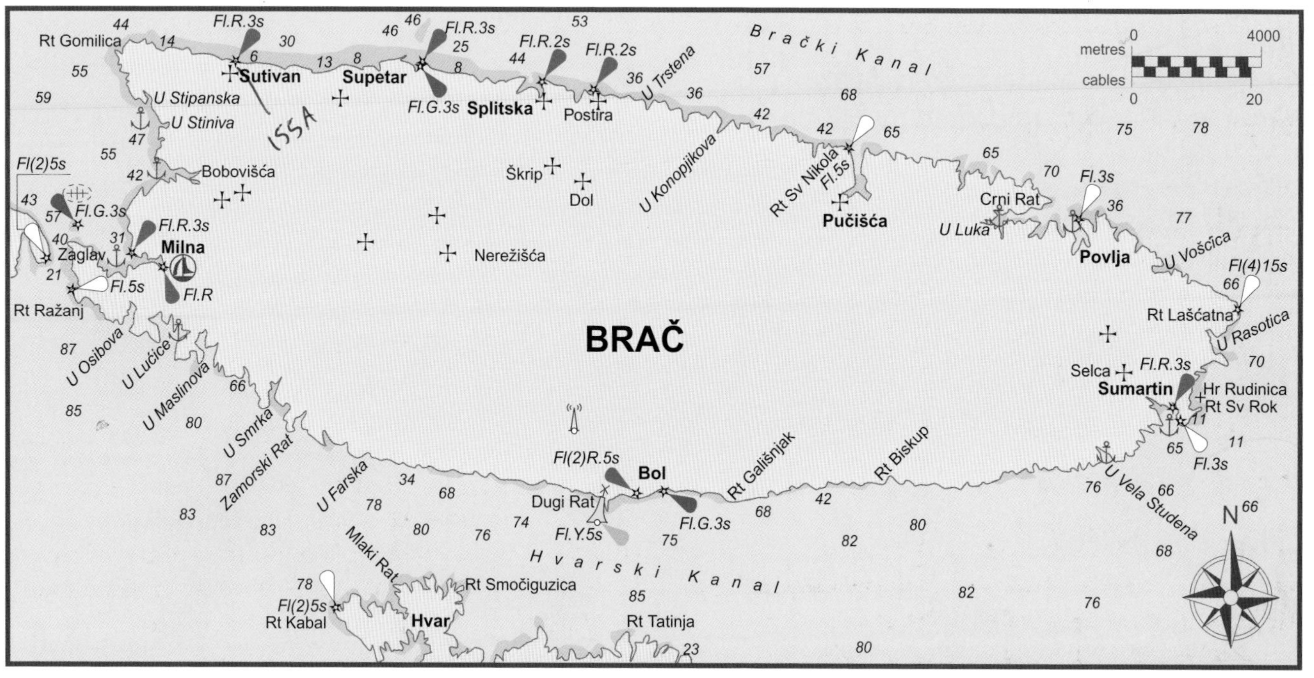

Pučišća, a traditional quarrying settlement, has a good town harbour, and Splitska, Sumartin and Povlja are well worth a stop. There are fuel stations at Milna, Bol and Sumartin. We start with Milna and work our way clockwise around the island.

TRANSPORT ON BRAČ

Supetar is the main ferry port, with up to 14 ferries a day linking it to Split. Alternatively, you can catch the ferry from Sumartin, at the other end of the island, to Makarska on the mainland (three to five services per day). From Bol you can get a ferry to Jelsa on Hvar or direct to Split (up to four services a day). Brač has a small airport but, as far as we are aware, it is mainly used by small private planes. The nearest airport is therefore Split. Local buses service the main settlements and ferry ports, and the various tourist offices should be able to find you a reasonable local taxi service if you need one. Car and bike rental details are given with each port wherever we found they were available.

Milna

Entrance to bay:
43°19'.68N
16°25'.94E

Approach to Milna: the canning factory (with tall chimney) is on the right, and the ACI marina follows after it

Milna has an ACI marina in the heart of town and a Dutch-owned marina, Marina Vlaška, just inside the entrance to the bay. It was hard to get much information out of the staff at Marina Vlaška when we visited and the prices they gave us were higher than those shown on their website. Our preference for facilities and service would be the ACI marina. Milna itself is a charming place and well worth an overnight stop. There are suggestions of a third marina planned for the town, on the site of the canning factory.

NAVIGATION

Charts: HHI MK-16 & MK-18; AC 2712, SC5767

Approaches: The approach is clear from all directions, apart from the small islet of Mrduja (Fl G 3s), which guards the entrance.

Pilotage: As the bay narrows, there's a red light (Fl R 3s) to port on Rt Bijaka, after which is an inlet, also to port, that is home to Marina Vlaška. You will then pass a canning factory to starboard, followed by the road inland and, lastly, the fuel station.

The head of the bay splits into two inlets. To port is an area for local boats while to starboard is the marina. On the shore, in the middle of these two areas, is a red light.

BERTHING

The ACI marina can be contacted on VHF Channel 17, Tel: 021 636 306. A Category II marina, it is open all year round, with 144 berths and 15 dry berths. Depths are between 2.5 and 7m.

Prices are €3.6 to €4 per metre per day for a 10 to 20m

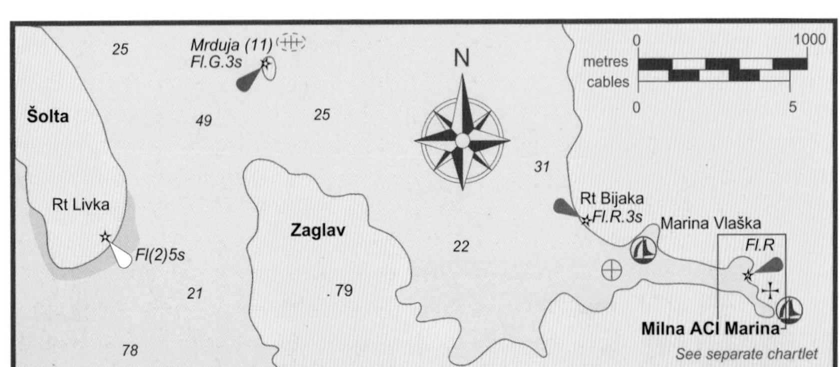

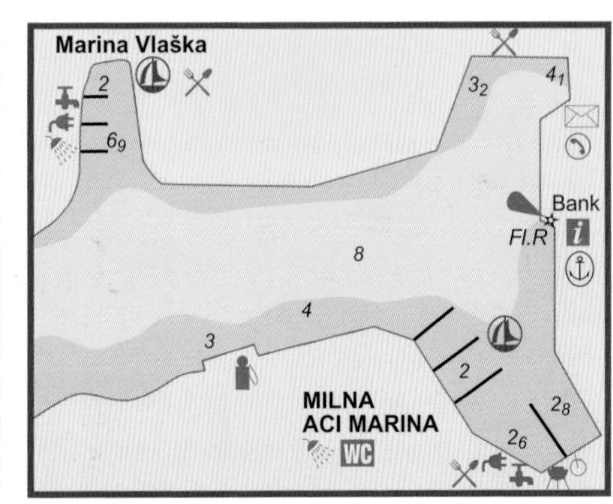

(33 and 66ft) boat plus 10% in July and August. Note that there is a relatively new pontoon bisecting the head of the inlet in a northwesterly direction, which may not appear in some guides.

The Bora blows strongly here but the bay, in different parts, is well protected in winds from all directions.

Milna ACI Marina

Useful information – Milna

FACILITIES

In addition to the standard ACI facilities, the marina has a **repair workshop**, a 10-ton **crane** and a 120-ton **slipway**. The nearby **shipyard** specialises in wooden boats. The **fuel** station, Tel: 021 636 340, has depths of 3m and is open off season (1 October to 31 May) from 0800 to 1200, Monday to Saturday, excluding Bank Holidays. During the season, its opening hours are from 0800 to 1300 and from 1700 to 2000, excluding Sundays and Bank Holidays when it is open between 0800 and 1300.

PROVISIONING

Most of the shops and facilities are around the head of the bay. The **tourist information centre** is next to Splitska **bank**, with the **post office** a little further north-west. There are plenty of **shops** and **supermarkets.** The **post office** is open from 0800 to 1200 and from 1800 to 2100 Monday to Saturday during the season and from 0700 to 1400 Monday to Friday at all other times.

EATING OUT

There are at least six restaurants and pizzerias in Milna and the ACI marina has a restaurant and bar. Fontana (Tel: 021 636 285) at the head of the northern inner inlet, is open all year round, but seemed a little clinical. We particularly liked Konoba Dupini (Tel: 098 180 6216) which has its tables and chairs laid out in a back street just behind the harbour.

ASHORE

The **tourist office**, Tel: 021 636 233; email: tzo-milna@st.htnet.hr, is open in the season between 0800 and 1500 Monday to Saturday, and from 1700 to 1900 on Sundays. There's plenty of literature and a book on Brač that you can buy. Nike, signposted from the shore as a 1,000m walk, offers tennis, a disco and a restaurant. Note that Milna is not an ideal place for swimming, so it is better to head to Bobovišća, about three miles further north.

OTHER INFORMATION

Harbourmaster: Next to Splitska Bank, Riva 7, 21405 Milna, Tel/fax: 021 636 205.
ACI marina: 21405 Milna, Tel: 021 636 306; Fax: 021 636 272; email: m.milna@aci-club.hr; website: www.aci-club.hr.
Marina Vlaška: Pantera bb, 21405 Milna, Tel/fax: 021 636 247; email: info@marinavlaska.com; website: www.marinavlaska.com. Basic facilities and if you drive there by car, be prepared for a lot of reversing on a narrow road when you return, as there's rarely anywhere to turn round.
Medical centre: Tel: 021 636 109, near the root of the new ACI marina pontoon.

The church at Milna

Bobovišća

Entrance to bay: 43°21'.23N 16°26'.52E
Charts: HHI MK-16, MK-18; AC 2712, SC5767

This is a quiet anchorage, although popular with the charter companies. The approach is clear from all directions and the bay can be identified by the disused quarry on the north shore. The inlet divides into two parts: the anchorage, where mooring buoys have also been laid, is in the northern inlet, while the village lies at the head of the southern inlet. Recently mooring buoys have been laid in this southern inlet as well as in the entrance to the bay, close to the northern shore. The anchorage is operated, on a concession, by local sports association Vrila. The holding here is good, on a mud bed, in depths of up to 5m.

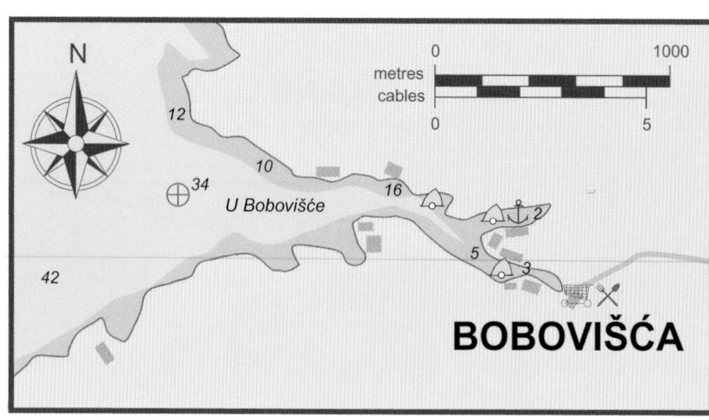

Small local craft at the quay in Bobovišća

The outer part of the inlet is exposed to the Bora and winds from the south-west, through west, to north-west. The inner part of the inlet is well protected, but southwesterly winds do cause a swell. Apart from a grocery shop and a couple of restaurants – Konoba Vala and Grill Rasa – there are not many other signs of life.

Uvala Stipanska

Entrance to bay: 43°22'.35N 16°26'.44E
Charts: HHI MK-16, MK-18; AC 2712, SC5767

Another popular anchorage in a bay with just one stone house, part of which is roofless. The approach is straightforward. A few mooring buoys have been laid but you can anchor on a sand and weed bed, which provides good holding in 2 to 4m. The bay is exposed to winds from the south, but is otherwise well protected.

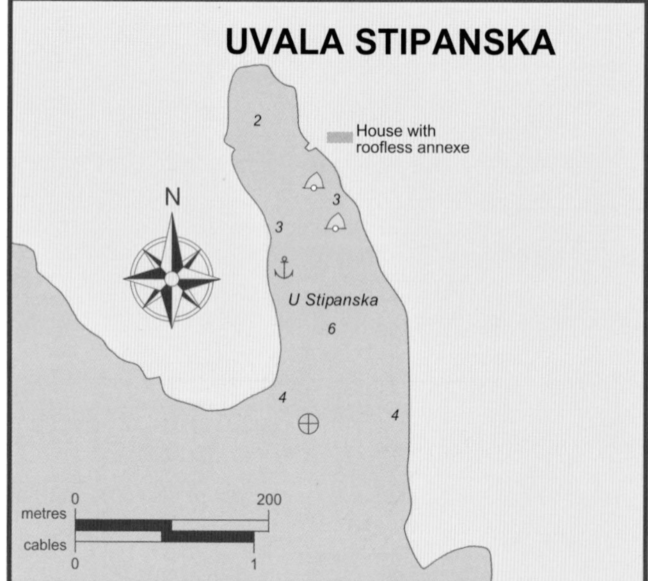

Sutivan

Harbour: 43°23'.30N 16°28'.61E
Charts: HHI MK-18; AC 2712, SC5767

Sutivan is clearly identified by its magnificent tall church spire with a cupola. It's a friendly port with plenty of life. There are no hazards on the approach and the harbour, with a red light (Fl R 3s) at the end of the breakwater, is close to the church. If space is available, you can berth bows- or stern-to at the breakwater in depths of around 2m. The main square has a post office, tourist office, supermarket and mini-market, and the place is dotted with restaurants and bars. There are also a number of shops, a bank, cash points and pharmacy. The tourist office can provide information on the various places of interest, including the Church of St Rok, which was

Sutivan Harbour

Sutivan's main café area around the harbour

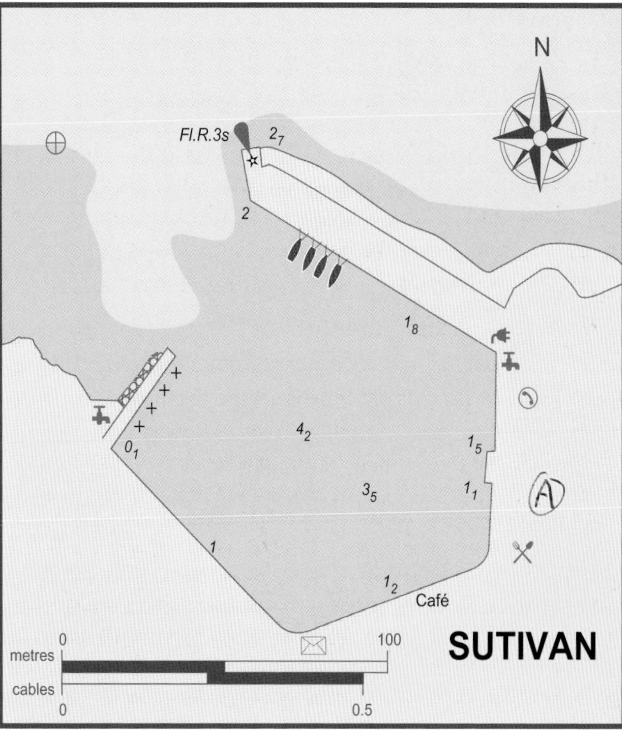

built in 1623, expanded in 1788 and had a bell tower added in 1879.

USEFUL INFORMATION

Tourist office: Blato bb, 21403 Sutivan, Tel: 021 638 357; Fax: 021 717 544; email: tzo-sutivan@inet.hr; website: www.sutivan.hr.
Post office: Sutivan bb, 21403 Sutivan. Opening hours are as Milna – see page 153.
Police: Tel: 021 631 145.
Pharmacy: Tel: 021 631 714.
Taxi: Tel: 098 264 619; 098 265 692.
Diving: Dive Centar Atlantis, Tel: 0989 455 930.
Beaches: Reasonable beaches can be found on either side of the town centre.

Supetar

Harbour: 43°23'.23N 16°33'.16E
Charts: HHI MK-18; AC 2712, SC5767

Although Supetar is both the main town and ferry port of Brač, and the island's principal tourist town, it's not a bad land base for a couple of days. The Riva bustles with bars and boutiques, the summer festival provides entertainment most nights in the high season and there are some decent beaches nearby. However, it's not a particularly comfortable harbour, with a good

The inner breakwater with green light (Fl G 3s)

deal of traffic from the ferries and day-tripper boats. The northerly wind blows strongly here and can cause a swell, while the Sirocco and Bora at times generate heavy seas in front of the harbour. The best place to berth, if there's any space, is alongside on the inner wall of the inner breakwater in depths of up to 3m. Water and electricity are available. The sign suggests that boats under 20m (66ft) will be charged 100 Kunas for electricity and 30 Kunas for water.

When approaching the harbour entrance there are no real hazards to watch out for. Landmarks include an impressive white mausoleum east of the town, built in 1927 and belonging to the Petrinović family, and the tall church tower, which is also clearly visible. The outer and inner breakwaters are marked by a red (Fl R 3s) and green light (Fl G 3s) respectively.

Ashore you'll find everything you need – a wide range of shops, a post office, a bank, cash points,

A few of the many bars and restaurants around Supetar's harbour

several restaurants and bars and some good beaches. Try Konoba Vinotoka, Jobova 6, Tel: 021 630 969, or Restaurant Dolac, Tel: 021 630 446, which has a large terrace and is a short walk up a side street just past the church. Both restaurants are well signposted from the town centre. Just over a mile from the centre, the old village of Mirca has some attractive traditional houses, though new developments have stretched the settlement down to the sea.

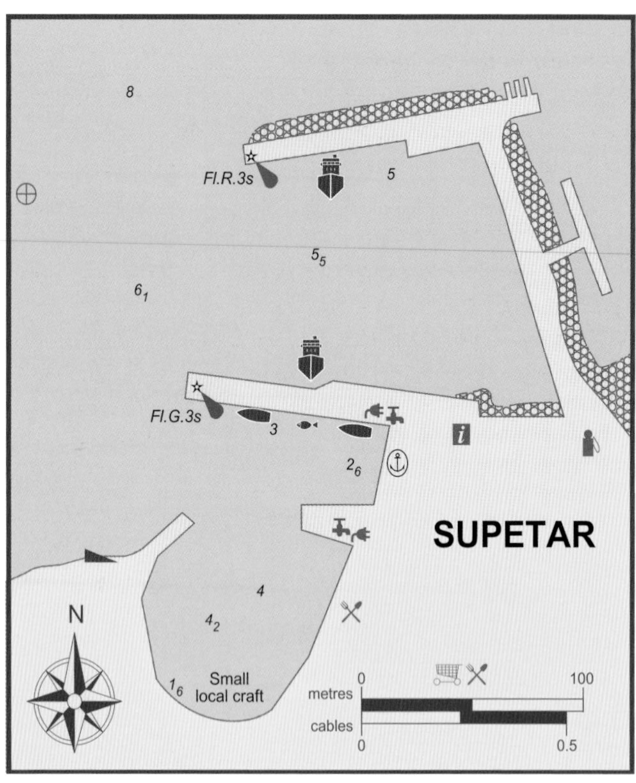

USEFUL INFORMATION

Harbourmaster: By the ferry pier, Porat 4, 21400 Supetar, Tel/fax: 021 631 116.

Tourist office: At the root of the ferry pier, Porat 1, 21400 Supetar, Tel: 021 630 551; email: tzg-supetar@st.htnet.hr; website: www.supetar.hr

Post office: Just west of the harbour, Vlačića 13, 21400 Supetar. Open from 0730 to 2100 Monday to Saturday in the season, otherwise from 0700 to 2000 Monday to Friday and from 0700 to 1300 on Saturdays.

Medical centre: Tel: 021 631 222.

Pharmacy: In the main square by the church.

Supermarket: Kerum in the main square and a few smaller stores. There's also a wine shop just off the main square.

Car/scooter hire: Gentours, Tel: 021 630 266, situated by the harbour.

Bike hire: Tel: 021 631 014/ 091 516 5126.

Splitska

Entrance to bay: 43°23'.06N 16°36'.17E
Charts: HHI MK-18; AC 2712, SC5767

Another classic Croatian settlement and the source of the stone used to build Diocletian's Palace in Split. The bay is divided into two inlets, with the village lying in the easternmost part. There are no approach hazards and the church tower is visible from a distance. The red light (Fl R 2s) on the east headland of the eastern inlet is not so easy to spot and was partially obscured by trees when we visited. You can either moor alongside

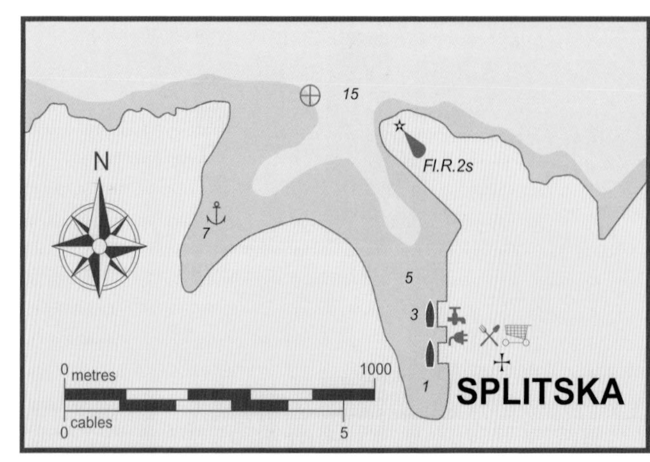

the quay in the eastern inlet, in depths of up to 3m, or anchor in the western inlet in depths of 4 to 10m. No anchoring is permitted in the eastern inlet where there are underwater cables. Electricity and water are available at the quay. Both locations are exposed to northerly winds, the anchorage is open to the Bora and the town quay is exposed to north westerlies. You'll find a couple of good restaurants, bars, a bakery and a supermarket ashore.

About two miles inland lies the village of Škrip, the oldest settlement on Brač. The museum of Brač is located in an old building belonging to the Radojković family and there are some lovely traditional houses and churches in the village.

Barbecue and café area around Splitska harbour

Postira

Harbour: 43°22'.79E 16°37'.57E
Charts: HHI MK-18; AC 2712, SC5767

Unfortunately Postira has become a little run down with even the town plan on the wall barely legible. It has a large, package-type hotel and some old fishing boats, but not much in the way of shops or restaurants. If you do decide to stop here the approach is clear and the red light (Fl R 2s) on the breakwater is distinguished by its square stone tower and red dome. You'll also see the hotel from a distance, currently painted royal blue and white, and a church tower that is much higher than the other buildings surrounding it. Local boats use the quay, while the fishing boats tend to stack up inside the breakwater with the odd tourist boat using the inner pier. It's best, therefore, to berth where you can, in depths of between 1.3 and 5m, looking out

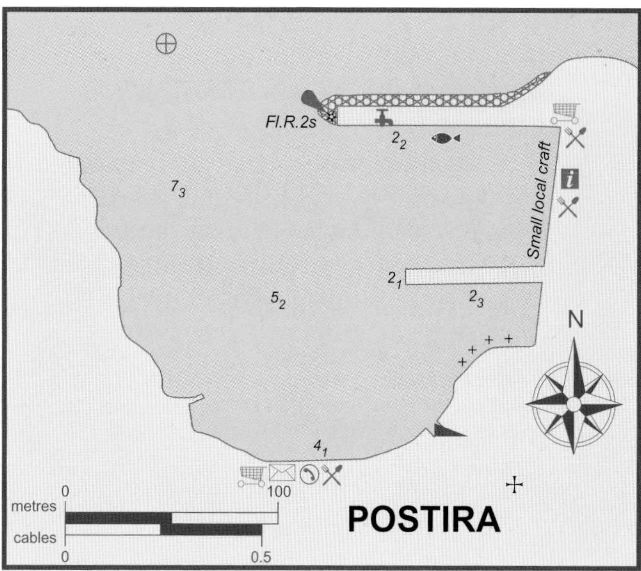

for rocks close to the quay. The harbour is exposed to winds from the north and north-west, which also cause

Yachts and fishing boats vying for space on the inner side of Postira's breakwater

a swell. Ashore, clustered around the harbour, you'll find a tourist office, a few restaurants and bars, a bank, a supermarket and a post office.

USEFUL INFORMATION

Tourist office: By the harbour, Tel: 021 632 966; Fax: 021 632 107.

Post office: Postira bb, 21410 Postira. Opening hours are the same as at Milna in the season; 0800 to 1500 Monday to Friday off-season.

Medical centre: Tel: 021 632 209.

Two of Postira's cafés and the somewhat faded town plan

Pučišća

Entrance to bay: 43°21'.75N 16°44'.30E

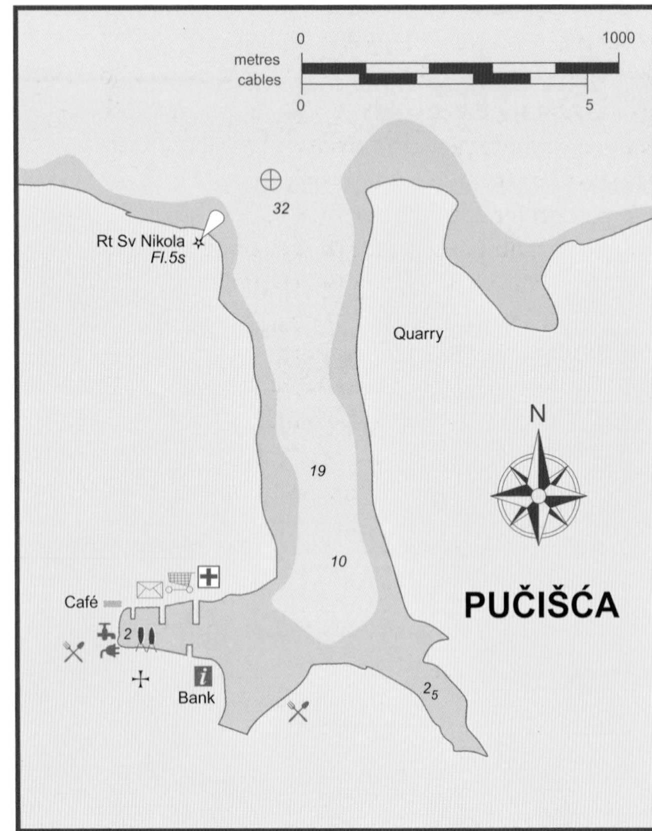

Pučišća was one of our favourite overnight stops, though the church bells were the loudest we've heard in Croatia. The entrance to the long inlet is readily identified by the stone quarry on the eastern headland and the village itself appears to be thriving on the profits of quarrying. Even the streetlights are made of white stone. The locals are therefore indifferent to tourists and you will be treated the same as everyone else.

NAVIGATION

Charts: HHI MK-18; AC 2712, SC5767

Approaches: The approach is straightforward. Once you have passed the quarry on the eastern side of the inlet and the lighthouse to the west of the entrance, it's about a mile to the harbour. The inlet divides into two and the harbour and town are in the western part. You'll see the church tower with a red cupola from a distance, similar in style to Sutivan's church. The visitors' berths are to port, inside the small breakwater, by the church.

BERTHING/FACILITIES

Berth bows- or stern-to, using the lazylines provided, in depths of about 3m. There are around 26 berths, and a 10m (33ft) yacht will cost about 150 Kunas per night. Electricity and water are available and rubbish bins have been installed.

Visitors' berths at Pučišća

ASHORE

There's a small private tourist agency next to Splitska bank on the south side of the inlet, heading east from the moorings. On the other side are a chemist, post office (opening hours as at Postira) and supermarket. We ate at Konoba Lado (Tel: 021 633 069) which, well signposted, is up some stone steps just off the head of the inlet. Perhaps a little more expensive than average, it offers good food and ambience. Otherwise there are a few other restaurants and pizzerias to try. The hotel bar is full of locals and you'll find a diving centre and a few shops around the bay.

BRAC

Povlja

Entrance to bay: 43°20'.72N 16°49'.53E
Charts: HHI MK-18; AC 1574; AC 2712, SC5767

Povlja itself is a small, quiet settlement with a new post office and tourist office, some bars, restaurants and a couple of shops.

The large bay divides up into several smaller inlets. The village and harbour lie at the end of the easternmost inlet but the westernmost inlet, Luka, provides a very well-sheltered anchorage. The approach to the bay is straightforward, though there is a shallow area around the eastern headland, which is lit (Fl 3s). Luka has three smaller inlets that afford a variety of options – lazylines at the quay by the restaurant, mooring buoys, or you can anchor on a sand and mud bed with good holding in depths of between 3 and 8m. Apart from the restaurant, there are no other facilities in the bay.

If you prefer a little more life then head for the village harbour, aiming for the tall church tower set back from the shore. The inner part of the quay shoals considerably on the western side, but depths by the quay and pier in the eastern part of the harbour are between 2 and 4m until very close to the quay. There's not always much space here, but water and electrics are available. The Bora blows strongly, although does not pose any problems; the harbour is exposed to winds from the north and north-west.

Povlja village looking towards the mainland

USEFUL INFORMATION

Tourist office: Tel: 021 639 252, is open in the season from 0800 to 1200 and 1800 to 2100 Monday to Friday.
Post office: Open weekdays only, Tel: 021 639 017.
Bank: The nearest bank is inland at Selca, but there is an ATM at the new fuel station at Sumartin.
Adria Diving Centre: Tel: 091 767 9463.

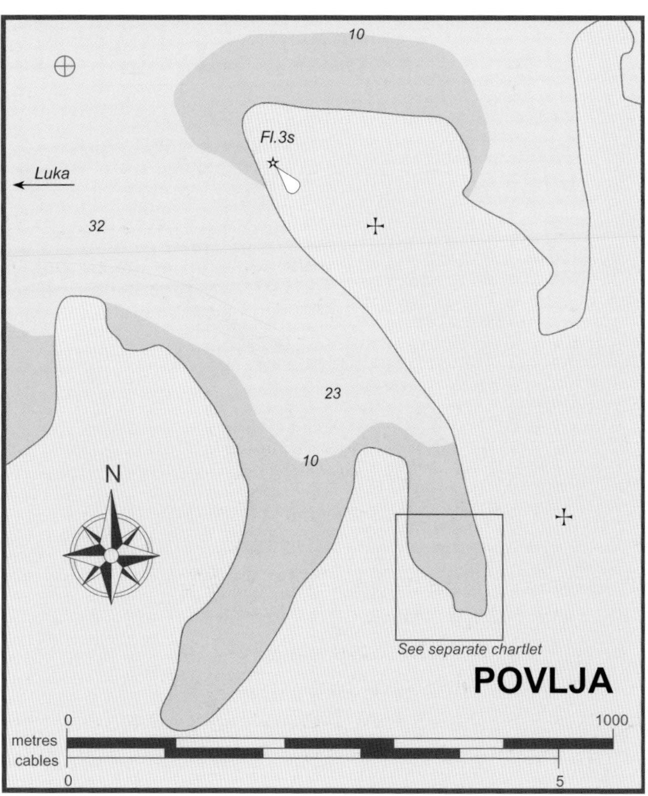

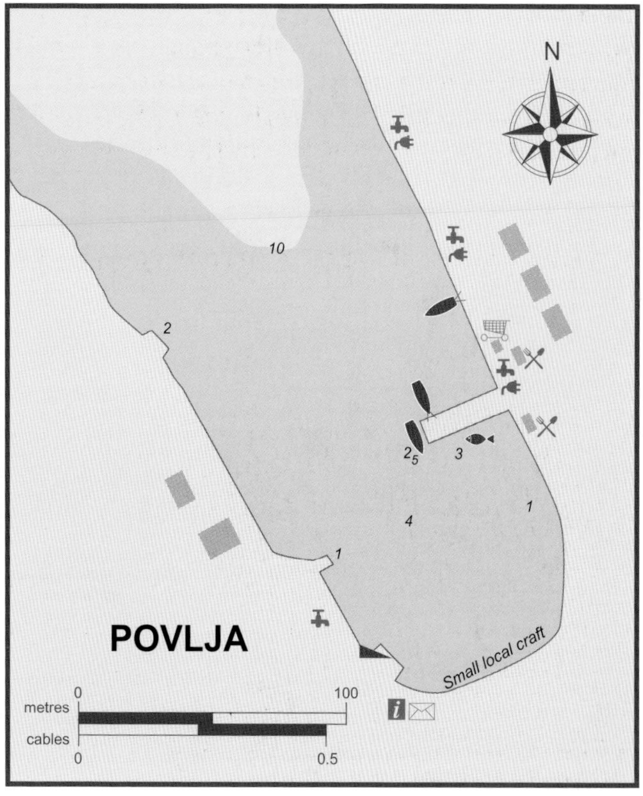

Uvala Rasotica

Anchorage: 43°18'.23N 16°53'.64E
Charts: HHI MK-18; AC 1574, SC5767

A lovely, secluded anchorage, with no facilities. Suitable really for just one boat to be at anchor, Uvala Rasotica should only be used in settled weather as it's exposed to the Bora and Sirocco. The sand and weed bed provides reasonable holding in depths of 2 to 8m.

Uvala Rasotica

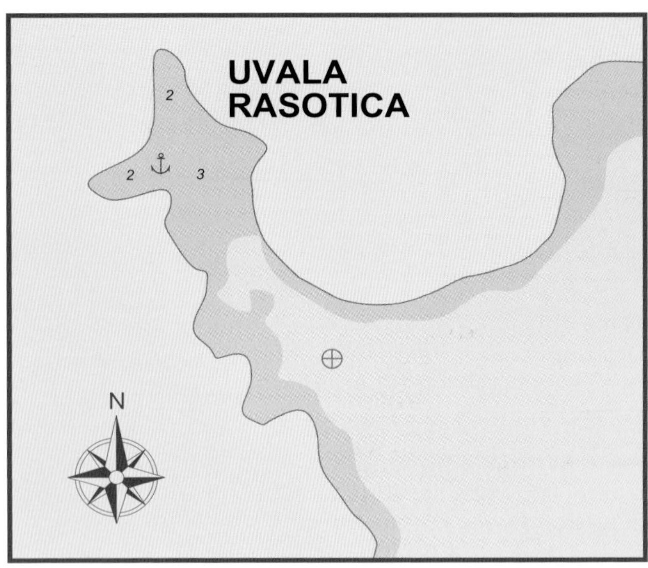

Sumartin

Harbour: 43°17'.04N 16°52'.24E
Charts: HHI MK-18; AC 1574, AC 2712, SC5767

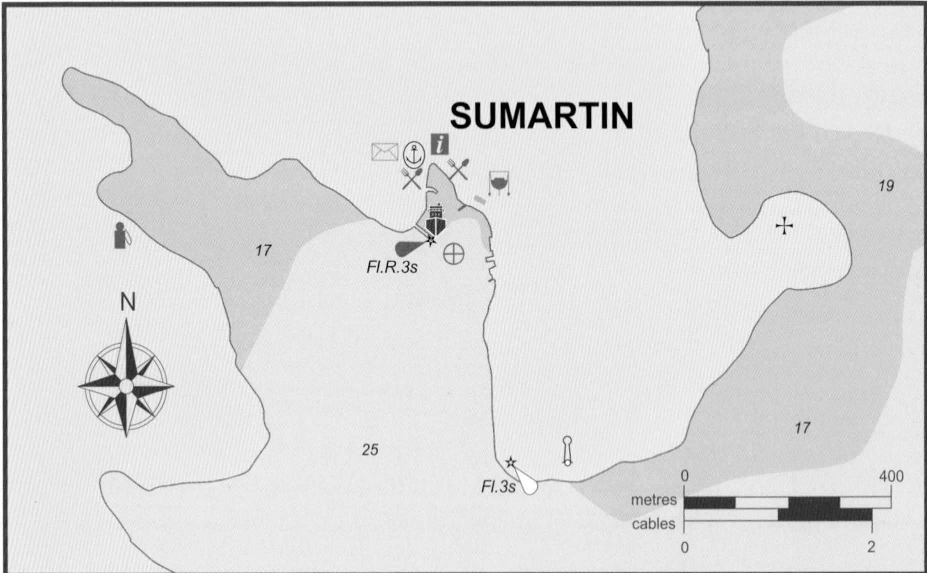

Situated on the south side of the east coast of Brač, Sumartin connects to the mainland at Makarska by ferry. It's a small settlement with a relatively large fishing fleet and a brand new fuel station cut into the rocks.

The approach is straightforward but, if coming from the north, do not hug the coastline as there is a rock and shallows just off the coast, half a mile north of Rt Sumartin. Useful landmarks include a church on Rt Sv Rok, to the east of Rt Sumartin, and a low-lying lighthouse on Rt Sumartin itself. The fuel station is to port as you enter the bay and has a cash point.

Berth bows- or stern-to in the main harbour, where you can find a space in depths of up to 3m. Winds from the south cause a swell and the Bora blows strongly in this area.

The tourist information office (Tel: 021 648 209) is at the head of the bay next to the post office (opening

The red light on Sumartin's outer breakwater

hours as at Postira on page 158) and there are three or four restaurants, an ice-cream parlour, a supermarket and a kiosk here. About two miles inland is the village of Selca, which has a bank, tourist office, pharmacy, medical centre and more shops.

Harbourmaster: Tel: 021 648 222.

Right: Sumartin's fuel station cut into the rocks

Bol and the south coast of Brač

The south coast of Brač is mostly inhospitable and uninhabited. Bol, in the centre of the south coast, is the exception, but is not an ideal place to stop in unsettled weather and can get very busy in the height of the season.

Perhaps the best way to visit Bol is to put into Jelsa on Hvar and make the short ferry passage across. There are two feasible anchorages on the south coast: Uvala Vela Studena, towards the eastern end of the island, and Uvala Lučice at the western end. Uvala Osibova, also at the western end, is mentioned in some guide books, but is really too deep for most pleasure vessels.

If you have time, it is worth looking at Uvala Smrka, otherwise known as James Bond Bay, which lies towards the western end of the south coast, where there is a well-concealed submarine cave.

Bol

Harbour: 43°15'.59N 16°39'.42E

Bol is a lovely place to spend a couple of days as a land-based tourist and there is always its famous beach, Dugi Rat (sometimes known as Zlatni Rat), to investigate, though it's about a mile west of the town. This must be the most photographed beach in Croatia and features in the majority of tourist brochures. Even close up it looks like sand, however, it is in fact a long, narrow pebble peninsula stretching out into the sea, which changes shape with the tides and currents and is a centre for all kinds of watersports, particularly windsurfing.

The breakwater/ferry pier has a green light (Fl G 3s) on the end of it and marks the eastern boundary of the harbour. The fuel station is just west of the most westerly pier. The visitors' moorings lie between the middle pier (red light – Fl (2) R 5s) and the most westerly pier.

Bol's visitors' berths with red and green lights in the background

NAVIGATION

Charts: HHI MK-18; AC 2712, SC5767

Approaches: The only hazards are the beach and the shallows around it, which are marked by a yellow isolated danger buoy, although this can be difficult to spot from a distance. Near to the beach is a white holiday apartment complex and, since Bol is the only settlement of any size on the south coast, it's hard to miss.

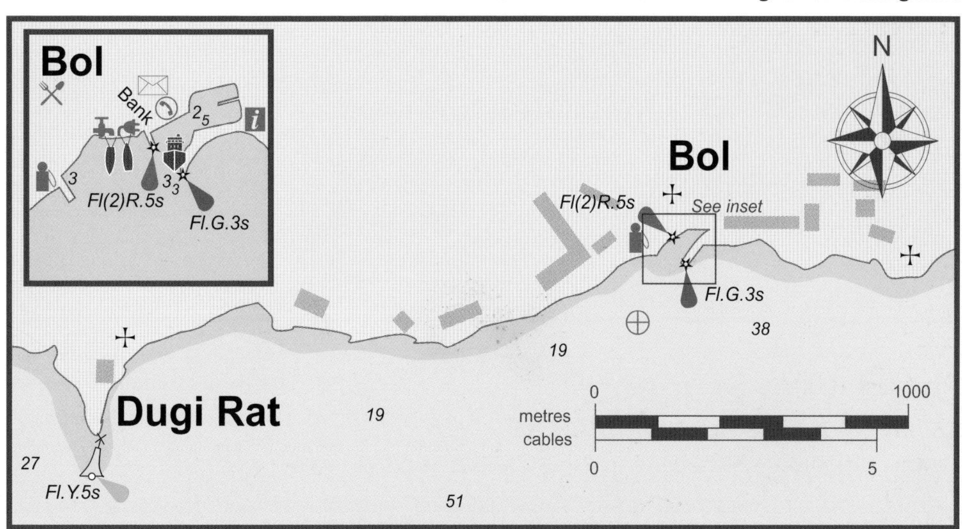

The compact and charming centre of Bol

Useful information – Bol

BERTHING/FACILITES

Moor bows- or stern-to at the quay in depths of 2 to 3m or alongside the inner side of the eastern breakwater. Berthing fees will be payable. A new quay has recently been laid west of the red light, and is fitted with lazylines as well as **electricity** and **water** pedestals. The **fuel** station (Tel: 021 635 119) has depths of 3.5m and is open from 0700 to 2000 Monday to Saturday and from 0700 to 1200 on Sunday between 1 June and 30 September, otherwise from 0800 to 1200 and 1600 to 1900 Monday to Saturday. The harbour is well sheltered except from the Bora and southwesterly winds, which can cause a swell.

ASHORE

Bol is a buzzing town with all the expected facilities and more. The **tourist office** (Tel: 021 635 638) is just east of the main breakwater. The **post office**, Uz Pjacu 5, 21420 Bol, is a couple of streets behind the middle pier and open from 0730 to 2100 Monday to Saturday in the summer, otherwise from 0800 to 1500 Monday to Friday and 0800 to 1300 on Saturdays. Splitska **bank** is near the post office and there are numerous **cash points**. The **supermarkets**, **bakeries**, **pharmacy** and **shops** are mostly just behind the harbour, a couple of streets in, while the **bars** and **restaurants** are concentrated directly around the seafront.

Restaurant Ribarska Kućica (Tel: 021 635 033) is an upmarket seafood restaurant with its own beach, a short walk east of the centre, although you don't have to walk far to find somewhere that suits you.

If you don't have the energy to walk to the main beach, there are some lovely small **beaches** just east of the centre and, further east, you will find a Dominican monastery **museum**. To the west of the town are the hotel and apartment complexes, as well as a large tennis centre that hosts international tournaments.

OTHER INFORMATION

Harbourmaster: Up the steps just behind the harbour, Tel: 021 635 903.
Car hire: Boltours, V Nazora 18, Tel: 021 635 693.
Medical centre: Porat Bolskih Pomoraca, 21420 Bol, Tel: 021 635 112.
Pharmacy: Porat Bolskih Pomoraca bb, 21420 Bol, Tel: 021 635 987.
Diving: Delfin Bol, Tel: 021 635 367; Big Blue Diving, Tel: 021 306 222.

Uvala Vela Studena

Entrance to bay: 43°16'.09N 16°50'.63E
Charts: HHI MK-18, MK-20; AC 1574, AC 2712, SC5767

A couple of miles west of Sumartin, this bay offers an anchorage that is protected from winds from the west, through north, to east.

Anchor in 6 to 10m near the head of the bay. The approach is straightforward, but note that there are no facilities in this bay at all.

Uvala Lučice

Entrance to bay: 43°18'.02N 16°26'.94E
Charts: HHI MK-16, MK-18; AC 2712, SC5767

Lučice is a large bay with smaller inlets at its head. Rt Križ, which forms the western boundary of the bay, has shallow water around it, but apart from that the approach is clear.

The westernmost inlet has mooring buoys, but you can anchor further out or in the middle inlet, in depths of up to 12m. Again, watch out for very shallow water around the inlets, particularly the western boundary of the most easterly cove.

Southwesterly winds cause heavy seas, but otherwise the anchorage affords good all-round protection depending on where you anchor or moor. There are no facilities.

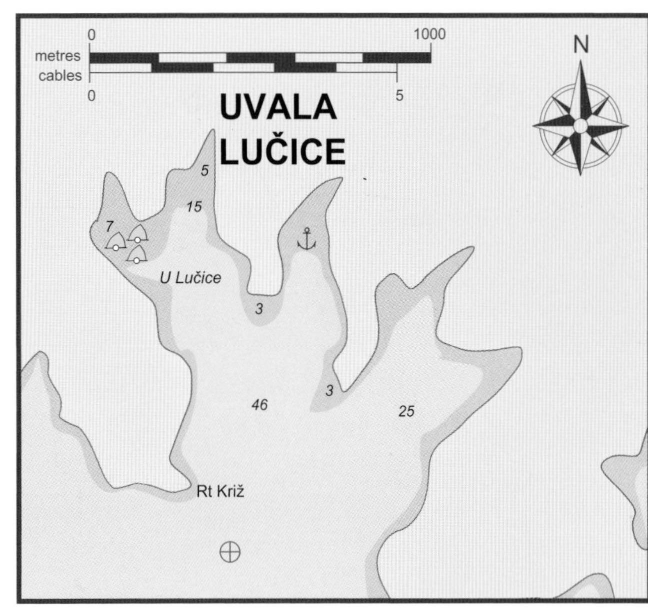

Hvar Island and the Pakleni Islands

Of all Croatia's islands, Hvar is probably the best known. It enjoys the most hours of sunshine in the region and its major town, Hvar, with its nightclub Carpe Diem, is popular with the jet set. The town has a great history and some lovely architecture, but it has become too commercial for us. Hvar Town harbour is a busy port full of tripper boats and yachts. If you manage to find a space, it can be quite bumpy with all the traffic. One alternative is the ACI marina about 2 miles away on the island of Sveti Klement, which has water taxis to and from Hvar Town. Sveti Klement is the largest of the Pakleni Islands and has a number of good anchorages. Marinkovak, east of Sv Klement, has two reasonable anchorages, while further east again is Jerolim, a naturist island with only two possible anchorages, although these are over 7m deep and generally roped off for swimmers. Navigating around the Pakleni Islands is definitely not recommended at night and even during the day some of the low-lying rocks are very difficult to spot, so be careful. Also be aware that currents can be strong in the channels between the islets, particularly in southerly winds. The majority of the settlements on Hvar are concentrated on the western half of the north coast. Stari Grad is a comfortable ferry port, Vrboska has a good municipal harbour and another ACI marina, and Jelsa is a fast-growing town with plenty of new restaurants opening up everywhere. East of Hvar, on the south coast, Milna is a small village with a secure anchorage and a few good restaurants. The western half of the south coast doesn't have much to offer in the way of shelter, but there are some anchorages as you head further east. At the eastern tip of Hvar is Sućuraj, a quiet, attractive village with a ferry connection to the mainland.

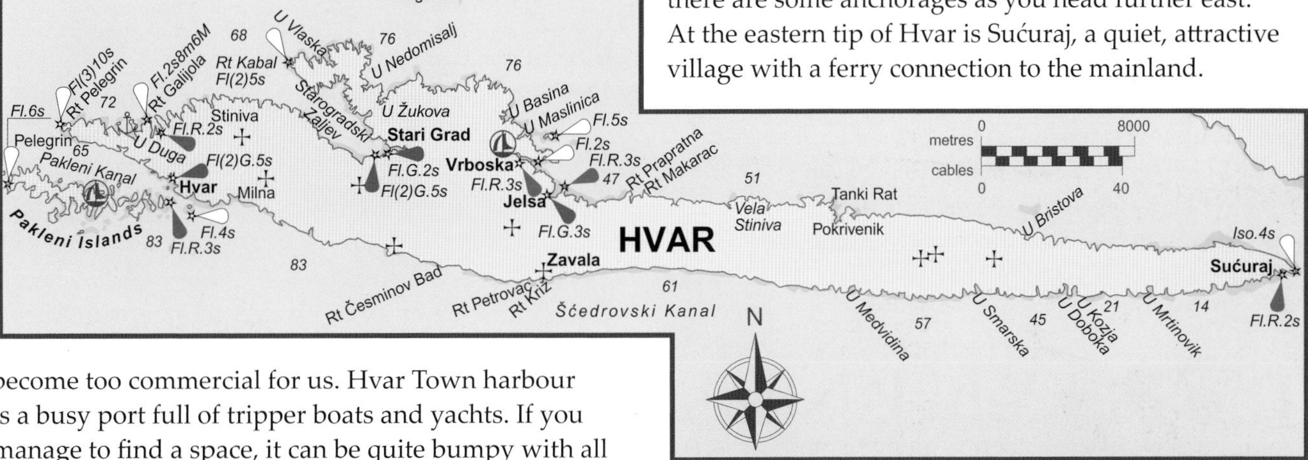

Starboard light on the ferry quay, as you enter Hvar bay

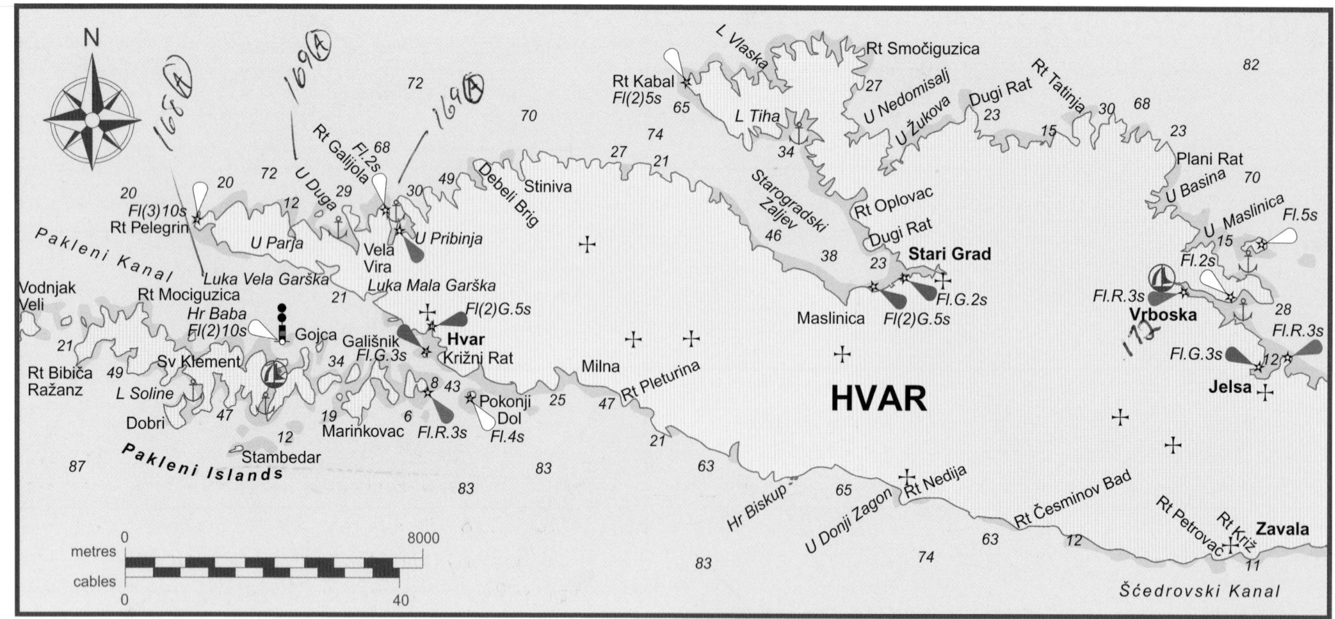

Scattered around are a number of smaller settlements and anchorages. In this chapter, we start with the Pakleni Islands and then, starting with Hvar Town, work our way clockwise around Hvar island. Fuel stations can be found both at Hvar Town and Vrboska (ACI marina).

TRANSPORT ON HVAR

The nearest airport is Split, with ferries connecting Hvar to Split from Hvar Town, Stari Grad and Jelsa (via Bol). There are three to five services a day depending on the season, but note that the services to Hvar Town and Jelsa are for foot passengers only. At the other end of the island, Sućuraj connects to Drvenik on the mainland and has up to 10 ferries a day. There are local ferries between Jerolim and Hvar and also between Hvar and Vis and Bol. Buses link the main settlements to the ferry ports and are timed accordingly.

Hvar Town

The Pakleni Islands

Charts: HHI 536, MK-19; AC 269, AC 2712, SC5767

By far the largest island is Sv Klement with its ACI marina. However, the surrounding small islets and the south coast of Sv Klement provide good shelter, and we explore the anchorages after detailing what's available in and around the marina.

As an alternative to the marina, there's a delightful and popular anchorage in the bay opposite it, Uvala Vinogradišće (see page 165), on the south coast of Sv Klement. The bay has access to the same great choice of restaurants and provides an idyllic and tranquil setting for a relaxing overnight stay.

The Pakleni Islands

Sv Klement Island, Palmižana

Entrance to bay: 43°09'.95N 16°23'.84E

NAVIGATION

Approaches: Approaching from the north, Hrid Baba, a low-lying rock, is situated just north of the entrance to the bay and is marked by an isolated danger beacon, lit at night (Fl (2) 10s). It has shallow water around it, so stay well clear. To the east, Gojca Islet has a 3m shoal surrounding it that extends approximately 500m south. There's an unmarked rock between Borovac and Planikovac islets and the waters around most of these islets are shallow, so watch depths carefully. Approaching from the south, between Borovac and Sv Klement, depths reduce to below 5m. The entrance to the marina is marked by an ACI sign.

BERTHING

The Category III marina is open from the beginning of April to the end of September and has 160 berths. Prices range from €3.8 to €4.35 per metre per day for a 10 to 20m (33 and 66ft) boat, plus 10% in July and August. The marina is well protected in all winds from all directions, and can be contacted on VHF Channel 17; Pakleni Otoci, 21450 Hvar, Tel: 021 744 995; Fax: 021 744 985; email: m.palmizana@aci-club.hr; website: www.aci-club.hr.

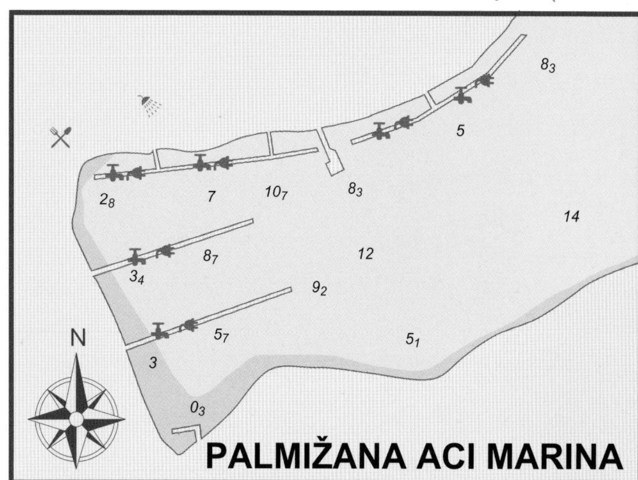

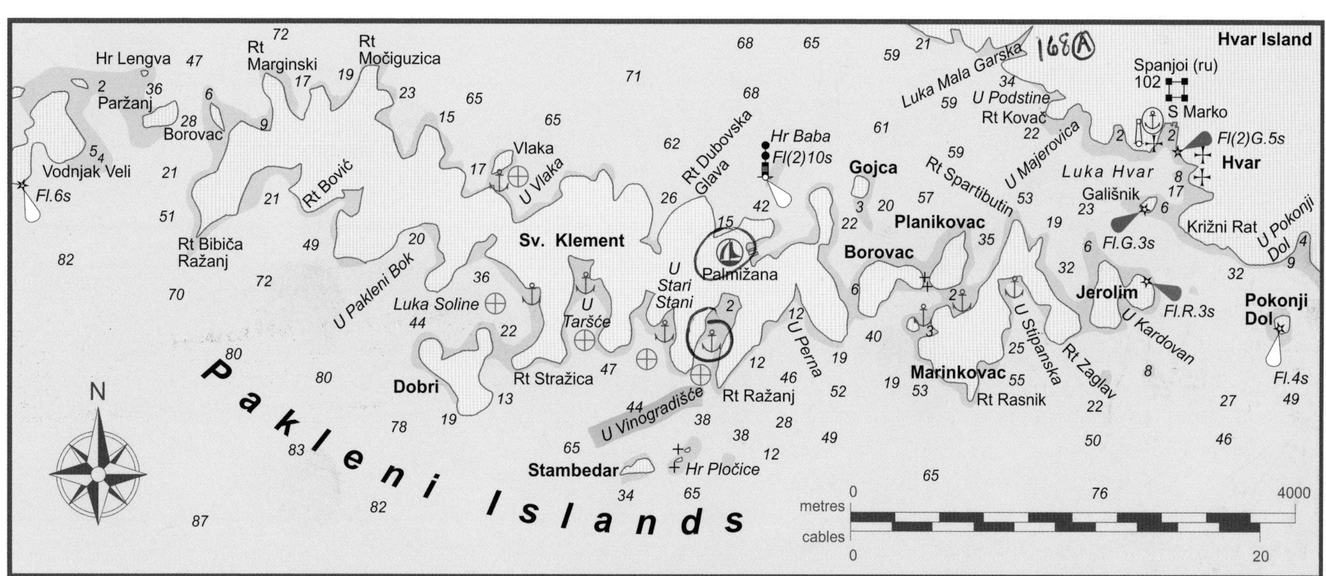

Useful information – Palmižana ACI Marina

FACILITIES

Facilities are more limited here than at other ACI marinas, as far as repairs are concerned, but it has a **shop** and **café**. There are **water taxis** to Hvar town for around 20 Kunas for a return ticket in July and August, Tel: 098 942 6155.

EATING OUT

A short walk over the hill to Uvala Vinogradišće, the bay on the other side of the island, will bring you to a number of excellent restaurants, mainly signposted from the head of the bay. With spectacular views from most of them, they all offer a varied menu. Prices are a little higher than on the mainland, but not extortionately so. We ate at Gostionica Zori, Tel: 021 718 231; email: info@zori.hr; website: www.zori.hr, but the others looked equally good.

Uvala Vinogradišće

Entrance to bay: 43°09'.08N 16°23'.21E

This bay, on the south of the island, shares the same restaurants as the ACI marina (see above) and is a popular anchorage. If approaching from the south, look out for Hrid Pločice with its surrounding shoals and rocks, which lie about 750m south of the entrance to the bay. To the west of Hrid Pločice is the islet of Stambedar.

The bay is exposed to winds and seas from the south, but offers good holding on a sand bottom in depths of 3 to 10m.

Uvala Stari Stani

Entrance to bay: 43°09'.19N 16°22'.87E

Immediately west of Uvala Vinogradišće, but without easy land access to the restaurants, this bay shares the same protection as its neighbour. Moderate holding on a sand and weed bed in depths of 2 to 12m.

Uvala Taršće

Entrance to bay: 43°09'.18N 16°22'.48E

Immediately to the west of Uvala Stari Stani, this anchorage has depths of 4 to 10m at the head of the bay. Similar hazards and weather protection as its neighbours above (see page 165).

Luka Soline

Centre of bay: 43°09'.48N 16°21'.71E

This large bay is protected from southerly winds by the islet of Dobri, but winds from the south, south-west and west can cause heavy seas. Anchoring is not permitted in the westernmost inlet, where underwater cables run to the island of Vis.

The inlet at the northern end of the eastern side of the bay provides the best protection. Here depths are between 2 to 10m, but the holding is poor. The immediate approach is straightforward. See page 165 if coming from the east.

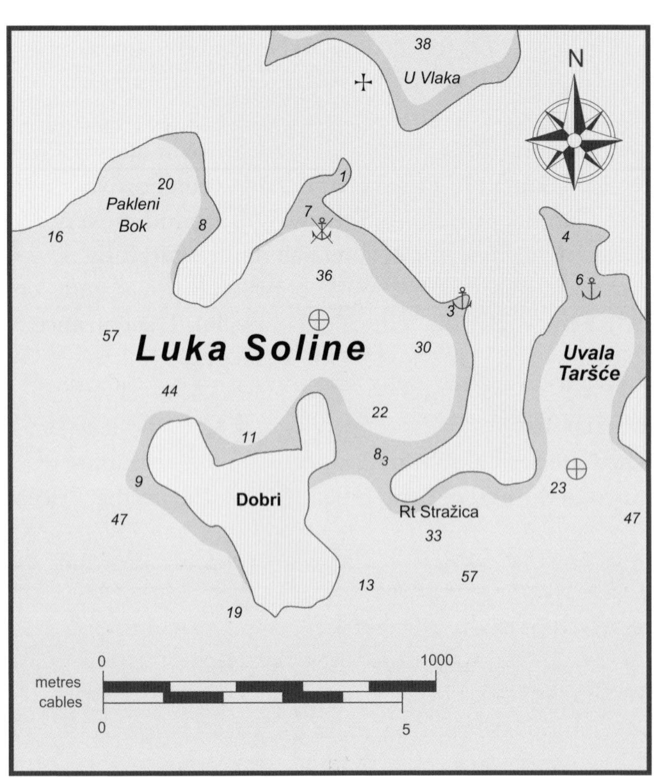

Uvala Vlaka

Entrance to bay: 43°10'.10N 16°22'.09E

Uvala Vlaka is on the north side of Sv Klement and has a clear approach, apart from the islet of Vlaka. The best anchorage is between this islet and Vlaka bay. Do not anchor further east as an underwater cable runs to Hvar. Anchor in depths of between 2 and 8m on a sand bed. The bay is not particularly well sheltered in any winds from the west, through north, to east.

Marinkovac Island, Uvala Ždrilca

Anchorage:
43°09'.49N 16°25'.01E

There are several possible anchorages on the north-west coast of Marinkovac, which is protected by two smaller islets. Two restaurants are situated roughly opposite the middle of the east coast of Planikovac Islet, and you can anchor here in depths of between 5 and 10m. Alternatively, head a little further south-west to a

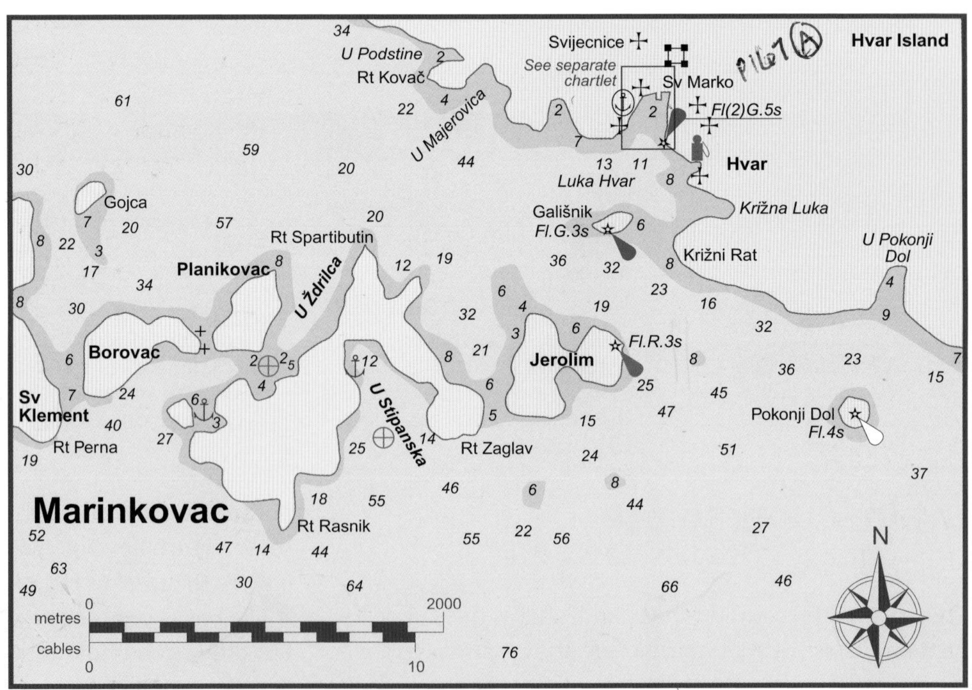

smaller anchorage just before Rt Mlin and anchor in 4 to 6m of water.

Do not pass between the islets of Planikovac and Borovac as there is a rock and a 1m shoal between them. The passage between Sv Klement and Borovac has a 5m depth. See the section on Sv Klement for other hazards in the vicinity on page 165. There is reasonable protection here in winds from all directions.

Uvala Stipanska

Entrance to bay: 43°09'.25N 16°25'.43E

This is a large, deep bay on the south coast of the island, with a bar and a swimming area to starboard as you enter. The approach is straightforward, and you can anchor on a sand and weed bed in depths of 10m. The bay is completely exposed to winds from the south.

Hvar Town

Entrance to bay: 43°10'.16N 16°26'.36E

If you do decide to go for the town harbour and the glitz of Hvar, get there early as it's one of the most popular ports in the region.

NAVIGATION

Charts: HHI 536, MK-19; AC 269, AC 2712, SC5767

Approaches: From the north-west, the approach is relatively straightforward if you head for the centre of the bay, avoiding the low-lying rock Baba, north of Sv Klement (see page 165), and the shallow areas around the islet of Gališnik, south of the bay. Approaching from the south, you will pass the lighthouse on Pokonji Dol and then leave the red light (Fl R 3s) on the islet of Jerolim to port, and the green light (Fl G 3s) on Gališnik to starboard. Give Gališnik a wide berth and do not pass between it and Hvar Island if you need depths of over 5m. Also do not attempt to take a short cut through the Pakleni Islands if approaching from the south-west as there are shallows and low-lying rocks. The town, with the fortress on the hill behind it, should be clearly visible from a distance.

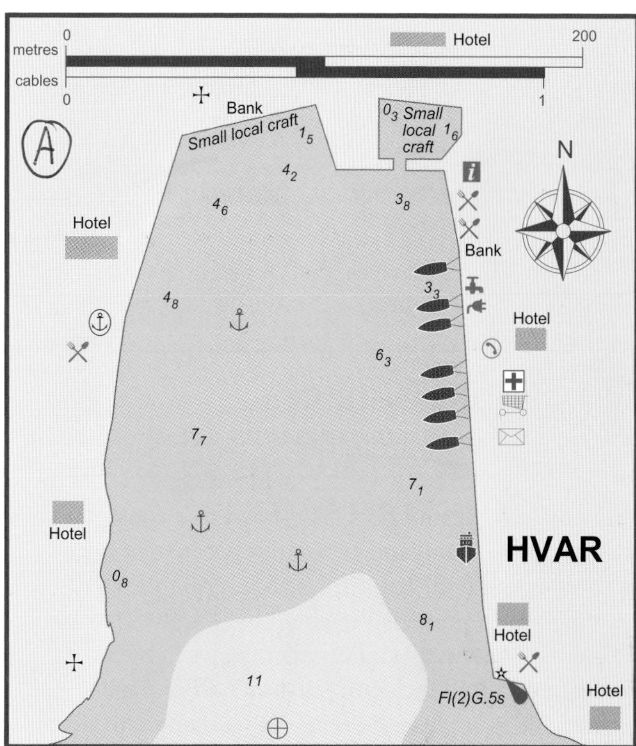

Hvar Town's busy harbour

BERTHING/ANCHORING

The ferries use the outer part of the east quay near the green light, but if you can find space elsewhere on this quay, berth bows- or stern-to on lazylines. A fee will be payable. Alternatively, anchor in the middle of the bay out of the ferry route, and watch out for other boats that may subsequently restrict swinging space. Avoid the western part of the bay in a Sirocco. The bay is exposed to winds from the south, through west, to west-north-west and these winds can cause a swell and make the bay a very uncomfortable place to be in.

One of the many local boats in Hvar bay offering trips to the islands

Useful information – Hvar Town

FACILITIES

Water and **electricity** are available and there is a **fuel** station in the inlet east of Gališnik Islet, Tel: 021 741 060. However, depths by the fuel station are only 1.8m and space for manoeuvring can be limited. Opening hours are 0700 to 2100, seven days a week from 1 June to 30 September, otherwise from 0800 to 1600 Monday to Saturday and 0800 to 1200 on Sundays.

PROVISIONING/ EATING OUT

Hvar has everything you need in close proximity to the harbour. The **post office** and **ferry ticket office** are beside the east quay and there are many **restaurants** to choose from, so take your pick. Unfortunately, Hvar Town provided us with our two experiences of being wilfully over-charged in Croatia.

ASHORE

The **tourist office** is just on the right as you enter the main square, which you will find by walking north along the east quay and turning right at the end. There's plenty to do and see in Hvar, which boasts the oldest Croatian theatre and claims to have one of Thomas à Becket's fingers in a glass bell in the church. We tried to follow this up with Canterbury Cathedral, but drew a blank. There are beaches either side of the port, plenty of excursions available, either via the various tourist agencies or on display in the harbour, and a myriad of **boat/car/bike hire** agencies to choose from. No cars are allowed in the town centre.

Hvar Town's main square

OTHER INFORMATION

Harbourmaster: Halfway along the west quay, Fabrika bb, 21450 Hvar, Tel/fax: 021 741 007.
Tourist office: Trg Sv Stjepana, 21450 Hvar, Tel: 021 741 059; Fax: 021 742 977; email: tzg-hvar@st.htnet.hr; website: www.tzhvar.hr.
Pharmacy: Pjaca bb, Tel: 021 741 002.
Medical centre: In the main square, Tel: 021 741 111.

Luka Mala Garška

Entrance to bay: 43°10'.61N 16°25'.18E
Charts: HHI MK-19; AC 269, AC 2712, SC5767

A mile north-west of Hvar, this bay has a conspicuous, package-style hotel and is popular because of its proximity to Hvar. The approach is straightforward and the bay is protected from all but southwesterly and westerly winds. Underwater cables to Sv Klement have been laid in the south-eastern half of the bay, but you can anchor close to the north-west shore in depths of 6 to 10m on a sand and weed bottom.

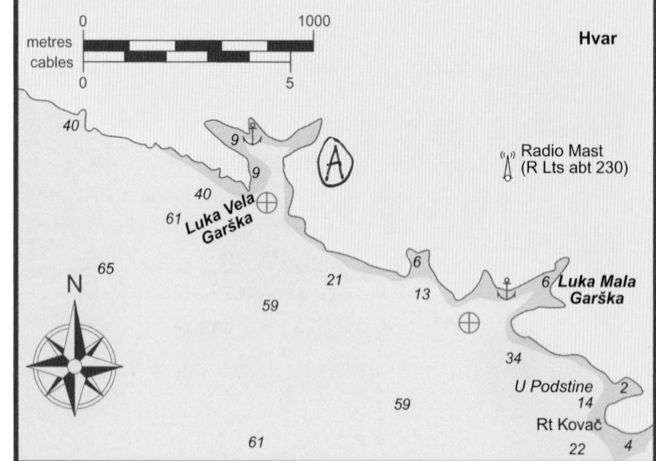

Luka Vela Garška

Entrance to bay: 43°10'.86N 16°24'.47E
Charts: HHI MK-19; AC 269, AC 2712, SC5767

This is less busy than its neighbouring bay and is protected from all but southerly winds. It provides an anchorage with good holding on a mud bed, depths 5 to 10m. Straightforward approach; no facilities.

Pelegrin

Entrance to bay: 43°11'.44N 16°22'.22E
Charts: HHI MK-19; AC 269, AC 2712, SC5767

A very deep bay, with limited space at the shallower head of the inlet, it is not recommended for anchoring. If you do have a look, watch out for the shallows around the western and southern side of Rt Pelegrin.

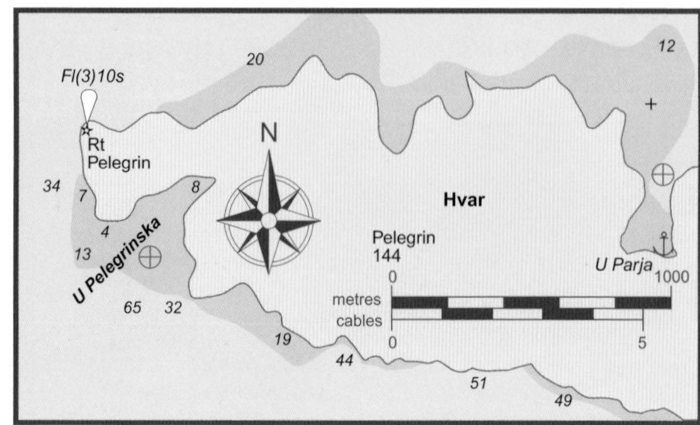

Uvala Parja

Entrance to bay: 43°11'.69N 16°23'.87E
Charts: HHI MK-19; AC 2712, SC5767

Uvala Parja is a well sheltered anchorage, although exposed to the Bora and winds from the north. Moreover, northerly and northwesterly winds can cause a swell. Beware of the rock and shallow water off the western headland. Anchor towards the head of the bay in depths of around 5m.

Uvala Duga

Entrance to bay: 43°11'.69N 16°24'.61E
Charts: HHI MK-19; AC 2712, SC5767

This large deep bay on the western end of Hvar's north coast affords good all-round shelter, particularly from the Bora and easterly winds, though northwesterly winds do cause a swell. You can anchor in depths of 3 to 20m, on a sand bed with good holding. The small islet of Duga, in the middle of the bay, provides a prominent landmark and the only other hazards to watch out for are the rock and shallow area just off the western headland of Uvala Parja. No facilities.

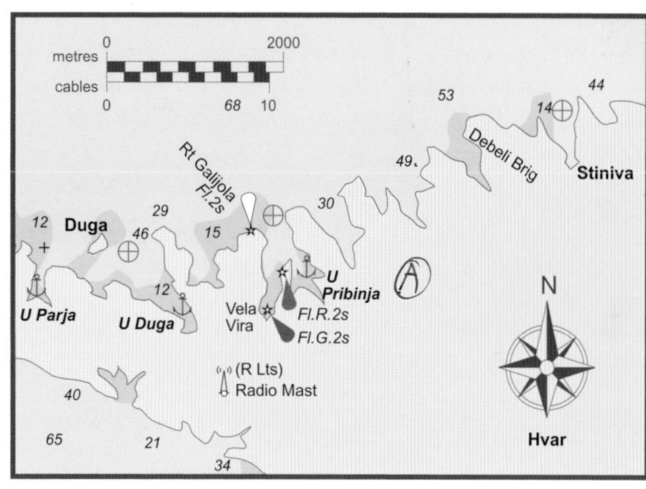

Uvala Pribinja

Entrance to bay: 43°11'.96N 16°25'.64E
Charts: HHI MK-19; AC 2712, SC5767

Another well-sheltered anchorage, although northwesterly winds create a swell here. A headland marked by a red light (Fl R 2s) splits the bay into two smaller bays. An underwater cable runs from just west of this headland to Brač. Ferries to Hvar berth alongside a pier (marked by a green light [Fl G 2s]) that extends from the middle of the western inlet.

You can anchor in the eastern inlet where holding is good on a sand bed in depths of 6 to 15m.

The approach is straightforward, with a white light (Fl 2s) on the western headland, Rt Galijola. Facilities include a restaurant, bars and shops.

Stiniva

Entrance to bay: 43°12'.54N 16°27'.96E
Charts: HHI MK-19; AC 2712, SC5767

Not to be confused with Vela Stiniva, which lies several miles further east along the coast of Hvar, Stiniva is a deep inlet situated 2 miles east of Uvala Pribinja, with a few houses at the head of the bay and a breakwater. The approach is clear from all directions.

You can either berth alongside the inner side of the breakwater or anchor further into the inlet in depths of 6 to 8m, where there is good holding on a mud bed. The breakwater provides limited protection from the Bora, but otherwise the inlet is exposed to all winds from the north-west, north and north-east.

Stari Grad

Entrance to inlet:
43°11'.07N 16°34'.92E

Stari Grad, the main ferry port for the island, is an attractive town with plenty of facilities, interesting architecture and a comfortable town harbour. The ferry terminal is just south-west of the inlet that leads to the town and the ferries moor up in the next bay west, Maslinica, while not in service.

Looking towards the entrance to Stari Grad's harbour

NAVIGATION

Charts: HHI 535, MK-19;
AC 269, AC 2712, SC5767

Approaches: The entrance into the large bay, Starogradski Zaljev, is clear of hazards and the eastern headland, Rt Kabal, has a white light (Fl [2] 5s) on it. As you proceed into the bay you will see a green light (green tower) and white light (white tower) to starboard, indicating the ferry pier, and another green light (Fl G 2s) to port on Rt Fortin (white tower), identifying the starboard side of the entrance into the inlet leading to the harbour and town. There's a large hotel to port just before the inlet narrows. Look out for the conical, unlit, green buoy to starboard as you enter the harbour, which marks a shallow area.

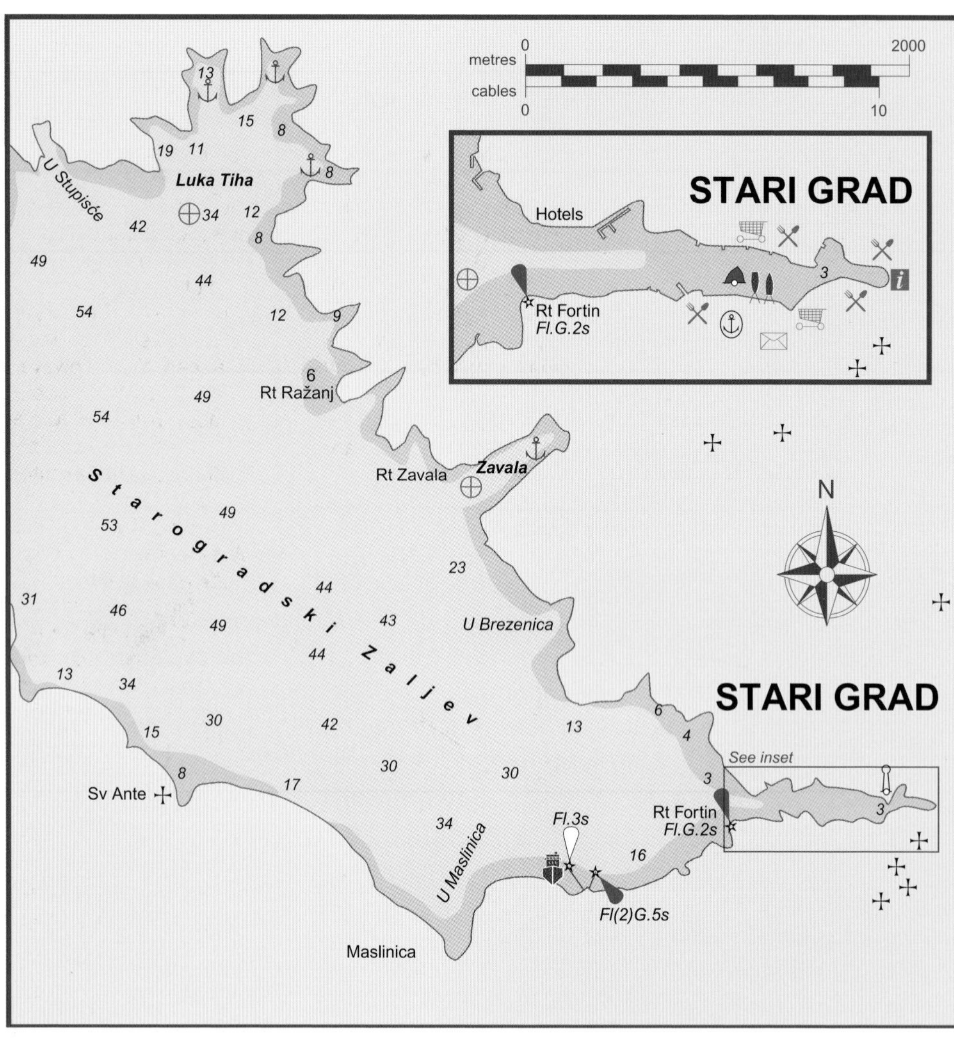

BERTHING

As you enter the outer harbour, the visitors' berths are to starboard. There's room for about 30 boats, moored bows- or stern-to using the lazylines provided, and a berthing fee will be payable. The harbour is well sheltered from all winds except those from the west and north-west.

Stari Grad's inner harbour, full of small local craft

Useful information – Stari Grad

FACILITIES

Electricity and **water** are available. The nearest fuel is in Vrboska, but there is a **nautical shop** at the head of the bay, Boltano, Tel: 021 766 211.

Nautical shop at the head of Stari Grad's bay

PROVISIONING

A large **supermarket** is situated at the head of the bay, near the **tourist office** and the **fruit and vegetable market.** Splitska **bank** is on the south side of the inlet and there are plenty of **cash points** around. The **post office** is a couple of streets back from the town hall, on the south side of the bay, Ulica Braće Biancini 2. It is open from 0730 to 2100 Monday to Saturday during the season, otherwise from 0800 to 1500 Monday to Friday. There is no shortage of small shops, bakeries, etc.

EATING OUT

A good choice of **restaurants** and **bars**, both by the seafront and up the back streets. Buffet Antika (Tel: 021 765 479) is a couple of streets back from the shore, on the south of the bay, and specialises in fish as well as having a good selection of cocktails. Alternatively, try Restauraunt Kod Barba Luke (Tel: 021 765 206) just north of the head of the bay.

ASHORE

The **tourist office**, Tel/fax: 021 765 763; email: tzg-stari-grad@st.tel.hr; website: www.stari-grad-faros.hr, is situated by Kerum supermarket at the head of the bay. It offers a wide range of literature, although we had to pay for a map. Note, however, that a good one does exist on the website. There are some reasonable **beaches** by the hotels in the outer part of the bay and plenty of agencies for **hiring cars, bikes** and **scooters.**

The ancient Greeks settled in Stari Grad in 385 BC and, later, the Romans made their mark. The architecture around the bay reflects a rich history and the back streets are equally enticing. Petar Hektorović (1487 – 1572), a famous Croatian poet, had his fortified summer residence, Tvrdalj, here and the ruins are well worth a visit. For scholars, one of his most famous works, *Fishing and Fisherman's Conversations*, has been translated into English and provides a rare insight into life during this period.

OTHER INFORMATION

Harbourmaster: Towards the ferry terminal on the southern side of the bay – Šetalište don Šime Ljubića bb, 21460 Stari Grad, Tel: 021 765 060.
Medical centre: Obala Žrtva Rata bb, Tel: 021 765 122.
Pharmacy: Obala Žrtava bb, Tel: 021 765 061.

Zavala

Entrance to bay: 43°11'.89N 16°34'.04E
Charts: HHI 535, MK-19; AC 269, AC 2712, SC5767

This deep, long, narrow inlet, halfway along the north-east coast of Starogradski Zaljev, provides good shelter from all but southwesterly winds and has a hazard-free approach (see chart on page 170).

Anchor on a sand and weed bed in depths of around 7m. There's a seasonal bar ashore.

Luka Tiha

Entrance to bay: 43°12'.66N 16°33'.11E
Charts: HHI 535, MK-19; AC 269, AC 2712, SC5767

A couple of miles further north from Zavala, this is a wide, deep bay with a number of smaller inlets. These provide, in different parts, good shelter from all but southwesterly winds. Keep well clear of the northern headland when approaching the bay, as there is a shallow area that extends from it. The holding is reasonable on a sand and weed bed, in depths of between 5 and 10m. No facilities.

Uvala Glavna

Entrance to bay: 43°13'.68N 16°31'.95E
Charts: HHI MK-19; AC 2712, SC5767

Half a mile east of Rt Kabal (white light), this anchorage provides good shelter from all winds except those from the north-west and north, and has posts ashore to secure ropes. Anchor on a sand bed in depths of 2 to 8m. Clear approach; no facilities.

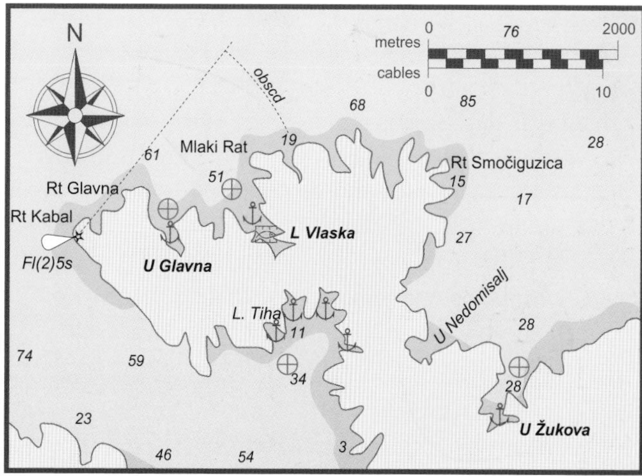

Luka Vlaska

Entrance to bay: 43°13'.77N 16°32'.54E
Charts: HHI MK-19; AC 2712, SC5767

Another long thin bay with just one house, no facilities and a small fish farm close to the shore. The approach is hazard free and it's protected from all winds except those from the north-west. Anchor in depths of 2 to 8m on a sand and weed bed.

Uvala Žukova

Entrance to bay: 43°12'.79N 16°35'.08E
Charts: HHI MK-19; AC 2712, SC5767

Although exposed to north and northeasterly winds, this bay provides good shelter from other directions and the eastern inlet affords partial protection from the Bora. Anchor on a sand and weed bottom in depths of 4 to 10m. No facilities, but a popular area for swimmers in the season.

Basina

Entrance to bay:
43°11'.98N 16°39'.96E
Charts: HHI MK-19;
AC 2712, SC5767

A mile north of Vrboska as the crow flies, this small settlement has a few houses and quays for shallow-draught boats. The bay is exposed to the north, north-east and east, but provides reasonable shelter and holding in depths of 4 to 10m. Watch out for the shallow area stretching about half a mile south-east from the south-eastern entrance to the bay and which extends 185m offshore. There are no facilities.

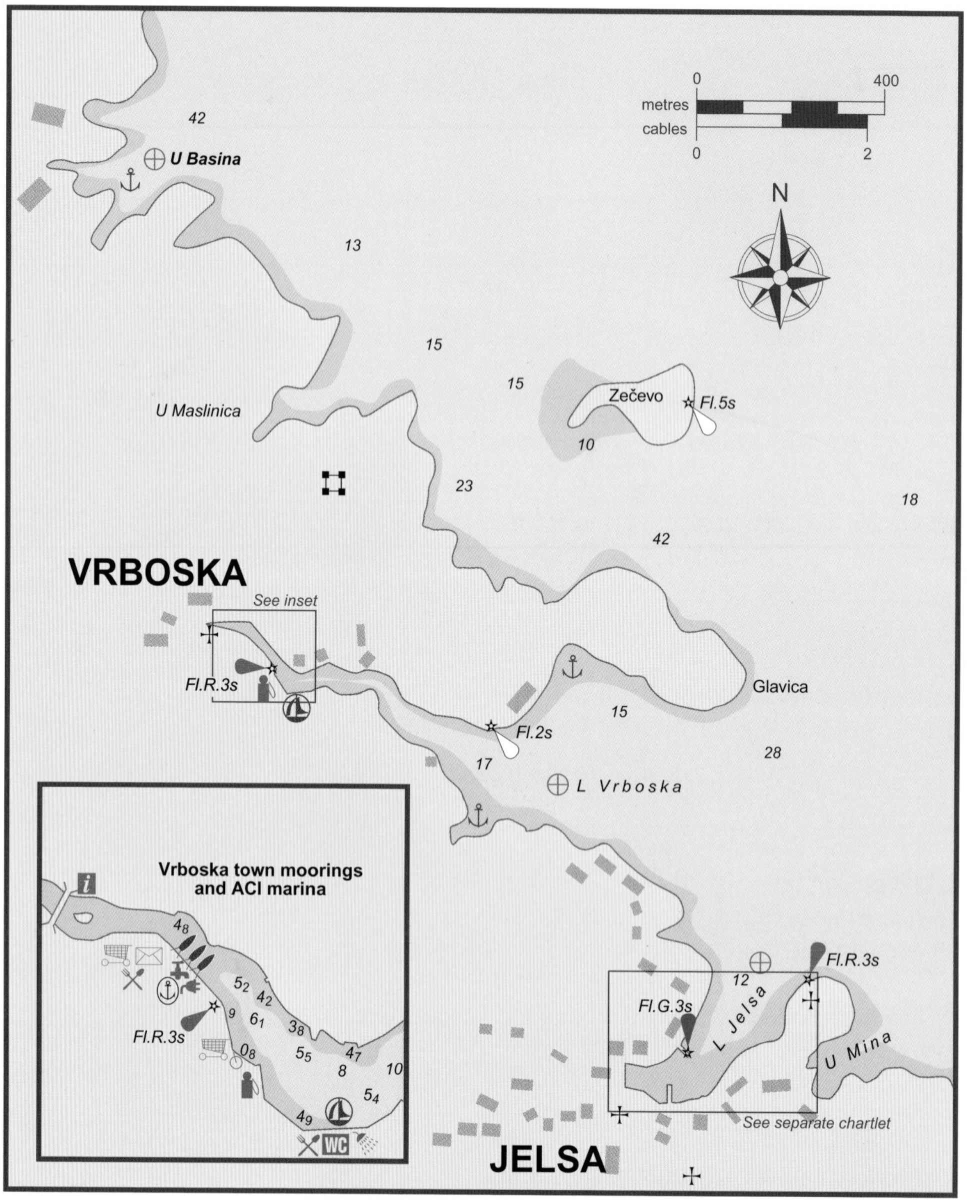

Vrboska

Entrance to inlet:
43°10'.52N 16°41'.32E

Vrboska was another of our favourite overnight stops, with the municipal moorings being run by a very enthusiastic harbourmaster who volunteered a potted history of the area and was adamant that we would be better off in his harbour than the ACI marina. To be fair, it is further into the inlet, so arguably it offers more shelter as well as an increased chance of finding a mooring. He was also optimistic about the time it takes to walk to nearby Jelsa – allow an hour – but it's an interesting walk past some pleasant beaches, hotels and attractive houses. It cost us 144 Kunas for an 11m (36ft) yacht and four people, with lazylines, electrics and water provided. Details of the ACI marina are below, but you can also anchor in the two inlets either side of the bay before you get to the marina.

Vrboska's town moorings, with the disused canning factory in the background

Vrboska is a charming village, sometimes ambitiously called 'Little Venice' on account of its many small stone bridges.

Vrboska's small island at the head of the bay

NAVIGATION

Charts: HHI 535, MK-19; AC 2712, SC5767

Approaches: The approach is straightforward and from the north-west you can go either side of Zečevo Islet, although it does have shallow water extending about 200m or so off its west coast. The ACI marina is to port as you head into the inlet, and the town harbour is further on. There's a white light (Fl 2s) to starboard, just as the bay starts to narrow, and then a red light (Fl R 3s) to port. This marks the quay beyond which visiting boats can berth on lazylines either bows- or stern-to. You'll see the canning factory with a tall chimney on the right as you get to the head of the bay.

BERTHING

This category II marina can be contacted on VHF Channel 17, Tel: 021 774 018. Open all year round, it has 84 berths and 25 dry berths, with depths of up to 5m. Prices are €3.8 to €4 per metre per day for a 10 to 20m (33 and 66ft) boat plus 10% in July and August.

Useful information – Vrboska

FACILITIES

As well as the standard amenities, there is a 5-ton **crane** and a **fuel** station, Tel: 021 774 220, depth 2m, opening hours 0800 to 1500. From 1 June to 30 September, these hours are valid seven days a week. Outside this period, the fuel station is closed on Sundays and Bank Holidays.

ASHORE

Better shops and facilities are available in Jelsa, but

A pizza restaurant at the head of the bay

Vrboska has a few good **restaurants** and **bars**, a **tourist office, grocery shops, cash points**, a **post office**, a private tourist agency and a fish museum. The restaurants are scattered in town and also on the walk out of town past the ACI marina. We ate well and at a reasonable price in Restaurant Mediteran, vl Domagoj Kraljević, Tel: 021 744 323.

OTHER INFORMATION

Tourist office: On the north shore, just west of the tiny islet in the centre of the channel, Tel: 021 774 137.

ACI Marina: 21463 Vrboska, Tel: 021 774 018; Fax: 021 774 144; email: m.vrboska@aci-club.hr; website: www.aci-club.hr.

Post office: On the southern shore, halfway between the municipal moorings and the ACI marina. Opening hours are from 0800 to 1200 and 1800 to 2100, Monday to Saturday in the season; otherwise from 0800 to 1500 Monday to Friday.

Jelsa

Entrance to bay: 43°10'.04N 16°42'.03E

Jelsa doesn't have the charm of Vrboska, but is a bustling town with an increasing tourist trade. The visitors' berths are very close to a clutch of restaurants, so if you want a quiet early night it's probably not the best spot to be. The bay is also fully exposed to the Bora, although the two breakwaters provide limited shelter. Regular ferries to Brač and Split.

Jelsa: Ferry terminal and church on the south side of the bay

NAVIGATION

Charts: HHI 535, MK-19; AC 2712, SC5767

Approaches: The first breakwater, to port on approach (Fl R 3s), is at the entrance to the bay. There are hotels on both sides and the tall church tower can be seen once you are in the bay. There are no real hazards, but stay clear of the breakwaters, which are surrounded by rocks, and look out for the marked swimming areas. The visitors' berths are just after the second breakwater, which lies to starboard and is marked by a green light (Fl G 3s).

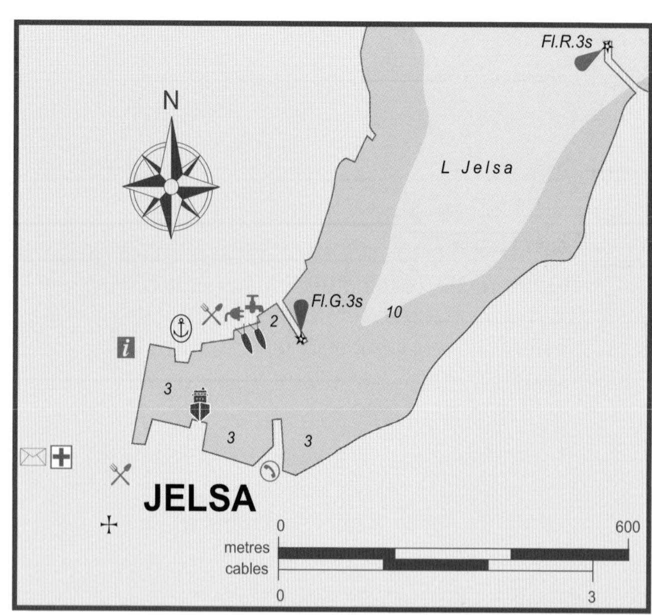

BERTHING

Berth bows- or stern-to on the lazylines provided outside Restaurant Napoleon. Electricity and water are available, but you will be asked to pay a fee. The bay is well protected from all winds except the Bora.

Useful information – Jelsa

PROVISIONING

A Konzum **supermarket** is located on the opposite side of the bay to the berthing area, along with plenty of other shops and a couple of **banks.** The **post office,** adjacent to the **pharmacy,** is a short walk west, away from the sea at the head of the bay, (Stossmayerovo, 21465 Jelsa). Opening hours are from 0730 to 2100 Monday to Saturday in the season, otherwise from 0800 to 1500 Monday to Friday and 0800 to 1300 on Saturdays.

Bustling cafés near the ferry terminal

EATING OUT

Due to a power cut when we stayed at Jelsa, Napoleon was the only restaurant that was still open for business, although we were restricted to pizzas. Nonetheless it appeared to offer a good, reasonably-priced menu.

An English-owned night club, Vertigo, can be found in the centre of town together with numerous bars, restaurants, pizzerias and cafés.

ASHORE

The **tourist office** is on the northern corner of the head of the bay and provides plenty of information – Obala bb, Tel/fax: 021 761 017; email: info@tzjelsa.hr; website; www.tzjelsa.hr and www.jelsa-online.com. There are private agencies all around town offering **car, boat, scooter** and **bike hire**, as well as a number of excursions, including trips to Bol on Brač Island. Divecentre Hvar Jelsa is on the road that heads to Vrboska, Tel: 021 761 822; Fax: 021 761 822; website: www.tauchinjelsa.de.

There are good **beaches** on either side of the bay and sports facilities in the hotel complexes, as well as on the road out of town towards Hvar.

OTHER INFORMATION

Harbourmaster: On the north side of the bay opposite the ferry terminal; 21465 Jelsa, Tel: 021 761 055; Fax: 021 761 055.
Pharmacy: Tel: 021 761 108.
Medical centre: Tel: 021 761 194.

Vela Stiniva

Entrance to bay:
43°09'.53N 16°48'.75E
Charts: HHI MK-19 & MK-20; AC 1574, AC 2712, SC5767

A small inlet with a few houses, a bar, a restaurant and a harbour that is usually full of local boats. The approach is clear and you can anchor west of the breakwater, in depths of 4 to 7m on a sand bed.

The bay is exposed to winds from the north-west, north and north-east.

The tranquil setting of Vela Stiniva

Pokrivenik

Entrance to bay: 43°09'.46N 16°53'.33E
Charts: HHI MK-19 & MK-20; AC 1574, SC5767

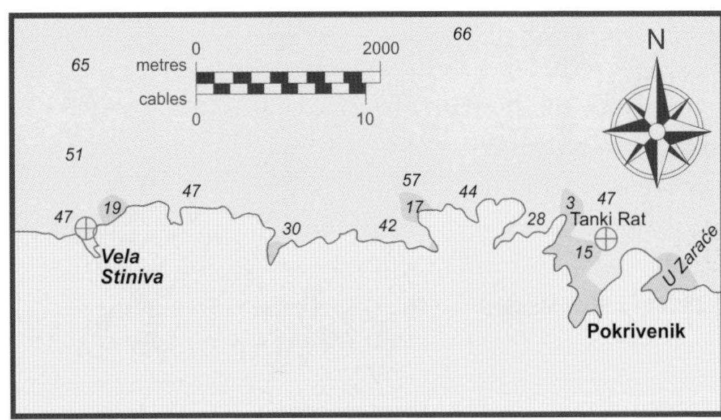

Although providing only partial protection, the south-east part of this bay offers the best shelter from the Bora along this section of the coast. It's a great place for a swim and has a newly-renovated hotel and restaurant, Hotel Timun, Pokrivenik, 21467 Hvar, Tel/fax: 021 745 140; email: info@hotel-timun.hr; website: www.hotel-timun.hr. Leave Tanki Rat and the two smaller headlands south of it well to starboard as they have shallow banks extending from them. Beware also of another shallow bank on the port side, just after the last one to starboard. A course of 191°T from an approach waypoint of 43°10'.00N 16°53'.34E will leave you clear of the shallows, but with not much room to spare. You can anchor in depths of between 5 to 10m on a sand bed, but there are rocks about and the holding is unreliable.

The view across Pokrivenik bay from Hotel Timun

Sućuraj

Harbour entrance: 43°07'.47N 17°11'.44E
Charts: HHI MK-20, MK-22; AC 1574, SC5767

The lighthouse on Rt Sućuraj

This small ferry port is one of the most photogenic villages we visited. Rt Sućuraj has a stone lighthouse right on the shore and the breakwater has a red light at the end (Fl R 2s). A shallow area stretches around Rt Sućuraj and to the west. The bay is narrow, so make sure you have a clear view on approach in order to spot the ferries in time. Berth alongside on the inner side of the breakwater in depths of 2 to 4m. The bay is exposed to the Sirocco and winds from the east and south-east can cause a swell, but otherwise the shelter is good.

ASHORE

Facilities comprise a selection of restaurants and bars (try Vlaka fish restaurant [Tel: 021 773 247] or Konoba Gusarka Luka [Tel: 021 773 214]), a harbourmaster, tourist office, post office, supermarket, medical centre, hotel and a few small shops. The ferry goes to Drvenik on the mainland.

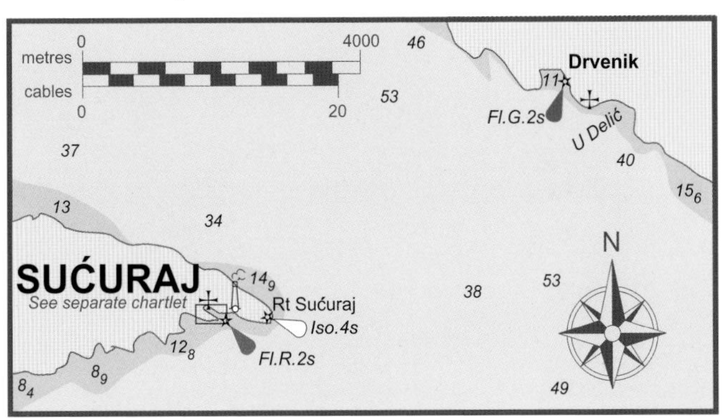

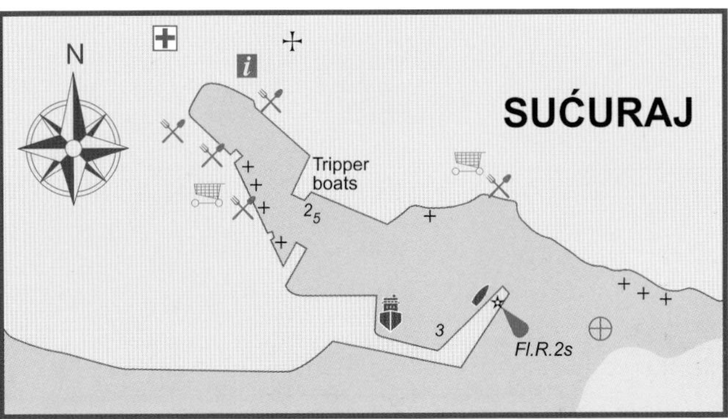

OTHER INFORMATION

Harbourmaster: By the ferry terminal and bus station – 21469 Sućuraj, Tel/fax: 021 773 228.
Post office: A couple of streets back from the north-east shore; opening hours as Vrboska.
Tourist office: Towards the head of the bay on the north-east shore; Tel/fax: 021 717288; email: tz.sucuraj@st.htnet.hr.
Medical centre: A short walk west-north-west of the tourist office, Tel: 021 773 210.

Sućuraj's inner harbour

Uvala Duboka

Entrance to bay: 43°06'.84N 17°02'.45E
Charts: HHI MK-20, MK-22; AC 1574, SC5767

Uvala Duboka is situated immediately west of Uvala Kozja, with similar protection and no hazards on approach.

There's a fish farm in the middle of the inlet, but you can anchor beyond it, on a sand and weed bed, in depths of 5 to 8m.

Uvala Kozja

Entrance to bay: 43°06'.75N 17°02'.83E
Charts: HHI MK-20, MK-22; AC 1574, SC5767

A straightforward approach to find a reasonable anchorage on a mud bed, in depths of around 10m, which offers shelter from winds from the west, through north, to the east.

There are no facilities, although the village of Zaglav is half a mile inland.

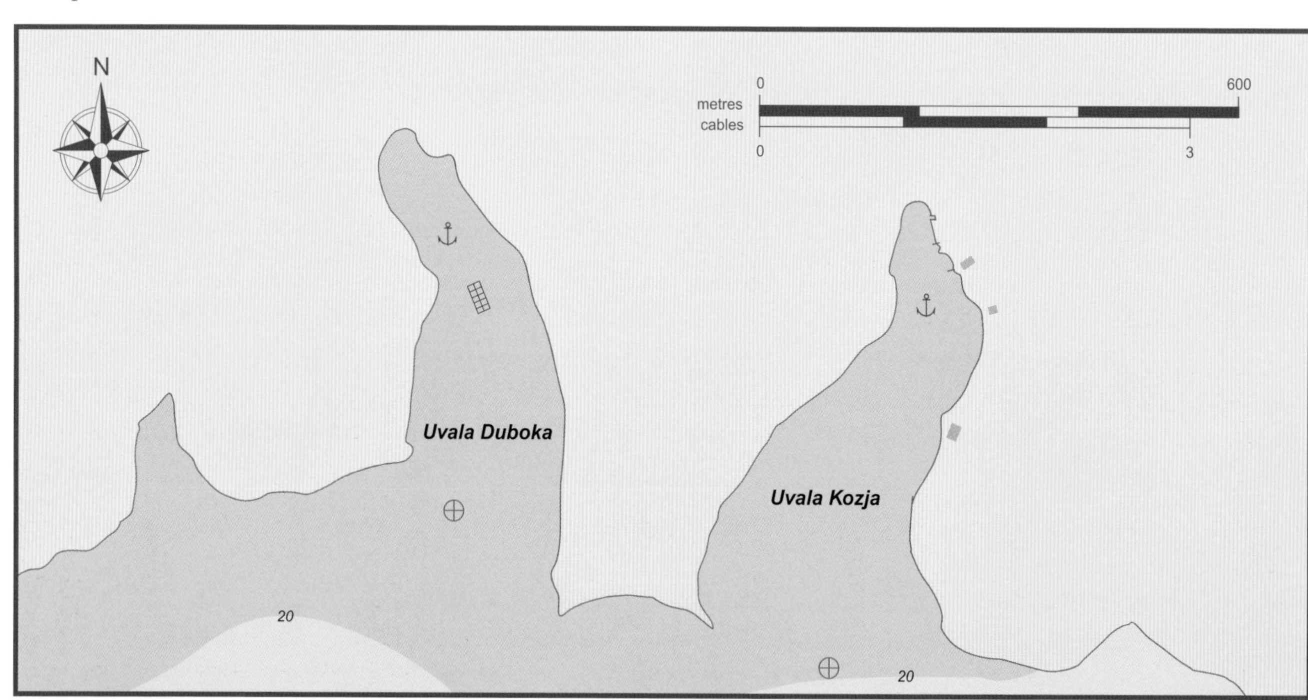

Zavala

Entrance to bay: 43°07'.20N 16°41'.45E
Charts: HHI MK-19; AC 2712, SC5767

On the south coast of Hvar, opposite the island of Šćedro, this bay has a popular beach and a café open during the season. You can berth alongside the small pier but protection is limited, especially if the wind is from a southerly direction.

Dubovica

Entrance to bay: 43°08'.54N 16°31'.89E
Charts: HHI MK-19; AC 2712, SC5767

This bay has a popular beach but no facilities. You can berth stern-to the quay, west of the beach. Alternatively, anchor in depths of 8 to 10m.

The bay is exposed to winds from the south-west, south and south-east.

Milna

Entrance to bay: 43°09'.51N 16°29'.03E

Not to be confused with its larger namesake on Brač, this is a small settlement with a few traditional restaurants. Mooring buoys have been laid by the restaurant Moli Ante; anchoring is prohibited because of underwater cables. The chapel, with a red-tiled roof, overlooks the village and is surrounded by trees. Beware of the shallows and above-water rocks to the west of the bay.

The bay is open to winds from the south-west, south and south-east, which cause a swell. Moli Ante, Tel: 021 745 025; email: antun.tudor@st.htnet.hr, is open from around Easter to mid-October (although its chef will cook a meal for visiting yachtsmen outside the season, given prior warning), and has air-conditioned rooms available.

A restaurant terrace overlooking the bay in Milna, Hvar

Šćedro Island

South of Hvar Island, Šćedro has a heavily-indented coast, with a number of possible stop-offs. The most popular anchorages are Lovišće and Manastir, immediately east of Lovišće, both of which lie on the north coast.

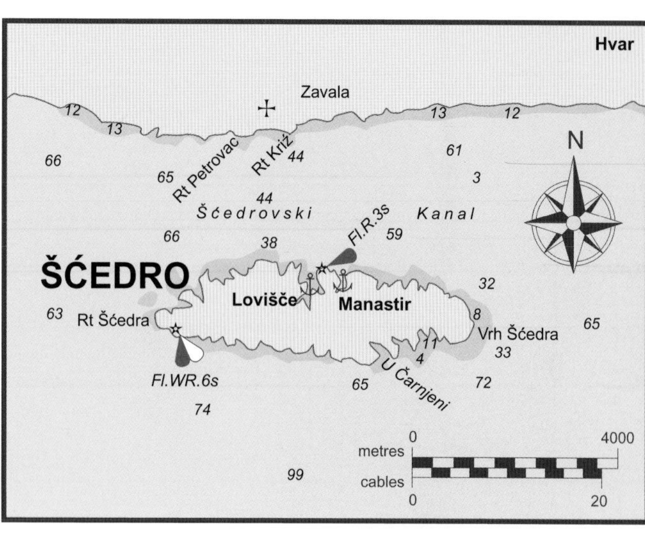

Lovišće

Entrance to bay: 43°06'.01N 16°41'.93E
Charts: HHI MK-19; AC 2712, SC5767

This large bay has several inlets where it is possible to obtain shelter from all winds except those from the north. Anchor in one of the inlets, depending on the direction of the wind, in depths of 2 to 12m on a sand and weed bed. The approach is straightforward, with a red light (Fl R 3s) marking the eastern headland. You will find a number of restaurants ashore.

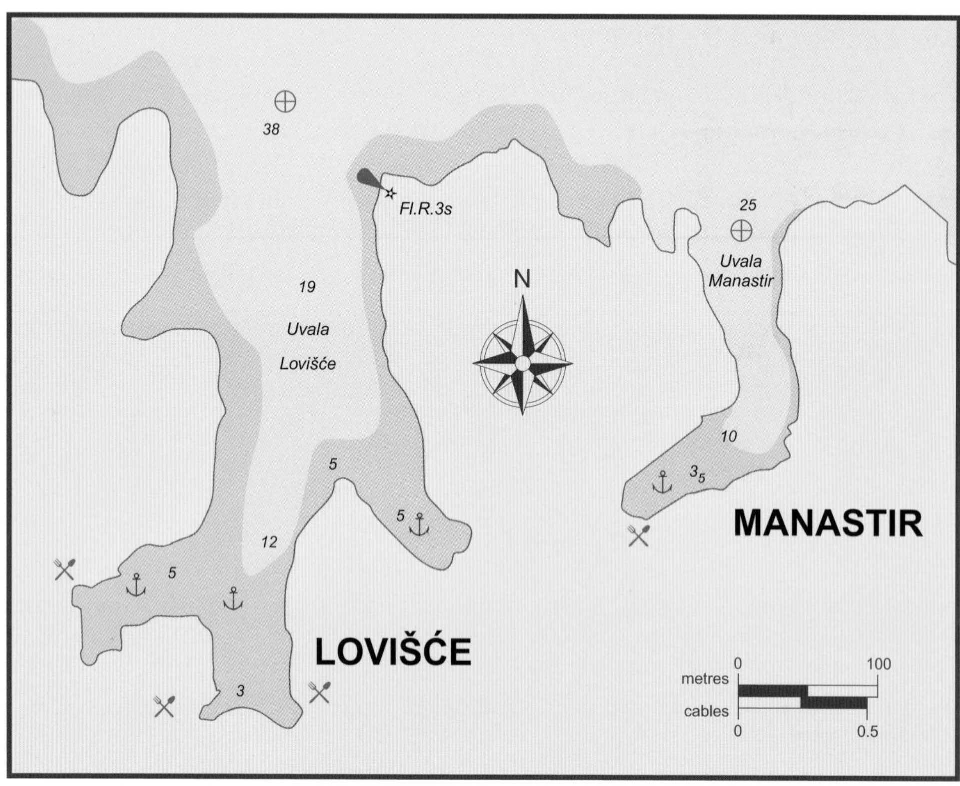

Manastir

Entrance to bay:
43°05'.86N 16°42'.40E

The ruins of a 15th century Dominican monastery lie on the south-eastern shore of this bay, which gives it its name. Anchor on a sand and weed bed in depths of 3 to 8m. Straightforward approach and similar protection to Lovišće. The restaurant ashore is run by the Kordić family (www.adventure-island.net).

Vis Island

Vis Island was Croatia's first main defence against aggression from the sea and there is much evidence of its wartime past. With old artillery posts high up on the hills and a number of submarine caves, it was Tito's stronghold during the Second World War and was the last Croatian island to open for tourism after the war. It has, therefore, stood still in time longer than its neighbouring islands and has a more British feel to it as a result of its history as an allied base. It's very popular in the summer, especially with superyachts, but is extremely quiet out of season – we spent Christmas there one year and were the only guests in the one hotel that was open! The island's two main settlements comprise the town of Vis, on the north side of the island, and Komiža on the west. Both are great places to stay, although we preferred the cosier feel of Komiža. There are also a few anchorages, but the coastline is not very indented and the waters are generally deep. We explore the two towns first and then the best of the rest.

Looking across from the visitors' berths at Vis Town towards the harbour entrance and the small peninsula on the north-west shore

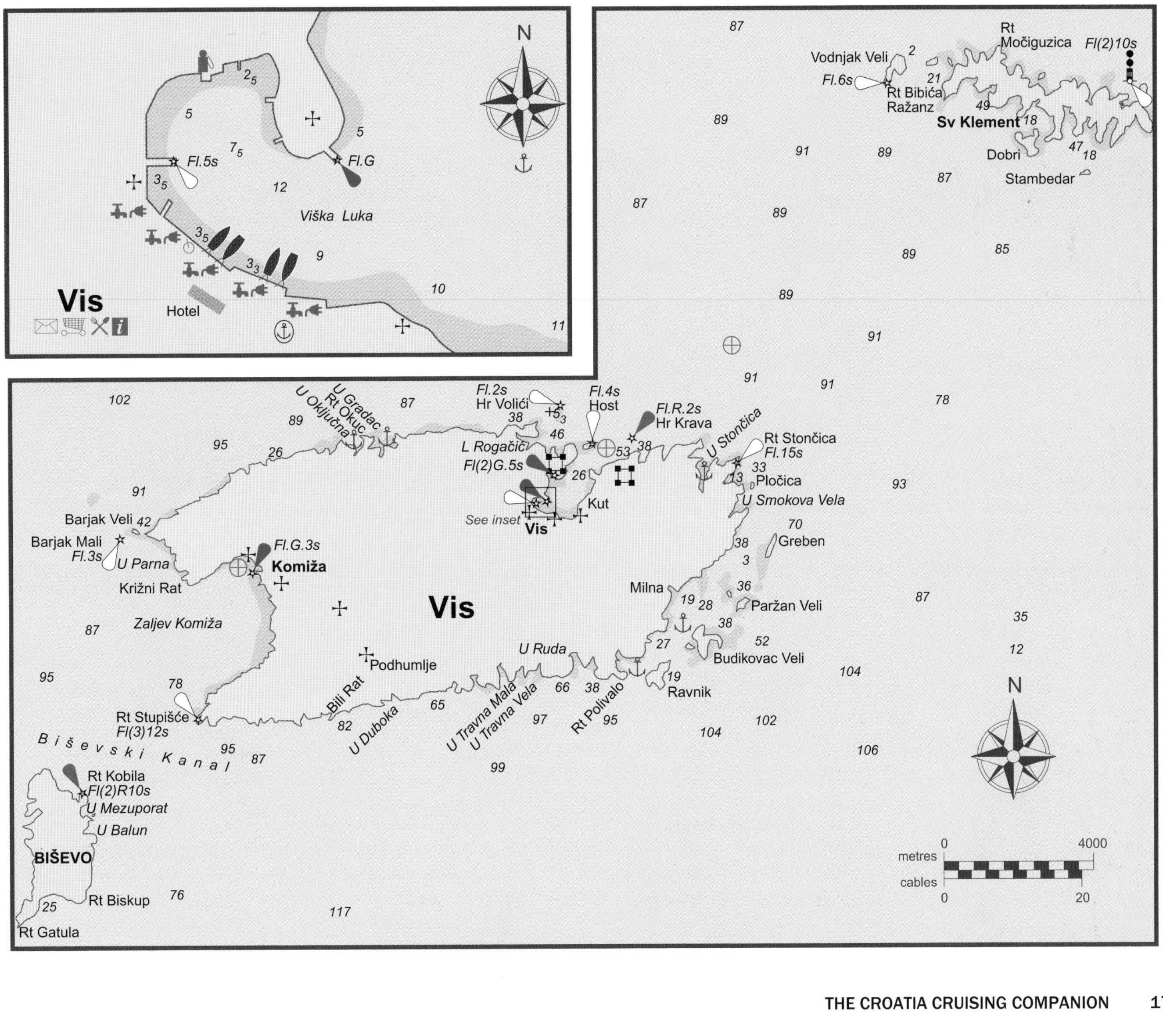

Vis Town

Entrance to bay: 43°04'.69N 16°12'.72E

The town is spread around the large bay and has a few relics of interest, including Roman baths, a British cemetery, Fort Wellington and the George III fortress. It is now the island's wine and agriculture centre.

NAVIGATION

Charts: HHI 535, MK-17; AC 2712, AC 2774, SC5767

Approaches: One and a half miles east of the entrance is the lighthouse on Rt Stončica (Fl 15s) and half a mile west of the entrance is the above-water rock, Hrid Volići, identified by a white light (Fl 2s) just north-east of it. The islet of Host, with its lighthouse (Fl 4s), lies to starboard at the entrance to the bay, while just before it to port is another above-water rock, Hrid Krava, with a red light (Fl R 2s). The fortresses should be visible on the hills. A small peninsula with a church on it extends from the north-west shore and is marked by a green light (Fl G).

Pilotage: A course of 219°T from an approach waypoint of 43°06'.50N 16°14'.71E will take you between Host and Hrid Krava and into the centre of the bay. The visitors' berths are in front of a Venetian-style building that forms part of Hotel Tamaris. The ferry pier (Fl 5s) is to starboard of these berths, with the fuel station beyond it.

BERTHING

Berth on lazylines, bows- or stern-to, in depths of up to 3.5m, with the deepest water at the centre of the western part of the inner bay. The berths are exposed to the Bora, which can cause heavy seas.

The view across Vis bay from the eastern shore

Useful information – Vis Town

FACILITIES

Water and **electricity** are available. The **fuel** station (Tel: 021 711 176) has depths of 2.5m alongside and is open in the season from 0700 to 2100 Monday to Saturday and from 0800 to 1200 on Sundays. Otherwise opening times are from 0700 to 1200 and 1700 to 1900, Monday to Saturday.

ASHORE

Vis has all the facilities you would expect for a town of this size. Mainly located close to the shore, these comprise **markets, banks, shops, post office**, etc, although there seemed to be fewer **restaurants** than the Croatian 'norm', probably due to Vis' 'late' discovery as a tourist destination.

We can recommend the pizzas at Dionis, which, open all year round, is about a five-minute walk east from the visitors' moorings, (Matije Gubca 1, Tel: 021 711 963; Fax: 021 711 126). The restaurant in Hotel Tamaris is convenient but lacking in atmosphere. Instead try Villa Kaliopa, near to the town museum on the eastern side of the bay (Vladimira Nazora 32, Kut, Tel: 021 771 755). It's not cheap, but the setting in a walled garden is superb. Also worth a try in Kut is the popular Konoba Vatrica, Kralja Krešimira IV bb, Tel: 021 711 574 and the more rustic Tezok, Kralja Krešimira IV bb, Tel: 021 711 271.

The best **beach** is by the Hotel Issa, west of

Useful information – Vis Town continued

the centre of town.

There are a couple of **ferries** per day between Split and Vis and you can **hire cars** and **scooters** via the numerous agencies advertising on the seafront. **Buses** run between Komiža and Vis to coincide with the ferries.

OTHER INFORMATION

Harbourmaster: Near the ferry terminal at Šetalište Stare Isse 6, 21480 Vis, Tel/fax: 021 711 111.

Tourist office: Situated near the ferry terminal at Šetalište Stare Isse 5, 21480 Vis, Tel: 021 717 017; Fax: 021 717 018; website: www.tz-vis.hr.

Post office: On the eastern side of the bay, Obala Svetog Jurja 25, 21480 Vis, open from 0730 to 2100 Monday to Saturday in the season, otherwise from 0700 to 1900 Monday to Friday and 0700 to 1300 on Saturday.

Medical centre: Located at Poljana Sv Duha 10, 21480 Vis, Tel: 021 711 633.

Pharmacy: Located at Vukovarska 2, 21480 Vis, Tel: 021 711 434.

Dodoro Diving Tours: Kranjevica 4, 21480 Vis, Tel/fax: 021 711 347; www.dodoro-diving.com.

Komiža

Harbour entrance: 43°02'.75N 16°04'.88E

Komiža is a conventional fishing village and famous for a traditional, sail-powered wooden fishing boat, the Gajeta Falkuša, built on Vis for over 300 years. It's another favourite overnight stop of ours for its lovely stone buildings, compact size and friendly atmosphere.

NAVIGATION

Charts: HHI MK-17; AC 2774, SC5767

Approaches: From the north-west, beware of the low-lying islets of Barjak Mali and Barjak Veli, with shallow waters and rocks around them. From the south, beware of a 3m shoal just after Rt Stupišće, close to the entrance to the bay. There are shallow waters and rocks all along the inner part of the bay.

Head for the inside of the pier, with the green light (Fl G 3s) at the end, where the visitors' moorings have been laid. The large church, south-east of the town and set back from the shore, is visible from a distance.

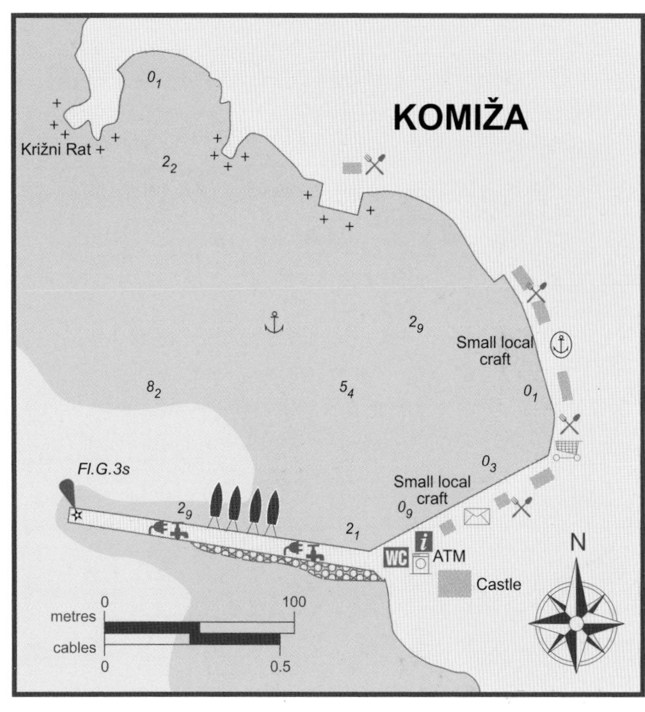

BERTHING

Berth bows- or stern-to on lazylines along the pier. The bay is not recommended in southwesterly and westerly winds, and the Sirocco causes a swell.

Komiza's castle housing the fishing museum; the breakwater providing visitors berths is in the background

Useful information – Komiža

FACILITIES

Electricity and **water** are available, and there are **toilets** and a **laundry** service just past the root of the pier.

ASHORE

The **tourist office** is just past the root of the pier, with a **cash point** adjacent to it. Walking a little further around the bay you'll pass the fishing museum and a number of **bars**, followed by the **market** and finally the **post office**. Konoba Bako is a great seafood restaurant, with its own small beach and a private archaeological collection – Gundulićeva 1, Tel: 021 713 008; website: www.konobabako.hr. There's also a wide choice of other **restaurants** here.

Trips to the **blue cave** on Biševo Island go from Komiža and the tourist office will give you all the necessary information. The ceremonial burning of a traditional fishing boat takes place on 6 December to mark the day of St Nicholas, the patron saint of travellers, sailors and fishermen. There is also a fisherman's night on the first Saturday in August.

Buses run between Komiža and Vis to coincide with the ferries.

OTHER INFORMATION

Harbourmaster: Škor 1, 21485 Komiža, Tel: 021 713 085; Fax: 021 713 085.
Tourist office: Riva 1, 21485 Komiža, Tel: 021 713 455; Fax: 021 713 095; email: tzg-komize@st.htnet.hr.
Post office: Hrvatskih Mučenika 8, 21485 Komiža. Open in the season from 0800 to 1200 and 1800 to 2100 Monday to Saturday, otherwise from 0800 to 1400 Monday to Friday and 0800 to 1300 on Saturdays.
Medical centre: San Pedra bb, 21485 Komiža, Tel: 021 713 122.
Pharmacy: Podspiljska bb, 21485 Komiža, Tel: 021 713 445.

Anchorages on Vis

Charts: HHI MK-17; AC 2774, SC5767

There are really only two feasible anchorages for pleasure craft (see chart on page 179), as most of the inlets are too deep, too exposed or both. However, as Vis is a fair distance from alternative protection, we'd recommend you stick to the two main towns for an overnight stop.

Uvala Stončica, on the north-east coast of the island, has a popular restaurant at the head of the bay and provides a reasonable, though deep, anchorage. It's exposed to the Bora and the Sirocco causes a swell.

Uvala Oključna and neighbouring Uvala Gradac, just west of the centre of the north coast, only give protection from winds from the south.

Biševo Island

Charts: HHI MK-17; AC 2774, SC5767

This small island, south-west of Vis, is most renowned for its 'blue cave' in Uvala Balun, where the sun enters the cave through an underwater gap, shines on the sea bed and the reflection casts an iridescent blue light through the water and around the cave. The effect is best around noon. There are regular trips to Biševo from Komiža on Vis and a connection to Hvar, Brač and the mainland. Understandably, but unfortunately, the authorities have stopped people visiting the cave independently, and the organised tours can become a bit of a free-for-all as those dropped off from the tourist boats fight for their turn to visit the cave in one of the small fishing boats or loiter around the open-air café.

There are a few small harbours and anchorages, but generally the waters are deep and protection is limited. Here are the best but none of them are recommended for an overnight stay.

Biševska Luka, situated on the west coast, has a quay with depths of up to 1.5m. It is not recommended in a Sirocco, but offers shelter from the Bora and easterly winds.

Uvala Salbunara, just north of Biševska Luka, has depths of up to 1m alongside the quay and provides similar protection to its neighbour.

Uvala Mezuporat, on the east coast, affords shelter from winds from the west and south-west and has a quay used by the boat service from Komiža. Look out for the above-water rock to the south of the bay.

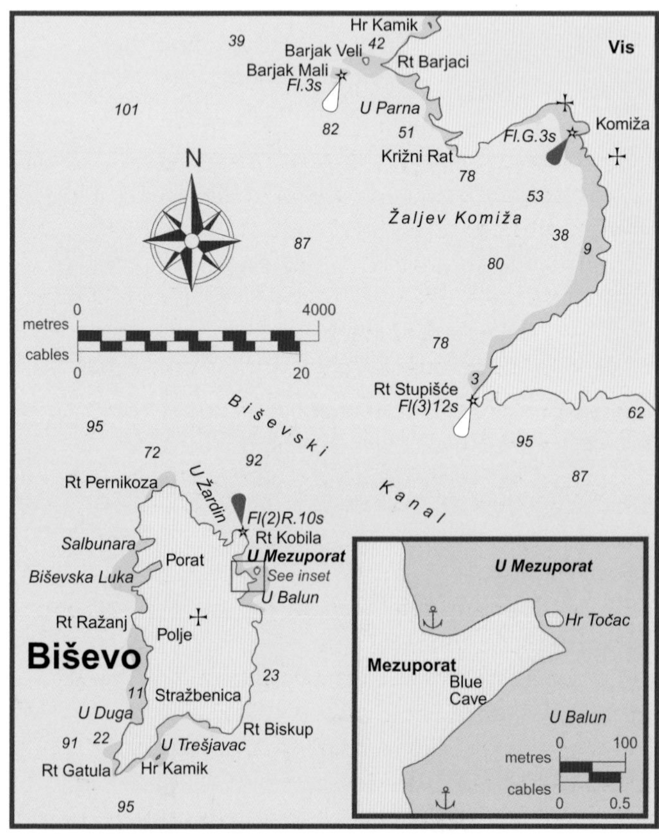

Orebić

Chapter six

The mainland south-east of Split and the Pelješac Peninsula

This is probably the least interesting area covered in this cruising companion, although there are still some noteworthy towns and villages. However, the nearby islands of Brač and Hvar provide far better stop-off opportunities. Furthermore, once you get past Gradac, just opposite the tip of Hvar, and anywhere beyond, you'll have to retrace your passage before you reach a dead-end. There's really not much to see past Gradac, apart from numerous shellfish farms, with the notable exception of Ston and Mali Ston, which are more easily reached from the other side of the Pelješac Peninsula.

Ploče, a big industrial town 10 miles south-east of Gradac, by the mouth of the Neretva River Delta, was one of the least inspiring places we have come across, although the surrounding wetlands are striking. Another 10 miles south-east of Ploče is the very short stretch of coastline belonging to Bosnia and Hercegovina, with the new town of Neum in the middle, also displaying little character.

Nearer to Split, and probably of most interest, is the town of Omiš. Semi-industrial on the outskirts, the mountain backdrop, close as it is to the town, is spectacular. There are some reasonable beaches around Omiš and the River Cetina flows to the sea through a gorge just north-west of the centre of town and attracts plenty of visitors to participate in the numerous river-rafting excursions.

The other major settlement is Makarska, which is very much a land-based tourist resort with a large beach. The 'Makarska Riviera' includes a number of smaller resorts, nearly all of the same package-holiday type style.

There is now a marina attached to Le Méridien Grand Hotel Lav in Podstrana, just east of Split. This new and lavish five star hotel opened its doors in February 2007 and the small marina is handy if you want to treat yourself to a slap up meal but, apart from the hotel complex, there's not much else around. You can also find a small marina at Baška Voda and another one at Tučepi, a couple of miles south-east of Makarska, but otherwise the harbours are normally busy with local and tripper boats and shelter is limited. Shore side fuel stations are located in Makarska and Ploče. The nearest airports are Split and Dubrovnik and buses connect all the towns along the coast.

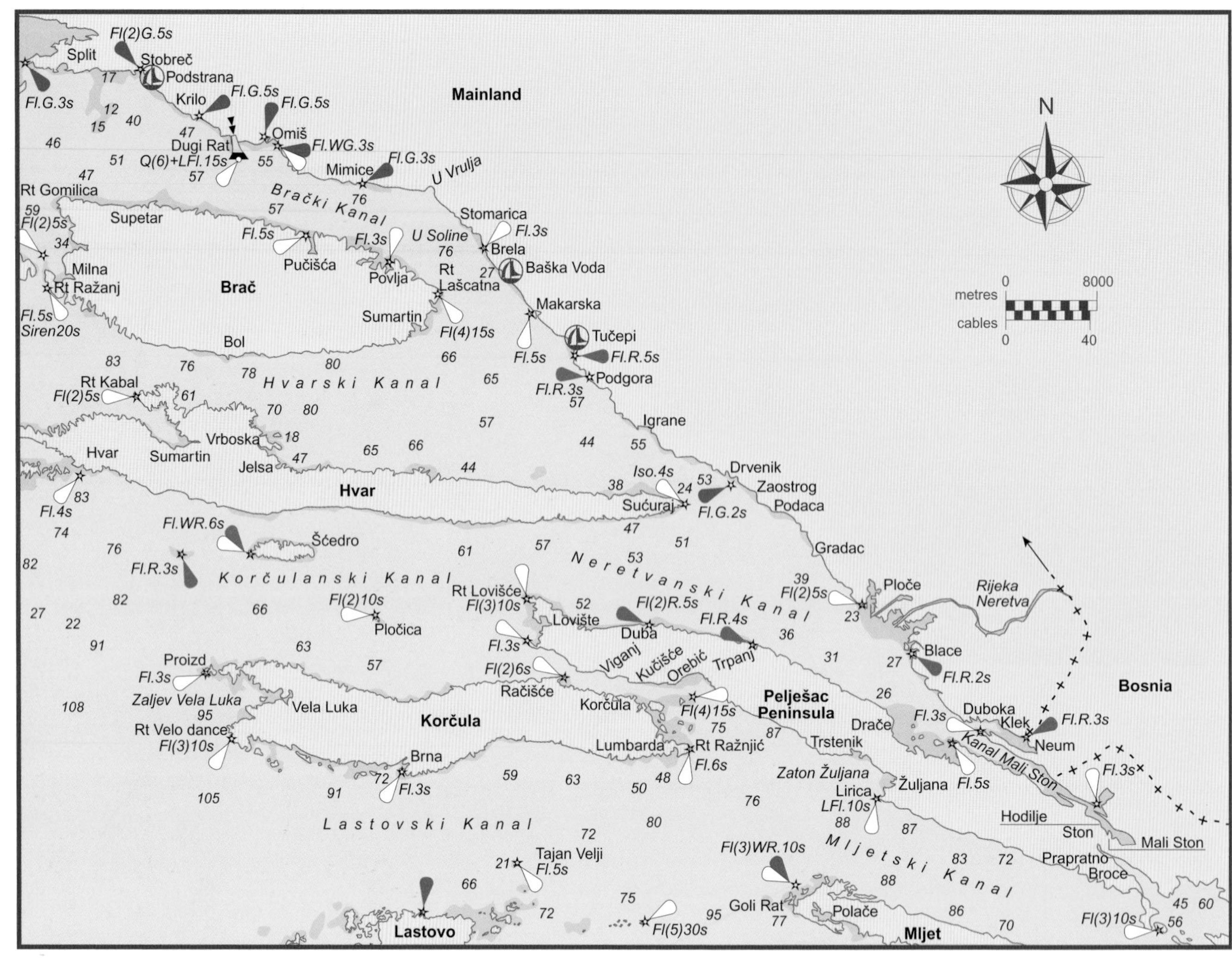

Stobreč

Entrance to bay: 43°29'.68N 16°31'.71E
Charts: HHI MK-18; AC 2712, SC5767

Stobreč is a small, sleepy settlement, at least compared with neighbouring Split, with a campsite, houses and a few bars and restaurants around the bay. On the eastern headland is a large hotel. On the west of the bay is the village harbour and on the east side a small local marina. Stay well clear of the breakwater on the west of the bay as there are a number of rocks, some below water, near the western headland and extending from the breakwater. No anchoring is permitted over the sewage pipe, which runs south-east then south from the land jutting out from the north-west shore.

The best place to berth is on the inner side of the breakwater in depths of around 3.5m, although it's normally full of local boats. The marina opposite is shallower. Alternatively, anchor north of the breakwater on a mud bottom in depths of around 3m, but make sure you stay clear of the sewage pipe.

The bay itself is not well protected, but the breakwater provides some shelter from winds from the south. The small marina has water and a crane, and you can find a supermarket, post office and tourist office in the village, as well as a bus service to Split. The post office is on Cetinska 22, 21311 Stobreč. Opening hours in the summer are from 0800 to 1200 and 1800 to 2100 Monday to Saturday, otherwise from 0700 to 1400 Monday to Friday.

Podstrana: Le Méridien Grand Hotel Lav – marina

Charts: HHI MK-18; AC 2712, SC5767

This luxury hotel complex opened in February 2007 to much national acclaim and publicity, as the first five star hotel in the Split area. Its 80 berth marina was almost completely fitted out in August 2007 and has electricity and water supplied to all berths. A formal price list and detailed information was yet to be published at the time of going to print, but you can follow the news and get

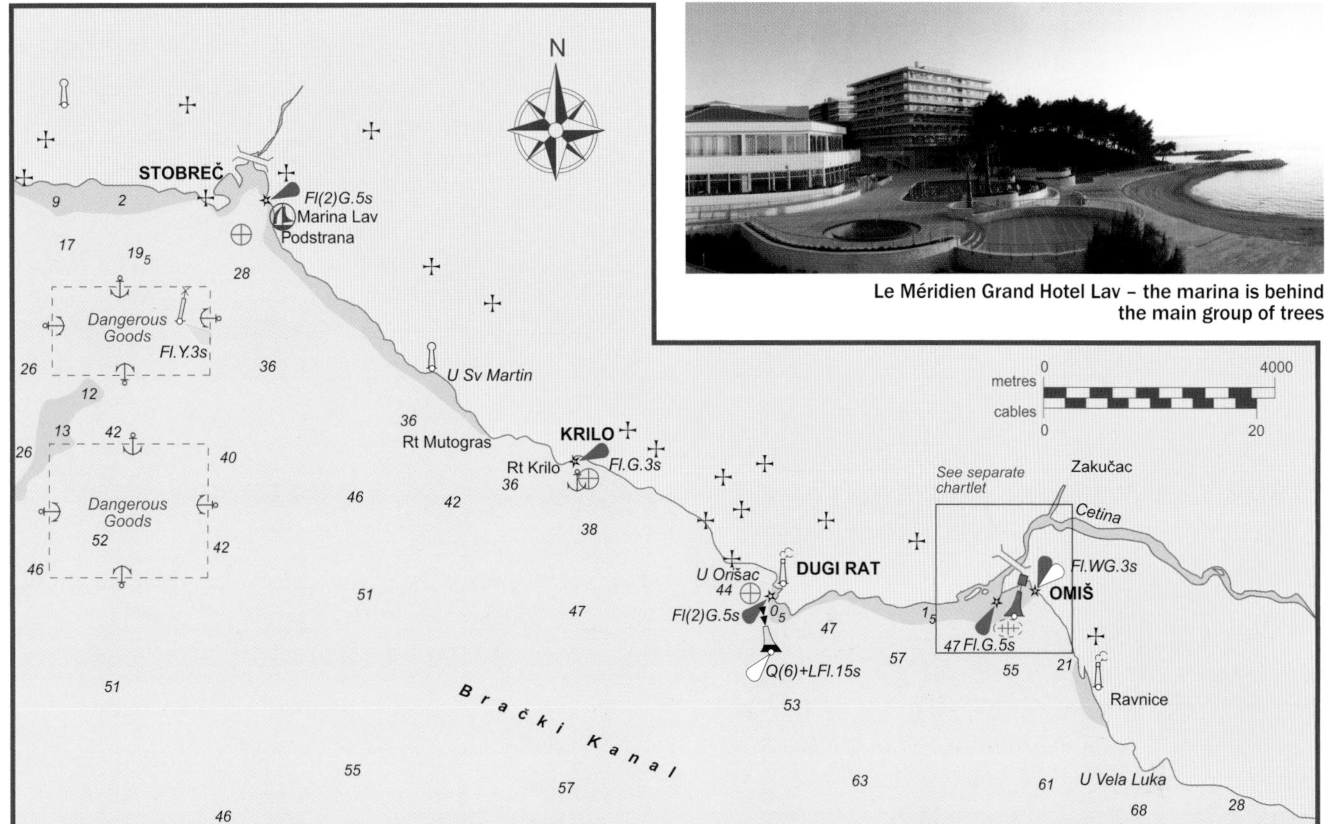

Le Méridien Grand Hotel Lav – the marina is behind the main group of trees

more information from the website www.lemeridien.com/split. Generally referred to as Hotel/Marina Lav (Croatian for 'lion'!), we've given the full name above as you'll see a number of permutations. To contact the hotel (Grljevačka 2a, 21312 Podstrana) call Tel: 021 500 500 or Fax: 021 500 705.

Krilo

Harbour entrance: 43°27'.55N 16°35'.94E
Charts: HHI MK-18; AC 2712, SC5767

Krilo has a small, busy, partially sheltered harbour, but offers a reasonable anchorage outside the port on a sand and weed bed in depths of around 5 to 7m. There's a bus service to Split and facilities are limited to a supermarket and a few bars and shops.

A flashing light (Fl G 3s) marks the end of the breakwater and the harbour lies on the western side of the bay.

Dugi Rat

Entrance to bay: 43°26'.51N 16°38'.00E
Charts: HHI MK-18; AC 2712, SC5767

Dugi Rat is presently a sprawling suburban settlement which grew up around a now disused steelworks. It has a few small beaches, bars and restaurants that come to life in the summer, and a small local harbour where you can berth in depths of around 4m. In just a few years time, it will be the site of a prestigious development, phase one of which includes a 300-berth marina. Follow progress on www.korenatpoint.com.

Watch out for the shoal south of Rt Dugi Rat, which is marked by a south cardinal buoy. The port is protected from the Bora but is otherwise exposed. Services include several bars, restaurants, shops and a post office.

Omiš

Harbour entrance: 43°26'.44N 16°41'.39E

Omiš is an unusual tourist town in that the long main high street is not right on the seafront. The mountains immediately behind the town, together with the crumbling remains of the fortress, lend themselves to great pictures, as does the River Cetina gorge.

NAVIGATION

Charts: HHI MK-18; AC 2712, SC5767

Approaches: See Dugi Rat if approaching from the west. The shallows off Dugi Rat extend up to about 550m

Omiš Town Quay

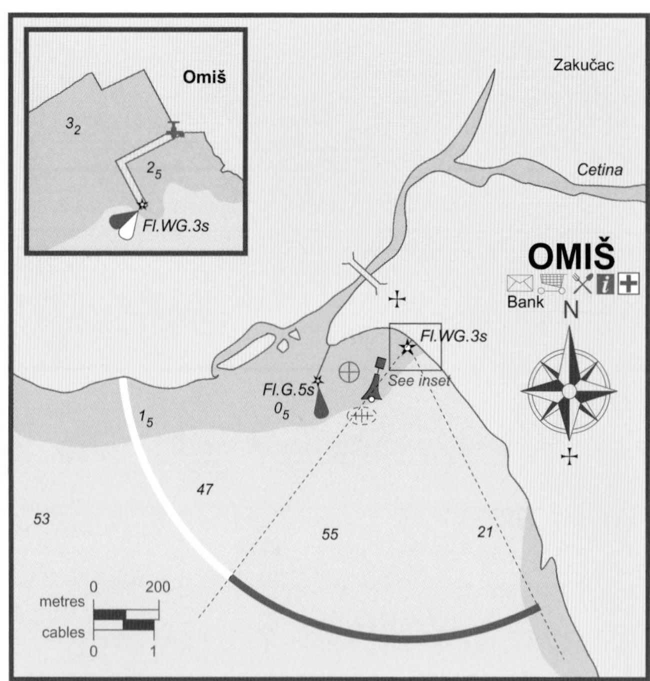

Omiš' crowded pier

from the coast, as far as Omiš, and change in shape at the mouth of the River Cetina. Buoys mark the 5m contour line along this stretch. You'll also need to avoid the sunken wreck at the southern end of the shallows just after passing the gorge, heading east. An unlit red buoy has been laid to the north-east of the wreck. The harbour itself is at the foot of a rocky mountain with some traditional buildings clearly visible by the pier, a small fortress above them and a tall chimney to the east. The end of the pier is marked by a flashing white and green light (Fl WG 3s).

BERTHING

Berth on either side of the pier or at the quay, as space permits. The Bora can be very strong here and funnels down the gorge. The Sirocco also blows hard in this area and at times generates heavy seas, while southwesterly winds produce a swell.

Useful information – Omiš

FACILITIES

There are a couple of **electricity** and **water** pedestals on the pier and a fee for using them may be payable.

PROVISIONING

Omiš has all the **shops**, **markets** and facilities you'd expect from a large town. The nearest **bank** is on the right of the main road roughly halfway between the harbour and the river, with the **post office** next to it - Fošal 1, 21309 Omiš. Opening hours for the post office in the season are 0730 to 2100 Monday to Saturday, off season 0730 to 1900 Monday to Friday, 0730 to 1400 on Saturdays. The various **markets** stretch along the main road.

EATING OUT

There are several restaurants and bars in town. Try Konoba u Našeg Marina, Knezova Kačića bb, Tel: 021 861 328, for local food in a rustic environment. Along the River Cetina are two restaurants, which can be reached by ferry in the high season for about 35 Kunas per person. Radmanove Mlinice (Tel: 021 862 073) is approximately four miles upstream, while Restoran Kaštil Slanica (Tel: 021 861 783) is a mile further upstream.

ASHORE/TRANSPORT

The **tourist office** is in Trg Kneza Miroslava, the last square on the left before you cross the River Cetina, as you walk west from the harbour – Tel: 021 861 350, email: tz-omis@st.htnet.hr, website: www.tz-omis.hr. Private tourist agencies can be found all around town and also along the banks of the River Cetina. Most of them offer **car** and **bike hire** as well as the normal trips; some of them even arrange mountain climbing. The **river-rafting** is well worth a try, although it's a lot more thrilling just outside the high season when there's more water. The mountain scenery along the canyon is particularly impressive and we were told by our rafting leader that a famous western film was shot there. We organised our trip through Atlas in Trogir (look at the website, www.atlas-croatia.com for branch details), but there are several different companies operating on the river. Try Adventure Sports

Useful information – Omiš continued

for a range of outdoor activities – Knezova Kačića bb, Tel: 021 863 015.
If you're not into rafting but want a swim in some fresh water surrounded by spectacular scenery, take a drive along the east bank of the river. You'll find the two restaurants mentioned above and plenty of small lay-bys where you can leave the car and stop for a swim, although watch out for canoes.

Omiš is famous for its Klapa (several part harmony singing) festival in the summer. Tel: 021 861 015 for more information or check out the website www.fdk.hr.

There are a number of good **beaches** situated just south-east of Omiš.

Buses run approximately every 30 minutes to Split, but the weekend traffic in the high season is a bit of a nuisance.

OTHER INFORMATION

Port authority: The harbour-master's office is on the same street as the **bank** and **post office** – Fošal 13, 21310 Omiš, Tel: 021 861 025; Fax: 021 861 025.
Medical: The hospital is east of the harbour, Tel: 021 862 035, and there are a number of **pharmacies** in the area.

Mimice

Entrance to bay: 43°24'.20N 16°48'.37E
Charts: HHI MK-18; AC 1574, AC 2712, SC5767

Three miles east of Omiš, Mimice is a small tourist village with a busy harbour, partially sheltered from winds from the north-west through north to south-east, although the Bora blows strongly in this area.

Beware of the rocks close to the shore one mile east of Mimice, as well as a wreck and more rocks to the west, by Rt Brcančeva. The breakwater has a green light (Fl G 3s) at the end. You can berth alongside the breakwater in depths of between 1.5 and 2.5m.

Ashore you'll find a post office, grocery shop, several bars and cafés, a couple of restaurants and a great pebble beach.

Uvala Vrulja

Entrance to bay:
43°23'.63N 16°52'.85E
Charts: HHI MK-18;
AC 1574, SC5767

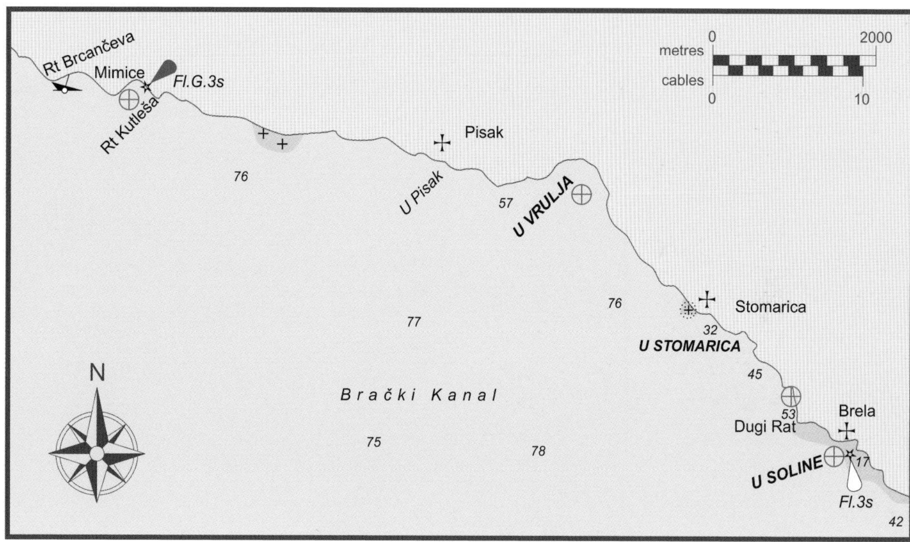

Uvala Vrulja lies 10 miles east of Omiš. Although this is one of the most indented bays along this stretch of coastline, do not be tempted to stop here unless you want to risk experiencing a sudden Bora at full strength. The location and positioning of the bay makes it an ideal funnel for occasionally hurricane-force squalls and this can occur at any time of the year.

Although the onset of a Bora is difficult to spot, look out for thin strips of cloud above the valley as you pass, which indicate the likelihood of one developing.

Uvala Stomarica

Harbour entrance: 43°22'.81N 16°54'.69E
Charts: HHI MK-18; AC 1574, SC5767

Situated 10½ miles east of Omiš, Uvala Stomarica has a small crumbling, partially-sheltered harbour with limited facilities, although it is possible, with caution, to berth alongside the breakwater. Facilities close to the shore are limited, and it's a longish walk to the village of Brela, so the bay is not recommended.

Uvala Soline (Brela)

Entrance to bay: 43°21'.93N 16°55'.88E
Charts: HHI MK-18; AC 1574, SC5767

Just over a mile south-east of Uvala Stomarica, Uvala Soline provides shelter from the Bora but is exposed to winds from the south. Southeasterly winds can cause heavy seas. Brela itself is thought to be the prettiest of the Makarska Riviera resorts and has some good beaches. The water is quite shallow either side of the bay. The breakwater has a white light (Fl 3s) and you can berth alongside the inner side of the breakwater or further into the harbour on lazylines. Electricity and water pedestals have been installed fairly recently. Shops, hotels, bars and cash points are in Brela. Other information is as follows:

Tourist office: Obala Kneza Domagoja bb, 21322 Brela, Tel: 021 618 455; Fax: 021 618 337; e-mail: tz-brela@st.t-com.hr; website: www.brela.hr.
Post office: Trg Alojzija Stepinca 1, 21322 Brela, open from 0800 to 1200 and 1800 to 2100, Monday to Saturday in the season, otherwise from 0700 to 1400, Monday to Friday.
Medical centre: Hotel Solone, 21322, Brela, Tel: 021 603 222.

Baška Voda

Marina entrance:
43°21'.42N
16°56'.88E

Baška Voda is another tourist resort in the old Yugoslavian style, with several hotels and some good beaches. The town harbour now comprises a small marina run by Baotić Yachting (www.baoticyachting.de) where you can berth on lazylines in depths of up to 4m. Electricity and water are available at the quay. The approach is clear, but the water shoals from quite a long way offshore. The breakwater has a red light (Fl R 5s) at its head and the hotels are visible from a distance.

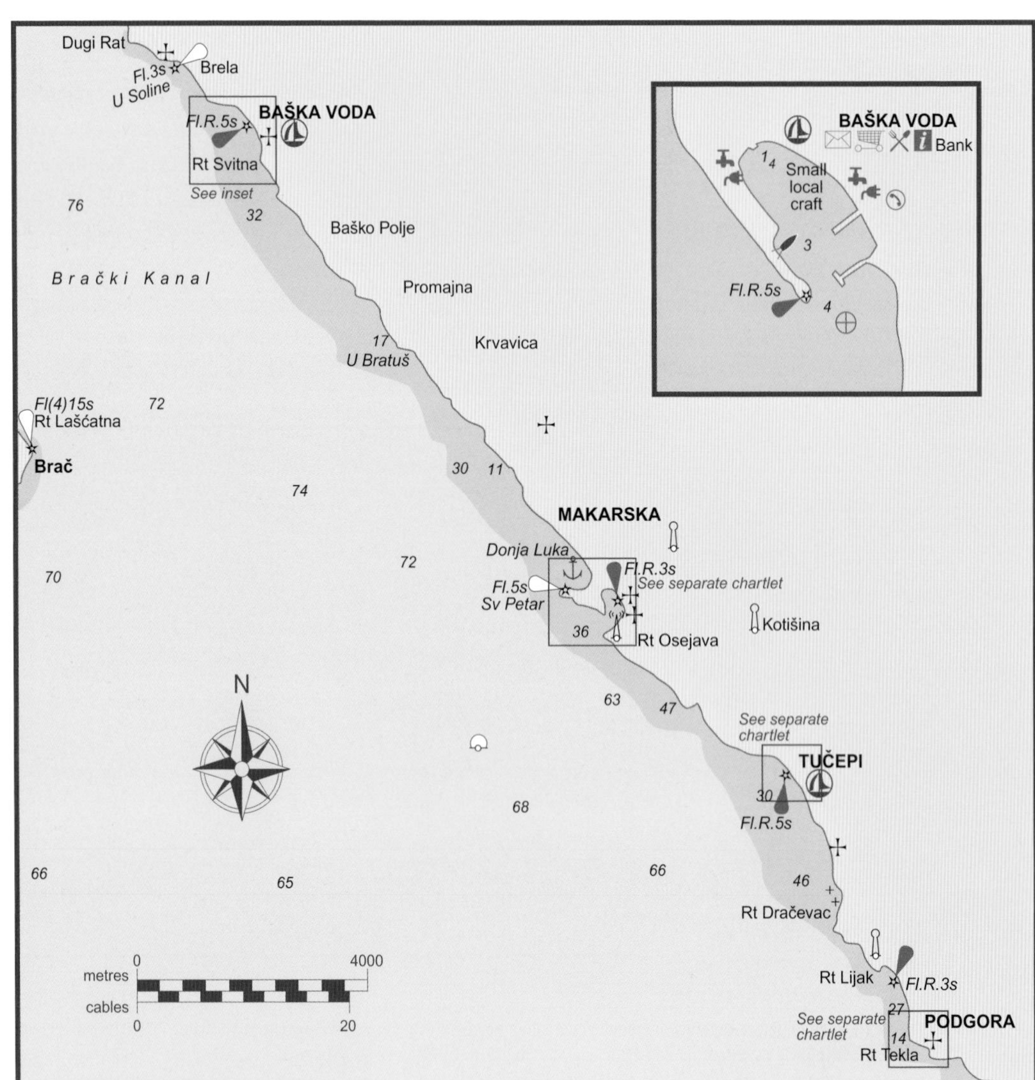

Baška Voda

The town incorporates a post office (on the main road running along the shore), banks, shops, markets, a supermarket, tourist office and many restaurants. The tourist office website has a good map of the town and harbour along with details of all the various land based sports and watersports available (Obala Sv Nikole 31, 21320 Baška Voda, Tel: 021 620 713; Fax: 021 620 713; email: info@baskavoda.hr; website: www.baskavoda.hr). The medical centre can be found in Podspiline bb, Tel: 021 620 133, while a pharmacy is situated in Obala Sv Nicola 29e, Tel: 021 620 077.

Makarska

Entrance to bay: 43°17'.37N 17°00'.76E

Makarska, at the foot of the Biokovo Mountain, is the centre of the package tourist industry in this area and is a favourite with Saga travellers. Its large, palm tree lined, semi-circular beach and streets provide all the facilities and entertainments you would expect from a busy tourist town. The ferry terminal, at the north end of the bay, connects to Sumartin on Brač Island and there is a fuel station just west of the ferry pier. The place is heaving with tourists in the summer, but the nearby Biokovo Nature Park is a great place for the energetic to explore in spring or autumn.

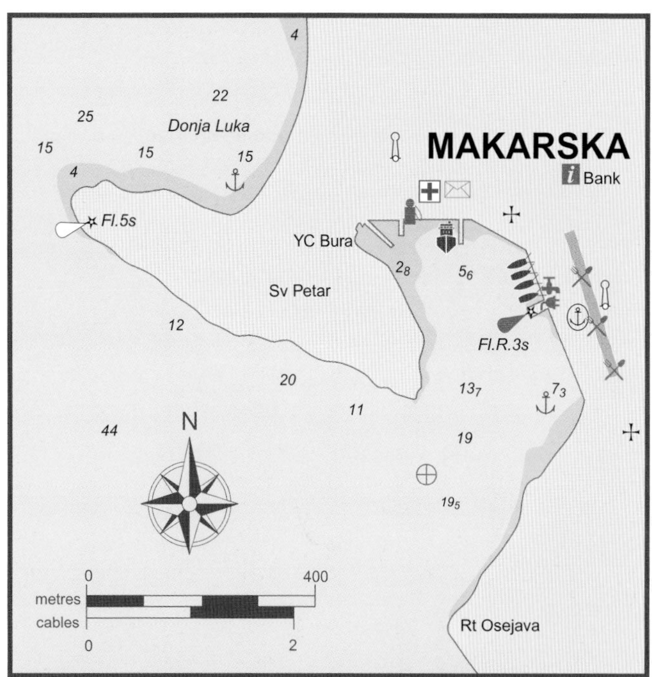

NAVIGATION

Charts: HHI 100-26, MK-20 (including detailed insert of Makarska); AC 1574, SC5767

Approaches: The town, with its mountain backdrop, is easy to spot. On the western tip of the peninsula that bounds the bay to the west is a white light (Fl 5s), while on the pier is a white metal tower, on top of which is a red light (Fl R 3s). You should stay clear of the swimming areas.

BERTHING/ANCHORING

Space permitting you can berth bows- or stern-to on lazylines at the quay, just east of the fuel station and car ferry. Expect to pay a fee, however. There's a private yacht club to the west of the harbour. Alternatively, you can anchor south of the pier on a mud bed in depths of around 6m, or in Donja Luka, north-west of the peninsula, although you will need to go close to the shore to find shallower water. Good holding on a shingle and sand bed. The Bora blows strongly here, but the harbour is well protected from all but southwesterly winds, which create a swell. Donja Luka is less protected and winds from the west, south-west or north-west cause a swell.

The north end of Makarska's wide bay

Makarska's ferry pier

Useful information – Makarska

FACILITIES

Electricity and **water** are available at the quay. The **fuel** station (Tel: 021 612 660) has depths of 3 to 5m alongside it. Its opening hours are from 0800 to 2000 every day in season and from 0800 to 1500 Monday to Saturday outside of it. There's a **slipway** to the west of the harbour, which is suitable for boats on trailers. The **harbourmaster's office** is at Kralja Tomislava 1a, 21300 Makarska, Tel: 021 611 977; Fax: 021 611 977.

PROVISIONING

The **post office**, situated at Trg 4 Svibanja 533 br 1, 21300 Makarska, is open from 0730 to 2100 Monday to Saturday in the season, otherwise from 0700 to 1900 Monday to Friday and 0700 to 1300 on Saturdays. A **pharmacy** can be found at Sv Ivičevića 2, 21300 Makarska, Tel: 021 612 288.

EATING OUT

There are scores of **restaurants** and **pizzerias** to choose from.

ASHORE

You'll be able to find most conceivable tourist offerings via the numerous private agencies in the town and there is plenty of entertainment in the summer evenings. The main **tourist office** is at Obala Kralja Tomislava 16, 21300 Makarska, Tel: 021 612 688; Fax: 021 615 352; email: info@turist-biro@makarska.com; website: www.turistbiro-makarska.com.

Contact details for the **nature park** are Tel: 021 616 924, website: www.biokovo.com, but Biokovo Activ Holidays organises tours and has information on the walks and mountain huts, Tel: 021 611 688. **Ferries** connect Makarska to Sumartin on Brač Island.

Buses run regularly to Split and Dubrovnik.

OTHER INFORMATION

Medical centre: Sv Ivičevića 2, 21300 Makarska, Tel: 021 612 033.

Tučepi

Marina entrance: 43°16'.17N 17°03'.17E

Two miles south-east of Makarska, Tučepi has some attractive pebble beaches and is a good place to visit if you want to hike up a mountain. It also has a small marina, now run by the municipality, which does not seem to feature in many of the brochures or guides on this area.

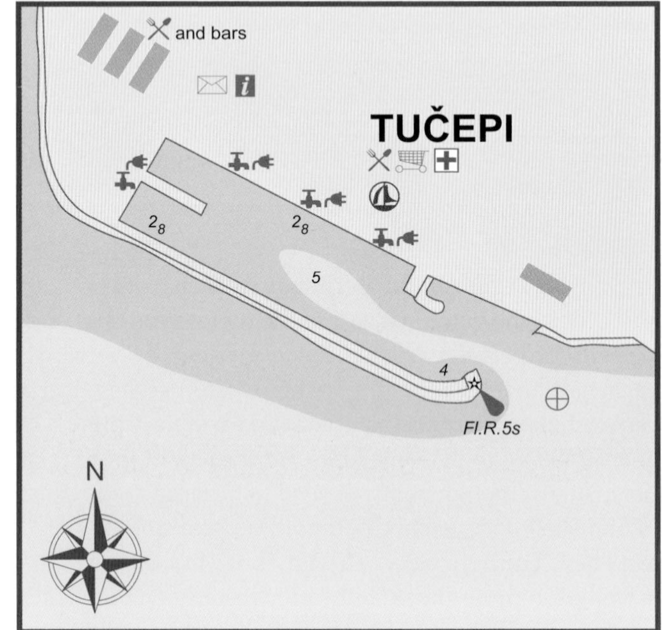

NAVIGATION

Charts: HHI MK-20; AC 1574, SC5767

Approaches: There are some rocks just offshore about a mile south-east of the harbour, but otherwise the approach is clear. The breakwater has a red light (Fl R 5s) on it and Makarska should be visible to the north-west.

BERTHING/FACILITIES

There are 45 berths for yachts up to 16m (52ft) in length. Berth bows- or stern-to using lazylines in depths of 2 to 7m. The marina (Kraj bb, 21235 Tučepi, Tel: 098 927 2785) is open from April to October and charges around 220 Kunas for a 10m (33ft) yacht for an overnight stay.

Facilities include electricity, water and telephone as well as cable TV connections laid on to all berths. The bay is not very well protected but the harbour provides shelter from most seas, although southerly winds can cause a swell.

Tučepi Marina

ASHORE

The tourist office is at Kraj 46, 21325 Tučepi, Tel: 021 623 100, e-mail: tz@tucepi.com, website: www.tucepi.com. The website has telephone numbers and addresses for most of the shops, restaurants, bars, tourist agencies and facilities. The post office (opening hours as Stobreč on page 185) and banks are all on the same street as the tourist office and there are a number of restaurants from which to choose.

Podgora

Harbour entrance: 43°14'.55N 17°04'.47E

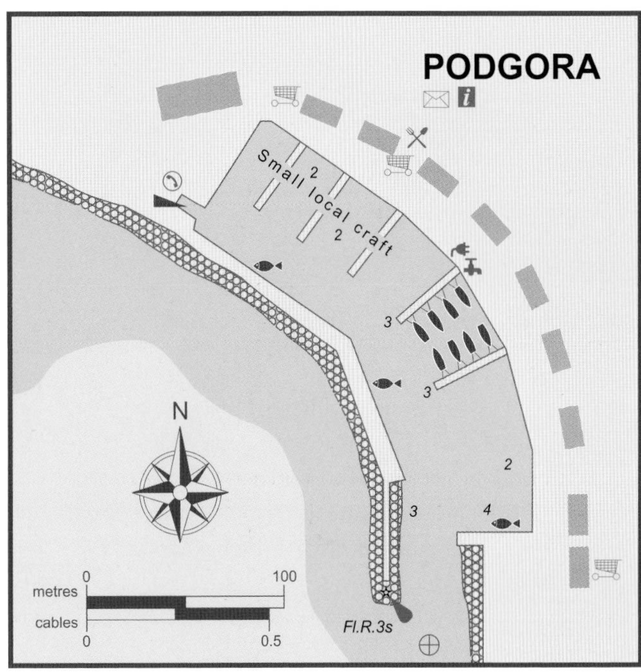

Four miles south-east of Makarska, Podgora is another traditional and busy tourist resort, with a distinctive statue on the top of the hill behind the town. The seagull's wings are a memorial to the town's role as a centre of resistance during the Second World War.

NAVIGATION

Charts: HHI MK-20; AC 1574, SC5767

Approaches: If you are hugging the coast from either direction, check the charts for rocks close to the shore, but a direct approach from the west is straightforward and you should see the statue from a distance. The main, recently refurbished, harbour has a red light (Fl R 3s) at the end of its breakwater.

BERTHING

The newer harbour has pontoons where you can berth bows- or stern-to on lazylines. Fishing boats tend to use the inside of the breakwater. The harbour is exposed to winds from the north-west, throught west, to south-east, and southwesterly winds can cause heavy seas. Electricity and water are available. Slightly further east, in Uvala Čaklje, is a small harbour that is mainly reserved for fishing boats.

ASHORE

Most of the shops and services are located on the main road by the sea. The post office is at Obala Kneza Branimira, 21327 Podgora, with a Splitska bank nearby, while a pharmacy is situated at Branimirova 87, Tel: 021 625 211. There are plenty of restaurants, bars and hotels from which to choose, as you would expect for a resort of this size.

The tourist office is at Branimirova 87, Tel/fax: 021 625 560; email: tz-podgora@st.htnet.hr; website: www.podgora.hr. The website has some useful contact numbers and addresses. You will also come across tourist agencies all over town, through which you can rent cars and bikes. Birgmaier Sub operates a diving centre from Branimirova 107, Tel: 021 625 134.

Podgora's distinctive monument on the hill and the harbour in the foreground

Drašnice

Approach to anchorage: 43°13'.03N 17°06'.23E
Charts: HHI MK-20; AC 1574, SC5767

Drašnice is a small settlement with a harbour that is really only suitable for shallow-draught boats. Although the approach is straightforward, it's quite exposed and not suitable for an overnight stop, but you can anchor near the breakwater on a sand bed, in depths of around 9m. The limited facilities include a post office.

Igrane

Harbour entrance: 43°11'.70N 17°08'.58E
Charts: HHI MK-20; AC 1574, SC5767

Igrane is a densely developed tourist resort built around a small bay. The approach is straightforward. There's a little harbour at the north-west end of the bay, but depths are well under 1m so find a space to berth alongside the inner wall of the breakwater in 2 to 3m of water.

Alternatively, anchor off the harbour in depths of 5 to 12m on a sand and mud bed, which has good holding. Note that there's an underwater cable running from the eastern tip of Rt Igrane to Hvar Island and most of the beach is roped off as a swimming area. The harbour is exposed to winds from the south, south-east and east.

Post office: Vrtina bb, 21329 Igrane, open in the season from 0800 to 1200 and 1800 to 2100 Monday to Saturday, otherwise from 0800 to 1500 Monday to Friday.

Tourist office: Tel: 021 627 801 (work)/021 627847 (home); email: tz-igrane@st.htnet.hr; website: www.igrane.com.

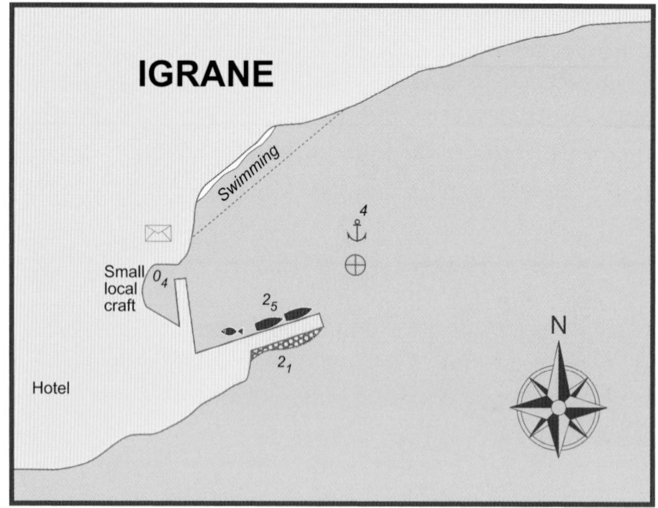

Drvenik

Entrance to Uvala Delić: 43°08'.95N 17°15'.45E
Charts: HHI MK-20; AC 1574, SC5767

Drvenik connects the mainland, by ferry, with Sućuraj on the eastern tip of Hvar Island. Apart from the ferry connection, a hotel, a post office and a few reasonable restaurants and bars around the beach,

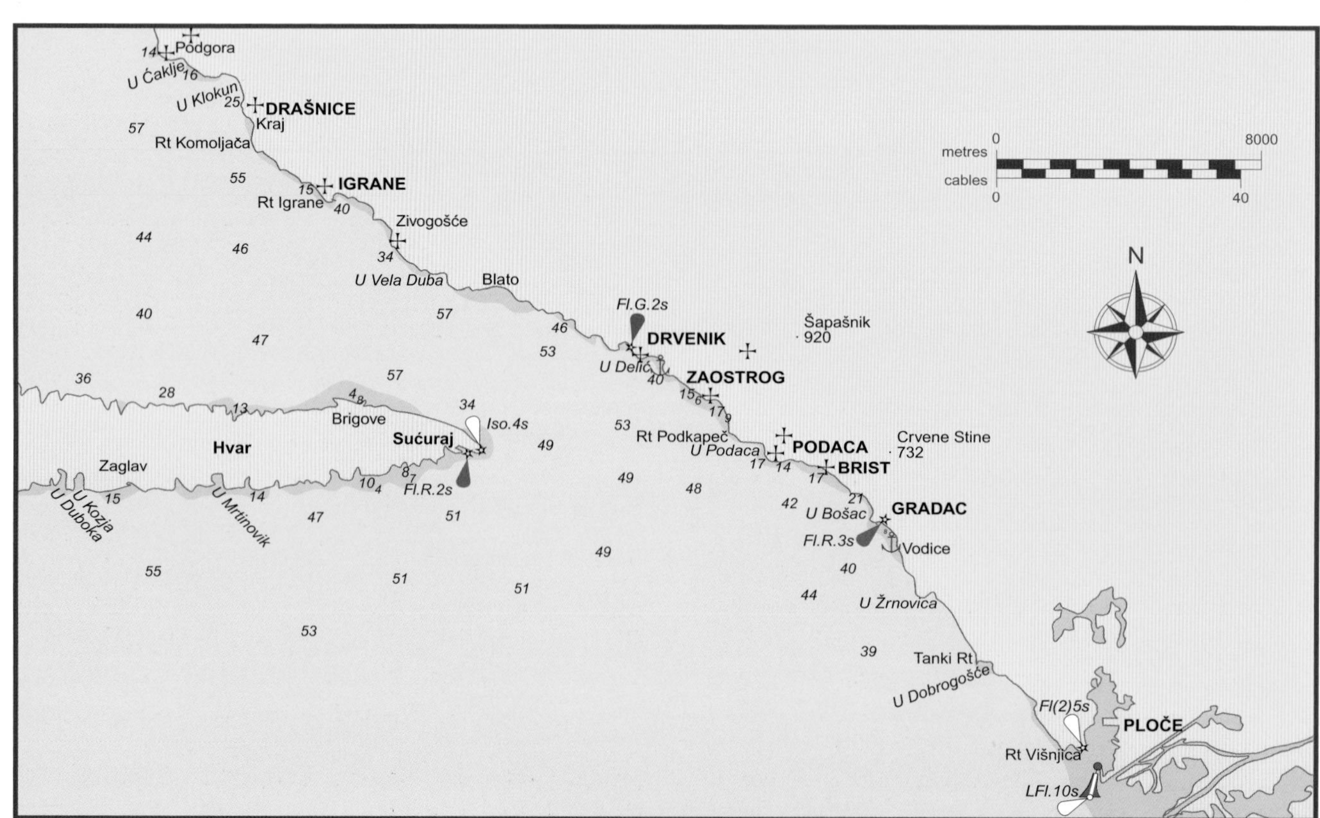

there's not a great deal going on here. The harbour is busy with local fishing boats and you need to stay clear of the ferry and swimming area, so anchor out of the traffic or, better still, in the adjacent bay, Uvala Delić. Protected from the Bora and winds from the east, it offers good holding on a mud bottom in depths of 5 to 10m. The approach is straightforward, but there are two settlements ahead of you: the ferry port and main beach are to the west, with a green light (Fl G 2s) at the end of the ferry pier, while the anchorage is to the east.

Post office: Donja Vala bb, 21333 Drvenik, opening hours as Igrane above on page 192.

Tourist office: Donja Vala bb, Tel: 021 623 100.

The ferry berthing at Drvenik

Drvenik's ferry port and main beach; the anchorage is to the east, in Uvala Delić

Zaostrog

Entrance to bay: 43°08'.13N 17°16'.86E
Charts: HHI MK-20; AC 1574, SC5767

Another little tourist resort, less developed than its neighbours, with a modest harbour that is really only suitable for small local boats and has an unlit breakwater. The approach is straightforward and you should be able to spot the belfry of the old monastery among the trees and the hotel complex to the west of it. It's quite exposed to seas and winds and not suitable for an overnight stay, but you can get some protection from the Bora and easterly winds close to the shore, in the eastern part of the bay. Good holding on a mud bottom in depths of 5 to 12m. Among the amenities ashore are bars, restaurants, cafés, shops, a post office (opening hours are the same as Igrane – see page 192) and an attractive beach.

Zaostrog's modest harbour

Podaca/Brist

Entrance to Uvala Podaca: 43°07'.45N 17°17'.74E
Centre of Brist bay: 43°06'.92N 17°19'.23E
Charts: HHI MK-20; AC 1574, SC5767

Podaca is a smaller resort with a busy pier. The bay provides partial shelter from the Bora but is otherwise exposed. This harbour is not suitable for an overnight stop, but facilities include a post office.

Alternatively, you can anchor at nearby Brist, which offers the same shelter, but has no post office.

Gradac

Harbour entrance: 43°06'.15N 17°20'.65E
Charts: HHI MK-20; AC 1574, SC5767

Located five miles south-east of Drvenik, and the south-eastern boundary of the Makarska Riviera, Gradac has a popular pebble beach just south of town. It's packed in the summer so watch out for swimmers. The belfry and statue on the hill above the harbour should be visible from a distance, while the hotel complex, north-west of the harbour, comes into view from closer in. The breakwater has a relatively new red light (Fl R 3s) that is not indicated on some charts and guides. You can either berth alongside the inner wall of the breakwater in depths of 2 to 3m, or anchor south-east of the harbour on a sand bed where there is good holding in depths of 5 to 10m. The breakwater provides shelter from all winds, although southerlies may cause a swell. The anchorage area is protected from the Bora and northerly winds, but is not suitable in southerly or westerly winds. Beware of strong currents, particularly when the River Neretva is running high, and in southerly or southeasterly winds.

Gradac's small harbour

Gradac's restaurants vying for trade

On shore are the standard resort tourist shops, bars, restaurants and facilities. Hotel Marco Polo on Obala 15 (Tel: 021 697 502) has a friendly terrace restaurant overlooking the beach. The tourist office situated at Stepana Radica 1, 21330 Gradac, can be contacted on Tel: 021 697 511, email: tzo-gradac@st.htnet.hr, website: www.gradac.hr. The post office's opening hours are the same as Podgora (see page 191).

Ploče

Entrance to channel:
43°02'.00N 17°24'.76E

Ploče is the largest port in the area, with a large amount of traffic for Bosnia and Hercegovina. The approach is complicated by shallows around the mouth of the channel. Currents can be strong here and there are also rocks to be avoided. While the harbour is well protected and has a fuel station, it's not the place to savour Croatia. We

Grey Ploče on a grey day

found it grey and industrial with few saving graces. We've included the most important points, but look at the charts carefully and follow the markers if you have to come here.

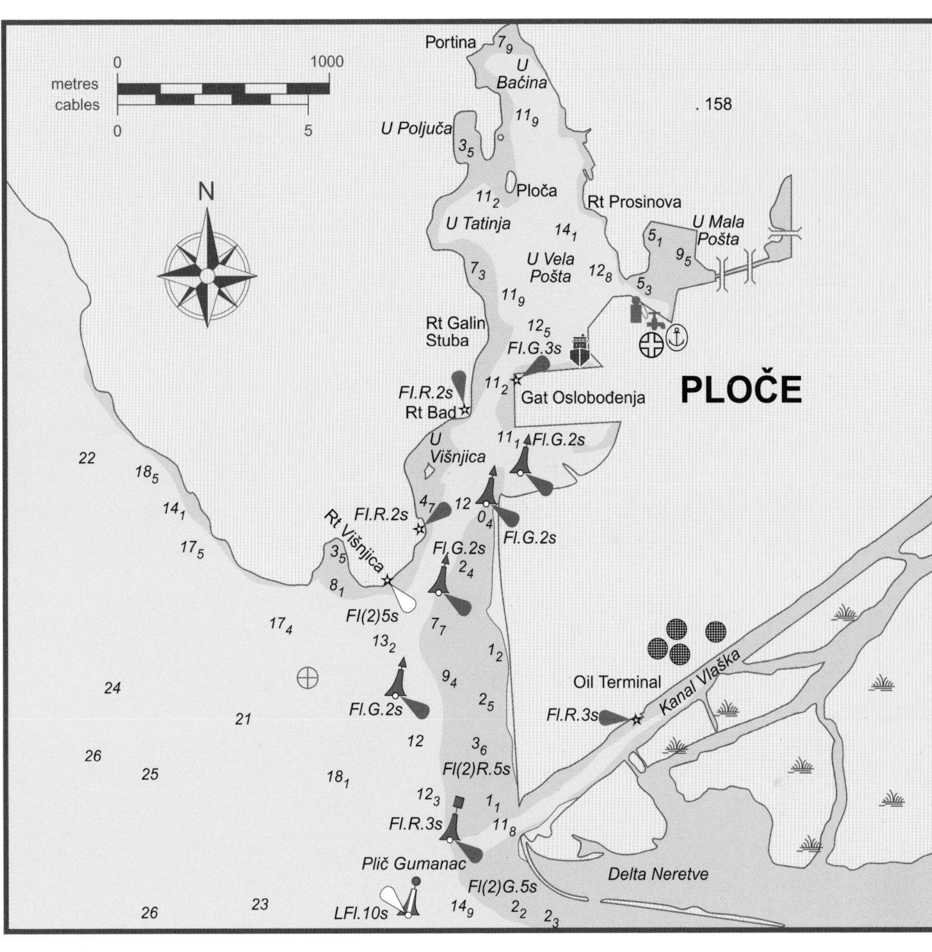

NAVIGATION

Charts: HHI 63, 154, MK-24; AC 269, AC 1574, SC5767

Approaches: Special regulations apply and the channel is well marked. If coming from the west, give Rt Višnjica, west of the channel and marked by a white light (Fl (2) 5s), at least a mile's clearance to be able to see into the channel and avoid traffic coming out. As you exit the channel, the maximum clearance is half a mile before turning to the west.

BERTHING

Head for the inner part of the harbour and berth bows- or stern-to the quay beyond the ferry pier and near to the fuel station. The Bora and the Sirocco blow strongly in this area, but the harbour is well protected.

Useful information – Ploče

FACILITIES

Water and **electricity** are available. The **fuel** station (at Neretvanskih Gusara 1, 20340 Ploče, Tel: 020 679 579) has depths of up to 8m and is open from 0600 to 2200 in the summer, seven days a week. Outside the summer season, the opening hours are 0600 to 2000 Monday to Saturday and 0700 to 1100 on Sundays and bank holidays. Nautical charts and maps can also be purchased here.

OTHER INFORMATION

Port authority: Based in Trg Kralja Tomislava 24, 20340 Ploče, Tel: 020 679 008. The harbourmaster's telephone number is 020 679 541.

Post office: Trg Kralja Tomislava, 20340 Ploče. Open 0700 to 2000 Monday to Friday, 0700 to 1300 on Saturdays, all year round.

Tourist office: V Nazora 26, 20340 Ploče, Tel: 020 679 510. No email address or website details were available.

Medical centre: Tel: 020 679 910.

Pharmacy: Tel: 020 671 889.

Bus and **train stations** and **ferries** to Trpanj, on the Pelješac Peninsula.

Right: Church and supermarket in Ploče

The Neretva River

Charts: HHI MK-24; AC 1574, SC5767

Perhaps most famous for the recently rebuilt bridge in Bosnia's Mostar, which lies much further upstream, the Neretva River is navigable, with caution, up to Metković by yachts drawing less than 4.5m and with an air height of less than 14m. Depths, however, can vary according to weather, currents and water levels. In the summer, the river is at its shallowest after long droughts and during southerly winds. In the winter, frosts and the Bora also reduce depths. The two main settlements are Opuzen, about 7 miles upstream, and Metković, a further 5 miles upstream, although there are also three smaller villages. You can take an organised trip

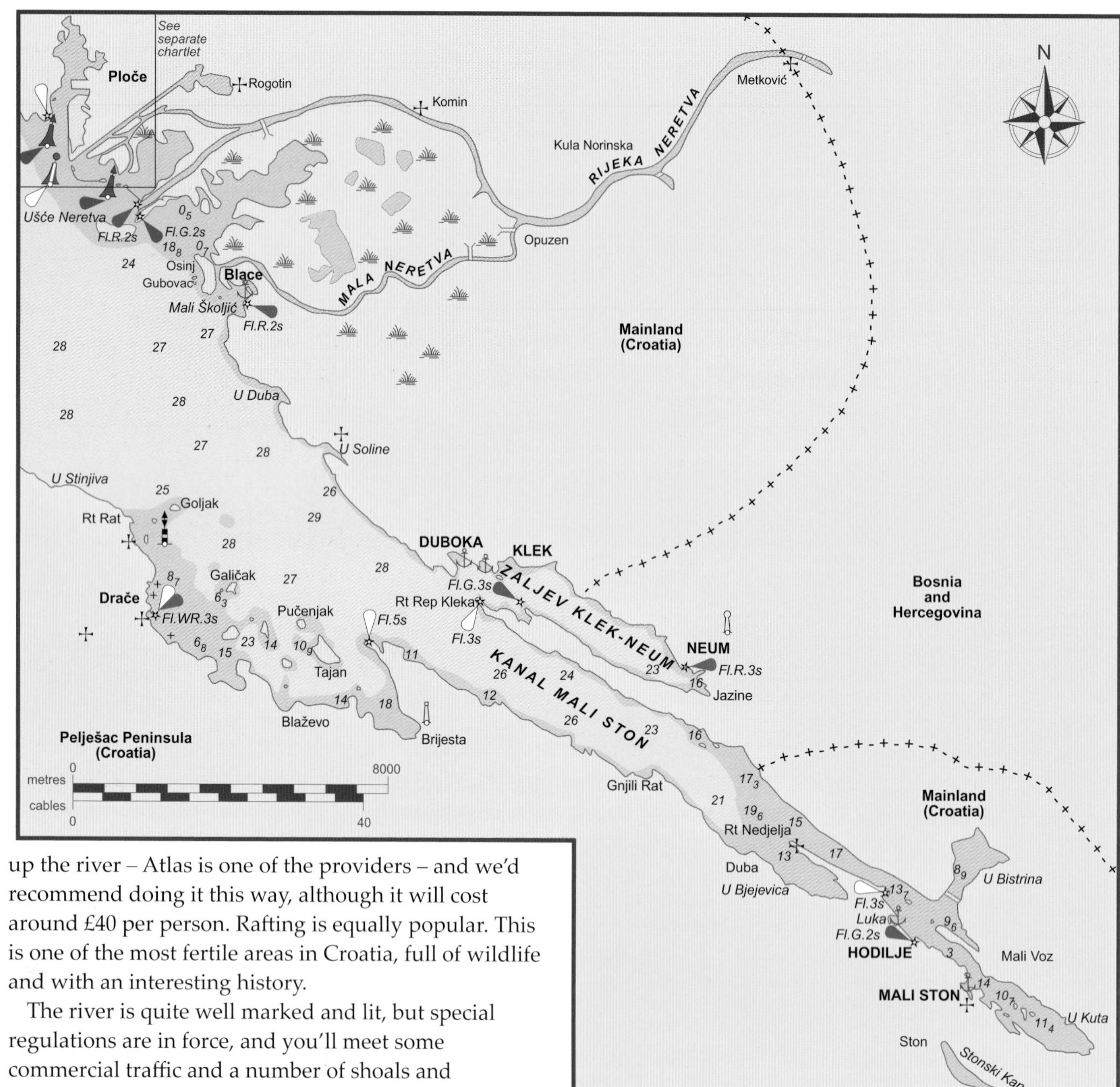

up the river – Atlas is one of the providers – and we'd recommend doing it this way, although it will cost around £40 per person. Rafting is equally popular. This is one of the most fertile areas in Croatia, full of wildlife and with an interesting history.

The river is quite well marked and lit, but special regulations are in force, and you'll meet some commercial traffic and a number of shoals and challenges if you decide to navigate it on your own. Both main settlements have quays to which you can berth, and Metković is a good-sized town.

For more information on the history of the delta and its main towns, look at www.metkovic.hr, which also has an interesting page on the traditional boats in use on the river. Try www.huck-finn.hr for details of rafting excursions on the river. Choose 'rafting' and then 'rafting Neretva'.

Blace

Entrance to bay: 42°59'.86N 17°28'.17E
Charts: HHI MK-24; AC 1574, SC5767

Lying two miles south-east of the mouth of the Neretva Delta, Blace is a small village with a shallow, well-protected bay, although the Bora blows strongly here. From the north-west, keep clear of the shallows around the river estuary. There is a small islet, Mali Školjić, with a red light (Fl R 2s) in the mouth of the bay. Depths are up to 2m between the mainland and the east coast of the islet, but reduce to 0.3m west of Mali Školjić, so leave the islet to port and head for the pier just beyond, to berth on the south-east side in depths of 2 to 3m. Look out for rocks north-west of the pier. Alternatively, anchor between the islet and the pier. The holding is good on a mud bed, with depths of around 6m. The inner part of the harbour shoals to 0.3m and there is an overhead power cable across the channel leading to the inner harbour, with a maximum air clearance of 8m. The village has a small shop, but not much else.

Zaljev Klek Neum

Charts: HHI MK-24; AC 1574, SC5767

Part of this large bay is in Bosnia and Hercegovina, but this is not a problem for visitors. It's a deep bay and not particularly suitable for anchoring. It's also being developed for tourism in a somewhat clinical way and therefore not ideal to visit. You can berth at Neum, in Bosnia and Hercegovina, using the quays by the hotel, or anchor at Duboka or Klek. Approaching the entrance to the bay is relatively straightforward and you will see a white light (Fl 3s) to starboard on Rt Rep Kleka. Immediately after entering the bay you need to look out for two low-lying, above-water rocks on either side. Hrid Klještac, off the north coast, has a small chapel on it, while Hrid Lopat, off the south coast, is marked by a green light (Fl G 3s).

Duboka

Entrance to bay: 42°56'.28N 17°33'.07E

Immediately to port on entering the bay, and before the two rocks, Duboka has a few houses but limited facilities. Anchor on a sand bed in depths of 5 to 10m where the holding is good. Note that it is exposed to the Sirocco, which can cause a swell.

Klek

Entrance to bay: 42°56'.46N 17°33'.73E

Klek lies on the north coast of the bay immediately after the low-lying rock. Anchor away from the swimming area in the middle of the bay, in depths of 6 to 10m. The holding is good until you get to the gravel closer to shore. Shelter is similar to Duboka.

Klek has a good beach, hotels, a campsite and 'holiday village' with tennis courts and mini golf, a post office (Klek bb, 20356 Klek, open 0700 to 1100 Monday to Friday all year round), tourist office (Trg Palmi 1, 20356 Klek), shops and a few bars and restaurants.

Neum

Quay: 42°55'.30N 17°36'.59E

Bosnia and Hercegovina's only port is a sprawling modern development. There appears to be no Customs formalities for visiting boats, although by car there are frontier controls. However, it is advisable to inform the police of your arrival, as soon as possible, at the police station by the quay. Berth at the quay in front of Hotel Zenit. The bay is exposed to westerly and southwesterly winds. Neum boasts all the facilities of a largish town. For more information, go to websites www.hotel-zenit.com or www.neum.ba.

Neum's less glamorous side

Kanal Mali Ston

Leading to a dead end, where the Pelješac Peninsula joins the mainland, the canal becomes shallow, rocky and narrow in several places. There are numerous shellfish farms, which makes many of the bays out of bounds to yachts. Adding to the challenges are the Bora and Sirocco, which can reach gale force and cause moderate seas. We follow the canal, heading south-east to the end, then north-west along the north-east coast of the Pelješac Peninsula to Rt Blaca. Mali Ston and the neighbouring (by road) Ston are well worth a visit, but it's a long trip and they might be better explored by land or, alternatively, from the other side of the peninsula.

Kapetanova Kuća, Mali Ston, one of Croatia's most well-known restaurants

NAVIGATION IN THE CANAL

Charts: HHI MK-24 and MK-25 for the whole area; AC 1574, SC5767

Three to four miles into the canal, a rock lies close to the north-east coast. Further in, by Duba, off the south-west coast, a shallow area extends about 400m offshore. Rt Nedjelja bisects the canal with the shallower water to its south and the fairway to the north. The northern fairway narrows significantly here and, just before it opens out again, there is another shoal and islet. The shoal is in the centre of the canal, with the white light (Fl 3s) on Rt Čeljen to the west-north-west. It's easiest to leave the shoal and the islet to starboard. Uvala Bistrina lies to port – a large shallow bay used for shellfish farming.

The settlement of Hodilje is situated to starboard and has a green light (Fl G 2s) on the breakwater. Continuing past Hodilje, the channel is well marked but depths reduce to 3m and there's a rock off the promontory, north-north-east of Hodilje. Mali Ston is to starboard, about a mile after passing Hodilje (see chartlet on page 196). You then reach Uvala Kuta where there are more shellfish farms, an islet and several rocks in the middle that are surrounded by shallow water.

Luka

Entrance to bay: 42°51'.75N 17°41'.15E

Luka, situated on the north-west end of the larger bay that it shares with Hodilje (see below), provides a reasonable anchorage but has no facilities apart from a fishing boat repair yard.

Anchor in the centre of the bay in depths of 2 to 5m. Holding is good on a mud bed and shelter is similar to that of Hodilje (see below).

Hodilje

Entrance to bay: 42°51'.61N 17°41'.41E

On the north coast of the peninsula, just before you get to the shallowest part of the canal, Hodilje is a small village with a few restaurants and shops on the south east of the bay that it shares with Luka.

Shellfish farms stretch from the centre of the bay, north-west to Luka, but you can berth along either side of the mole (Fl G 2s) in depths of between 1 and 3.5m. Alternatively, anchor north of the mole in about 8m on a mud bed where the holding is good. It is protected from all winds and seas except the Bora, which blows strongly here.

Mali Ston
(and Ston 'Ashore')

Entrance to bay: 42°50'.94N 17°42'.54E

Mali Ston and Ston are half a mile apart by road, but you'd need to circumnavigate the whole of the Pelješac Peninsula to travel between the two by boat. Mali Ston is at the root of the Kanal Mali Ston on the south-eastern extremity of the north-east coast of the peninsula, and Ston lies at the end of a large inlet off the southern tip of the peninsula. The two settlements are joined together by the still impressive remnants of a 14th century wall that was part of the main fortification protecting the peninsula from mainland marauders. Each village was also fortified individually, and there was a total of 3½ miles of walls and 40 towers, of which about half remain today. Ston has been described as a mini Dubrovnik without the crowds. There was widespread destruction during the Homeland War as well as the 1996 earthquake, and many of the buildings are now damaged and/or empty. Mali Ston is famous for its oysters and other shellfish, as is Ston, which is also known for its salt. Boasting a couple of good hotels, Ston is also developing a reputation for romantic getaways, helped no doubt by the aphrodisiac qualities of its oysters.

NAVIGATION/BERTHING

See above for general navigation in the canal. You should make out the stone walls and towers from a distance, both in the town and up on the hills south-west of the village. As you pass through the shallowest part of the canal, heading south-east and about a mile past Hodilje, Mali Ston is the first bay to starboard. There are shellfish farms on either side of the bay and a breakwater across the harbour. Depths vary considerably, but the eastern wall of the harbour has up to 3m of water at its outermost end, by the tower. Depending on the volume of traffic and the proximity of the shellfish farms, it may be possible to anchor north of the breakwater. You will find good holding on a mud bed in depths of 3 to 5m. It is sheltered from all winds except the Bora, which blows strongly here but does not cause heavy seas. Very rarely a sudden change in the sea level can occur, sometimes by up to 2m, which is usually caused by unexpected southerly winds or gales.

Useful information – Mali Ston/Ston

EATING OUT
Most things are available in either Ston or Mali Ston. There are some great restaurants, as you would expect. Kapetenova Kuća in Mali Ston has a reputation throughout Croatia and specialises in oysters and fish, Tel: 020 756 264; e-mail: ostrea.info@ostrea.hr; website: www.ostrea.hr. Restaurants in Ston are less exclusive and generally cheaper. Try Tavern Bacchus (Tel: 020 754 270).

ASHORE
The **tourist office** is on the main street in Ston, Tel: 020 754 452. It does not seem to have a website yet, but you can find out a little more about the area by looking at www.visitdubrovnik.hr and choosing Ston. There are marked walks around the town walls and a summer festival that starts in late July and continues for most of August.

TRANSPORT
There are two **buses** a day to Dubrovnik and two to Orebić, coinciding with the **ferries** from Orebić to Korčula.

OTHER INFORMATION
Harbourmaster, Ston: Od Stovišta 1, 20230 Ston, Tel: 020 754 661.
Post office: Gundulićeva Poljana, 20230 Ston. Opening hours: Monday to Friday 0700 to 1300, Saturday 0700 to 1200, all year round.
Pharmacy: Ston, Tel: 020 754 034.
Medical centre: Ston, Tel: 020 754 004.

The Pelješac Peninsula, anti-clockwise from Drače

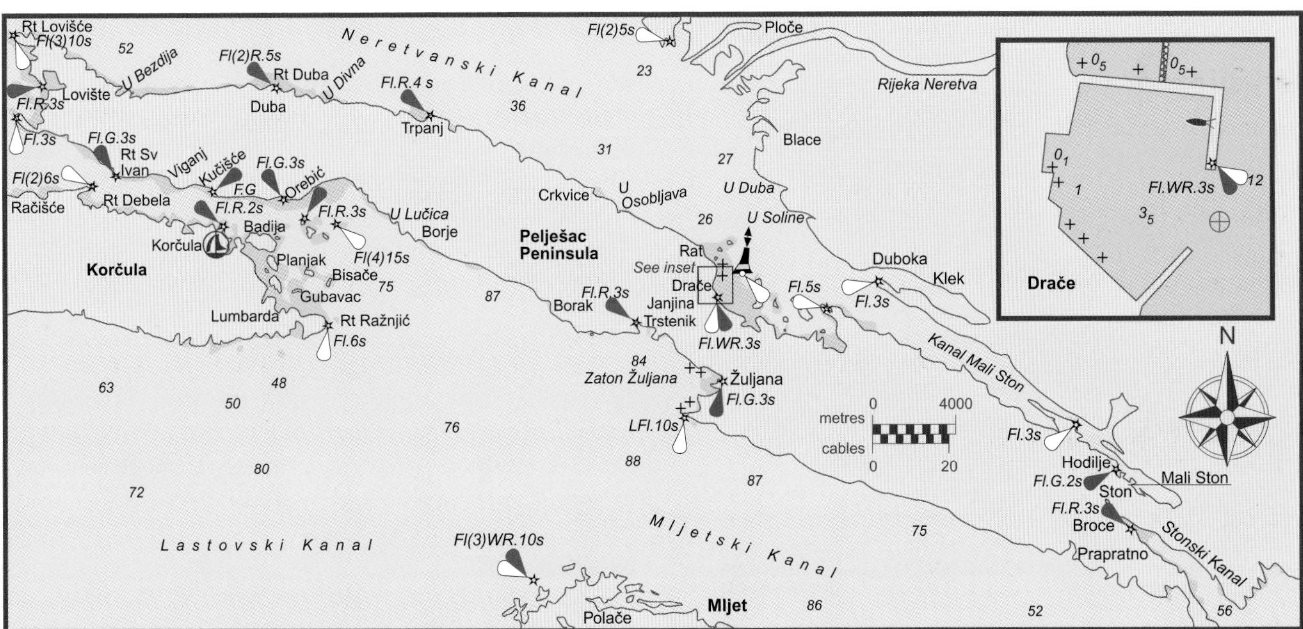

The Pelješac Peninsula is famous for wine, olives and shellfish and is very pretty in parts. However, both by sea and road it's a long way to go, with settlements few and far between.

We've covered Ston and Mali Ston above, and now we work our way anticlockwise from Drače on the north-east coast, around the western tip, and then south-east along the south-west coast. Much of the coastline is inhospitable, but there are a few interesting settlements within easy reach if you are visiting the islands of Korčula or Mljet, or passing the south-west coast of the peninsula on your way between Dubrovnik and Split.

Drače

Harbour entrance: 42°55'.73N 17°27'.10E

Drače lies in a large shallow bay with a number of rocks close to the shore (see inset above). It's a popular summer swimming destination and has a couple of seasonal bars and a fish restaurant. The bigger settlement of Janjina lies about a mile inland along the road up the hill.

NAVIGATION

Charts: HHI MK-24; AC 1574, SC5767

Approaches: The bay is full of islets, shoals and rocks, and becomes shallow from 500 to 800m offshore. There are a number of different approaches between the hazards, but look at the charts carefully to avoid the rocks, and head straight for the harbour entrance from out at sea rather than hugging the coastline on either side. If you are passing the bay by, stay close to the south-west coast of the mainland rather than the peninsula. You should be able to see on the hill the belfry in Janjina and the breakwater has a red and white light (Fl WR 3s) at its head.

BERTHING

Depths in the harbour vary from 1 to 3m, the deepest water being along the inner side of the breakwater. The bay is exposed to the Bora and partly to the Sirocco. The breakwater, which was improved a couple of years ago, affords protection from the Bora, but the Sirocco still causes a swell. There are plans to provide electricity and water.

ASHORE

There's a tourist office at Janjina – Tel: 020 741 130; Fax: 020 741 005; email: tzo-janjina@du.htnet.hr. It has no official website as yet, but we found a good alternative at www.janjina@croatia1.com. Janjina also has a medical centre (Tel: 020 741 231) and a post office.

Drače has two restaurants, one pizzeria, two cafés, a grocery shop and a private tourist agency.

Uvala Osobljava

Entrance to bay: 42°58'.11N 17°23'.46E
Charts: HHI MK-24; AC 1574, SC5767

This bay has a small quay with depths of 1 to 2m alongside or, alternatively, you can anchor in depths of 3 to 10m on a sand bed that provides good holding.

The approach is straightforward, but there are no facilities, and protection from the winds and sea, especially the Bora, Sirocco and northwesterlies, is limited.

Crkvice

Harbour entrance: 42°58'.56N 17°22'.61E
Charts: HHI MK-24; AC 1574, SC5767

Crkvice is a small settlement with a breakwater and local boats berthed along home-made jetties by the shore. The approach is straightforward and landmarks include a small white cross on the top of the hill and some houses around the breakwater. You can berth alongside on the inner side of the breakwater, in depths of up to 3m.

Anchoring is not recommended as an underwater cable runs from just inside the south-east headland to the mainland. Shelter as Uvala Osobljava above.

Trpanj

Harbour entrance: 43°00'.82N 17°15.'77E

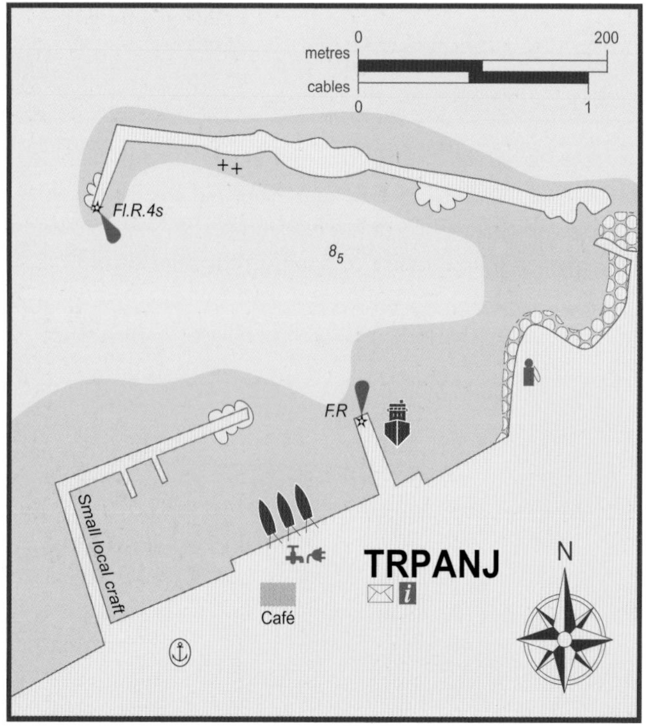

Trpanj is the primary ferry port in the area, connecting with Ploče on the mainland, and is a busy tourist town. Don't be tempted to try Luka, the bay immediately east of Trpanj, as it is very rocky.

NAVIGATION

Charts: HHI MK-22; AC 1574, SC5767

Approaches: The approach is straightforward (although note that a 3.6m shoal lies just off the bay) and Trpanj is difficult to miss, being the only settlement of any size in the area. The main breakwater has a red light (Fl R 4s) as does the ferry pier, which is situated further into the harbour.

BERTHING/FACILITIES

Berth at the quay or in the south-west part of the harbour in depths of between 2 and 4m. Lazylines are provided and water and electricity are available. There's a fuel station on the eastern part of the quay, but no berthing facilities so you'll need to take jerry cans ashore.

The harbour itself is well protected, but the bay is exposed to westerly and northwesterly winds, the Bora and the Sirocco, all of which can cause heavy seas or swell.

ASHORE

You will find a bank and shops ashore. Useful telephone numbers include:
Harbourmaster: Ribarska Obala 14, 20240 Trpanj, Tel: 020 743 542.
Post office: Kralja Tomislava 24, 20240 Trpanj; open in the season from 0800 to 1200 and 1800 to 2100, Mon to Sat, otherwise from 0800 to 1500, Mon to Fri.
Tourist office: Žalo 7, 20240 Trpanj, Tel: 020 743 433; Fax: 020 742 920; email: tzo-trpanj@du.htnet.hr.
Medical centre: Tel: 020 743 404.
Pharmacy: Tel: 020 743 435.

Uvala Divna

Entrance to bay: 43°01'.24N 17°12'.10E
Charts: HHI MK-22; AC 1574, SC5767

A small, shallow bay, 3 miles west of Trpanj, with a lovely beach ('Divna' being Croatian for beautiful). A suitable lunchtime anchorage, although it's only sheltered from the west, through south, to east. Anchor in depths of between 5 and 10m, where you will find good holding on a sand bed. There's a small islet off the west side of the bay, with shallow water between it and the peninsula. You may find a beach bar but not much else, apart from the summer residence of the 16th century Dubrovnik poet Dinko Ranjna.

Duba

Harbour entrance: 43°01'.56N 17°10'.39E
Charts: HHI MK-22; AC 1574, SC5767

Duba, opposite the eastern tip of Hvar Island, has a reputation for a large number of its native-born citizens emigrating to America. A few have returned, but there are still plenty of empty houses in the village, which lies half a mile inland. There is, therefore, normally ample room in the harbour. Depths drop to below 10m about 200m out from the shore either side of the harbour, but there are no hazards on the approach. You'll see a chapel at the root of the western breakwater and a red light (Fl (2) R 5s) at the head of the northern breakwater. Berth on the inside of either breakwater in depths of 1.2 to 2.7m. The Sirocco causes a swell and the bay is exposed to the Bora, which generates heavy seas. Don't count on the shop being open.

Lovište

Entrance to bay: 43°01'.33N 17°01'.06E

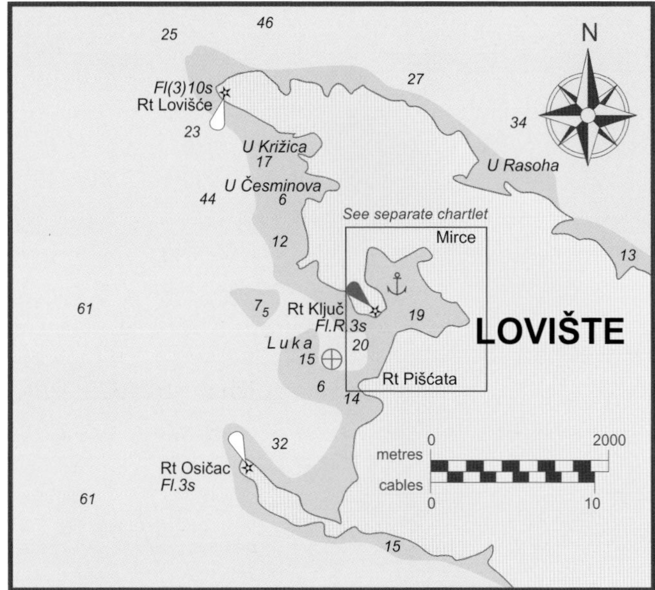

Lovište lies in a large bay in the middle of the western tip of the Pelješac Peninsula. It's a busy harbour and anchorage in the summer, so you may be charged a fee.

NAVIGATION

Charts: HHI MK-22; AC 1574, SC5767

Approaches: The northern boundary of the west coast of the peninsula, Rt Lovišće, has a white light (Fl (3) 10s), as does the southern boundary, Rt Osičac (Fl 3s). The water shoals to below 10m about 200m offshore all along the western coast. As you approach the entrance to the bay you will see a red light to port on Rt Ključ (Fl R 3s). Lovište is in the south-east part of the bay, while a smaller settlement and harbour, Mirce, lies in the northern inlet.

BERTHING/FACILITIES

You can berth bows- or stern-to the quay in depths of about 2 to 4m. Alternatively, anchor in the northern part of the bay. There is good holding on a sand and

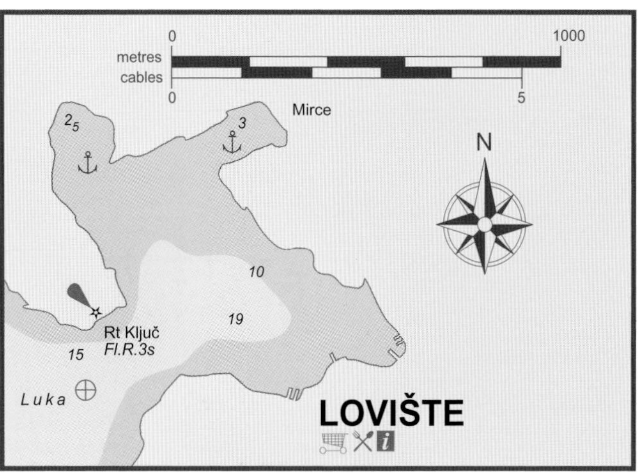

mud bed in depths of 3 to 10m. The anchorage is well protected from all winds and seas, but the harbour is subject to swell in strong westerly and southwesterly winds.

ASHORE

There's not much at Mirce, but Lovište has a tourist office (Tel: 020 718 051), hotel, post office, restaurants, bars and shops.

Viganj

Entrance to bay: 42°58'.85N 17°05'.81E
Charts: HHI MK-22; AC 683, SC5767

Viganj is marked on the charts as a deep-water anchorage for large ships, but it is possible to anchor in shallower water or, for very shallow draught boats, to berth by the pier. However, this is the second most popular windsurfing beach in Croatia after Bol and it's not very well sheltered, so it's probably best to give it a miss. Facilities ashore include a tourist office (Tel: 020 719 295), restaurants, bars and shops as well as a windsurfing school at Camping Liberan, Tel: 020 719 330.

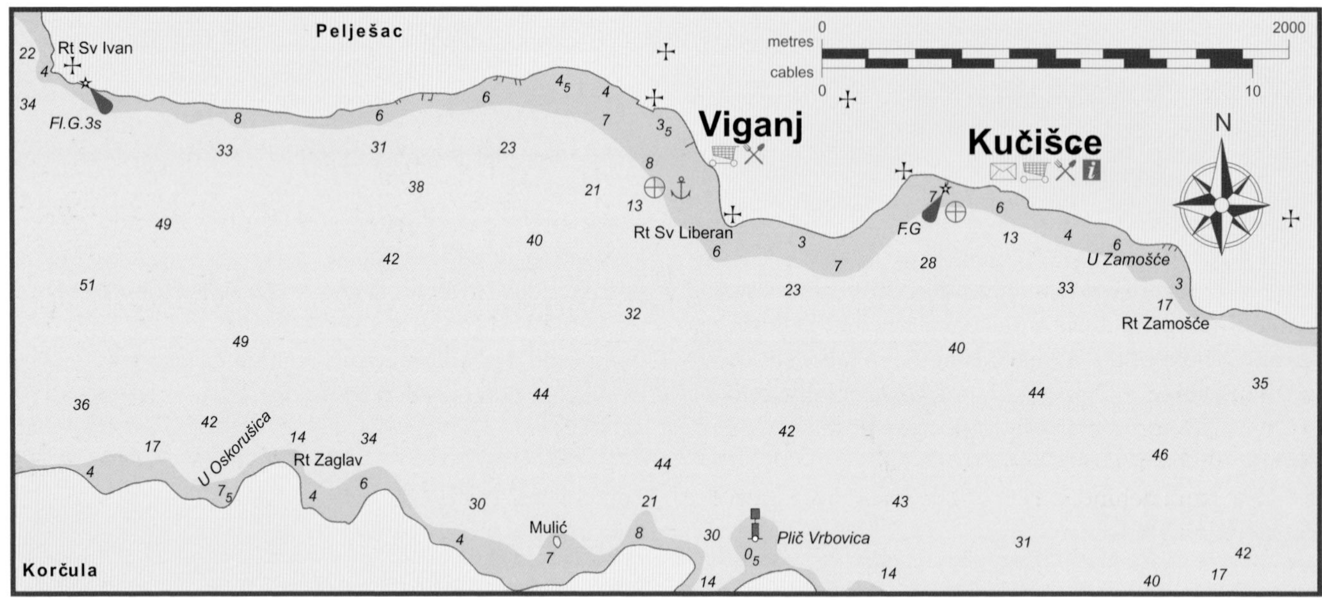

Kučišće

Entrance to pier: 42°58'.68N 17°07'.01E
Charts: HHI MK-22; AC 683, SC5767

Kučišće is another deep-water anchorage with slightly better protection than Viganj, although shallow draught boats can berth at the pier (F G).

Ashore you will find a tourist office (Tel: 020 719 123), post office, restaurant, bars and shops.

Orebić

Harbour entrance:
42°58'.49N 17°10'.42E

Orebić is a classic, and very pretty, Dalmatian settlement with a good-sized harbour. It's popular both as a resort in its own right and as the ferry port for reaching Korčula Town on Korčula Island.

Orebić's inner harbour for shallow draught boats

NAVIGATION

Charts: HHI MK-22; AC 683; AC 1574, SC5767
Approaches: If you are approaching

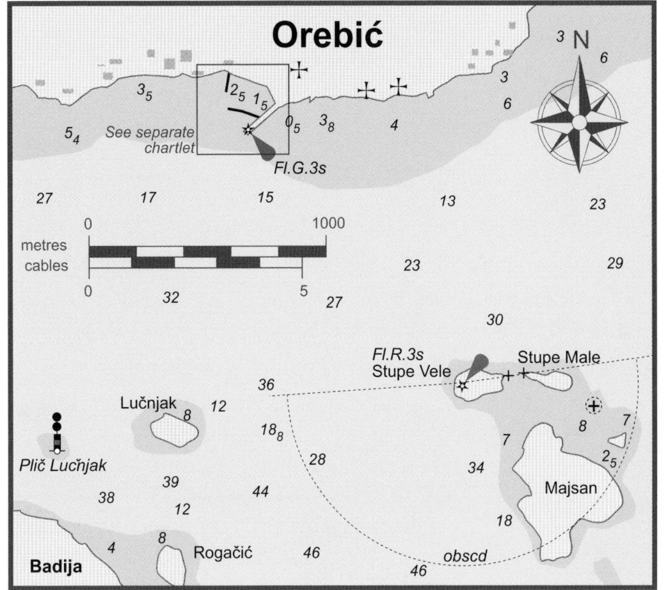

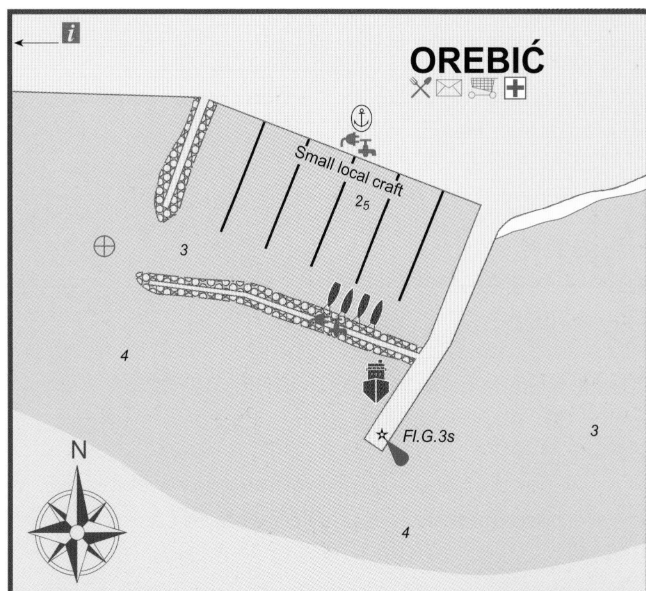

from the south, there's a group of islets, rocks and shoals to watch out for, but plenty of clear water lies between them, so plot your route carefully on the chart. From the west there are no dangers, while from the south-east, as long as you stay about half a mile from the peninsula, you will avoid the islets and other obstacles. Depths reduce to below 10m about 350m out from the shore, south of Orebić, and about 550m from the shore, east of Orebić. There's a green light (Fl G 3s) at the end of the easterly breakwater, and the top half of the church is visible from behind the rows of houses at the foot of the mountain.

BERTHING

Ferries use the north-west side of the seaward end of the main pier. Just beyond the ferry pier is a breakwater, where you can berth on lazylines stern- or bows-to the inner side in depths of 2 to 4m. The inner part of the harbour is for shallow draught local boats. Southerly and westerly winds cause heavy seas, although the breakwater provides some protection. The Bora can blow very strongly in the area.

Orebić's tall church, visible from a distance

Orebić harbour from the east. Ferries run between here and Korčula Island

Useful information – Orebić

FACILITIES

Water and **electricity** are both available.

PROVISIONING/ EATING OUT

The **post office** is on Obala Pomoraca 30, 20250 Orebić. Opening hours in the summer are 0730 to 2100 Monday to Friday, 0800 to 1200 and 1800 to 2100 on Saturday otherwise 0800 to 1500 Monday to Friday and 0800 to 1300 on Saturday. Plenty of **shops, cash points** and a **market**, plus a number of good **restaurants**. Try Restoran Babilon, a short walk up the back streets but signposted from the seafront, Tel: 020 713 352.

Food and music, but no prices!

ASHORE

The tourist office is on the first street away from the sea – Trg Mimbelli bb, Tel/fax: 020 713 718; email: tz-orebic@du.htnet.hr; website: www.tz-orebic.com. The Maritime Museum is in the same square and there's also a Franciscan monastery, with a museum, 20 minutes' walk away, offering a great view over the peninsula from the terrace. For the very energetic, there are even better views from the top of Sveti Ilija, the mountain behind the town. The marked path takes four hours to the top.

OTHER INFORMATION

Pharmacy: Tel: 020 713 019.
Medical centre: Tel: 020 713 025.

Trstenik

Entrance to bay: 42°54'.79N 17°24'.17E
Charts: HHI MK-24; AC 1574; AC 1580, SC5767

Trstenik is situated in the north-west corner of a large bay, Zaton Žuljana, about 11 miles south-east of Orebić, and is noted for its Dingac wine. The immediate approach is straightforward, though don't hug the coast too much when entering the bay from either direction as there is an islet just off both headlands. The south-eastern islet of Lirica is marked by a white tower with a light (L Fl 10s). You can berth alongside the pier or at the quay in depths of 3 to 5m, but make sure you stay clear of the ferry area. Alternatively, anchor north-east of the head of the breakwater. Good holding on a mud bed in 4 to 10m of water. The Bora blows strongly here and southwesterlies and the Sirocco can cause a swell, but the harbour provides sufficient protection.

Ashore you will find a tourist office (Tel: 021 741 291) a post office (open in the summer from 0900 to 1200 and 1900 to 2100 Monday to Friday, otherwise from 0800 to 1230 Monday to Friday), shops, bars and restaurants, and a ferry service to Polače on Mjlet island. There is also a diving centre, which can be contacted on Tel: 098 564 878, email: diving@freaky-diving.com, website: www.freaky-diving.com.

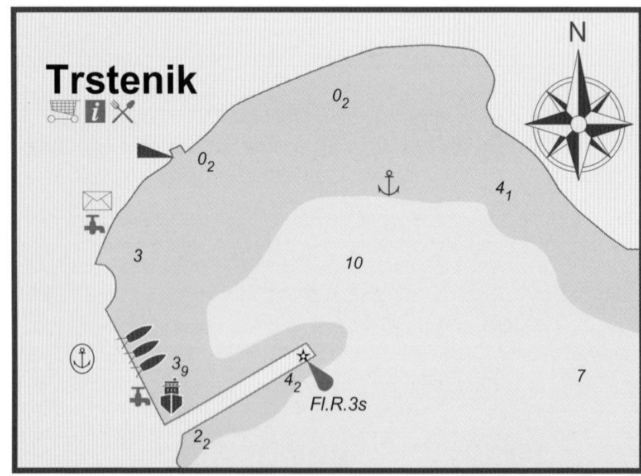

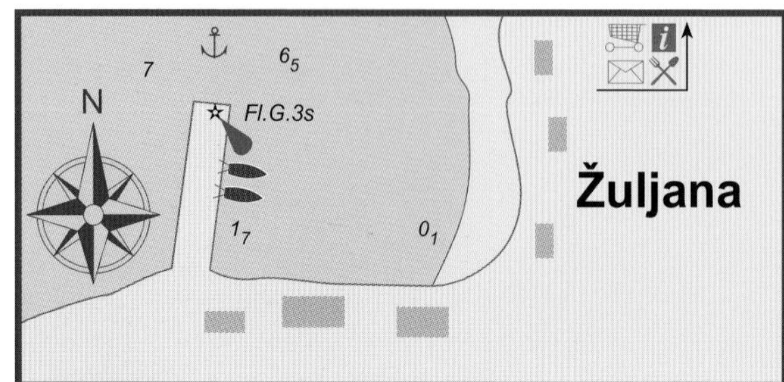

The islet of Lirica, marked by a prominent white light (L Fl 10s), lies to the south-west of Žuljana

Žuljana

Entrance to bay: 42°53'.52N 17°26'.95E
Charts: HHI MK-24; AC 1574, AC 1580, SC5767

Žuljana is situated in the north-east corner of Zaton Žuljana. It has a popular campsite as well as being a regular stop for flotillas, which means it can get quite crowded in the summer. The islet of Lirica lies just off the eastern entrance of the large bay and has a tall white tower (L Fl 10s) on the top of it. There is a shallow area between the islet and the peninsula, and about half a mile east-south-east of Lirica is a 3.1m shoal. After entering the bay you will need to plot a course between two tiny islets, some shallows and a number of rocks, so look at the charts carefully and keep your eyes open. There's a green light (Fl G 3s) at the end of the breakwater and a few houses at the head of the bay. You can berth on the inner side of the breakwater in depths of between 1.5 and 4m, or anchor on a sand bottom north of the breakwater in depths of around 7m.

The harbour is well sheltered from all winds and seas, but westerly winds cause a swell and the Bora tends to funnel down the valley so can blow very strongly here.

Facilities include a shop, tourist office, bars, restaurants and some good beaches. Contact details for the tourist office are Žuljana Tourist Board, Kraj bb 20247, Žuljana, Tel/fax: 020 756 227; email: tzmzuljana@hotmail.com.

Žuljana's breakwater and beach

Prapratno

Entrance to bay: 42°48'.54N 17°40'.34E
Charts: HHI MK-24, MK-25; AC 1580, SC5767

Luka Prapratna is a deep bay and not a particularly suitable anchorage. The sand bed provides poor holding and there are two underwater cables running to Mljet Island from the south-eastern shore of the inner bay. However, if you do decide to stop here, anchor in depths of 4 to 10m in the very inner part of the head of the bay.

The Bora blows hard in the area and the bay is exposed to southwesterly winds and seas. The approach is straightforward, but there are no facilities.

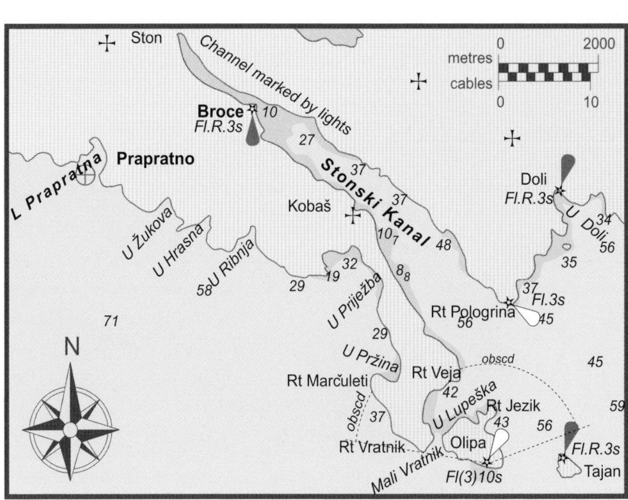

The south-west coast of the Pelješac Peninsula, south-east of Prapratno

This five-mile stretch of coastline has a number of bays, but they are all relatively inhospitable. The waters are deep and there's limited shelter, so plan for somewhere else to stop off at.

Ston, Broce and the Stonski Kanal

Charts: HHI 525, MK-25; AC 1580, SC5767

NAVIGATION IN THE STONSKI CANAL

We've covered the onshore delights of Ston on page 198, with its neighbour Mali Ston. To get to it by sea you'll need to sail north-west along the 5-mile Stonski Kanal, past Broce. Depths in the canal reduce considerably within half a mile of Broce, and there are various reports about just how deep the inner channel is, and how often and effectively it is dredged to keep it navigable. Suggestions are that minimum depths can be anything between 2 and 4m and depths do vary with currents and weather conditions.

The fairway is well marked, but we'd suggest you phone the harbourmaster at Ston to check depths if you draw more than 2m, or perhaps check at Broce before you go on to Ston. Note that vessels leaving the channel heading south-east have priority, and you need to wait at Broce until the channel is clear. Similarly, you should not leave Ston if another vessel has already entered the channel. Finally, note that there is a submerged obstruction in the fairway entrance, about 90m north-north-west of the light on the pier in Broce harbour, so stay close to the pier.

Broce

Broce is a pretty village with a few houses, a campsite and a shop.

It has a small harbour where you can berth at the outer end of either of the two piers in depths of between 1 and 2.5m. The most easterly pier has a red light (Fl R 3s) at the end. The harbour is sheltered from all winds except the Sirocco.

Ston

Refer to Mali Ston on page 198 for information on what is available ashore, including harbourmaster details. See immediately above for approach notes. There's a quay with a red light (Fl R 3s) where you can berth in depths of up to 2m.

Ston provides good shelter from all winds and seas; however, the inlet acts like a funnel for the Bora and Sirocco.

Ston – renowned for its oysters and shellfish

Korčula Town and marina

Chapter seven
The islands of Southern Dalmatia

As you head further south, the islands become greener, less developed and generally have fewer facilities: cash points, for example, become much more scarce. Korčula Island (particularly Korčula Town) is one of the 'must-see' places in Croatia. Korčula Town is a stunning example of classic architecture and ambience packed into a small space, with stone steps leading up the hill to a maze of alleys and a spectacular view. Korčula Island has plenty of other charming places to visit. Mljet, the next largest island in this area, is one of the lushest places in Croatia, with saltwater lakes and a vast National Park. Ubli, on Lastovo, has made a big effort to try and accommodate nautical visitors, while the Elaphite Islands around Dubrovnik have the sort of low-key tourism that appeals to anyone who wants to get away from it all, with the added benefit of an almost total ban on cars.

The ACI marina in Korčula Town is the only marina in the area, apart from Dubrovnik on the mainland (see page 241 of chapter eight), although there are good moorings at Lumbarda. The four fuel stations in the area are at Sobra on Mljet Island, Korčula and Vela Luka on Korčula Island and Ubli on Lastovo Island.

Our coverage of this area starts with Korčula Island,

which lies just south of the Pelješac Peninsula. We then head to Lastovo and Sušac, further south, before heading south-east to Mljet and the Elaphite Islands. Lokrum Island, just south-east of Dubrovnik, and the islets around Cavtat are covered on pages 245 and 247 of chapter eight.

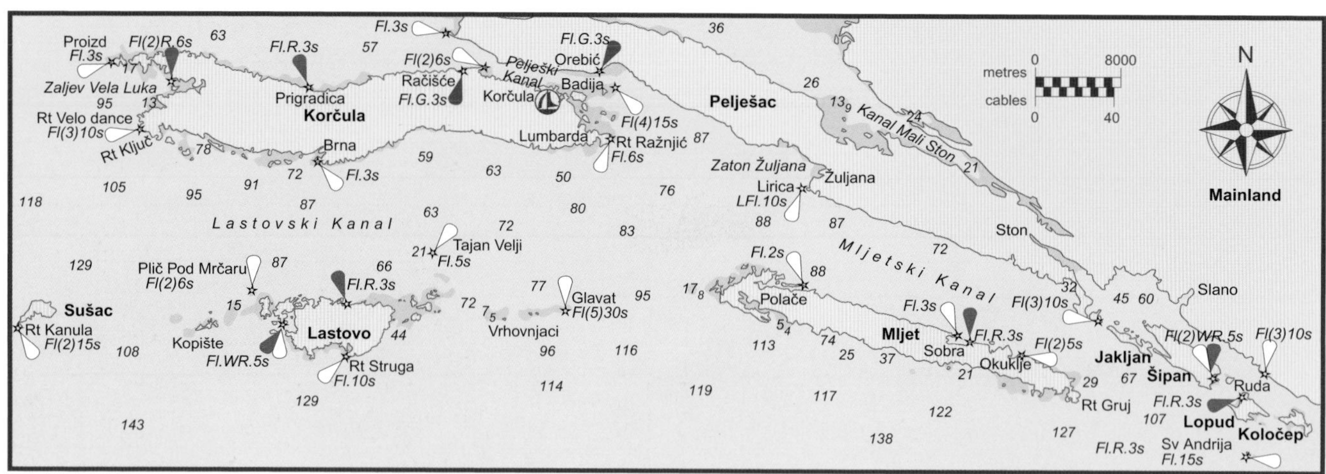

Korčula Island

(including the off-lying islets)

Korčula Island is long, thin and densely wooded. It is particularly noted for the three main wines produced here – Pošip, Marastina and Grk – and for the Moreška sword dance. The striking town of Korčula juts out into the sea, with its fortifications around the peninsula and the imposing cathedral on top of the hill dominating the scene. The rest of the settlements on the island can't quite match up to the delights of the eponymous town, but have charms of their own.

Vela Luka, situated at the western end of the island, gets short shrift in many of the guide books, but we found it to be a town of some stature and charm. Some good beaches can be found near Lumbarda at the eastern end of the island, while Brna, on the south coast, has a popular anchorage.

Little or no shelter exists along the eastern half of the south coast between Lumbarda and Brna, as well as along significant stretches of the north coast. We start with Korčula Town and then head clockwise around the island, taking in the off-lying islets as we go round.

TRANSPORT

Should you want to explore inland, there are around six buses a day running the length of the island. Ferries and catamarans operate between Split and Vela Luka or Korčula Town, while car ferries sail frequently between Orebić, on the Pelješac Peninsula, and Dominče, near Korčula Town. Alternatively, there are foot passenger ferries direct to the town, and a daily bus service linking Dubrovnik and Korčula Town. Water taxis operate from the eastern harbour of Korčula Town to Lumbarda and Badija Islet.

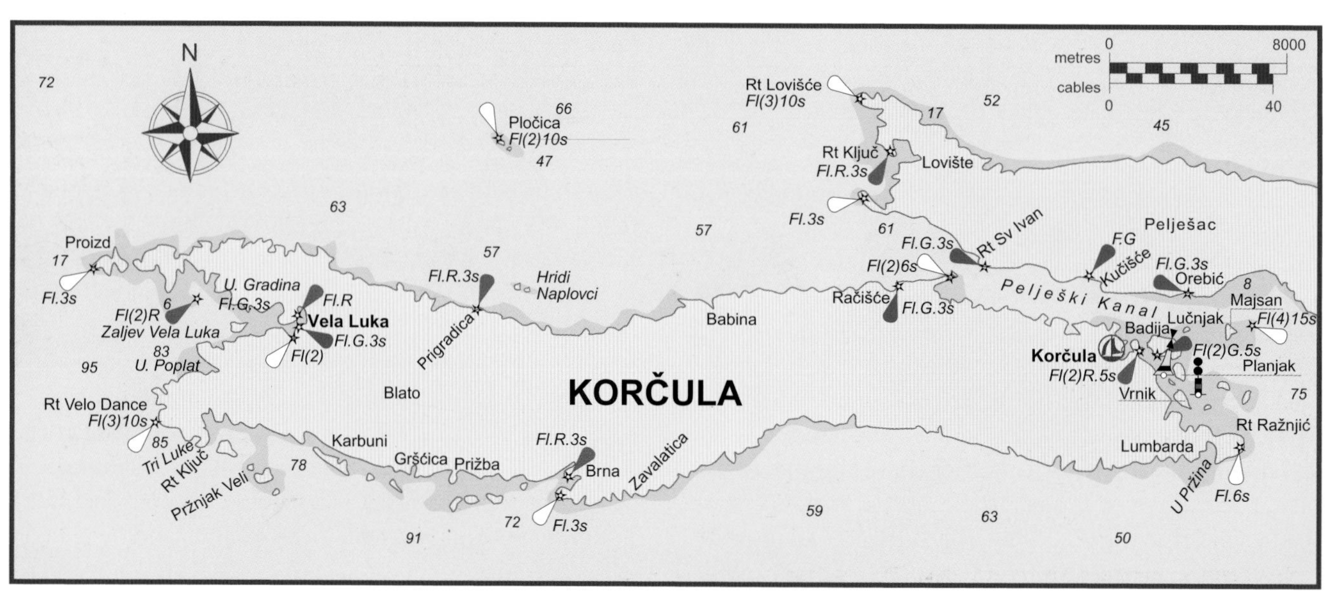

Korčula Town

Marina entrance: 42°57'.46N 17°08'.29E

One of Dalmatia's best preserved medieval town centres and allegedly the birthplace of explorer Marco Polo, Korčula oozes with history, character and charm. It's very popular in the summer, so you'll need to get there early if you want a space in the marina. Four of the 15th century cylindrical towers, part of the fortifications built to protect the town against the Turkish invasion, are still standing.

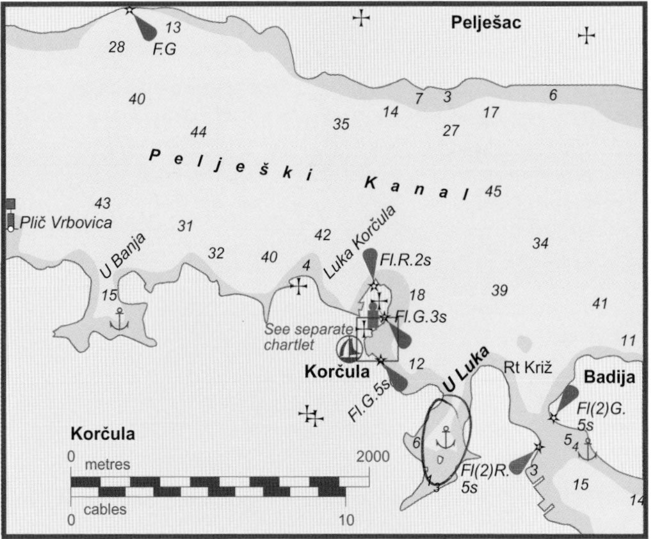

NAVIGATION

Charts: HHI MK-22; AC 683, AC 1574, SC5767

Approaches: (For approaches from the east, see chartlets on page 211). From the east, 1.2 miles from the town, there is an unlit beacon marking a rock and shallow patch. Further in, half a mile from the town, is a 4.5m shoal, Pličina Križ. To the south-east and east, the islets of Badija, Planjak, Vrnik, Gubavac, Sutvara, Bisače, Majsan, Gojak and Sestrica are surrounded by shallow waters and a number of rocks and hazards, so check the charts carefully. Approaching from the west, 1½ miles from the town, is another unlit beacon marking Pličina Vrbovica, a rock and a shoal with depths of 0.5m of water over them.

Korčula is a busy port, with a ferry terminal and tripper boats on the north-west side of town and the marina to the south, so keep an eye-out for traffic. The town is easily visible from a distance, with a red light (Fl R 2s) situated on the ferry pier and a green light (Fl G 5s) installed at the end of the main marina pier/breakwater.

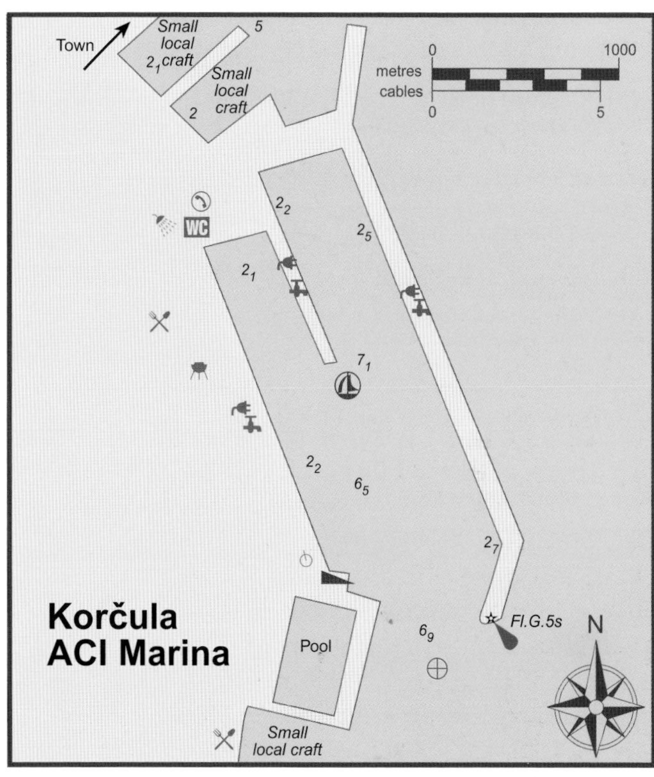

Korčula's ferry terminal and local boat harbour. The Old Town is in the background

BERTHING

The marina can be contacted on VHF Channel 17, Tel: 020 711 661. Open all year round and listed as a Category II marina, it has 159 berths and 16 dry berths. Prices are €3.8 to €4.35 per metre per day for a 10 to 20m (33 to 66ft) boat, plus 10% in June, July, August and September.

The bay is exposed to the Bora, but the breakwater provides adequate protection. The Sirocco causes a swell.

Useful information – Korčula Town

FACILITIES

The **showers** don't have a temperature control, which can be a little irritating. On top of the standard facilities, the marina has a **supermarket**, a **service/repair workshop** and a 10-ton **crane. Fuel** is available by the ferry pier – Dubrovračka Cesta bb, 20260 Korčula, Tel: 020 711 017 – depth 3.5m. Opening hours from 0700 to 2100 every day in the summer, otherwise from 0700 to 1900 Monday to Saturday and 0700 to 1100 on Sundays and Bank Holidays. In the marina complex is an **engine repair workshop:** AD Mehanic Nauta, Tel: 091 507 4635.

PROVISIONING

The old town is crammed full of shops and boutiques, with **banks** and **cash points** widely available too. The **fruit and vegetable market** is halfway up the hill and the **supermarkets** in town are better value than the one in the marina. There are a couple of **pharmacies** in the centre. The **post office** is at Trg Kralja Tomislava 1 and open from 0730 to 2100 Monday to Saturday in the summer, otherwise from 0730 to 1900 Monday to Friday and from 0730 to 1400 on Saturday.

EATING OUT

You are spoilt for choice in Korčula, with scores of pizzerias and restaurants. Adio Mare (Tel: 020 711 253) on Svetog Roka, just by the alley that leads to Marco Polo's house, is very popular with tourists and has the queues to match – a quality traditional menu served in a rustic room. Planjak (Tel: 020 711 015) on Plokata 19 Travnja, offers reasonably priced food inside or on a terrace overlooking a small square. Popular with locals and tourists alike, the atmosphere is cosy and informal. If you like pastries, don't miss Cukarin, Hrvatske Bratske Zajednice bb, Tel: 020 711 055, and for budget-priced tortilla wraps, smoothies and cocktails, try Fresh's kiosk on Kod Kina Liburne 1, Tel: 091 799 2086; website: www.igotfresh.com. Korčula is buzzing with bars and cafés, but most of them tend to shut at around 2300.

ASHORE/TRANSPORT

The **tourist office** is on the seafront next to Hotel Korčula – Obala Dr FranjeTuđmana bb, Tel: 020 715 867; Fax: 020 715 866; email: tzg-korcule@du.htnet.hr; website: www.korculainfo.com or www.korcula.net – and a town museum is situated opposite the cathedral. There are several private travel agencies, mostly by the ferry pier, where you can hire **bikes, boats, cars** and **scooters**, as well as finding **taxis**. The island is particularly suitable for cycling as it is relatively flat.

The town is famous for a traditional sword dance called the Moreška. The main celebration of this is on 29 July, St Theodore's Day, but now there's a weekly event every Thursday evening in the summer. Go to Marco Polo Tours, situated by the ferry terminal, for tickets and more information. Jan and Steve Collett, originally from England, run Dupin Diving Centre, Tel: 020 716 247; website: www.croatiadiving.com. There are up to 18 ferries a day between Orebić, on the Pelješac Peninsula, and Korčula.

OTHER INFORMATION

Harbourmaster: On the west side of the old town, all year round port of entry – Obala Vinka Palentina 176, 20260 Korčula, Tel: 020 711 178; Fax: 020 711 178.
Korčula ACI Marina: 20260 Korčula, Tel: 020 711 661; Fax: 020 711 748; email: m.korcula@aci-club.hr; website: www.aci-club.hr.
Medical centre: Ulica 59, 20269 Korčula, Tel: 020 711 137.

Korčula's Medieval Old Town. In the foreground are two of the four remaining 15th century cylindrical towers, built to protect the town from invasion by the Turks

Uvala Luka

Entrance to bay: 42°57'.48N 17°08'.59E
Charts: HHI MK-22; AC 683, AC 1574, SC5767

This deep, sheltered bay lies about half a mile south-east of Korčula Town. See approach notes for Korčula Town on page 209 and look out for the rocky islet in the centre of the bay, which is level with the quay.

Either berth at the quay on the west side of the bay, in a minimum depth of 1.5m, or anchor on a mud bed in depths of 5 to 10m. An underwater pipeline runs out to sea from just north of the quay, so keep to the centre of the outer part of the bay or south of the islet in the inner part of the bay.

Around the shore are a campsite, bars and restaurants, and it's just a short walk into Korčula Town.

Badija Islet

Anchorage: 42°57'.02N 17°09'.74E
Charts: HHI MK-22; AC 683, AC 1574, SC5767

You'll find a peaceful, sheltered anchorage off the south coast of Badija Islet, by the old Franciscan abbey. The approach, however, needs to be treated with caution as only some routes are safe.

The best approach is from the north, between Badija and Korčula, passing over a 4.5m shoal. The channel from the east, between Badija and Planjak, is shallow and rocky and not suitable for yachts. The safest approach from the south is between Vrnik and Korčula, avoiding the islet and rocks to the south-west and west of Planjak. This channel has depths of 5m.

Anchor on a sand and weed bed in depths of between 5 and 10m. This anchorage offers good all-round protection.

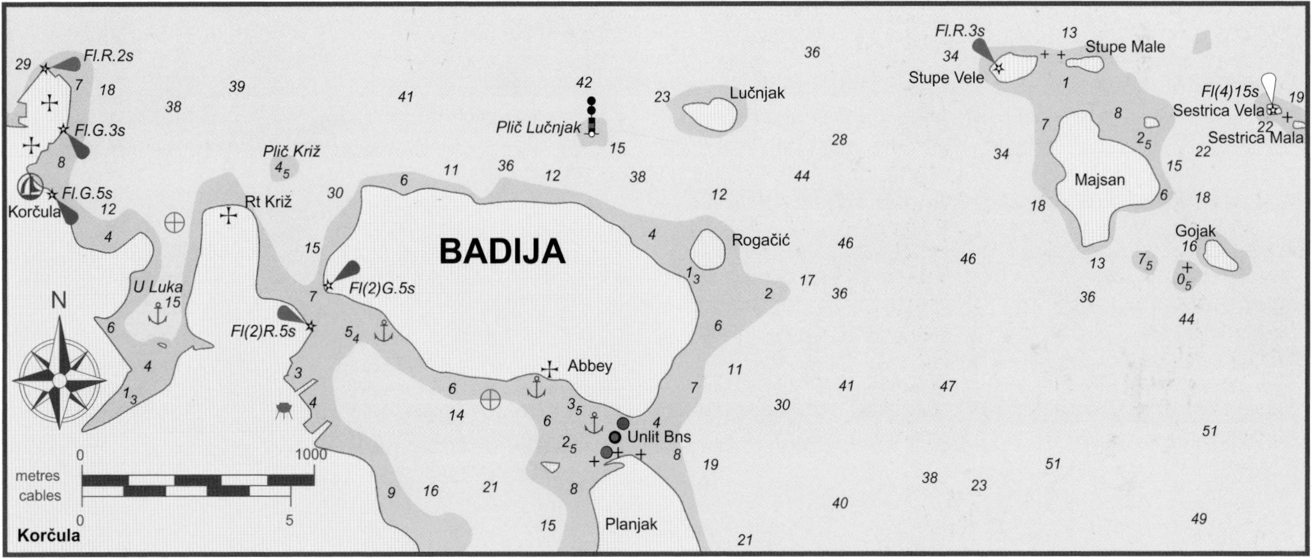

Vrnik Islet

Lying north of Lumbarda and separated from the mainland by a channel, about 200m wide with depths of around 5m, Vrnik is a rocky island with many stone quarries, but has a small quay on its north-west side with depths of 0.2 to 1.7m. Alternatively, anchor off the south-west side of the islet in depths of around 7m. There are a few good pebble beaches nearby.

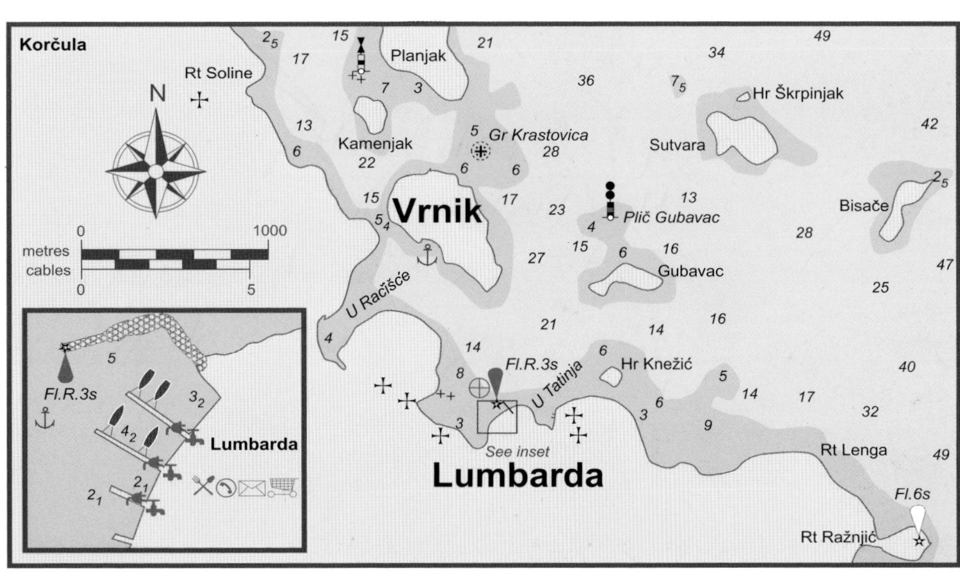

Lumbarda

Harbour entrance: 42°55'.62N 17°10'.31E

Although Lumbarda has a marina sign on the Croatian charts, it's a little bit of a hybrid at the time of writing and we would suggest just 'good berths' in 2007, although we understand that showers and toilets have recently been built and more improvements are on the way. At a distance of two miles south-east of Korčula Town, it would certainly take the pressure off Korčula Marina.

NAVIGATION

Charts: HHI MK-22, MK-23; AC 683, AC 1574, SC5767

Approaches: (See page 211 for chartlet of Lumbarda). There's an above-water rock (Hr Knežić) half a mile east of the bay, a 5m shoal about 400m further east, and the water shallows to below 5m up to 400m off the shores east of Lumbarda and around Rt Ražnjić. Therefore, from the east, stay between the islet of Gubavac and Hrid Knežić.

From the north, beware of shallow water all around Gubavac, which extends north to a point marked by an unlit isolated danger mark. Just north of Vrnik Islet is a rock, Grebena Krastovica, and a shallow area, so take a course due south in the centre of the channel between Vrnik and Gubavac. From the north-east, head between the islets of Sutvara and Bisače, avoiding the rock Hrid Skirpinjak off the north coast of Sutvara and the shallows around it.

From the south, Rt Ražnjić is a narrow, low-lying point surrounded by shallows, but marked by a white light (Fl 6s). There's a red light (Fl R 3s) on the breakwater and, as you enter the bay, look out for the rock and 1.8m shoal, west of the breakwater light, which is marked by an unlit beacon.

BERTHING/ANCHORING

Wait for someone to find you and take you to a berth where you can tie up bows- or stern-to on lazylines. Up to date prices are not published so contact the operators, details below, for more information. Alternatively, you can anchor in depths of 3 to 5m on a sand bed. A strong Sirocco causes a swell and the Bora can create a moderate sea here.

A tripper boat waiting for customers alongside Lumbarda's breakwater

Useful information – Lumbarda

FACILITIES

Electricity and **water** are available on the piers. **Showers** and **toilets** have recently been installed. Contact: Lučica Lumbarda, 20263 Lumbarda, Tel: 020 712 489; Fax: 020 712 479; email: lucica-lumbarda@htnet.hr

ASHORE

In the summer the **post office** is open from 0800 to 2100 Mon to Fri and from 0800 to 1200 and 1800 to 2100 on Sat, otherwise from 0800 to 1500 Mon to Fri. The **tourist office** details are Tel: 020 712 005/020 712 490; email: tz-lumbarda@du.htnet.hr; website: www.korculainfo.com. Lumbarda has a couple of hotels, a **supermarket** and **shops**, a few **restaurants** and **bars**, and some great **beaches** nearby.

Lazyline berthing at Lumbarda, Korčula

Uvala Pržina

Entrance to bay: 42°54'.75N 17°10'.95E
Charts: HHI MK-22, MK-23; AC 1574, SC5767

On the south coast of Korčula, connected to Lumbarda by a track onshore, Uvala Pržina's shallow bay makes for a popular and busy beach. You can anchor in depths of around 5m on a sand bed. The shelter is good from the west, through north to east. Straightforward approach; no facilities except a bar.

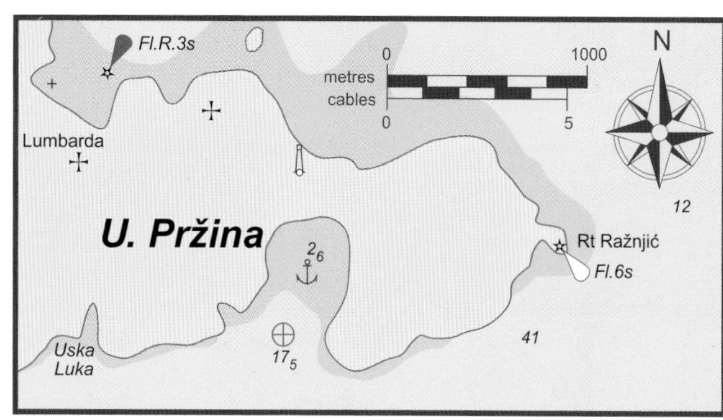

Uvala Pržina: anchorage and a popular beach in the summer

Zavalatica

Entrance to bay: 42°54'.62N 16°55'.96E
Charts: HHI MK-21, MK-22 and MK-23; AC 1574, SC5767

Situated about halfway along the south coast of the island, Zavalatica comprises a small boat harbour and village that are rapidly growing with the increase in the tourism trade. The new building developments on Dugi Rat, the point immediately east of the bay, should be visible from a distance.

You can berth inside the breakwater in depths of 2 to 5m. Southerly and southwesterly winds produce heavy seas in the area, and the Sirocco causes a significant swell. Among the facilities ashore are restaurants, bars and a supermarket.

Space is often limited for visiting yachts, with a number of small local boats taking up much of the harbour. If you find this to be the case, perhaps try anchoring in the bay immediately east, Uvala Žitna. Bear in mind, however, that without protection from a breakwater, you will be completely exposed to the winds and seas mentioned above.

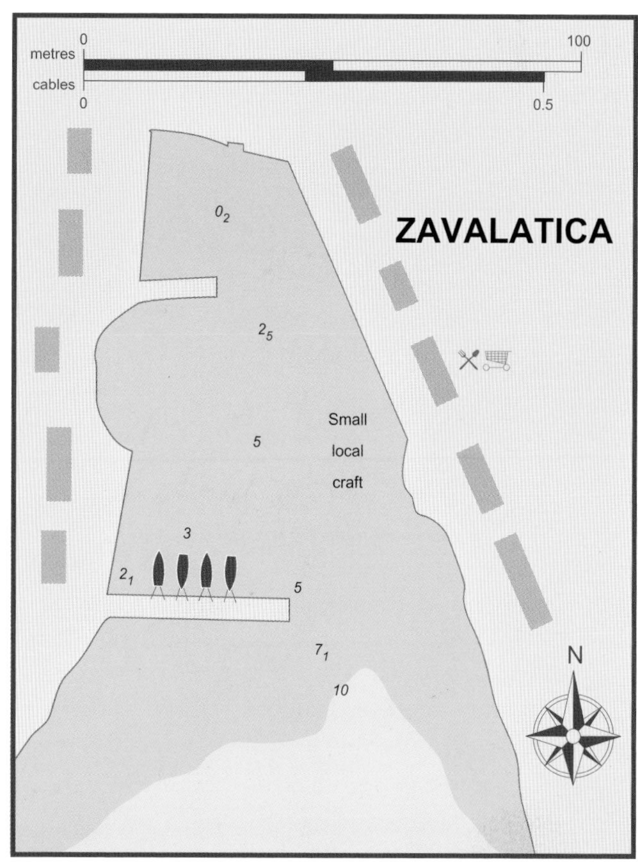

Brna

Entrance to bay: 42°53'.92N 16°50'.32E

Brna is a pleasant village for an overnight stop and has a friendly and helpful tourist office. The bay has two inlets; the village and moorings are in the easterly inlet and there is an anchorage in the more sheltered westerly inlet.

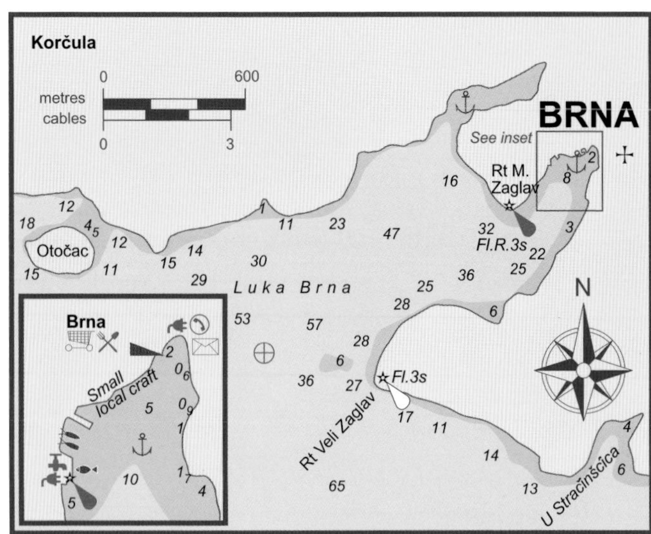

NAVIGATION

Charts: HHI 535, MK-21, MK-22, MK-23; AC 1574, AC 2712, SC5767

Approaches: Approaching from the west, beware of a rock just off the headland at Prižba and a number of islets and shoals. From the east or south there are no hazards to watch out for, although note that the water shoals to 6m off Rt Veli Zaglav (Fl 3s). You'll see a conspicuous white hotel on the headland between the two bays and, as you head towards the village, the small pier has a red light (Fl R 3s) on it, beyond which are the moorings.

A fishing boat monopolising the mole (red light), with yachts moored at the quay behind

BERTHING/ANCHORING

No lazylines have been installed as yet so you have to berth stern-to the quay using your anchor. Depths are around 2m, but watch out for a protruding ledge underwater and shallow water near the quay.

Alternatively, anchor at the head of the bay or, better still, in the western inlet in depths of 5 to 10m. Good holding on a sand bed. Southwesterly winds cause a heavy swell.

Useful information – Brna

FACILITIES

Water and **electrics** were available to commercial vessels when we visited.

ASHORE

The Hotel Feral was refurbished a couple of years ago and boasts great views across the water, a sandy beach and a sports centre. The mud from the nearby bay of Istruga is supposed to be good for treating rheumatic illnesses. Contact details for the **tourist office** are Tel/fax: 020 832 255; email: tzo-smokvice@du.htnet.hr; website: www.brna.hr. The **post office** opening times displayed were more extensive than the official ones we received and suggest that in the season opening hours are from 0800 to 1200 and 1900 to 2100 Monday to Friday and from 0800 to 1200 on Saturday. It is closed off season. Other facilities include a **supermarket, grocery shops** and a few **restaurants** and **bars.** Pizzeria Zal will also rent you a scooter, Tel: 020 832 219/098 512 864.

Prižba

Entrance to bay: 42°54'.29N 16°47'.23E
Charts: HHI 535, MK-21, MK-22, MK-23; AC 1574; AC 2712, SC5767

Prižba is easily recognisable by its peninsula, which juts out to sea giving it a coastline of some 2.5 miles. To the south and south-east of this harbour are four small deserted islands that protect it from some of the elements. The islets have shallow water in between them (minimum depth 6m) and shoals around them (minimum depth 5m). Note that there is a rock about 400m south-south-west of the end of the peninsula. See page 215 (Gršćica) if approaching from the west past the islet of Kosor.

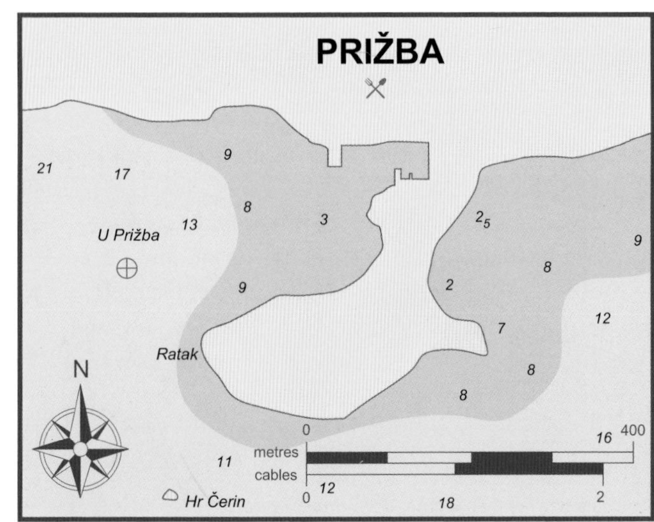

You can berth at the mole in the north-east part of the bay, in depths of 2 to 3m, but look out for boulders east of the mole. The rocky bottom makes the bay unsuitable as an anchorage. The Sirocco causes a swell and southwesterly winds produce heavy seas. The settlement has a couple of seasonal restaurants: Prižba (Tel: 020 861 222) and Riva 1 (Tel: 020 861 260), but otherwise facilities are limited.

Holiday accommodation in Uvala Prižba

Gršćica

Entrance to bay: 42°54'.26N 16°46'.25E
Charts: HHI 535, MK-21, MK-22, MK-23; AC 1574, AC 2712, SC5767

Gršćica has a little harbour, mainly used by small local boats. There are a number of islets, shoals and rocks around the entrance to the bay. In particular, the islet of Kosor has a rock just off its north-east tip, another rock about 500m west of the first, and a 3.5m shoal off its south-east tip. See Prižba on page 214 above for hazards approaching from the east. Also watch out for an unmarked submerged rock (clearance 1.2m) and the rocky shoal that extends eastwards from it towards the eastern inlet, in the centre of the outer bay. The quay at the head of the cove has depths of between 0.5m and 2m alongside or you can anchor, in calm weather, at the entrance to the bay in depths of 10 to 20m. However, you will need to make sure you are well clear of the rock, so it's not recommended. The inner part of the bay is well protected, while the outer part is exposed to the south and south-west and the Sirocco causes a swell. You'll find a restaurant and a small shop ashore.

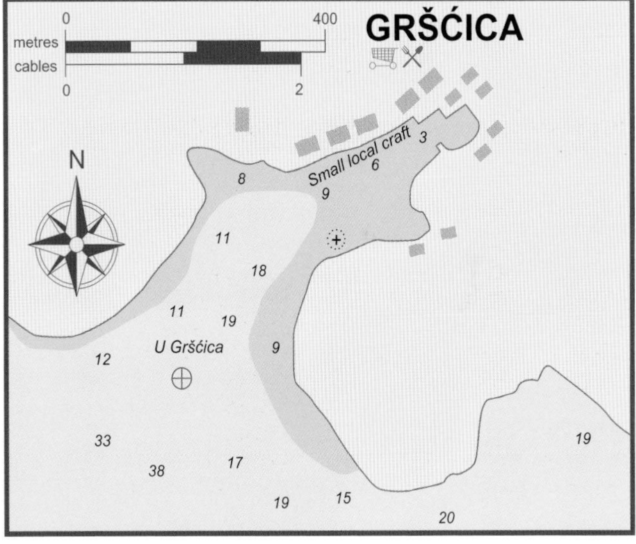

Gršćica's bay, with an increasing number of holiday apartments

Karbuni

Anchorage: 42°54'.67N 16°44'.04E
Charts: HHI 535, MK-21, MK-22; AC 2712, SC5767

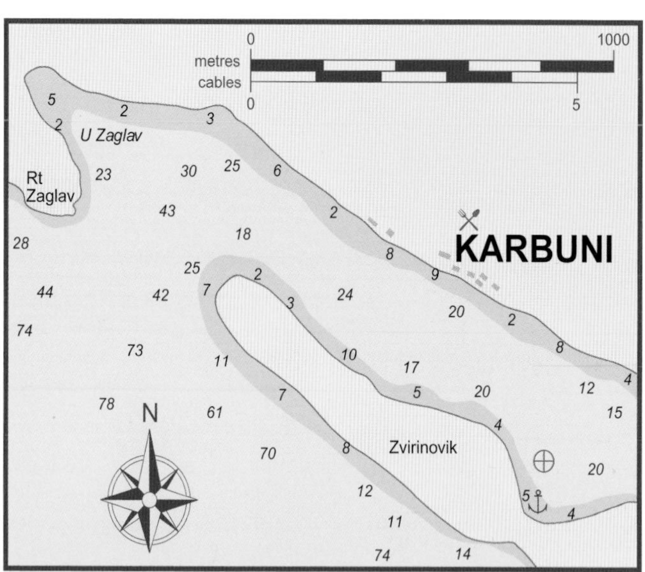

A small settlement with a number of concrete piers for local boats as well as a restaurant, Karbuni is sheltered by the long thin islet of Zvirinovik. As the water off Karbuni is quite deep, it's best to anchor off Zvirinovik in depths of around 8m. The anchorage is exposed to winds and seas from the south-east.

If approaching from the east, see Gršćica on page 215 for details of the rocks and shoals around the islet of Kosor. From the south-west, look out for Hrid Gradica off the east coast of Pržnjak Veli and the shallows around Pržnjak Veli, Pržnjak Mali and Hrid Gradica (see chart on page 217).

Karbuni, where there are a number of small concrete jetties for local boats

Uvala Tri Luke

Entrance to main bay: 42°55'.27N 16°40'.24E
Charts: HHI MK-21; AC 2712, SC5767

Just before you round Rt Ključ to head north along the short west coast of Korčula, there are three quite deep inlets, collectively known as Uvala Tri Luke (the bay of three ports). The islet of Trstenik provides some additional protection. The immediate approach is relatively straightforward but look out for the shallows and rock around the islet of Pržnjak Veli, to the south-east.

All three inlets afford good holding on sand beds in depths of 3 to 8m, as well as providing shelter from winds from the west through north to east, although the two most westerly bays offer greater protection from southwesterly winds. The outer parts of the bays are exposed to the Sirocco and, in these conditions, you will find better shelter if you anchor off the north coast of Pržnjak Veli. There are no facilities in Uvala Tri Luke.

Uvala Zaklopatica

Entrance to bay: 42°54'.98N 16°39'.40E
Charts: HHI MK-21; AC 2712, SC5767

Uvala Zaklopatica is an uninhabited bay immediately west of Uvala Tri Luke and Rt Ključ. It was a busy anchorage when we visited it in calm weather. However, it seems very exposed, particularly to the west through south to south-east. Depths are approximately 8m.

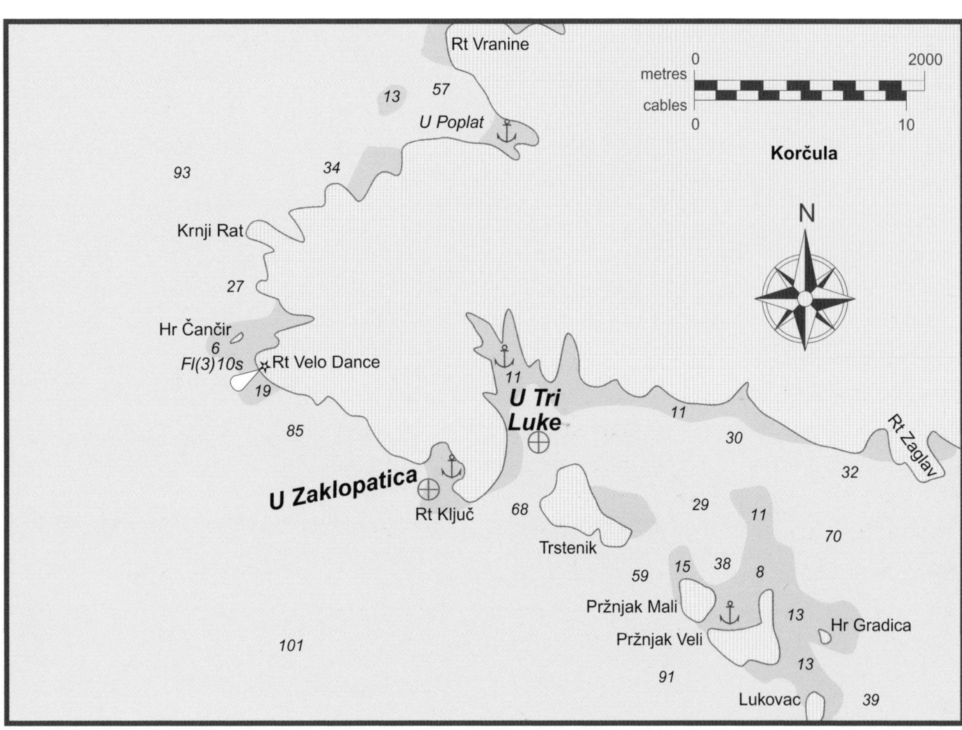

Uvala Poplat

Entrance to bay: 42°55'.82N 16°38'.24E
Charts: HHI MK-21; AC 2712, SC5767

A wide bay at the western end of Korčula Island that is exposed to winds and seas from the west and north-west. Anchor in depths of 5 to 10m towards the head of the bay, on a sand and weed bed. You will find a few houses here, but no facilities. From the south, stay well clear of Rt Velo Dance (Fl [3] 10s) as well as the shoals and islet just north and north-east of the light. Otherwise the approach is straightforward.

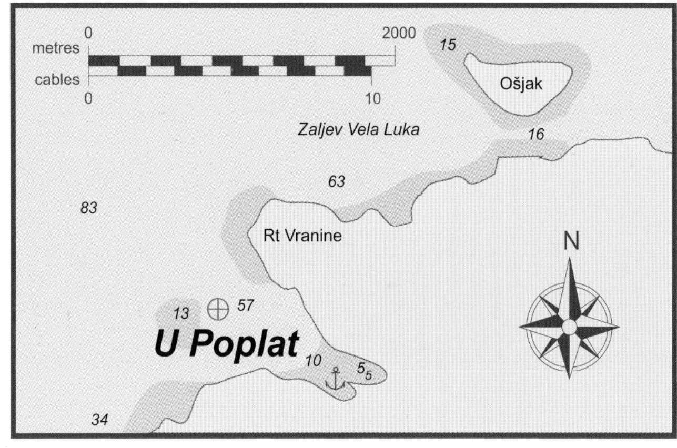

Vela Luka

Entrance to inner inlets: 42°57'.76N 16°41'.76E

Having read some general guide books on Vela Luka prior to our visit, we certainly envisaged finding a bit of a dump, but were pleasantly surprised. The architecture is a little formidable in places, but it's a big town with a good deal of charm and the inner inlet is very well sheltered.

Vela Luka approach: green light and fuel station

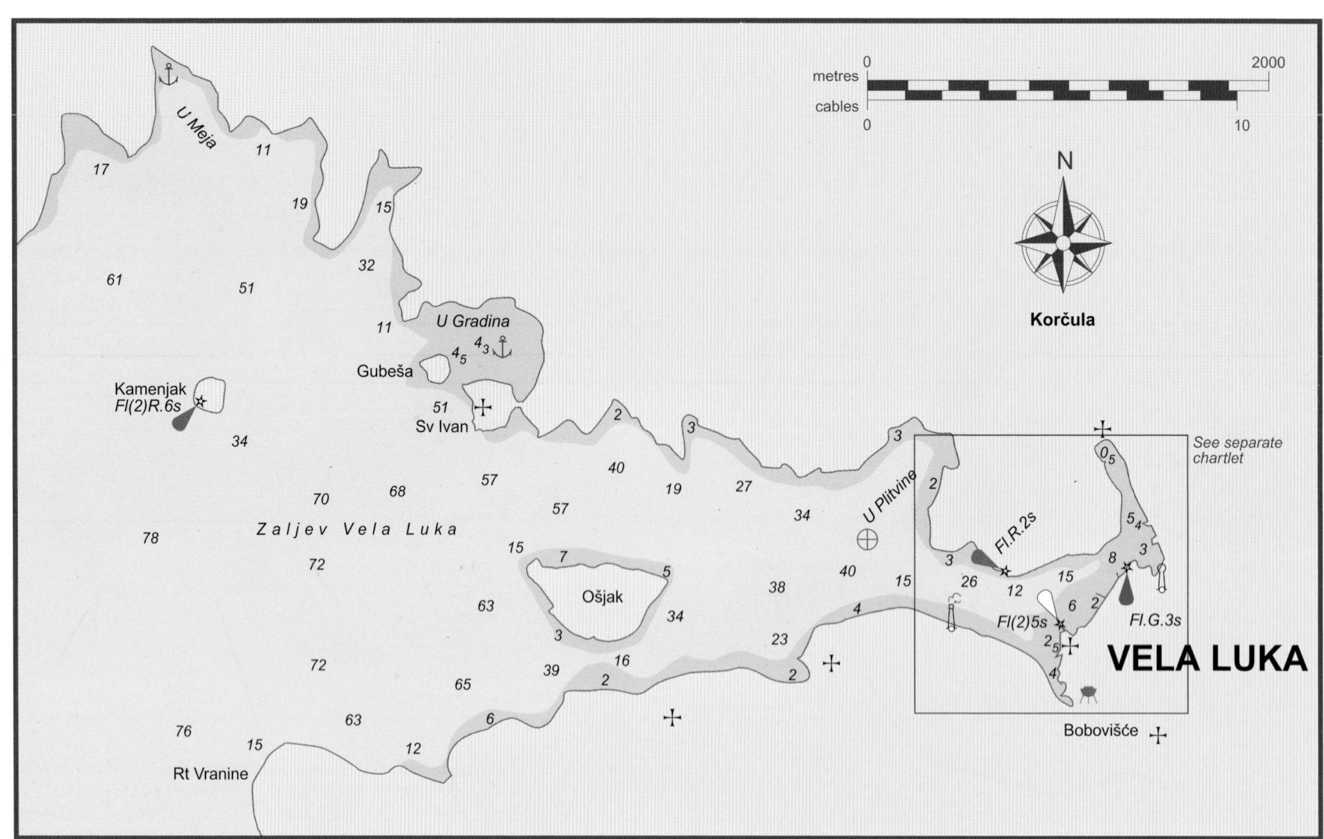

NAVIGATION

Charts: HHI 535, MK-21; AC 269; AC 2712, SC5767

Approaches: From the west, it's easiest to head south of the red light (Fl [2] R 6s) on the islet of Kamenjak and north of the larger islet of Ošjak. There are two small islets surrounded by shallow water off the north-west coast of the bay, about half a mile east-north-east of Kamenjak, (see Uvala Gradina on page 219), and a 6m shoal about a quarter of a mile west-south-west of the red light. The easterly islet, Sv Ivan, is joined to the mainland by a causeway.

From the south-west, it is possible to pass between Korčula Island and Ošjak but stay in the middle of the channel in the deeper water. See Uvala Poplat on page 217 for hazards to the south-west off Rt Velo Dance. As you head towards the inner bay, you'll see a red light to port (Fl R 2s) and a white light (Fl [2] 5s) and boatyard to starboard, followed by a green light (Fl G 3s). The white light marks the end of the ferry pier for ferries to Lastovo, Split and Hvar, while the green light identifies the end of the ferry pier for trips to the islets of Ošjak and Proizd. The fuel station is on the western side of the innermost ferry pier. Head past it for the visitors' berths at the quay.

BERTHING

There are no lazylines as yet so drop your anchor and berth stern-to or go alongside if there's room. You will probably have to pay a fee for an overnight stay. Note that the bay is exposed to winds from the west, which can cause a swell.

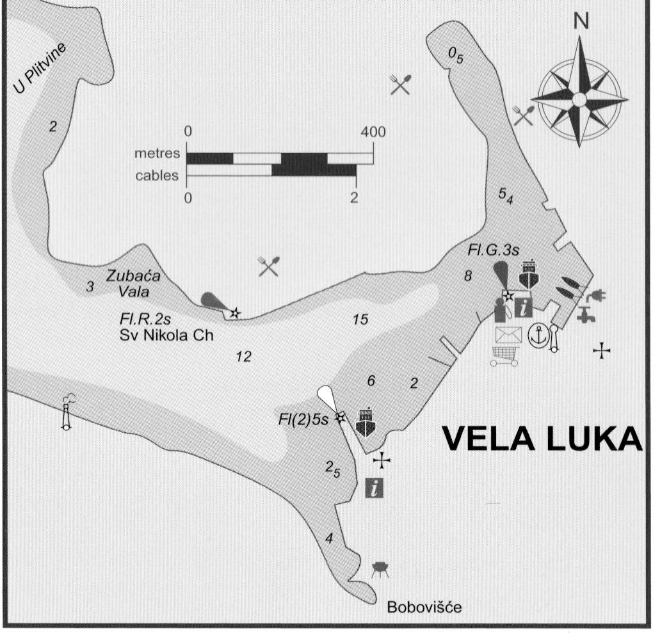

Vela Luka: fuel station and visitors' berths in the background

Useful information – Vela Luka

FACILITIES

Electricity and **water** are available. The **fuel station** (Tel: 020 812 910) has depths of 2 to 3m alongside and is open from 0700 to 2000 every day in the season, otherwise from 0700 to 1900 Monday to Saturday, 0700 to 1200 on Sunday and closed on Bank Holidays. **Shipyard** Leda, Tel: 020 711 002; website: www.shipyard-leda.hr, formerly known as Inkobrod, is by the outermost ferry pier and specialises in naval architecture. It has a 100-ton **crane**, manufactures sections for larger shipyards, has acquired a reputation for modifications to hatches, ramps, etc, and builds and refits smaller boats. There's also an **engine repair/ service facility** at Agromehanika, Ulica 43 10, Tel: 020 813 489.

PROVISIONING

The **market** is a short walk away from the shore from Obala 3, by the visitors' moorings, with **grocery shops**, a **bank** and a **supermarket** nearby. The **pharmacy** is a little further north-west around the bay, while the **medical centre** and **specialist hospital** (see below) are at the end of the north-west inner inlet. The **post office**, situated on Obala 2, br 1, is open in the summer from 0700 to 2100 Monday to Friday, 0800 to 1200 and 1800 to 2100 on Saturdays, otherwise from 0800 to 1200 and 1600 to 1900, Monday to Friday, and 0800 to 1300 on Saturdays.

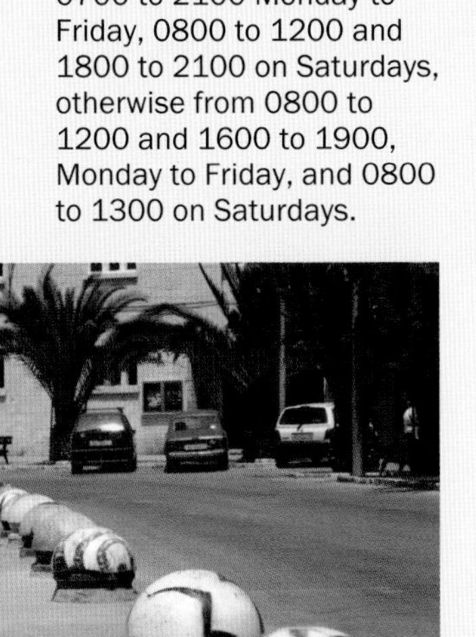

Vela Luka's artistic bollards surrounding the harbour

EATING OUT

There are at least seven restaurants around the bay, along with several bars and cafés. We had a good and very reasonably-priced meal at Pod Bore, Obala 2/3 Tel: 020 812 123, an imposing building right on the front.

ASHORE/TRANSPORT

The **tourist office** is off Obala 3, not far from the market, Ulica 41, br 11, 20270 Vela Luka, Tel/fax: 020 813 619; email: tzo-vela-luka@du.htnet.hr. It doesn't have its own website yet, but there is a private one that is reasonably helpful: www.apartments-vela-luka.com.

The **town museum** is next to the tourist office, while the main hotels, **beach** and **diving centre** are on the north-west side of the bay. The specialist hospital mentioned above is called Kalos and seems to be a cross between a health spa and an alternative medicine clinic. It claims to treat a number of ailments, from stress to rheumatism, mostly using the special properties of the mud found in the area.

There are at least two **ferries** a day between Vela Luka, Hvar, Lastovo and Split.

One of Vela Luka's imposing churches

OTHER INFORMATION

Harbourmaster: Obala 3 br 16, 20270 Vela Luka, Tel: 020 812 023; Tel/fax: 020 711 178.
Pharmacy: Tel: 020 812 032.
Medical centre: Tel: 020 812 040.
Specialist Hospital Kalos: Obala 3, br 3, Tel: 020 812 422 (see above).
Taxi Jure: Tel: 091 511 4096.

Uvala Gradina

Anchorage: 42°58'.32N 16°40'.41E
Charts: HHI MK-21; AC 269, AC 2712, SC5767

Between the north coast of Zaljev Vela Luka, the small islet of Sv Ivan and the even smaller islet of Gubeša, is a shallow area that provides a good anchorage. Oddly enough, it is only the smaller of the two islets that is named on Chart HHI MK-21, although there is a more detailed chart available.

See Vela Luka on page 218 for approaches and note that Sv Ivan is joined to Korčula by a causeway. Good holding on a sand bed in depths of 2 to 6m. The anchorage is exposed to winds from the west and south-west, which can cause a swell. There are no facilities here.

Prigradica

Harbour entrance: 42°58'.15N 16°48'.51E
Charts: HHI MK-21, MK-22; AC 1574; AC 2712, SC5767

This village has a small harbour where you can berth either on the inside of the breakwater (marked with a red light – Fl R 3s) in depths of 3 to 4m, or by the quay in depths of 2.5 to 3m. It's exposed to the Bora and winds from the east, which can cause heavy seas. Strong northwesterly winds generate a swell.

Approaching from the north, give the islet of Pločica, four miles out, a wide berth. It has a white light (Fl (2) 10s) on its north-west tip and is surrounded by shallows and rocks.

From the east, beware of a 2m shoal lying 3.2 miles east of Prigradica, immediately off Rt Prihodišće. Also note that just under a mile west of that, 2.3 miles east of the bay, is a marked but unlit rock off Rt Blaca, which is surrounded by shallow water, while half a mile east of Prigradica, a quarter of a mile off the coast of Korčula, are two small islets encircled by shallow water.

From the west, the approach is straightforward.

Prigradica has a beach at the head of the bay, a seasonal bar/restaurant and a supermarket.

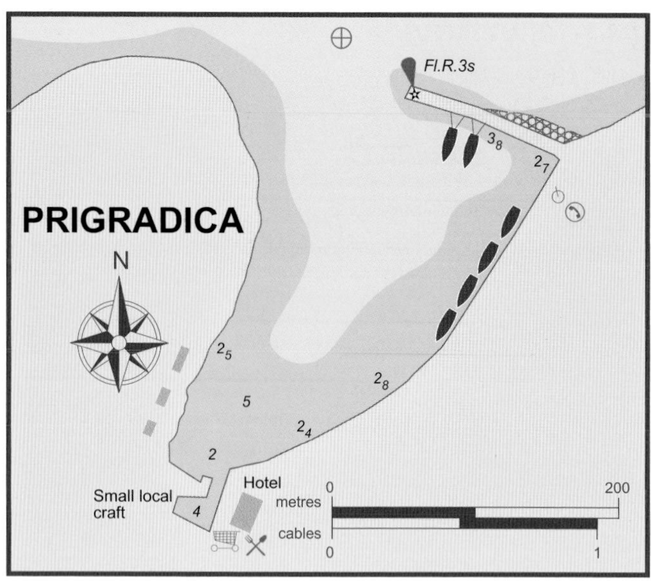

Račišće

Harbour: 42°58'.63N 17°01'.05E
Charts: HHI MK-22; AC 1574, SC5767

Račišće is a compact village opposite the western tip of the Pelješac Peninsula, with probably the best beach

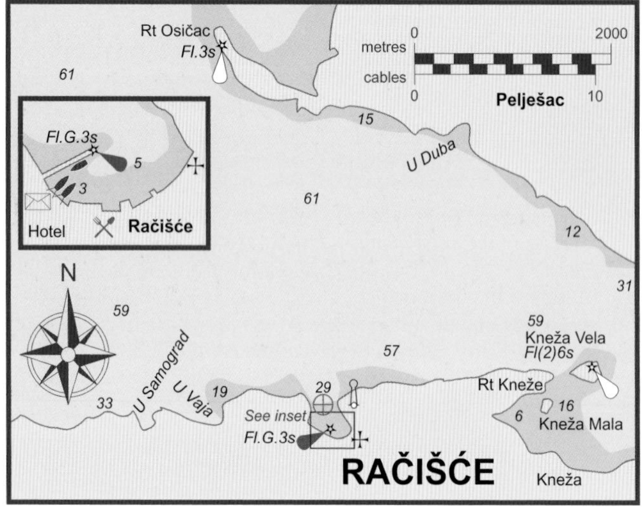

on the island – Vaja – a 15-minute walk north of the harbour. The approach from the north and west is straightforward. From the east, stay clear of Kneža Vela (Fl [2] 6s), the small islet east of Rt Kneža. Depths between Kneža Vela and Korčula are 4m. The smaller island of Kneža Mala lies about 400m south-west of the larger islet and there is only 0.3m of water between Kneža Mala and Korčula.

The breakwater has a green light (Fl G 3s) and the church, in the eastern corner of the head of the bay, should be visible among the trees once you have a complete view of the bay. Berth on the inner side of the breakwater in depths of 2.8 to 5m, or bows- or stern-to at the quay in depths of 0.2 to 3m, with the deeper water nearer the breakwater. Anchoring is not advised as there are underwater cables running to Pelješac. The bay offers good protection other than from the north-west when waves sometimes crash over the breakwater.

Among the facilities are a post office (open in the season from 0800 to 2100 Monday to Friday and from 0800 to 1200 and 1800 to 2100 on Saturday), shop, hotel with restaurant, café/grill and bar.

Kneža

Anchorage: 42°58'.58N 17°02'.76E
Charts: HHI MK-22; AC 683, AC 1574, SC5767

A small settlement with a few houses and a shop. See Račišće above for approach notes on the immediate area and also be aware that there is an unlit beacon marking a rocky shoal 2.5 miles east of the bay. Remember to avoid passing between Mala Kneža and Korčula, and anchor west or west-south-west of Kneža Mala in depths of between 3 and 9m. Good holding on a sand and mud bed. The anchorage is exposed to the Bora and Sirocco, which can cause heavy seas as the winds funnel through the Pelješac Canal.

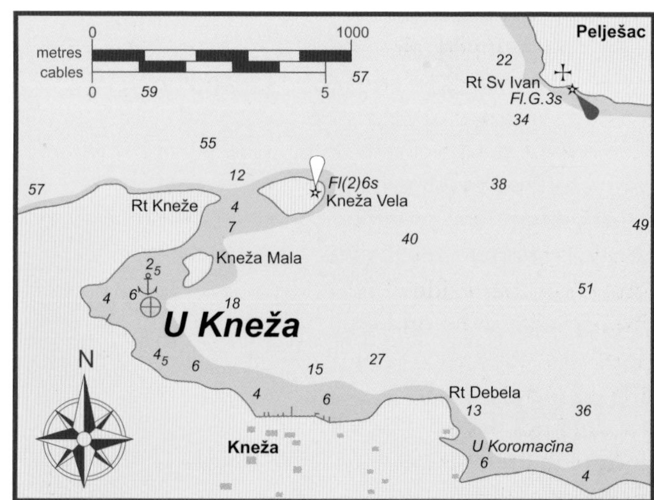

Uvala Vrbovica

Entrance to bay:
42°57'.93N 17°06'.23E
Charts: HHI MK-22; AC 683, AC 1574, SC5767

This anchorage is easily identified by the unlit red marker that indicates a rocky shoal with depths of 0.4m over it. The shoal is about 200m from the entrance to the bay and it is possible to pass between it and Korčula, but safer to pass north of it.

Anchor in either of the inlets in depths of 4 to 9m. The Sirocco causes a swell and the bay is exposed to the Bora. No facilities.

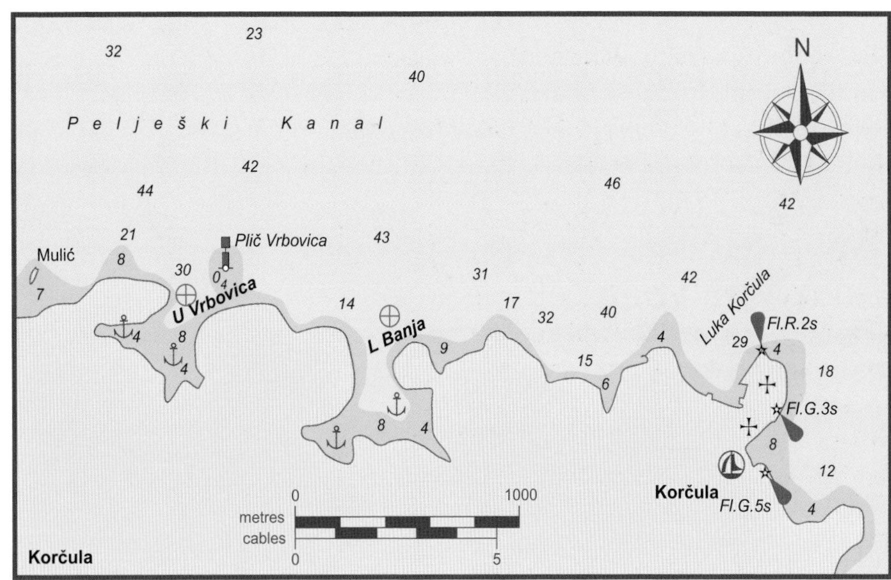

Luka Banja

Entrance to bay: 42°57'.92N 17°06'.84E
Charts: HHI MK-22; AC 683, AC 1574, SC5767

The last anchorage before heading east to Korčula Town, Luka Banja provides good shelter apart from in winds and seas from the north.

If approaching from the west, see Uvala Vrbovica above for details of the shoal, and see Korčula Town on page 209 if approaching from the east. The holding is good on a sand bed in depths of between 5 and 12m. Facilities comprise a shop and a bar.

Lastovo Island

Like the island of Vis, Lastovo is geographically strategic to Croatia's defence and was therefore out of bounds to visitors for many years. The submarine caves still remain as a reminder. Again, like Vis, this has resulted in it remaining very undeveloped, although things are starting to change. Lastovo is joined on its north-west coast to the island of Prežba by a small road bridge. There's a good anchorage and a few berths on the northern side of the bridge, with more on the southern side. The owner of the hotel in Pasadur, who has laid down the moorings, is hoping to improve the facilities in the future.

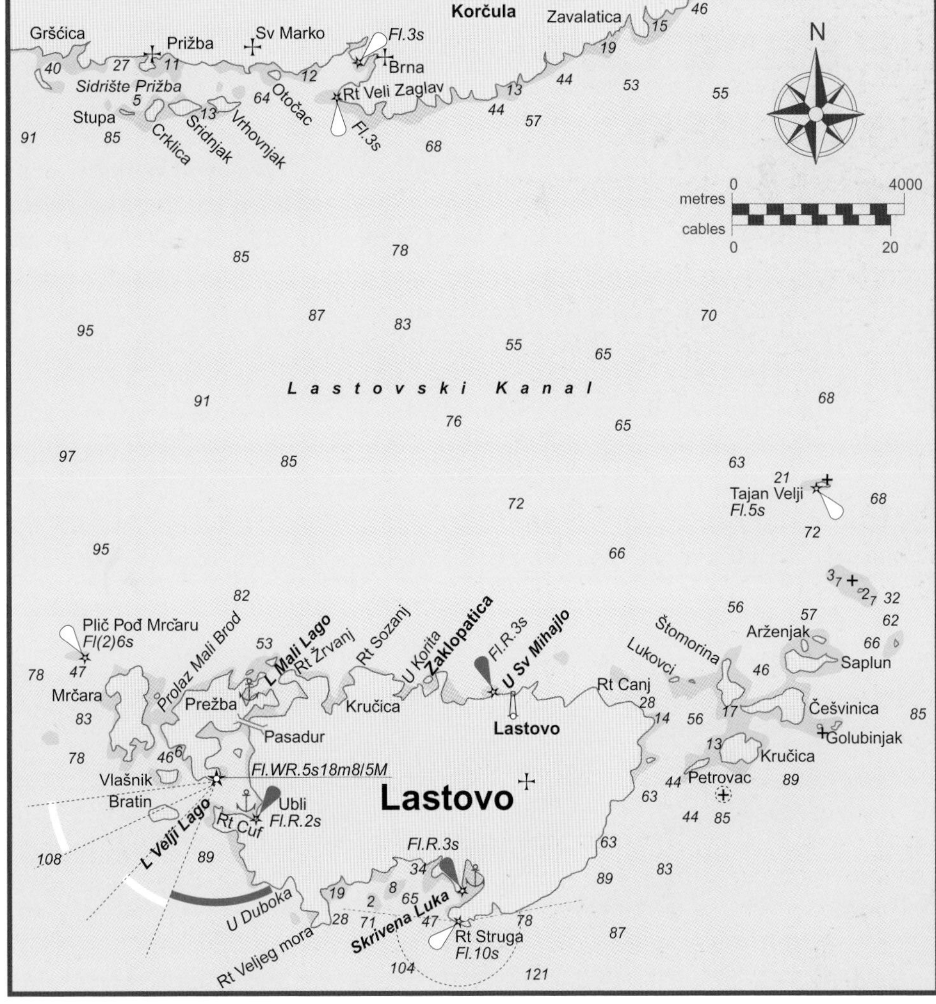

We start with Luka Mali Lago, on the north side of the Pasadur bridge, and head anticlockwise around Lastovo. Fuel is available in Ubli, situated roughly in the middle of the west coast of Lastovo, which is also the island's ferry terminal. We didn't manage to spot any cash points on the island, although there is a bank at Ubli.

North-east of Lastovo is an archipelago of about 40 islets and rocks. Protection is limited and navigation can be tricky, but the islet of Saplun is well worth a visit for its sandy beach.

Luka Mali Lago

Entrance to bay: 42°46'.44N 16°49'.79E
Charts: HHI MK-21, MK-23; AC 1574, AC 2712, SC5767

This is a shallow, well-protected anchorage that is very popular in the summer. Pension Ladesta, the hotel on the other side of the road bridge, has laid some berths near the bridge, with water and electricity provided. You can expect to pay a fee similar to normal marina rates for use of the facilities.

Approaching from the north, head between the east coast of Maslovnjak Veli Island and Lastovo, as there are low-lying rocks west and south-west of Maslovnjak Veli.

If coming from the west, keep clear of the rock and shoal 750m north-west of the north coast of Mrčara. Note that the Bora does blow strongly in the area but shelter can be found from all winds in various parts of the bay. See Ubli's Useful Information section on page 223 for details of facilities.

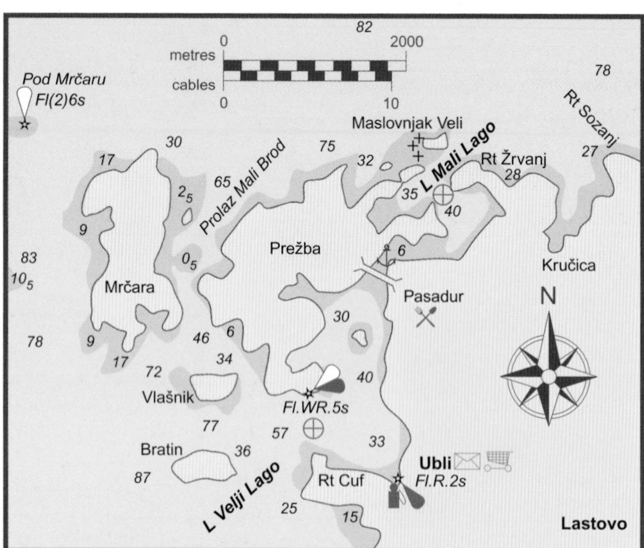

Ubli and Luka Velji Lago

Entrance to bay: 42°45'.12N 16°48'.50E

Luka Velji Lago is a large bay formed by most of the west coast of Lastovo and the indented south-east coast of Prežba. Ubli, the island's ferry terminal, is in the south-east corner of the bay and, in the north-east corner, south of the road bridge that separates Luka Velji Lago from Luka Mali Lago, is the hotel Pension Ladesta and about 30 berths run by the hotel.

NAVIGATION

Charts: HHI 535, MK-21, MK-23; AC 1574, AC 2712, SC5767

Approaches: From the north, it is safest to pass to the west of the islet of Mrčara but look out for the two shoals about 800m north-west of the north coast of Mrčara. The easterly shoal surrounds a rock with a white light (Fl [2] 6s). Once you have left Mrčara behind, turn to port between the islets of Vlašnik and Bratin and head for the centre of the bay, taking care to avoid the shallow water around the promontory of Rt Cuf on the south coast of the bay. Ubli is straight ahead with its red light (Fl R 2s), ferry pier and fuel station to starboard. Turn to port towards Pasadur for the berths, avoiding the small

The road bridge between Lastovo and Prežba. The visitors' moorings south of the bridge, in Pasadur, are on the right

islet near the head of the northern part of the bay. From the south, take the centre of the channel between the islet of Bratin and Lastovo and don't turn to starboard until you are well past Rt Cuf and its shallows.

BERTHING

Berth on lazylines, as directed by a member of staff who will normally be watching out for new visitors, sometimes with a free drink to greet you. Expect to pay around €40 per day for a 10m (33ft) boat. The hotel and moorings are usually only open/available between 1 May and 30 September. but contact Pension Ladesta, also known as Hotel Solitudo, for more information on Tel: 020 802 100/098 220 120.

Visitors' berths in front of Pension Ladesta's restaurants

Useful information – Ubli and Luka Velji Lago

FACILITIES
Water and **electricity** are available and you can use the **showers** and **toilets** in the **hotel**, which also has exchange facilities, a **bar**, a **restaurant** and a **diving centre**. Email: info@diving-paradise.net; website: www.diving-paradise.net. The **fuel** station in Ubli (Tel: 020 805 034) has depths of up to 2.5m and is open from 0700 to 2000 every day in the summer, otherwise from 0700 to 1200 and 1700 to 2000 every day except Bank Holidays.

ASHORE
Ubli itself has a **ferry terminal** and **café** by the shore, as well as a **post office** and **supermarket** on the road towards Lastovo. The post office address is Trg Sv Petra bb, 20289 Ubli. Opening hours are from 0800 to 1200 and 1800 to 2100 Monday to Saturday in season, otherwise from 1700 to 2000 Monday to Friday. In Pasadur, the hotel restaurant looked fine, but we ate at Konoba Frenki by the bridge, Tel: 020 805 091.

Skrivena Luka

Entrance to bay: 42°43'.73N 16°52'.90E
Charts: HHI MK-23; AC 1574, SC5767

The name translates as 'Hidden Harbour' because the bay is so difficult to spot from the open sea. It's a very well protected anchorage on the south side of the island, with a restaurant ashore but not much else.

The entrance to the bay has maximum depths of 6.1m. A red light (Fl R 3s) is situated on the northern side of the entrance to the bay, with a lighthouse (Fl 10s) on Rt Struga, further south. Look out for the rock and shoals to the west of the entrance.

Anchor in 7 to 10m on a mud and weed bed that provides reasonable holding. The restaurant Konoba Potorus (Tel: 020 801 261) has a terrace and berths for shallow draught boats.

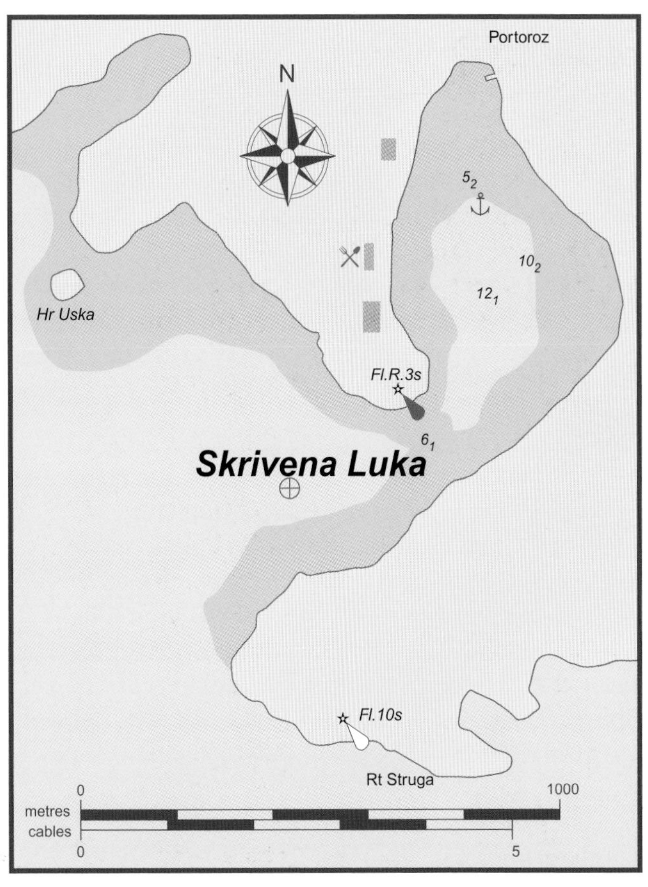

Zaklopatica

Entrance to bay: 42°46'.63N 16°52'.57E
Charts: HHI MK-23; AC 1574, SC5767

This is a classic island bay, on the north coast of Lastovo, with two good restaurants, both with lazyline berths, and a shop. A small islet partially blocks the entrance to the bay and you should enter to the east of this islet, in depths of 6m, rather than to the west where depths are less than a metre. Otherwise the approach is straightforward. Of the two restaurants, Triton (Tel: 020 801 161) is thought to be the best, but August Insula (Tel: 020 801 167) has electricity and water pedestals. Depths at the quay are about 2.5m. It's approximately half a mile's walk to Lastovo town. The bay is well sheltered apart from when the Bora blows.

Restaurant August Insula's owner holding up a lazyline to entice visitors to his moorings

Useful information – Lastovo Island

Lastovo, inland on the north side, is the main settlement for the island and has road connections to Ubli, Zaklopatica and Skrivena Luka. Facilities include a bank, pharmacy, post office, medical centre, tourist office and a few shops. The houses, dating from the 15th century, are dotted around narrow alleys and stone stairways, and many have unusual chimneys shaped like minarets. A big carnival takes place each year on Shrove Tuesday.

HARBOURMASTER (Ubli): **Tel:** 020 805 006.

PHARMACY: Lastovo, **Tel:** 020 801 276.

TOURIST OFFICE: Lastovo, **Tel:** 020 801 018; **email:** tz-lastovo@du.htnet.hr; **website:** www.lastovo-tz.net.

MEDICAL CENTRE: **Tel:** 020 801 270.

BEACHES: Uvala Sv Mihovil lies close to Lastovo and has a concrete quay with easy access to the water and a summer bar. Saplun, one of the islets north-east of Lastovo, has a lovely bay with a sandy beach.

TRANSPORT ON THE ISLAND

There is one ferry a day to and from Split, via Hvar and Korčula, total journey time around five hours. A daily catamaran also operates the same route, for foot passengers only, journey time just under three hours. A bus runs between Ubli and Lastovo to coincide with the ferry arrivals and departures. Between mid-July and mid-September the bus route includes Skrivena Luka.

Sušac Island

This island, lying about 13 miles west of Lastovo, is not to be confused with Susak Island in North Croatia. Don't be confused either by the fact that it looks like two separate islands from a distance.

Sušac is isolated with no facilities, but has accommodation available to let in its lighthouse on the southern tip of the island. On the south-east coast are some well-indented bays, which are good for swimming, although only suitable for a temporary stop in anything other than a shallow-draught boat. Given this and the lack of protection, we wouldn't recommend a special trip to Sušac.

See www.privateislandsonline.com/susac-island.htm for more information on the island and its lighthouse accommodation.

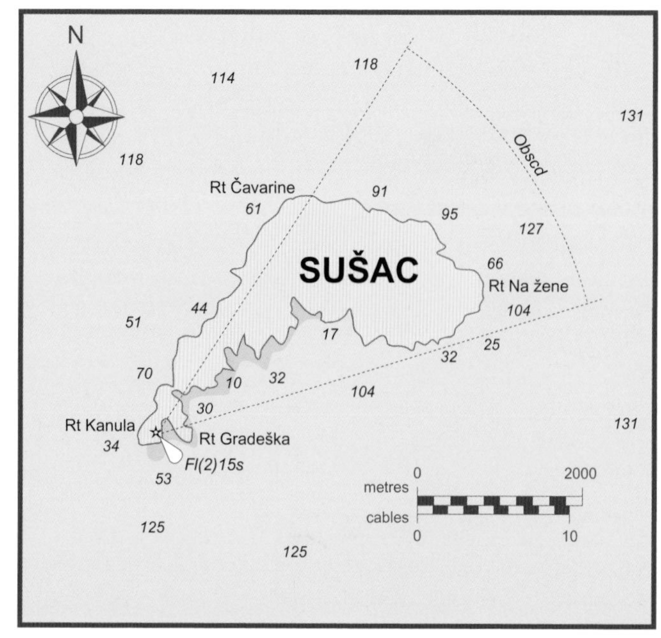

Mljet Island

The east end of Mljet's south coast looking from the north over the National Park and the bigger of the two saltwater lakes, Veliko Jezero

Mljet is probably the lushest, greenest island in the Adriatic and the most southerly of the larger populated islands. The majority of its coastline is inhospitable. However, there are notable exceptions, particularly the National Park area with its saltwater lakes, covering about a third of the island from the western end. Mljet's discovery as an idyllic holiday destination has been slow, so it is still relatively unspoilt and well worth a visit. We start with Pomena, on the west coast, and work our way clockwise around the north coast of the island, finishing with details of the National Park and useful information on the island.

The south coast has little to offer: it is very exposed to southerly winds and seas, barely indented and surrounded by deep water, and there are a number of rocks, islets and shoals off the coast, making navigation hazardous.

As we mentioned at the start of this chapter, facilities become more limited in the southern islands. On Mljet these are concentrated in Sobra where there is a fuel station, harbourmaster's office and ferry service to the mainland.

Right: Tourists exploring the convent on the small islet on Veliko Jezero

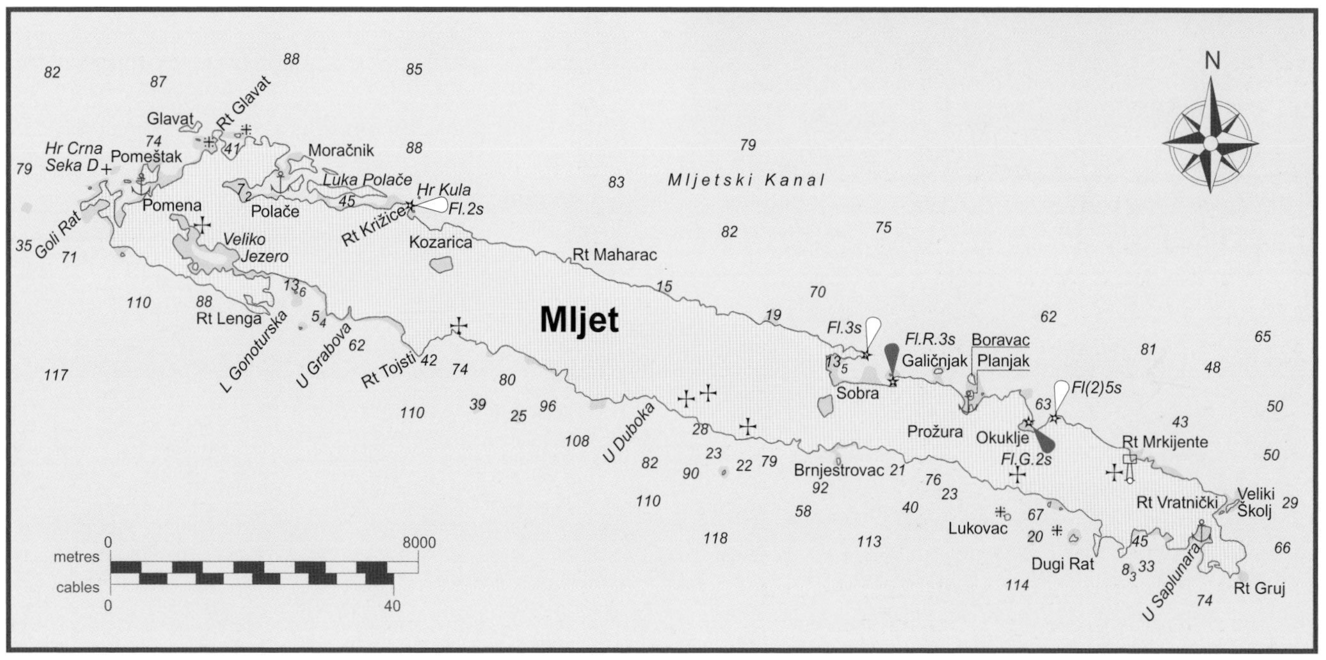

Pomena

Entrance to bay: 42°47'.38N 17°20'.57E

At the north-west end of the island, Pomena is probably the most tourist-orientated settlement on Mljet, with several moorings, a hotel complex and a number of daytripper boats going in and out. The two saltwater lakes of the National Park are within walking distance or you can join one of the many organised trips.

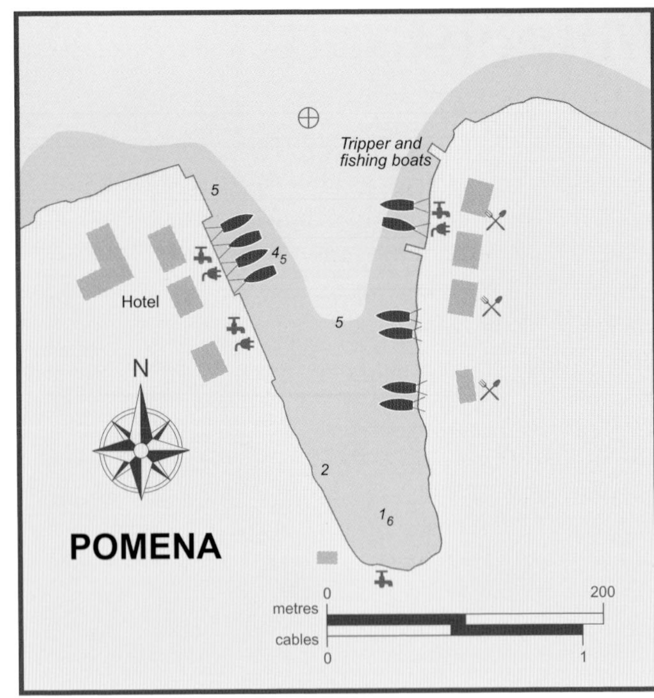

NAVIGATION

Charts: HHI MK-24; AC 1574, AC 1580, SC5767

Approaches: There are a number of rocks and shoals around the entrance to Pomena. The best approach is from the north-west, avoiding the rock Hr Sij, west of Sparožni Rat. Then stay close to Sparožni Rat, leaving the rocks Hr Crna Seka Donja and Hr Galicija to port. The channel between Mljet and the islet of Pomeštak is 6m deep in the centre, but avoid passing between Pomeštak and the small islet west of it (Galicija). If approaching from the north or east, give Rt Glavat and the islet of Glavat a wide berth as there are rocks and shoals close to the coast. Also be aware of the 2.7m shoal off the north-eastern tip of Pomeštak Islet.

Konoba Galija, Pomena, and its lazyline berths

BERTHING/ANCHORING

You can berth on lazylines by the hotel, on the western side of the bay, or by the restaurants opposite, on the eastern side. The hotel berths have access to water and electricity, as do some of the restaurant berths, notably Konoba Galija, Tel: 020 744 029, and Konoba Nine, Tel: 020 744 037. Although the Bora blows strongly in the area, the berths are well protected from all winds and seas. Alternatively, anchor south of Pomeštak Islet or in the deep bay west of Pomena.

ASHORE

Apart from the attractions of the National Park, the Hotel Odisej (Tel: 020 362 111; Fax: 020 744 042; email: info@hotelodisej.hr; website: www.hotelodisej.hr) has a range of activities on offer, including diving, canoeing, kayaking, sailing, windsurfing, excursions and car and bike hire. There's also a good choice of restaurants, but you will be expected to use the restaurant that has provided you with a berth. Konoba Nine is well known for its lobsters, which you can select live from the pool outside.

Pomena approach with the rock Crna Seka D in the foreground

Polače

Entrance to inner bay/anchorage:
42°47'.37N 17°23'.29E

The settlement of Polače lies in a deep, well-sheltered bay with a large and popular anchorage that can become quite busy in the summer. Polače is also within walking distance of the saltwater lakes, but the less energetic may prefer an organised trip by coach, departing from near the castle.

NAVIGATION

Charts: HHI 100-27, MK-24; AC 1574, AC 1580, SC5767

Approaches: From the west, beware of the underwater rock about 500m east of Rt Glavat and the rocks and shoals immediately west of Rt Glavat. There are a number of easily-visible islets in Luka Polače itself and, approaching from the east, a rock, Hr Kula, which is marked by a white light (Fl 2s).

Entering the western side of the bay by Rt Stupa, watch out for a small, above-water rock Školjić. Between the southern tip of Moračnik Islet and Mljet is a shoal, with barely visible rocks close to the shore, so stay in the middle of the channel. Inside the bay, note that depths reduce to 2m just north-east of the castle.

BERTHING/ANCHORING

As you enter the bay, you will see a cluster of restaurants with stern-to moorings available to port, while in the southern corner of the bay is the ferry terminal.

For best protection, anchor on the north side of the bay, avoiding the rocky area north-east of the castle ruins. The holding is good on a mud bed, with depths of 2 to 12m. The biggest problem might be the number of other boats in the anchorage so make sure you have adequate room to swing. Expect to pay a fee in the high season.

Facilities include an electricity supply on the ferry pier and a water tap near the castle ruins.

ASHORE

The tourist office (Tel: 020 744 086) is by the ferry quay where you will also find a kiosk for buying tickets for the National Park trip. There's a wide choice of restaurants here, but the prices are higher than on the mainland. Try Stella Maris (Tel: 020 744 059), Bourbon (Tel: 020 744 090) or Ankora (Tel: 020 744 159). Other amenities include a selection of supermarkets and shops.

During the summer a twice-daily ferry service runs to Trstenik on the Pelješac Peninsula. The excursions to the lakes operate hourly.

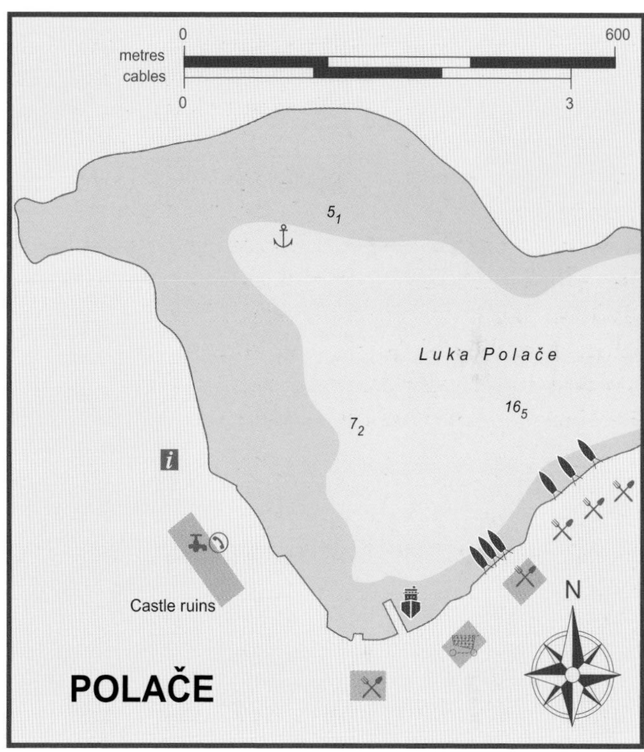

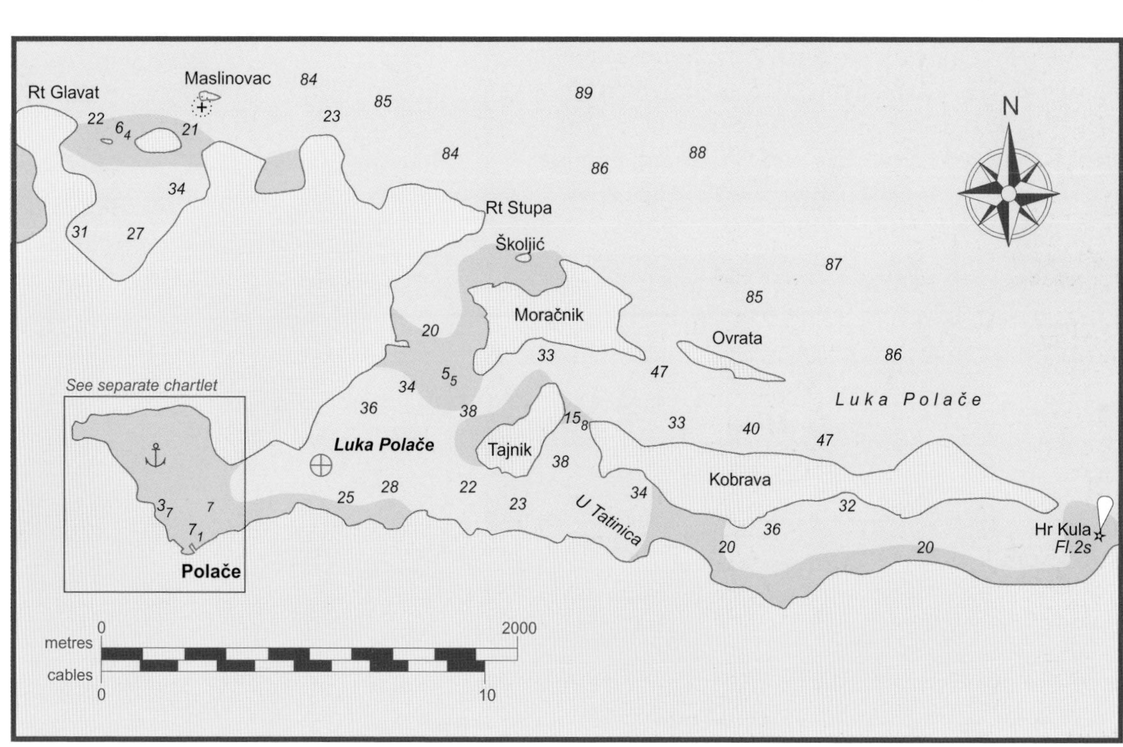

Polače's anchorage and castle ruins

Sobra

Entrance to bay: 42°44'.63N 17°37'.00E
Charts: HHI MK-24, MK-25; AC 1580, SC5767

The small settlement of Sobra lies in a large bay that is really too deep to provide a good anchorage and is exposed to the Bora, Sirocco and winds from the east. However, it is possible to berth alongside the harbour wall by the café, in the south-west part of the bay in depths of around 4 to 6m.

Apart from the fuel station, the harbourmaster's office and ferry terminal to the mainland, there's not a lot going on here so you'd do better elsewhere on the island. Beware of a reef just off Pusti Rt and another rock inside the bay just off the middle of the west coast.

Off the eastern headland of the bay is a small islet joined to the mainland. The ferry quay and fuel station are immediately after it. We've had different reports on the opening times of the fuel station (Tel: 020 746 226). When we visited recently we were told that the opening hours were from 1000 to 1800 every day except Sundays and Bank Holidays all year round. However, in reality it seems that the hours are more limited in the winter. Depths are around 5m.

Facilities ashore include a restaurant, shop and a couple of cafés. There's a daily ferry service to and from Dubrovnik and a fast daily catamaran for foot passengers only, in the summer. Buses run along the island, timed to meet ferry departures and arrivals.

Konoba Lanterna, by the ferry quay in Sobra

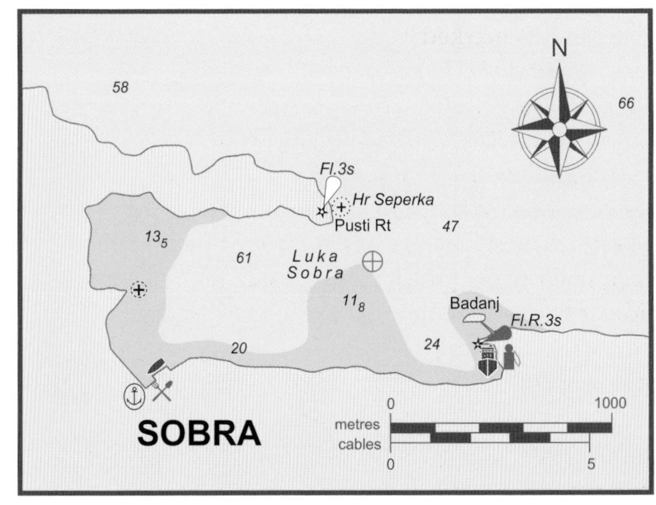

Prožura

Entrance to bay: 42°44'.32N 17°38'.75E
Charts: HHI MK-24, MK-25; AC 1580, SC5767

Two islets help to protect this popular anchorage. Four berths are also available in front of one of the restaurants in the bay, Marijina Konoba (Tel: 020 746 113), which is famed for its squid dishes and goats cheese. Enter the bay to the west of Planjak Islet as the channel east of the islet is shallow and has an above-water rock. You can anchor in good holding in the centre of the bay in depths of 4 to 6m. The restaurant's berths have lazylines and depths of 1.7 to 2.5m. The Bora and easterly winds cause a swell, but otherwise the bay is well protected. The restaurant owners stay on the island during the winter and will provide meals outside the summer season by arrangement.

Seasonal restaurant in Prožura

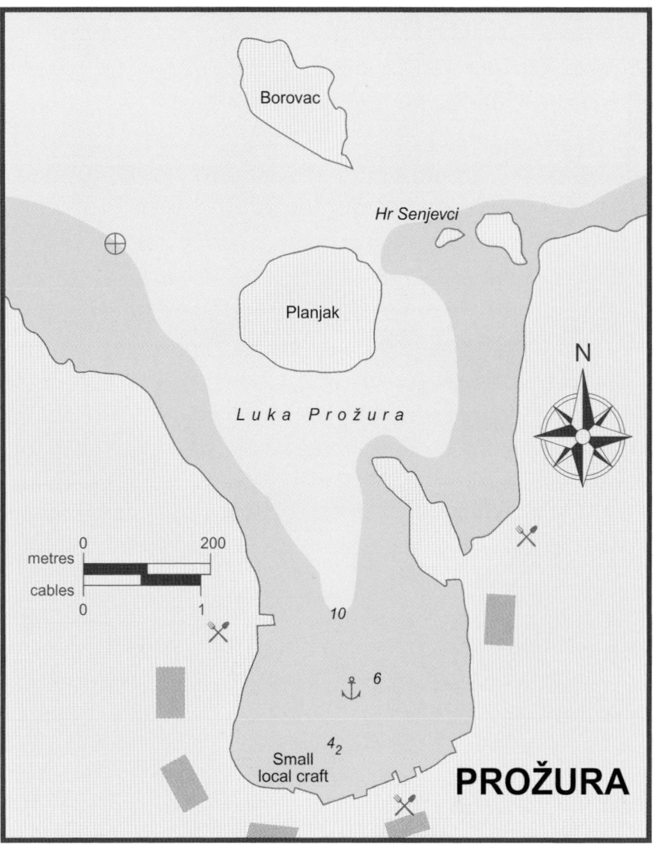

Okuklje

Entrance to bay: 42°43'.79N 17°40'.66E
Charts: HHI MK-24, MK-25; AC 1580, SC5767

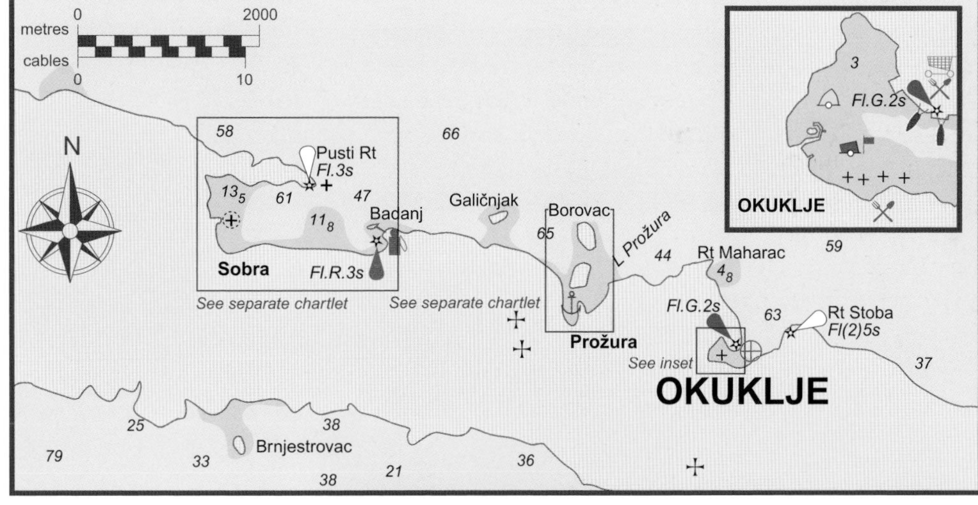

Okuklje lies in a well-protected bay and has become a popular overnight stop. It is memorable for the small, above-water rock (red marker) in the middle of the bay. Rt Stoba, situated on Okuklje's eastern headland, is marked by a white light (Fl [2] 5s) and, as you enter the bay, you will see a green light (Fl G 2s) to starboard on Rt Okuklje. Either pick up a mooring buoy or a lazyline by one of the restaurants. The bottom is rocky and not suitable for anchoring. Also be careful going ashore in a tender as the water is very shallow over the jagged rocks on the south side of the bay. We moored at a buoy belonging to Restoran Maestral, so that's where we ate – good food at reasonable island prices. However, there are plenty of other restaurants to choose from and there's also a small shop by the green light. No electricity and water pedestals as yet.

Okuklje, a popular anchorage on Mljet

Uvala Saplunara

Entrance to bay: 42°41'.58N 17°44'.10E
Charts: HHI MK-25; AC 1580, SC5767

Located on the southeastern tip of Mljet Island, this bay provides partial shelter, but the Sirocco causes a swell and southwesterly winds produce heavy seas.

The approach is straightforward and you can anchor at the head of the bay on a sand bed. Good holding in depths of between 3 and 8m. The buoy and jetty are reserved for naval vessels.

This bay is renowned for its sandy beaches and there are a number of holiday houses here, as well as a small hotel and restaurant Villa Mirosa, Tel: 020 746 133; email: srdjan.basica@du.t-com.hr; website: www.villa-mirosa.com.

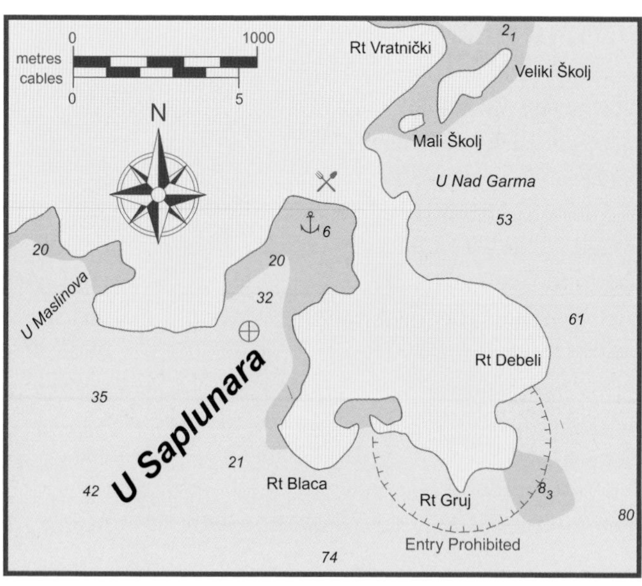

National Park Mljet

Although the whole area of the park is one of diverse beauty, flora and fauna, the main attractions of the park are its two saltwater lakes Veliko Jezero and Malo Jezero. In fact these lakes are bays, as the larger lake connects to the sea via a small channel, and the smaller one connects to the larger one via an even smaller channel, with an old stone bridge across it. In the most southeasterly cove of the larger lake is St Mary's Islet, with a 12th century Benedictine monastery that serves as a restaurant in the summer and forms part of the organised tours. The park is a great place to walk or cycle around, and the brackish water is ideal for swimming as it stays a few degrees warmer than the sea. The best swimming area is right next to the stone bridge.

It costs 90 Kunas per person to enter the park, which should include a short bus ride from Pomena or Polače and a boat trip to the island and monastery. The website www.np-mljet.hr will give you full details of what's included and more information about the park and facilities.

Alternatively, write to Nacionalni Park Mljet, 20 226 Goveđari, Pristanište 2, Croatia, Tel: 020 744 041; Fax: 020 744 043 or email: np-mljet@np-mljet.hr. Mali Raj (Tel: 020 744 115), a seasonal restaurant, has a terrace overlooking Veliko Jezero.

Restaurant and Benedictine monastery on St Mary's Islet in Veliko Jezero, the larger of Mljet National Park's two saltwater lakes

Useful information – Mljet

The main town of Babino Polje is situated inland from Sobra, and there are some other interesting settlements away from the coast. The cave where Odysseus is said to have held the nymph Calypso captive is on the south coast of the island, near Babino Polje.

HARBOURMASTER'S OFFICE (Sobra): 20225 Babino Polje, Sobra 25, **Tel:** 020 745 040.

TOURIST OFFICE (Babino Polje): 20225 Babino Polje, Zabrijezje 2, **Tel/fax:** 020 746 025; **email:** tzinfo@mljet.hr; **website:** www.mljet.hr.

POST OFFICE: Sršenovići 46, 20225 Babino Polje. The only post office on the island, it is open from 0800 to 1000 Monday to Friday, all year round.

CAR HIRE: Based in Sobra, Mini Brum will offer you cars for hire with a difference – mainly small convertibles decorated with spots or made to look like cats! Contact 20225 Babino Polje, Mljet, **Tel:** 020 745 084/098 285 566; **email:** mini.brum@du.htnet.hr; **website:** http://www.mljet.hr/mini_brum1.asp.

The Elaphite Islands

The name derives from the Greek word *elafos*, meaning deer. There are some suggestions that the name may have originated from the fact that the island grouping looked like antlers, rather than that the islands were populated by deer, and there are certainly no deer on the islands any more. Close to the mainland, unspoilt, predominantly car-free and with a number of good bays, the Elaphite Islands are a popular weekend destination for Dubrovnik city dwellers. There are a few seasonal restaurants and the larger islands are inhabited all year round, but facilities are limited so make sure you are well stocked with supplies. The smaller and most northwesterly Elaphite Islands of Olipa and Tajan have little in the way of shelter so we start with the island of Jakljan and work our way south-east.

Luka on Šipan Island

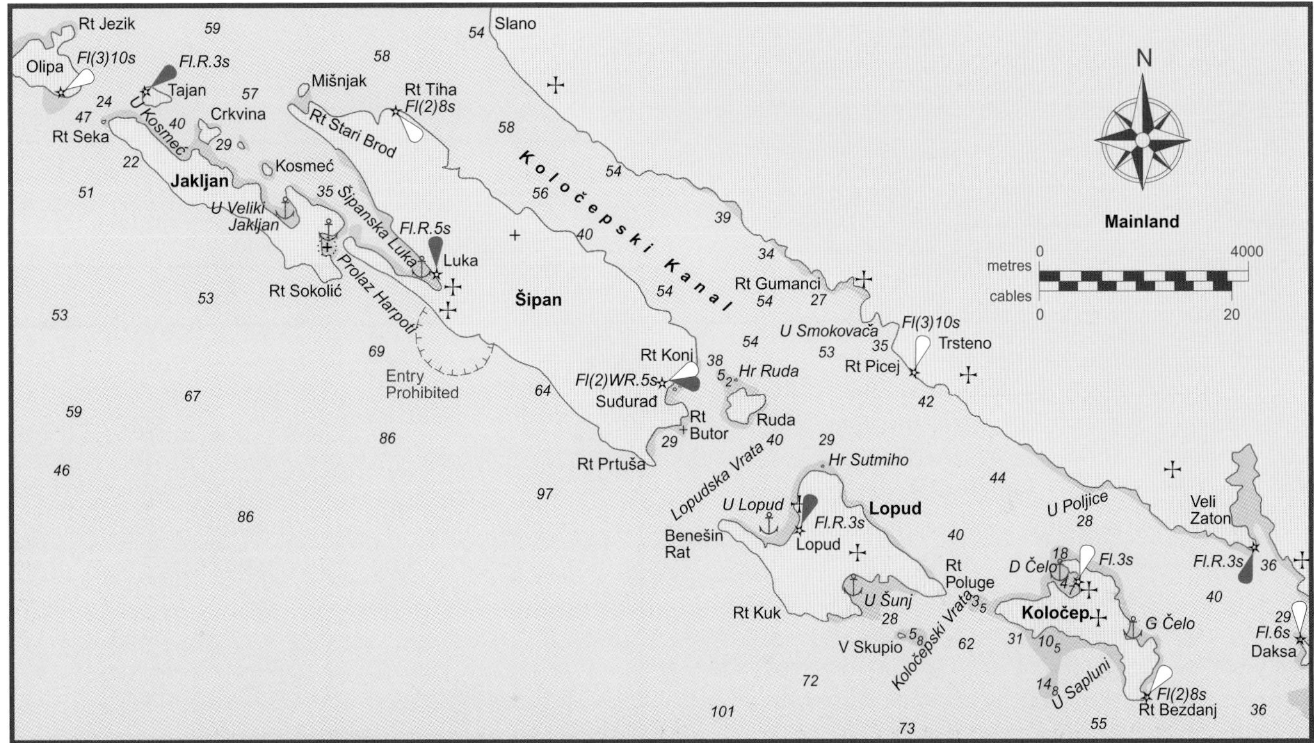

Jakljan Island

Charts: HHI 50-20 (for Prolaz Harpoti – see below), MK-25; AC 1580, SC5767

The south-west coast is steep, rocky and offers no protection. There is a large, wooded bay off the north-east coast, Uvala Veliki Jakljan, which, apart from a few swimmers in the roped-off swimming area at its head and a couple of small boats tied up at the pier, was deserted when we passed it in July. Two coves are situated on the south-eastern tip of the island in Prolaz Harpoti where anchoring is also possible.

The Serbian Government originally rented the buildings on this island from the Croatian Privatisation Fund on a 10 year lease that expired in 2005, and the main building in Uvala Veliki Jakljan was used as a children's summer camp. There appears to be an ongoing dispute as to the status of the title to the property, which may explain why it was so deserted when we visited.

Deserted children's summer camp in Uvala Veliki Jakljan

Uvala Veliki Jakljan

Entrance to bay: 42°44'.55N 17°49'.54E

The entrance to the bay is fairly straightforward and you can pass either side of the small islets to the north-west. A white cross can be seen at the head of the bay, while a wooded area runs close to the shore.

No anchoring is permitted at the entrance to the bay where there is an underwater cable. However, you can anchor in the centre of the bay on a sand bed in depths of 3 to 7m. Good protection and holding. No facilities were available at the time of our visit, no doubt a result of the problems mentioned above. Once these are resolved, and it may take some time, there are plans on the table for a luxury hotel.

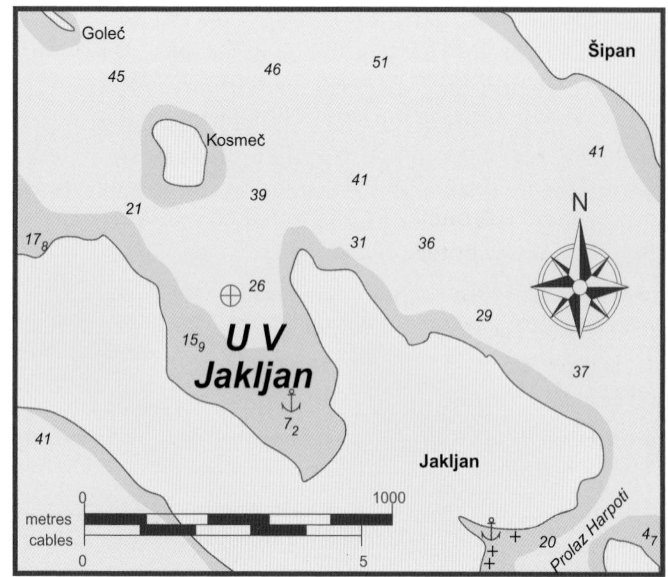

Prolaz Harpoti

Entrance to bay: 42°44'.02N 17°50'.28E

Prolaz Harpoti is the channel between the north-west-facing peninsula on the south coast of Šipan and the south-eastern tip of Jakljan. The two anchorages off Jakljan are narrow inlets with a number of rocks on either side of the entrance, so care is required. Also be aware of shallows around the tip of the Šipan peninsula, depth 4.5m, and a high voltage cable over the channel with air clearance of 46m. Anchor on a sand and weed bed in depths of 10 to 12m. Winds from the south, south-west and south-east may cause heavy seas. There are no facilities.

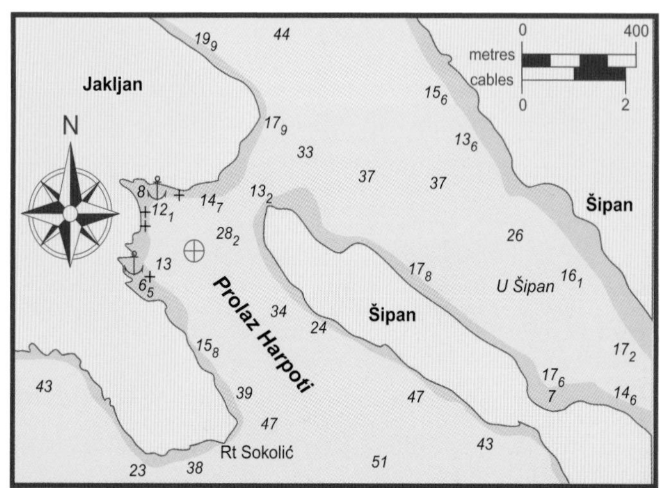

Šipan Island

Charts: HHI 50-20 (for Luka – see below), MK-25; AC 1580, SC5767

Šipan is the largest and most populated island of the group and was a favourite place for Dubrovnik noblemen of the 15th and 16th centuries to build their summer-houses. Much of the island is cultivated and there are a number of interesting ruins.

The two main coastal settlements are Luka, lying in a deep inlet on the south-west coast of the island, and Suđurađ, on the south-east coast. Apart from these two anchorages, there's a shallow area between the north-western tip of Šipan and the islet of Mišnjak, which could provide a suitable anchorage for a lunchtime stop in calm weather.

Note that several underwater cables and pipelines run from the mainland to Šipan and from Šipan to surrounding islands.

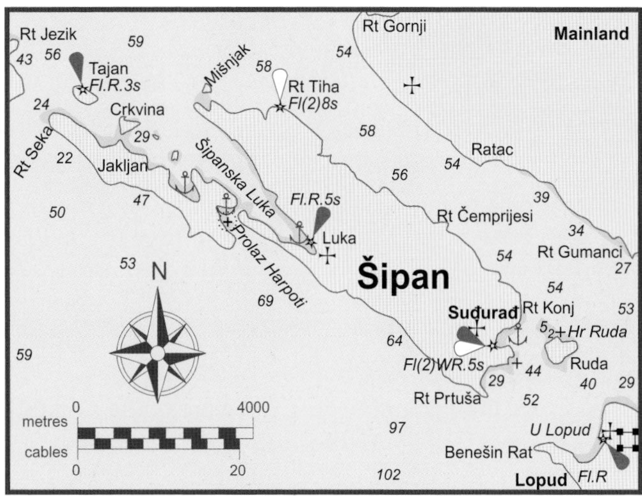

Luka

Entrance to inner bay: 42°43'.80N 17°51'.40E

See Prolaz Harpoti on page 232 if approaching Luka from the south. Approaching from the north-west, give the north-western tip of Šipan a wide berth to avoid the islet and shallow area. The houses are clearly visible from a distance and there's a red light on the pier. The one hotel on the island, Hotel Šipan (website: www.hotelsipan.com), is by the church. Anchor towards the head of the bay in depths of 1 to 6m, leaving plenty of room for the ferry to turn. The holding is good on a sand and weed bed. Alternatively, berth stern-to the quay, just past the pier, as you head into the bay. The hotel has a few berths at the head of the bay, but depths are only 1 to 2m here. The inlet is generally well protected, but northwesterly winds, which funnel down the Stonski Kanal, can cause heavy seas.

Luka has a tourist office (Tel: 020 758 084), shop, post office and a few bars and restaurants – try Kod Marka (Tel: 020 758 007) or More (Tel: 098 565 027).

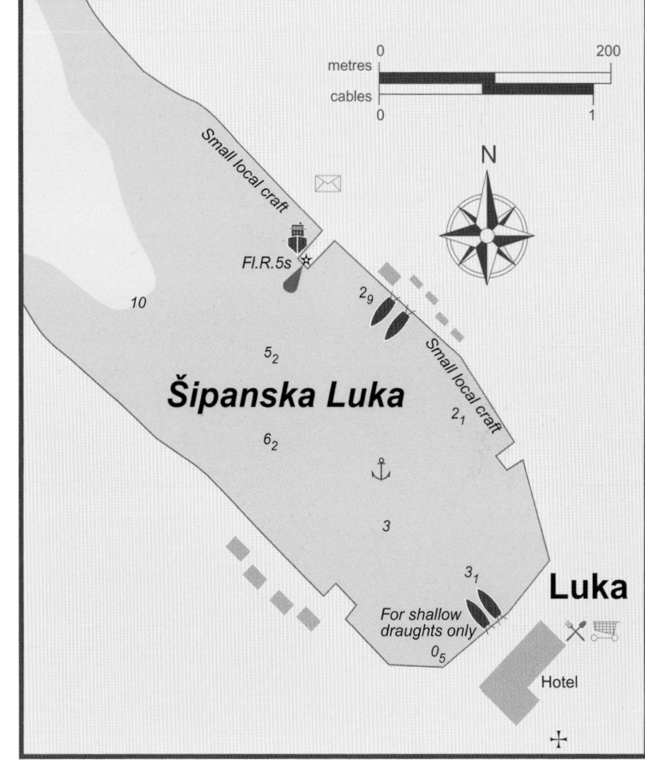

Šipanska Luka's red light (Fl R 3s), behind which are the visitors' berths

Suđurađ

Entrance to bay: 42°42'.54N 17°54'.95E

Suđurađ has a small harbour where you can berth alongside or stern-to, inside the main breakwater in depths of up to 3m. Note that a new ferry pier has been constructed just outside the harbour. Alternatively, anchor in the bay, staying clear of the ferry route.

The bay is exposed to winds from the south, south-east, east and north-east.

If approaching from the north, beware of the above-water rock and shoal off the north-west coast of the islet of Ruda and, if approaching from the south, a rock and shoal off Rt Botor.

The bay itself has a series of rocks and shoals

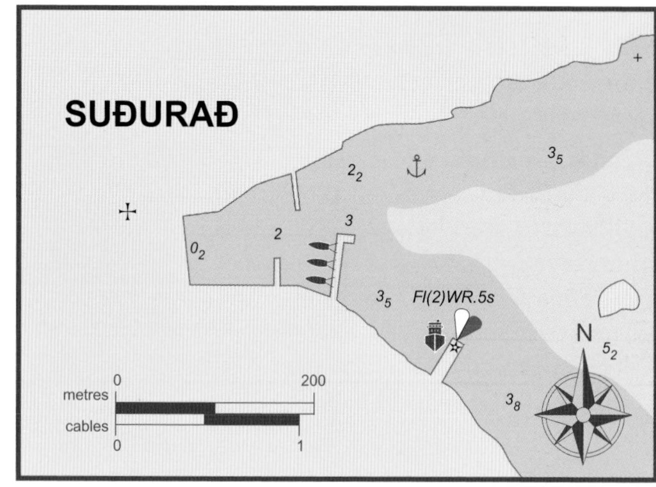

extending from the middle of the bay to the north shore. Facilities include a shop and a restaurant.

TRANSPORT ON ŠIPAN

A foot ferry regularly sails between Gruž Harbour, Dubrovnik and Luka in the summer, but less frequently in the winter, while a car ferry runs approximately twice a week from Gruž to Suđurađ on its way to Mljet. Both services are operated by Jadrolinija.

Buses connect the two main coastal towns. Local boat owners will also sometimes provide transport or excursions.

Lopud Island

Lopud is probably the most popular of the Elaphite Islands, mainly for its sandy beaches. As with Šipan, it was also a sought-after place for Dubrovnik noblemen to build their summer-houses. It is reputed to have had 30 churches in its heyday and there are a variety of ruins, the most notable of which is a Franciscan monastery that dates back to 1483.

The island incorporates two large bays: Lopud Town lies in the bay on the north-west side of the island and Uvala Šunj is on the south-east side. You can walk the footpath between the two bays in about 20 minutes. There are reasonably frequent ferries connecting to the mainland.

Lopud

Centre of bay: 42°41'.40N 17°56'.14E

Lopud is a lovely, unspoilt settlement with a large sandy beach and was one of our favourite discoveries.

NAVIGATION

Charts: HHI MK-25 & MK-26; AC 1580, SC5767

Approaches: Approaching from the east or north, there's an above-water rock, Sutmiho, just off the most northerly tip of the island. Otherwise the approach is straightforward. The church is visible as you enter the bay and the quay is marked with a red light (Fl R 3s).

ANCHORING

Keeping clear of the ferry pier, anchor off the beach in depths of 4 to 8m. There is good holding in a sand bed. The small harbour is mostly taken up with local

Lopud's sandy beach and small local boats packed into the harbour

boats and has depths of 1 to 4m. The bay is exposed to winds and seas from the west through north to north-east, but otherwise is well protected.

ASHORE

Lopud has a tourist office (Tel: 020 759 086), post office, medical centre (Tel: 020 759 202), hotel, shops, restaurants and cafés. The post office, adjacent to the hotel in Obala Ivana Kuljevana, Lopud 20222, is open from 0800 to 1200 and 1800 to 2100 Monday to Friday in the season, otherwise from 0900 to 1300 Monday to Friday.

Right: A clutch of cafés around Lopud's tourist office

Uvala Šunj

Entrance to bay: 42°40'.58N 17°57'.82E
Charts: HHI MK-25 & MK-26; AC 683, AC 1580, SC5767

This may be a great place to swim, with its sandy beach and shallow waters, but it doesn't make for an ideal anchorage and there's really not a huge amount to see except deckchairs and a couple of beach bars. It's crowded with swimmers in the summer and not very well protected, but if you do visit Uvala Šunj, stay clear of the shoal and islets, including Velo Skupio, which make a line south-east from the south-western boundary of the bay, and the 3.5m shoal between Čelo and Lopud.

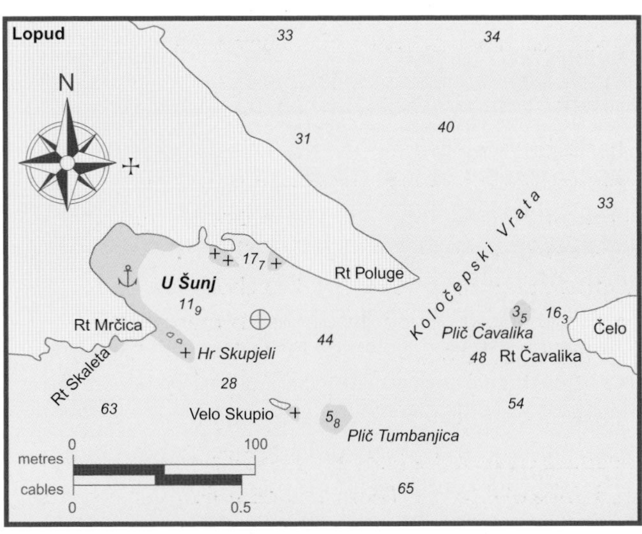

Koločep Island

Charts: HHI MK-25 & MK-26; AC 683, AC 1580, SC5767

The smallest of the Elaphite Islands, with a tradition for coral diving, Koločep is also the closest to Dubrovnik. It has two quiet settlements lying in pretty bays, which are linked together by a footpath.

Donje Čelo, on the north-west coast, has the best beach, right by a modern hotel. There are fairly frequent ferry connections to Gruž Harbour, Dubrovnik, and the locals provide a watertaxi service in the season.

Donje Čelo

Entrance to bay: 42°40'.88N 18°00'.00E

This shallow bay offers a reasonably well-protected anchorage. There is a 3.5m shoal in the narrowest part of the channel between Lopud and Koločep and see Uvala Sunj on page 235 if coming from the west, but otherwise the approach is straightforward. The ferry pier is marked by a white light (Fl 3s). Anchor in depths of between 4 and 10m on a sand and weed bed, avoiding the swimming area and the ferry pier. The bay is exposed to northwesterly winds and the Bora causes heavy seas on the southern side of the bay.

Ashore you will find a post office (open from 0800 to 1200 and 1800 to 2100, Monday to Saturday in the season, otherwise from 0900 to 1230, Monday to Friday), a tourist office (Tel: 020 757 060), a supermarket, restaurants, bars and a hotel.

Café and post office in Donje Celo

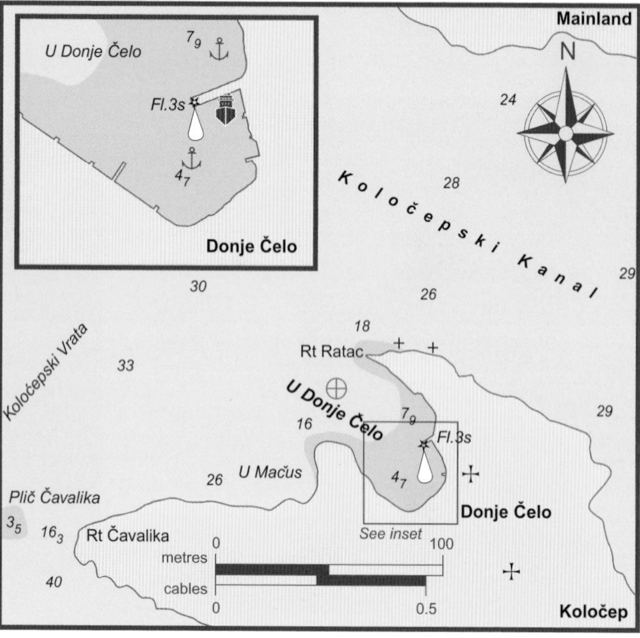

Donje Čelo's ferry pier and white light

Gornje Čelo

Entrance to bay: 42°40'.30N 18°01'.19E

Situated on the eastern side of the island, this bay has a large hotel close to the shore. There are no hazards on the approach. An underwater pipeline runs east from the northern headland of the bay.

Anchor in 3 to 5m of water on a sand and weed bed. The bay is exposed to winds and seas from the north, north-east, east and south-east. Ashore you will find a restaurant and café as well as the hotel. Gornje Čelo's main church, St Anthony of Padova, was built in the 11th and 12th centuries and is one of a handful of pre-Romanesque churches on the island.

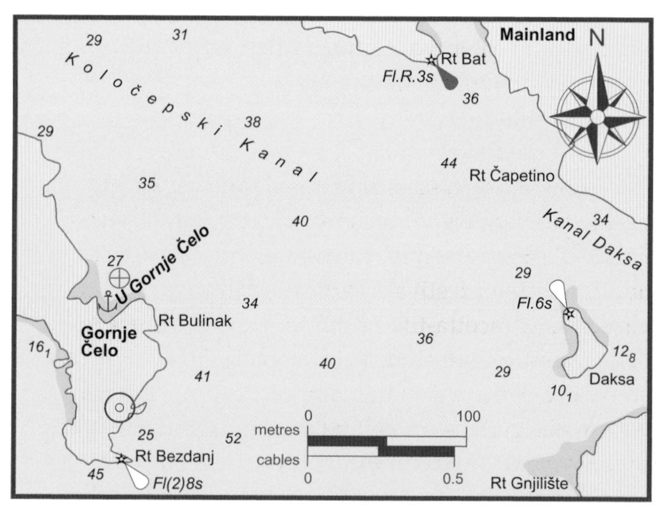

Cavtat

Chapter eight

The mainland coast, south-east of the Pelješac Peninsula, and Lokrum Island

This last chapter of our cruising companion takes us from Doli, the first port east of the Stonski Kanal, to Molunat, the last bay before entering Montenegro. We've covered the Elaphite Islands in Chapter seven, but in this chapter we include the island of Lokrum, which lies off Dubrovnik.

There's not much that hasn't already been said about the medieval walled town of Dubrovnik, but it's certainly worth spending a few days exploring it and walking around the city walls. You will find a wealth of history, some beautiful architecture and a vibrant summer festival. Within the city's defensive walls, the terracotta-tiled roofs of the densely packed houses have all been lovingly restored since the town was badly damaged in the Homeland War. If you visit Dubrovnik in the summer, be prepared for a very busy town, overflowing with tourists, cruise ship passengers and an increasing number of holiday home-owners. Dubrovnik, unlike much of the rest of Croatia, has been well and truly discovered!

Cavtat, on the other hand, is still a picturesque but sleepy tourist town and a favourite destination for superyachts. It's much easier to go through Customs formalities in Cavtat than Dubrovnik and the pace is more relaxed. It's also very close to Dubrovnik airport. Molunat, a small settlement further south-east, is even sleepier.

There's just one marina in the area, the Dubrovnik ACI marina, deep in the estuary of the River Dubrovačka and a 10-minute car ride from the town. The marina has a fuel station, as does Yacht Club Orsan, located in the inlet to Gruž harbour. Dubrovnik's port of Gruž is in the heart of the city, but it's a busy commercial port and not the most tranquil of places to stay. Both the marina and the port can get very crowded in the summer.

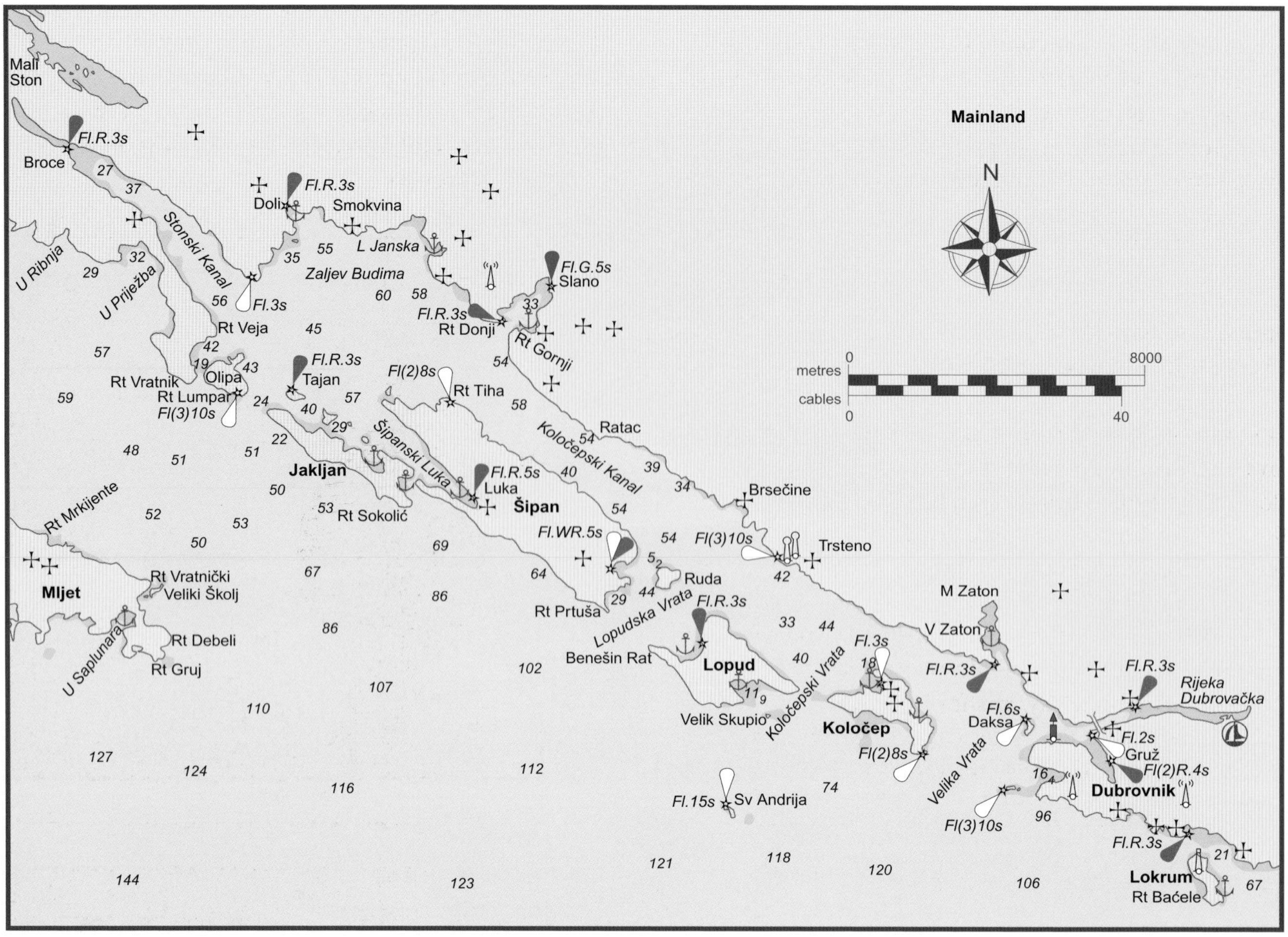

Dubrovnik

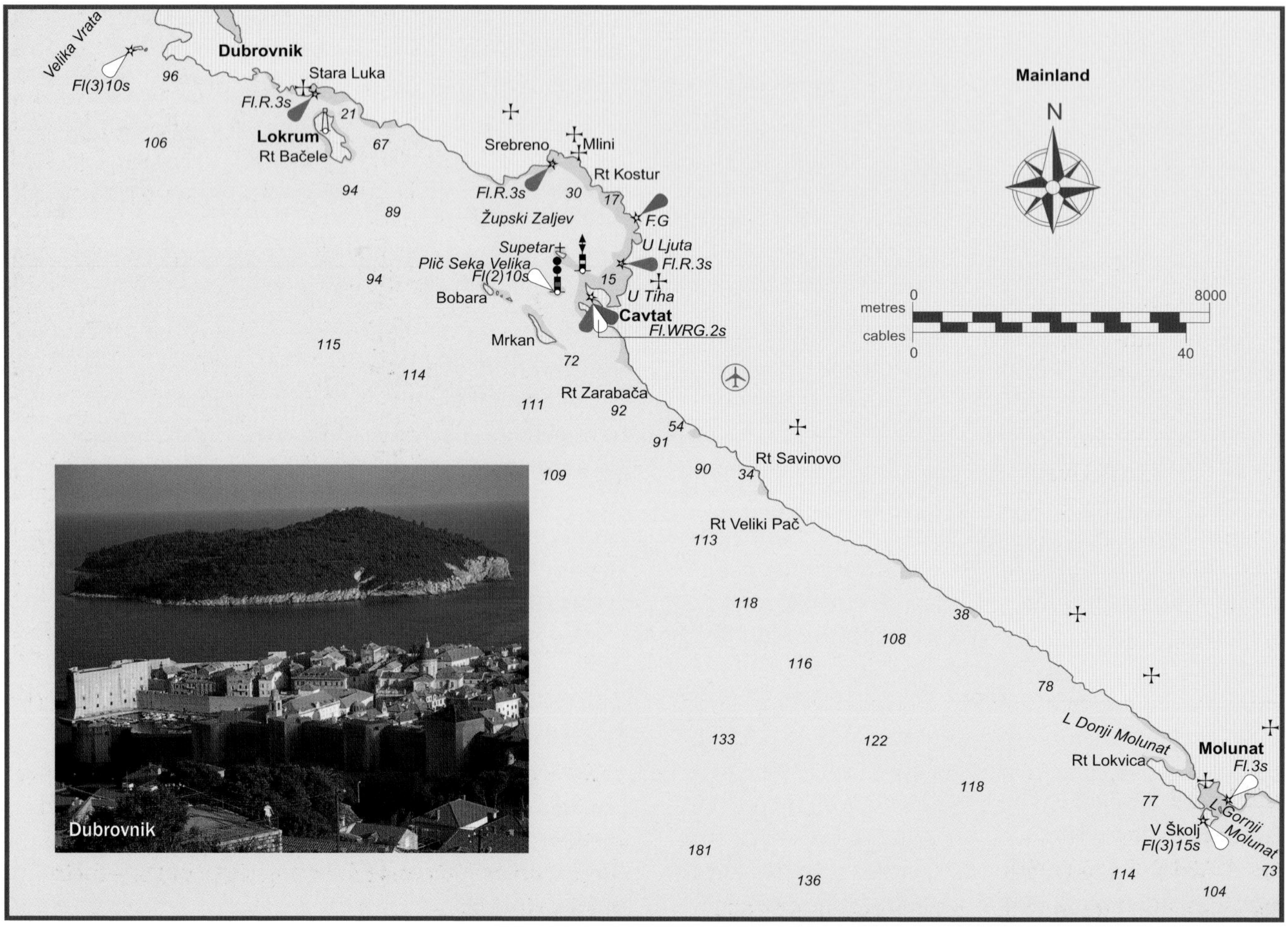

TRANSPORT FOR THE AREA

Buses link all the main settlements between Split and Dubrovnik and coaches operate regularly between the principal Croatian cities, including Zagreb.

Dubrovnik airport is near Cavtat, about a 40-minute drive from Dubrovnik, and there is an increasing number of international routes operating to and from this airport.

Dubrovnik has regular ferry services to Rijeka, Zadar, Split, Stari Grad on Hvar, Korčula, Sobra on Mljet, the Elaphite Islands and, internationally, to various ports in Italy. There's also a watertaxi between Cavtat and Dubrovnik.

Doli

Entrance to bay: 42°48'.13N 17°47'.98E
Charts: HHI MK-25; AC 1580, SC5767

Doli is a small settlement with a town harbour and a restaurant. Beware of the islet of Bogutovac, which lies south of the headland on the western side of the bay, as well as the shallow rocky area that extends from the islet to Doli's breakwater (Fl R 3s).

Either berth on the inside of the breakwater or on the outer end of the breakwater in depths of 2.5 to 4m. Alternatively, anchor in the centre of the bay in depths of about 6m. Southeasterly winds cause a heavy swell but otherwise the bay is well protected.

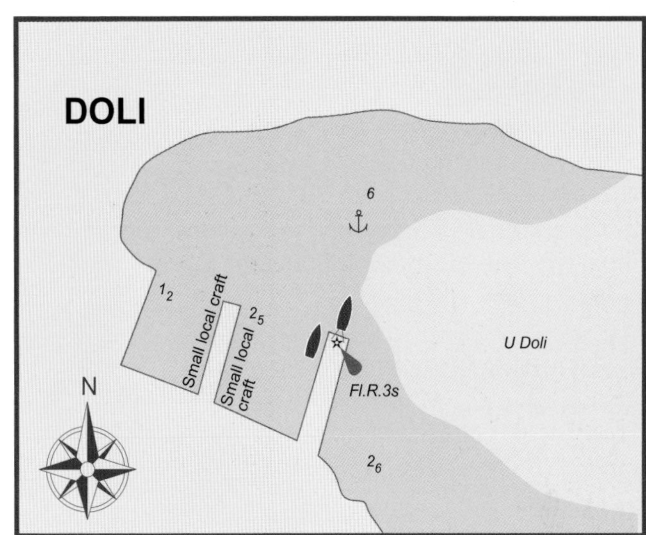

Luka Janska

Entrance to bay:
42°47'.69N 17°50'.64E
Charts: HHI MK-25;
AC 1580, SC5767

A sheltered bay with no hazards on approach, where you can anchor on a mud bed. Good holding in depths of 4 to 15m. Luka Janska is exposed to winds from the south-west, which can cause a swell. There are no facilities.

Immediately north-west of Luka Janska is Uvala Budima, which has a good pebble beach and provides a suitable lunchtime stop, although it is right by the main coast road.

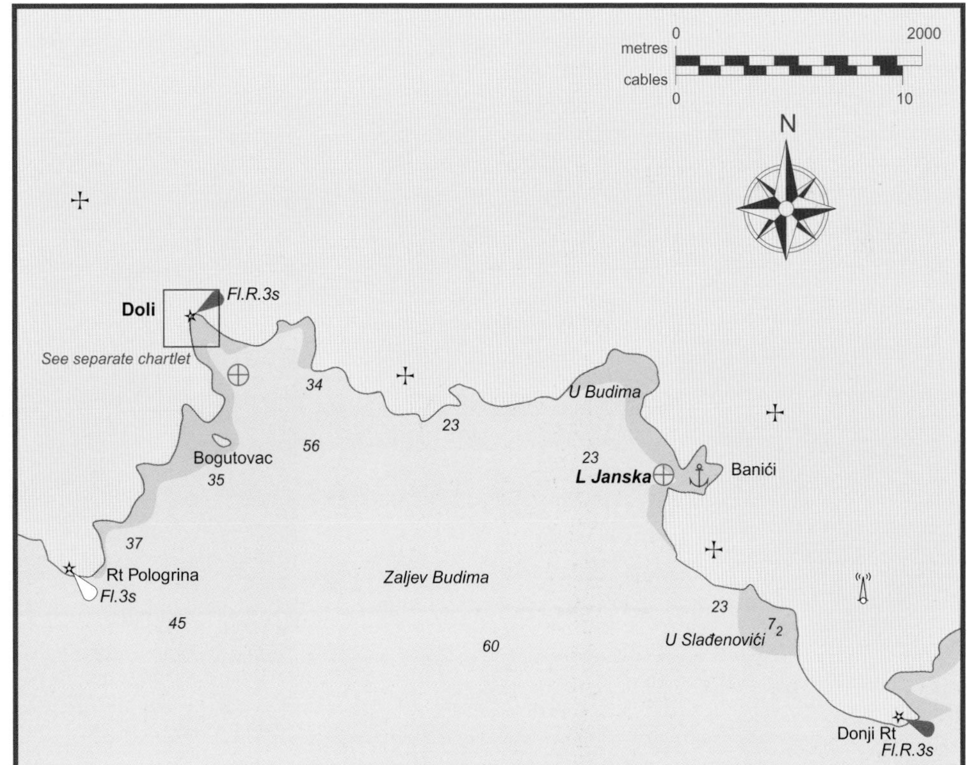

Slano

Entrance to bay:
42°46'.31N 17°52'.09E

Slano is a quiet town with a good beach, a big hotel and a well-protected bay. It was badly damaged during the Homeland War and an earthquake in 1996 caused further destruction. However, when we visited Slano there were no obvious remaining signs of the effects of these incidents.

NAVIGATION

Charts: HHI 50-20, HHI 100-27, MK-25; AC 1580, SC5767

Approaches: There are no hazards in the immediate approach and the red light (Fl R 3s), with a small stone house behind it, on Donji Rt, the headland north-west of the bay, helps to identify the entrance. The big hotel lies in the first small cove to port as you enter the main bay. Visitors' berths have been laid on the quay at the head of the bay near the green light (Fl G 5s).

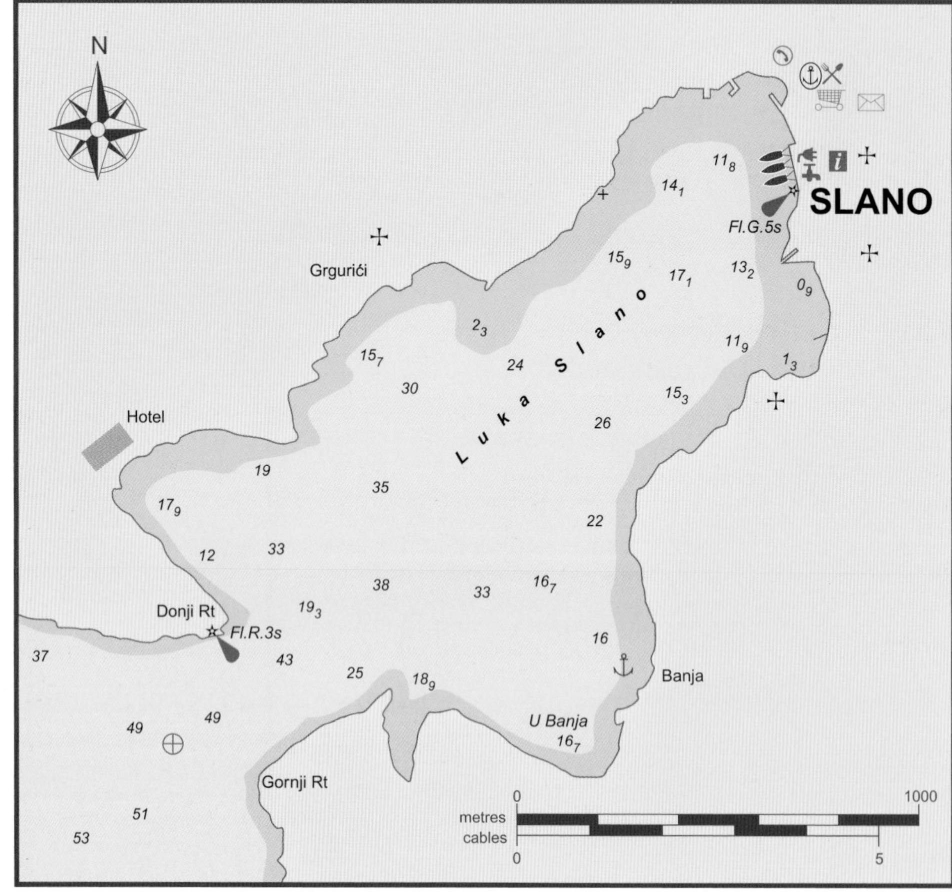

BERTHING/ANCHORING

The bay is popular with flotillas but, if space permits, berth on lazylines at the quay where water and electricity are available. Alternatively, the best anchorage is in Uvala Banja, in depths of 5 to 15m, where the holding is good on a mud bed. The small bay, immediately to starboard as you enter, has a rocky bed, as does the bay in front of the hotel, and the holding in front of the quay is unreliable. The bay is well protected from winds and seas from all directions except the south-west, although the Bora can blow strongly.

ASHORE

The tourist office, mini-market, harbourmaster's office, a couple of bars and a restaurant are all clustered together a short walk inland from the quay. This is one of the few mainland settlements of any size where we could not find a cash point, but that may have changed by now. There's a regular bus service to Dubrovnik.

Harbourmaster: Trg Ruđera Boškovića bb, 20232 Slano, Tel: 020 871 177.
Tourist office: Obala Stjepana Radića 1, 20232 Slano, Tel: 020 871 236.
Post office: Trg Ruđera Boškovića, 20232 Slano. Open in the summer from 0730 to 2100 Monday to Friday, 0800 to 1200 and 1800 to 2100 Saturday, otherwise from 0800 to 1500 Monday to Friday.
Medical centre: Tel: 020 871 227.
Restaurants: Mirakul Tel: 020 871 020; Bacchus Tel: 020 871 185.
Scooter hire: Tel: 098 965 4597.
Taxis: Tel: 098 161 7916.

Yachts berthed at the northern end of Slano's quay

Brsečine

Entrance to bay: 42°43'.38N 17°57'.06E
Charts: HHI MK-25; AC 1580, SC5767

A small bay incorporating a harbour with depths of 2 to 4m and an anchorage with poor holding. The bay is completely exposed to winds from the south and is therefore not recommended.

Trsteno

Entrance to bay: 42°42'.57N 17°58'.40E
Charts: HHI MK-25, MK-26; AC1580, SC5767

The small harbour at Trsteno is not well protected and is not recommended for anything other than a short stop in calm weather. However, it is worth mentioning the Trsteno Arboretum, one of the oldest Gothic-Renaissance gardens in Croatia. Unfortunately, the garden was a victim of the Homeland War in 1991 and a fire in 2000, but it has been replanted and still merits a visit.

Luka Zaton

Entrance to bay: 42°40'.97N 18°02'.91E
Charts: HHI MK-26; AC 683; AC 1580, SC5767

In a long narrow inlet north-west of Dubrovnik are three villages: Veliki Zaton, Mali Zaton and Štikavica. There's a harbour at Veliki Zaton where you can berth in depths of around 2 to 4m in the outer part. Note that there is a 4.5m shoal on the approach to Veliki Zaton harbour where depths are otherwise around 20m. In calm weather you can anchor at the head of the bay or by Štikavica, both in depths of around 6m. However, the inlet is very exposed and not recommended for anything other than a short stop. At Veliki Zaton you will find a post office, tourist office (Starčevićeva Obala 6, Tel: 020 891 230) and supermarket, while Mali Zaton has a good local restaurant, Gverović-Orsan (Štikavica 42, Tel: 020 891 267), with moorings provided on the outside of the L-shaped concrete quay where depths are around 4m.

Looking towards the northern end of Luka Zaton

Dubrovnik ACI Marina (Rijeka Dubrovačka)

Entrance to marina inlet: 42°40'.04N 18°04'.67E

Although not in the heart of the town, the marina is a well-equipped place to stay, with easy transport to the centre. It is possible for small boats to anchor further upstream, but this is not recommended as the Bora can blow at gale force along the inlet. Useful information for the whole of the Dubrovnik area is included on pages 244–245 (Dubrovnik City).

NAVIGATION

Charts: HHI 83, MK-26; AC 683, AC 1580, SC5767
Approaches: You'll see the fairly spectacular suspension road bridge, which has an air height of 49m (161ft),

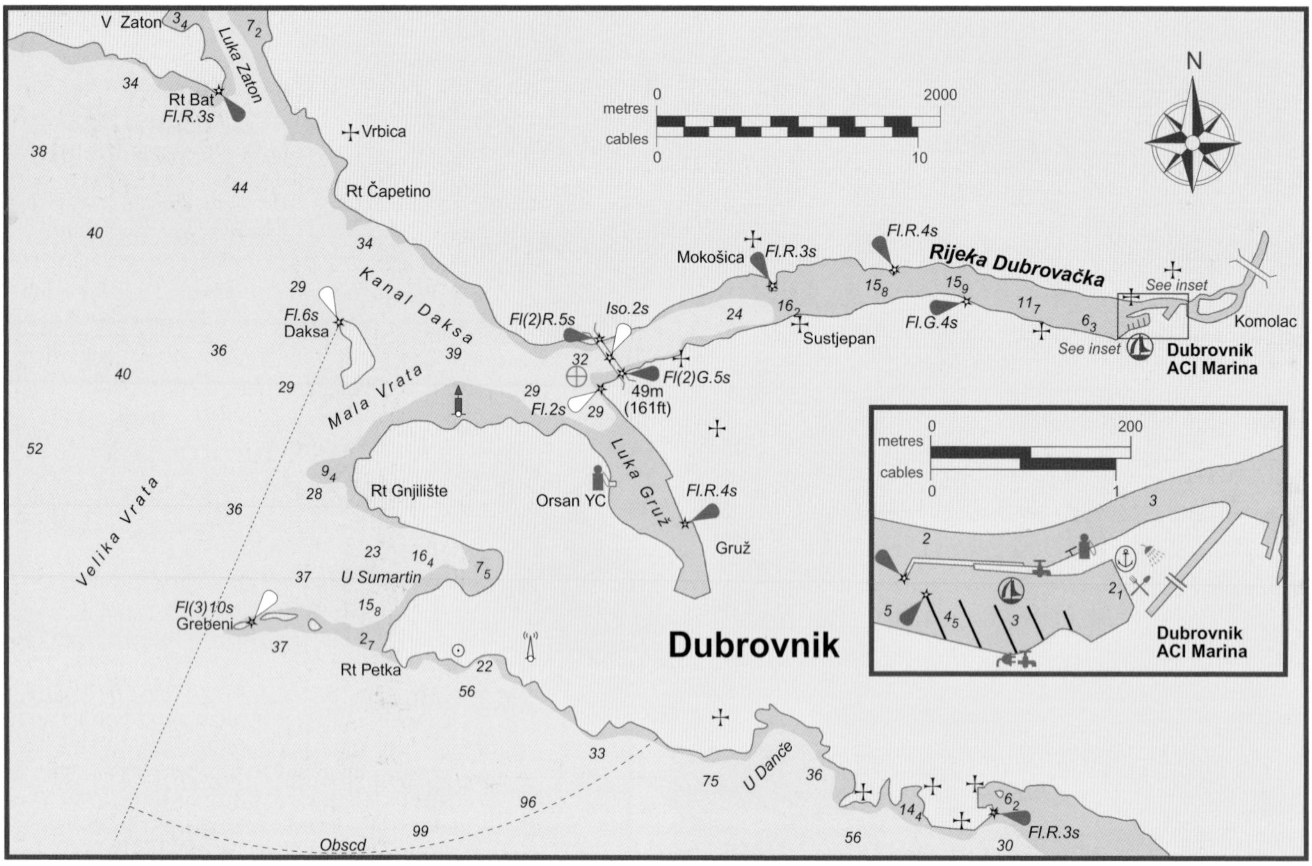

straddling the river estuary from a long way off. You need to pass under the bridge for the marina and take the inlet to starboard just before the bridge for Gruž harbour. From the south or south-east, there are shallows and a rock off the southern headland of Uvala Sumartin and, about 400m further west, a series of islets with a lighthouse on the most westerly of them. The safest route is therefore west of the lighthouse. From the north-west, the islet of Daksa, with a white light (Fl 6s) on its northwestern tip, should be left to starboard. Just after passing Daksa, you will see, to starboard, an unlit beacon marking a shoal. Pass under the bridge and keep in the centre of the channel – after about two miles you will find the marina to starboard.

BERTHING

The marina can be contacted on VHF Channel 17; Tel: 020 455 020.

It is best to call ahead to make sure there is a spare berth, especially in July and August, and you will normally be met by someone who will direct you to your berth. There are 425 berths and 140 dry berths, and the marina is Category II. You will pay €3.4 per metre per day for a 10m boat, with a 10% surcharge in July and August. The marina is well protected, although the Bora can blow very strongly in the inlet.

View to port approaching Dubrovnik ACI Marina

Useful information – Dubrovnik ACI Marina (Rijeka Dubrovačka)

FACILITIES

The marina reception and facility buildings are modern, but the charter companies have their offices in a lovely old summer palace surrounded by fishponds and palm trees.

All berths are supplied with **water** and **electricity**, and marina facilities include the normal **toilets**, **showers** and **reception**, plus **restaurants** and **bars**, **supermarket**, tennis courts, a swimming pool, **nautical shop**, **laundry** service, **gas** bottle filling station, **workshop** and 60-ton **travel hoist**. The **fuel** station (just past the entrance to the marina; depth 4m, Tel: 020 454 142) is open 0800 to 2000 every day in the summer and as required off season.

Alternatively, try Orsan Yacht Club: Tel: 020 435 965. Open 0700 to 2000 every day in the summer and 0700 to 1800 every day outside the season,

Useful information – Dubrovnik ACI Marina continued

except Bank Holidays. Depths 3.7 to 4m.

ASHORE

We cover the city of Dubrovnik separately on page 244, after Gruž harbour.

A **restaurant** is situated further upstream, and you will normally be handed a flyer with the offer of a lift by **water taxi** to get there.

A **bus** service operates to the city centre and Gruž, while a **post office** can be found in Komolac.

OTHER INFORMATION

Harbourmaster: Dubrovnik ACI Marina: Tel: 020 452 421.

Dubrovnik ACI Marina: 20236 Mokošika-Dubrovnik, Tel: 020 455 020; Fax: 020 451 922; email: m.Dubrovnik@aci-club.hr; website: www.aci-club.hr.

Part of the Dubrovnik ACI Marina complex: the charter company offices are housed in the old summer palace

Gruž

Centre of inlet:
42°39'.62N 18°04'.93E

The busy commercial port of Gruž is not recommended as an overnight stop on account of the traffic and noise, but is used by big yachts and motorcruisers.

If you want to clear Customs then Cavtat, further south-east, is a better bet. The local yacht club, Orsan (Tel: 020 435 922), halfway along the western shore, may accept passing visitors and has a fuel station (depth 3.7m, Tel: 020 435 965).

NAVIGATION/BERTHING

Charts: HHI 83, MK-26; AC 683; AC 1580, SC5767

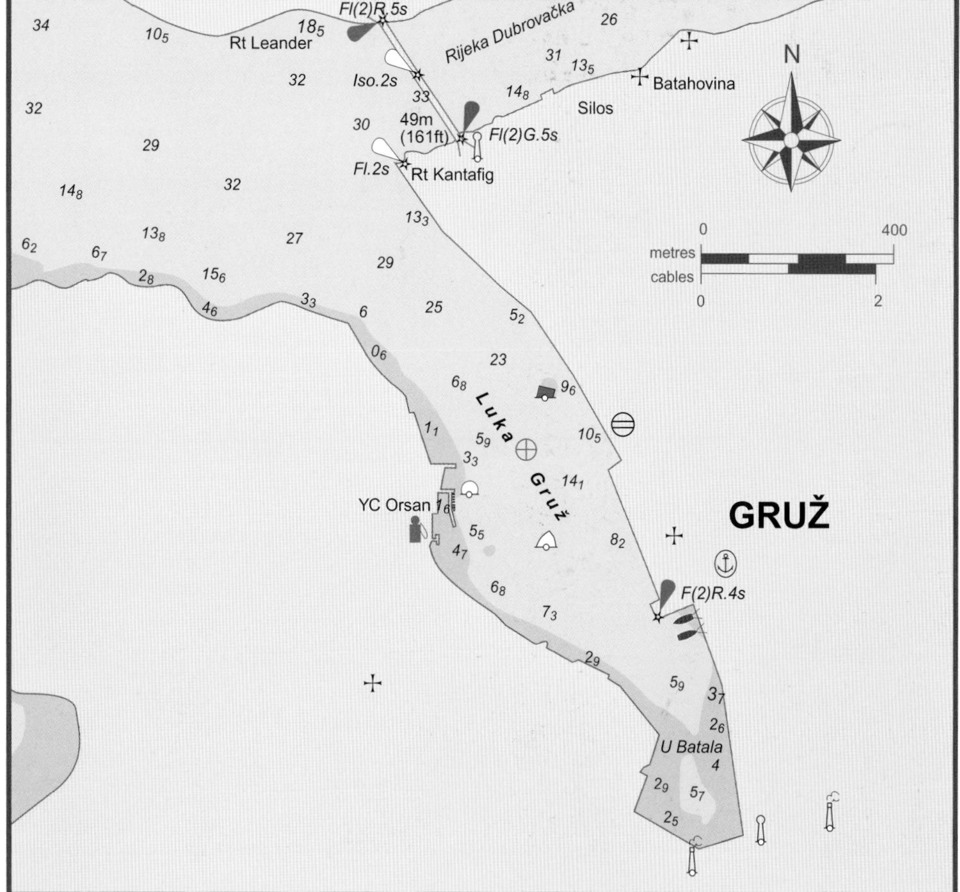

Gruž – port hand light and berthing area

Approaches: See page 242 for the approach to the inlet. Most of the eastern side of the inlet is normally reserved for commercial boats and ferries. A buoy situated about halfway along the eastern quay marks a 4.5m shoal. You may find a mooring at the head of the bay after the red light (Fl [2] R 4s). The harbourmaster's office is located next to this red light, while the Custom's building can be found adjacent to the ferry quay.

ASHORE

See Dubrovnik City below, although you'll come across nearly every kind of shop and service you need very close to the quay. The Yacht Club Orsan (Tel: 020 455 933) has a good fish restaurant.

Dubrovnik City

Dubrovnik has so much to offer that it's difficult to do it justice in a small space. The city centre is a mixture of squares, with polished stone walkways, and small alleyways full of buzzing restaurants, bars and boutiques. Moreover it is, of course, surrounded by the magnificent city walls. The summer festival carries on for most of July and August with an eclectic variety of entertainment, and it is one of the few places in Dalmatia that has a life all year round.

Useful information – Dubrovnik City

PROVISIONING

You will probably want to stock up close to your boat in either the ACI marina **supermarket** or Gruž but, in the city itself, the supermarkets are generally just outside the city walls, with the specialist shops and boutiques in the centre.

EATING OUT

There's certainly no shortage of choice in Dubrovnik, although you'll find the prices a bit higher than elsewhere. Below is a sample of restaurants to try:
Tabasco, a pizzeria (Hrvatska 42, Tel: 020 429 595) has a great location inside the city walls.
Atlas Club Nautika (Brsalje 3, Tel: 020 442 526/020 442 573) is frequently touted as the best restaurant in Dubrovnik. Housed in a 19th century building just outside the city walls, it's a relatively formal restaurant with good meat and fish dishes.
Steak House Domino (Od Domina 6, Tel: 020 432 832/020 323 103) in the old town offers a change if you've overdosed on fish.
Mea Culpa (Za Rokom 3, Tel: 020 424 819), inside the city walls, is said to provide the best pizzas in town.
Škola (Antuninska 1, 20000 Dubrovnik, Tel: 020 321 096) is renowned for its sandwiches lovingly made with a variety of local ingredients and home-made bread.

ASHORE

If you're staying for

Dubrovnik Old Town from the south-east

Useful information – Dubrovnik City

any length of time in Dubrovnik, then visit the **tourist office** as soon as possible for the wealth of literature available and the latest programme of events (Contact: Cvijete Zuzorić 1/2, pp 258, 20000 Dubrovnik, Tel: 020 323 887/020 323 889/020 323 907; Fax: 020 323 725; email: info@tzdubrovnik.hr; web: www.tzdubrovnik.hr). A walk around the city walls is good for orientation, spectacular views and absorbing the atmosphere, after which you can then pick the sights you want to see. If all the hustle and bustle is too much for you, you can take a water taxi to the **islet of Lokrum** for a swim. On the mainland there is a good pebble **beach** in Lapad Cove, near Hotel Zagreb.

The **Dubrovnik Summer Festival** runs from mid-July until the end of August (website: www.dubrovnik-festival.hr), and includes opera, classical and folk music, theatre and a number of fringe events. Outside the summer festival period you can visit the **National Theatre** for drama, opera or classical music, but most performances will be in Croatian. The Dubrovnik Sunday Shows, mainly comprising folk music and dance, start in late April and are held at 11am in front of the **Church of St Blaise**.

If you like to party into the small hours then your choices are limited, as most of the bars are closed by midnight. Bepap, situated at Kneza Damjana Jude in the old town, is one of the few that may still be open.

As you can imagine, there are plenty of private travel agencies around that are only too happy to organise any conceivable tour, excursion, sporting activity or vehicle hire. Atlas (Tel: 020 442 222) and Generalturist (Tel: 020 432 974) are both large, established organisations and can therefore be relied upon, along with many of the smaller operators.

INFORMATION ON THE DUBROVNIK AREA

Harbourmaster: Gruž: Obala Stjepana Radića 37, PP. 31, 20000 Dubrovnik, Tel: 020 418 988/ 020 418 989/020 413 222; Fax: 020 418 987.
Hospital: Roko Mišetića bb, Tel: 020 431 777.
Medical centre: Dr A Starčevića 45, Tel: 020 429 044.
Pharmacy Gruž: Gruška Obala, Tel: 020 418 990.
Pharmacy Kod Zvonika: Placa, Tel: 020 321 503.

Lokrum Islet

Charts: HHI 83, MK-26; AC 683; AC 1580

Given its proximity to Dubrovnik, Lokrum is clearly very popular with city dwellers who want to get away from it all. The 10-minute boat trip runs every half hour in the summer. It's known locally as the 'King of Islands' and has a Botanical Garden and a small saltwater lake, 'Mrtvo More', or the 'Dead Sea' in English. Uvala Portoč at the southern end of the east coast, is the main bay, with the jetties being used by the day-tripper boats. The best beaches and the salt-water lake are on the south-west side of the island.

The approach is straightforward, but the bay shelves rapidly and the shallow area extends to the southern tip of the island. You can anchor in around 8 to 12m, but the holding is unreliable, the bay is only protected from winds and seas from the west and north-west, and there's a large amount of traffic, so you would do better to take one of the local boats from Dubrovnik.

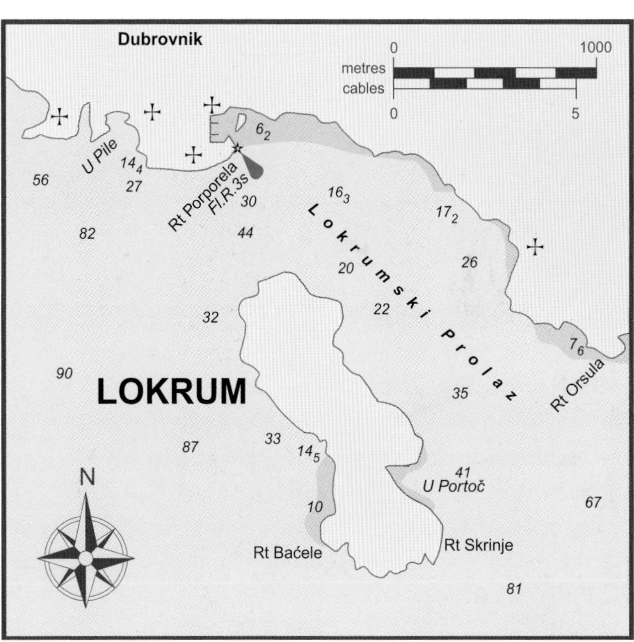

Županski Zaljev

Entrance to bay: 42°37'.13N 18°12'.19E
Charts: HHI MK-26; AC 1580

This large bay is quite exposed but has two possible stop-off places – Mlini and Srebreno – both on the northern side of the bay and within walking distance of each other. Mlini has more shops and facilities than Srebreno and, as well as the normal interconnecting bus services, there's a local ferry to Cavtat and Dubrovnik. Ideally, use Cavtat or Dubrovnik marina as an overnight stop, although we do include brief details of both harbours below.

The main hazards on the approach to the bay are the string of islets west and south-west of Cavtat, the islet and rock north-west of Cavtat and two shoals. The larger shoal, Pličina Seka Velika, is about 600m north-west of the entrance to Cavtat Luka and marked by an isolated danger beacon and light (Fl [2] 10s). The smaller shoal, Pličina Seka Mala, has depths of less than 2m over it and extends north from Sveti Rok to the northern tip of this headland. Navigation is hazardous at night and the safest route at any time if approaching from the south or south-east is to leave the Cavtat islets (and all the other hazards) well to starboard.

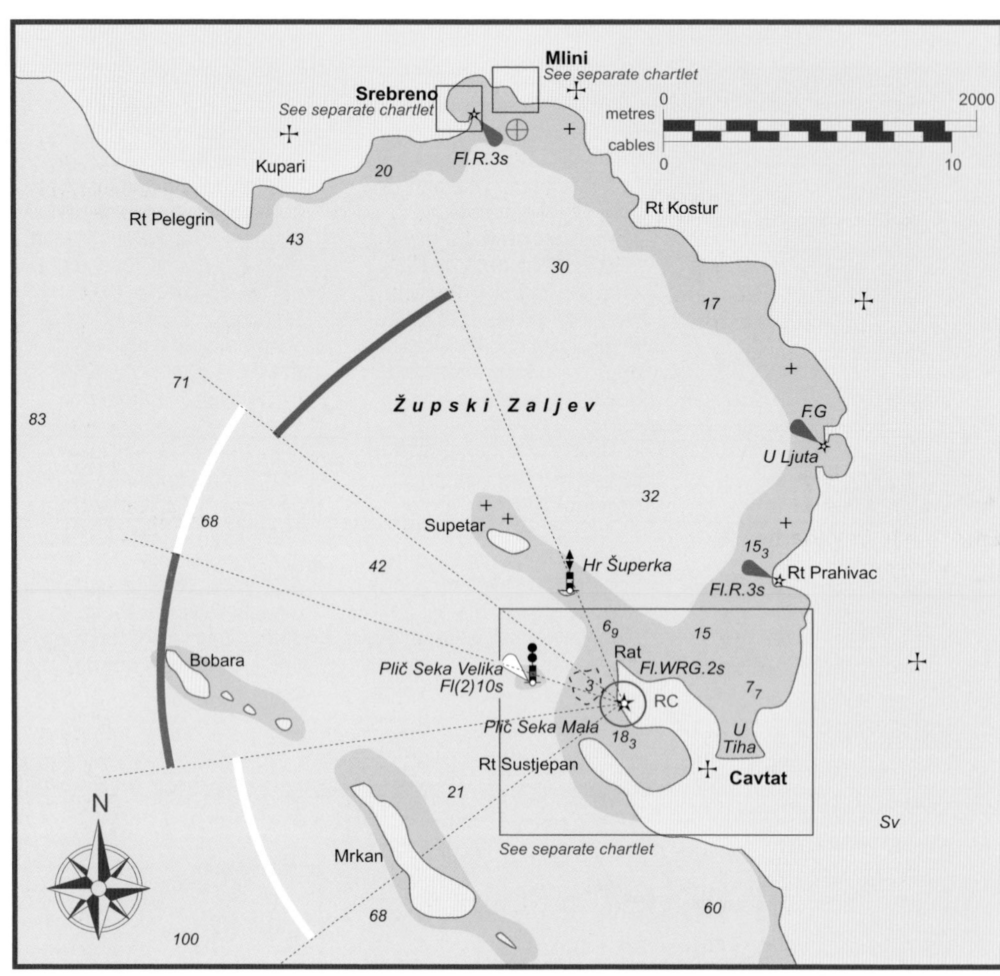

Srebreno

Srebreno is a busy tourist destination with hotels and a large beach that is predominantly roped-off for swimmers. There are no hazards in the immediate approach, the breakwater has a red light (Fl R 3s), and you should head for the quay where you can berth alongside or stern-to in depths of 2 to 4m. The bay is not protected from the Bora, which can cause heavy seas and make the berths unsafe. Southwesterly winds produce a swell, but otherwise the berths are well protected.

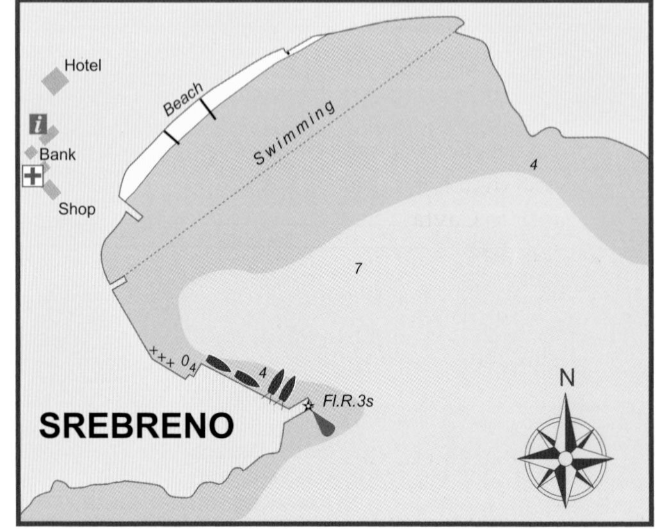

Mlini

The western side of the bay has some loose boulders and south-east of the breakwater are above-water rocks. The inner harbour has depths of less than a metre, but there is deeper water by the breakwater head. A water tap is situated at the foot of the breakwater. The bay is not suitable in winds with any south in them and westerly and northwesterly winds can cause a swell.

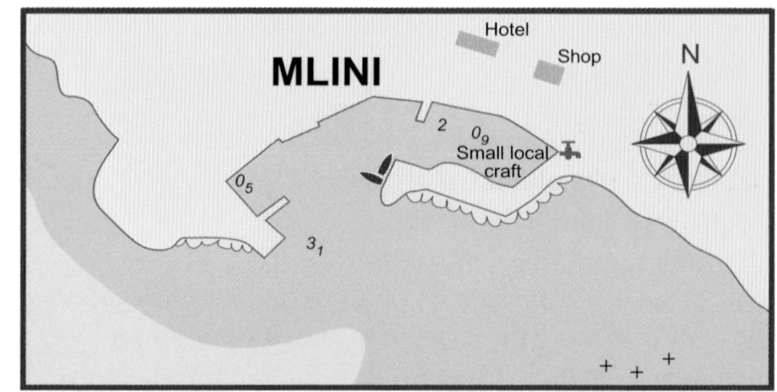

Useful information – Mlini and Srebreno

TOURIST INFORMATION OFFICE: 20207 Mlini, Srebreno **Tel:** 020 486 254; **Fax:** 020 487 003; **email:** tz-zupa-dubrovavacka@du.htnet.hr

POST OFFICE: Brašina uz Magistralu, 20207 Mlini. Open 0730 to 2100 Monday to Friday, 0800 to 1200 and 1800 to 2100 on Saturdays in the summer, otherwise from 0730 to 1900 Monday to Friday and 0730 to 1400 on Saturdays.

PHARMACY SREBRENO: 20207 Mlini, Srebreno, **Tel:** 020 487 014.

TAVERN CIPARIS: 20207 Mlini, Srebreno, **Tel:** 020 485 750.

KONOBA MLINI: Šetalište Marka Marojice b.b. Mlini, **Tel:** 098 699 613; **email:** vivado@du.htnet.hr.

SOLARIS DIVING CENTRE: Plat bb Mlini, **Tel:** 020 313 105; **Fax:** 020 313 106; **email:** shipping@solaris-tours.com; **website:** www.solaris-group.hr.

Cavtat

Entrance to bay (harbour):
42°35'.07N 18°12'.56E

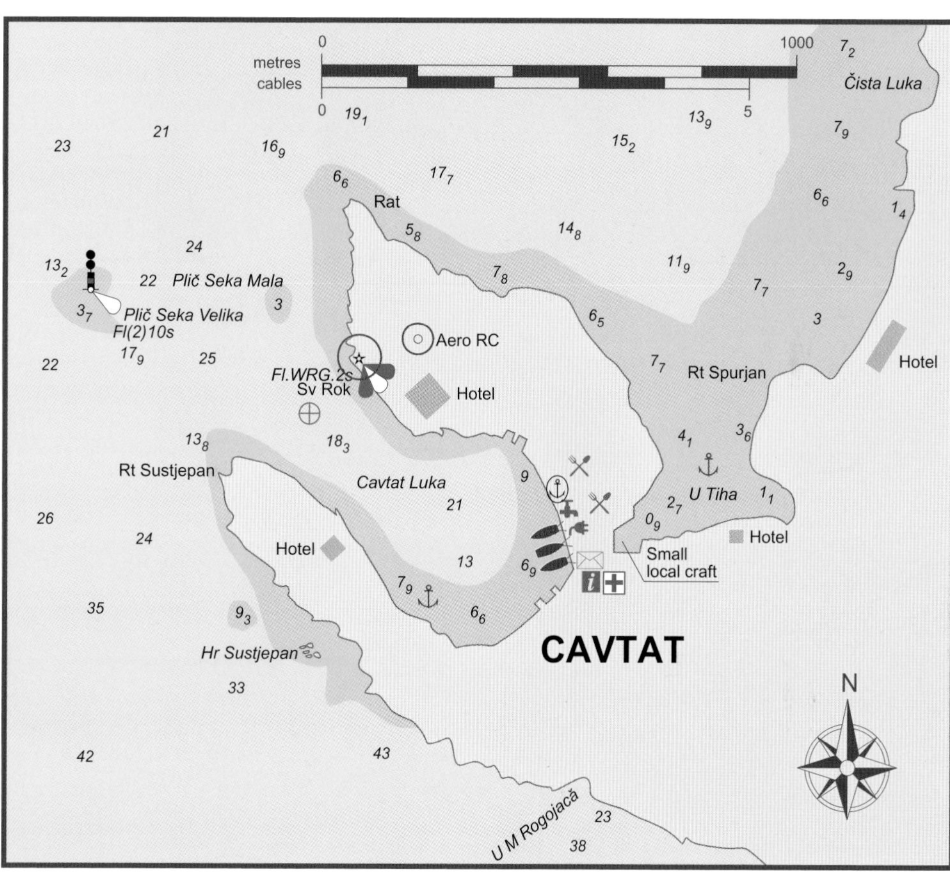

Cavtat is a well-cared for and prosperous fishing village that has expanded with the increase in tourism and its close proximity to Dubrovnik International Airport. It has become a more popular place to clear Customs than Dubrovnik and you'll frequently see luxury yachts taking in its ambience.

NAVIGATION

Charts: HHI 100-28, MK-26; AC 1580

Approaches: See pages 245–246 for hazards in the Župski Zaljev, immediately around the entrance to Cavtat Luka. The local and day-tripper boats tend to berth in Uvala Tiha, east of the town centre, with ferries and visiting yachts using the main bay, Cavtat Luka.

BERTHING/ANCHORING

In Cavtat Luka, you can berth, usually bows- or stern-to, in depths of 2 to 4m and will probably be directed by the harbourmaster. Water and electricity are available on the quay, although use is restricted. In Uvala Tiha, depths are up to 3m, but there is no water or electricity as yet. You will normally be expected to pay a fee, particularly in Cavtat Luka.

You can anchor in either the southern part of Cavtat Luka in depths of 5 to 10m, or in the centre of Uvala Tiha, away from the moorings and in depths of 3 to 7m, although the holding is reported to be unreliable here. Winds from the west and north-west can cause a heavy swell in Cavtat Luka, and Uvala Tiha is not protected from winds from the north.

Cavtat is a popular destination for luxury yachts

Useful information – Cavtat

ASHORE

Cavtat is a lovely place to relax for a couple of days, with all the **shops**, **restaurants** and **bars** that you will need. It also has its fair share of **museums**, ancient buildings and beaches. The **tourist office** (Tiha 3, Tel: 020 479 025; Fax: 020 478 025; email: info@tzcavtat-konavle.hr; website: www.tzcavtat-konavle.hr) is just east of the head of the main bay, immediately west of which are the **pharmacy** and **post office**. Post office opening times are the same as Mlini – see page 247.

Leut (Trumbičev Put 11, Tel: 020 478 477) in the centre of town is a good fish restaurant. If you don't mind getting a taxi or hiring a car, Konavoski Dvori (Ljuta, Konavle, Tel: 020 791 039) is a very popular restaurant, with waitresses dressed in traditional costumes. Situated 19 miles east of Cavtat by a watermill on the River Ljuta, it's probably best to call ahead before making the trip, as it's a favoured spot for tour groups. The best **beaches** are in Uvala Tiha but, compared with many places, you're spoilt for choice.

A few of the many island excursions on offer in Cavtat

OTHER INFORMATION

Harbourmaster: Obala Ante Starčevića 10, 20210 Cavtat, Tel: 020 478 065.
Medical centre: Tel: 020 478 352.
Pharmacy: Pharmacie Mišetić, Trumbićev put 2, Tel: 020 478 262.
Diving centres: Diving Centre Epidaurum, Šetalište Žal bb, Tel: 020 471 444; website: www.epidaurum-diving-cavtat.hr.
Diving Club Konavle, Trumbićev put 25, Tel: 020 478 774/098 2511 326.

Molunat

Entrance to bay:
42°26'.73N 18°26'.41E

After all we'd heard about Molunat and following our visit to nearby Cavtat, we were surprised just how undeveloped it actually was. It is really just a couple of large bays with some campsites, plenty of rooms to let and a handful of bars and restaurants.

Two bays flank the narrow piece of land that joins the peninsula to the mainland. The northwesterly bay, Luka Donji Molunat, is too deep for anchoring, although there are some mooring posts on the shore and it's the only bay in the area that provides protection in winds

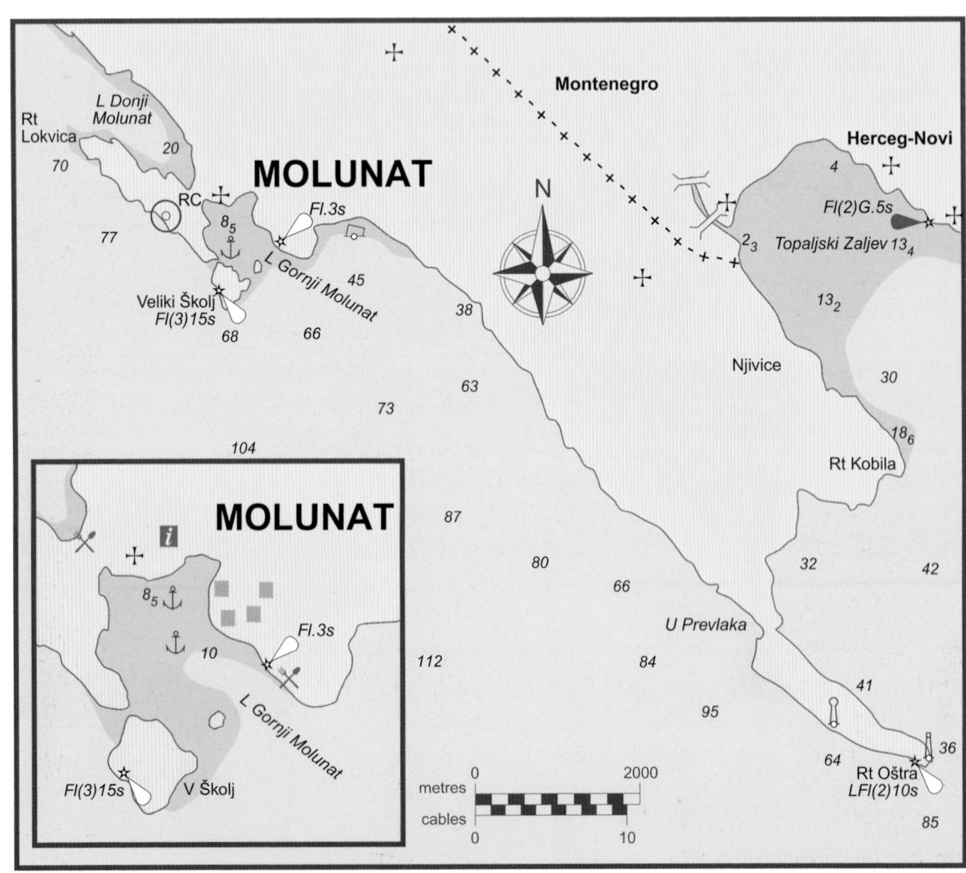

from the south and south-west. The notes below refer to the southeasterly bay, Luka Gornji Molunat, which affords a good anchorage in most conditions.

NAVIGATION

Charts: HHI 100-28, MK-26, MK-27; AC 1582

Approaches: The larger islet, Veliki Školj, with a white light (Fl [3] 15s) on its south-western tip, lies off the south-eastern end of the peninsula, while a smaller islet is situated just north-east of its south-eastern end. There are rocks around the smaller islet and shallows encircle both islets, so the best approach is close to the mainland by the white light (Fl 3s) on the north-eastern side of the bay. Look out for rocks extending from the shore as you enter the bay.

ANCHORING

Anchor in depths of 7 to 10m in the westerly part of the bay, avoiding the underwater cable, which runs north-west across the piece of land joining the peninsula to the mainland, just north-east of the head of the bay. Southeasterly winds cause a heavy swell in the bay and the Bora can blow strongly here, although it does not produce a swell. The anchorage provides good protection from winds and seas from other directions.

ASHORE

The local tourist office details do not appear to be listed as yet, but you will find some information on Molunat on the website for the Cavtat tourist office; see page 248. There's a small shop in the village along with a post office, where the opening hours in the summer are from 0800 to 1200 and 1800 to 2100 Monday to Saturday, closed in the winter.

Molunat's popular rocky beach

Molunat's shallow inner bay, with plenty of holiday accommodation dotted around

CROATIAN PHRASEBOOK

Basics

Yes	da
No	ne
Good morning	dobro jutro
Good day (hello – formal)	dobar dan
Good evening	dobra večer
Good night	laku noć
Hello and goodbye (informal)	bok or bog
Please	molim
Thank you	hvala
Excuse me	oprostite
I'm sorry	žao mi je
Pleased to meet you	drago mi je
Do you speak English?	govorite li engleski?
I don't speak Croatian	ne govorim hrvatski
I don't know	ne znam
I don't understand	ne razumijem
What's your name?	kako se zovete?
My name is....	zovem se ....
When?	kada?
How much is it?	koliko košta?
Where is?	gdje je?
Where to?	kamo?
Here	ovdje
There	tamo
Right	desno
Left	lijevo
Straight	pravo
Back/backwards	natrag
Forwards	naprijed
What time is it?	koliko je sati?
Today, tomorrow, yesterday	danas, sutra, jučer
In the morning	ujutro
In the evening	uvečer
Early	rano
Late	kasno

Eating out

[Nearly all menus will be translated into English]

I'd like a table for two please	molim stol za dvoje
The menu please	molim vas jelovnik
I'm a vegetarian	ja sam vegetarijanac
The bill please	račun molim
Water	voda

CROATIAN PHRASEBOOK continued

Numbers

Unfortunately the number endings change according to case and gender so you may hear *dvije* instead of *dva* and *jedno* or *jedna* instead of *jedan*, etc.

1	jedan
2	dva
3	tri
4	četiri
5	pet
6	šest
7	sedam
8	osam
9	devet
10	deset
11	jedanaest
12	dvanaest
13	trinaest
14	četrnaest
15	petnaest
16	šesnaest
17	sedamnaest
18	osamnaest
19	devetnaest
20	dvadeset
21	dvadeset i jedan
30	trideset
40	četrdeset
50	pedeset
60	šezdeset
70	sedamdeset
80	osamdeset
90	devedeset
100	sto

Days of the week

Monday	ponedjeljak
Tuesday	utorak
Wednesday	srijeda
Thursday	četvrtak
Friday	petak
Saturday	subota
Sunday	nedjelja

Months of the year

January	siječanj
February	veljača
March	ožujak
April	travanj
May	svibanj
June	lipanj
July	srpanj

CROATIAN PHRASEBOOK

August	kolovoz
September	rujan
October	listopad
November	studeni
December	prosinac

Sailing

Berth	vez
Boat	brod
Sailing boat	jedrilica
Speedboat	gliser
Bow	pramac
Drop anchor	baciti sidro
Dock/pier	pristanište
Fender	bokobran
Harbour	luka
I need a berth for two days?	treba mi vez na dva dana?
What is the depth of your pier?	koja je dubina na pristaništu?
What are your rates?	kolike su vaše cijene?
Where can I moor my boat?	gdje mogu privezati brod?
Does the berth have a water and power supply?	ima li vez vodu I struju?
Does your marina have a 15 ton crane?	Ima li vaša marina petnaesttonsku dizalicu?
Is there a sheltered harbour near by?	Postoji li u blizini zaštićena luka?
Where is the harbour master's office?	Gdje je lučka kapetanija?

Croatian names on charts and maps

The Croatian charts, Admiralty charts, local maps and this companion use Croatian proper names throughout. Where, for example, 'saint' (*sveti*), 'island' (*otok*) or 'bay' (*uvala*) are part of a proper name then we have used the Croatian word. Below is a brief glossary of such words, together with other Croatian words that you may see on local charts, maps or elsewhere. There seem to be plenty of Croatian words for mud! Note again that adjectives change their endings according to gender, number and case so, for example, for 'white' you may see *bijel*, *bijelo*, or *bijela*, and for black you may see *crn*, *crna* or *crno*. The plural of *greben* (rock) is *grebeni*, but plural endings are also different according to gender and case.

CROATIAN PHRASEBOOK continued

Bijel	white
Blato	mud
Brdo	hill
Carina	customs office
Cjevovod	pipeline
Crkva	church
Crn	black
Crven	red
Dolina	valley
Donji	lower (normally applied to place names) as in lower Seget or upper Seget
Dvorac	castle or villa
Gat	bank, dyke, embankment, mole, pier
Gaz	ford
Gaz broda	draught
Geodetski datum	chart datum
Glib	mud
Gospa	Our Lady (church of…)
Gorivo	fuel
Gornji	upper (see *donji* above)
Grad	city or town
Greben	submerged rock, reef, ridge
Hrid	rock (above water)
Hum	hillock, mound
Istok	east
Izvor	spring, source, well
Jezero	lake
Jug	south
Kabel	cable
Kabeli i cjevovodi	cables and pipelines
Kamen, kamenje	stone, stones
Kanal	canal or channel
Kapela	chapel
Konoba	informal, family-run restaurant
Kopno	land
Kuća	house

CROATIAN PHRASEBOOK

Kula	tower
Laguna	lagoon
Lučica	small harbour
Luka	harbour, port
Lukobran	breakwater
Mali	small
Manastir/Samostan	monastery, nunnery, convent
Marina	marina
Mjesto	small town or village, literally place
More	sea
Morska trava	seaweed
Most	bridge
Mulj	mud
Naselje	settlement or community
Navigacijska oznaka	navigational mark
Navoz	slipway
Novi	new
Obala	quay, shore
Otočić	islet
Otok	island
Pijesak	sand
Planina	mountain
Pličina	shoal
Plitvac	rock, reef
Plutača	buoy
Podrtina	wreck
Poluotok	peninsula
Pontonski gat	pontoon
Pošta	post office
Potok	stream
Pristan	landing place, quay
Pristanište	landing place, port
Prolaz	passage
Prometne veze	communications
Propisi	regulations
Put	road, path, way
Rat	cape
Razina mora	sea level
Restoran	restaurant
Rijeka	river
Rječica	small river or stream

CROATIAN PHRASEBOOK continued

Rt	cape, point, headland
Rtić	small cape or point
Ruševina	ruin
Samostan	monastery or convent
Selo	village
Sidrište	anchorage
Sjever	north
Školj, školjić	islet, reef
Školjke	shells, mussels
Slapovi	waterfalls
Šljunak	pebbles
Spomenik	monument
Srednji	middle, centre
Star	old
Šuma	forest, wood
Sveti	saint
Svjetionik	lighthouse
Svjetlo	light
Tjesnac	strait or channel
Točka	point
Trajekt	ferry
Upozorenje	warning, caution
Upute za plovidbu	sailing directions
Ušće	river mouth
Utvrda	fort, castle
Uvala	bay, inlet
Uvalica	small bay, inlet or cove
Veli	large, great
Velik	large, great
Vez	berth
Voda	water
Vrata	passage, gate (literally/commonly door)
Vremenske prilike	local weather
Vrh	peak, top
Zabranjeno sidrenje	anchoring prohibited
Zaklonište	shelter
Zaljev	gulf, bay, basin
Zapad	west
Zastavno koplje	flagstaff, flagpole
Zaton	bay
Zelen	green
Žut	yellow